Business Statistics by Example

Terry Sincich
University of Florida

Dellen Publishing Company
San Francisco and Santa Clara, California

On the cover: The work on the cover is a collage and acrylic painting on canvas by Robert Natkin. His work is in many private and public collections, among them the Museum of Modern Art, the Guggenheim Museum, the Metropolitan Museum of Art, and the Los Angeles County Museum. Natkin's work may be seen at the Tortue Gallery in Santa Monica, California, and at the Gimpel and Weitzenhoffer Gallery in New York City.

© Copyright 1982 by Dellen Publishing Company, 3600 Pruneridge Avenue, Santa Clara, California 95051

Printed in the United States of America
10 9 8 7 6 5 4 3 2 1

Library of Congress Cataloging in Publication Data

Sincich, Terence L.
  Business statistics by example.

  Includes index.
    1. Commercial statistics.   2. Commercial
statistics—Case studies.   3. Statistics.
  I. Title.
HF1017.S53   519.5   81-17450
ISBN 0-89517-035-3   AACR2

Contents

Four   Probability   93

Five   Opinion Polls and the Binomial Probability Distribution   135

Twelve   Simple Linear Regression and Correlation   373

Thirteen   Multiple Regression   427

Preface

This introductory college business statistics text is designed for a one-semester or one-quarter course for students who have only a high school background in mathematics as a prerequisite. It differs from most other business texts in two ways:

1. Explanations of basic statistical concepts and methodology are based on and motivated by the use of real data sets.
2. Concepts and statistical methods are explained in examples. These examples arise as questions posed about the data sets.

We think that this practical orientation helps the student to relate statistics to real-life problems and, hopefully, will develop a pattern of thought that will persist after the student enters the business world.

The text contains four data sets; the first two are heavily used as instructional vehicles. These data sets are:

Appendix A. The set of actual assessed values and sale prices for all properties sold in 1978 in a midsized city.

Appendix B. The assessed values and sale prices (extracted from Appendix A) for six neighborhoods which differ in their economic and sociological characteristics.

Appendix C. The daily closing prices and daily changes of the Standard & Poor's Stock Index, 1975–1979.

Appendix D. Supermarket customer checkout times for mechanical and automated checkers.

Although all of the data sets are used to develop the notion of a population and a sample, the real estate assessed values and sale prices (Appendices A and B) are used to demonstrate the need for data description; to develop the notion of a sampling distribution; and to motivate the inferential methods commonly studied in an introductory business statistics course.

In addition to teaching via data sets and by example, this text contains the following features:

1. Definitions are boxed.
2. Steps for constructing bar graphs, performing statistical calculations, and conducting statistical tests are listed and boxed for each procedure.
3. Key words, which must be added to a student's vocabulary, are listed (and boxed) at the end of each chapter.
4. Warnings, indicating situations where a student might misuse a statistical technique, are presented in boxed form. The student is directed to specific alternative methods.
5. The basic concepts of probability and their relation to statistical inference are presented in an easy-to-understand manner and are developed around the game of blackjack. Problem solving for the sake of problem solving is avoided.
6. The use of computer program packages is introduced in the presentation of the analysis of variance (Chapter 11) and multiple regression analysis (Chapter 13). The computer printouts for three different program packages, Minitab, SAS, and SPSS, are presented for the analyses of identical sets of data.
7. Case studies that detail specific current events in business are used at the end of each chapter to pose questions for the student. These case studies, extracted from business news articles and journals, demonstrate to the student the relevance of statistics to the solution of current practical business problems.
8. The data sets can be used by the instructor to illustrate the concept of a sampling distribution and the concepts of estimation and tests of hypotheses.
9. The data sets can be entered into computer storage and can be accessed by students for sampling and statistical inference. The student can then access the data sets for the demonstration of statistical concepts and for realistic statistical exercises.

In addition to the features described above, the text is accompanied by the following supplementary material:

1. A student's exercise solutions manual that presents the solutions for half the exercises contained in the text.
2. A study guide for the student which will provide additional worked examples.

I wish to acknowledge the many individuals who provided their invaluable assistance to this project. Their efforts are much appreciated. In particular, I thank the following for providing helpful suggestions and advice on the writing of the manuscript: John S. Bowdidge, Southwest Missouri State University; John Cameron, Rockhurst College; Geoffrey B. Holmewood, Hudson Valley Community College; Thomas B. Laase, University of Southern Colorado; James T. McClave, University of Florida; William Mendenhall, University of Florida; Susan Reiland, North Carolina State University; and John B. Rushton, Metropolitan State College. Susan Reiland deserves special recognition for her excellent line-by-line reviews, during both the writing and the production of the text. I am very grateful to Info Tech, Inc., for providing data on the 1978 real estate sales, and to Venus Wong, who patiently spent long hours at the supermarket recording customer checkout times. Also, I thank Robert Fordham and Jim Yucha for preparing answers to the exercises, and I thank the excellent group of typists, June Hubert, Diane Lamich, Cecily Noble, Carol Rozear, and in particular, Brenda Dobson, who had the added responsibility of proofreading, correcting, and organizing the typed copy. Phyllis Niklas took great care in supervising the production of the text, and her work is much appreciated.

Finally, I owe very special thanks to William Mendenhall and James T. McClave who, together, suggested the concept of this text and then provided me with the opportunity to write the manuscript. Without their guidance and encouragement this text would never have been completed.

One   **Introduction**

Have you ever thought of the difficulty that you would encounter if you tried to audit the inventory of a large hospital? The inventory shown in computerized records will be larger than the actual inventory because of poor record keeping, loss or theft of supplies, etc. Think of the massive task of actually counting and recording the values of all items in supply, and the attendant errors associated with that procedure. Then think of sampling! How you can use sampling and the science of statistics to solve this and other problems is the subject of this chapter and this text. The hospital inventory problem is discussed in greater detail in Case Study 1.3.

Contents:

1.1   What Is Statistics?

You know from contact with the news media and with business literature that statistics involves numbers, data description, and sampling. Consequently, a good way to develop an understanding of the word *statistics* is to examine a real data set and the phenomenon which it purports to describe. We have chosen data that should be of interest to both business and nonbusiness majors, namely data concerned with the appraisal of the value of real or personal property (used automobiles, diamonds, real estate, corporate stock, etc.).

For our purposes, we have chosen to examine the appraised values of residential properties in a specific mid-Florida city. Appendix A gives the location, appraised values, and sale prices for all 2,862 residential properties sold in 1978 in the city.* Sketches of the city are shown in Figures 1.1 and 1.2.

Examining Figure 1.1, you will see that the area encompassing the city and its surroundings is divided into large squares, each square identified by a particular Range number (which varies in the horizontal direction) and Township number (which varies in the vertical direction). Each of these squares is subdivided into 36 Sections, numbered as shown in the inset.

Figure 1.2 is an enlargement of the four squares of Figure 1.1 that contain the business and residential sections of the city. It also shows the locations of the industrial parks and shopping malls. Although there are many different residential neighborhoods in the city, we have identified six that are located on the sketch by the symbols A, B, C, D, E, and F. Within a given neighborhood, the properties are similar in age, construction, and price and the residents possess similar sociological characteristics. Neighborhoods A, B, and F contain properties that tend to be higher priced, and the residents are older and established in business, government, or the professions. Neighborhoods C, D, and E contain smaller, lower priced homes, many with younger residents who are just embarking on their careers. Even though A, B, and F are similar, they contain some differences, as do neighborhoods C, D, and E.

Each row of the data set, Appendix A, pertains to a single 1978 residential sale and gives the following information:

1. Location of the Property: The three values in this column give the Township, Range, and Section for the property.
2. Appraised Value of the Land
3. Appraised Value of Improvements
4. Sale Price of the Property
5. Ratio of Sale Price to the Total of Appraised Value of Land and Improvements

The appraised land and improvement values and the sale prices for all residential properties sold in 1978 in the six neighborhoods A, B, C, . . . , F were extracted from the data set, Appendix A, and are given in Appendix B. This will enable you to compare appraised values and sale prices for six different neighborhoods in the city.

---

*The data were obtained from the city tax assessor.

Location of sections within
a Range-Township block

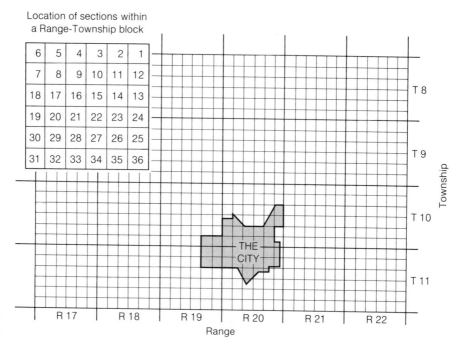

FIGURE 1.1
Location of the City and
Surrounding Areas

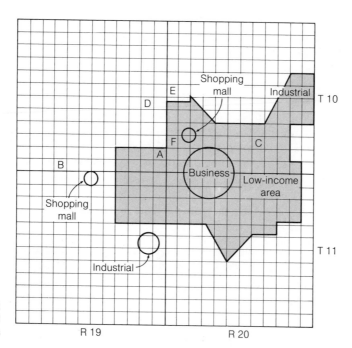

FIGURE 1.2
The City (Shaded) and
Adjacent Areas

What practical phenomena are characterized by the data sets, Appendices A and B? The set of residential property sale prices, Column 7 of Appendix A, characterizes the values of residential properties in the city—at least of those that were sold. The complete set of ratios of sale price to appraised value, Column 8, characterizes the ability of the tax assessor to properly appraise city property values for purposes of taxation. Particularly, for a 100% assessment, the ratios should be near 1. Each of the six data sets, Appendix B, characterizes the sale prices of residential properties sold in one of the six neighborhoods. Thus, we have given three of many possible phenomena that the data sets characterize.

When you examine a data set in the course of your business, you will be doing so because the data characterize some phenomenon of interest to you. The data set which is the target of your interest is called a **population.** Notice that a population does not refer to people, it refers to a collection of data.

DEFINITION 1.1

A **population** is a collection (or set) of data that describes some phenomenon of interest to you.

The objects upon which measurements are made are called **experimental units.** For example, each property sold in 1978 is an experimental unit. Measurements taken on this collection of units produced the populations of Appendices A and B. It is not uncommon for people to use the word *population* in two ways: to characterize the collection of experimental units upon which the measurements are made, as well as to characterize the data set itself. The particular meaning attached to the word will be clear from the context in which it is used.

Now that you know what we mean by the word *population*, let us return to the notion that a population characterizes some phenomenon of interest to you. Who defines a population? You do! Consequently, if you are interested in some phenomenon, you must be sure that your population really does characterize it. For example, if you take the complete set of all ratios of sale price to total appraised value as a measure of the city property appraiser's ability to perform his or her job, you should be certain that this data set does, in fact, characterize the appraiser's ability. To illustrate:

EXAMPLE 1.1   Do the sale price data, Appendix A, characterize residential property values in the city in 1978?

Solution   To a certain extent they do characterize 1978 residential property values in the city, but they do not do so completely. To properly characterize this phenomenon, we would need to know the values* of all properties in the city, not only those that were sold but also those that were not offered for sale. This population, i.e., the set of all sale

---

*We will assume for the purposes of this discussion that the sale price of a property is equal to the property's value.

prices that would have been generated if every property in the city had been sold, would (in our opinion) characterize the 1978 residential property values in the city.

EXAMPLE 1.2 Refer to Example 1.1. Why is the set of residential sale prices, Appendix A, inadequate for characterizing 1978 residential property values in the city?

Solution The data set, Appendix A, represents only a subset of the residential property values in the city. Thus, it represents a *sample* selected from the totality of all property values. If this sample possesses characteristics that are very close to those of the complete set of all property values, you might be safe in using it to characterize residential property values. But this situation is unlikely. The properties that sell in any one year will be those whose owners tend to be mobile. Not all types of property may appear in your sample. For example, the owners of the most expensive properties may be older and less mobile. Consequently, the distribution of sale prices in the sample may vary substantially from the distribution of all residential property values.

DEFINITION 1.2

A *sample* is a subset of data selected from a population.

EXAMPLE 1.3 Can the data set, Appendix A, be either a sample or a population?

Solution Remember, you are the one who defines the population. Presumably, it is a data set that characterizes some phenomenon of interest to you. If you are interested only in the sale prices of properties sold in the city in 1978, then the data set, Appendix A, characterizes this phenomenon and it would be the population. In contrast, if you are interested in characterizing the property values of all residential properties in the city in 1978, then, as explained in Example 1.2, the data set, Appendix A, is a sample selected from the complete set of all property values in the city. Whether a data set is a sample or a population depends upon the phenomenon that you wish to characterize.

EXAMPLE 1.4 Research* by faculty at the Virginia Polytechnic Institute suggests that the 2-drink lunch decreases the output of laborers. Particularly, a team of researchers found that a normal person needs about 19% more time to accomplish a relatively simple task if the person's blood alcohol level reaches 0.07%. This level is produced (approximately) by two mixed drinks or two 16-ounce glasses of beer. The sample data produced by this research included the times required for a group of persons to assemble a common water tap under two conditions, at alcohol blood levels of 0% and 0.07%, and the percentage increase in the length of assembly time.

    a. Describe the population of data from which this sample was selected.
    b. What phenomenon does the population characterize?

---

*Reported in the Orlando *Sentinel Star*, May 18, 1980.

Solution   **α.**   The sample consists of a set of percentages corresponding to the increase in the lengths of times for a group of volunteer persons to assemble a common water tap. Consequently, the population is conceptual (existing in our minds), and consists of the percentage increases for the collection of all workers similar to those who volunteered for the study and who could be required to assemble a common water tap.

        b.   The population, part a, characterizes the percentage increase in time to assemble a common water tap for assemblers with physical abilities (coordination, strength, etc.) and experience comparable to the volunteers employed in the researchers' experiment and who have had a 2-drink lunch. Most of us would like to extrapolate and imagine that the population characterizes the percentage increases in assembly time for any and all assembly workers and for any and all assembly operations. This, of course, is not the case, but it is easy to believe that similar experiments with almost any type of worker in any assembly operation would produce data that are similar to that obtained by the researchers at the Virginia Polytechnic Institute. The average percentage increase in assembly times induced by an alcohol level of 0.07% in the blood of assembly workers may vary, depending on the type of worker and on the assembly operation, but we would expect the percentage change in assembly time to be positive and sufficiently large to affect worker productivity.

1.2   How Can Statistics Be of Value in Business?

The data sets, Appendices A and B, and the preceding discussion identify the two ways that the body of knowledge called *statistics* can be of value to managers and others involved in business operations. We will assume that you are interested in some phenomenon associated with some aspect of a business and that you have identified a population of data that characterizes this phenomenon. Then statistics can be of value in two ways:

1.   If you have the population in hand, i.e., if you have every measurement in the population, then statistical methodology can help you describe this typically large set of data. That is, we will find graphical and numerical ways to make sense out of a large mass of data. The branch of statistics devoted to this application is called *descriptive statistics.*

DEFINITION 1.3

The branch of statistics devoted to the summarization and description of data sets is called *descriptive statistics.*

---

2.   It may be too expensive to obtain every measurement in the population or, as in the case of the residential property values, it may be impossible to acquire them.

Then we will wish to select a sample of data from the population and use the sample to infer the nature of the population.

DEFINITION 1.4

The branch of statistics concerned with using sample data to make an inference about a population of data is called *inferential statistics.*

A careful analysis of most data sets will reveal that they are samples from larger data sets that are really the object of our interest. Consequently, most applications of statistics involve sampling and using the information in the samples to make inferences about the sampled population. To illustrate, if the residential sale prices, Appendix A, really comprise a representative* sample of all 1978 residential property values in the city, then we could use the characteristics of the sample to infer the characteristics of the population. The "average" sale price in the sample would be an estimate of the "average" of all 1978 city property values. The spread of the sample sale prices would be a rough indicator of the dispersion of the population property values.

EXAMPLE 1.5 Would the "average" of the sample sale prices equal the "average" of all city property values?

Solution The answer is "not likely," and this pinpoints the major contribution of statistics to real estate appraisers, managers, or other business personnel. *Anyone can examine a sample and calculate an estimate of some population characteristic. But statistical methodology enables you to go one step further. When the sample is selected in a specified way from the population, statistical methodology will enable you to say how accurate your sample estimate will be.* Statistical methodology not only tells you how to make an inference about a population based upon sample data, but it also tells you how reliable your inference will be.

To illustrate the value of possessing a measure of reliability for a particular inference, consider the following situation: Suppose that you would like to know the value of a particular piece of residential property. You can hire only one of two appraisers. Both appraisers are supposed to be "good," but the properties of Appraiser #2's appraisal error are known—records show that this appraiser is within $2,000 of the sale price 99% of the time. You have no information on the appraisal errors of Appraiser #1. Which appraiser would you choose? We think that you would choose Appraiser #2 because you would attach a very real value to knowing how much reliability you could place in the appraisal. The appraisals of Appraiser #1 may be better or worse than those of Appraiser #2, i.e., they might fall within $500 of the

---

*We use this term loosely. We will have more to say about sampling in later discussions.

sale prices of appraised properties—or they might fall within $5,000—but, either way, it is a great disadvantage not to know how large this error is apt to be. This example points to the major contribution of statistics, one that a nonstatistical method does not possess: statistical methods provide measures of reliability for each inference obtained from a sample.

The key facts to remember in this section are:

THE OBJECTIVE OF STATISTICS:

1. To describe data sets
2. To use sample data to make inferences about a population

THE MAJOR CONTRIBUTION OF STATISTICS:

Provides a measure of reliability for every statistical inference

---

1.3 Summary

This chapter identified the types of problems for which statistical procedures are useful, describing data sets and using sample data to make inferences about a sampled population. Basic to the application of these techniques is the identification of a population of data that truly characterizes the phenomenon of interest to you.

Most statistical problems involve sampling and using a sample to make inferences about the sampled population. For example, the ratios of sale prices to total appraised values for the six neighborhoods, Appendix B, could be viewed as samples of the ratios of property values to appraised values for their respective neighborhoods. Do these sample values suggest a difference in the distributions of the ratios of property value to appraised value among the six neighborhoods? Statistical methods (to be covered later) will help us answer this question and will provide us with a measure of reliability for our decision.

The remainder of this course will examine some basic statistical procedures for describing data sets and giving them meaning. More important, we will learn how to use sample data to infer the nature of the sampled population and to do so with a known degree of reliability.

KEY WORDS

Population	Inference
Sample	Reliability

EXERCISES **1.1** Appendix D contains the checkout times for 500 grocery shoppers at each of two supermarkets, supermarket A and supermarket B. *Customer checkout time* is defined here as the total length of time required for service personnel to check the prices of the customer's food items, total the prices, accept payment, and return change.

The checking of food items at supermarket A is conducted in the usual manner; the cashier searches for the price marked on each item and manually punches in the price on the cash register. Supermarket B, however, employs automated checkers. With automated checkers, the cashier need only brush the item across a scanning window located on the counter. A laser beam is then activated which reads the price code several times, verifies its accuracy, and transmits the price to the checkstand to be printed on the receipt tape. Thus, the data of Appendix D provide us with an opportunity to compare customer checkout times at supermarkets using manual and automated checkers.

a. Suppose that you were to view the two sets of customer checkout times as two different populations. What phenomenon do the supermarket A checkout times characterize? The supermarket B checkout times?

b. Do the data sets actually represent the populations you described in part a, or do they represent samples selected, respectively, from the totality of all customer checkout times at supermarket A and supermarket B? Explain.

c. Suppose that you were to use the average of the 500 supermarket A customer checkout times to estimate the average checkout time of all customers who shop at supermarket A. Would the sample average equal the average for the population? Explain.

1.2 A real estate appraiser is in the process of appraising the total value of all 1-, 2-, or 3-bedroom apartments located within a city's limits. Since a major university (enrollment: 30,000 students) is situated near the center of the city, the appraiser will base the appraisal partly upon the proportion of the city's 1-, 2-, or 3-bedroom apartments which currently house university students. In order to estimate this proportion, the appraiser randomly selects fifty 1-, 2-, or 3-bedroom apartments located within the city and counts the number of these apartments which currently house university students.

a. What is the population of interest to the real estate appraiser?

b. What phenomenon does the population characterize?

c. Describe the sample in this problem.

d. Suppose that 31 of the 50 randomly selected apartments currently house university students. Thus, the appraiser estimates that 62% of all 1-, 2-, or 3-bedroom apartments within the city house university students. Do you believe that this estimate is equal to the proportion for the entire population? Explain.

1.3 One of the keys to operating and expanding a successful restaurant chain is the careful selection of a location for a new franchise. A fast-food chain which specializes in fried chicken is considering locating a franchise in a large residential neighborhood. However, the final decision will be made after an examination of the annual incomes of households in the neighborhood.

a.   Suppose that you view the set of annual incomes of households in the residential neighborhood as a population. What phenomenon do they characterize?

b.   The fast-food chain has determined that the final decision on locating a franchise in the neighborhood can be properly made by examining the annual incomes of 30 households randomly selected from all the households in the neighborhood. What does the set of these 30 annual incomes represent?

c.   Suppose that the fast-food chain will use the average annual income of the 30 households to estimate the average of the population. Will the average of the 30 households equal the population average? Explain.

1.4   An assembly line which produces automobile gear shifts is considered to be operating successfully if less than 1% of the gear shifts manufactured per day are defective. If 1% or more of the gear shifts are defective, the line must be shut down and proper adjustments made. Since a halt in the production process for even as little as 5 minutes could cost the manufacturer millions of dollars in lost revenue, the line should be shut down only if the true proportion of defective gear shifts produced is 1% or larger. However, to check every gear shift as it comes off the line each day would be not only time-consuming, but also very costly. As a solution, quality control inspectors randomly select 100 gear shifts from a day's production and test for defects. The decision on whether to shut down the line is then made according to the proportion of defectives in the 100 gear shifts.

a.   Describe the population of interest to the manufacturer of the automobile gear shifts. What phenomenon does it characterize?

b.   Describe the sample.

c.   If the sample proportion of defectives is larger than 1%, is it necessarily true that the actual proportion of defective gear shifts produced per day is larger than 1%? Explain.

1.5   A national magazine is interested in comparing the amount of money kept in savings accounts by people residing in the financially booming city of Houston with the amount kept in similar accounts by people residing in the financially troubled city of Cleveland. With the permission of the proper authorities, the magazine was able to obtain 150 savings account numbers in various Houston banks and 150 savings account numbers in various Cleveland banks, along with the respective amount deposited in each account. This information will be used to estimate the difference between the average amount kept in Houston savings accounts and the average amount kept in Cleveland savings accounts.

a.   Consider the totality of Houston savings account deposits and the totality of Cleveland savings account deposits as two distinct populations. What phenomena do the populations characterize?

b.   Would you expect the samples of 150 savings account deposits in each city to adequately represent the corresponding population you described in part a?

c.   Explain how the national magazine could use the sample information to estimate the difference in the averages of the two populations described in part a.

1.6   A successful discount clothing store, in business for 30 years, must order Levi's blue jeans from the manufacturer one month in advance. In order to avoid large losses, the store needs to be able to predict the monthly demand for blue jeans for each month of the year. Suppose that the store has ready access to the monthly sales records (i.e., the number of blue jeans sold by the store during each month) for the past 10 years. This information will be used to project monthly demand.

a. If the discount store views the monthly blue jean sales data over the past 10 years as a population, what phenomenon does it characterize?

b. If the discount store views the monthly blue jean sales data over the past 10 years as a sample selected from a population, describe the population.

c. Suggest a way in which the discount clothing store could use the monthly sales records over the past 10 years to project monthly blue jean demand.

1.7 The high cost of fuel oil and the diversion of low-cost natural gas from power plants to home heating are often cited as the principal reasons for the record high January 1981 utility bills registered across the country.* To partially ease the burden of payment on the customer, many utility companies allowed their customers to pay only half of January's bill initially, and then to pay the balance over the next 90 days. For example, customers of Gainesville (Florida) Regional Utilities whose January 1981 electric bills were twice as much or more than in January 1980 were declared eligible for a deferred-payment plan. Suppose that the director of utilities in a city which had a January 1981 deferred-payment plan wished to estimate the true proportion of the utility's residential customers who qualified for the plan (i.e., whose January 1981 bill was at least two times as much as their January 1980 bill). To obtain this estimate, the director randomly sampled 200 customers, compared their January 1980 and January 1981 utility bills, and recorded the number who qualified for the deferred-payment plan.

a. What is the population of interest to the director?

b. What is the sample?

c. What type of inference does the director desire to make?

1.8 Refer to Exercise 1.7. Suppose that the utility director also wished to estimate the difference between the average January 1981 utility bill and the average January 1980 utility bill of the utility's customers. Then the problem is to compare the averages of two populations, where the first population, say population A, is the collection of all January 1981 utility bill amounts issued by the utility, and the second population, say population B, is the collection of all January 1980 utility bill amounts issued by the utility.

a. What phenomenon does population A characterize?

b. What phenomenon does population B characterize?

c. Suggest how the director could use the information collected on the January utility bills for the sample of 200 customers to estimate the difference between the averages of the populations.

d. Would you expect the difference in the sample averages to equal the difference in the population averages? Explain.

---

*Gainesville *Sun*, February 4, 1981.

1.9 Manufacturers of low-tar, low-nicotine cigarettes claim that smokers who switch to their brands will be better off physically than those who continue to smoke regular cigarettes. However, in his annual survey of smoking, the U.S. Surgeon General reported* that low-yield brands reduce the risk of developing lung cancer only slightly, and reduce the risk of heart disease, emphysema, and bronchitis not at all. In addition, some of the additives (e.g., cocoa) which manufacturers have been using to enhance the weaker flavor of the low-tar, low-nicotine cigarettes turn into cancer-causing substances when burned. In view of these facts, let us suppose that a manufacturer of low-yield cigarettes is interested in determining the fraction of smokers of low-tar, low-nicotine cigarettes who are aware of the U.S. Surgeon General's report.

a. What is the population of interest to the manufacturer?

b. What phenomenon does it characterize?

c. Do you believe that the manufacturer could actually determine the true fraction of smokers of low-yield cigarettes who are aware of the report? Explain.

d. Suggest a way in which the manufacturer could obtain an estimate of the true fraction.

1.10 Suppose that you are interested in comparing the annual salaries of one-company insurance agents and independent insurance agents. A *one-company agent* is an insurance agent who represents and offers the policies of the insurance company from which he or she draws a salary. An *independent agent* is self-employed, independent, and licensed by a particular state to provide insurance services to the public. The independent agent is free to represent several insurance companies.

a. What phenomenon does the collection of annual salaries for all one-company insurance agents characterize?

b. What phenomenon does the collection of annual salaries for all independent agents characterize?

c. Do each of the collections of annual salaries described in parts a and b constitute a population?

d. Explain how samples collected from each population could be used to obtain an estimate of the difference in average annual salaries of the two groups of insurance agents.

e. Do you believe the estimate of part d will equal the difference between the population averages? Explain.

CASE STUDY 1.1
**The Standard &
Poor's Stock
Index**

The Standard & Poor's Corporation has been in business since 1860 and is now a major publisher of business and financial information on publicly held U.S. and foreign corporations and municipalities. In 1966, all of Standard & Poor's common stock was acquired by McGraw-Hill, a major publishing company, and currently Standard & Poor's operates as a wholly owned subsidiary of this company.

One of the many services provided by Standard & Poor's over the years has been the assignment of credit ratings to corporate bonds, municipal bonds, and

Time, January 26, 1981.

commercial paper. These credit ratings provide investors with an informative and meaningful symbol of the credit quality of a possibly unknown issuer (of commercial paper, bonds, etc.). However, ratings are of value only as long as they are credible, and it is this credibility as a rating agency that Standard & Poor's has strived to maintain year after year.

Appendix C contains the daily indices (closing prices) and daily changes in closing prices of Standard & Poor's common stock for the years 1975 to 1979. In one sense, we can think of this data as representing a measure of Standard & Poor's credibility as a rating agency over the 5 years. For example, suppose that at some point during these 5 years, Standard & Poor's began to function as an investment banker or financial advisor (this did not actually occur). Performance of such a role would ultimately impair Standard & Poor's credibility by leaving the corporation open to a charge of rating the issues it structures. We would expect this credibility loss to be reflected by a severe drop in the stock's daily closing prices. Of course, there are many other economic and market variables which influence the movement of the stock market, and these certainly should not be ignored when examining the changes in daily closing prices. (For instance, the economy was in the final stages of an economic upswing at the end of 1978, inflation was rising, and the prime interest rate was 11.5%. In contrast, the economy was on the brink of a steep recession at year-end 1979, the inflation rate had increased greatly, and the prime interest rate had moved to 15.3%.)

a. Suppose that you were to view the totality of daily closing prices in Appendix C as a population. What phenomenon do they characterize?

b. Suppose that you were to view the totality of the daily changes in closing prices in Appendix C as a population. When phenomenon do they characterize?

c. Suppose that you were to view each year's daily closing prices as a distinct population. What phenomena do the five populations characterize?

d. Select ten 1979 daily closing prices from the listing, Appendix C. Would this constitute a sample from the population you described in part c? Explain.

e. Suppose that you were to use the average value of the ten daily closing prices (part d) to estimate the average daily closing price of Standard & Poor's stock during the year 1979. Would the sample average equal the average for the population? Explain.

CASE STUDY 1.2
Cruising: How
Foresters
Estimate Timber
Weights

Paper and lumber companies pay for timber by the weight per truckload of 16-foot logs. Consequently, an investor in forest land needs to estimate the total weight of logs that can be produced by a property. This is done by "cruising the property" and counting the total number* of trees capable of producing 16-foot logs. A random sample of trees (usually 10% of the total number) is selected from this group and the diameter at chest height and the number of logs per tree (a visual guess) are recorded for each. A forester can then use the diameter and logs-per-tree measurements to calculate the *approximate* weight for each tree.

---

*This number is usually close to, but not actually equal to, the exact number of trees. For the purposes of this discussion, we will assume that it is an exact count.

For use in this and later case studies, we were able to obtain data of this type for an actual 40-acre tract of short-leaf pine timber located in Western Arkansas.* Twenty ⅕-acre plots were sampled (i.e., a total of 4 acres were "cruised"), and the chest height diameters and logs per tree were measured for each of the 117 trees on these plots. The trees were then grouped according to diameter (10, 11, . . . , 15, or 16 inches), and an estimate of the weight per tree in each diameter group (based on the average of the logs-per-tree measurements) was calculated. The "grouped" data are reported in Table 1.1.

TABLE 1.1
Diameters and Estimated Weights for a Sample of 117 Short-Leaf Pine Trees

DIAMETER AT CHEST HEIGHT (INCHES)	ESTIMATED (AVERAGE) WEIGHT IN POUNDS PER TREE	NUMBER OF TREES
10	580	38
11	750	34
12	1,100	21
13	1,800	15
14	2,000	5
15	2,660	3
16	3,000	1
		117

a. Describe the population of measurements from which the sample of tree-weight measurements was selected.

b. What phenomenon does the population, part a, characterize?

c. What will the average of the sample of tree weights estimate? Do you think that this estimate will equal or be close to the quantity that you have estimated? Explain.

CASE STUDY 1.3
Auditing Hospital Inventory

Consider the problem of auditing the inventory of a large hospital and assessing the value on hand of the very large number of items that are in daily use. Some items, such as drugs, adhesive tape, bandages, etc., are expended daily in large amounts while others, such as stethoscopes, scissors, typewriters, etc., are lost due to wear, damage, or theft.

Theoretically, auditing this inventory might appear to be easy. Thus, the hospital records (usually stored in a computer) should contain the number and dollar value on hand for each of this large number of items stocked by the hospital. In practice, however, the auditing problem is not so easy because the actual number and dollar value on hand for any given item will usually be less than the numbers shown in the hospital records. This discrepancy may be due to the failure to record the use or destruction of an item or, for many small disposable items (tape, gauze, etc.), it may be due to theft.

An auditor envisions two populations of data. The first population, population A (stored in the computer), is the collection of the recorded dollar values of all items held

*Timber data and information courtesy of Delton F. Price, Fort Smith, Arkansas.

in inventory. The second population, population B (whose values are unknown to us), is the collection of the actual dollar values of all items held in inventory.

a. What phenomenon does population A characterize?

b. What phenomenon does population B characterize?

c. How is the goal of the auditor related to the two populations?

d. Suppose an auditor decided to base an estimate of the total value of inventory on a complete count of the number on hand and dollar value for each and all of the items listed in the hospital records. Aside from the fact that this procedure would be very costly, explain why the total dollar value of all items in inventory obtained by this method would be subject to error, i.e., differ from the true dollar value of the inventory.

e. Suppose that you were to conduct a complete count and calculate the dollar value on hand for a sample of 50 items selected from the complete list of items held in inventory. Can you suggest a way to use these sample values to obtain an estimate of the total value of the inventory on hand? Explain why this estimate would be subject to error.

REFERENCES   *Careers in Statistics*, American Statistical Association and the Institute of Mathematical Statistics, 1974.

Tanur, J. M., Mosteller, F., Kruskal, W. H., Link, R. F., Pieters, R. S., & Rising, G. R. *Statistics: A guide to the unknown*. San Francisco: Holden-Day, 1978.

Two

Graphical Methods for Describing Data Sets

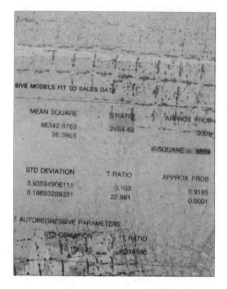

Why do women seem to be facing an uphill battle for success (and attendant promotion) as industrial buyers? A recent article in *Purchasing* magazine (October 5, 1976) sought an answer to this question by surveying the opinions of 1,000 buyers. A graphical method for summarizing and making sense of this mass of data is the topic of Case Study 2.1. Graphical methods that rapidly convey the information contained in a data set are discussed in this chapter.

Contents:

2.1 The Objective of Data Description

The objective of data description is to summarize the characteristics of a data set. Ultimately, we wish to make the data set more comprehensible and meaningful. In this chapter we will show you how to construct charts and graphs that convey the nature of a data set. The procedure that we will use to accomplish this objective will depend upon the type of data that you wish to describe.

2.2 Types of Data

You will recall that Appendix B contains the sale and appraisal data for residential property sold in 1978 in six neighborhoods of a mid-sized Florida city. If you examine Appendix B, you will see that it contains two different types of data. To illustrate, we show in Table 2.1 data pertaining to each of 10 properties randomly selected from Appendix B.

TABLE 2.1

A Sample of Data from Appendix B

OBSERVATION NUMBER	APPRAISED LAND VALUE	APPRAISED IMPROVEMENT VALUE	SALE PRICE	NEIGHBORHOOD
533	4,300	28,480	40,900	D
147	3,400	14,380	28,200	C
649	6,000	17,090	33,000	E
337	4,100	20,020	34,900	D
488	5,400	33,060	49,900	D
62	5,500	35,660	57,000	B
862	8,100	47,710	66,900	F
31	6,500	40,950	55,600	A
129	3,540	18,430	36,800	C
593	3,490	19,100	38,000	E

The first three pieces of information (Appraised land value, Appraised improvement value, Sale price) represent *quantitative data,* data which take values on a numerical scale. The fourth (Neighborhood) is an example of *qualitative data.* Qualitative data are those which take values that are nonnumerical; they can only be classified. For example, the observation that property #533 is in neighborhood D is a qualitative observation. We can classify each property according to neighborhood, but we cannot represent a neighborhood as a numerical quantity.

DEFINITION 2.1

Quantitative data are observations measured on a numerical scale.

> **DEFINITION 2.2**
>
> Nonnumerical data which can only be classified into one of a group of categories are said to be *qualitative.*

The four columns of data, Table 2.1, represent measurements (or observations) on variables. For example, appraised land value varies from property to property. It is called a *quantitative variable* because the data obtained by observing appraised land value are quantitative. For similar reasons, neighborhood may vary from property to property and is called a *qualitative variable.*

EXAMPLE 2.1 Suppose that the following types of data were available for the properties, Appendix A. Classify the data according to whether they are quantitative or qualitative.

a. Number of bathrooms per residence
b. Type of roofing on a residence
c. Square feet of floor space per residence

Solution Number of bathrooms and square feet of floor space are measured on a numerical scale. Typical values for the number of bathrooms would be 1, 1½, 2, 2½, 3, etc. Similarly, square feet of floor space could take any one of a very large number of values. Consequently, both of these are quantitative data sets. In contrast, type of roofing (wooden shingles, asphalt, tin, etc.) cannot be measured on a quantitative scale; it can only be classified. Consequently, data on type of roofing are qualitative.

EXAMPLE 2.2 State whether the following variables are quantitative or qualitative.

a. Prime interest rate
b. Annual sales of a corporation
c. Foreman in charge of a production shift in a manufacturing plant
d. Number of accounting errors per page in a ledger
e. Person's race

Solution The variables a, b, and d are quantitative because the values that the variables can assume are numerical, i.e., they are measured on a numerical scale. In contrast, the two variables c and e are qualitative. For example, suppose that the manufacturing plant in c operates on three shifts, using a different foreman for each shift. Thus, the foreman varies from shift to shift, but the values that the variable Foreman in charge can assume cannot be quantified. We can identify a foreman only by giving his or her name. Similarly, Person's race may vary from person to person, but the values that this variable can assume cannot be quantified. We can identify people as Caucasian, black, etc., but cannot locate these "values" on a numerical scale.

EXAMPLE 2.3 New issues (stocks for newly created companies) were in great demand in the 1960's. A recent Securities and Exchange Commission (SEC) study of 500 randomly selected issues that went public in 1961 and 1962 revealed that only 20% had shown profitability up to the time of the study, and that 43% had gone bankrupt.* Clearly, the purpose of this study was to examine the current financial conditions of all (number unknown) of the new companies which went public during 1961 and 1962. The experimental units, the objects upon which observations were taken, are the individual companies. Suppose that for each company we record whether it showed profitability by 1980. Describe the variable observed for each company and explain whether it is a quantitative variable.

Solution   One way to view this situation is to note that the variable that is being measured, Profitability, can assume one of two conditions. A company can either be profitable or it cannot. From this point of view, profitability is a qualitative variable.

A second way to view the response would be to convert the qualitative response into a meaningful quantitative response by assigning a number, 1, to all companies that are profitable and a 0 to those that are not. Then the sum of all of the 0's and 1's in the sample will equal the total number of companies in the sample that showed profitability by 1980. (For example, if there were 5 companies in the sample with 2 that did and 3 that did not show profitability by 1980, then the sample data would be 1, 1, 0, 0, 0. The sum of these observations would equal 2, the number of companies in the sample that showed profitability by 1980.) Qualitative variables cannot always be converted into meaningful quantitative variables, but it can be done (as shown above) when the number of categories into which the observations fall is equal to 2. Then for a (0, 1) assignment to the two categories, the sum of the observations will always equal the number of observations falling in the "1" category.

EXERCISES   2.1   Examine the following variables and state whether they are quantitative or qualitative.
a.   Number of acres in a plot of land
b.   Zoning for a property
c.   Type of residential water heating system

2.2   Futures (commodities) markets are often used in forecasting business activity. State whether each of the market variables given below is quantitative or qualitative.
a.   Level of yield on interest rate futures
b.   Price of a bushel of wheat, deliverable in May
c.   Month during which gold futures were most actively traded

2.3   List the variables that you consider before you purchase a new automobile. State whether each is qualitative or quantitative.

2.4   Classify the following business variables as either quantitative or qualitative.
a.   Political affiliation of a chief executive whose firm is listed in the *Fortune* 500
b.   Geographical region with the highest percentage of single-family housing starts in the United States

*Source: *Forbes,* October 27, 1980. p. 202.

c. Gas mileage attained by an automobile powered by alcohol
d. Number of machine breakdowns per day at a car company
e. Store department where the most shoplifting occurs

2.5 List the variables that a bank or other lending institution considers before granting a loan. State whether each is qualitative or quantitative.

2.3 Graphical Descriptions of Qualitative Data

Bar graphs and *pie charts* are two of the most widely used graphical methods for describing qualitative data sets. Essentially, they show how many observations fall into each qualitative category.

The observations for the qualitative variable Foreman in charge in part c of Example 2.2 could fall into one of a number of categories or *classes.* If three foremen were used in the manufacturing operation, then the number of classes would equal 3. If the variable Foreman in charge was observed on a number of shifts, we would find that foreman #1 was in charge a certain number of times, say n_1 times, foreman #2, n_2 times, and foreman #3, n_3 times.

The summary information that we seek on qualitative variables is either the number of observations falling into each class or the proportion of the total number of observations falling into each class. Bar graphs can be constructed to show either of these types of information. Pie charts usually show the proportions or percentages of the total number of measurements falling into the classes.

EXAMPLE 2.4 Figure 2.1 (p. 22) is a bar graph that allows you to visually compare the frequencies of sales for the six neighborhoods of Appendix B. Notice that the figure contains a rectangle or *bar* for each neighborhood and that the height of a particular bar is proportional to the number of sales for its neighborhood. You can rapidly compare the sales for the six neighborhoods by visually comparing the heights of the bars.

DEFINITION 2.3

The *frequency* for a particular class is the number of observations falling in that class.

DEFINITION 2.4

The *relative frequency* for a particular class is equal to the class frequency divided by the total number of observations.

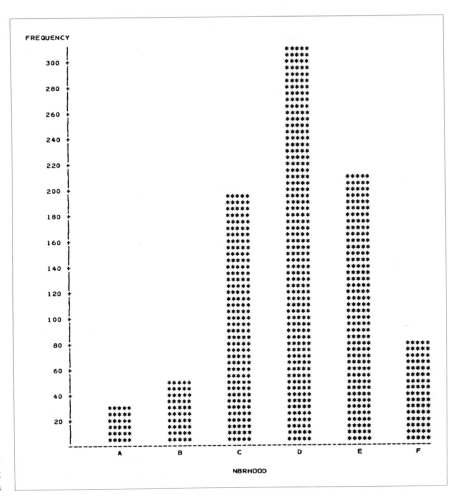

FIGURE 2.1
A Bar Graph Showing
Frequency of Sales for Six
Neighborhoods

The class frequencies, the number of sales for each of the six neighborhoods, are shown in Table 2.2. The class relative frequencies, obtained by dividing each class frequency by the total number of sales, 877, are also shown in Table 2.2.

TABLE 2.2
Frequencies and Relative
Frequencies of Sales for
the Six Neighborhoods of
Appendix B

NEIGHBORHOOD	CLASS FREQUENCY	RELATIVE FREQUENCY
A	31	.035
B	52	.059
.	.	.
.	.	.
.	.	.
F	80	.091
TOTAL	877	1.0

The bar graph that permits a comparison of sales can be constructed in several different ways. The heights of the bars can be measured in units of frequency (see Figure 2.1) or relative frequency (see Figure 2.2). It is also common to reverse the axes and display the bars in a horizontal fashion as shown in Figure 2.3.

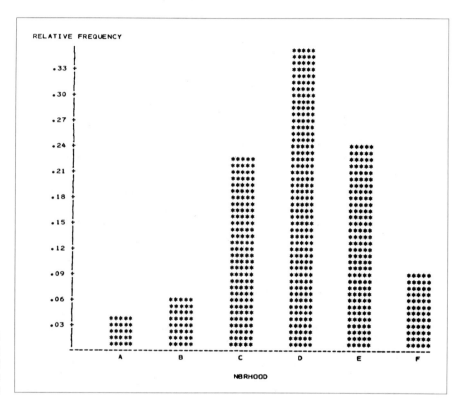

FIGURE 2.2
A Bar Graph Showing Relative Frequency of Sales for Six Neighborhoods

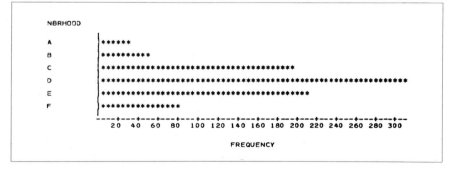

FIGURE 2.3
A Horizontal Bar Graph Showing Frequency of Sales for Six Neighborhoods

EXAMPLE 2.5   Figure 2.4 (p. 24) is a pie chart that conveys the same information as the bar chart in Figure 2.2. The total number of sales for the six neighborhoods, the pie, is split into six pieces. The size (angle) of the slice assigned to a neighborhood is proportional to the relative frequency for that neighborhood. It is common to show the percentage of measurements in each class on the pie chart as indicated.

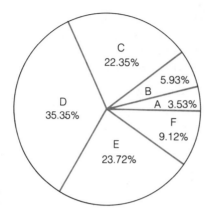

EXAMPLE 2.6 *Business Week* magazine (July 21, 1980) reported on the 1978 *Economic Impact Study of the Japanese Business Community in the U.S.* One facet of the study was designed to investigate the employment impact of Japanese firms in the U.S.; i.e., how many U.S. jobs are created directly or indirectly through Japanese firms. In 1978, Japanese firms in the U.S. had a total employment effect of 624,500. Figure 2.5 gives the breakdown in the type of employment (directly or indirectly) related to Japanese firms for the 624,500 jobs. Interpret the figure.

Solution Each of the 624,500 jobs created directly or indirectly by Japanese firms in the U.S. has been classified according to type of employment. Note that Type of employment is a qualitative variable. The five types of employment, or classes, are shown in the figure. The percentage given in each section of the pie (i.e., the percentage of the

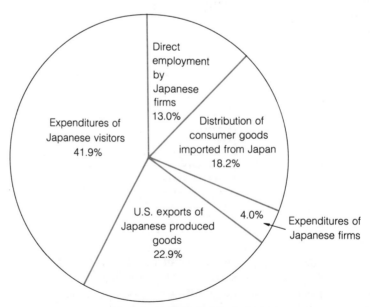

FIGURE 2.5
Pie Chart Showing the
1978 Proportion of
Japanese Firm Related
Jobs in Each Area of
Employment

measurements corresponding to each class) represents the proportion of the 624,500 jobs which fall under the corresponding type of employment. For example, 4.0% of the 624,500 jobs (i.e., 24,980 jobs) are related to expenditures of Japanese firms, while 22.9% (143,010 jobs) are related to U.S. exports of Japanese produced goods. An interesting observation is that 41.9% of the 1978 Japanese firm related jobs are related in some way to the expenditures of Japanese visitors in the U.S.

EXAMPLE 2.7 A recent advertisement claims that by virtue of their sensible design, unmatched safety record, and network of factory-owned service centers, the Cessna *Citation* has become the world's best-selling business jet. Cessna presents as evidence of the *Citation*'s leader status the bar graph shown in Figure 2.6. Discuss the information provided by the graph. Does it lend support to the Cessna claim?

FIGURE 2.6 Frequency of 1979 Worldwide Deliveries of Business Jets (Total number of deliveries = 400)

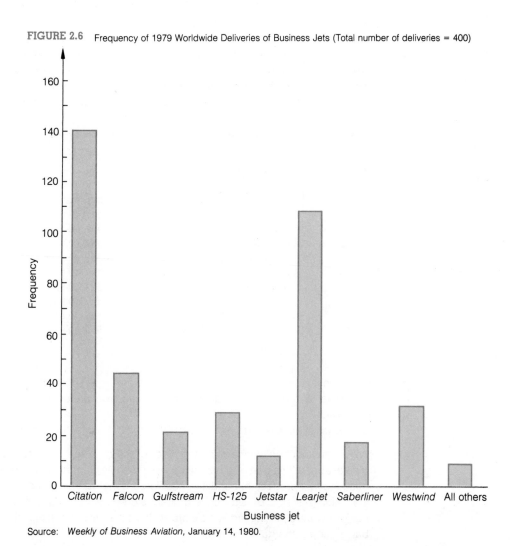

Source: *Weekly of Business Aviation,* January 14, 1980.

Solution   Each of the 400 business jets delivered throughout the world in 1979 has been
classified according to model type. The height of the vertical bar above each jet model
is proportional to the number of worldwide deliveries for that particular model. Since
the height of the bar above *Citation* is 140, we conclude that 140 of the 400 business
jets delivered worldwide in 1979 were Cessna *Citations*. Cessna's nearest competitor
is *Learjet,* whose 1979 worldwide deliveries were (approximately) 110. Figure 2.6 thus
supports Cessna *Citation*'s claim to be the world's best-selling business jet, at least in
1979.

EXERCISES   **2.6**   During August, 1980, hundreds of thousands of Poland's workers walked off the
job, protesting the country's poor labor conditions. One of their demands, eventually
negotiated with the government through the independent Polish labor union Solidarity,
was the reduction of a mandatory 6-day, 48-hour work week to a 5-day, 40-hour week.
In the United States, many corporations are considering instituting a 4-day, 40-hour
work week or a 3-day, 40-hour work week. Suppose that a company surveyed its
employees concerning the type of work week they would prefer: a 6-day, 48-hour work
week; a 5-day, 40-hour work week; a 4-day, 40-hour work week; or a 3-day, 40-hour
work week. Twenty-five employees responded as shown in the table.

EMPLOYEE	WORK WEEK	EMPLOYEE	WORK WEEK
1	5-day, 40-hour	14	4-day, 40-hour
2	5-day, 40-hour	15	6-day, 48-hour
3	3-day, 40-hour	16	4-day, 40-hour
4	6-day, 48-hour	17	5-day, 40-hour
5	4-day, 40-hour	18	5-day, 40-hour
6	4-day, 40-hour	19	5-day, 40-hour
7	5-day, 40-hour	20	4-day, 40-hour
8	3-day, 40-hour	21	3-day, 40-hour
9	6-day, 48-hour	22	5-day, 40-hour
10	5-day, 40-hour	23	3-day, 40-hour
11	4-day, 40-hour	24	4-day, 40-hour
12	5-day, 40-hour	25	5-day, 40-hour
13	4-day, 40-hour		

a.   Construct a bar graph for the data on work-week preferences.
b.   What is the relative frequency of workers who prefer a 5-day, 40-hour work
week?
c.   What is the relative frequency of workers who prefer a 3-day, 40-hour work week?

2.7   How much influence does the color of the package of a product have on its
market appeal? As part of a marketing experiment, a laundry detergent manufacturer
packaged its product in four different colored boxes of identical design and placed
the packages side by side on a grocery store shelf. During one week, 30 of the
packages were purchased at the store, with the results given in the table. Construct a
bar graph for the data. Interpret your results.

PACKAGE COLOR	NUMBER PURCHASED
Blue	6
Orange	11
White	9
Green	4
TOTAL	30

2.8 In order to gain insight on how well the law works to compensate the victims of automobile accidents, an elaborate study of auto accidents was undertaken. The resulting distribution of reparations is given in the table.

SOURCE OF REPARATION TO INJURED PARTY	PERCENT OF TOTAL DOLLARS
Liability of third parties who had negligently caused the accident	55
Injured's own insurance:	
Accident	22
Hospital and medical	11
Life and burial	5
Social Security	2
Employer and Workmen's Compensation	1
Other	4
TOTAL	100%

a. Illustrate the distribution of reparations with a pie chart.

b. Many auto drivers assume that liability law is overwhelmingly the most important source of compensation for accident victims. Does the pie chart (part a) support this belief?

2.9 *Time* magazine (January 26, 1981) reported that Jimmy Carter's "farewell" 1982 budget "does little to reverse the federal spending machine. Outlays in fiscal 1982 are

Reprinted by permission from *Time*, The Weekly Newsmagazine, Copyright Time Inc. 1981.

slated to rise by 11.5%, to $739 billion, leaving a projected deficit of $27.5 billion" for President Ronald Reagan's administration. *Time* illustrated the areas of increased federal spending with pie charts which are reproduced here.

a. Compute the percentage of the federal budget allocated to each of the spending areas for both the 1981 and 1982 budgets.
b. Interpret the percentages you computed in part a.
c. Which area had been allocated the largest increase in federal spending, relative to the total 1982 budget?

2.10 Many worldwide industries currently use, or are planning to use, newly designed robots to perform certain assembly tasks which often require as many as ten people to complete. Information on the estimated number of industrial robots currently being utilized in each of 11 countries is given in the table.

COUNTRY	NUMBER OF INDUSTRIAL ROBOTS
Finland	130
France	200
Great Britain	185
Italy	500
Japan	10,000
Norway	200
Poland	360
Sweden	600
United States	3,000
U.S.S.R.	25
West Germany	850
TOTAL	16,050

Source: *Time*, December 8, 1980. Figures are 1979 estimates. Reprinted by permission from *Time*, The Weekly Newsmagazine; Copyright Time Inc. 1980.

a. Construct a bar graph to describe the distribution of industrial robots in the 11 countries.
b. Interpret the bar graph in part a.

2.4 Graphical Descriptions of Quantitative Data

You will recall that Appendix A contains the 2,862 residential property sales recorded in a mid-sized Florida city during 1978. Turn to Appendix A and examine the set of 2,862 sale prices and, as you do so, keep in mind that these prices provide an indicator of the value of residential properties in the city. How could we provide a graphical description of this data set?

To answer this question, we shall extend the procedure employed in describing qualitative data sets. That is, we shall classify the prices by forming intervals, say $10,000 to $14,999, $15,000 to $19,999, $20,000 to $24,999, etc. Then we shall count the sale prices falling within each interval (or *class*) and form a figure similar to the bar graph of Section 2.3. The bars can be constructed so that their heights are proportional to either the class *frequencies* or to the class *relative frequencies.* The corresponding graphs are called *frequency distributions* and *relative frequency distributions,* respectively.*

The *relative frequency distribution* that describes the 2,862 residential sale prices is shown in Figure 2.7 (p. 30). The classes are marked off in intervals of $5,000 along the horizontal axis of the graph. Notice that the *class intervals* are of equal width and that we have essentially divided the sale price axis into 21 equal class intervals. The heights of the bars constructed over the intervals are proportional to the relative frequencies of the respective classes.

Figure 2.7 provides a good graphical description of the 2,862 residential sale prices. You can see how the sale prices are *distributed* along the sale price axis. The sale prices tend to pile up near $35,000 (notice that the class, $32,500 to $37,500, has the greatest relative frequency). None of the sale prices was less than $7,500, the *lower class boundary* of the lowest price class, or larger than $112,500, the *upper class boundary* of the highest price class. [*Note:* Extremely large and extremely small sale prices, and their respective class intervals, are not shown in Figure 2.7. Since these prices, representing nonhousing sales (e.g., farms and vacant lots), account for only 1% of the 2,862 sales, Figure 2.7 can be said to represent, for all intents and purposes, the relative frequency distribution of all 2,862 residential sale prices.]

Because the classes are of equal width, the area of the bar associated with a particular class is proportional to its class relative frequency. Consequently, we can visually guess the proportion of prices falling within any particular price interval by comparing the area of bars over that interval with the total area of all the bars.

EXAMPLE 2.8 Examine Figure 2.7 and visually estimate the proportion of the total number of sale prices that lie between $22,500 and $42,500.

Solution Shade the bars lying above the interval, $22,500 to $42,500, as indicated in Figure 2.8 (p. 31). You can see that this shaded portion represents approximately .55 (actually, .555) of the total area of the bars for the complete distribution. This tells us that approximately 55% of the sale prices were in the interval, $22,500 to $42,500. A more precise (but less rapid) answer could be obtained by recording and summing the relative frequencies for the classes in the interval, $22,500 to $42,500.

Now that we know what a relative frequency distribution is and the type of information that it conveys, let us examine the details of its construction. We will use a sample of data from Appendix A to illustrate the procedure.

---

*The proper term is *histogram* but the word *distribution* conveys a better notion of the functional use of the graph.

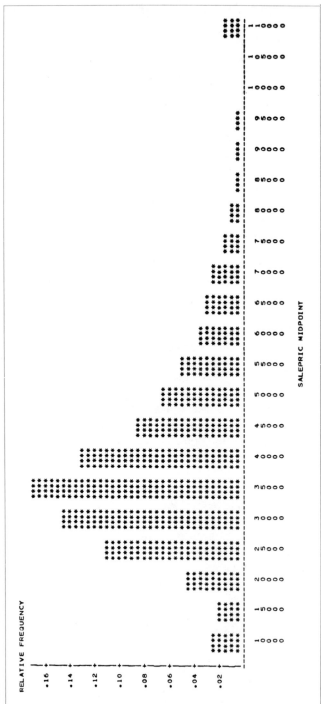

FIGURE 2.7   A Relative Frequency Distribution for the 2,862 Residential Sale Prices of Appendix A

FIGURE 2.8 Proportion of the 2,862 Residential Sale Prices That Lie between $22,500 and $42,500

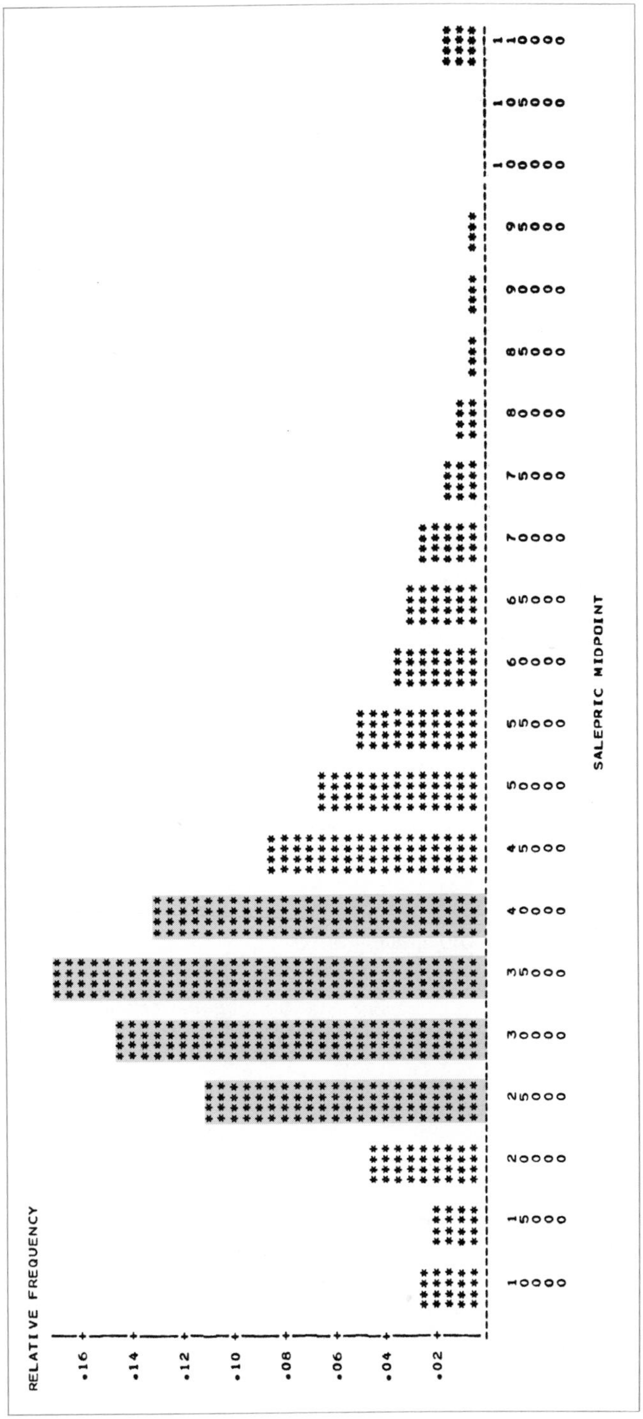

EXAMPLE 2.9   Table 2.3 gives the sale prices for 50 properties selected at random from the 2,862 sale prices of Appendix A.

TABLE 2.3
The Sale Prices for a
Sample of 50 Properties
Selected from Appendix A

52,000	38,500	23,900	42,300	52,500
36,900	37,300	37,800	26,200	37,800
42,400	56,400	30,900	35,100	37,000
45,000	34,900	27,000	53,000	72,000
67,500	27,700	125,000	37,900	70,000
58,500	29,700	36,300	57,500	37,000
25,500	45,800	31,000	36,900	26,000
33,500	29,500	39,000	30,900	55,000
51,300	40,000	34,600	18,200	90,000
36,800	32,900	38,800	30,900	43,800

The first step in constructing the relative frequency distribution for this sample is to define the *class intervals.* To do this, we need to know the smallest and largest sale prices in the data set. These prices are $18,200 and $125,000, respectively. Since we want the smallest price to fall in the lowest class interval and the largest price to fall in the highest class interval, we shall want the class intervals to span sale prices in the interval, $18,200 to $125,000.

The next step is to choose the *class interval width,* and this will depend upon how many intervals we wish to use to span the sale price range. The sale price range is equal to

$$\text{Range} = \text{Largest measurement} - \text{Smallest measurement}$$

$$= \$125,000 - \$18,200$$

$$= \$106,800$$

Suppose that we choose to use 11 class intervals.* Then the class interval width should approximately equal

$$\text{Class interval} \approx \frac{\text{Range}}{\text{Number of class intervals}}$$

$$\approx \frac{106,800}{11}$$

$$\approx \$10,000$$

We shall start the first class slightly below the smallest observation, $18,200, and choose the point so that no observation can fall on a class boundary. Since sale prices are recorded to the nearest hundred dollars, we can do this by choosing the lower class boundary of the first class interval to be $15,050. [*Note:*   We could just as easily have chosen $15,025, $16,050, $17,050, or any one of many other points below and near $18,200.] Then the class intervals would be $15,050 to $25,050, $25,050 to $35,050, etc. The 11 class intervals are shown in the second column of Table 2.4.

---

*We shall discuss the selection of an appropriate number of class intervals later in this section.

The next step in constructing a relative frequency distribution is to obtain each class frequency, i.e., the number of observations falling within each class. This is done by examining each sale price in Table 2.3 and recording by tally (as shown in the third column of Table 2.4) the class in which it falls. The tally for each class gives the class frequencies shown in Column 4 of Table 2.4. Finally, we calculate the class relative frequency as

$$\text{Class relative frequency} = \frac{\text{Class frequency}}{\text{Total number of observations}}$$

$$= \frac{\text{Class frequency}}{50}$$

These values are shown in the fifth column of Table 2.4.

TABLE 2.4
Tabulation of Data for the
50 Sale Prices, Table 2.3

CLASS	CLASS INTERVAL	TALLY	CLASS FREQUENCY	CLASS RELATIVE FREQUENCY
1	15,050— 25,050	//	2	.04
2	25,050— 35,050	### ### ###	15	.30
3	35,050— 45,050	### ### ### ////	19	.38
4	45,050— 55,050	### /	6	.12
5	55,050— 65,050	///	3	.06
6	65,050— 75,050	///	3	.06
7	75,050— 85,050		0	.00
8	85,050— 95,050	/	1	.02
9	95,050—105,050		0	.00
10	105,050—115,050		0	.00
11	115,050—125,050	/	1	.02
			50	1.00

The final step in constructing a relative frequency distribution is to draw the graph. Mark off the class intervals along a horizontal line, as shown in Figure 2.9.

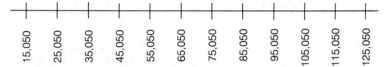

FIGURE 2.9
Class Intervals for the
Data, Table 2.4

Then construct over each class interval a bar with the height proportional to the class relative frequency. The resulting relative frequency distribution is shown in Figure 2.10 (p. 34).

If you had any question about how to construct a relative frequency distribution, you would probably ask why we chose 11 class intervals for Figure 2.10. Why not 5, 10, 15, or 20? The answer is that there is no "best" number, but 11 seemed to be a good choice. Remember, the reason for constructing the graph is to obtain a figure that visually tells us how the observations are distributed along the sale price axis. You can

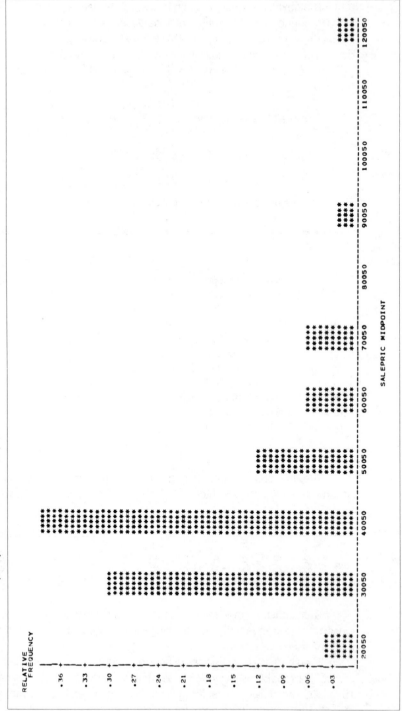

FIGURE 2.10   Relative Frequency Distribution for the Data, Table 2.3

see at a glance that most of the residential properties in the sample of 50 fell between $25,050 and $45,050; and you can obtain an approximate value for the proportion of sale prices in this interval by comparing the area of the two bars over the interval, $25,050 to $45,050, to the total area of all the bars. This ratio is approximately ⅔. None of the sale prices was less than $15,050, but several large sales caused the distribution to be *skewed* to the right. Suppose that you had spanned the range with 3 classes instead of 11. Almost all of the observations would have fallen in a single class and the resulting relative frequency distribution would not have been nearly as informative as Figure 2.10. Or suppose that you had chosen to span the interval, $18,200 to $125,000, with 50 classes. Then many classes would have contained only a few observations and others would have been empty. Again, this figure would not have been as informative as Figure 2.10.

The rule of thumb in deciding on the number of class intervals is to use a small number when you wish to describe a small amount of data, say 5 or 6 classes for up to 25 or 30 observations. You can increase the number of classes (as we did) for 50 observations, and you may wish to use 15 or 20 classes for large amounts of data. (See the relative frequency distribution, Figure 2.7, for the 2,862 observations of Appendix A.) Remember, the objective is to obtain a graph that rapidly conveys a visual picture of the data. If your first choice of class interval width is not satisfactory, you may wish to choose a different interval width and try again.

The steps employed in constructing a relative frequency distribution are summarized in the box.

STEPS EMPLOYED IN CONSTRUCTING A RELATIVE FREQUENCY DISTRIBUTION

1. Examine the data to obtain the smallest and the largest measurement.
2. Divide the interval between the smallest and the largest measurement into between five and twenty equal subintervals called *classes*. These classes should satisfy the following requirement:

    Each measurement falls into one and only one subinterval

    Note that this requirement implies that no measurement falls on a boundary of a subinterval. Although the choice of the number of classes is arbitrary, you will obtain a better description of the data if you use a small number of subintervals when you have a small amount of data and a large number of subintervals for a large amount of data.
3. Compute the proportion (relative frequency) of measurements falling within each subinterval.*
4. Using a vertical axis of about three-fourths the length of the horizontal axis, plot each relative frequency as a rectangle over the corresponding subinterval.

---

*Note that *frequencies* rather than relative frequencies may be used in constructing a frequency distribution. The frequency is the actual number of measurements in each interval.

The important concept to use in visually interpreting a relative frequency distribution is as follows:

INTERPRETING A RELATIVE FREQUENCY DISTRIBUTION

The percentage of the total number of measurements falling within a particular interval is proportional to the area of the bar that is constructed above the interval. If 30% of the area under the distribution lies over a particular interval, then 30% of the observations fell in that interval.

EXERCISES   **2.11**   Hospitals are required to file a yearly Cost Report in order to obtain reimbursement from the state for patient bills paid through the Medicare, Medicaid, and Blue Cross programs. Many factors contribute to the amount of reimbursement that the hospital receives. One important factor is bed size (i.e., the total number of beds available for patient use). The data below represent the bed sizes for 54 hospitals which were satisfied with their Cost Report reimbursements last year. Construct a relative frequency distribution for the bed size data using ten classes to span the range.

303	550	243	282	195	310	288	188	190	335
473	169	292	492	200	478	182	172	231	375
171	262	198	313	600	264	311	371	145	242
278	183	215	719	519	382	249	350	99	218
300	450	337	330	252	400	514	427	533	930
319	210	550	488						

2.12   Repeat Exercise 2.11, but use only three classes to span the range. Compare with the relative frequency distribution you constructed in that exercise. Which is more informative? Why does an inadequate number of classes limit the information conveyed by the relative frequency distribution?

2.13   Repeat Exercise 2.11, but use 25 classes. Comment on the information provided by this graph as compared to that of Exercise 2.11.

2.14   Given below are last year's total deposits (in $ billions) for a random selection of 35 members of the Association of Bank Holding Companies. Construct a relative frequency distribution for the data.

1.90	2.70	1.16	32.41	0.52	1.41	0.62	8.46
24.92	1.62	35.83	20.89	0.33	11.47	2.45	11.21
17.50	2.75	3.55	13.17	16.97	0.87	1.22	0.12
1.28	21.21	1.36	18.75	1.59	1.39	2.21	7.82
11.10	6.10	0.47					

2.15   Examine the relative frequency distribution (Figure 2.7) for the sale prices of all 2,862 residential properties of Appendix A. By visually comparing the area under the distribution to the left of $37,500 to the total area under the distribution, estimate the proportion of sale prices less than or equal to $37,500.

2.5 Summary

The method for describing data sets of both qualitative and quantitative variables is based upon the same concept. Qualitative data, by their very nature, fall into specific categories or classes. Similarly, the values associated with quantitative data can be subdivided into classes. Then, to describe the data, we calculate the number of observations falling into each class and construct a bar graph where the height of the bar constructed for each class is proportional to the number of observations falling within that class. Alternatively, the height of the bar may be proportional to the proportion of the total number of observations falling within that class.

The difference between a bar graph and a relative frequency distribution is that the classes of a qualitative variable are unrelated. In contrast, the classes for a quantitative variable are intervals on a real line which are connected; the upper class boundary of one interval is the lower class boundary of the next.

If the bars are constructed so that they are of equal width, then the area of a bar, in comparison to the total area of all the bars, is proportional to the proportion of the total number of observations falling within that class interval. This enables you to examine a relative frequency distribution and visually estimate the proportion of the total number of measurements falling within specific intervals. In brief, bar graphs, pie charts, and relative frequency distributions provide for a rapid description of qualitative and quantitative data sets.

KEY WORDS

Quantitative data	Bar graph
Quantitative variable	Pie chart
Qualitative data	Class interval
Qualitative variable	Class boundaries (lower and upper)
Class	Frequency distribution
Class frequency	Relative frequency distribution
Class relative frequency	Skewed distribution

SUPPLEMENTARY EXERCISES

2.16   Classify each of the following variables as either quantitative or qualitative.

a.   Number of 1982 federal income tax returns which are filed incorrectly with the Internal Revenue Service

b.   Brand of toothpaste with the largest yearly sales

c.   Time (in hours) between failures of a certain brand of aircraft radio

d.   Neighborhood (of a city) with the lowest crime rate
e.   Type of heating fuel used in a rural home
f.   Actual weight of a bag of sugar marked *Net Wt. 5 lb.*
g.   Price (per gallon) of unleaded gasoline at a self-service station
h.   Professional sport with the highest average attendance per game

2.17 *Sales and Marketing Management (S&MM)* magazine publishes the total number of U.S. plants and shipments in each type of manufacturing industry as part of its annual *Survey of Industrial Purchasing Power.* To the trained eye, these figures can provide insights into the total customer-base (plants) available to the marketer's sales force, and the potential market demand (shipments). In each industry, plants are classified by primary product, and only those plants employing 20 or more workers are included in the total.

Data on the total number of plants in the leather industry for 1980 are recorded in the table.

PRIMARY PRODUCT	NUMBER OF PLANTS
Leather tanning and finishing	252
Boot and shoe cut stock and findings	167
House slippers	59
Men's nonathletic footwear	173
Women's nonathletic footwear	196
Nonrubber footwear n.e.c.	233
Leather gloves and mittens	78
Luggage	113
Women's handbags & purses	181
Personal leather goods n.e.c.	130
Leather goods n.e.c.	172
TOTAL	1,754

n.e.c. = not elsewhere classified

Source: *S&MM,* April 28, 1980.

a.   State whether the variable of interest, Leather plant's primary product, is qualitative or quantitative.
b.   Use one of the graphical methods described in this chapter to summarize the leather industry data.
c.   Use the graph to visually estimate the proportion of leather plants producing nonathletic footwear as the primary product.

2.18 The U.S. Environmental Protection Agency (EPA) performs fuel economy tests on all makes and models of automobiles each year. An important variable that is measured on each car is Miles per gallon (mpg). Listed at the top of the next page are the EPA highway estimates of mpg for thirty 1980 model automobiles. Construct a relative frequency distribution for the data using six class intervals.

AMC Spirit	18	Lincoln Continental	15
Buick LeSabre	17	Jaguar XJ	14
Buick Skylark	20	Olds Cutlass	20
Cadillac Eldorado	14	Ford Thunderbird	18
Chevy Malibu	19	Honda Civic	36
Chrysler Cordoba	17	Olds Omega	22
Datsun 310	31	Plymouth Arrow	29
Datsun 210SX	26	Plymouth Champ	37
Chevy Chevette	25	Pontiac Firebird	20
Audi 4000	22	Porsche 924	19
Dodge Aspen	17	Toyota Corolla	26
Dodge Colt	30	Triumph Spitfire	21
Fiat Brava	20	Rolls Royce/Bentley	10
Ford LTD	17	Plymouth Volare	17
Mazda GLC	27	VW Diesel Rabbit	42

Source: *The World Almanac & Book of Facts,* 1980 ed. Copyright © Newspaper Enterprise Association, 1981, New York, N.Y. 10166.

2.19 Each year the National Soft Drink Association (NSDA) presents a review of the industry's sales performance based upon a survey of the association's members. The survey provides an estimate of annual industry growth that is reconciled with the U.S. Department of Commerce's Census of Manufacturers.

The NSDA reported the information given in the table on the 1977 market share of regular (nondiet) soft drink flavors.

SOFT DRINK FLAVOR	PROPORTION OF ALL PACKAGED SALES IN 1977
Cola	.622
Lemon Lime	.121
Orange	.035
Ginger Ale	.015
Root Beer	.030
Grape	.016
Other	.161
	1.000

Source: NSDA 1977 Sales Survey of the Soft Drink Industry.

a. Construct a bar graph for the 1977 market share data.

b. What was the predominant flavor of soft drink in terms of packaged sales in 1977?

c. Estimate the 1977 percentage of packaged sales of noncola soft drinks.

2.20 Since 1972, the total number of business failures per year has slowly declined. The Business Economics Division of the U.S. Department of Labor classifies each business failure into one of the following eight categories: failure due to (1) neglect; (2) fraud; (3) lack of experience in the line; (4) lack of managerial experience; (5) unbalanced experience; (6) incompetence; (7) disaster; (8) unknown reasons. These classifications are based on the opinions of informed creditors and information in Business Economics Division reports.

A summary of 1,463 failures of construction enterprises in 1977 is given in the table.

UNDERLYING CAUSE	RELATIVE FREQUENCY
1. Neglect	.008
2. Fraud	.002
3. Lack of line experience	.076
4. Lack of managerial experience	.161
5. Unbalanced experience	.215
6. Incompetence	.477
7. Disaster	.004
8. Reason unknown	.057
	1.000

a.   Use an appropriate graphical method to describe the 1977 construction business failures.

b.   Visually estimate the percentage of construction businesses which failed due to inadequate experience or incompetence.

2.21   A traditional pulse rate of the economic health of the accommodations (hotel-motel) industry is the trend in room occupancy. (The *room occupancy* at a hotel or motel is determined by dividing the number of rooms occupied at the hotel or motel by the total number of inservice rooms available.) Given below are the room occupancies for 30 Miami, Florida, hotels (motels) during a randomly selected day in August. Construct a relative frequency distribution for the data.

.68	.93	.55	.70	.58	.60	.81	.48	.39	.43
.71	.80	.67	.52	.60	.92	.41	.59	.91	.85
.53	.77	.68	.66	.33	.62	.60	.82	.69	.67

2.22   The vitality of the minicomputer/small business computer market is evidenced by annual sales growths of 30–40% in recent years, well above the average for the computer industry in general. Recently the *Wall Street Journal,* with the cooperation of nine leading minicomputer manufacturers, undertook a survey of customers and manufacturers in the minicomputer/small business computer industry. One of the many variables investigated was Company revenue. The 1977 company revenues for the 198 minicomputer equipment manufacturers who responded to the survey are reported in the table.

a.   Classify the variable of interest, Company revenue, as qualitative or quantitative.

COMPANY REVENUE	NUMBER OF MANUFACTURERS
Under $1 million	77
$1 — 1.9 million	18
$2 — 4.9 million	21
$5 — 9.9 million	18
$10 — 24.9 million	13
$25 — 49.9 million	8
$50 — 99.9 million	9
$100—249.9 million	7
$250—499.9 million	7
$500—999.9 million	4
$1 billion or more	16
TOTAL	198

Source: *Minicomputers & Small Business Computers: A Market Survey*, 1979.

b. Based on your answer to part a, what type of graphical method could be used to summarize the revenue data?

c. Explain why we are unable to correctly use one of the graphical methods discussed in this chapter to describe the company revenue data in the form that it is given.

2.23 The palatability of a new food product can often be determined by preliminary market taste tests. Experience has shown that having as few as 50 people taste and evaluate a new product under controlled conditions is adequate to reveal a major problem in consumer acceptability, if one exists. Suppose that 50 randomly selected individuals agreed to participate in a taste test for a new product, chocolate peanut butter. After tasting the product, each person was asked to mark a ballot rating overall acceptability on a scale from -3 to $+3$ ($-3 =$ "terrible," $-2 =$ "very poor," $-1 =$ "poor," $0 =$ "average," $+1 =$ "good," $+2 =$ "very good," and $+3 =$ "excellent"). The results are displayed in the graph.

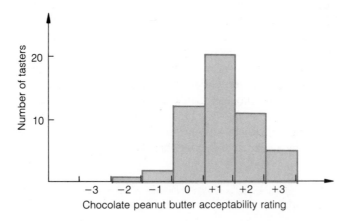

Chocolate peanut butter acceptability rating

a. What type of graphical tool is used to describe the results of the taste test?
b. What information is conveyed by the graph?
c. What proportion of the 50 tasters rated the new chocolate peanut butter as "terrible"?

2.24 In his essay *Making Things Right,* W. Edwards Deming considered the role of statistics in the quality control of industrial products.* In one example, Deming examined the quality control process for a manufacturer of steel rods. Rods produced with diameters smaller than 1 centimeter fit too loosely in their bearings and ultimately must be rejected (thrown out). To determine if the diameter setting of the machine which produces the rods is correct, 500 rods are randomly selected from the day's production and their diameters are recorded. The distribution of the 500 diameters for one day's production is shown in the figure. Note that the symbol LSL in the figure represents the 1-centimeter lower specification limit of the steel rod diameters.

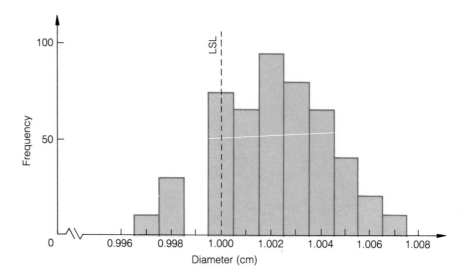

a. What type of data, quantitative or qualitative, does the figure portray?
b. What type of graphical method is being used to describe the data?
c. Use the figure to estimate the proportion of rods with diameters between 1.0025 and 1.0045 centimeters.
d. There has been speculation that some of the inspectors are unaware of the trouble that an undersized rod diameter would cause later on in the manufacturing process. Consequently, these inspectors may be passing rods with diameters that were barely below the lower specification limit, and recording them in the interval centered at 1.000 centimeter. According to the figure, is there any evidence to support this claim? Explain.

---

*From J. Tanur et al., eds. 1978. *Statistics: A guide to the unknown.* San Francisco: Holden-Day. pp. 279–281.

2.25 Refer to the supermarket customer checkout time data of Appendix D.

a. Classify the variable Supermarket customer checkout time as qualitative or quantitative.

b. Use one of the graphical methods described in this chapter to depict the distribution of checkout times for the 500 customers at supermarket A.

c. Repeat part b for the 500 customer checkout times at supermarket B. Place the figure on the same axes as the figure for part b so that the distribution of customer checkout times for the two supermarkets can be compared.

2.26 Refer to Exercise 2.25, part c. Explain how the manager of supermarket A could use these results as an aid in determining whether to authorize a switch from mechanical checking to automated checking. What is your recommendation if the manager is only interested in speeding up the customer checkout process at the supermarket?

CASE STUDY 2.1
The Biggest Problem Facing Women in Industrial Purchasing

Traditionally, the field of industrial purchasing has been male-dominated. A recent article in *Purchasing* magazine (October 5, 1976)* reported on the growing number of women who are opting for a career as an industrial buyer. Some of these women, however, face an uphill struggle against male bias and substandard salaries. The opinion of one female purchaser, who is responsible for buying some $14 million of metals per year, is that "women can never let down. They must put far more time and effort into the job than their male counterparts." Another wryly states that "a woman may command equal pay for equal performance, but she won't get it."

Purchasing conducted a survey on the subject of female buyers. Of the 1,000 randomly selected buyers who were surveyed, 368 responded. One of the many questions asked of the buyers was the following: "In your opinion, what is the biggest problem facing women in industrial purchasing?" The results are given in Table 2.5.

TABLE 2.5

THE BIGGEST PROBLEM FOR WOMEN IN INDUSTRIAL PURCHASING	RELATIVE FREQUENCY
1. Difference in sex puts them on the defensive	.19
2. Not tough enough to drive a hard bargain	.13
3. Don't have good business sense	.04
4. Have more trouble making a decision	.09
5. Other problems	.14
6. No real difference between a man and a woman	.41

a. Construct a bar graph for the data of Table 2.5.

b. What fraction of the respondents feel that the biggest problem for female buyers is either their lack of good business sense or their indecisiveness?

c. Estimate the percentage of all buyers who feel that women in industrial purchasing face problems in addition to those faced by a male.

---

*D. Brookman. "The biggest problem facing women in industrial purchasing." *Purchasing*, October 5, 1976, 32–37. Reprinted from *Purchasing Magazine*. Copyright by Cahners Publishing.

d. Refer to your answer to part c. Comment on the reliability of your inference. [*Hint:* Consider that of the 1,000 buyers surveyed, only 368 responded. Do you believe the 368 responses are representative of the set of responses for the population of all industrial buyers? If not, explain how inferences derived from a survey conducted in this manner could be misleading.]

CASE STUDY 2.2
Trouble beneath the Sidewalks of New York— Subways Deep in Debt

An article in *Railway Age* (May 12, 1980) describes the problems of New York's subways as follows:

> The nation's busiest passenger railroad, the 230-mile system that operates mainly beneath the sidewalks of New York, was back in business April 11 [1980] after a crippling 11-day strike by the Transit Workers Union. For New Yorkers, the return of their trains marked the end of a crisis—one that brought them not to their knees but to their feet, as millions walked, bicycled, and even roller-skated to work.
>
> But for the New York City Transit Authority (NYCTA), business as usual meant problems as usual.

Steven Kauffman, NYCTA's senior executive officer and general manager, hopes to solve their equipment shortage by acquiring hundreds of millions of dollars worth of new and rebuilt cars (in 1980), and is trying to correct the shortage of knowledgeable workers with a new personnel development program. However, the NYCTA is currently faced with "a deepening financial crisis that tends to shove [these and] all other problems to the back burner." Kauffman estimates that the NYCTA will need to spend $18 billion over the next 10 years to rebuild itself.

The severity of the NYCTA's debt for the fiscal year ending June 30, 1980, is illustrated by the pie charts shown in Figures 2.11(a) and 2.11(b).

FIGURE 2.11   NYCTA Funds for Fiscal Year Ending June 30, 1980 (Excludes Transit Police, Capital Engineering, Debt Service)

(a) Income: $1,249,000,000   (b) Outgo: $1,260,600,000

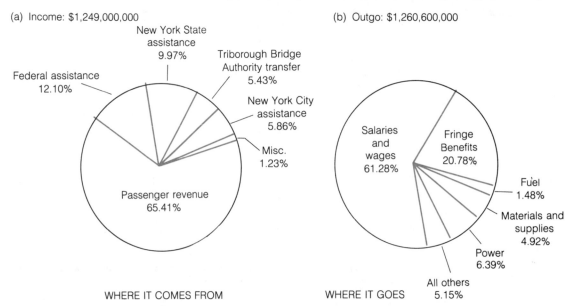

a. What proportion of incoming NYCTA funds were generated by passenger revenue during this fiscal year?
b. What proportion of incoming NYCTA funds were generated through the federal, New York State, or New York City assistance programs?
c. What proportion of outgoing NYCTA funds were allocated to employees' salaries, wages, or fringe benefits?

CASE STUDY 2.3
The OBG
Specialist's
Hectic Work
Week

"Although the national birth rate has been declining steadily since the beginning of the decade, obstetrics/gynecology (OBG) is still a very profitable specialty." So states the December 10, 1979, issue of *Medical Economics.** Surveys show that OBG specialists have higher net earnings than office-based doctors in private practice but, since 1974, the earnings edge has been narrowing. This "is surprising in view of the fact that more obstetrical cases are going to specialists these days. [General practitioners], particularly the older ones, are getting out of the time-consuming, schedule-disrupting baby-delivering business, and patients themselves have become more attuned to seeking specialists' care. . . . OBGs did 69% of all U.S. deliveries 10 years ago; today they do 82%."

Genetic counseling, treatment of infertility problems, increased availability of abortions, and new means of treating high-risk pregnancies, along with the fact that more women are inclined to view their gynecologist as their primary physician, have all contributed to the increased workload of OBGs. "The typical OBG specialist . . . puts in more hours a week than any other specialist except the general surgeon."

Figure 2.12, reproduced from the *Medical Economics* article, serves to illustrate

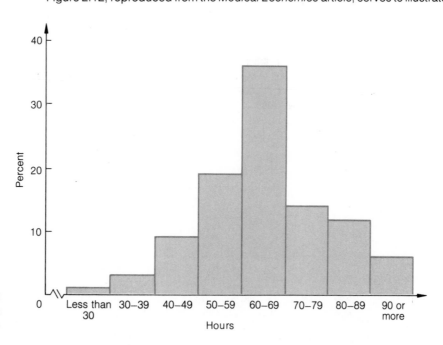

FIGURE 2.12
Hours Worked per Week
by % of OBGs

the OBG specialist's hectic work week. The figure represents a relative frequency distribution of the hours worked per week by those OBG specialists included in the *Medical Economics* survey. Note that the length of each rectangle is proportional to the number of OBGs who work, per week, the hours indicated.

α. What percentage of those OBGs sampled work between 40 and 69 hours per week?

b. What percentage of those OBGs sampled work less than 40 hours per week?

c. Estimate the percentage of all OBGs who work at least 70 hours per week.

REFERENCES   Alexander, C. "Carter's farewell budget." *Time,* January 26, 1981, 50–51.

Brookman, D. "The biggest problem facing women in industrial purchasing." *Purchasing,* October 5, 1976, 32–37.

Chou, Ya-lun. *Statistical analysis.* 2d ed. New York: Holt, Rinehart, and Winston, 1975. Chapter 2.

Dow Jones & Co., Inc. *Minicomputers and small business computers: A market survey, 1979,* 32.

Friedrich, O. "The robot revolution." *Time,* December 8, 1980, 72–78, 83.

McClave, J. T., & Benson, P. G. *Statistics for business and economics.* 2d ed. San Francisco: Dellen, 1982.

Mattera, M. D. "OBG a top-earning specialty loses some of its edge." *Medical Economics,* December 10, 1979, 91–92, 94–95.

Miller, L. S. "New York subways: Business (& crises) as usual." *Railway Age,* May 12, 1980, 37–40.

National Soft Drink Association. "NSDA 1977 sales survey of the soft drink industry." 1–16.

Neter, J., Wasserman, W., & Whitmore, G. A. *Fundamental statistics for business and economics.* 4th ed. Boston: Allyn and Bacon, 1973. Chapter 3.

"Special edition: Japan & America." *Business Week,* July 21, 1980, 31.

Tanur, J. M., Mosteller, F., Kruskal, W. H., Link, R. F., Pieters, R. S., & Rising, G. R. *Statistics: A guide to the unknown.* San Francisco: Holden-Day, 1978.

Taylor, T. C. "Putting profitable sales into perspective." *Sales and Marketing Management,* April 28, 1980, 7–16.

Three

Numerical Methods for Describing Quantitative Data

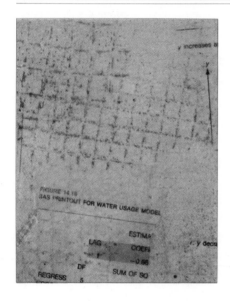

Timber is sold by weight. Suppose that you planned to invest in a piece of timberland and, to aid you in assessing its value, you grouped logs by weight for a sample of 117 trees selected from the property. How could you describe the weights of these logs with a single number that would characterize the weights of the sample of 117 logs? We will show you in this chapter how numbers (called *numerical descriptive measures*) can be used to describe the characteristics of a set of measurements, and we will apply this to the timber-sampling problem in Case Study 3.3. Ultimately, we would like to use the sample numerical descriptive measures to estimate the total weight of all logs on the property.

Contents:

3.1 Why We Need Numerical Descriptive Measures

It is probably true that a picture is worth a thousand words, and it is certainly true when you wish to describe a quantitative data set. But sometimes you will want to discuss the major features of a data set and it may not be convenient to produce the relative frequency distribution for the data. When this situation occurs, we seek a few summarizing numbers, called *numerical descriptive measures,* that conjure in our minds a picture of the relative frequency distribution.

3.2 Types of Numerical Descriptive Measures

Examine the relative frequency distribution for the 2,862 residential sale prices, Appendix A, that is reproduced in Figure 3.1. If you were allowed to choose two numbers that would help you to construct a mental image of the distribution, which two would you choose?

We think that you would probably choose

1. A number that is located near the "center" of the distribution (see Figure 3.2(a))
2. A number that measures the "spread" of the distribution (see Figure 3.2(b))

A number which would describe the "center" of the distribution would be visually located near the spot where most of the data seem to be concentrated. Consequently, numbers that fulfill this role are called *measures of central tendency.* We will define and describe several measures of central tendency for data sets in Section 3.4.

The amount of "spread" in a data set is a measure of the variation in the data. Consequently, numerical descriptive measures that perform this function are called *measures of variation* or, sometimes, *measures of dispersion.* As you will subsequently see (Section 3.5), there are several ways to measure the variation in a data set.

Measures of central tendency and data variation are not the only numerical descriptive measures for describing data sets. Some are constructed to measure the *skewness* of a relative frequency distribution, the tendency of the distribution to tail out to the right (or left). For example, the relative frequency distribution, Figure 3.1, shows that most of the sale prices were concentrated near $35,000 but that a few properties sold for much larger prices. A distribution that tends to spread unusually far to the high side is said to be *skewed to the right* or *positively skewed.* Similarly, distributions of data are said to be *skewed to the left* or *negatively skewed* if they tend to spread unusually far to the low side.

We will concentrate in this chapter on measures of central tendency and measures of variation. As you read this material, keep in mind our goal of using a pair of numbers to create a mental image of a relative frequency distribution. Relate each numerical descriptive measure to this objective and verify that it fulfills the role it is intended to play.

FIGURE 3.1 The Relative Frequency Distribution for the 2,862 Sale Prices of Appendix A

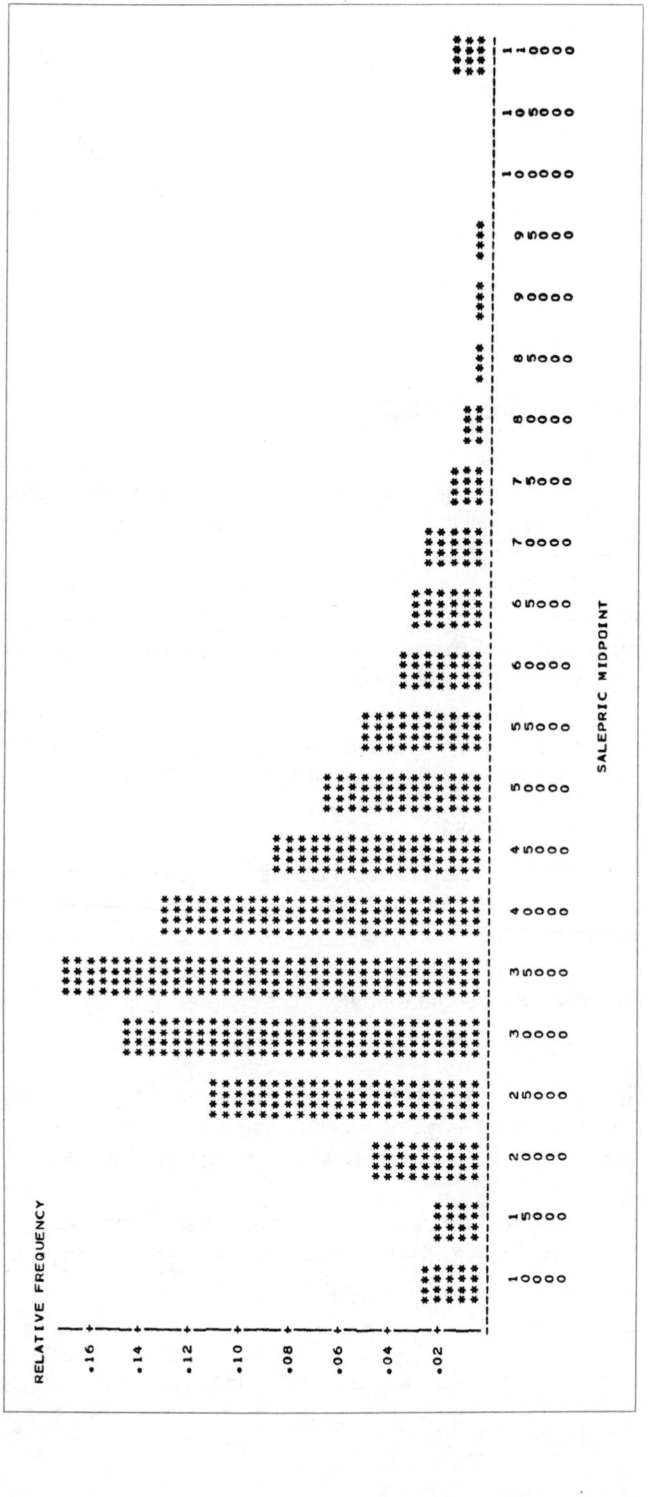

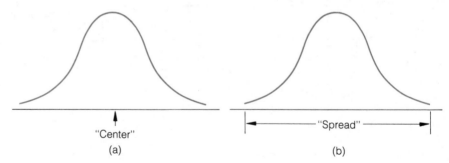

FIGURE 3.2
Numerical Descriptive
Measures

"Center"
(a)

"Spread"
(b)

3.3 Summation Notation

Explaining how to find specific numerical descriptive measures, particularly some measures of variability, often requires so much verbal explanation that the procedures may become lost in the verbiage. Consequently, we need to express the procedures in terms of formulas.

Suppose that a data set was obtained by observing a quantitative variable, x. For example, x may represent the quantitative sale prices of residential properties. By observing x (sale prices) for the 2,862 properties of Appendix A, we obtained the data set consisting of 2,862 sale prices.

If we want to represent a particular observation in a data set, say the 26th one, we represent it by the symbol x with a subscript 26. For example, you can see that the 26th observation in Appendix A is \$38,500. Therefore,

$$x_{26} = \$38,500$$

The complete data set would be represented by the symbols $x_1, x_2, x_3, \ldots, x_{2,862}$.

Most of the formulas that we shall use require the summation of numbers. For example, we may want to sum the observations in a data set, or we may want to square each observation and sum the squares of all observations in the data set. The sum of the observations in a data set will be represented by the symbol

$$\Sigma x$$

This symbol is read "summation x." The symbol Σ (sigma), the capital letter "S" in the Greek alphabet, is giving you an instruction. It is telling you to sum a set of numbers. The variable to be summed, x, is shown to the right of the Σ symbol.

EXAMPLE 3.1 Suppose that the variable x is used to represent the number of bathrooms in a given residence. Five residential properties are examined and the value of x is recorded for each. These observations are 2, 1, 3, 2, 3.

a. Find Σx.   **b.** Find Σx^2.

Solution **a.** The symbol Σx tells you to sum the x-values in the data set. Therefore,

$$\Sigma x = 2 + 1 + 3 + 2 + 3 = 11$$

b. The symbol Σx^2 tells you to sum the squares of the x-values in the data set. Therefore,

$$\Sigma x^2 = (2)^2 + (1)^2 + (3)^2 + (2)^2 + (3)^2$$
$$= 4 + 1 + 9 + 4 + 9 = 27$$

EXAMPLE 3.2 Refer to Example 3.1.

a. Find $\Sigma(x-3)$.   b. Find $\Sigma(x-3)^2$.

Solution a. The symbol $\Sigma(x-3)$ tells you to subtract 3 from each x-value and then sum. Therefore,

$$\Sigma(x-3) = (2-3) + (1-3) + (3-3) + (2-3) + (3-3)$$
$$= (-1) + (-2) + 0 + (-1) + 0 = -4$$

b. The symbol $\Sigma(x-3)^2$ tells you to subtract 3 from each x-value in the data set, square these differences, and then sum them as follows:

$$\Sigma(x-3)^2 = (2-3)^2 + (1-3)^2 + (3-3)^2 + (2-3)^2 + (3-3)^2$$
$$= (-1)^2 + (-2)^2 + (0)^2 + (-1)^2 + (0)^2$$
$$= 1 + 4 + 0 + 1 + 0 = 6$$

MEANING OF SUMMATION NOTATION Σx

Sum observations on the variable that appears to the right of the summation (i.e., the sigma) symbol.

EXERCISES **3.1** A data set contains the observations 5, 1, 3, 2, 1. Find:
a. Σx b. Σx^2 c. $\Sigma(x-1)$ d. $\Sigma(x-1)^2$

3.2 Suppose that a data set contains the observations 3, 8, 4, 5, 3, 4, 6. Find:
a. Σx b. Σx^2 c. $\Sigma(x-5)^2$ d. $\Sigma(x-2)^2$

3.3 Refer to Exercise 3.1. Find:
a. $\Sigma x^2 - \dfrac{(\Sigma x)^2}{5}$ b. $\Sigma(x-2)^2$

3.4 Refer to Exercise 3.2. Find:
a. $\Sigma x^2 - \dfrac{(\Sigma x)^2}{7}$ b. $\Sigma(x-5)^2$

3.5 A data set contains the observations 6, 0, −2, −1, 3. Find:
a. Σx b. Σx^2 c. $\Sigma x^2 - \dfrac{(\Sigma x)^2}{5}$

3.4 Measures of Central Tendency

The word *center,* as applied to a relative frequency distribution, is not a well-defined term. In our minds, we know vaguely what we mean: a number somewhere near the "middle" of the distribution, a single number that tends to typify the data set. The measures of central tendency that we define often generate different numbers for the same data set but all will satisfy our general objective. If we visually imagine a hump-shaped relative frequency distribution, all measures of central tendency will fall near the middle of the hump.

The most common measure of the central tendency of a data set, one that is familiar to you, is the **arithmetic mean** of the data. The arithmetic average, or arithmetic mean, is defined as follows:

DEFINITION 3.1

The **arithmetic mean** of a set of n observations, $x_1, x_2, \ldots, x_n$, is denoted by the symbol $\bar{x}$, and is computed as:

$$\bar{x} = \frac{\text{Sum of the } x\text{-values}}{\text{Number of observations}} = \frac{\Sigma x}{n}$$

(the symbol $\bar{x}$ is read "x-bar")

EXAMPLE 3.3   Find the mean for the data set, 5, 1, 6, 2, 4.

Solution   You can see that the data set contains $n = 5$ observations. Therefore,

$$\bar{x} = \frac{\Sigma x}{n} = \frac{5 + 1 + 6 + 2 + 4}{5} = \frac{18}{5} = 3.6$$

EXAMPLE 3.4   Find the mean for the 2,862 sale prices of Appendix A. Locate it on the relative frequency distribution, Figure 3.1. Does the mean fall near the center of the distribution?

Solution   We summed the sale price observations in Appendix A by computer and divided this sum by the number of observations, 2,862, to obtain

$$\bar{x} = \$42,040$$

This mean or average sale price should be located near the center of the relative frequency distribution for the 2,862 sale prices, Figure 3.1. If you examine Figure 3.1, you will see that the mean $\bar{x}$ does indeed fall near the center of the mound-shaped portion of the distribution. If we did not have Figure 3.1 available, we could reconstruct the distribution in our minds as a mound-shaped figure centered in the vicinity of $\bar{x} = \$42,040$.

A second measure of central tendency for a data set is the **median**. The **median** for a data set is a number chosen so that half of the observations are less than the median and half are larger. Since the areas of the bars used to construct the relative

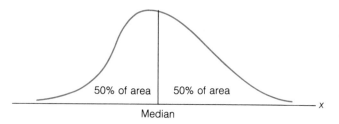

FIGURE 3.3
The Median Divides the
Area of a Relative
Frequency Distribution
into Two Equal Portions

frequency distribution are proportional to the numbers of observations falling within the classes, it follows that the median is a value of x that divides the area of the relative frequency distribution into two equal portions. Half of the area will lie to the left of the median (see Figure 3.3) and half will lie to the right. For example, the median for the 2,862 sale prices, Figure 3.1, is $37,000. You can see from Figure 3.1 that this sale price divides the data into two sets of equal size. Half of the 2,862 sale prices will be less than $37,000; half will be larger.

EXAMPLE 3.5 Find the median for the data set, 7, 4, 3, 5, 3.

Solution We first arrange the data in increasing (or decreasing) order:

3, 3, 4, 5, 7

Since we have an *odd number* of measurements, the choice for the median is easy; we will choose 4. Half of the measurements are less than 4 and half are greater than 4.

EXAMPLE 3.6 Suppose that you have an *even number* of measurements in the data set, say 5, 7, 3, 1, 4, 6. Find the median.

Solution If we arrange the data in increasing order, we obtain

1, 3, 4, 5, 6, 7

You can see that there are now many choices for the median. Any number between 4 and 5 will divide the data set into two groups of three each. There are many ways to choose this number, but the simplest is to choose the median as the point halfway between the two middle numbers when the data are arranged in order. Thus,

Median = 4.5

DEFINITION 3.2

The **median** of the n observations in a data set is defined as follows:

If n is odd: the middle observation when the data are arranged in order.
If n is even: the number halfway between the two middle observations when the data are arranged in order.

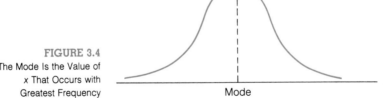

FIGURE 3.4
The Mode Is the Value of
x That Occurs with
Greatest Frequency

A third measure of central tendency for a data set is the *mode.* The *mode* is the value of x that occurs with greatest frequency (see Figure 3.4). If the data have been grouped into classes, we will define the mode as the center of the class with the largest class frequency (or relative frequency). For example, you can see from Figure 3.1 that the modal sale price is $35,000.

DEFINITION 3.3

The *mode* of a data set is the value of x that occurs with greatest frequency.

The mean, median, and mode are shown (Figure 3.5) on the graph of the relative frequency distribution for the 2,862 sale prices, Appendix A. Which is the best measure of central tendency for this distribution? The answer is that it depends upon the descriptive information that you desire. If the distribution figure were made of plywood and balanced on a line, that line would coincide with the mean. The median is a point that equally divides the area of the distribution, and the mode is located beneath the point at which the highest frequency occurs. If your notion of a typical or "central" sale price is one that is larger than half of the sale prices and less than the remainder, then you will prefer the median to the mean or mode.

The mean is sensitive to very large or very small observations. Consequently, the mean will shift toward the direction of skewness. The median is often preferred as a measure of central tendency because it is insensitive to skewness. If the relative frequency of occurrence of values of x can be viewed as a measure of customer preference (for example, the greatest frequency of sales occurred in the $32,500 to $37,500 class), then the mode might be the preferred measure of central tendency. You may regard these differences in the mean, median, and mode to be rather minor when you examine Figure 3.5. Notice that there is little difference in the numerical values of these three measures of central tendency and that all three accomplish their objective. Knowing the value of any one of the three would help you mentally locate the "center" of a relative frequency distribution.

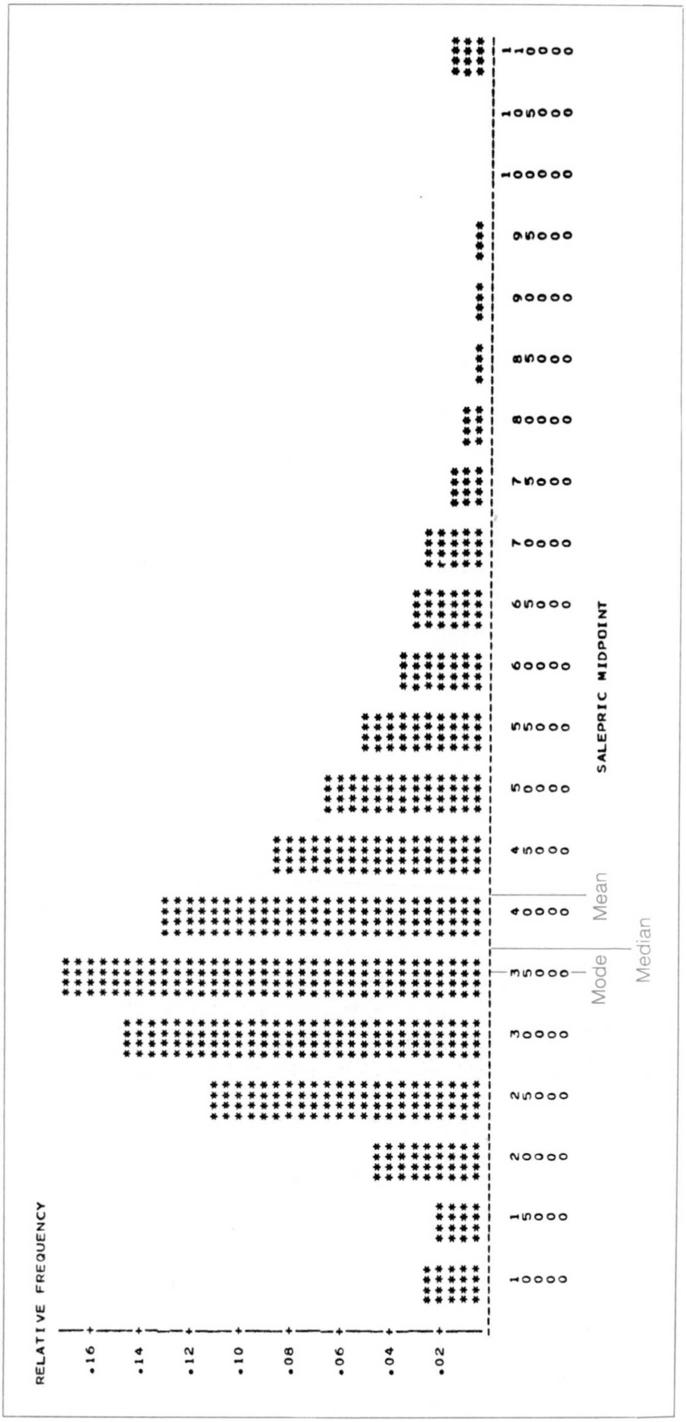

FIGURE 3.5 Locations of the Mean, Median, and Mode for the Sale Price Data, Appendix A

EXERCISES   **3.6**   Find the mean and median for the data set consisting of the five measurements, 3, 9, 0, 7, 4.

3.7   Find the mean and median for the sample of $n = 6$ measurements, 7, 3, 4, 1, 5, 6.

3.8   Find the mean and median for the $n = 50$ sale prices of Table 2.3 (p. 32). Locate the mean and median on the relative frequency distribution for the data set (see Figure 2.10). Notice that they fall near the center of the distribution.

3.9   Find the *modal class* (the class in which the mode occurs) for the relative frequency distribution, Figure 2.10. Take the mode to be the midpoint of this class interval. Compare your answer with the mean and median obtained in Exercise 3.8.

3.10   Suppose that a distribution of data is skewed to the right. Would you expect the mean of this data set to be larger or smaller than the median? See if your answer agrees with the results of Exercise 3.8.

3.11   Appendix B contains the sale prices for properties sold in six specific residential neighborhoods. These data were extracted from Appendix A. The mean sale prices (to the nearest dollar) for the six data sets are shown in the accompanying table. Use these measures of central tendency to construct a mental picture of the relative locations of the relative frequency distributions for the six data sets.

NEIGHBORHOOD	MEAN SALE PRICE
A	$62,797
B	69,419
C	30,524
D	41,233
E	37,791
F	52,325

3.5 Measures of Data Variation

Just as measures of central tendency locate the "center" of a relative frequency distribution, measures of variability measure its "spread." Examine the relative frequency distribution for the 2,862 sale prices, Figure 3.5, and think how you might describe its spread. The first thought that probably comes to mind is the *range*.

DEFINITION 3.4

The *range* of a quantitative data set is equal to the difference between the largest and the smallest measurements in the set.

EXAMPLE 3.7   Find the range for the data set, 3, 7, 2, 1, 8.

Solution   The smallest and largest members of the data set are 1 and 8, respectively. Therefore,

$$\text{Range} = \text{Largest measurement} - \text{Smallest measurement} = 8 - 1 = 7$$

FIGURE 3.6

Two Relative Frequency
Distributions That Have
Equal Ranges, but Show
Differing Amounts of Data
Variation

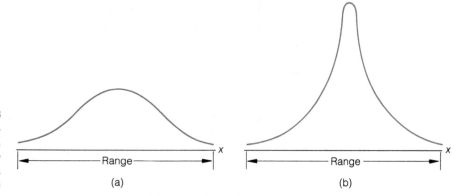

(a)   (b)

The range of a data set is easy to acquire, but it is an insensitive measure of variation and is not very informative. To demonstrate insensitivity, examine Figure 3.6. Both relative frequency distributions possess the *same range,* but it is clear that the relative frequency distribution, Figure 3.6(b), indicates much less data variation than the distribution, Figure 3.6(a). Most of the observations, Figure 3.6(b), lie close to the mean. In contrast, most of the observations, Figure 3.6(a), deviate substantially from the center of the distribution. Since the ranges for the two distributions are equal, it is clear that the range is a fairly insensitive measure of data variation. It was unable to detect the differences in data variation for the data sets represented in Figure 3.6.

To demonstrate the fact that the range is not very informative, examine the relative frequency distribution, Figure 3.5, and note that most of the data fall between $7,500 and $97,500, i.e., visually, we see the range as approximately $90,000. But if we examine the set of all 2,862 sale prices, Appendix A, you will find that the smallest observation is $1,500, the largest is $770,000, and the range is really $768,500. In other words, the range for the data set quantifies the spread of the extreme largest and smallest members of the data set. *What would be more useful is a range within which most of the data would lie.* This, along with the mean or median, would help us construct a mental image of the relative frequency distribution, Figure 3.5.

The magical measure that will perform this chore for us is known as the **standard deviation** of a data set. The standard deviation of a data set is based on how much the observations deviate from their mean. Notice that most of the observations, Figure 3.6(b), deviate very little from the mean of the distribution. In contrast, most of the observations, Figure 3.6(a), deviate substantially from the mean of that distribution.

The deviation between an observation x and the mean $\bar{x}$ of a data set is the difference,

$$x - \bar{x}$$

If a quantitative data set contains n observations, the **variance** of the data set is equal to the sum of the squares of the deviations from the mean of all n observations, divided by $(n - 1)$. That is, the variance, denoted by the symbol s^2, is

$$s^2 = \frac{\Sigma (x - \bar{x})^2}{n - 1}$$

The standard deviation, s, is the square root of this quantity. Before we give practical significance to the standard deviation, we will show you how it is computed for a small data set.

DEFINITION 3.5

The **variance, s^2,** of a set of n measurements is equal to the sum of squares of deviations of the measurements about their mean, divided by $(n - 1)$, i.e.,

$$s^2 = \frac{\Sigma (x - \overline{x})^2}{n - 1}$$

DEFINITION 3.6

The **standard deviation** of a set of n measurements is equal to the square root of the variance, i.e.,

$$s = \sqrt{\frac{\Sigma (x - \overline{x})^2}{n - 1}}$$

EXAMPLE 3.8 Find the standard deviation for the data set, 3, 7, 2, 1, 8.

Solution The five observations are listed in the first column of Table 3.1. You can see that $\Sigma x = 21$ and, therefore,

$$\overline{x} = \frac{\Sigma x}{n} = \frac{21}{5} = 4.2$$

This value of $\overline{x}$, 4.2, is subtracted from each observation to determine how much each observation deviates from the mean. These deviations are shown in the second column of Table 3.1. A *negative* deviation means that the observation fell *below* the mean; a *positive* deviation indicates that the observation fell *above* the mean. *Notice that the sum of the deviations equals 0. This will be true for all data sets.*

TABLE 3.1
Data and Computation Table

OBSERVATION x	$x - \overline{x}$	$(x - \overline{x})^2$
3	−1.2	1.44
7	2.8	7.84
2	−2.2	4.84
1	−3.2	10.24
8	3.8	14.44
TOTALS 21	0	38.8

The squares of the deviations are shown in Column 3 of Table 3.1. The total at the bottom of the column gives the sum of squares of deviations,

$$\Sigma (x - \bar{x})^2 = 38.8$$

Then the *variance* is

$$s^2 = \frac{\Sigma (x - \bar{x})^2}{n - 1} = \frac{38.8}{4} = 9.7$$

and the *standard deviation* is

$$s = \sqrt{s^2} = \sqrt{9.7} = 3.1$$

The procedure illustrated in Example 3.8 for calculating a standard deviation is tedious and often leads to rounding errors in finding the sum of squares of deviations, $\Sigma (x - \bar{x})^2$. A shortcut procedure for calculating the sum of squares of deviations is illustrated in the following example.

EXAMPLE 3.9   Use the **shortcut procedure** to calculate the sum of squares of deviations, $\Sigma (x - \bar{x})^2$, for the data set, Example 3.8.

Solution   The shortcut procedure provides an easy way to calculate $\Sigma (x - \bar{x})^2$. Instead of calculating the deviation of each measurement from the mean, we calculate the squares of the observations, as shown in Table 3.2.

TABLE 3.2
Table for Calculating a Standard Deviation: The Shortcut Procedure

OBSERVATION	
x	x^2
3	9
7	49
2	4
1	1
8	64
TOTALS 21	127

Then it can be shown (proof omitted) that $\Sigma (x - \bar{x})^2$ is equal to

$$\Sigma (x - \bar{x})^2 = \Sigma x^2 - \frac{(\Sigma x)^2}{n}$$

Substituting the sum of squares Σx^2 and the sum Σx of the observations into this formula, we obtain

$$\Sigma (x - \bar{x})^2 = \Sigma x^2 - \frac{(\Sigma x)^2}{n} = 127 - \frac{(21)^2}{5}$$

$$= 127 - 88.2 = 38.8$$

This is exactly the same total that you obtained for the sum of squares of deviations in Table 3.1.

SHORTCUT PROCEDURE FOR CALCULATING $\Sigma(x - \bar{x})^2$

$$\Sigma(x - \bar{x})^2 = \Sigma x^2 - \frac{(\Sigma x)^2}{n}$$

Now that you know how to calculate a standard deviation, we will demonstrate with examples how it can be used to measure the spread or variation of a relative frequency distribution.

EXAMPLE 3.10 The mean and standard deviation of the 2,862 sale prices of Figure 3.5 were calculated by computer and found to be

$$\bar{x} = \$42,040$$

$$s = \$28,322$$

Form an interval by measuring one standard deviation on either side of the mean, i.e., $\bar{x} \pm s$. Also, form the intervals $\bar{x} \pm 2s$ and $\bar{x} \pm 3s$. The intervals $\bar{x} \pm s$ and $\bar{x} \pm 2s$ are shown on the relative frequency distribution for the data, Figure 3.7. Find the proportions of the total number (2,862) of measurements falling within these intervals.

Solution It is too tedious to check by hand each of the sale prices in Appendix A to determine whether they fall within the three intervals, so we did it by computer. The proportions of the total number of sale prices falling within the three intervals are shown in Table 3.3. You can see that the proportions of the total area under the relative frequency distribution, Figure 3.7, that lie over the three intervals agree with these proportions.

TABLE 3.3
Proportions of the Total Number of Sale Prices in Intervals $\bar{x} \pm s$, $\bar{x} \pm 2s$, and $\bar{x} \pm 3s$

INTERVAL			PROPORTION IN INTERVAL
$\bar{x} \pm s$	or	($13,718, $70,362)	0.90
$\bar{x} \pm 2s$	or	(−$14,604, $98,684)	0.98
$\bar{x} \pm 3s$	or	(−$42,926, $127,006)	0.99

Will the proportions of the total number of observations falling within the intervals $\bar{x} \pm s$, $\bar{x} \pm 2s$, and $\bar{x} \pm 3s$ remain fairly stable for most distributions of data? To examine this possibility, consider the following example:

EXAMPLE 3.11 Calculate the mean and standard deviation of the following data sets (Appendix A):

a. The 2,862 appraised land values
b. The 2,862 appraised property improvement values
c. The 2,862 ratios of sale price to total appraised property value

Solution Because of the large amounts of data involved, we computed the means and standard deviations on a computer. They are shown in Table 3.4. The relative frequency

FIGURE 3.7   Relative Frequency Distribution for the 2,862 Sale Prices of Appendix A

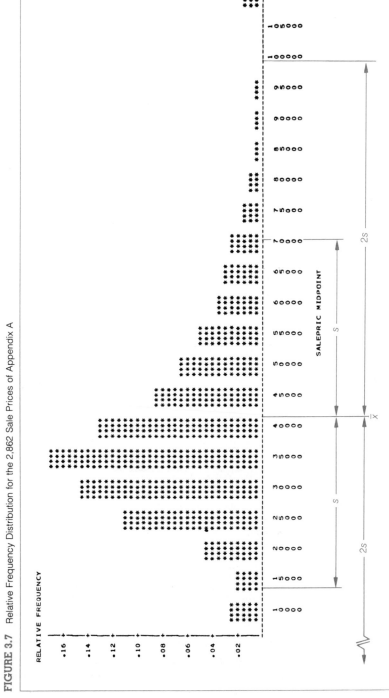

distributions for the three data sets are shown in Figures 3.8, 3.9, and 3.10, respectively (see pp. 63–65).

(see pp. 63–65)

DATA SET	MEAN $\bar{x}$	STANDARD DEVIATION s
Appraised land value	$ 4,220	$ 2,629
Appraised improvement value	$24,638	$14,590
Ratio, sale price to total appraised value	1.56	.84

The means and standard deviations of Table 3.4 were used to calculate the intervals $\bar{x} \pm s$, $\bar{x} \pm 2s$, and $\bar{x} \pm 3s$ for each data set, and we obtained a computer count of the number and proportion of the total number of observations falling within each interval. These proportions are presented in Tables 3.5(a), (b), and (c).

TABLE 3.5
Proportions of the Total
Number of Observations
Falling within $\bar{x} \pm s$,
$\bar{x} \pm 2s$, and $\bar{x} \pm 3s$

(a) Appraised Land Value

INTERVAL		PROPORTION IN INTERVAL
$\bar{x} \pm s$	or ($1,591, $6,849)	0.80
$\bar{x} \pm 2s$	or (−$1,038, $9,478)	0.98
$\bar{x} \pm 3s$	or (−$3,667, $12,107)	0.99

(b) Appraised Improvement Value

INTERVAL		PROPORTION IN INTERVAL
$\bar{x} \pm s$	or ($10,048, $39,228)	0.80
$\bar{x} \pm 2s$	or (−$4,542, $53,818)	0.98
$\bar{x} \pm 3s$	or (−$19,132, $68,408)	0.99

(c) Ratio, Sale Price to Total Appraised Value

INTERVAL		PROPORTION IN INTERVAL
$\bar{x} \pm s$	or (.72, 2.4)	0.94
$\bar{x} \pm 2s$	or (−.12, 3.24)	0.98
$\bar{x} \pm 3s$	or (−.96, 4.08)	0.99

Tables 3.3 and 3.5(a), (b), and (c) demonstrate a property that is common to many data sets. The percentage of observations that lie within one standard deviation of the mean $\bar{x}$, i.e., in the interval ($\bar{x} \pm s$), is fairly large and variable, usually from 60% to 80% of the total number, but the percentage can reach 90% or more for highly skewed distributions of data. The percentage within two standard deviations of $\bar{x}$, i.e., in the interval ($\bar{x} \pm 2s$), is close to 95% but, again, this percentage will be larger for highly skewed sets of data. Finally, the percentage of observations within three standard

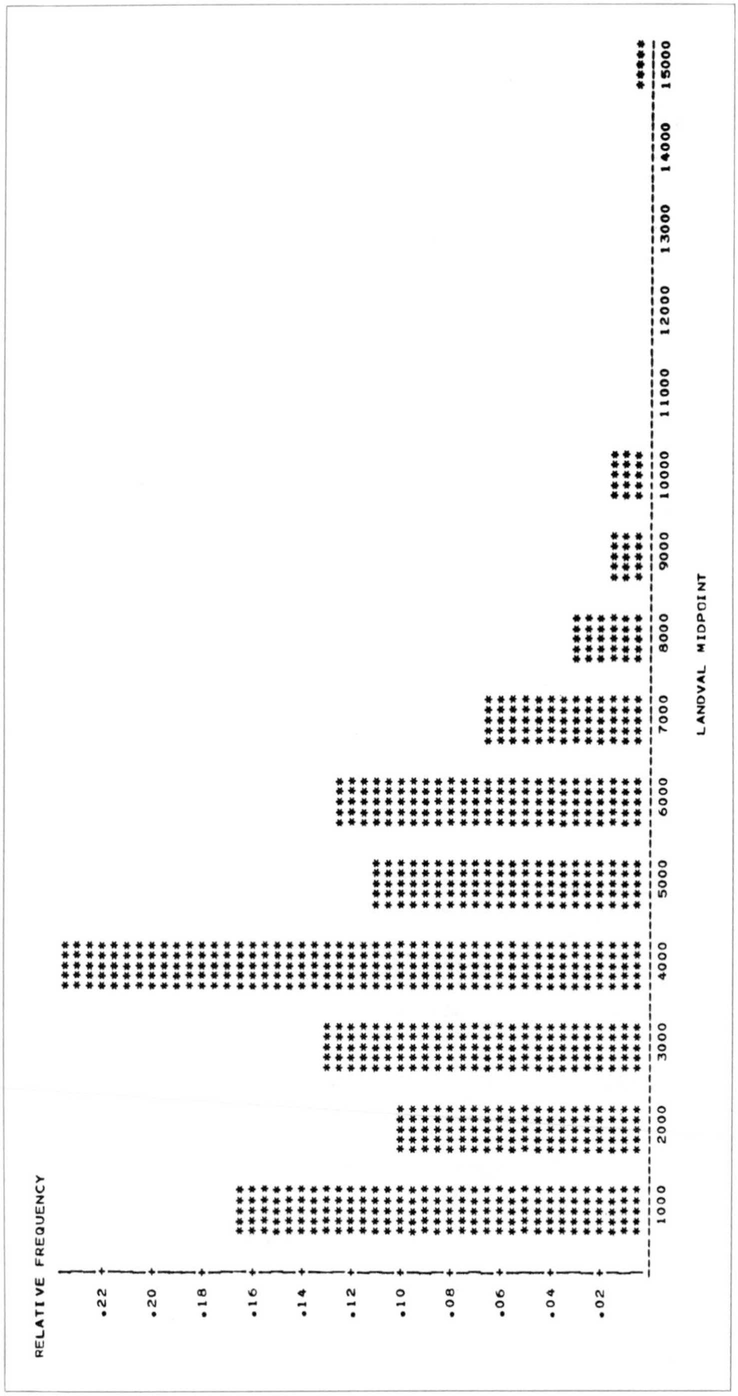

FIGURE 3.8   Real Estate Analyses, 1978 Appraised Value

FIGURE 3.9   Real Estate Analyses, 1978 Appraised Improvements

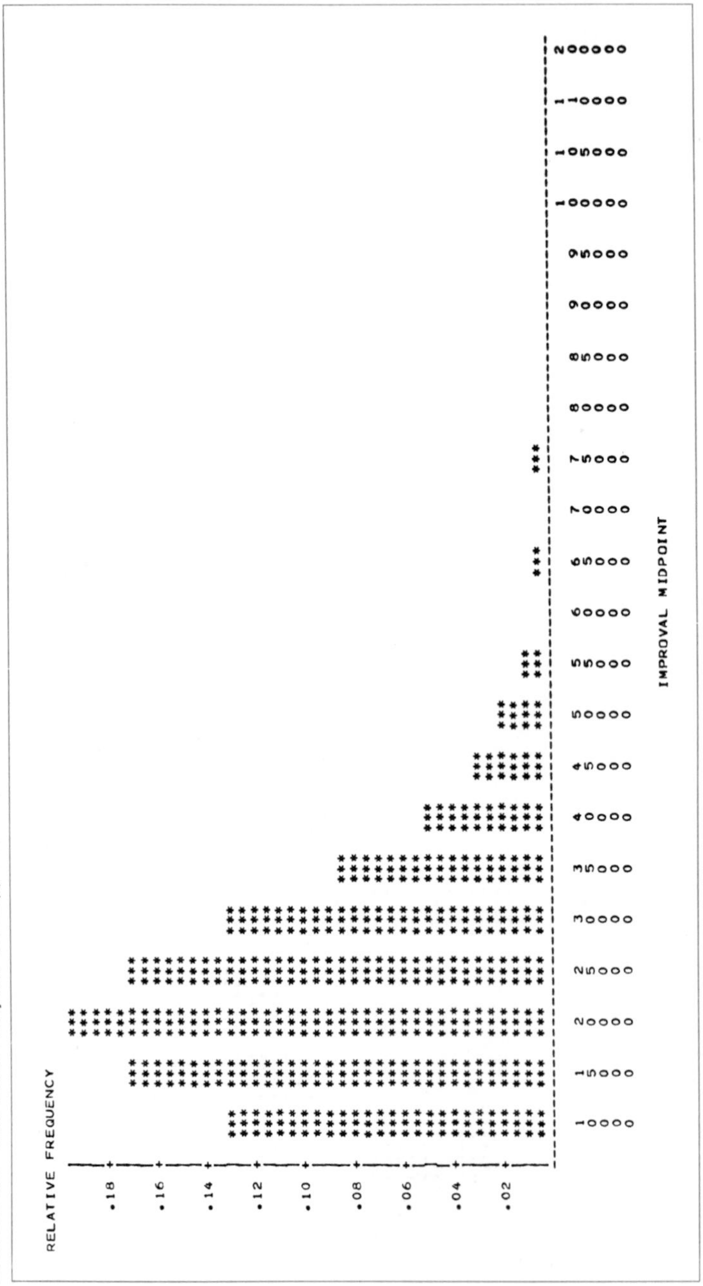

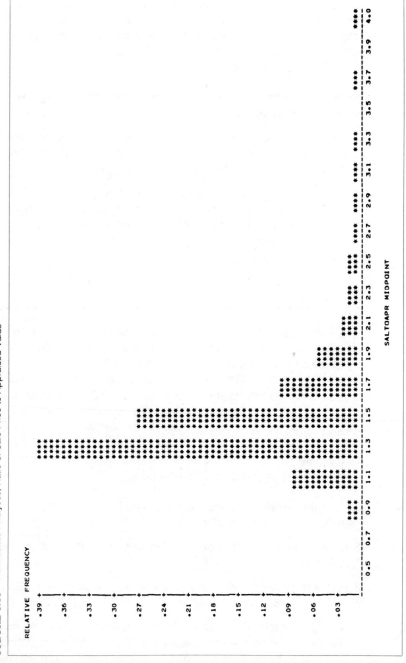

FIGURE 3.10 Real Estate Analyses, Ratio of Sale Price to Appraised Value

deviations of $\bar{x}$, i.e., in the interval $(\bar{x} \pm 3s)$, is almost 100%, meaning that almost all of the observations in a data set will fall within this interval. This property, which seems to hold for most data sets which contain at least 20 observations, is called the *Empirical Rule.* The Empirical Rule provides a very good rule of thumb for forming a mental image of a distribution of data when you know the mean and standard deviation of the data set. Calculate the intervals $\bar{x} \pm s$, $\bar{x} \pm 2s$, and $\bar{x} \pm 3s$ and then picture the observations grouped as follows:

THE EMPIRICAL RULE

If a relative frequency distribution of data has mean $\bar{x}$ and standard deviation s, then the proportions of the total number of observations falling within the intervals $\bar{x} \pm s$, $\bar{x} \pm 2s$, and $\bar{x} \pm 3s$ are as follows:

$\bar{x} \pm s$: Usually 60% to approximately 80%. The percentage will be larger (near 90%) for highly skewed distributions. The percentage will be near 70% for distributions that are mound-shaped and nearly symmetric.

$\bar{x} \pm 2s$: Close to 95%

$\bar{x} \pm 3s$: Near 100%

If you examine the relative frequency distribution of sale prices, Figure 3.7 (or any of the distributions, Figures 3.8, 3.9, and 3.10), you will see that most of the sale prices are concentrated in a mound-shaped distribution lying between $10,000 and $75,000. The distribution then skews to the right, and even contains one sale price as large as $770,000 and several in the range of $200,000 to $300,000 (see the original data set, Appendix A). These very large sale prices create a high degree of skewness in the distribution which inflates the value of the standard deviation, s. For this reason, the percentages of observations falling within the intervals $\bar{x} \pm s$, $\bar{x} \pm 2s$, and $\bar{x} \pm 3s$ for the distributions, Figures 3.7, 3.8, 3.9, and 3.10, will tend to be on the high side of the range of values given by the Empirical Rule.

EXERCISES **3.12** Find the range, variance, and standard deviation for the data set, 3, 9, 0, 7, 4. (Use the shortcut procedure to calculate $\Sigma(x - \bar{x})^2$.)

3.13 Find the range, variance, and standard deviation for the $n = 6$ measurements, 7, 3, 4, 1, 5, 6.

3.14 Find the range, variance, and standard deviation for the $n = 25$ measurements, 2, 1, 7, 6, 5, 3, 8, 5, 2, 4, 5, 6, 3, 4, 4, 6, 9, 4, 3, 4, 5, 5, 7, 3, 5.

3.15 Refer to the data, Exercise 3.14. Construct the intervals $\bar{x} \pm s$, $\bar{x} \pm 2s$, and $\bar{x} \pm 3s$. Count the number of observations falling within each interval and find the corresponding proportions. Compare your results to the Empirical Rule.

3.16 Use the information, Exercise 3.15, to construct a sketch of the relative frequency distribution for the data set, Exercise 3.14. Then construct a relative frequency distribution for the data using class intervals .5 to 1.5, 1.5 to 2.5, . . . , 8.5 to 9.5. Compare your sketch with the relative frequency distribution for the data set, Exercise 3.14.

3.17 The National Advisory Committee on Criminal Justice Standards and Goals compiles yearly reports on the cost and resource implications of correctional standards related to halfway houses. The main purpose of these reports is to provide state and local decision makers with cost information on the many kinds of activities carried out by halfway houses. One variable included in the report is Yearly per bed rental costs. Given below are the yearly per bed rental costs (in dollars) for a random sample of 35 halfway houses:

417	282	280	303	400	76	643	480	472
317	264	384	205	257	136	250	100	732
750	402	422	373	325	408	345	749	313
791	196	891	283	186	693	137	52	

Compute $\bar{x}$ and s for this sample, then find the intervals $\bar{x} \pm s$, $\bar{x} \pm 2s$, and $\bar{x} \pm 3s$. Count the number of yearly per bed rental costs in each interval and construct a table similar to Table 3.3. Compare your results with the Empirical Rule. Do you agree that the values of $\bar{x}$ and s, in conjunction with the Empirical Rule, provide a reasonably good description of the data set?

3.18 Worker productivity is often gauged by the amount that a company invests in capital equipment divided by the number of workers at the company. Recent studies show that office productivity lags far behind the productivity figures for industry and agriculture. The means and standard deviations of Company investment per worker in capital equipment for the three types of workers as reported by a major consulting firm are shown in the accompanying table.

	OFFICE WORKER	INDUSTRIAL WORKER	FARM WORKER
Mean productivity	$2,000	$25,000	$35,000
Standard deviation	500	7,000	8,000

a. Use the above information, in conjunction with the Empirical Rule, to sketch your mental images of the three relative frequency distributions. Construct them on the same graph so that you can see how they appear relative to each other.

b. Estimate the proportion of companies which invest between $11,000 and $39,000 in capital equipment per industrial worker.

c. Estimate the proportion of companies which invest between $27,000 and $43,000 in capital equipment per farm worker.

3.6 Measures of Relative Standing

You may want to describe the relative position of a particular measurement in a data set. For example, suppose that a property in the data set, Appendix A, sold for $80,000. You might want to know whether this is a relatively small or large sale price, etc. What percentage of the sale prices were less than $80,000; what percentage were larger? Descriptive measures that locate the relative position of a measurement, in relation to the other measurements, are called *measures of relative standing.* One that expresses this position in terms of a percentage is called a *percentile* for the data set.

DEFINITION 3.7

Let x_1, x_2, ..., x_n be a set of n measurements arranged in increasing (or decreasing) order. The *pth percentile* is a number x such that $p\%$ of the measurements fall below the pth percentile and $(100 - p)\%$ fall above it.

The sale price, $80,000, falls at the 96.5 percentile of the sale price data, Appendix A. This tells you that 96.5% of the sale prices were less than $80,000 and $(100 - 96.5)\% = 3.5\%$ were greater.

Another measure of relative standing is the *z-score* for a measurement. For example, suppose that you were told that $80,000 lay 1.34 standard deviations above the mean for the 2,862 sale prices of Appendix A. Knowing that most of the sale prices will be less than 2 standard deviations from the mean and almost all will be within 3, you would have a good idea of the relative standing of the $80,000 sale price.

The distance that a measurement, x, lies above or below the mean, $\bar{x}$, of a data set, measured in units of the standard deviation, s, is called the *z-score* for the measurement. Negative z-scores indicate that the observation lies to the left of the mean; positive z-scores indicate that the observation lies to the right of the mean.

DEFINITION 3.8

The *z-score* for a measurement, x, is

$$z = \frac{x - \bar{x}}{s}$$

EXAMPLE 3.12 We have noted that the mean and standard deviation for the 2,862 sale prices, Appendix A, are $\bar{x} = \$42,040$ and $s = \$28,322$. Use these values to find the z-score for a sale price of $80,000.

Solution   Substituting the values of x, $\bar{x}$, and s into the formula for z, we obtain

$$z = \frac{x - \bar{x}}{s} = \frac{\$80,000 - \$42,040}{\$28,322}$$

$$= 1.34$$

Since the z-score is positive, we conclude that the $80,000 sale price lies a distance of 1.34 standard deviations above (to the right of) the mean of $42,040.

EXERCISES   **3.19**   The 70th percentile for the 2,862 residential sale prices, Appendix A, is $45,000. Interpret this value.

3.20   Refer to the 50 sale prices, Table 2.3 (p. 32). The mean and standard deviation are $\bar{x} = \$42,728$ and $s = \$18,246$. Find the z-score for a property selling for:
a. $27,000   **b.** $56,400
What is the interpretation of negative z-scores?

3.21   The relative frequency distribution of the daily single-room lodging rates for a sample of 68 motels and hotels in Las Vegas, Nevada, is summarized by the following numerical descriptive measures:

$$\bar{x} = \$31.25 \qquad s = \$6.50 \qquad \text{Median} = \$28.75$$

a.   Find the 50th percentile for the 68 single-room lodging rates.
b.   A Las Vegas motel, selected at random from the 68, advertises its daily single-room lodging rate as $23.97. Find the z-score for this motel rate and interpret its value.
c.   If the median for a set of data has a z-score which is positive, the relative frequency distribution is skewed to the left; a negative z-score implies that the relative frequency distribution is skewed to the right. Find the z-score for the median Las Vegas single-room lodging rate. Interpret this value.

3.22   An electric company serving a mid-sized central Florida city reported that the number of kilowatt-hours (KWH) used by 1,200 apartment dwellers during the month of September had a mean of 630 and a standard deviation of 80.
a.   September utility statements showed that the 97th percentile for the set of 1,200 electric meter readings was 782 KWH. Interpret this value.
b.   The September utility bill for one of the 1,200 apartments was selected at random from the company's files. The number of KWH used by this apartment was recorded as 874. Find the z-score for this electrical usage value.
c.   Refer to your answer to part b. Assuming that the mean and standard deviation reported by the company were correct, would you expect an apartment with a September kilowatt usage as high as 874 KWH? [*Hint:* Apply the Empirical Rule.] Does this suggest that the mean and/or standard deviation of the 1,200 kilowatt usages may have been incorrectly reported? Explain.

3.23 Chamber of Commerce groups from 400 U.S. cities were surveyed and the number of tourists who visited each of the cities last year was recorded. The mean number of tourists per city for the 400 cities and the standard deviation were computed to be $\bar{x} = 1{,}500{,}000$ and $s = 400{,}000$.

a. Use the Empirical Rule to help you sketch the relative frequency distribution for the number of tourists per city for the 400 U.S. cities last year.

b. Records show that the city of Jacksonville, Florida, one of the 400 cities surveyed, had 2,300,000 tourists last year. Locate this observation on your sketch and compute its z-score.

c. Would you expect many of the 400 U.S. cities to have z-scores larger than the z-score for Jacksonville, Florida?

3.7 Numerical Descriptive Measures for Populations

Remember, when you analyze a data set, you are doing so for a reason. Presumably, you want to use the information in the data set to infer the nature of some larger set of data, a population. For example, we might want to know something about the complete set of 1978 property values for all properties in the mid-sized Florida city described in Section 1.1. If we take the value for each property to be the sale price that the owner *would have received* in 1978 (if the property had been sold), then the conceptual set of sale prices for all residential properties in the city would be the population of interest to us. However, most of the properties in the city *were not sold* in 1978 and, consequently, we can never obtain the sale prices for all residential properties in the population. We do know that the entire population of sale prices possesses a relative frequency distribution (the exact form of which is unknown to us), and we will want to infer the nature of this distribution based on the sample of 2,862 sale prices contained in Appendix A. It is natural that we would want to use the descriptive measures of this sample to infer the nature of the population relative frequency distribution.

The numerical descriptive measures that characterize the relative frequency distribution for a population are called **parameters.** Since we will often use the numerical descriptive measures of a sample to estimate the corresponding unknown numerical descriptive measures of the population, we will need to make a distinction between the numerical descriptive measure symbols for the population and for the sample.

In our previous discussion, we used the symbols $\bar{x}$ and s to denote the mean and standard deviation, respectively, of a sample of n observations. Similarly, we will use the symbol μ (mu), the Greek letter "m," to denote the mean of a population, and the symbol σ (sigma), the Greek letter "s," to denote the standard deviation of a population. As you will subsequently see, we will use the sample mean $\bar{x}$ to estimate the population mean μ, and the sample standard deviation s to estimate the population standard deviation σ. In doing so, we will be using the sample to help us infer the nature of the population relative frequency distribution.

SAMPLE AND POPULATION NUMERICAL DESCRIPTIVE MEASURES

Sample mean: $\bar{x}$

Population mean: μ

Sample standard deviation: s

Population standard deviation: σ

Sample z-score: $z = \dfrac{x - \bar{x}}{s}$

Population z-score: $z = \dfrac{x - \mu}{\sigma}$

3.8 Calculating a Mean and Standard Deviation from Grouped Data (Optional)

In Sections 3.4 and 3.5 we gave formulas for computing the mean and standard deviation of a data set. However, these formulas apply only to *raw* data sets, i.e., those in which the value of each of the individual observations in the data set is known. If your data have already been grouped into classes of equal class width and arranged in a frequency table, you must use an alternative method to compute the mean and standard deviation.

EXAMPLE 3.13 Refer to Example 2.9 (p. 32). Calculate the mean and standard deviation for the sale price data, Table 2.3, using the grouping shown in the frequency table, Table 2.4.

Solution Since the data of Table 2.3 are raw, i.e., the sale prices for each of the 50 properties selected from Appendix A are given, we could compute the sample mean sale price and sample standard deviation of sale prices directly, using the formulas of Sections 3.4 and 3.5. For the purposes of illustration, however, we will assume that we have access only to the grouped data of Table 2.4. The formulas for calculating $\bar{x}$, s^2, and s from grouped data are given in the box on the next page.

The eleven class intervals, midpoints, and frequencies of Table 2.4 are reproduced in Table 3.6 (p. 73). Substituting the class midpoints and frequencies into the formulas, we obtain:

$$\bar{x} = \frac{\sum x_i f_i}{n} = \frac{(20,050)(2) + (30,050)(15) + (40,050)(19) + \cdots + (120,050)(1)}{50}$$

$$= \frac{2,152,500}{50} = 43,050$$

$$s^2 = \frac{\sum x_i^2 f_i - \frac{(\sum x_i f_i)^2}{n}}{n-1}$$

$$= \frac{\{(20,050)^2(2) + (30,050)^2(15) + \cdots + (120,050)^2(1)\} - \frac{(\sum x_i f_i)^2}{50}}{50 - 1}$$

Since we found $\sum x_i f_i = 2,152,500$ when calculating $\bar{x}$, we have

$$s^2 = \frac{\{(20,050)^2(2) + (30,050)^2(15) + \cdots + (120,050)^2(1)\} - \frac{(2,152,500)^2}{50}}{49}$$

$$= \frac{(107,915,125,000) - (92,665,125,000)}{49} = 311,224,489.8$$

and

$$s = \sqrt{311,224,489.8} = 17,641.556$$

Thus, using the grouped data method, we have $\bar{x} = \$43,050$ and $s = \$17,641.556$.

FORMULAS FOR CALCULATING A MEAN AND STANDARD DEVIATION FROM GROUPED DATA

x_i = Midpoint of the ith class

f_i = Frequency of the ith class

k = Number of classes

n = Total number of observations in the data set

$$\bar{x} = \frac{(x_1 f_1 + x_2 f_2 + x_3 f_3 + \cdots + x_k f_k)}{n}$$

$$= \frac{\sum x_i f_i}{n}$$

$$s^2 = \frac{(x_1^2 f_1 + x_2^2 f_2 + x_3^2 f_3 + \cdots + x_k^2 f_k) - \frac{(\sum x_i f_i)^2}{n}}{n-1}$$

$$= \frac{\sum x_i^2 f_i - \frac{(\sum x_i f_i)^2}{n}}{n-1}$$

$$s = \sqrt{s^2}$$

TABLE 3.6
Class Intervals, Midpoints,
and Frequencies for the
50 Sale Prices, Table 2.4

CLASS	CLASS INTERVAL	CLASS MIDPOINT x_i	CLASS FREQUENCY f_i
1	15,050—25,050	20,050	2
2	25,050—35,050	30,050	15
3	35,050—45,050	40,050	19
4	45,050—55,050	50,050	6
5	55,050—65,050	60,050	3
6	65,050—75,050	70,050	3
7	75,050—85,050	80,050	0
8	85,050—95,050	90,050	1
9	95,050—105,050	100,050	0
10	105,050—115,050	110,050	0
11	115,050—125,050	120,050	1
			$n = 50$

The values of $\bar{x}$, s^2, and s based on the formulas for grouped data will usually not agree exactly with those obtained using the raw or ungrouped data. Applying the formulas of Sections 3.4 and 3.5 to the raw data of Table 2.3, we obtain $\bar{x} = 42,728$ and $s = 18,246.018$. These values are different from those computed above because, in the grouped data method, we have substituted the value of the class midpoint for each value of x, Sale price, in a class interval. Only when every value of x in each class is equal to its respective class midpoint (which is rarely the case) will the formulas for grouped and for ungrouped data give identical values of $\bar{x}$, s^2, and s. Therefore, the formulas for grouped data are approximations to these numerical descriptive measures.

EXERCISES

3.24 Refer to the yearly per bed rental cost data of Exercise 3.17.

a. Using the six class intervals, 51.5—191.5, 191.5—331.5, ..., 751.5—891.5, construct a frequency table similar to Table 3.6.

b. Compute $\bar{x}$ and s from the grouped data formulas. Compare these values to the values of $\bar{x}$ and s you obtained in Exercise 3.17 using the raw data.

3.25 Refer to Exercise 2.14.

a. Calculate the mean and standard deviation for the sample of 35 Bank Holding Companies' deposits, using the raw data.

b. Repeat part a, but use the grouped data method. Use the class intervals that you formed in Exercise 2.14.

3.26 The Federal Communications Commission (FCC) is investigating a New York radio station for irregularly broadcast radio commercials. The distribution of the lengths of time for 50 randomly selected commercials broadcast during the station's early morning programming period is given in the table on p. 74. Compute the mean and standard deviation for the distribution of 50 radio commercial time lengths.

LENGTH OF TIME (IN SECONDS)	NUMBER OF RADIO COMMERCIALS
0.5— 6.5	0
6.5—12.5	3
12.5—18.5	18
18.5—24.5	2
24.5—30.5	1
30.5—36.5	10
36.5—42.5	0
42.5—48.5	0
48.5—54.5	2
54.5—60.5	14
	50

3.27   Many of the top producers in the liquor industry saw little growth in the consumption of their brand during 1979. Information on the percent change in sales volume from 1978 to 1979 for the 35 highest ranked brands of liquor is given in the table. Compute $\bar{x}$, s^2, and s for the percent change in sales volume data, using the grouping given in the table.

PERCENT CHANGE IN SALES VOLUME, 1978 TO 1979	NUMBER OF BRANDS
−8.05 to −3.55	8
−3.55 to +0.95	3
+0.95 to +5.45	16
+5.45 to +9.95	2
+9.95 to +14.45	4
+14.45 to +18.95	1
+18.95 to +23.45	0
+23.45 to +27.95	1
	35

Source: *Advertising Age,* March 31, 1980. Copyright 1980 by Crain Communications Inc. Reprinted with permission.

3.9   Summary

Numerical descriptive measures enable us to construct a mental image of the relative frequency distribution for a data set. The two most important types of numerical descriptive measures are those that measure central tendency and data variation.

Three numerical descriptive measures are used to locate the "center" of a relative frequency distribution: the mean, median, and mode. Each conveys a special piece of information. In a sense, the mean is the balancing point for the data. The median divides the data; half of the observations will be less than the median, and half will be larger. The mode is the value of x that occurs with greatest frequency. It is the value of x that locates the point where the relative frequency distribution achieves its maximum relative frequency.

The range and the standard deviation measure the spread of a relative frequency distribution. Particularly, we can obtain a very good notion of the way data are distributed by constructing the intervals $\bar{x} \pm s$, $\bar{x} \pm 2s$, and $\bar{x} \pm 3s$ and referring to the Empirical Rule. The percentages of the total number of observations falling within these intervals will be approximately as shown in the accompanying table.

INTERVAL	PERCENTAGE
$\bar{x} \pm s$	60% to 80%
$\bar{x} \pm 2s$	95%
$\bar{x} \pm 3s$	Almost 100%

KEY WORDS

Numerical descriptive measures	Variance
Measures of central tendency	Standard deviation
Measures of data variation or spread	Empirical Rule
Measures of relative standing	Percentile
Mean	z-Score
Median	Parameters
Mode	Raw data*
Skewness	Grouped data*
Range	

*From the optional section.

KEY SYMBOLS

For a sample:
  Mean: $\bar{x}$
  Variance: s^2
  Standard deviation: s
  z-Score: $z = \dfrac{x - \bar{x}}{s}$

For a population:
  Mean: μ
  Variance: σ^2
  Standard deviation: σ
  z-Score: $z = \dfrac{x - \mu}{\sigma}$

SUPPLEMENTARY EXERCISES

[*Note:* Starred (*) exercises refer to the optional section in this chapter.]

3.28   Compute Σx, Σx^2, and $(\Sigma x)^2$ for each of the following data sets:
α.   7, 8, 4, −2, 12, 8
b.   123, 247, 0, 100
c.   −3, 4, −2, 0, −3, −2, −4
d.   17, 17, 20, 23, 12

3.29 Compute the mean, median, and mode for each of the data sets in Exercise 3.28.

3.30 Compute the range, s^2, and s for each of the data sets in Exercise 3.28.

3.31 Calculate $\bar{x}$, s^2, and s for each of the following data sets:
a. $\Sigma x^2 = 13.3$, $\Sigma x = 7.6$, $n = 10$ **b.** $\Sigma x^2 = 863$, $\Sigma x = 112$, $n = 27$
c. $\Sigma x^2 = 45$, $\Sigma x = 8$, $n = 4$

3.32 For each of the following data sets, compute $\bar{x}$, s^2, and s:
a. 14, 7, 0, 0, 9, 0   **b.** −8, −6, 10, 16
c. −4, −2, −2, 1, 1, 8, 6, 4, 6   **d.** 1,242, 1,793, 485, 480

3.33 Give a realistic business example for which the best measure of central tendency of a quantitative data set is provided by:
a. The mean   **b.** The median   **c.** The mode

3.34 What is the best measure of the variability of a quantitative data set? Why?

3.35 Give two different methods of measuring the relative standing of an observation within a set of measurements. How are they different? How are they alike?

3.36 In an attempt to reduce the revenue lost due to passengers who have reserved a seat but fail to show, most major airlines frequently overbook their flights. *Overbooking* is the practice of selling more ticket reservations for a flight than there are seats available on the plane. Thus, at times, more passengers with reservations show up for a flight than there are seats available, and some must wait until the next available flight before departing (they have been *bumped*). The following data represent the number of passengers who were bumped from a Chicago to Atlanta flight due to overbooking on 10 randomly selected days:

     3, 0, 0, 1, 4, 2, 1, 1, 0, 2

a. Determine the mean, median, mode, range, variance, and standard deviation for this data set.
b. Which of the numerical descriptive measures in part a are measures of variability, and which are measures of central tendency?

3.37 An important factor in an oil company's decision on whether to continue drilling in a certain region is the productivity of the oil wells currently in use in the region. A major oil company now operates one oil well in a flatland region of Texas. The decision on whether to drill for more wells in the region will be based upon the daily production of the oil well for the 25 days that it has been in operation. These daily productions (in hundreds of barrels) are given below. Compute $\bar{x}$, s^2, and s for this data set.

82	91	43	75	88	28	57	74	76
44	55	83	94	93	37	77	86	68
93	42	58	78	49	63	63		

3.38 Suppose that you have a choice of three stocks in which to invest. The only information available to you is the mean daily gain in price and the standard deviation of price gains of each stock for the past 30 days. This information is given in the accompanying table. [*Note:* A negative gain denotes a loss.] Sketch your mental images of the three relative frequency distributions. (The Empirical Rule will help you do this.) Is there one stock that appears to be the superior investment? The inferior investment?

STOCK	MEAN DAILY GAIN (dollars)	STANDARD DEVIATION (dollars)
1	1.40	.22
2	5.00	2.35
3	−2.50	.50

3.39 The start of the 1980–81 television ratings race among the three major TV networks was delayed due to a strike by the Guild of Screen and Television Actors in September 1980. Items under negotiation with television producers included higher minimum salaries and more fringe benefits for the actors. At the time of the strike, salaries were structured so that the majority of TV actors earned from $30,000 to $100,000 per year, while a few "big-name" actors earned millions of dollars annually.

a. Based on this salary information, discuss possible skewness in the pre-strike distribution of TV actors' salaries.

b. Which measure of central tendency of TV actors' salaries—the mean or the median—should the actors use in an attempt to convince TV producers that they (the actors) are deserving of higher salaries and more fringe benefits? Explain.

c. Which measure of central tendency of TV actors' salaries should the producers quote in order to rebuff the actors' demands? Explain.

3.40 Buckingham Cutty Sark brand liquor falls in the 68th percentile of the 1979 sales volume distribution of the country's 35 top-selling liquor brands. Describe Cutty Sark's ranking within the 1979 liquor sales volume distribution.

3.41 The "ad volumes" of various business publications are made available quarterly by *Industrial Marketing* magazine. Listings include the total number of full-run advertising display pages during the period for each publication. The accompanying data set (from *Industrial Marketing*, November 1980) shows the number of full-run display pages for a random selection of forty business publications during the third quarter of 1980.

156	181	162	124	47	674	205	162	135	219
49	174	82	405	215	85	188	175	269	93
194	373	163	343	91	101	256	133	238	174
222	349	161	90	192	120	70	214	597	79

a. Compute the mean of the data set.

b. Find the median of the data set.

c. Find the mode of the data set.

3.42   Refer to Exercise 3.41. Find the range, variance, and standard deviation of the data set. (Use the shortcut procedure to calculate $\Sigma (x - \bar{x})^2$.)

3.43   Refer to Exercises 3.41 and 3.42. Construct the intervals $\bar{x} \pm s$, $\bar{x} \pm 2s$, and $\bar{x} \pm 3s$. Count the number of observations falling within each interval and find the corresponding proportions. Compare the results to the Empirical Rule.

3.44   Refer to Exercise 3.41. Find the 10th percentile for the ad volume data set.

3.45   Market-demand studies indicate that the typical wine-purchasing household has a higher income, fewer members, and more education than average. A random sample of 4,500 wine-purchasing households showed incomes with an average of $16,039 and a standard deviation of $5,010; a sample of 7,000 nonpurchasing households showed incomes with an average of $13,126 and a standard deviation of $3,102.
  a.   Roughly sketch on a piece of graph paper the relative frequency distributions for the purchasing and nonpurchasing household incomes.
  b.   What is the approximate proportion of wine-purchasing households in the sample with incomes between $6,019 and $26,059?
  c.   What is the approximate proportion of nonpurchasing households in the sample with incomes larger than $16,228 or smaller than $10,024?

3.46   Five applicants for real estate appraisal training, two from Oregon and three from Florida, have submitted their scores on different real estate appraisal aptitude exams. The two from Oregon had taken the Pacific Appraisers' Aptitude Test (PACAT), while the three from Florida had taken the Southeastern Appraisers' Aptitude Test (SEAT). Scores on the PACAT have a mean of 50 and a standard deviation of 10, while scores on the SEAT have a mean of 120 and a standard deviation of 15. The applicants and their scores are listed in the table.

APPLICANT	EXAM TAKEN	SCORE
#1	PACAT	60
#2	PACAT	45
#3	SEAT	130
#4	SEAT	115
#5	SEAT	110

  a.   Find the respective z-scores for each of the applicants.
  b.   If the five applicants are ranked from highest to lowest entirely on the basis of who had the best appraisal aptitude test score *in relation to the type of exam taken* (highest score receiving rank 1, and so forth), which applicant would have the highest rank? The lowest? [*Hint:*   Use your results from part a.]

3.47   Full-time manufacturing workers in the Jacksonville, Florida, Standard Metropolitan Statistical Area (SMSA) earned, on the average, $273.51 in June 1980. Assume that the standard deviation of the June salaries is $78.35.
  a.   Use the Empirical Rule to describe the relative frequency distribution of the June salaries for all full-time manufacturing workers in the Jacksonville SMSA.

b. Approximately what proportion of full-time Jacksonville manufacturing workers earned between $116.81 and $430.21 in June 1980?

c. The median June 1980 salary for full-time Jacksonville manufacturing workers was $270.88. What proportion of workers earned less than $270.88 during this period?

d. A manufacturing worker from northern Florida indicates to you that he earned $450 during June 1980. Do you believe that this worker is employed in the Jacksonville SMSA? Explain.

3.48   Refer to the sale prices of residential properties in the six neighborhoods of Appendix B. The means and standard deviations of the sale prices of the six data sets are shown in the table.

NEIGHBORHOOD	MEAN SALE PRICE	STANDARD DEVIATION
A	$62,797	$20,072
B	69,419	12,900
C	30,524	9,815
D	41,233	8,995
E	37,791	5,321
F	52,325	15,506

a. Use them, in conjunction with the Empirical Rule, to sketch your mental images of the six relative frequency distributions. Construct them on the same graph so that you can see how they appear relative to each other.

b. Construct tables similar to Table 3.3 for the sale price data for each of the six neighborhoods. Do the proportions agree with the Empirical Rule? [*Note:* The relative frequency distributions for these six data sets are shown in Figures 3.11 to 3.16, pp. 80–85, respectively.]

3.49   An all-news cable television network claims that the distribution of the number of homes reached nightly by their prime-time (8:00 PM) newscast has a mean of 2.7 million homes and a standard deviation of .35 million homes. Assume that the claim is true and also that the distribution is mound-shaped.

a. Approximately what proportion of the prime-time newscasts would you expect to reach between 2.0 and 3.4 million homes?

b. Approximately what proportion of the prime-time newscasts would you expect to reach between 1.65 and 3.75 million homes?

3.50   Refer to Exercise 3.49. A potential advertiser questions the validity of the cable network's claim concerning the mean number of homes reached nightly by the prime-time newscast. Specifically, the advertiser believes the claimed mean of 2.7 million homes is too high. In an attempt to support this belief, the advertiser hires a rating service that uses the same rating system as the cable network. Suppose that the rating service found that, for one randomly selected night, the prime-time newscast was viewed by 1.5 million homes.

a. Compute the z-score for the observation, 1.5 million homes, assuming that the information provided by the cable network is correct. Interpret its value.

FIGURE 3.11   Real Estate Analyses, 1978 Sale Price

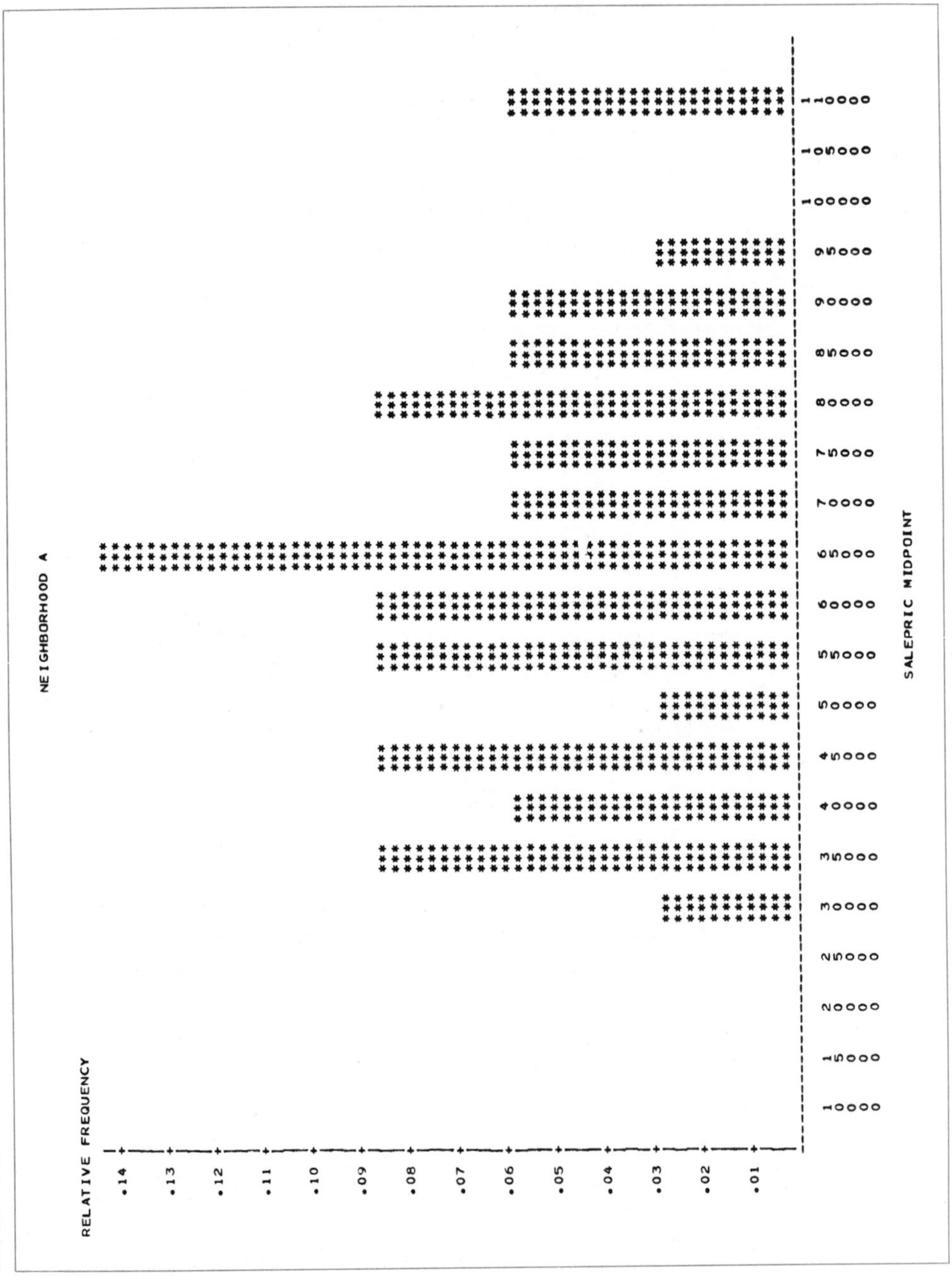

FIGURE 3.12 Real Estate Analyses, 1978 Sale Price

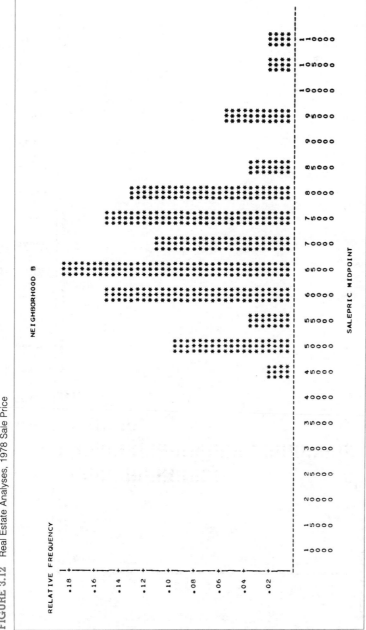

FIGURE 3.13   Real Estate Analyses, 1978 Sale Price

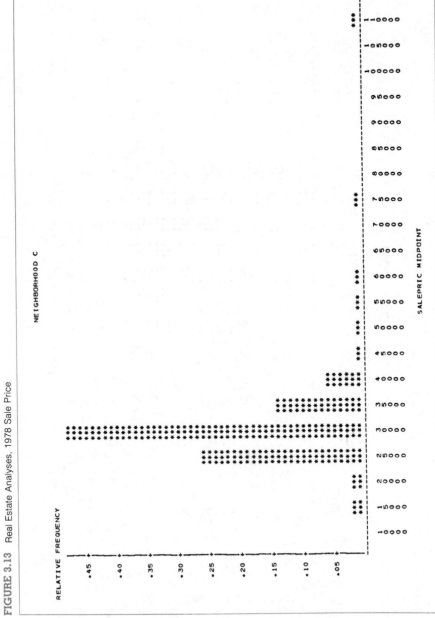

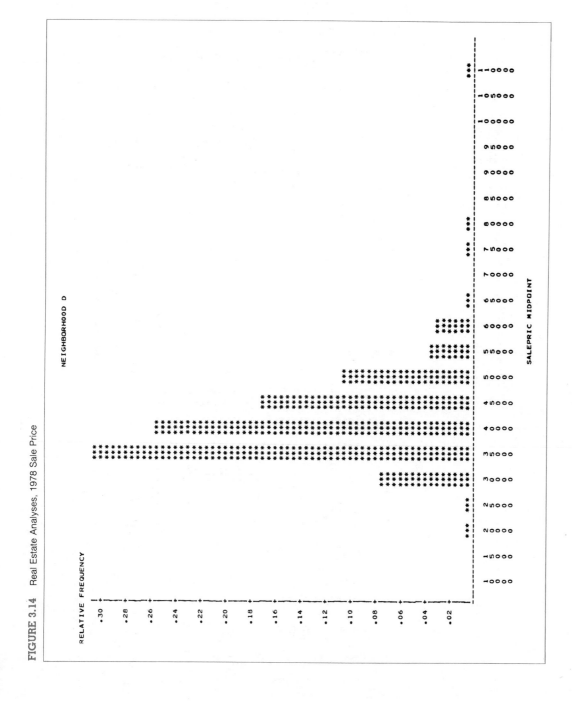

FIGURE 3.14 Real Estate Analyses, 1978 Sale Price

FIGURE 3.15   Real Estate Analyses, 1978 Sale Price

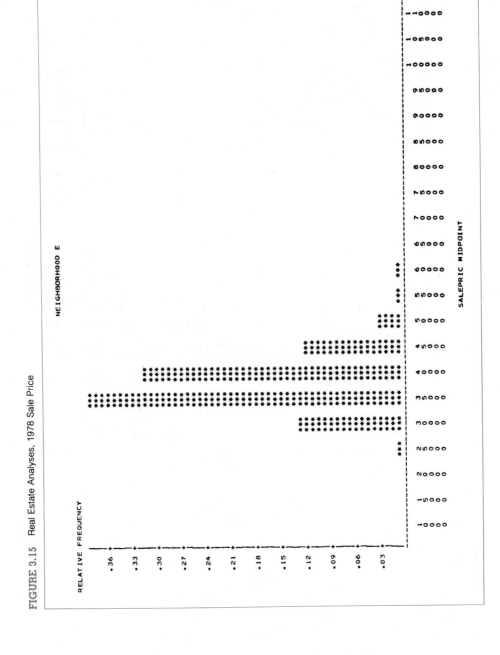

FIGURE 3.16   Real Estate Analyses, 1978 Sale Price

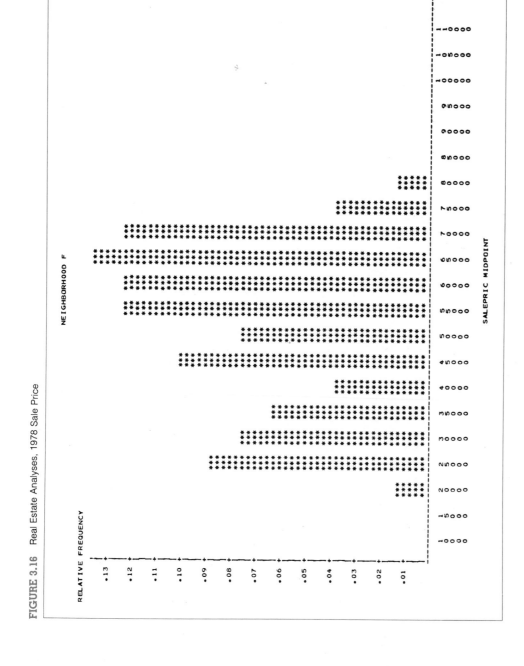

b.   On the basis of the rater's findings and your knowledge of the Empirical Rule, do you believe that the cable network has overstated the mean number of homes reached by their prime-time newscast? Explain.

*3.51   An important part of human resource planning by an organization's personnel department is an analysis of labor force trends. In order to assess the supply of labor during the next decade, a company obtained U.S. labor force projections, by age group, for 1990. The data are presented in grouped form in the accompanying table.

AGE GROUP	PROJECTED NUMBER IN THE LABOR FORCE IN 1990 (THOUSANDS)
15—24	22,139
25—34	32,301
35—44	28,532
45—54	18,733
55—64	11,218
	112,923

Source: U.S. Department of Labor, *Employment and Training Report of the President,* 1977.

a.   Compute the approximate mean projected age of persons in the U.S. labor force in 1990.
b.   Compute the approximate standard deviation of the projected ages of persons in the U.S. labor force in 1990.

*3.52   The time patients spend waiting in a physician's office before they receive health care services, i.e., *patient waiting time,* plays an important role in the efficient operation of the physician's practice (see Case Study 7.2). The number of minutes (after their appointment times) that each of a sample of 55 patients had to wait in a dentist's office before being served are shown in the accompanying table.

WAITING TIME (MINUTES)	NUMBER OF PATIENTS
0— 3.5	12
3.5— 7.0	11
7.0—10.5	7
10.5—14.0	15
14.0—17.5	6
17.5—21.0	3
21.0—24.5	1
	55

a.   Calculate approximate values for the mean waiting time and standard deviation of waiting times from this sample.
b.   Form the interval $\bar{x} \pm 2s$. Using the frequency table, determine the number of patients in the sample with waiting times in this interval.
c.   Compare the results of part b with the Empirical Rule.

3.53 Arizona's housing market has recently become one of the nation's strongest. This is due to the steady stream of new residents fleeing harsh northern winters, along with former Californians searching for a relatively less-populated area in which to live. In a random sample of forty new homes sold in Arizona this year, the average cost was $83,350 and the standard deviation was $7,650.

a. Describe the relative frequency distribution of the costs of the forty Arizona homes.

b. Estimate the fraction of the forty Arizona homes which cost between $75,700 and $91,000.

c. One of the homes in the sample, located in Flagstaff, Arizona, had a cost of $73,787. Compute the z-score for the cost of this home.

d. If an Arizona home were chosen at random from the sample of forty, is it more likely that the cost of the home would be greater than $73,787 or less than $73,787? Refer to your answer to part c.

3.54 A chemical manufacturing plant, under investigation by the Environmental Protection Agency (EPA) for possible violation of air pollution standards, reports that the distribution of the amount of dangerous chemicals in the plant's air emissions is approximately mound-shaped, with a mean of 5 parts per million (ppm) and a standard deviation of 1.5 ppm.

a. Use the Empirical Rule to describe the distribution of the amount of dangerous chemicals in the plant's air emissions.

b. The EPA sets a limit of 10 ppm on dangerous chemicals in plant air emissions. Plants found exceeding this standard more than once per year are required to install expensive air pollution control devices. Based upon your description of the air emissions distribution of part a, do you believe that the chemical plant is in violation of air quality standards? Explain.

*3.55 The accompanying table gives the distribution of hourly wage rates of 200 welders employed by an electric transformer manufacturing company.

HOURLY WAGE RATE (DOLLARS)	NUMBER OF WELDERS
6.55—6.85	10
6.85—7.15	15
7.15—7.45	38
7.45—7.75	42
7.75—8.05	30
8.05—8.35	46
8.35—8.65	11
8.65—8.95	5
8.95—9.25	3
	200

a. Find the modal class of the grouped data.

b. Compute the approximate mean and standard deviation of the data set, based on the grouping shown in the table.

c. Estimate the percentage of welders with hourly wage rates within 2 standard deviations of the mean hourly wage rate.

3.56 The accompanying data set represents the sales volume (in shares) of the 15 most active stocks on the New York Stock Exchange for Tuesday, February 10, 1981.

Prime Cm	790,300	Texaco Inc.	391,000	TW Corp	326,100
Exxon	666,300	Cont. Air Lines	385,500	Twc Fox	304,400
Sony Corp	523,900	US Air	375,700	Gillette Co.	303,600
Boeing	420,900	Whirlpool	341,000	K Mart	303,000
IBM	392,600	AT&T	329,500	Standard Oil	301,400

a. Compute $\bar{x}$, s^2, and s for the sample.
b. Compute the median and the range.
c. Find the z-score for IBM's sales volume. Interpret this value.
d. Find the stock which falls in the 80th percentile of the sales volume distribution of the 15 most active stocks.
e. Compute the intervals $\bar{x} \pm s$, $\bar{x} \pm 2s$, and $\bar{x} \pm 3s$. Count the number of stock sales volumes which fall within each interval and compare the interval percentages to those of the Empirical Rule.

3.57 Suppose that the average loss payment per insurance claim by a sample of 1,000 motorcycle owners is $615 and the standard deviation is $85. Assume that the distribution of loss payment per claim is approximately mound-shaped.
a. Form a mental image of the distribution of loss payments for this sample. Sketch your image on a piece of graph paper.
b. Estimate the percentage of the loss payments in the interval $445 to $785.
c. Would you expect to observe a loss payment in the sample as large as $900?

*3.58 Refer to Exercise 3.41. Construct a frequency table for the ad volume data, using 10 class intervals. Compute $\bar{x}$, s^2, and s using the grouped data method, and compare these values to your previous results (Exercises 3.41 and 3.42).

3.59 Refer to Exercise 2.18.
a. Calculate $\bar{x}$, s^2, and s for the EPA estimated highway mileage data.
b. Use the numerical measures of part a to describe the relative frequency distribution of the data.
c. Compute a measure of the relative standing of Pontiac Firebird's estimated mpg of 20.

3.60 A Las Vegas tourist hotel has recently experienced problems with people who reserve rooms for a nonholiday weekend but fail to show up. These "no shows" cost the hotel thousands of dollars in lost revenue. An examination of hotel records for a random selection of 35 nonholiday weekends indicated that the number of empty rooms (per weekend) due to "no shows" had a mean of 8.5 and a standard deviation of 2.0.
a. Describe the distribution of the number of empty rooms due to "no shows" on nonholiday weekends at the Las Vegas hotel.

b. Suppose that for an upcoming nonholiday weekend, after all the rooms were reserved, 4 additional reservations were accepted by the hotel. Management thus expects that there will be enough "no shows" (in fact, 4 or more) so that the hotel can honor all of its reservations. Based upon your description of the distribution in part a, do you think it is very likely that the hotel will be able to honor all of its reservations? Explain.

CASE STUDY 3.1
Using Growth Rates to Measure the Cost of Capital

On determining the cost of common equity capital, David F. Scott, Jr., et al., write:*

One of the most critical aspects of the corporate budgeting process is the determination of a proper "hurdle rate" or "cut-off" rate to employ in the screening of proposed uses of funds. This hurdle rate is now commonly referred to in both industry and the literature of financial management as the cost of capital. General agreement on how to measure the equity component of the cost of capital (i.e., the cost of common equity) has not yet been achieved by either practitioners or theorists. A unique approach . . . involves quizzing directly a sample of the corporation's existing common stockholders as to their dividend and capital gain expectations. Proper interpretation of the responses can provide top corporate management with an estimate of the cost of equity capital, as represented by the returns (expected) by shareholders.

The methodology of this new approach to measuring the cost of capital depends upon the shareholders' perceptions of growth rates for the firm's (1) common stock price, (2) cash dividends per share, and (3) earnings per share. (The growth rate, defined over a 10–15 year period, is the average percent at which the firm's common stock price, cash dividends, and earnings per share *increase* each year.)

In early 1977, questionnaires were sent to the owners of Apex (a pseudonym) Industries, Inc. common stock. Each shareholder was asked to estimate the growth rate in each of the three categories defined above.

A total of 229 responses were returned in usable form. This information can be broken into three distinct data sets: the data set consisting of the 229 estimated common stock price growth rates; the data set made up of the 229 estimated cash dividends per share growth rates; and the data set containing the 229 estimated earnings per share growth rates. Summary measures of the respective data sets are provided in the accompanying table.

Growth Rate Estimates (%)

ITEM	MEAN	STANDARD DEVIATION
1. Common stock price	16.82	13.64
2. Cash dividends per share	16.17	20.76
3. Earnings per share	28.29	23.46

*D.F. Scott, Jr., J.W. Petty, & C.W. Shepherd. "Determining the cost of common equity capital: The direct method." *Journal of Business Research,* March 1980, *8,* 89–103. Copyright 1980 by Elsevier North Holland, Inc. Reprinted by permission.

On the average, the firm's shareholders are projecting a 16.82% stock price rise per year, accompanied by a 16.17% rise in dividends and a 28.29% rise in earnings. Scott, et al. use growth rate means to compute an estimate of the cost of equity capital for Apex. They theorize that if the true growth rate for each item is known, a fairly accurate estimate of the cost of capital can be computed. However, since these growth rates cannot be precisely predicted, Scott, et al. obtain the average "guess" of the particular growth rate by the firm's shareholders and use these means to obtain an estimate of the company's cost of capital.

a. Construct the interval $\bar{x} \pm 2s$ for each of the three Apex stock items. (A negative growth rate implies an annual decrease in the stock item.)
b. Assume that the estimated growth rate for each item has a relative frequency distribution which is nearly mound-shaped. Approximate the proportion of the measurements which fall within the interval $\bar{x} \pm 2s$ for each of the three data sets.
c. Considering the wide range of the intervals you computed in part a, would you feel comfortable using the mean projected growth rate of the sample to estimate the true growth rate for each of the respective stock items? Is it possible that the sample mean projected growth rates could lead to poor cost of capital estimates? (We give a detailed discussion on the reliability of the sample mean as an estimate of the population mean in Chapters 7 and 8.)

CASE STUDY 3.2
Consumer
Complaints: Due
to Chance or
Specific Causes?

The degree of sensitization on the part of a firm to the needs and wants of its consumers is frequently an important factor in determining the firm's overall success. Jean Namias* presents a procedure for achieving such sensitivity. This procedure uses the rate of consumer complaints about a product to determine when and when not to conduct a search for specific causes of consumer complaints. This rate may change or vary merely as a result of chance or fate, or it may be due to some specific cause, such as a decline in the quality of the product. Concerning the former, Namias writes:

> In any operation or production process, variability in the output or product will occur, and no two operational results may be expected to be exactly alike. Complete constancy of consumer rates of complaint is not possible, for the vagaries of fate and chance operate even within the most rigid framework of quality or operation control.

Namias has determined that the complaint rate of a product (e.g., the number of customer complaints per 10,000 units sold) has a relative frequency distribution which is approximately mound-shaped. This leads to a *Decision Rule* with which to determine when the observed variation in the rate is due to chance and when it is due to specific causes.

The reasoning is that if there are no problems with the production and distribution of the product, 95% of the time the rate of complaint should be within 2 standard deviations of the mean rate. If the production and distribution process were

---
*J. Namias, "A method to detect specific causes of consumer complaints." *Journal of Marketing Research*, August 1964, 63–68.

DECISION RULE

If the observed rate is 2 standard deviations or less away from the mean rate of complaint, it is attributed to chance. If the observed rate is farther than 2 standard deviations above the mean rate, it is attributed to a specific problem in the production or distribution of the product.

---

operating normally, it would be very unlikely for a rate higher than 2 standard deviations above the mean to occur. Instead, it is more likely that the high complaint rate is caused by abnormal operation of the production and/or distribution process, i.e., something specific is wrong with the process.

Namias recommends searching for the cause (or causes) only if the observed variation in the rate of complaints is determined by the rule to be the result of a specific cause (or causes). The degree of variability due to chance must be tolerated. Namias says:

> As long as the results exhibit chance variability, the causes are common, and there is no need to attempt to improve the product by making specific changes. Indeed, this may only create more variability, not less, and may inject trouble where none existed, with waste of time and money. . . . On the other hand, time and money are again wasted through failure to recognize specific conditions when they arise. It is therefore economical to look for a specific cause when there is more variability than is expected on the basis of chance alone.

Namias collected data from the records of a beverage company for a 2-week period to demonstrate the effectiveness of the rule. Consumer complaints primarily concerned chipped bottles that looked dangerous. For one of the firm's brands, the complaint rate was determined to have a mean of 26.01 per 10,000 bottles sold and a standard deviation of 11.28. The complaint rate observed during the 2 weeks under study was 93.12 complaints per 10,000 bottles sold.

a. Compute the z-score for the observed rate of 93.12.
b. Make a general interpretation of its value.
c. Use the Namias Decision Rule to determine whether the observed rate is due to chance or whether it is due to some specific cause. (In actuality, a search for a possible problem in the bottling process led to a discovery of rough handling of the bottled beverage in the warehouse by newly hired workers. As a result, a training program for new workers was instituted.)

CASE STUDY 3.3

Estimating the Mean Weight of Short-Leaf Pine Trees—Grouped Data Method

Consider the problem of estimating the true mean weight of short-leaf pine trees in the 40-acre tract of land located in western Arkansas (Case Study 1.2, p. 13). How can we use the sample information given in Table 1.1 to obtain this estimate? From our discussion in this chapter, we need to compute the sample mean, i.e., the mean weight of the sample of 117 trees in the 20 ⅕-acre plots which were "cruised." However, recall that the actual weight of each tree had to be estimated, based upon the diameter of the tree at chest height and the number of 16-foot logs the tree was capable of producing. This was best accomplished by grouping the trees according to diameter and assigning the same estimated weight to each tree in a particular group. For example, the 38 trees which had chest height diameters measured at 10 inches had all been assigned the estimated weight of 580 pounds, while the 34 trees with 11-inch diameters had all been assigned a weight of 750 pounds (see Table 1.1). In one sense, we can think of these weights as representing the midpoints of various weight class intervals. The weight of 580 pounds could represent the midpoint of the class interval 579.5—580.5, 750 pounds the midpoint of the class interval 749.5—750.5, etc. Notice that there are numerous class intervals (e.g., 580.5—581.5, 581.5—582.5, . . . , 748.5—749.5) which have a class frequency of 0.

α. Use the formulas given in Section 3.8 to compute the approximate sample mean weight $\bar{x}$ and the sample standard deviation s from the grouped data of Table 1.1.

b. Suppose that the tree weights were given in raw data form and that the estimated weights in Table 1.1 were the actual weights of the trees. If you were to compute $\bar{x}$ and s from the raw data, how would these values compare to those computed in part a?

REFERENCES   "Ad pages decline 3rd quarter." *Industrial Marketing,* November 1980, 91–92, 94–96.

Hamburg, M. *Statistical analysis for decision making.* 2d ed. New York: Harcourt Brace Jovanovich, 1977. Chapter 1.

Levine, R. I. *Statistics for management.* Englewood Cliffs, N. J.: Prentice-Hall, 1978. Chapters 3 and 4.

Maxwell, J. C., Jr. "Higher prices driving consumers from liquor." *Advertising Age,* March 31, 1980, 64.

Mendenhall, W. & Reinmuth, J. E. *Statistics for management and economics.* 2d ed. North Scituate, Mass.: Duxbury, 1974. Chapter 3.

Namias, J. "A method to detect specific causes of consumer complaints." *Journal of Marketing Research,* August 1964, 63–68.

Scott, D. F., Jr., Petty, J. W., & Shepherd, C. W. "Determining the cost of common equity capital: The direct method." *Journal of Business Research,* March 1980, *8,* 89–103.

Four   **Probability**

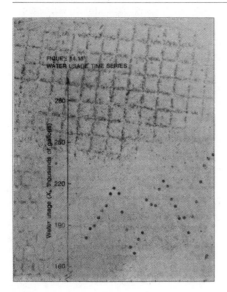

How would you like to strike it rich with a $10 stake (Case Study 4.3), or obtain a winning edge in blackjack (Case Study 4.4)? And what do either of these ventures have to do with statistics? The answer is *uncertainty.* The return in real dollars on most investments cannot be predicted with certainty. Neither can we be certain that an inference about a population, based on the partial information contained in a sample, will be correct. In this chapter we shall learn how probability can be used to measure uncertainty, and we shall take a brief glimpse at its role in assessing the reliability of statistical inferences.

Contents:

4.1   Blackjack, Investing, and Statistics

If you play blackjack, a popular gambling game, whether you win in any one game is an outcome that is very uncertain. Similarly, investing in bonds, stock, a new business, etc., is a venture whose success is, again, subject to uncertainty. (In fact, some would argue that investing is a form of educated gambling, one in which knowledge, experience, and good judgment can improve the odds of winning.*)

Much like blackjack and investing, inferences based on sample data are also subject to uncertainty. A sample rarely tells a perfectly accurate story about the population from which it was selected. There is always a margin of error (as the pollsters tell us) when sample data are used to estimate the proportion of people in favor of a particular political candidate, some consumer product, or some political or social issue. There is always uncertainty about how far the sample estimate will depart from the true population proportion of affirmative answers that you are attempting to estimate. Consequently, a measure of the amount of uncertainty associated with an estimate (which we called *the reliability of an inference* in Chapter 1) plays a major role in statistical inference.

How do we measure the uncertainty associated with events? Anyone who has observed a daily newscast can answer that question. The answer is *probability.* Thus, it may be reported that the probability of rain on a given day is 20%. Such a statement acknowledges that it is uncertain whether it will rain on the given day and indicates that the forecaster measures the likelihood of its occurrence as 20%.

In this chapter we will examine the meaning of probability and develop some properties of probability that will be useful in our study of statistics. We will do so by building our discussion around a game of chance, namely blackjack, and then we will apply our knowledge to the solution of some practical business problems.

4.2   The Game of Blackjack

Blackjack (or Twenty-One as it is sometimes called) is a game played by two or more players using an ordinary 52-card bridge deck. Each card is assigned a value. Cards numbered from 2 to 10 are assigned the values shown on the card. For example, a 7 of spades has a value of 7; a 3 of hearts has a value of 3. Face cards (kings, queens, and jacks) are each valued at 10, and an ace can be assigned a value of either 1 or 11, a decision that is at the discretion of the player holding the card.

The essence of the game is that you are dealt two cards and you may request more. The objective is to acquire cards whose total value is as near as possible to, but not exceeding, 21. If the sum of the initial two cards is equal to 21, you have drawn a "blackjack," in most circumstances a winning hand. Each player bets and plays against one of the players who is designated as the "dealer." You win the bet if the total value of your hand exceeds the total value of the dealer's hand. If the total value of the

---

*One can also utilize sample data (experience) to improve the chances of winning at blackjack. The *Wall Street Journal* (October 24, 1980) reports that the Treasury Hotel Casino in Las Vegas offers seminars on a "surefire method for beating the house" in blackjack.

FIGURE 4.1
Some Typical Two-Card
Draws and Their Values

19   7   21   20

Blackjack

cards in your hand exceeds 21, you automatically lose; if you hold 5 cards and their total value is 21 or less, you automatically win; if you tie the dealer, you lose. Some typical initial draws are shown in Figure 4.1.

The game is played as follows: The dealer distributes two cards, face down, to each player and two cards to himself, one face up and one face down. You see the total value of your hand and, seeing **one** of the dealer's two cards, you have some information on the total value of the cards in the dealer's hand. The next move belongs to you. You can decide to face the dealer with the total value of the two cards contained in your initial draw, or you can elect to draw one or more new cards, hoping to push the total value of your hand nearer to, but not exceeding, 21. If additional draws lead to a total exceeding 21, you lose. If not, presumably at some draw, you decide to face the dealer with the total value that you then hold in your hand.

After you and the other players finish playing, the dealer must decide whether to face you with the total value contained in his initial pair of cards (if the initial pair is a blackjack, the dealer automatically wins) or whether to draw additional cards in an attempt to increase the total value of his hand.* In doing so, he risks the possibility of drawing a card whose value will push the total value of his hand over 21. If this were to occur, the dealer would lose to all players still in the game.

When the dealer concludes his draw, he displays his cards face up. If the total value of your cards exceeds the total value of the dealer's cards, you win. If not, you lose. Naturally, you hope to draw an ace and a 10 or a face card on the initial draw. This draw, "blackjack," is an automatic win for you unless the dealer matches your feat.

Now that you have a basic understanding of the game of blackjack, we are ready to use this game of chance to illustrate some important and useful probability concepts.

4.3 Experiments and Events

In the language employed in a study of probability, the word **experiment** possesses a very broad meaning. In this language, an experiment is a process of making an observation. For example, dealing a pair of cards in the game of blackjack could be

---

*Different variations of the game are played in casinos throughout the world. For example, "blackjack" is an automatic win for a player in Las Vegas. Also according to Las Vegas rules, the dealer has no decision on a "hit." If the total value of the dealer's cards is 16 or less, he must "hit" (draw another card). If his hand has a total value of 17 through 21, he must "stick" (play the cards in his hand).

viewed as an experiment. Counting the number of defective light bulbs produced per hour in a manufacturing process is an experiment. Similarly, recording the annual sales of a corporation is an experiment. Observing the annual average inflation rate is an experiment. Note that most experiments result in outcomes which cannot be predicted with certainty in advance.

DEFINITION 4.1

The process of making an observation is called an *experiment.*

EXAMPLE 4.1 Consider the following experiment: You are dealt a pair of cards in the game of blackjack. List some possible outcomes of this experiment that cannot be predicted with certainty in advance.

Solution Some possible outcomes of this experiment that cannot be predicted with certainty in advance are:

a.   You draw an ace of hearts and a 3 of clubs.
b.   You draw an 8 of diamonds and a 9 of hearts.
c.   You draw a blackjack—an ace and a card whose value is 10 (a total value of 21).
d.   You do not draw a blackjack.

EXAMPLE 4.2 Consider the following experiment: A sample of 500 is selected from among a large number of home buyers to determine the proportion who plan to install microwave ovens in their homes. The response of each of the home buyers is recorded. List some possible outcomes of this experiment that cannot be predicted with certainty in advance.

Solution Some of the very large number of outcomes of this experiment are as follows:

a.   Exactly 387 of the 500 home buyers plan to install microwave ovens.
b.   Exactly 388 plan to install microwave ovens.
c.   A particular home buyer, the Jones family, plans to install a microwave oven.

Clearly, we could define many other outcomes of this experiment that cannot be predicted in advance.

In the language of probability theory, outcomes of experiments are called *events.* One particular property of events can be seen in Examples 4.1 and 4.2. Two events are said to be *mutually exclusive* if, when one occurs, the other cannot occur. To illustrate, the events listed under parts c and d of Example 4.1 are mutually exclusive. You cannot conduct an experiment and "draw a blackjack" (the event listed under part c) and at the same time "not draw a blackjack" (the event listed under part d). If one of these two events occurs when an experiment is conducted, the other event cannot have occurred. Therefore, we say that they are mutually exclusive events.

DEFINITION 4.2

Outcomes of experiments are called **events.** [*Note:* In order to simplify our discussion, we will use italic capital letters, A, B, C, . . . , to denote specific events.]

DEFINITION 4.3

Two events are said to be **mutually exclusive** if, when one of the two events occurs in an experiment, the other cannot occur.

EXAMPLE 4.3   Refer to Example 4.2 and define the following events:

    A: Exactly 387 of the 500 home buyers plan to install microwave ovens.
    B: Exactly 388 plan to install microwave ovens.
    C: A particular home buyer, the Jones family, plans to install a microwave oven.

State whether the pairs of events, A and B, A and C, B and C, are mutually exclusive.

Solution a. Events A and B are mutually exclusive because if you have observed precisely 387 home buyers who plan to install microwave ovens, then you could not, at the same time, have observed precisely 388.

        b. Events A and C are **not** mutually exclusive because the Jones family may be one of the buyers among the 387 buyers in event A who plan to install microwave ovens. Therefore, it is possible for both events A and C to occur simultaneously.

        c. Events B and C are not mutually exclusive for the same reason given in part b.

EXAMPLE 4.4   Suppose that an experiment consists of two players (you and the dealer) being dealt the initial two cards in a game of blackjack. Define the following events:

    A: You draw a blackjack (21).
    B: The dealer draws a blackjack.

Are A and B mutually exclusive events?

Solution   A and B are not mutually exclusive because both could occur when the cards are dealt. That is, both you and the dealer could each draw a blackjack (21). If both events A and B occurred, you would be in a tie with the dealer and the dealer would win. (At some casinos, the play is a "standoff" and the bet is canceled.)

      As you will subsequently learn, mutually exclusive events play an important role in calculating the probability of an event. The concept of the probability of an event is the topic of our next section.

EXERCISES   **4.1**   Consider the following experiment: You invest in three stocks and, after 12 months, you record the gain (or loss) in price for each. We will define the following events:

  A: All three stocks rise in price.
  B: Stock #1 rises in price.
  C: Stock #2 experiences a $4.75 drop in price.

Explain whether the pairs of events, *A* and *B, A* and *C, B* and *C*, are mutually exclusive.

4.2   Consider the following experiment: A production manager observes and records the monthly inventory level of a bearing that is used in the manufacture of electric motors. We will define the following events:

  A: The monthly inventory shows 30,310 bearings.
  B: The monthly inventory level is less than 30,000 bearings.
  C: The monthly inventory level exceeds the minimum monthly inventory needed to sustain the manufacturing operation, namely 30,000 bearings.

Explain whether the pairs of events, *A* and *B, A* and *C, B* and *C*, are mutually exclusive.

4.3   The loan officer of a bank performs the following experiment: Observe the size of a loan request and the financial characteristics (as they relate to credit risk) of the applicant. If the experiment is conducted once (the loan officer observes the characteristics described above for a single loan application), some of the events he or she might observe are:

  A: The loan request exceeds $100,000.
  B: The loan request exceeds $60,000.
  C: The applicant's net worth is $185,000.

Explain whether the pairs of events, *A* and *B, A* and *C, B* and *C*, are mutually exclusive.

4.4   The owner of two television cable networks, an all-movie station and an all-sports station, is interested in the following experiment: Observe the year-end profit (or loss) generated by each of the cable networks. Consider the following events:

  A: The all-sports station turns a profit of $200,000.
  B: Each cable network turns a profit.
  C: The all-news station turns a profit, but the all-sports station experiences a loss.

Explain whether the pairs of events, *A* and *B, A* and *C, B* and *C*, are mutually exclusive.

4.5   A housewife is asked to rank three brands of laundry detergent, Wisk, Era, and Shout, according to her preference. Consider the following experiment: Observe the rankings (1st, 2nd, and 3rd) of the three brands.
  a.   Give two of the many different events which could be observed.
  b.   Are the two events you listed in part a mutually exclusive? Explain. If not, define a pair of mutually exclusive events.

4.4 The Probability of an Event

The outcome for each of the experiments described in the preceding sections was shrouded in uncertainty; i.e., prior to conducting the experiment, we could not be certain whether a particular event would occur. This uncertainty is measured by the *probability* of the event.

EXAMPLE 4.5

Suppose that we define the following experiment: Toss a coin and observe whether the upside of the coin is a head or a tail. If an event H is defined by

H: Observe a head

what do we mean when we say that the probability of H, denoted by $P(H)$, is equal to ½?

Solution

We mean that, in a very long series of tosses, we believe that approximately half would result in a head. Therefore, the number, ½, measures the likelihood of observing a head on a single toss of the coin.

Stating that the probability of observing a head is $P(H) = $ ½ does not mean that exactly half of a number of tosses will result in heads. For example, we do not expect to observe exactly 1 head in 2 tosses of a coin or exactly 5 heads in 10 tosses of a coin. Rather, we would expect the proportion of heads to vary in a random manner and to approach closer and closer the probability of a head, $P(H) = $ ½, as the number of tosses increases. This property can be seen in the graphs, Figure 4.2, pp. 100–101.

Figure 4.2(a) shows the proportion of heads observed after $n = 25, 50, 75, 100, 125, \ldots, 1,450, 1,475, 1,500$ repetitions of a coin-tossing experiment simulated by the author. The number of tosses is marked along the horizontal axis of the graph, and the corresponding proportions of heads are plotted on the vertical axis above the values of n. We have connected the points by line segments to emphasize the fact that the proportion of heads moves closer and closer to .5 as n gets larger (as you move to the right on the graph).

The results of a similar experiment ($n = 10, 11, 12, \ldots, 99, 100$) are shown in Figure 4.2(b). You can see that the proportions of heads for a given value of n may differ from Figures 4.2(a) to 4.2(b), but the proportion of heads, for both experiments, moves closer and closer to ½ as n gets larger (as you move to the right along the horizontal axes).

We conducted a similar experiment to determine the approximate probability of drawing a blackjack when two cards are dealt from a well-mixed standard deck of bridge cards. Figure 4.3 (p. 102) shows the proportion of times a blackjack is observed when the deal is repeated $n = 100, 200, 300, 400, \ldots, 9,800, 9,900,$ and 10,000 times. The proportions are plotted in Figure 4.3 for each value of n. Notice that the proportion of times a blackjack is observed moves closer and closer to 0.048 as n gets larger (as you move to the right along the horizontal axis). We will show how to calculate the exact probability of drawing a blackjack, 0.04826546, in Section 4.6.

Although most people think of the probability of an event as the proportion of times the event occurs in a very long series of trials, some experiments can never be

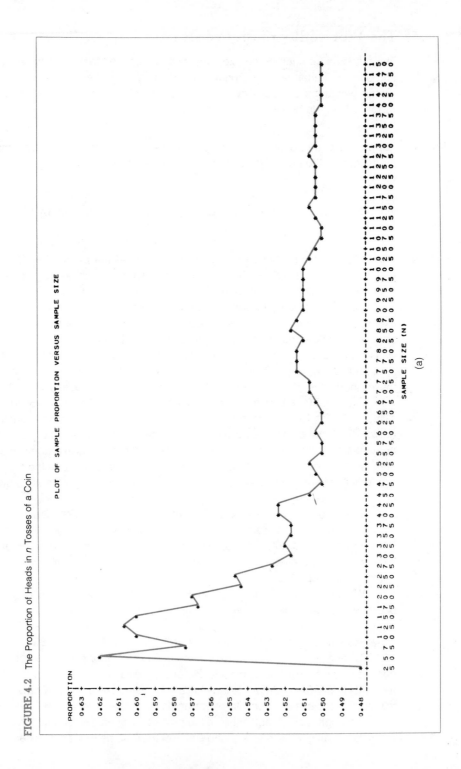

FIGURE 4.2   The Proportion of Heads in *n* Tosses of a Coin

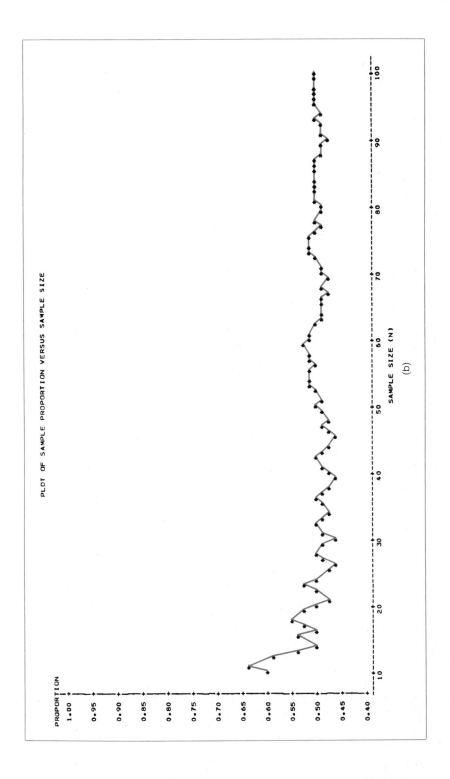

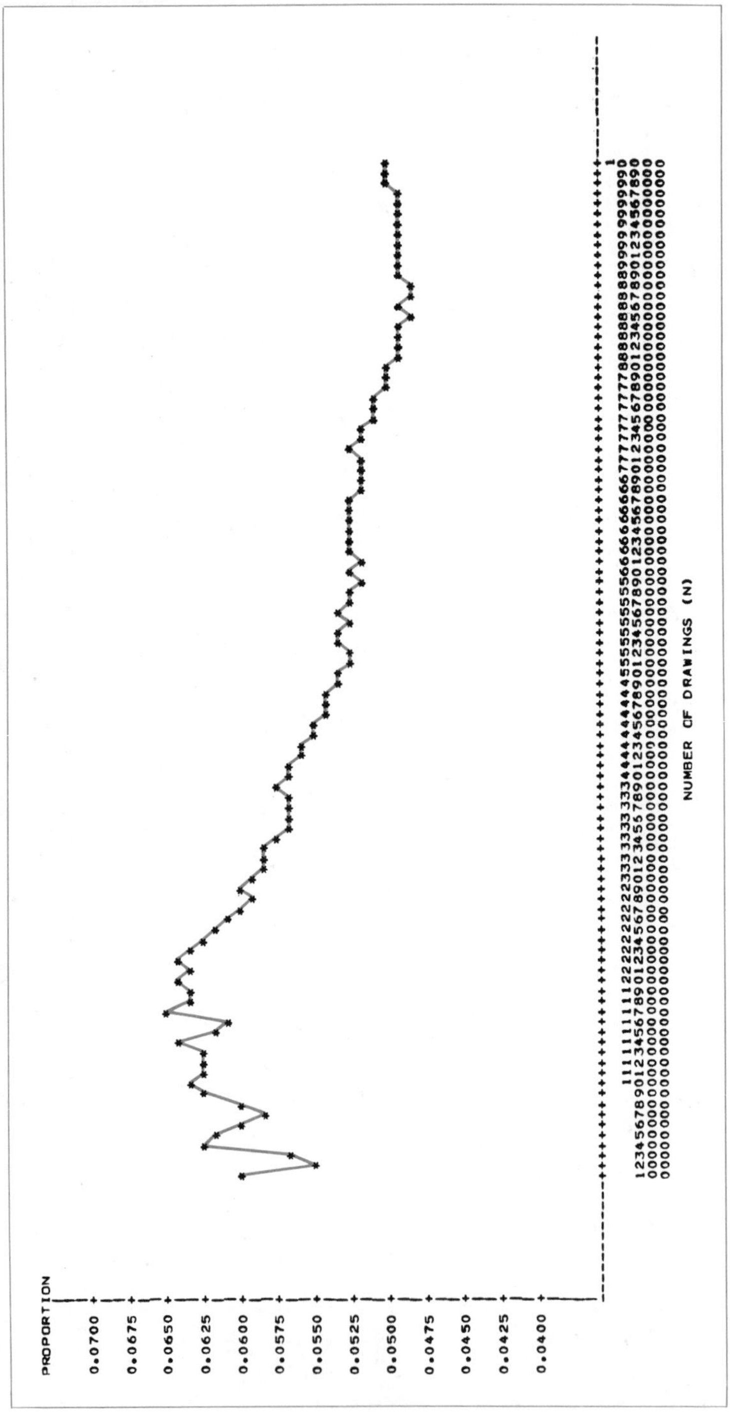

FIGURE 4.3 The Proportion of Times Blackjack Is Observed in *n* Drawings of Two Cards from a Well-Mixed Bridge Deck

repeated. For example, if you invest $50,000 in starting a new business, the probability that your business will survive five years has some unknown value that you will never be able to evaluate by repetitive experiments. The probability of this event occurring is a number that has some value, but it is unknown to us. The best that we could do, in estimating its value, would be to attempt to determine the proportion of similar businesses that survived five years and take this as an approximation to the desired probability. In spite of the fact that we may not be able to conduct repetitive experiments, the relative frequency definition for probability appeals to our intuition.

DEFINITION 4.4

The *probability of an event A,* denoted by $P(A)$, is the proportion of times that A is observed when the experiment is repeated a very large number of times.

EXERCISES   **4.6**   Consider the following experiment: Thirteen cards are dealt face up from a standard, well-mixed, 52-card bridge deck and their suits (hearts, spades, clubs, and diamonds) are observed. Define the event A as follows:

   A: 4 hearts, 4 spades, 3 clubs, and 2 diamonds are observed.

It can be shown that the probability of A is .01796, i.e., $P(A) = .01796$. What do we mean by the statement, "$P(A) = .01796$"?

4.7   A power plant which discharges its waste into a nearby gulf performed the following experiment each day for a period of one year (365 days): A water sample is selected from an area near the plant's discharge, analyzed for the presence of PCB (a dangerous chemical), and the amount of PCB (in parts per million) in the sample is recorded. Suppose that the power plant observed that the amount of PCB in the water samples exceeded government pollution standards on two of the days. Find the approximate probability of A, where A is the event that, on any randomly selected day, the amount of PCB in the water sample will exceed the standard.

4.8   Your broker has informed you that if you invest in gold futures now, there is a "high" probability (say, near .90) that your investment will return a profit. What is your interpretation of your broker's statement?

4.9   The U.S. government estimates that unemployment in the labor force will reach 8% by year-end 1981 (Board of Economics, *Time,* January 19, 1981). That is, of all those who are considered to be eligible workers by year-end 1981, 8% will be unemployed. Suppose that we select one eligible worker at random from the labor force at the end of 1981 and determine that person's employment status. Based on the government estimate, what is the probability that we will find this person unemployed?

4.5 The Additive Probability Rule for Mutually Exclusive Events

If two events, A and B, are mutually exclusive, the probability that *either A or B* occurs is equal to the sum of their probabilities. We will illustrate with an example.

EXAMPLE 4.6

Consider the following experiment: You toss two coins and observe the upper faces of the two coins. What is the probability that you toss exactly one head?

Solution

The experiment can result in one of four mutually exclusive events. One possibility is that you will observe a head on coin #1, call it H_1, and a head on coin #2, H_2. We could denote this event as H_1H_2. Similarly, we could observe a head on coin #1 and a tail on coin #2, call this H_1T_2. The other two possible outcomes are a tail on coin #1 and a head on coin #2, T_1H_2, or tails on both coins, T_1T_2. These four events are shown diagrammatically in Figure 4.4.

Since the chance of tossing either a head or a tail on each coin is $\frac{1}{2}$, we would expect each of the four mutually exclusive outcomes of Figure 4.4 to occur with approximately equal relative frequency, $\frac{1}{4}$, if the coin-tossing experiment were repeated over and over again a large number of times. Since you will observe exactly one head *only if T_1H_2 occurs or if H_1T_2 occurs,* and these events are mutually exclusive, either one or the other of these events will occur $(\frac{1}{4}) + (\frac{1}{4}) = \frac{1}{2}$ of the time. Therefore, the probability of observing exactly one head in a toss of a pair of coins is equal to the probability of observing *either T_1H_2 or H_1T_2,* which is $\frac{1}{2}$. You can verify this result experimentally, using the procedure employed in Section 4.4.

PROBABILITY RULE #1

The Additive Rule for Mutually Exclusive Events   If two events, A and B, are mutually exclusive, the probability that *either A or B* occurs is equal to the sum of their respective probabilities; i.e.,

$P(\text{either } A \text{ or } B \text{ occurs}) = P(A) + P(B)$

FIGURE 4.4
Four Mutually Exclusive
Outcomes When Tossing
a Pair of Coins

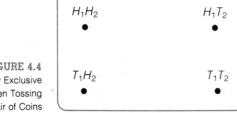

You can now see why the concept of mutually exclusive events is important. We will illustrate with another example.

EXAMPLE 4.7   Consider the following experiment: A pair of dice is tossed and the number of dots on the upper faces of the dice are observed. Find the probability that the sum of the two numbers is equal to 7 (a winning number in the game of craps).

Solution   Mark the dice so that they are identified as die #1 and die #2. Then there are $6 \times 6 = 36$ distinctly different ways that the dice could fall. You could observe a 1 on die #1 and a 1 on die #2; a 1 on die #1 and a 2 on die #2; a 1 on die #1 and a 3 on die #2, etc. In other words, you can pair the 6 values (shown on the six sides) of die #1 with the 6 values of die #2 in $6 \times 6 = 36$ mutually exclusive ways. These combinations are shown in Figure 4.5.

Since there are 36 possible ways the dice could fall and, since these ways should occur with equal frequency, the probability of observing any one of the 36 events listed above is $\frac{1}{36}$. Then to find the probability of tossing a 7, we only need to add the probabilities of those events corresponding to a sum on the dice equal to 7.

If we denote the event that you observe a 6 on die #1 and a 1 on die #2 as $(6, 1)$, etc., then as shown in Figure 4.5, you will toss a 7 if you observe a $(6, 1)$, $(5, 2)$, $(4, 3)$, $(3, 4)$, $(2, 5)$, or $(1, 6)$. Therefore, the probability of tossing a 7 is

$$P(7) = P[(6, 1) \text{ or } (5, 2) \text{ or } (4, 3) \text{ or } (3, 4) \text{ or } (2, 5) \text{ or } (1, 6)]$$
$$= P(6, 1) + P(5, 2) + P(4, 3) + P(3, 4) + P(2, 5) + P(1, 6)$$
$$= \frac{1}{36} + \frac{1}{36} + \frac{1}{36} + \frac{1}{36} + \frac{1}{36} + \frac{1}{36} = \frac{6}{36} = \frac{1}{6}$$

Example 4.7 suggests a modification of Probability Rule #1 when an experiment can result in one and only one of a number of equally likely (equiprobable) mutually exclusive events.

Die #1

	⚀	⚁	⚂	⚃	⚄	⚅
⚀	2	3	4	5	6	7
⚁	3	4	5	6	7	8
⚂	4	5	6	7	8	9
⚃	5	6	7	8	9	10
⚄	6	7	8	9	10	11
⚅	7	8	9	10	11	12

Die #2

FIGURE 4.5
The Sum of the Dots for the 36 Mutually Exclusive Outcomes in the Tossing of a Pair of Dice

---

PROBABILITY RULE #2

The Probability Rule for an Experiment That Results in One of a Number of Equally Likely Mutually Exclusive Events   Suppose that an experiment can result in one and only one of M equally likely mutually exclusive events and that m of these events result in event A. Then the probability of event A is

$$P(A) = \frac{m}{M}$$

EXAMPLE 4.8   Two prospective managers are randomly selected from among four candidates who appear to be equally qualified. If two are really better than the others, what is the probability that at least one of these two will be selected?

Solution   Identify the four candidates as C_1, C_2, C_3, and C_4, and let C_3 and C_4 be the two best candidates. Then the six distinctly different and mutually exclusive ways that the two candidates may be selected from the four are:

$$C_1C_2 \quad C_1C_3 \quad C_1C_4 \quad C_2C_3 \quad C_2C_4 \quad C_3C_4$$

Since the candidates were randomly chosen, we would expect the likelihood that any one pair would be chosen would be the same as for any other pair. Then, since $M = 6$ and since $m = 5$ of the pairs result in the choice of either C_3 or C_4 or both, the probability of drawing at least one of these two candidates is

$$P(\text{at least one of } C_3 \text{ or } C_4) = \frac{m}{M} = \frac{5}{6}$$

Examples 4.6, 4.7, and 4.8 identify the properties of the probabilities of all events, as shown in the box.

PROPERTIES OF PROBABILITIES

1. The probability of an event always assumes a value between 0 and 1.
2. If two events A and B are mutually exclusive, then the probability that *either A or B* occurs is equal to $P(A) + P(B)$.
3. If we list all possible mutually exclusive events associated with an experiment, then the sum of their probabilities will always equal 1.

Before concluding this section, we will comment on two important mutually exclusive events and their probabilities. Consider, once again, the game of blackjack and define the following two events:

A: The first two cards dealt result in a blackjack.
$\overline{A}$: The first two cards dealt do not result in a blackjack.

Thus $\overline{A}$ is the event that A ***does not*** occur. You can see that A and $\overline{A}$ are mutually exclusive events and, further, that if A occurs $p\%$ of the time in a long series of trials, then $\overline{A}$ will occur $(100 - p)\%$ of the time. In other words,

$$P(A) + P(\overline{A}) = 1$$

DEFINITION 4.5

The ***complement*** of an event A, denoted by the symbol $\overline{A}$, is the event that A ***does not*** occur.

Complementary events are important because sometimes it is difficult to find the probability of an event A but easy to find the probability of its complement, $\overline{A}$. In this case, we can find $P(A)$ using the relationship

$$P(A) = 1 - P(\overline{A})$$

EXERCISES

4.10 Refer to Examples 4.6, 4.7, and 4.8 and verify that property 3 (shown in the box that lists the properties of probabilities) holds for each of these examples.

4.11 Suppose that an experiment involves tossing two coins and observing the upper faces of the coins. Find the probabilities of:
a. A: Observing exactly two heads
b. B: Observing exactly two tails
c. C: Observing at least one head
d. Describe the complement of event A and find its probability.

4.12 Two dice are tossed and the upper faces of the dice are observed. Use Figure 4.5 to find the probability that the sum shown on the dice is equal to:
a. 12   **b.** 5   **c.** 11

4.13 Refer to the dice-tossing experiment, Exercise 4.12. Find the approximate probability of tossing a total of 7 by conducting an experiment similar to the experiments illustrated in Figure 4.2: Toss a pair of dice a large number of times and record the proportion of times a 7 is observed. Compare your value with the exact probability, $\frac{1}{6}$.

4.14 An investor has decided to purchase two from among a group of four oil stocks. If the investor has no prior knowledge that any one stock will outperform the others, and consequently selects two at random, what is the probability that the investor selects the two stocks that will achieve the best performances?

4.6 Random Sampling and the Probability of Blackjack

Most samples are selected from populations that contain a finite number of experimental units. For example, two candidates were selected from among a total of four candidates in Example 4.8. Similarly, polls conducted by the Gallup, Harris, and other polling organizations select a sample of opinions from a population that contains a finite number of people. If the sample is selected in such a way that every different sample of size *n* has an equal probability of being selected, the procedure is called *random sampling* and the sample is called a (simple) *random sample* of size *n*.

DEFINITION 4.6

A *random sample* of *n* experimental units is one that is selected in such a way that every different sample of size *n* has an equal probability of selection.

Dealing two cards from a well-mixed bridge deck is equivalent to selecting a sample of 2 from a population containing 52 experimental units. Therefore, finding the probability of drawing a blackjack is just a generalization of Example 4.8.

EXAMPLE 4.9   Find the probability of drawing a blackjack.

Solution   Since every possible pair of cards is as likely to be drawn as any other, we will use Probability Rule #2 to find the probability of drawing a blackjack.

1. The first step is to find *M*, the number of distinctly different samples of 2 cards that can be selected from a deck of 52. We will use the formula in the box (proof omitted), which gives the number of ways for selecting *n* objects from a total of *N*.

COMBINATORIAL RULE FOR DETERMINING THE NUMBER OF DIFFERENT SAMPLES THAT CAN BE SELECTED FROM A POPULATION

The number of different samples of *n* objects that can be selected from among a total of *N* is

$$C_n^N = \frac{N!}{n!(N-n)!}$$

where

$$N! = N(N-1)(N-2)(N-3)\ldots(3)(2)(1)$$
$$n! = n(n-1)(n-2)(n-3)\ldots(3)(2)(1)$$
$$0! = 1$$

For this problem, we are selecting $n = 2$ cards from $N = 52$. Therefore, the total number of different pairs of cards that could be dealt is

$$M = C_n^N = \frac{N!}{n!(N-n)!} = \frac{52!}{2!50!} = \frac{(52)(51)(50)\ldots(3)(2)(1)}{[(2)(1)][(50)(49)(48)\ldots(3)(2)(1)]}$$

or

$$M = \frac{(52)(51)}{2} = 1,326$$

2. The second step in solving the problem is to find the number m of samples that result in a blackjack (21). We can find m by considering the pairs of cards that could produce a total of 21. We will first list the cards valued 10 that could be paired with the ace of hearts. These are:

$$\left. \begin{array}{llll} K\,\heartsuit, & Q\,\heartsuit, & J\,\heartsuit, & 10\,\heartsuit \\ K\,\diamondsuit, & Q\,\diamondsuit, & J\,\diamondsuit, & 10\,\diamondsuit \\ K\,\clubsuit, & Q\,\clubsuit, & J\,\clubsuit, & 10\,\clubsuit \\ K\,\spadesuit, & Q\,\spadesuit, & J\,\spadesuit, & 10\,\spadesuit \end{array} \right\}$$ The 16 cards that could be matched with the ace of hearts to produce blackjack

You can see that the ace of hearts could be paired with any of 16 different cards, each valued 10, to produce a blackjack. Likewise, the same 16 cards could be paired with either the ace of diamonds, the ace of spades, or the ace of clubs. Therefore, there are $m = (4)(16) = 64$ pairs of cards that could result in a blackjack.

3. In step 3, we apply Probability Rule #2. We found in step 1 that $M = 1,326$ and in step 2 that $m = 64$. Therefore, the probability of drawing a blackjack is

$$P(\text{blackjack}) = \frac{m}{M} = \frac{64}{1,326} = .04826546$$

or, approximately 1 chance in 20.

EXAMPLE 4.10   A case of wine contains 12 bottles of which two are improperly sealed and therefore spoiled. If two bottles are selected from the case, what is the probability that both are spoiled?

Solution   Step 1.   We are sampling $n = 2$ bottles from a total of $N = 12$. Therefore, there are

$$M = C_n^N = C_2^{12} = \frac{12!}{2!10!} = \frac{(12)(11)(10)\ldots(3)(2)(1)}{[(2)(1)][(10)(9)\ldots(3)(2)(1)]}$$

$$= 66$$

different pairs of bottles that could be selected.

Step 2.   There is only $m = 1$ way of selecting two spoiled bottles from the case since the case contains only two bottles which are spoiled.

Step 3.   Therefore, the probability of drawing the two spoiled bottles of wine is

$$P(\text{draw two spoiled bottles}) = \frac{m}{M} = \frac{1}{66}$$

EXAMPLE 4.11   Consider the following problem in statistical inference: Regard the 12 wine bottles in the case in Example 4.10 as a population, and suppose you now think that the case contains at most 2 spoiled bottles. You sample 2 bottles from the 12 and observe that both are spoiled. What would you infer about the population (i.e., the case) of 12 bottles?

Solution   You have a theory that the population contains at most 2 spoiled bottles, and you have sampled 2 bottles to see if the sample data disagree with your theory. If your theory is true and, at worst, the population contains 2 spoiled bottles, the chance of observing a sample of 2 spoiled out of 2 sampled is very small; i.e., only 1/66 or 0.0152. Naturally, the probability of drawing 2 spoiled bottles in a sample of 2 is much higher if the case contains a larger number of spoiled bottles. For example, if 6 are spoiled, the probability of drawing 2 spoiled out of 2 is (proof omitted) 15/66 = .2273. Consequently, we can reach one of two conclusions.

1.   Our theory is correct. The number of spoiled bottles in the case does not exceed 2. The fact that we drew 2 spoiled in a sample of 2 was an unlucky and rare event.
2.   Our theory is incorrect. The case contains more than 2 spoiled bottles, a situation that makes the observed sample more probable.

      Which of these two conclusions would you choose? We think that you will choose the second one. In doing so, you have used the probability of an observed sample to infer the nature of a population. If you choose the first one, you are implying that the observed sample is an unlucky and rare event, with only a 1/66 chance of occurring. The fact that the event did occur leads you to believe that its probability of occurring was much higher, i.e., that the case contains more than 2 spoiled bottles.

EXERCISES   4.15   In Example 4.8, we found that one could choose six different samples of 2 candidates from a group of 4. Use the Combinatorial Rule to arrive at this result.

4.16   How many different samples of size $n = 3$ can be selected from a population containing $N = 5$ elements?
a.   Use the Combinatorial Rule to acquire the answer.
b.   Suppose that the $N = 5$ elements are denoted as A, B, C, D, E. List the different samples (for example, one sample would be A, B, C; another would be A, B, E, etc.).

4.17   A federal agency recently claimed that each of five grant applicants received equal consideration in awarding two grants and that, in fact, the recipients were randomly selected from among the five. Three of the applicants were large corporations and two were small businesses. Suppose that both grants were awarded to large corporations.

α. What is the probability of this event occurring if, in fact, the federal agency's claim is true?

b. Is the probability, part a, inconsistent with the agency's claim that the selection was at random?

4.18 In order to ensure delivery of its raw materials, a company has decided to establish a pattern of purchases with at least two potential suppliers. If five suppliers are available, how many choices (options) are available to the company? [*Hint:* If the five suppliers are denoted as $A, B, C, D,$ and $E,$ one option would be to use two suppliers, A and $B.$ Another would be to use four suppliers, $A, B, C,$ and $D.$]

4.19 Refer to Exercise 4.18. Suppose that the supplier options available to the company are equiprobable, i.e., one choice of suppliers is as likely to occur as any other choice. Find the probability that both supplier A and supplier E are chosen to deliver raw materials for the company.

4.20 Two differently styled blue jeans, A and $B,$ are being considered for mass production by a large clothing manufacturer. A marketing experiment is to be run in a local department store to determine if the public has a preference for one of the two styles. Each of four randomly selected customers will be shown a pair of style A blue jeans and a pair of style B blue jeans, and asked to voice their preference. The four responses are then observed.

α. List the possible outcomes for this experiment.

b. If the public has no preference for one style over the other, then the events you listed in part a are equiprobable. Assuming equally likely events, what is the probability that all four customers will prefer style A?

c. Suppose that the experiment is run and, in fact, all four customers voice their preference for style $A.$ Use your answer to part b to infer whether the public has a preference for one of the two styles of blue jeans.

4.7 Conditional Probability and Independence

The *Wall Street Journal* (October 24, 1980) reports that the Treasury Hotel Casino in Las Vegas offers seminars on a "surefire method for beating the house" in blackjack. The system that will "beat the house" is based on the observation of cards dealt by the dealer.

To give a simple example, we found the probability of drawing a blackjack from a well-mixed deck of cards to be equal to 0.04826546. But suppose that the deck has not been newly shuffled, and that we have already seen 10 cards fall on the table: 3 aces, 4 tens, and 3 cards with values less than 10. Now what is the probability that you will draw blackjack in the next pair of cards dealt to you? Intuitively, you will realize that the probability will be less than when drawing from a complete deck because now the deck contains only 1 ace. In fact, given that 10 cards have been removed from the deck, including 3 aces and 4 tens, the probability of drawing blackjack on the next pair of cards is only $^{12}\!/_{861}$ or 0.0139373.

The probability of drawing blackjack from a mixed complete deck is called the *unconditional probability* of that event. In contrast, the probability of drawing a blackjack, *given that you know some other event has already occurred,* is called the *conditional probability* of the event.

DEFINITION 4.7

The probability of an event *A,* given that an event *B* has occurred, is called the *conditional probability of A given B* and is denoted by the symbol

$P(A|B)$

[*Note:* The vertical bar between *A* and *B* is read "given."]

EXAMPLE 4.12   A box contains three fuses, one good and two defective. Two fuses are drawn in sequence, first one and then the other.

   a.   What is the probability that the second fuse is defective?
   b.   What is the probability that the second fuse is defective if you know, for certain, that the first fuse drawn is defective?

Solution   **a.**   We will denote the good fuse by the letter *G* and the two defective fuses as D_1 and D_2. If the fuses are drawn at random from the box, the six possible orders of selection are:

G, D_1 G, D_2 D_1, G D_1, D_2 D_2, G D_2, D_1

   Step 1.   Since these six mutually exclusive events are equally likely and comprise all possible outcomes of the draw, we have $M = 6$.
   Step 2.   Next, we must find the number of selections in which a defective is selected in the second draw. You can see from the listed draws that $m = 4$.
   Step 3.   Using Probability Rule #2, the unconditional probability of obtaining a defective fuse on the second draw is

$$P(\text{defective fuse on the 2nd draw}) = \frac{m}{M} = \frac{4}{6} = \frac{2}{3}$$

   b.   The probability of observing a defective on the second draw, given that you have observed a defective on the first draw, is a conditional probability, $P(A|B)$, where:

   A: Observe a defective fuse on the second draw.
   B: Observe a defective fuse on the first draw.

If the first fuse drawn from the box is defective, then the box now contains only two fuses, one defective and one nondefective. This means that you have a fifty-fifty chance of drawing a defective fuse on the second draw, given that a defective fuse has already been drawn. That is,

$$P(A|B) = \frac{1}{2}$$

The probability obtained in part a, the unconditional probability of event *A*, was equal to ⅔. Clearly, the probability has changed when we know that event *B* has occurred.

EXAMPLE 4.13 A balanced coin is tossed 10 times, resulting in 10 tails. If the coin is tossed one more time, what is the probability of observing a head?

Solution We are asked to find the conditional probability of event *A*, given that event *B* has occurred, where

    A: The 11th toss results in a head.
    B: The first ten tosses resulted in 10 heads.

Intuitively, it seems reasonable to expect the probability of observing a head on the 11th toss (given that the ten previous tosses resulted in heads) to be greater than ½, but such is not the case. If the coin is truly balanced and is tossed in an unbiased manner, the probability of observing a head on the 11th toss is still ½. (This has been verified both theoretically and experimentally.) Therefore, this is a case where the conditional probability of an event *A* is equal to the unconditional probability of *A*.

Example 4.13 illustrates an important relationship that exists between some pairs of events. If the probability of one event does not depend upon whether a second event has occurred, then the events are said to be *independent*.

DEFINITION 4.8

Two events *A* and *B* are said to be *independent* if

    $P(A|B) = P(A)$

or if

    $P(B|A) = P(B)$

[*Note:* If one of these equalities is true, then the other will also be true.]

The notion of independence is particularly important when we want to find the probability that *both* of two events will occur. When the events are independent, the probability that both events will occur is equal to the product of their unconditional probabilities.

PROBABILITY RULE #3

The Probability That Both of Two Independent Events A and B Occur   If two events, A and B, are independent, the probability that *both A and B* occur is equal to the product of their respective unconditional probabilities; i.e.,

$$P(\text{both } A \text{ and } B \text{ occur}) = P(A)P(B)$$

EXAMPLE 4.14   Find the probability of observing two heads in two tosses of a balanced coin.

Solution   Define the following events:

> A: Observe a head on the first toss.
> B: Observe a head on the second toss.

Since we know that events A and B are independent and that $P(A) = P(B) = \frac{1}{2}$, the probability that we observe two heads, i.e., both events A and B is

$$P(\text{observe two heads}) = P(A)P(B)$$

$$= \left(\frac{1}{2}\right)\left(\frac{1}{2}\right) = \frac{1}{4}$$

You can see that this answer agrees with our reasoning in Example 4.6.

EXAMPLE 4.15   Experience has shown that a manufacturing operation produces, on the average, only 1 defective unit in 10. These are removed from the production line, repaired, and returned to the warehouse. Suppose that during a given period of time you observe 5 defective units emerging from the production line in sequence.

a.   If prior history has shown that defective units usually emerge randomly from the production line, what is the probability of observing a sequence of 5 consecutive defective units?

b.   If the event in part a really occurred, what would you conclude about the process?

Solution   **a.**   If the defectives really occur randomly, then whether any one unit is defective should be independent of whether the others are defective. Second, the unconditional probability that any one unit is defective is known to be $\frac{1}{10}$. We will define the following events:

> D_1:   The first unit is defective.
> D_2:   The second unit is defective.
> .
> .
> .
> D_5:   The fifth unit is defective.

Then,

$$P(D_1) = P(D_2) = P(D_3) = P(D_4) = P(D_5) = \frac{1}{10}$$

and the probability that all 5 are defective is

$$P(\text{all 5 are defective}) = P(D_1)P(D_2) \ldots P(D_5)$$

$$= \left(\frac{1}{10}\right)\left(\frac{1}{10}\right)\left(\frac{1}{10}\right)\left(\frac{1}{10}\right)\left(\frac{1}{10}\right)$$

$$= \frac{1}{100,000}$$

b. We do not need a knowledge of probability to know that something must be wrong with the production line. Intuition would tell us that observing 5 defectives in sequence is highly improbable (given past history), and we would immediately infer that past history no longer describes the condition of the process. In fact, we would infer that something is disturbing the stability of the process.

EXERCISES   **4.21** Find the probability of throwing a pair of 4's when tossing a pair of dice. Compare your answer with the answer that you would obtain from Figure 4.5.

4.22 A manufacturer guarantees that the failure rate of its new solar-powered battery is only 1 in 20. A new system to be used in a space vehicle operates on one of these batteries. To increase the reliability of the system, three batteries are installed, each designed to operate if the preceding batteries in the chain fail. If the system is operated in a practical situation, what is the probability that all three batteries would fail?

4.23 Responding to complaints of spoiled milk being served to customers of a late-night diner, the Food and Drug Administration (FDA) has sent an official government inspector to the diner. Suppose that 10 of the 50 bottles of milk the diner currently has on hand contain spoiled milk. The FDA official randomly selects 5 bottles from the 50 (drawn in sequence) for inspection and testing.
a. What is the probability that the first bottle selected contains spoiled milk?
b. If the first bottle selected does not contain spoiled milk, what is the probability that the second bottle selected will contain spoiled milk?
c. Suppose that none of the first four bottles selected contain spoiled milk. What is the probability that the last (fifth) bottle selected will contain spoiled milk?

4.24 A large-volume retailer of high fidelity stereo needles boasts that only 1% of the needles he sells need to be replaced after five years of continuous use (i.e., on the average, 1 in every 100 needles sold needs to be replaced after five years of use). Four customers are randomly chosen from among those customers who have recently purchased stereo needles from the retailer.
a. If the retailer's claim is true, what is the probability that all four customers will need to replace their stereo needles after five years of continuous use?

b. Suppose that the event, part a, actually occurs. What could you infer about the retailer's claim?

4.25 The game of craps is played with two dice. A player throws both dice, winning unconditionally if he produces either of the outcomes 7 or 11 (the sum of the numbers showing on the two dice) which are designated as "naturals." If the player casts the outcomes 2, 3, or 12—referred to as "craps"—he loses unconditionally.
a. Find the probability of a player throwing a "natural."
b. Find the probability of a player throwing "craps."
c. Suppose that a "hot" player has thrown five "naturals" in a row. What is the probability that the player throws a "natural" on his next toss?
d. Suppose that a "cold" player has thrown five "craps" in a row. What is the probability that the player throws "craps" on his next toss?

4.8 The Additive and Multiplicative Laws of Probability (Optional)

Probability Rule #3 (Section 4.7) gave a formula for finding the probability that both events A and B occur for the special case where A and B were independent events. We can also give a formula, called the *Multiplicative Law of Probability,* that applies in general; i.e., regardless of whether A and B are independent events. Although this law is not needed for a study of the remaining material in this text, it (along with the *Additive Law of Probability* which we will subsequently present) is needed to complete an introductory coverage of probability.

THE MULTIPLICATIVE LAW OF PROBABILITY

The probability that *both* of two events, A and B, occur is

$P(\text{both } A \text{ and } B \text{ occur}) = P(A)P(B|A)$
$\qquad = P(B)P(A|B)$

EXAMPLE 4.16   Refer to Example 4.12 where we selected two fuses from a box that contained three, two of which were defective. Use the Multiplicative Law of Probability to find the probability that you first draw defective fuse D_1 and then draw D_2.

Solution   Define the following events:

A: The second draw results in D_2.
B: The first draw results in D_1.

The probability of event B is $P(B) = 1/3$. Also, from Example 4.12, the conditional probability, $P(A|B) = 1/2$. Then, the probability that both events A and B occur is

$$P(\text{both } A \text{ and } B \text{ occur}) = P(B)P(A|B) = \left(\frac{1}{3}\right)\left(\frac{1}{2}\right) = \frac{1}{6}$$

You can verify this result by rereading Example 4.12.

An additive probability rule, Probability Rule #1, was given for the event that either A or B occurs, but it applied only to the case where A and B were mutually exclusive events. A rule that applies in general is given by the *Additive Law of Probability.*

THE ADDITIVE LAW OF PROBABILITY

The probability that *either* an event A *or* an event B or *both* occur is

P(*either* A or B or *both* occur) = P(A) + P(B) − P(both A and B occur)

EXAMPLE 4.17　Suppose that an experiment consists of tossing a pair of coins and observing the upper faces. Define the following events:

　　A: Observe at least one head.
　　B: Observe at least one tail.

Use the Additive Law of Probability to find the probability of observing either A or B or both.

Solution　We know the answer to this question before we start because the probability of observing at least one head or at least one tail is 1; i.e., the event is a certainty. To obtain this answer using the Additive Law of Probability, we could use the method of Example 4.6 to find:

$$P(A) = P(\text{at least one head}) = \frac{3}{4}$$

$$P(B) = P(\text{at least one tail}) = \frac{3}{4}$$

The event "both A and B occur"—observing at least one head and at least one tail—is the event that you observe exactly one head and exactly one tail. We found this probability in Example 4.6 to be ½. Therefore,

$$P(\text{either } A \text{ or } B \text{ or both occur}) = P(A) + P(B) - P(\text{both } A \text{ and } B \text{ occur})$$

$$= \frac{3}{4} + \frac{3}{4} - \frac{1}{2} = 1$$

This answer confirms what we already knew, that the probability of the event is equal to 1.

EXAMPLE 4.18　A survey of 1,000 small business ventures classified each according to the profitability of the business (profitable or unprofitable), and according to whether the business had been in operation less than 2 years, 2 to 5 years, or more than 5 years. The percentages of businesses falling in the six categories are shown in Table 4.1. Suppose that we use the percentages contained in the table to give the approximate probabilities that a single business would fall in the respective category. We will define the following events:

> A: The business is profitable.
> B: The business has been in existence for more than 5 years.

a. Find the probability that both A and B occur.
b. Find the conditional probability that A will occur given that B has occurred.
c. Find the probability that A will not occur.
d. Find the probability that either A or B or both occur.

	LENGTH OF TIME IN BUSINESS (YEARS)			TOTALS
	Less than 2	2–5	More than 5	
PROFITABLE	2	8	14	24
UNPROFITABLE	16	35	25	76
TOTALS	18	43	39	100

Solution

a. We can see from the table that 14% of the businesses were both profitable (A) and had survived more than 5 years (B). Therefore,

$$P(\text{both } A \text{ and } B \text{ occur}) = .14$$

b. Again, examining Table 4.1, we find that 24% of all the businesses were profitable and 39% had survived more than 5 years. Therefore,

$$P(A) = .24 \quad \text{and} \quad P(B) = .39$$

To find $P(A|B)$, we substitute the answer to part a and the value of $P(B)$ into the formula for the Multiplicative Law of Probability. Thus,

$$P(\text{both } A \text{ and } B \text{ occur}) = P(B)P(A|B)$$

or

$$.14 = (.39)P(A|B)$$

Solving for $P(A|B)$ yields

$$P(A|B) = \frac{.14}{.39} = .359$$

c. The event that A does not occur is the complement of A, denoted by the symbol $\overline{A}$. Since A is the event that a business is profitable, $\overline{A}$ is the event that a business is unprofitable. Recall that $P(A)$ and $P(\overline{A})$ bear a special relationship to each other; i.e.,

$$P(A) + P(\overline{A}) = 1$$

From part b, we have $P(A) = .24$. Therefore,

$$P(\overline{A}) = 1 - .24 = .76$$

which can be verified by examining Table 4.1.

d. The probability that either A or B or both occur is given by the Additive Law of Probability. From parts a and b we know that

$$P(A) = .24, \qquad P(B) = .39$$

and

$$P(\text{both } A \text{ and } B \text{ occur}) = .14$$

Then,

$$P(\text{either } A \text{ or } B \text{ or both occur}) = P(A) + P(B) - P(\text{both } A \text{ and } B \text{ occur})$$
$$= .24 + .39 - .14 = .49$$

EXERCISES   4.26 Experience has shown that 10% of the oil-drilling attempts in a certain region strike oil and, of these, 80% produce commercial quantities of oil. Define the following events:

A: A single oil-drilling attempt strikes oil.
B: A single oil-drilling attempt produces commercial quantities of oil.

a. Give the unconditional probability of event A.
b. Give the probability of event B, given that event A has occurred.
c. Find the probability that a single drilling will produce commercial quantities of oil.

4.27 A recent survey of the American public showed that a majority believed that when they retired their retirement income (from Social Security, company retirement plans, etc.) would be inadequate. A breakdown of the percentages in each category is shown in the table. Assume that the percentage of the total number of people who fall in a given cell of the table gives the approximate probability that a person selected at random will fall in that cell category. Define the following events:

A: A person believes that his or her retirement income will be inadequate.
B: The major source of retirement income will be a Social Security pension.
C: The major source of retirement income will be a job pension.

Find:

a. $P(A)$
b. $P(B)$
c. $P(C)$
d. $P(\text{both } A \text{ and } B)$
e. $P(\text{both } B \text{ and } C)$
f. $P(\text{either } A \text{ or } B \text{ or both})$
g. $P(B \mid A)$

| | | PRIMARY TYPE OF RETIREMENT SUPPORT | | | | TOTALS |
		Social Security	Job Pensions	Personal Savings	Other	
BELIEVE SUPPORT WILL BE	Adequate	16	9	11	1	37
	Inadequate	41	12	4	6	63
TOTALS		57	21	15	7	100

4.28   Your broker has set up a deal which involves two separate investments, London gold and American silver. You are informed that the gold investment has a .95 chance of being successful and the silver investment has a .80 chance of being successful. However, the deal is worked so that if either the gold or silver investment is a success, then your overall investment will also be a success. If the success of the gold investment is independent of the success of the silver investment, find the probability that your overall investment will be a success. [*Hint:*   Use the Additive Law of Probability and Probability Rule #3.]

4.29   The family-oriented "400 Club" has a membership of 400 people and operates facilities that include an outdoor Olympic-sized swimming pool and indoor racquetball courts. Before the decision on whether to build a new, smaller indoor pool and additional racquetball courts was made, the club manager surveyed members to determine the percentages who regularly use each facility. The survey showed that 60% of the members regularly use the swimming pool and, of these, 25% also regularly use the racquetball courts. Consider the following events:

   A: A randomly selected club member regularly uses the swimming pool.
   B: A randomly selected club member regularly uses the racquetball courts.

a.   Define the event, (both *A* and *B*), in the words of the problem.
b.   Find *P*(both *A* and *B*).
c.   Define the event, (either *A* or *B* or both), in the words of the problem.
d.   If the unconditional probability of event *B* is .45, find *P*(either *A* or *B* or both). (Use your answer to part b.)

4.30   A manufacturer of businessmen's sports coats and travel equipment produces three kinds of travel bags: bargain (low-priced); standard (medium-priced); and deluxe (high-priced). Each bag produced requires the following operations: (1) cutting and dyeing of materials; (2) sewing; (3) finishing; and (4) inspection and packaging. Last month, 1,000 travel bags were returned to the company because of defects, and each defect was traced to one of the four production operations. A breakdown of the percentages in each category is given in the accompanying table. Suppose that a travel bag is selected at random from the 1,000 returned defectives, and assume that the percentage of defective bags corresponding to a cell of the table gives the approximate probability that the randomly selected bag will fall in that cell category.

		PRODUCTION OPERATION				TOTALS
		Cutting & Dyeing	Sewing	Finishing	Inspection & Packaging	
TYPE	Bargain	15.0	24.2	1.6	10.7	51.5
OF	Standard	.3	13.3	1.0	29.8	44.4
BAG	Deluxe	.1	2.7	0	1.3	4.1
TOTALS		15.4	40.2	2.6	41.8	100.0

α. Given that a bargain bag is selected, what is the probability that the defect occurred in the sewing process?
b. What is the probability that a deluxe bag with a finishing defect is selected?
c. What is the probability that a standard bag with a cutting and dyeing defect is selected?
d. What is the probability that a bargain bag or a bag with inspection and packaging defects is selected?
e. What is the probability that a bag with sewing or finishing defects is selected?
f. What is the probability that a deluxe or bargain bag is selected?

4.9 Summary

In this chapter we introduced the notion of experiments whose outcomes could not be predicted with certainty in advance. The uncertainty associated with these outcomes (events) was measured by their probabilities—the relative frequencies of their occurrence in a very large number of repetitions of the experiment.

PROBABILITY RULES

1. **Additive Rule:** If two events A and B are mutually exclusive then

   P(either A or B occurs) $= P(A) + P(B)$

   In general,*

   P(either A or B or both occur) $= P(A) + P(B) - P$(both A and B occur)

2. **Modified Additive Rule for Equally Likely Mutually Exclusive Events:** If an experiment results in one and only one of M equally likely mutually exclusive events of which m of these result in an event A, then

   $$P(A) = \frac{m}{M}$$

3. **Multiplicative Rule:** If two events, A and B, are independent then

   P(both A and B occur) $= P(A)P(B)$

   In general,*

   P(both A and B occur) $= P(A)P(B \mid A) = P(B)P(A \mid B)$

Other Helpful Rules:

4. **Rule of Complements:** $P(A) = 1 - P(\overline{A})$
5. **Combinatorial Rule:** The number of different samples of n objects that can be selected from a total of N is

   $$C_n^N = \frac{N!}{n!(N - n)!}$$

---

*These rules are from the optional section in this chapter.

We presented three rules for finding the probabilities of events. Rules 1 and 2 enabled us to find the probability that either one or the other of two events would occur when the events were mutually exclusive (Probability Rule #1), and when all possible outcomes of the experiment were both mutually exclusive and equiprobable (Probability Rule #2). Rule 3 provides a formula for finding the probability that both of two events will occur when the two events are independent. In the optional section of this chapter we gave probability rules which apply in general—the Multiplicative Law of Probability and the Additive Law of Probability. (These probability rules are summarized in the box.)

Finally, we suggested in several of the examples how probability plays a role in statistical inference. We drew a sample from a population and then, based on the probability of observing the sample under various assumptions about the population, we made a decision concerning the nature of the sampled population.

We will not be using our probability rules to solve probability problems in the succeeding chapters because the sample probabilities that we need are too difficult to obtain (that is, their calculation is beyond the scope of this text). Nevertheless, the basic concepts of probability covered in this chapter will be of considerable benefit in understanding how probability plays a role in the inferential methods that follow.

KEY WORDS

Uncertainty	Mutually exclusive events
Experiment	Complementary events
Event	Conditional probability
Probability	Independent events

SUPPLEMENTARY EXERCISES

[Starred (*) exercises refer to the optional section in this chapter.]

4.31   A full-service bank provides two drive-in service windows for its customers, one for business deposits only, and one for personal checking and savings accounts. Suppose that a customer arrives at the bank's drive-in windows and a transaction is completed. Define the events A, B, C, and D as follows:

   A: The customer uses the business deposits window.
   B: The customer withdraws $1,000 from his checking account.
   C: The customer deposits $500 in his savings account.
   D: The customer deposits between $400 and $1,000.

Which pair(s) of events are mutually exclusive?

4.32   Rexford Manor is an apartment complex which rents both furnished and unfurnished 1-, 2-, and 3-bedroom units. Currently, the apartment complex has only one unit available for rent. Define the events A, B, and C as follows:

   A: The unit is an unfurnished apartment.
   B: The unit is a 1-bedroom, furnished apartment.
   C: The unit is a 2- or 3-bedroom apartment.

Explain whether the pairs of events, A and B, B and C, A and C, are mutually exclusive.

4.33   The positions of president and vice-president of a large labor union are vacant. In the upcoming election, union members are to choose from among four men to fill the positions: Anson (A), Bostock (B), Carrithers (C), and Dennison (D). The highest vote-getter is awarded the presidency and the runner-up is awarded the vice-presidency.
a.   List all possible outcomes of the election.
b.   Assuming that the events of part a are equiprobable, what is the probability that Bostock is elected president?
c.   Assuming that the events of part a are equiprobable, what is the probability that Dennison is elected to one of the two positions?

4.34   Suppose that a new printing company plans to purchase two word processors from a minicomputer distributor. The distributor has four word-processing systems available. However, unknown to the printing company, one is a "lemon," i.e., one word processor will need frequent repair. If the printing company makes its selection at random, what is the probability that the company will purchase the "lemon"? [*Hint:*   Denote the "lemon" by L and the "good" word processors by G_1, G_2, and G_3.]

4.35   As part of an advertising campaign to attract new listeners, an AM radio station conducts a cash jackpot drawing each weekday morning. Every morning a name is chosen at random from the local phone directory (residential phones only) and that person is called for a chance to win money. A housewife, whose last name begins with a "Y," calls the radio station and inquires about her chance of being selected. She is informed that since there are 26 letters in the alphabet, the probability of choosing a last name beginning with "Y" is $\frac{1}{26}$. Is this probability correct? Explain.

4.36   Most major New York banks now charge holders of their Visa and MasterCard credit cards a $15 annual fee. One New York bank reduces the card fee to $7.50 a year for customers who open interest-paying checking accounts and keep a minimum balance of $500. Suppose that 62% of this bank's Visa and MasterCard holders maintain a minimum balance of $500 in their interest-paying checking accounts. If one of the bank's card holders is randomly selected, what is the probability that the holder pays the reduced card fee of $7.50 per year?

4.37   A study of the urban mass transportation habits of a city's workers revealed the following: Fifteen percent of the city workers regularly drive their own car to work. Of those who do drive their own car to work, 80% would gladly switch to public mass transportation if it were available. Forty percent of the city workers live more than three miles from the center of the city.
      Suppose that one city worker is chosen at random. Define the events A, B, and C as follows:

   A: The person regularly drives their own car to work.
   B: The person would gladly switch to public mass transportation if it were available.
   C: The person lives within three miles of the center of the city.

Find:
a. P(A)   b. P(B | A)   c. P(C)
d. Explain whether the pairs of events, A and B, A and C, B and C, are mutually exclusive.

*4.38   Each year, American income earners must file a tax report with the Internal Revenue Service (IRS). The IRS has simplified the tax-filing process for many income earners by developing a short income tax form (Form 1040A). Workers earning less than $20,000 if single ($40,000 if filing a joint return) may be eligible to file the short form. Workers earning over this amount are required to file the long income tax form (Form 1040) and may also choose to itemize tax deductions. The accompanying table shows the number of correctly and incorrectly filed tax forms for a random sample of 500 forms examined by the IRS last year. Suppose that one filed tax form is selected at random from the 500 and examined. Define the events A, B, C, and D as follows:

A: The tax form was filed incorrectly.
B: The tax form was a short form (1040A).
C: The tax form was a long form (1040).
D: The tax form was a long form (1040) with no itemized deductions.

	Short Form (1040A)	Long Form (1040) No Itemized Deductions	Long Form (1040) Itemized Deductions	TOTALS
INCORRECT	10	61	19	90
CORRECT	115	206	89	410
TOTALS	125	267	108	500

Find:
a. P(Ā)   b. P(B)   c. P(C)
d. P(either A or B)   e. P(either B or C)   f. P(both A and D)
g. P(both B and D)   h. P(A | B)   i. P(C | A)
j. Are A and D independent events? Explain.
k. Are B and C mutually exclusive events? Explain.

*4.39   During negotiations with management, telephone craft union officials indicate that there is a .75 chance that a strike of craft employees will be called. If in fact a strike is called, the probability that the telephone craft employees will agree to strike is .90. What is the probability that the employees do indeed strike?

4.40   A weekly business periodical operates with two high-speed printing presses (presses #1 and #2). The manufacturer of these high-speed presses claims that, when operating properly, the machines shut down for repairs on only 1% of the operating days. Suppose that the presses operate independently, i.e., the chance of one press breaking down is in no way influenced by the current operating condition of the other. One operating day is randomly selected and the performance of the presses observed.

a. What is the probability that press #1 will be shut down for repairs?

b. What is the probability that press #2 will not need to be shut down for repairs?

c. What is the probability that both presses will be shut down for repairs?

d. Suppose that both presses actually do need to be shut down for repairs during the operating day. Based on this observation, what would you infer about the printing press manufacturer's claim?

4.41 One of the most popular card games among Americans is the game of poker. Each player in the game is dealt 5 cards from a standard 52-card bridge deck. The player with the best (as defined by the rules of the game) 5-card hand is declared the winner. Use the Combinatorial Rule to determine the number of different 5-card poker hands which can be dealt from a 52-card deck.

4.42 Advertisers often hire television, movie, and sports personalities to endorse their products. Suppose that a controversial sports personality is being considered to endorse a new product developed by a consumer-oriented company. As a result of this proposed advertising campaign, market strategists have determined that only one of three possible events would occur. These events and their predicted probabilities of occurring are given below.

		Probability
A:	The majority of consumers identify with the personality, and the advertising campaign is a huge success—product sales increase tremendously.	.30
B:	The majority of consumers do not identify with the personality but continue to buy the product, resulting in a moderate increase in sales.	.60
C:	The majority of consumers are antagonized by the personality and refuse to buy the product, which causes an immediate decrease in sales.	.10

Suppose that the company decides to use the controversial sports personality to endorse their product. Based on the market strategists' predictions, find:

a. The probability that the advertising campaign will increase sales tremendously

b. The probability that the advertising campaign will not cause an immediate decrease in sales

4.43 Researchers at a major oil company have developed a new oil-drilling device. Six drilling sites are being considered as potential testing sites for the new device, each in a different state—Arizona, California, Louisiana, New Mexico, Oklahoma, and Texas. Due to the high cost of experimenting with this new device, only three testing sites will be used. These three sites will be chosen randomly from the six states.

a. Use the Combinatorial Rule to determine the number of different three-state selections which the oil company can make.

b. List the different outcomes of part a.

c. What is the probability that both Arizona and Texas are selected for testing the new device?

d. What is the probability that California or Louisiana or both are selected for testing the new device?

e. Given that New Mexico is selected, what is the probability that Oklahoma is also selected?

4.44 Recently, teenage unemployment hit a four-year high of 19% (i.e., 19% of all teenagers who seek work remain unemployed). Congress is considering a bill designed to provide incentive for employers to hire disadvantaged youths. The bill, if passed, would allow employers to pay teenage workers (16 to 19 years old) less than the minimum wage for six months. The bill is supported by the National Restaurant Association, which reports that 16% of all working teenagers are employed by the food service industry. Suppose that a teenager is selected at random from all teenagers who are seeking or have obtained work.

a. What is the probability that the teenager is employed?

b. What is the probability that the teenager works in the food service industry?

4.45 An independent service station owner buys gasoline weekly from three different major oil companies, X, Y, and Z. Referring to orders placed on *two* successive weeks, (X, Z) denotes the event that the order for the first week was given to company X and the order for the second week was given to company Z.

a. List the different ways in which the two weekly orders may be placed with the oil companies. [*Note:* The same company may receive the order for both weeks.]

b. If the service station owner randomly selects the oil companies to fill the orders, what is the probability that company X gets at least one of the two orders?

c. If the service station owner randomly selects the oil companies to fill the orders, what is the probability that the same oil company gets both orders?

4.46 Refer to Exercise 4.42. A group of 50 potential television advertisers was asked to identify the television broadcaster who they believe the majority of consumers identify with and would thus be ideally suited to endorse the product they sell. The

BROADCASTER	NUMBER OF VOTES
Dan Rather, CBS News	13
Max Robinson, ABC News	10
Howard Cosell, ABC Sports	8
Dick Enberg, NBC Sports	5
Tom Brokaw, NBC News	4
Brent Musberger, CBS Sports	4
Mike Wallace, CBS News	4
Barbara Walters, ABC News	2
	50

*The *Wall Street Journal*, February 9, 1981

results of the survey are given in the table. Consider the broadcaster identified by an advertiser randomly selected from the group of 50 surveyed.

a.   What is the probability that the advertiser favors a sportscaster?

b.   What is the probability that the advertiser favors a broadcaster from CBS?

c.   What is the probability that the advertiser favors a newscaster or an NBC broadcaster or both?

d.   What is the probability that the advertiser favors a sportscaster from ABC?

e.   Given that a newscaster is selected, what is the probability that the newscaster is from CBS?

4.47   A survey of 100 members of Congress produced the breakdown given in the table according to political affiliation and position on continuation of the grain embargo against the Soviet Union. Suppose that one congressional member is randomly chosen from the group of 100 surveyed.

a.   What is the probability that the member is a Republican?

b.   What is the probability that the member is a Democrat and opposes the grain embargo?

c.   What is the probability that the member is an Independent or favors the grain embargo or both?

d.   Given that the congressional member is a Republican, what is the probability that the member opposes the grain embargo?

	REPUBLICAN	DEMOCRAT	INDEPENDENT	TOTALS
Favor grain embargo	22	31	7	60
Oppose grain embargo	18	12	10	40
TOTALS	40	43	17	100

4.48   Recently, the stock market has gained publicity through the "Witches of Wall Street." These "witches" are people who predict whether a stock will go up or down using Tarot cards, astrological readings, or other supernatural means. One such "witch" claims that she can correctly predict a daily increase or decrease in price for any stock 60% of the time. In order to test the "witch," a broker selects three stocks at random from the New York Stock Exchange and asks the "witch" to predict the next day's increase or decrease in price for each. Assume that the "witch's" three predictions are independently made.

a.   What is the probability that the "witch" correctly predicts an increase or decrease in price for all three stocks? (Assume that the "witch's" claim is true.)

b.   What is the probability that the "witch" makes an incorrect prediction for all three stocks? (Assume that the "witch's" claim is true.)

c.   Suppose that you observe three incorrect predictions by the "witch." Considering your answer to part b, do you believe that the "witch's" claim is true? Explain.

*4.49   A brewery utilizes two bottling machines, but they do not operate simultaneously. The second machine acts as a back-up system to the first machine, and operates only when the first breaks down during operating hours. The probability that the first machine breaks down during operating hours is .20. If in fact the first breaks down, then the second machine is turned on and has a probability of .30 of breaking down.

a.   What is the probability that the brewery's bottling system is not working during operating hours? [*Hint:*   The system is not working when both bottling machines break down during operating hours. Use the Multiplicative Law of Probability.]

b.   The reliability of the bottling process is the probability that the system is working during operating hours. Find the reliability of the bottling process at the brewery. [*Hint:*   Use your answer to part a and the notion of complementary events.]

4.50   Five $1 bills, four $5 bills, and one $20 bill are placed in a box and shuffled. You are permitted to reach blindly into the box and pull out one bill. If your selection is a $1 bill or a $20 bill, the game ends and you keep the bill. If you select a $5 bill, you may replace it and try again.

a.   What is the probability that you choose a $1 bill on the first attempt?

b.   Given that your first selection was a $5 bill and you have opted to play again, what is the probability that you will select the $20 bill on the second attempt?

*4.51   A county welfare agency employs twelve welfare workers who interview prospective food stamp recipients. The welfare supervisor suspects that two of the twelve have been giving illegal deductions to applicants, although the identity of the two is unknown. Suppose that the supervisor examines the forms completed by two randomly selected workers to audit for illegal deductions.

a.   What is the probability that the first worker chosen has been giving illegal deductions?

b.   Given that the first worker chosen has been giving illegal deductions, what is the probability that the second worker chosen has also been giving illegal deductions?

c.   What is the probability that both of the workers chosen have been giving illegal deductions? [*Hint:*   Use the Multiplicative Law of Probability and your answers to parts a and b.]

d.   Suppose the supervisor observes that both workers chosen have been giving illegal deductions. If in fact only two of the twelve workers have been giving illegal deductions, is the observed event considered rare? (Use your answer to part c.) Is there evidence that more than two workers are giving illegal deductions?

4.52   Food labelled as "low calorie" is required by law to contain no more than 40 calories per serving. The Food and Drug Administration (FDA) suspects a company of marketing illegally labelled cans of "low calorie" chocolate pudding, i.e., the cans contain more than 40 calories per serving even though they are labelled as "low calorie." From a supermarket shelf containing ten cans of "low calorie" chocolate pudding, the FDA randomly selects three for inspection. Unknown to the FDA, exactly seven of the ten cans contain more than 40 calories per serving.

α. In how many different ways can the FDA randomly select three of the ten cans for inspection? [*Hint*: Apply the Combinatorial Rule.]

b. What is the probability that the FDA observes all three cans to be legally labelled, i.e., the cans contain no more than 40 calories per serving?

c. What is the probability that the FDA observes at least one of the three cans to be illegally labelled? [*Hint*: The complement of the event "at least one of three cans is illegal" is the event "all three cans are legal."]

d. If the event of part b actually occurred, would you consider it to be a rare event, given the condition that seven of the ten cans are illegally labelled?

4.53 There are two identical job openings at an accounting firm. Out of five applicants for the jobs, one is a woman. Since the applicants are equally qualified, the openings will be randomly filled.

α. List the different ways in which the two jobs can be filled. Use the notation M_1, M_2, M_3, and M_4 for the four male applicants and F for the female applicant. [*Hint*: Apply the Combinatorial Rule to determine the number of outcomes in your list.]

b. What is the probability that the woman is hired?

4.54 The U.S. Census Bureau hopes to achieve at least 90% accuracy with the long form of the census. That is, the form is designed so that at least 90% of all those who receive the long form will complete the entire form correctly. To check the accuracy, a random sample of three households that received the long form in the last census is selected, and a follow-up interview is conducted to determine the accuracy of the completed forms. Define the events *A*, *B*, and *C* as follows:

A: All three households complete the form correctly.

B: Households #1 and #2 complete the form correctly, but household #3 completes the form incorrectly.

C: All three households complete the form incorrectly.

Assuming a 90% accuracy rate, find:

α. $P(A)$ b. $P(B)$ c. $P(C)$

d. P(either A or B) e. P(both B and C) f. $P(A|B)$

g. If event C is observed, do you think that the U.S. Census Bureau has achieved at least 90% accuracy with the long form of the census? Explain.

4.55 A broker is contemplating a $10,000 stock investment. If the investment is made, only one of four possible events will occur. These events and their corresponding probabilities are given in the accompanying table.

EVENT	PROBABILITY
A: The investment results in a net loss of $10,000.	.10
B: The investment is a "break-even" venture, a net gain (or loss) of $0.	.45
C: The investment results in a net gain of $10,000.	.40
D: The investment results in a net gain of $100,000.	.05

a. What is the probability that the investment will result in a net gain of at least $10,000? [*Hint:*   Find *P*(either *C* or *D*).]

b. What is the probability that the investment will not result in a net loss of $10,000? [*Hint:*   Consider the complementary event.]

c. What is the probability that the investment will result in both a net loss of $10,000 and a net gain of $0?

4.56   Refer to Exercise 4.25. In the two-dice game of craps, a player wins if he throws a "natural" (a 7 or 11) and loses if he throws "craps" (a 2, 3, or 12). However, if the sum of the two dice is 4, 5, 6, 8, 9, or 10 (each of these is known as a "point"), the player continues throwing the dice until the same outcome (point) is repeated (in which case the player wins), or the outcome 7 occurs (in which case the player loses). For example, if a player's first toss results in a 6, the player continues to toss the dice until a 6 or 7 occurs. If a 6 occurs first, the player wins. If a 7 occurs first, the player loses.

a. What is the probability that a player throws a "point" on his first toss? [*Hint:*   Find *P*(either 4 or 5 or 6 or 8 or 9 or 10).]

b. If a player throws a "point" of 6 on his first toss, what is the probability that the player wins the game on his next toss?

c. If a player throws a "point" of 6 on his first toss, what is the probability that the player loses the game on his next toss?

4.57   Refer to Exercises 4.25 and 4.56. From the information provided by these exercises, there are basically three events which result in a win for the craps player:

A: The player throws a 7 on his first toss.
B: The player throws an 11 on his first toss.
C: The player throws a "point" on his first toss, and throws the same "point" on a subsequent toss before throwing a 7.

Since the events *A, B,* and *C* form pairs of mutually exclusive events, the probability that the player wins the game, i.e., the probability of "making a pass," is simply *P*(*A*) + *P*(*B*) + *P*(*C*). It can be shown (proof omitted) that the probability of a player "making a pass" is .493.

a. Interpret this win probability.

b. In most casinos, betting that a player "makes a pass" pays off at "even odds," i.e., for every $1 bet, you win $1 if the player "makes a pass." Considering the .493 probability of winning, do you think that the even payoff odds are "fair," that is, if you repeatedly bet on a player to "make a pass," would you expect to win as much money as you lose? [*Hint:*   When the payoff odds for a winning bet are "even," the game is deemed "fair" if the probability of winning the bet is .50.]

CASE STUDY 4.1
The Illegal
Numbers Game

Forbes magazine (October 27, 1980) reports on the illegal "numbers game" which it describes as the poor man's alternative to the gambling playgrounds of Atlantic City. The numbers game, one of organized crime's largest sources of revenue, operates in the following manner: A player selects a three-digit number, such as 987, 243, etc., and then places a bet with an agent, who might be a shopkeeper, an office worker, newsstand operator, etc. These bets are picked up by a "runner" (who receives a commission of between 10% and 25%) who passes the money on to the numbers "bank" which finances the operation and pays off the winners.

In New York, the winning number is usually based on "the handle," the total dollar amount bet on each of the third, fifth, and seventh races at one of the local racetracks. The winning number is obtained by taking the last digit of the handle for each of the three races. Bets can be as small as 50 cents or a dollar, and the payoff to a winner is 500 to 1. For example, if you bet $1 and win, your return is $499 ($500, less the dollar placed with the agent).

Suppose that a person played the lottery and selected the number 139.

a. What is the probability that the winning first digit will be a 1?
b. What is the probability that the winning second digit will be a 3? The winning third digit will be a 9?
c. What is the probability that a person selecting one three-digit number will win?
d. Considering your answer to part c, do you think the payoff rate is reasonable for the player?

CASE STUDY 4.2
The Iranian
Hostage Rescue
Mission

According to an article in the Orlando *Sentinel Star* (April 29, 1980), a House of Representatives Subcommittee Chairman stated on April 28, 1980, that his panel would investigate "last week's attempt by American commandos to rescue the U.S. hostages in Iran." According to the report, Representative Samuel S. Stratton, Democrat, N.Y., said that the purpose of the inquiry by the House Armed Services Investigations Subcommittee would be to find out why three out of eight helicopters in the mission failed. It was estimated, prior to embarking on the mission, that at least six helicopters were needed to provide a reasonable probability of success.

Specifically, Stratton said, "The failure rate of three out of eight doesn't match the record. The President said this was practiced 20 times and the whole thing ran perfectly. We need to find out what the problem was and how it can be prevented in the future." Representative Stratton went on to say that he was not sure if the investigation will be public. (If Representative Stratton's investigation was public, and if he found a reasonable answer to the probabilistic inconsistency described above, it has received little attention by the press.)

A complete examination of the inconsistency between an observed failure rate of 3 helicopters out of 8 during the week of April 21 and a zero failure rate for 8 helicopters, each flown on 20 missions, is beyond the scope of this chapter, but we do have the tools to make some comments on the inconsistency noted by Representative Stratton, i.e., to see whether a "failure rate of 3 out of 8 doesn't match the record."

Suppose that the helicopters were very reliable (which would disagree with a failure rate of 3 out of 8 helicopters—or even 1 out of 8). For example, suppose that the probability that a single helicopter would fail on a single flight was only 1 chance in 100, i.e., $P(\text{failure of 1 helicopter}) = \frac{1}{100}$, and that this probability is the same for all 8 helicopters.

a. Assume that the helicopters were serviced between flights and that the failure on any one flight is independent of failure on any other flight. What is the probability that a single helicopter would be able to successfully complete two flights?

[*Hint:* If P(failure on a single flight) $= p = \frac{1}{100}$, then P(success on a single flight) $= 1 - p = 1 - \frac{1}{100} = \frac{99}{100}$. Then use Probability Law #3.]

b. Refer to part a. What is the probability that the helicopter would be able to successfully complete 3 flights?

c. 160 flights? [*Note:* You will need a pocket calculator to find this probability.]

d. You will note from part c that the probability of successfully completing 160 flights is very small, assuming $p = P$(failure on a single flight) is as small as .01. Does this result suggest that P(success on a single flight) is larger or smaller than .99?

e. Since the probability of failure p on a single flight is a *very* small number, is it reasonable to assume that, on the day of the rescue attempt, you would observe 3 failures among the 8 helicopters? Does this suggest that the value of p on the day of the rescue mission differed from the value that existed during the training flights? Explain.

CASE STUDY 4.3
Oil Leases:
Striking It Rich
with a $10 Stake

How would you like to be an oil baron? Jeffrey Zaslow, in an article* entitled "Striking It Rich with a $10 Stake," explains how you might be able to do it.

> Since 1960, parcels of land that may contain oil have been placed in a lottery with the winner receiving leasing rights for 10 years. Any U.S. citizen older than 21 can play by paying a $10 filing fee to the Bureau of Land Management. If you win—and if an oil company is interested in drilling on the parcel you obtain—a large sum of money could be tossed your way.

The parcels, most of which are located in Wyoming or New Mexico, are auctioned each month by the Bureau of Land Management. Only one entry is allowed per person or per company, and the winner is permitted to lease the land from the U.S. government for $1 per acre per year for a period of up to 10 years. Not all parcels contain oil but, if you are a lucky winner, some oil company will want to buy your lease. Zaslow mentions four particular winners who sold their leases to oil companies: "An army veteran won $63,000. A real-estate broker won $128,000. A shopkeeper in Texas won $166,000. And an Iowa newspaper circulation manager won $265,000."

Since not many Americans participate in the lottery, and because you have the same chance of winning as Exxon or Phillips Petroleum, this lottery provides the "little guy" with a real opportunity to strike it rich. Zaslow states that, "According to Chuck Wheeler, Department of Interior paralegal specialist, the probability of finding oil on the good parcels—the ones commanding $35,000 to $200,000 on initial sale—is usually a 1-in-20 shot." You can get some guidance on which parcels are the "good ones" by seeking the services of one of the many companies that not only provide this information but will also, for a fee, file the subscriber cards with the Bureau of Land Management.

As you might suspect, some problems associated with the lottery have emerged. Some of the service companies are knowledgeable and others are not. In addition, there have been some suspected cases of "hanky-panky" in the conduct of the lottery and, for several months in 1980, the lottery was suspended. One case

---

*Orlando *Sentinel Star*, October 12, 1980.

reported by Zaslow involved a player who won three times in one month. The three parcels had 1,836, 1,365, and 495 entries, respectively. In this particular case, an Interior Department audit stated that "federal workers did a poor job of shaking the drum before the drawing."

a. Find the probability that a player would win on three parcels involving 1,836, 1,365, and 495 entries.

b. Is this probability consistent with the Interior Department's explanation of this particular event?

c. Based on your knowledge of probability and "rare events," would you make the same inference as that made by the auditor? Explain.

CASE STUDY 4.4
The Blackjack
Victory of the
Seven Samurai

Since we commenced this chapter with a discussion of the game of blackjack, it is only appropriate that we terminate with the thoughtful consideration of a problem faced by gambling houses. Is card counting by blackjack players a threat to the house? And, if so, what can be done about it? To stimulate your thinking on the subject, we offer the following article from the November 18, 1980, issue of the *Wall Street Journal*.

Card counters—the bane of American casino operators—have turned up in Macao. And the house has been screaming for a new deal.

Seven touring gamblers from the U.S. and Austria, dubbed the Seven Samurai, until this past weekend were winning big at Macao's blackjack tables by memorizing cards to get a better jump on the odds. They hinted their net winnings were running $50,000 a week.

"We're just using our heads," said Gabriel Tirado, a 29-year-old recording studio operator from San Francisco, while his friends nodded in agreement.

"This is nonsense," fumed Stanley Ho, managing director of Macao Tourism & Amusement Co., which owns four casinos and has a monopoly on gambling in this Portuguese territory that is tucked under China about 40 miles from Hong Kong. "In all casinos in the world these people aren't welcome," Mr. Ho said.

While the seven didn't admit it, observers say the gamblers were winning by using a variation of a counting system.

In blackjack, players try to beat the dealer by accumulating cards that total as close to 21 as possible without exceeding it. If the player's count is higher than the dealer's, the player wins.

In card counting, the player memorizes the cards dealt from the pack to determine when the remaining pile is rich in picture cards, which are counted as 10, or in low numbers.

Casinos in Nevada and New Jersey bar counters because they can seize as much as a 1% to 1½% advantage over the house. But Macao's laws prevent Mr. Ho from barring anyone.

Mr. Ho has been trying to get the law changed and has altered some of the blackjack rules, including ordering the casino to shuffle the cards after each hand to frustrate the counters. But that switch in procedure worked only briefly before the counters were back to winning again.

The youngest of the crew is 22-year-old Harold Zima, a post-graduate mathematics student from Vienna. Besides Mr. Tirado, the others are Americans who say they are "involved in real estate."

Four members of the group were traveling in Europe when they met Mr. Zima at a casino in Baden-Baden, West Germany. At the casino's blackjack tables their common interest became apparent. The five, along with two other friends, decided to play Asia's casinos because "it is commonly known that Asian casinos are easier to play in," Mr. Tirado said.

About seven weeks ago, the group began arriving separately in Macao. They pretended they didn't know one another. Casino employees spotted several of the counters immediately. But the house didn't know they were working together. Eventually the size of their bets gave them all away. "We put a lot of money in action," said Joseph Maly, one of the seven. "And we would do that for eight to 10 hours at a time."

The casino encouraged them to leave and even threatened them, the gamblers said. Finally, it was hotel space—or the lack of it—that forced the seven out. The players had to leave Macao this past weekend because all the rooms were booked in advance for an annual auto race.

Whether the players will be allowed back is anybody's gamble—and, on this bet, the odds favor the house.

REFERENCES   Baker, T. "Reality takes the wheel." *Forbes,* October 27, 1980, 133–134.

Daniel, W., & Terrell, J. *Business statistics: Basic concepts and methodology.* 2d ed. Boston: Houghton Mifflin, 1979. Chapter 3.

Epstein, R. A. *The theory of gambling and statistical logic.* Rev. ed. New York: Academic Press, 1977.

Feller, W. *An introduction to probability theory and its applications.* Vol. I. New York: Wiley, 1957. Chapters 1, 4, and 5.

McClave, J. T., & Dietrich, F. H. *Statistics.* 2d ed. San Francisco: Dellen, 1982. Chapter 3.

Parzen, E. *Modern probability theory and its applications.* New York: Wiley, 1960. Chapters 1 and 2.

Spaeth, A. "Blackjack victory of 'Seven Samurai'." *Wall Street Journal,* November 18, 1980.

Zaslow, J. "Striking it rich with a $10.00 stake." Orlando *Sentinel Star,* October 12, 1980.

Five

Opinion Polls and the Binomial Probability Distribution

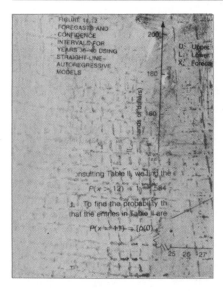

According to some stock market analysts, insider activity—the buying and selling of corporate stock by company officers—provides a signal indicating a possible rise or fall in stock fortunes. Thus, according to insider theory, the number x of stock purchases or sales by insiders provides a signal that indicates an upward or a downward trend in the stock's price. What values of x, the number of purchases (or, alternatively, the number of sales), signal an abnormal or rare event and a rise (or fall) in the stock's price? In this chapter we will learn how to answer questions of this type, and will specifically address the questions concerning "insider theory" in Case Study 5.1.

Contents:

5.1 Random Variables

In a practical business setting, an experiment (as defined in Chapter 4) involves selecting a sample of data consisting of one or more observations on some variable. For example, we might survey 1,000 consumers concerning their preferences for toothpaste and record x, the number preferring a particular brand. Or we might randomly select a single property from Appendix A and record its total appraised value, x. Since we can never know with certainty the exact value that we will observe when we record x for one experimental unit, we call x a *random variable.*

DEFINITION 5.1

A *random variable* is a variable which, when observed, assumes numerical values which are associated with events.

The two random variables described above are examples of two different types of random variables, ***discrete*** and ***continuous.*** The number x of consumers in a sample of 1,000 who prefer a particular brand of toothpaste is said to be a discrete random variable because it can assume only a countable number of values, 0, 1, 2, 3, . . . , 999, 1,000. In contrast, the appraised value of a property could theoretically assume any one of an infinite number of values, any value from $0 upwards. Of course, in practice we record appraised value to the nearest dollar but, *in theory,* the appraised value of a property could assume any value, say $51,144.13471.

A good way to distinguish between discrete and continuous random variables is to imagine the values that they may assume as points on a line. Discrete random variables may assume any one of a countable number (say 10, 21, 100, etc.) of values corresponding to points on a line. In contrast, a continuous random variable can assume *any* value corresponding to the points in one or more intervals on a line. For example, theoretically, the appraised value of a property could be represented by any of the infinitely large number of points on some portion of the positive half of a line.

DEFINITION 5.2

A *discrete random variable* is one that can assume only a countable [*Whole*] number of values.

DEFINITION 5.3

A *continuous random variable* can assume any value in one or more intervals on a line.

5.2 Probability Models for Populations

We learned in Chapter 4 that we make inferences based on the probability of observing a particular sample outcome. Since we never know the *exact* probability of some event, we must construct probability models for the values assumed by random variables. For example, if we toss a die, we assume that the values 1, 2, 3, 4, 5, and 6 represent equiprobable events, i.e., $P(1) = P(2) = P(3) = \cdots = P(6) = \frac{1}{6}$. In doing so, we have constructed a probabilistic model for the relative frequency distribution for the number of dots x that we would observe if we tossed the die thousands and thousands of times and recorded x for each toss. It is unlikely that a perfectly balanced die exists, but most dice would produce relative frequencies very close to $\frac{1}{6}$; and a relative frequency distribution of the results of a large number of tosses would appear as shown in Figure 5.1.

FIGURE 5.1
The Probability
Distribution for *x*, the
Number of Dots Observed
[*Note:* All the Probability
Is Concentrated at the
Midpoint of the Interval
beneath Each Rectangle.]

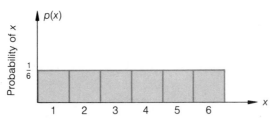

Figure 5.1, which gives the relative frequency for each value of x in a very large number of tosses of a die, is called the *probability distribution for the discrete random variable x.*

DEFINITION 5.4

The *probability distribution for a discrete random variable x* is a table, graph, or formula that gives the probability of observing each value of x. We shall denote the probability of x by the symbol $p(x)$.

EXAMPLE 5.1   Consider the following consumer-sampling situation: Draw a random sample of $n = 5$ consumers from a very large number, say 10,000, and record the number x of consumers who favor toothpaste brand X. Suppose that 2,000 of the consumers actually prefer brand X. Replace the 5 consumers in the population and randomly draw a new sample of 5 consumers. Record the value of x again. Repeat this process over and over again 100,000 times and construct a relative frequency distribution for the 100,000 values of x.

Solution   We simulated (on a computer) the drawing of 100,000 samples of 5 people from 10,000. Table 5.1 gives the possible values of x (0, 1, 2, 3, 4, and 5), the frequency (the number of times we observed a particular value of x), and the relative frequency (frequency/100,000) for each of these values. The relative frequency distribution is shown in Figure 5.2 (p. 138).

TABLE 5.1

Relative Frequencies for 100,000 Observations on x, the Number of People in a Sample of 5 Who Prefer Brand X

x	FREQUENCY	RELATIVE FREQUENCY	$p(x)$
0	32,891	.32891	.32768
1	40,929	.40929	.40960
2	20,473	.20473	.20480
3	5,104	.05104	.05120
4	599	.00599	.00640
5	4	.00004	.00032

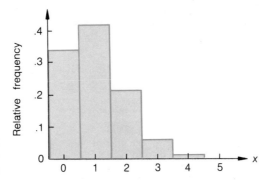

FIGURE 5.2

Relative Frequency Distribution for x

Figure 5.2 provides a very good approximation to the probability distribution for x, the number of people in a sample of 5 who prefer brand X (assuming that 20% of the people in the population prefer brand X).

In the next section, we will show you how to find a good model for this probability distribution. As you will subsequently learn, this model will give the probabilities, $p(x)$, shown in Table 5.1.

5.3 The Binomial Probability Distribution

Consumer preference and opinion polls are conducted so frequently in business and industrial situations that it is useful for us to know the probability distribution of the number x in a random sample of n experimental units (people) that prefer some specific proposition. This probability distribution, known as a *binomial probability distribution,* is applicable when the sample size n is small relative to the number N of experimental units in the population (see the box at the top of the next page).

EXAMPLE 5.2   Use the binomial probability distribution to calculate the probabilities for the sampling experiment, Example 5.1.

Solution   For this sample survey, $n = 5$ and p, the proportion of people in the population preferring toothpaste brand X, is .2. We will substitute these values of n and p and each value of x into the formula for $p(x)$,

$$p(x) = C_x^n p^x q^{n-x} = \frac{n!}{x!(n-x)!} p^x q^{n-x}$$

THE BINOMIAL PROBABILITY DISTRIBUTION

$$p(x) = C_x^n p^x q^{n-x} = \frac{n!}{x!(n-x)!} p^x q^{n-x}$$

where n = sample size

x = number in the sample who favor the proposition

p = proportion in the population that favor the proposition

$q = 1 - p$

Assumption: The sample size n is small relative to the number N of elements in the population, say, n/N smaller than $\frac{1}{20}$.

Then, remembering that $0! = 1$ and $q = 1 - p$,

$$P(x = 0) = p(0) = C_0^5 (.2)^0 (.8)^5$$

$$= \frac{5!}{0!5!}(.2)^0(.8)^5 = (1)(1)(.32768)$$

$$= .32768$$

Similarly,

$$P(x = 1) = p(1) = C_1^5 (.2)^1 (.8)^4 = \frac{5!}{1!4!}(.2)^1(.8)^4 = .40960$$

$$P(x = 2) = p(2) = C_2^5 (.2)^2 (.8)^3 = \frac{5!}{2!3!}(.2)^2(.8)^3 = .20480$$

$$P(x = 3) = p(3) = C_3^5 (.2)^3 (.8)^2 = \frac{5!}{3!2!}(.2)^3(.8)^2 = .05120$$

$$P(x = 4) = p(4) = C_4^5 (.2)^4 (.8)^1 = \frac{5!}{4!1!}(.2)^4(.8)^1 = .00640$$

$$P(x = 5) = p(5) = C_5^5 (.2)^5 (.8)^0 = \frac{5!}{5!0!}(.2)^5(.8)^0 = .00032$$

Example 5.2 illustrates an important property of discrete probability distributions: The sum of the probabilities for all values of x equals 1. Thus,

$$p(0) + p(1) + p(2) + \cdots + p(5) = .32768 + .40960 + .20480 + \cdots + .00032 = 1$$

PROPERTY #1 FOR ALL DISCRETE PROBABILITY DISTRIBUTIONS

The sum of the probabilities $p(x)$, $x = 0, 1, 2, \ldots, n, \ldots$ for all values of x is always equal to 1, i.e.,

$$\Sigma p(x) = 1$$

EXAMPLE 5.3   Refer to Example 5.2 and find the probability that 3 or more persons in the sample prefer brand X.

Solution   The values that a random variable x can assume are always mutually exclusive events, i.e., you could not observe $x = 2$ and, at the same time, observe $x = 3$. Therefore, the event "$x = 3$ or more" (the event that $x = 3$ or $x = 4$ or $x = 5$) can be found using Probability Rule #2 (Chapter 4). Thus,

$$P(x = 3 \text{ or } 4 \text{ or } 5) = P(x = 3) + P(x = 4) + P(x = 5) = p(3) + p(4) + p(5)$$

Substituting the probabilities found in Example 5.2, we obtain

$$P(x = 3 \text{ or } 4 \text{ or } 5) = .0512 + .0064 + .00032 = .05792$$

Example 5.3 illustrates a second important property of discrete probability distributions: The probability that $x = a$ or b is equal to $p(a) + p(b)$.

PROPERTY #2 FOR ALL DISCRETE PROBABILITY DISTRIBUTIONS

The probability that $x = a$ *or* $x = b$ is equal to $p(a) + p(b)$, i.e.,

$$P(x = a \text{ or } x = b) = p(a) + p(b)$$

We have defined a binomial probability distribution in the context of opinion polling, but the distribution possesses much wider applications—any that satisfy a set of five conditions characterizing a *binomial experiment.* These conditions are listed in the box.

CONDITIONS REQUIRED FOR A BINOMIAL EXPERIMENT

1.   A sample of n experimental units is selected from a population.
2.   Each experimental unit possesses one of two characteristics. We conventionally call the characteristic of interest a "success" and the other a "failure."
3.   The probability that a single experimental unit possesses the "success" characteristic is equal to p. This probability is the same for all experimental units.
4.   The outcome for any one experimental unit is independent of the outcome for any other experimental unit (i.e., the draws are independent).
5.   The random variable x counts the number of "successes" in a sample of size n.

The binomial probability distributions for a sample of $n = 10$ and

a. $p = .1$ **b.** $p = .3$ **c.** $p = .5$ **d.** $p = .7$ **e.** $p = .9$

are shown in Figure 5.3. Note that the probability distribution is skewed to the right for

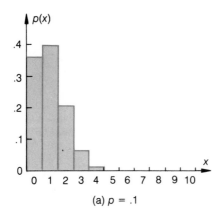

(a) $p = .1$

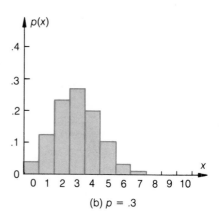

(b) $p = .3$

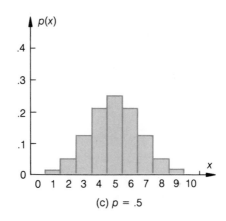

(c) $p = .5$

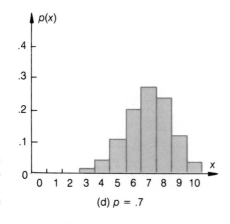

(d) $p = .7$

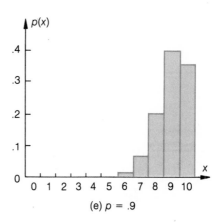

(e) $p = .9$

FIGURE 5.3
Binomial Probability
Distributions for $n = 10$,
$p = .1, .3, .5, .7, .9$

small values of p, skewed to the left for large values of p, and is symmetric for $p = .5$.

As you work the exercises in this chapter, you will encounter several nonsurvey applications of the binomial experiment. Check each to convince yourself that the five characteristics of a binomial experiment are satisfied.

EXERCISES   5.1   A coin is tossed 10 times and the number of heads is recorded. To a reasonable degree of approximation, is this a binomial experiment? Check to see whether each of the five identifying characteristics of a binomial experiment is satisfied.

5.2   Four coins are selected without replacement from a group of five pennies and five dimes. Let x equal the number of pennies in the sample of four coins. To a reasonable degree of approximation, is this a binomial experiment? Check to see whether each of the five identifying characteristics of a binomial experiment is satisfied.

5.3   A parachutist selects two parachutes from among a group of five. Unknown to the parachutist, two of the five are defective and will fail to open. Let x equal the number of defective parachutes in the parachutist's sample of two. To a reasonable degree of approximation, is this a binomial experiment? Check to see whether each of the five identifying characteristics of a binomial experiment is satisfied.

5.4   Suppose that the parachutist, Exercise 5.3, had chosen two parachutes from among a group of 1,000, of which 400 are defective and will fail to open. To a reasonable degree of approximation, is this a binomial experiment? Explain.

5.5   Suppose that you have invested $10 in each of three oil lease lotteries of the type described in Case Study 4.3. Let x equal the number of lotteries in which you will be the winner. To a reasonable degree of approximation, is this a binomial experiment? Explain.

5.6   A random sample of 1,200 people is selected, and each person is asked to choose the news magazine that he or she prefers. Let x equal the number who select the *U.S. News and World Report.* To a reasonable degree of approximation, is this a binomial experiment? Explain.

5.7   A random sample of 100 persons was selected to make a visual comparison of two floor waxes, A and B. Two hundred 9-inch squares of floor tile were used for the experiment and were randomly divided into two groups of 100 tiles each. The first group received a coat of floor polish A, the second group received a coat of floor polish B, and the tiles were marked so that they could be identified only by the person conducting the experiment. The tiles were then assigned, one of each type, to each of the 100 evaluators. Each evaluator chose the tile that he or she preferred, and the experimenter tabulated the number of persons preferring each of the two waxes. Suppose that x is the number of persons preferring floor wax A.

α.   Is x a binomial random variable? [*Hint:* Check to see if each of the five characteristics of a binomial experiment is satisfied.]

b. Suppose that the majority of persons inspecting pairs of tiles receiving polishes A and B prefer polish A. What does this imply about the value of p?

c. Suppose that the two waxes are, in fact, identical. What does this imply about the value of p?

5.8 Use the formula for the binomial probability distribution to find the probabilities for $n = 4$, $p = .5$, and $x = 0, 1, 2, 3,$ and 4.

5.9 Repeat the instructions of Exercise 5.8 for $n = 4$ and $p = .2$.

5.10 Construct graphs similar to Figure 5.3 of the two probability distributions, Exercises 5.8 and 5.9.

5.11 Refer to Exercise 5.8 and find the probability that:

a. x is less than 2.

b. x is less than or equal to 2.

c. Locate the probabilities, parts a and b, on the graph that you constructed in Exercise 5.10.

d. Verify that (except for rounding) the sum of the probabilities for $x = 0, 1, 2, 3,$ and 4 equals 1.

5.12 Refer to Exercise 5.9 and find the probability that:

a. x is less than 2.

b. x is equal to 2 or more.

c. How are the events, parts a and b, related?

d. What relationship must the probabilities, parts a and b, satisfy?

5.13 A door-to-door salesperson has found that her success rate in selling is .2, i.e., the probability of making a sale on a single contact is .2. If the salesperson contacts three prospects, what is the probability that:

a. She sells to all three?

b. She sells to exactly 1?

c. She sells to *at least* 1? [*Hint:* The event "at least 1" is equivalent to "$x = 1$ or $x = 2$ or $x = 3$."]

5.14 In Exercise 5.13, a "success" was defined as the event that the salesperson made a sale on a single contact. In contrast, suppose we define a "success" as the event that the salesperson does not make a sale on a single contact.

a. What is the value of p for this binomial experiment?

b. Define x in terms of the problem.

c. What value of x corresponds to the event that she sells to all 3 contacts?

d. What value of x corresponds to the event that she sells to exactly 1 out of 3?

e. What values of x correspond to the event that she sells to at least 1 out of 3?

5.15 In Exercise 5.4, we selected two parachutes from among a group of 1,000, of which 400 were defective. Let x equal the number of parachutes in a sample of 2 that open.

a. What is meant by a "success" in the context of this problem?
b. What is the value of p?
c. Find the approximate probability that $x = 1$.

5.16   Refer to Exercise 5.15. Let x equal the number of parachutes in a sample of 2 that fail to open.

a. What is meant by a "success" in the context of this problem?
b. What is the value of p?
c. Find the approximate probability that $x = 1$.

5.4   Tables of the Binomial Probability Distribution

As you can see from the preceding section, the calculation of binomial probabilities is often very tedious. In practice, we would refer to one of the many tables that give the computed values of $p(x)$ for a wide range of values of n and p. To aid you in using these tables, we have included binomial probability tables for $n = 5, 6, 7, 8, 9, 10, 15, 20, 25$. These are listed in Table 1, Appendix E. References to more extensive sets of tables are listed at the end of the chapter.

The tabulated binomial probability distribution for $n = 5$ (Table 1, Appendix E) is reproduced in Table 5.2.

TABLE 5.2   A Reproduction of Table 1, Appendix E: The Binomial Probability Distribution, $n = 5$

N=5														
x	0.01	0.05	0.1	0.2	0.3	0.4	0.5	0.6	0.7	0.8	0.9	0.95	0.99	x
0	.9510	.7738	.5905	.3277	.1681	.0778	.0313	.0102	.0024	.0003	.0000	.0000	.0000	0
1	.0480	.2036	.3280	.4096	.3601	.2592	.1563	.0768	.0283	.0064	.0005	.0000	.0000	1
2	.0010	.0214	.0729	.2048	.3087	.3456	.3125	.2304	.1323	.0512	.0081	.0011	.0000	2
3	.0000	.0011	.0081	.0512	.1323	.2304	.3125	.3456	.3087	.2048	.0729	.0214	.0010	3
4	.0000	.0000	.0004	.0064	.0283	.0768	.1563	.2592	.3601	.4096	.3280	.2036	.0480	4
5	.0000	.0000	.0000	.0003	.0024	.0102	.0313	.0778	.1681	.3277	.5905	.7738	.9510	5

Examining Table 5.2, you note that the values of p are given in the top row of the table, and the values that x can assume, $x = 0, 1, 2, 3, 4, 5$, are shown in the first column. To find the binomial probability for some value of p, say $p = .2$, move across the top row of the table to $p = .2$. The values of $p(x)$ appear in the column beneath this value of p. We will illustrate with an example.

EXAMPLE 5.4   Find the probability that $x = 1$ for a binomial random variable with $n = 5$ and $p = .2$.

Solution   Move down the column beneath $p = .2$ until you reach the row corresponding to $x = 1$. The value of $p(1)$ is given as .4096. This value is shaded in Table 5.2. Compare this and the tabulated values of $p(x)$ for $x = 0, 2, 3, 4,$ and 5 with the values that we computed (using the formula for $p(x)$) in Example 5.2.

EXERCISES 5.17 Refer to the binomial probability table for $n = 6$, Table 1, Appendix E.
a. Find $p(2)$ when $p = .30$.　　　　　　b. Find $p(3)$ when $p = .50$.
c. Find $p(5)$ when $p = .10$.

5.18 Refer to the binomial probability distribution for $n = 10$, Table 1, Appendix E.
a. Find $p(0)$ when $p = .1$.　　　　　　b. Find $p(1)$ when $p = .1$.
c. Find $p(2)$ when $p = .1$.
d. Compare these tabulated values with the values shown on the graph, Figure 5.3.

5.19 Refer to the binomial probability distribution for $n = 10$, Table 1, Appendix E.
a. Find $p(3)$ when $p = .5$.　　　　　　b. Find $p(4)$ when $p = .5$.
c. Find $p(5)$ when $p = .5$.
d. Compare your answers, parts a, b, c, with the values shown on the graph, Figure 5.3.

5.20 Construct graphs of the binomial probability distributions for:
a. $n = 6$, $p = .2$　　　　b. $n = 6$, $p = .5$　　　　c. $n = 6$, $p = .8$

5.21 Construct graphs of the binomial probability distributions for:
a. $n = 15$, $p = .1$　　　　b. $n = 15$, $p = .5$　　　　c. $n = 15$, $p = .9$

5.5 Cumulative Binomial Probability Tables

Sometimes we will want to compare an observed value of x obtained from an opinion poll (or some other binomial experiment) with some theory or claim associated with the sampled population. Particularly, we will want to see if the observed value of x represents a "rare event," assuming that the claim is true.

EXAMPLE 5.5 A manufacturer of photographic flash cubes claims that 95% of all flash cubes that it produces will function properly. Suppose that you purchase a box of ten of these flash cubes and find that only six flash. Is this sample outcome highly improbable (a "rare event"), if in fact the manufacturer's claim is true?

Solution If p really does equal .95 (or some larger value), then observing a small number, x, of flash cubes that function properly would represent a rare event. Since we observed $x = 6$, we want to know the probability of observing a value of $x = 6$ or some other value of x even more contradictory to the manufacturer's claim, i.e., we want to find the probability that $x = 0$ or $x = 1$ or $x = 2 \ldots$ or $x = 6$. Using the additive rule for values of $p(x)$, we obtain

$$P(x = 0 \text{ or } x = 1 \text{ or } x = 2 \ldots \text{ or } x = 6) = p(0) + p(1) + p(2) + p(3) + p(4) + p(5) + p(6)$$

when $n = 10$ and $p = .95$. Referring to Table 1, Appendix E, for these values of $p(x)$ and substituting, we find

$$P(x = 0 \text{ or } x = 1 \text{ or } x = 2 \ldots \text{ or } x = 6)$$
$$= .0000 + .0000 + .0000 + .0000 + .0000 + .0001 + .0010$$
$$= .0011$$

This small probability tells us that observing as few as 6 good flash cubes in a pack of 10 is indeed a rare event, if in fact the manufacturer's claim is true. Such a sample result suggests either that the manufacturer's claim is false or that the 10 flash cubes in the box do not represent a random sample from the manufacturer's total production. Perhaps they came from a particular production line that was temporarily malfunctioning.

Solving practical problems of the type illustrated in Example 5.5 requires us to sum values of $p(x)$. Partial sums of the values of $p(x)$, called *cumulative probabilities*, are given for $n = 5, 6, 7, 8, 9, 10, 15, 20,$ and 25 in Table 2, Appendix E.

A reproduction of the cumulative binomial probability table for $n = 5$ is shown in Table 5.3.

TABLE 5.3   A Reproduction of a Portion of Table 2, Appendix E: The Cumulative Binomial Probability Distribution, $n = 5$

N=5						P							
x	0.01	0.05	0.1	0.2	0.3	0.4	0.5	0.6	0.7	0.8	0.9	0.95	0.99	x
0	.9510	.7738	.5905	.3277	.1681	.0778	.0313	.0102	.0024	.0003	.0000	.0000	.0000	0
1	.9950	.9774	.9185	.7373	.5282	.3370	.1875	.0870	.0308	.0067	.0005	.0000	.0000	1
2	1.0000	.9988	.9914	.9421	.8369	.6826	.5000	.3174	.1631	.0579	.0086	.0012	.0000	2
3	1.0000	1.0000	.9995	.9933	.9652	.9130	.8125	.6630	.4718	.2627	.0815	.0226	.0010	3
4	1.0000	1.0000	1.0000	.9997	.9976	.9898	.9687	.9222	.8319	.6723	.4095	.2262	.0490	4

EXAMPLE 5.6   Consider a binomial experiment with $n = 5$ and $p = .2$. Find the sum of the binomial probabilities $p(x)$ for $x = 0, 1, 2$; i.e., find $P(x = 0$ or $x = 1$ or $x = 2)$.

Solution   In general, to find the sum of the binomial probabilities $p(x)$ for $x = 0, 1, 2, \ldots, a$ from Table 2, Appendix E, search for the tabled entry corresponding to the row $x = a$ under the appropriate column for p. The cumulative sum of probabilities for this example is given in the column corresponding to $p = .2$ and the row corresponding to $x = 2$. Therefore,

$$P(x = 0 \text{ or } x = 1 \text{ or } x = 2) = p(0) + p(1) + p(2) = .9421$$

This value is shaded in Table 5.3.

EXAMPLE 5.7   If you toss a balanced coin 10 times, what is the probability that you will observe 8 or more heads?

Solution   First, suppose that we define a success to be a head. Then, the probability of a success is .5, and

$$P(x = 8 \text{ or more}) = P(x = 8 \text{ or } x = 9 \text{ or } x = 10) = p(8) + p(9) + p(10)$$

Remember that Table 2, Appendix E, gives cumulative sums, and that the sum of the values of $p(x)$ over all values of x is equal to 1, i.e., $\Sigma p(x) = 1$. Therefore,

$$P(x = 8 \text{ or } x = 9 \text{ or } x = 10) = p(8) + p(9) + p(10) = 1 - [p(0) + p(1) + \cdots + p(7)]$$

where the partial sum $p(0) + p(1) + \cdots + p(7)$ is represented by the symbol

$$\sum_{x=0}^{7} p(x)$$

The next step is to turn to the cumulative binomial probability table in Table 2, Appendix E, for $n = 10$ and find

$$\sum_{x=0}^{7} p(x) = p(0) + p(1) + \cdots + p(7)$$

The tabulated value in the $p = .5$ column and the row corresponding to $x = 7$ is .9453. Then, the probability of tossing 8 or more heads in 10 tosses of a balanced coin is

$$P(x = 8 \text{ or } x = 9 \text{ or } x = 10) = 1 - \sum_{x=0}^{7} p(x) = 1 - .9453 = .0547$$

EXAMPLE 5.8   Find the probability of tossing 8 or more heads, Example 5.7, by defining a success as observing a tail.

Solution   If a success is observing a tail, then the probability of a success is still $p = .5$, and x is the number of tails in 10 tosses of the coin. The next step is to define the event "observe 8 or more heads" in terms of x, the number of tails. This event will occur if the number of tails is 0, 1, or 2. Therefore,

$$P(\text{observe 8 or more heads}) = P(x = 0 \text{ or } x = 1 \text{ or } x = 2) = \sum_{x=0}^{2} p(x)$$

We can read this cumulative sum directly from Table 2, Appendix E, in the table corresponding to $n = 10$. Looking in the column corresponding to $p = .5$ and the row corresponding to $x = 2$, we read

$$P(\text{observe 8 or more heads}) = P(x = 0 \text{ or } x = 1 \text{ or } x = 2) = \sum_{x=0}^{2} p(x) = .0547$$

This is exactly the same answer as was obtained in Example 5.7.

EXERCISES   **5.22**   Refer to the cumulative binomial probability table for $n = 5$, Table 2, Appendix E.

α.   Find $\displaystyle\sum_{x=0}^{2} p(x) = p(0) + p(1) + p(2)$ when $p = .3$.

b. Find $\sum_{x=0}^{4} p(x)$ when $p = .3$.

c. Find $\sum_{x=0}^{5} p(x)$ when $p = .3$.

5.23 Refer to the cumulative binomial probability table for $n = 10$ and $p = .4$, Table 2, Appendix E.
a. Find the probability that x is less than or equal to 8.
b. Find the probability that x is less than 8.
c. Find the probability that x is larger than 8.

5.24 If x is a binomial random variable with $n = 10$ and $p = .1$, use Table 2, Appendix E, to:
a. Find the probability that x is less than or equal to 2.
b. Locate the probability rectangles in Figure 5.2 that correspond to the probability, part a.
c. Find the probability that x is greater than 2.

5.25 If you flip a balanced coin 5 times, what is the probability that:
a. You will toss 3 or fewer heads?
b. You will toss more than 3 heads?
c. You will toss at most 1 head?
d. You will toss fewer than 3 heads?

5.26 A manufacturer ships electric fuses in boxes each containing 2,000 fuses. If only 5% of the fuses in a box are defective and you sample $n = 10$ from the box, find the probability that the number x of defective fuses in the sample is:
a. Less than 1   **b.** Less than or equal to 1
c. Less than 2   **d.** More than 1

5.27 According to union organizers, 80% of the 10,000 employees of a company will vote in an upcoming election for union representation. To check the situation, management selected a random sample of 25 employees from the 10,000 and recorded x, the number favoring union representation. If the union is correct in its assertion, what is the probability that:
a. x is less than 20?   **b.** x is less than 15?   **c.** x is more than 15?
d. What would you think about the union's assertion if the observed value of x is less than 15? Explain.

5.28 As we suggested in Chapter 4, investing may be viewed as a form of educated gambling where knowledge and experience will change your odds (chance) of winning. Suppose that the probability of your winning in a single venture is .6 and that you repeat the process for a total of $n = 20$ independent ventures. What is the probability that:

a. You will win on at least half of the ventures (i.e., $x = 10$ or more)?
b. You will win on at least 60% of the ventures (i.e., $x = 12$ or more)?
c. You will win on at least 80% of the ventures?

5.6 The Mean and Standard Deviation for a Binomial Probability Distribution

The samples collected in most sample surveys (or other binomial experiments) are usually quite large. For example, the Gallup and Harris survey results reported in the news media are usually based on samples from $n = 1,000$ to $n = 2,000$ people. Since we would not wish to calculate $p(x)$ for values of n this large, we need an easy way to describe the probability distribution for x to help us decide whether an observed value of x represents a rare event. To do this, we need to know the mean and standard deviation for the distribution. Then we can describe it using the Empirical Rule of Chapter 3.

In general, the probability distribution for a discrete random variable is a theoretical frequency distribution for a population. Consequently, we can describe it by finding its mean μ and standard deviation σ. These quantities are found using the following definitions:

DEFINITION 5.5

The *mean μ* (or *expected value*) of a discrete random variable x is equal to the sum of the products of each value of x and the corresponding value of $p(x)$, i.e.,

$$\mu = \Sigma \, xp(x)$$

DEFINITION 5.6

The *variance σ^2* of a discrete random variable x is equal to the sum of the products of $(x - \mu)^2$ and the corresponding value of $p(x)$, i.e.,

$$\sigma^2 = \Sigma \, (x - \mu)^2 p(x)$$

DEFINITION 5.7

The *standard deviation σ* of a random variable x is equal to the positive square root of the variance.

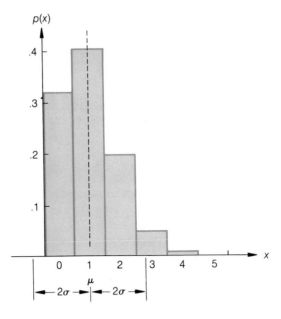

FIGURE 5.4
The Binomial Probability
Distribution
$n = 5$, $p = .2$

EXAMPLE 5.9 The formulas given in Definitions 5.5, 5.6, and 5.7 provide numerical measures (μ and σ) that will describe the location and spread of a discrete probability distribution. We shall demonstrate this by finding the mean and standard deviation for the binomial probability distribution with $n = 5$, $p = .2$. The graph of this probability distribution is shown in Figure 5.4.

Solution By Definition 5.5, the mean, μ, is given by

$$\mu = \Sigma\, xp(x)$$

The values of $p(x)$ are given in Table 1, Appendix E, for $n = 5$ and $p = .2$. Since x can take values, $x = 0, 1, 2, \ldots, 5$, we have

$$\mu = 0p(0) + 1p(1) + 2p(2) + \cdots + 5p(5)$$
$$= 0(.32768) + 1(.4096) + 2(.2048) + 3(.0512) + 4(.0064) + 5(.00032)$$
$$= 1.0$$

Similarly, by Definition 5.6,

$$\sigma^2 = \Sigma\, (x - \mu)^2 p(x) \qquad \text{where} \quad \mu = 1.0$$
$$= (0 - 1.0)^2 p(0) + (1 - 1.0)^2 p(1) + (2 - 1.0)^2 p(2) + \cdots + (5 - 1.0)^2 p(5)$$
$$= (0 - 1.0)^2(.32768) + (1 - 1.0)^2(.4096) + (2 - 1.0)^2(.2048)$$
$$\quad + (3 - 1.0)^2(.0512) + (4 - 1.0)^2(.0064) + (5 - 1.0)^2(.00032)$$
$$= .80$$

and by Definition 5.7, the standard deviation, σ, is given by

$$\sigma = \sqrt{\sigma^2} = \sqrt{.80} = .894$$

EXAMPLE 5.10   Locate the interval $\mu \pm 2\sigma$ on the graph of the binomial probability distribution for $n = 5$, $p = .2$. Confirm that most of the (theoretical) population falls within this interval.

Solution   Figure 5.4 gives the graph of the binomial probability distribution when $n = 5$, $p = .2$ (the actual probabilities are given in the table corresponding to $n = 5$, Table 1, Appendix E). Recall that $\mu = 1.0$ and $\sigma = .894$. Then,

$$\mu - 2\sigma = 1.0 - 2(.894) = -.788$$
$$\mu + 2\sigma = 1.0 + 2(.894) = 2.788$$

The interval $-.788$ to 2.788, shown in Figure 5.4, includes the values of $x = 0$, $x = 1$, and $x = 2$. Thus, the probability (relative frequency) that a population value falls within this interval is

$$p(0) + p(1) + p(2) = .3277 + .4096 + .2048$$
$$= .9421$$

This certainly agrees with the Empirical Rule, which states that approximately 95% of the data will lie within 2σ of the mean μ.

You can show (proof omitted), using the formulas in Definitions 5.5, 5.6, and 5.7, that the mean, variance, and standard deviation for a binomial probability distribution are as follows:

MEAN, VARIANCE, AND STANDARD DEVIATION FOR A BINOMIAL PROBABILITY DISTRIBUTION

$$\mu = np$$
$$\sigma^2 = npq$$
$$\sigma = \sqrt{npq}$$

where n = Sample size

p = Probability of a success on a single trial

= Proportion of experimental units in a large population that are "successes"

$q = 1 - p$

EXAMPLE 5.11   Although one primary objective is to describe binomial probability distributions based on large samples (i.e., when n is large), we can see how well μ and σ characterize the binomial probability distributions shown in the graphs, Figure 5.3. Find μ and σ for a binomial probability distribution with $n = 10$, $p = .1$, and find the theoretical proportion of the population which lies within the interval $\mu \pm 2\sigma$. Does this result agree with the Empirical Rule, which states that approximately 95% of the measurements in the distribution should lie within this interval?

Solution   Using the formulas for μ and σ, we obtain

$$\mu = np = (10)(.1) = 1$$
$$\sigma = \sqrt{npq} = \sqrt{(10)(.1)(.9)} = .949$$

Then,

$$\mu - 2\sigma = 1 - 2(.949) = -.898$$
$$\mu + 2\sigma = 1 + 2(.949) = 2.898$$

The values of x in the interval, $-.898$ to 2.898, are $x = 0, 1,$ and 2. To find the sum of the probabilities in the interval $\mu \pm 2\sigma$ (i.e., $-.898$ to 2.898), we need to find $p(0) + p(1) + p(2)$. The easy way to find this partial sum is to refer to the cumulative binomial probability table for $n = 10$ and $p = .1$. This gives

$$\sum_{x=0}^{2} p(x) = p(0) + p(1) + p(2) = .9298$$

You can see from this value, .9298, that the sum of the probabilities for values of x in the interval $\mu \pm 2\sigma$ agrees very closely with the Empirical Rule. You can see this graphically in Figure 5.5.

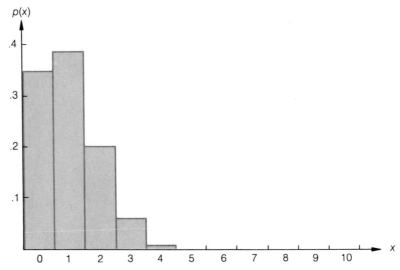

FIGURE 5.5
The Binomial Probability
Distribution
$n = 10, p = .1$

EXAMPLE 5.12   Describe a binomial probability distribution for $n = 1,000$ and $p = .4$.

Solution   We will use the formulas to find μ and σ:

$$\mu = np = (1,000)(.4) = 400$$
$$\sigma = \sqrt{npq} = \sqrt{1,000(.4)(.6)} = \sqrt{240} = 15.49$$
$$\mu - 2\sigma = 400 - 2(15.49) = 369.02$$
$$\mu + 2\sigma = 400 + 2(15.49) = 430.98$$

Therefore, we envision a distribution that centers about $\mu = 400$ with (from the Empirical Rule) approximately 95% of the distribution lying between 369.02 and 430.98. Since x can assume only integer values, this means that approximately 95% of the probability lies within the interval $x = 370$ to $x = 430$.

EXAMPLE 5.13   Refer to Example 5.12. Is it likely that x could assume a value as large as 450?

Solution   Not likely! We know that most (approximately 95%) of the distribution lies in the interval $x = 370$ to $x = 430$. A value of $x = 450$ lies outside this interval. In fact, the z-score (discussed in Chapter 3) corresponding to $x = 450$ is

$$z = \frac{x - \mu}{\sigma} = \frac{450 - 400}{15.49} = 3.23$$

Therefore, $x = 450$ lies 3.23 standard deviations above $\mu = 400$. The probability of observing a value of x this far above the mean μ is very small (almost negligible).

EXAMPLE 5.14   One hundred thousand early votes have been counted in a national election. If candidate Anderson has only 49,000 of the votes, does this imply that his opponent will win?

Solution   We cannot answer this question unless we can be fairly certain that the 100,000 early votes represent a random sample from the entire voting population. If we are willing to make this assumption, and if in fact Anderson will receive 50% of all the votes, then $p = .5$ and $q = .5$, and

$$\mu = np = (100,000)(.5) = 50,000$$
$$\sigma = \sqrt{npq} = \sqrt{(100,000)(.5)(.5)} = 158.1$$

Then, if Anderson really has 50% of *all* votes (i.e., if $p = .5$), we would expect the number of voters favoring Anderson to fall in the interval

$$\mu - 2\sigma = 50,000 - 2(158.1) = 49,683.8$$

to

$$\mu + 2\sigma = 50,000 + 2(158.1) = 50,316.2$$

If Anderson has only $x = 49,000$ votes in a sample of 100,000, you can see that this value of x is highly improbable (assuming $p = .5$). It lies a long way outside the interval $\mu \pm 2\sigma$. The z-score for this value of x is

$$z = \frac{x - \mu}{\sigma} = \frac{49,000 - 50,000}{158.1} = -6.33$$

If Anderson is to win (i.e., if $p = .5$ or larger), the probability that the number, x, of voters in a sample of 100,000 favoring him is as small as 49,000 is almost 0. Therefore, we are inclined to believe (based on the sample value, $x = 49,000$) that the proportion of voters favoring Anderson is much less than $p = .5$.

EXERCISES   **5.29**   Calculate μ and σ for a binomial probability distribution with
a. $n = 15, p = .1$ **b.** $n = 15, p = .5$

5.30 Since a probability distribution is a theoretical model for a population relative frequency distribution, what proportion of the total probability would you expect to lie within the interval $\mu \pm 2\sigma$? [*Hint:* Use the Empirical Rule, Chapter 3.]

5.31 Refer to Exercise 5.29. Locate the interval $\mu \pm 2\sigma$ on the graphs of the probability distributions, Exercise 5.21, parts a and b. For each graph, find the probability that x lies within the interval $\mu \pm 2\sigma$. Do these probabilities agree with your answer to Exercise 5.30?

5.32 Find the mean and standard deviation for the following binomial probability distributions:
a. $n = 100, p = .99$ b. $n = 100, p = .8$ c. $n = 100, p = .5$
d. $n = 100, p = .2$ e. $n = 100, p = .01$

5.33 Use the values of μ and σ calculated in Exercise 5.32 to construct rough sketches of the five binomial probability distributions.

5.34 Find the means and standard deviations for the following binomial probability distributions:
a. $n = 900, p = .99$ b. $n = 900, p = .8$ c. $n = 900, p = .5$
d. $n = 900, p = .2$ e. $n = 900, p = .01$

5.35 Use the values of μ and σ calculated in Exercise 5.34 to construct rough sketches of the five binomial probability distributions.

5.36 A manufacturer of perfume claims that 10% of all women aged 18 to 30 favor its brand. You select a random sample of 1,200 women in that age bracket.
a. What is the expected number who would prefer the manufacturer's brand?
b. Within what limits would you expect x, the number favoring the manufacturer's brand, to fall? [*Hint:* Find the interval $\mu \pm 2\sigma$.]
c. Suppose that the number, x, in the sample of 1,200 who favor the brand is equal to 89. If the manufacturer's claim is true, would this represent a rare event? Would you doubt the manufacturer's claim? Explain.

5.37 Many people perceive themselves as "middle class," but the term is difficult to define. According to the *Wall Street Journal* (February 10, 1981), New York's Mayor Koch earns $60,000 per year and "definitely" considers himself middle class. John Shannon of the Advisory Commission on Intergovernmental Relations, in defining "middle class," states that "it's that group of damned irritated people who receive no direct federal aid but aren't rich enough to work any sophisticated tax angles." Joseph Minarik of the Brookings Institution argues that the middle class live on income derived from labor (as opposed to dividend, other investment income, or government support), and that 98% of all American households received more than 90% of their income from labor in 1977. Suppose we accept the theory that approximately 98% of us view ourselves as middle class, and that a random sample of 2,000 adults is asked whether they perceive themselves in that category or not. Let x be the number of people in the sample who consider themselves middle class.
a. What is the expected number in the sample who will consider themselves to be middle class?

b. What is the standard deviation of x?

c. Within what limits would you expect x to fall if in fact 98% of all people view themselves as middle class?

d. Suppose that the number in the sample of 2,000 who consider themselves as middle class is 1,850. Does this contradict the theory that 98% of all people view themselves as middle class? Explain.

5.38   Refer to Exercise 5.37. Suppose that each member of your class is asked to write on a slip of paper whether or not they regard themselves as middle class. Let x equal the number in the class who consider themselves middle class.

a. Find the mean and standard deviation of x. Assume that 98% of all Americans consider themselves middle class.

b. Find the interval $\mu \pm 2\sigma$.

c. Is the value of x observed for your class consistent with the 98% theory? Explain. [*Note:* Regardless of the outcome of your survey, remember that your class is not a random sample from the population about which the inference is being made.]

5.39   Refer to Exercise 5.37. According to the *Wall Street Journal,* the median income of unemployed heads of households in 1979 was approximately $14,200. You randomly select 1,000 unemployed heads of households.

a. What proportion would you expect to have incomes exceeding $14,200? [*Hint:* If the median is known to be $14,200, then the probability that an unemployed head of household has an income exceeding $14,200 is .5.]

b. What are the mean and standard deviation of the number x who have incomes exceeding $14,200 in the sample of 1,000?

c. Within what range would you expect x to lie? [*Hint:* Use the Empirical Rule.]

5.7 Summary

This chapter utilizes a very practical business sampling problem, a public opinion poll, as a vehicle for discussing discrete random variables and the binomial probability distribution. We are first led to a discussion of random variables, particularly discrete random variables, which are those that can assume a countable number of values. A complete list (or graph or formula) that gives the probabilities associated with each value of a random variable x is called its probability distribution.

The number, x, of people (consumers, voters, etc.) in a random sample of n people from a large population who favor some proposition follows a binomial probability distribution. Other random variables that possess the same probability distribution are those that satisfy the five conditions that describe a binomial experiment. The formula for a binomial probability distribution (along with the binomial probability tables) enables us to calculate the probabilities about x. Particularly, in a practical situation, we can determine whether an observed sample value of x is a highly improbable event.

When the sample size n is large, it is difficult to calculate the values of $p(x)$ but it is easy to describe the binomial probability distribution by finding the mean μ and standard deviation σ of the distribution. Then we can use the Empirical Rule to describe $p(x)$ and to identify values of x that are improbable.

Keep in mind that this chapter is written about a very practical sampling situation, opinion polling, and that the binomial probability distribution gives the probability of observing a specific number x of people who favor some proposition. As you will subsequently see, we will use these probabilities to make an inference about the proportion p of people in the population who favor the proposition.

KEY WORDS

Random variable
Discrete random variable
Continuous random variable
Binomial random variable
Binomial probability distribution
Binomial experiment
Cumulative binomial probabilities
Rare event

SUPPLEMENTARY EXERCISES

5.40 Use the formula for the binomial probability distribution to find the probabilities for $n = 3$, $p = .1$, $x = 0$, 1, 2, 3. Graph this probability distribution.

5.41 Repeat Exercise 5.40 for $n = 3$, $p = .3$.

5.42 Repeat Exercise 5.40 for $n = 3$, $p = .5$.

5.43 Repeat Exercise 5.40 for $n = 3$, $p = .7$.

5.44 Repeat Exercise 5.40 for $n = 3$, $p = .9$.

5.45 A coin is tossed 8 times and the number x of heads is recorded. Find the probability that:
a. $x = 4$ **b.** x is larger than 4   **c.** x is less than 2

5.46 A company claims that only 1 out of 20 of its minicomputers develops defects within a one-year guarantee period. Suppose you purchase 9 of the systems and find that 2 develop defects within the one-year period.
a. Find the probability of observing as many as 2 defective computers in a group of 9 if, in fact, the company's claim is true.
b. Would the observed sample result be regarded as a rare event?
c. Would your answer to part b cause you to doubt the company's claim?

5.47 An accounting firm claims that the probability that it makes one or more errors on an income tax return is only one chance in 10 (i.e., $p = .1$). The firm has completed

the tax returns for four of your acquaintances and two of the four are found to contain errors.
a. What is the probability of observing 2 or more erroneous returns in a sample of 4 if, in fact, p is as small as .1?
b. Do you doubt the firm's claim that the probability that it will produce an erroneous return is only .1? Explain.
c. Can you think of a good reason why you might observe as many as 2 erroneous returns in a sample of 4 even if p really is equal to .1?

5.48 A bottling company randomly samples one bottle of a popular drink from the production line every 6 minutes and conducts a test of its contents. Each sampled bottle is then rated as acceptable or unacceptable. At the end of two hours, 20 bottles have been tested. Is x, the number of unacceptable bottles in the sample of 20, a binomial random variable? Justify your answer.

5.49 A group of 20 college graduates contains 10 highly motivated persons, as determined by a company psychologist. Suppose that a personnel director selects 10 persons from among this group of 20 for employment. Let x equal the number of highly motivated persons included in the personnel director's selection. Is this a binomial experiment? Explain.

5.50 In a long series of free-throws, a basketball player has a record of 80% successes. At the conclusion of an important game, the player is fouled and given two free-throws. With one successful free-throw out of two, his team wins the game.
a. Do you think that the probability of a basket on the first free-throw is equal to .8?
b. Is the outcome on the second free-throw likely to be independent of the outcome on the first free-throw?
c. Considering your answers to parts a and b, is it likely that the two free-throws constitute a binomial experiment?

5.51 Ten percent of the MBA graduates of a particular university, although not identifiable at graduation, will develop into outstanding managers. A large company has selected 10 MBA graduates from the university for employment. What is the probability that:
a. All 10 will develop into outstanding managers?
b. At least 3?
c. At least 1?

5.52 A production process produces, on the average, 1% defective electronic switches. If a random sample of 20 switches is selected from the production line, what is the probability of observing 1 or more defective switches in the sample?

5.53 Find the probabilities associated with a binomial probability distribution with $n = 6$ and $p = .5$. Graph $p(x)$.

5.54 Refer to Exercise 5.53.
a. Find μ and σ for the binomial probability distribution.
b. Construct the interval $\mu \pm 2\sigma$ and find the probability that x will fall within this interval. How does this result compare with the Empirical Rule?

5.55 A bank accepts 20% of its personal loan applications. If it receives 25 loan applications on a given day, what is the probability that:

α. It accepts 5 or more?

b. It accepts 8 or more?

c. It accepts fewer than 3?

5.56 Fifteen percent of the applicants at a large corporation are minorities. The corporation provides an equal opportunity for minorities and is planning to hire 500 individuals for immediate employment in a new facility.

α. What is the expected number of minorities that should appear among the number hired?

b. If x is the number of minority applicants hired, what is the standard deviation of x?

c. Could the company be suspected of discrimination if the number of minorities hired is less than 55?

5.57 A 1980 *Wall Street Journal*—Gallup survey (*Wall Street Journal,* November 21, 1980) of 282 corporate chief executives of the nation's largest firms found that 59% believed that their managers were more likely to fire an incompetent worker than they were a few years ago (see Case Study 14.1).

α. If you were to randomly select 5 corporate chief executives from this group and obtain their opinions on this question, where x is the number in the sample who believe their managers are more likely to fire incompetent workers, would x be (to a reasonable degree of approximation) a binomial random variable? Explain.

b. What is the probability that all five executives would believe that their managers are more likely to fire incompetent workers?

c. Fewer than 5?

d. More than 3?

5.58 Refer to Exercise 5.57. The 282 firms were selected from among 1,300 large corporations listed by *Fortune* magazine. Suppose that the actual proportion of chief executives in the entire population of 1,300 companies who believe that their managers are more likely to fire incompetent workers is equal to p. Would this survey of 282 firms from a total of 1,300 be, to a reasonable degree of approximation, a binomial experiment? Explain.

CASE STUDY 5.1
Signalling the Rise or Fall of the Stock Market: Corporate Insider Theory

Is the stock market going up or down in the immediate future? If you plan to invest, you may want to observe the behavior of those in the know—the corporate insiders. Insiders are officers, directors, or investors who hold 10% or more of a company's stock and, according to the Orlando *Sentinel Star,** whose buying behavior may signal a pending rise or fall in stock prices. The theory is that when insiders buy, they do so to make money: they expect their company's earnings to rise. When they sell, they see a drop in future earnings and their selling signals foul weather for their company.

According to one theory, an analysis of corporate insider stock transactions can be used to signal the future behavior of the stock market. If the proportion p of insider

*Orlando *Sentinel Star,* November 12, 1980

transactions which are buys increases from one time period (say one month) to another, the increase suggests a future rise in stock prices. If the proportion decreases, it portends a future decline in stock prices.

Let p_1 denote the probability that an insider transaction during the current month is a buy, and let p_2 denote the probability of the same event during the next month. Thus, according to the "insider theory," if $p_2 > p_1$ then the market is likely to rise, and if $p_2 < p_1$ then the market is likely to fall.

Suppose that n insider trades are observed next month and the number x of buys is recorded.

a. If conditions motivating the stock market's behavior are identical to last month's, within what limits would you expect x to fall? [*Hint:* Use the Empirical Rule, Chapter 3.]

b. How could you use the information obtained in part a to provide a signal, an indicator of a potential market rise or fall? Explain.

CASE STUDY 5.2
The Probability of a Successful Helicopter Flight during the Iran Rescue Mission

In Case Study 4.2, we discussed the ill-fated April 28, 1980, helicopter attempt to rescue the American hostages held by Iran. Particularly, we noted that the government (presumably, the Department of Defense) claimed that the 8 helicopters each flew 20 missions without malfunction, a total of 160 missions. On the day of the rescue mission, however, 3 of the 8 helicopters that embarked on the mission failed.

Some members of the public, including Congressional Representative Samuel S. Stratton, thought that the data collected on the day of the rescue attempt disagreed with the Department of Defense's claim. In fact, it seemed extremely doubtful that helicopters capable of flying 160 successful missions out of a total of 160 could produce 3 malfunctions in a sample of $n = 8$ flights.

Use the data to show that the probability that a single helicopter would complete a successful flight was probably much less during the rescue attempt than during the pre-raid training period. Explain why this might have been the case.

CASE STUDY 5.3
Expected Gains in the Oil Lease Lottery

In Case Study 4.3, we introduced you to the oil lease lottery conducted by the Bureau of Land Management. Given various probabilities of winning, it is interesting to compute the expected gain associated with a single $10 entry.

For example, it is estimated that the probability of winning on a parcel worth $25,000 to $150,000 is approximately $1/5,000$.

a. Use the values presented above to calculate the expected gain associated with a single $10 entry.

b. Suppose that you enter the lottery for three parcels of land. If the probability that you will win $25,000 on a single entry is $1/5,000$, what is the expected gain for the $30 investment in the three parcels? [*Hint:* The gain can assume one of four values depending upon whether x, the number of wins, is 0, 1, 2, or 3.]

REFERENCES

Allis, S. "Era of middle-class has arrived but it's hard to say who's in it." *Wall Street Journal,* February 10, 1981.

McClave, J. T., & Benson, P. G. *Statistics for business and economics.* 2d ed. San Francisco: Dellen, 1982.

Mendenhall, W. *Introduction to probability and statistics*. 5th ed. North Scituate, Mass.: Duxbury, 1979. Chapters 5 and 6.

Parzen, E. *Modern probability theory and its applications*. New York: Wiley, 1960. Chapters 3. 4, 6, and 7.

Summers, G., Peters, W., & Armstrong, C. *Basic statistics in business and economics*. 3d ed. Belmont, Ca.: Wadsworth, 1981. Chapter 5.

U.S. Department of Commerce, National Bureau of Standards. *Tables of the binomial probability distribution*. Applied Mathematics Series, Vol. 6, 1952.

Six

The Normal Distribution

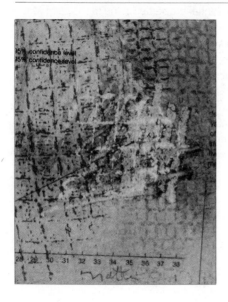

According to one theory of stock price behavior, publicized and popularized by B. G. Malkiel's book, *A Random Walk Down Wall Street* (Case Study 6.2), stock prices actually change (walk) upward and downward in a random manner and produce a relative frequency distribution of changes in price that possesses a familiar bell-shaped curve known as a *normal distribution.* Does the real world of stock price changes agree with this theory? For reasons that you will subsequently learn, many random variables possess normal relative frequency distributions. Consequently, we shall study the characteristics of normal distributions in this chapter and, particularly, learn how to identify improbable or rare events. This will help us decide whether the real world of stock prices disagrees with the random walk theory of stock price changes.

Contents:

6.1 Probability Models for Continuous Random Variables

Suppose that you want to predict your company's annual sales, its profit, the sale price of a home, the annual return on an investment, or an evening's winnings at blackjack. If you do, you will need to know something about continuous random variables.

You will recall that continuous random variables are those that, at least in theory, can assume any of the infinitely large number of values contained in an interval. Thus, we might envision a population of the sale prices of houses, the annual returns on a large number of similar investments, or the gains (or losses) of many evenings of blackjack. Since we shall want to make inferences about a population based on the measurements contained in a sample, we shall need to know the probability that the sample values (or sample statistics) assume specific values.

For example, suppose that all the residential properties in the mid-sized Florida city (of Chapter 1 and Appendix A) were sold in 1978, instead of only the 2,862 sales recorded in Appendix A. Then the resulting set of sale prices would be the population that characterizes the net worth of residential properties in the city. What is the probability that a single property selected at random will sell for less than $50,000? To answer this question, we need to know the proportion of all properties that sold (or would sell) for less than $50,000. This proportion is given by the shaded area under the population relative frequency distribution that lies to the left of $50,000 in Figure 6.1. For example, if this area is equal to seven-tenths of the total area, then the probability that a randomly selected single property would sell for less than $50,000 is .7.

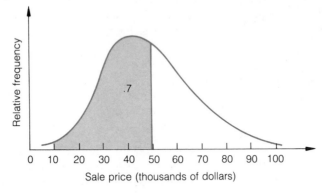

FIGURE 6.1
Relative Frequency
Distribution of Sale Prices
of Properties in the City in
1978

The problem, of course, is that not all of the properties in the city were sold in 1978, and hence we do not know the exact shape of the population relative frequency distribution, i.e., we can talk about Figure 6.1 but its exact shape is unknown. Then, as in the case of a coin-tossing experiment, we postulate a model, i.e., we select a smooth curve (similar to the one shown in Figure 6.1) as a *model* for the population relative frequency distribution. To find the probability that a particular observation, say a sale price, will fall in a particular interval, we use the model and find the area under the curve that falls over that interval.

Of course, in order for this approximate probability to be realistic, we need to be fairly certain that the smooth curve, the model, and the population relative frequency distribution are very similar. In Chapter 7 we shall show why we believe that the models we use are good approximations to reality.

In the following section, we shall introduce one of the most important and useful models for population relative frequency distributions and show how it can be used to find probabilities associated with specific sample observations.

6.2 The Normal Distribution

One of the most useful models for population relative frequency distributions is known as the *normal distribution.* A graph of the normal distribution, often called the *normal curve,* is shown in Figure 6.2.

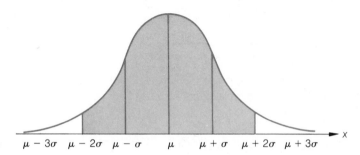

FIGURE 6.2
The Normal Curve

You can see that the mound-shaped normal curve is symmetric about its mean μ. Furthermore, approximately 68% of the area under a normal curve lies within the interval, $\mu \pm \sigma$ (see Figure 6.2). Approximately 95% of the area lies within the interval $\mu \pm 2\sigma$ (shaded in Figure 6.2), and almost all (99.7%) lies within the interval $\mu \pm 3\sigma$. Note that the mound-shaped normal curve agrees with the Empirical Rule of Section 3.5. This is because the Empirical Rule is based on consideration of a normal distribution.

Remember that areas under the normal curve have a probabilistic interpretation. Thus, if a population of measurements has approximately a normal distribution, then the probability that a randomly selected observation falls within the interval $\mu \pm 2\sigma$ is approximately .95.

The areas under the normal curve have been computed and they appear in Table 3 of Appendix E. Since the normal curve is symmetric, we need give areas on only one side of the mean. Consequently, the entries in Table 3 are areas between the mean and a point x to the right of the mean. This area is shaded in Figure 6.3.

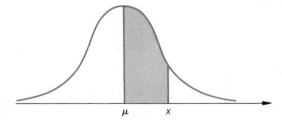

FIGURE 6.3
Tabulated Area Given in
Table 3, Appendix E

Since the values of μ and σ will vary from one normal distribution to another, the easiest way to express a distance from the mean is in terms of a z-score (see Section 3.6), the number of standard deviations between the mean and the point x. Thus,

$$z = \frac{x - \mu}{\sigma}$$

is the distance between x and μ expressed in units of σ.

EXAMPLE 6.1   Suppose that a population has a relative frequency distribution with mean $\mu = 500$ and standard deviation $\sigma = 100$. Give the z-score corresponding to x = 650.

Solution   You can see that x = 650 lies 150 units above $\mu = 500$. This distance, expressed in units of $\sigma (\sigma = 100)$, is 1.5. We can get this answer directly by substituting x, μ, and σ into the formula for z. Thus,

$$z = \frac{x - \mu}{\sigma} = \frac{150 - 100}{100} = \frac{150}{100} = 1.5$$

A partial reproduction of Table 3, Appendix E, is shown in Table 6.1. The entries in the complete table give the areas to the right of the mean for distances z = 0.00 to z = 3.09.

TABLE 6.1   Reproduction of Part of Table 3, Appendix E

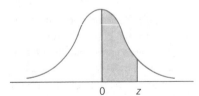

z	.00	.01	.02	.03	.04	.05	.06	.07	.08	.09
0.0	.0000	.0040	.0080	.0120	.0160	.0199	.0239	.0279	.0319	.0359
0.1	.0398	.0438	.0478	.0517	.0557	.0596	.0636	.0675	.0714	.0753
0.2	.0793	.0832	.0871	.0910	.0948	.0987	.1026	.1064	.1103	.1141
0.3	.1179	.1217	.1255	.1293	.1331	.1368	.1406	.1443	.1480	.1517
0.4	.1554	.1591	.1628	.1664	.1700	.1736	.1772	.1808	.1844	.1879
0.5	.1915	.1950	.1985	.2019	.2054	.2088	.2123	.2157	.2190	.2224
0.6	.2257	.2291	.2324	.2357	.2389	.2422	.2454	.2486	.2517	.2549
0.7	.2580	.2611	.2642	.2673	.2704	.2734	.2764	.2794	.2823	.2852
0.8	.2881	.2910	.2939	.2967	.2995	.3023	.3051	.3078	.3106	.3133
0.9	.3159	.3186	.3212	.3238	.3264	.3289	.3315	.3340	.3365	.3389
1.0	.3413	.3438	.3461	.3485	.3508	.3531	.3554	.3577	.3599	.3621
1.1	.3643	.3665	.3686	.3708	.3729	.3749	.3770	.3790	.3810	.3830
1.2	.3849	.3869	.3888	.3907	.3925	.3944	.3962	.3980	.3997	.4015
1.3	.4032	.4049	.4066	.4082	.4099	.4115	.4131	.4147	.4162	.4177
1.4	.4192	.4207	.4222	.4236	.4251	.4265	.4279	.4292	.4306	.4319
1.5	.4332	.4345	.4357	.4370	.4382	.4394	.4406	.4418	.4429	.4441

EXAMPLE 6.2 Find the area under a normal curve between the mean and a point $z = 1.26$ standard deviations to the right of the mean.

Solution To locate the proper entry, proceed down the left (z) column of the table to the row corresponding to $z = 1.2$. Then move across the top of the table to the column headed .06. The intersection of the .06 column with the 1.2 row contains the desired area, .3962. This area is shaded in Figure 6.4.

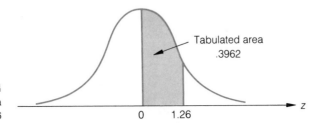

FIGURE 6.4
The Tabulated Area
Corresponding to $z = 1.26$

The normal distribution of the z statistic (as shown in Figure 6.4) is called the **standard normal distribution.** The mean of a standard normal distribution is 0 ($z = 0$ when $x = \mu$); the standard deviation is equal to 1. Since the mean is 0, z-values to the right of the mean are positive; those to the left are negative.

EXAMPLE 6.3 Find the area beneath a normal curve between the mean and the point, $z = -1.26$.

Solution The best way to solve a problem of this sort is to draw a sketch of the distribution (see Figure 6.5). Since $z = -1.26$ is negative, we know that it lies to the left of the mean, and the area that we seek will be the shaded area shown.

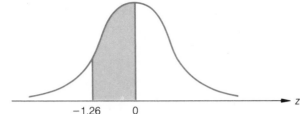

FIGURE 6.5
Standard Normal
Distribution: Example 6.3

Since the normal curve is symmetric, the area between the mean 0 and $z = -1.26$ is exactly the same as the area between the mean 0 and $z = +1.26$. We found this area in Example 6.2 to be .3962. Therefore, the area between $z = -1.26$ and $z = 0$ is .3962.

EXAMPLE 6.4 Find the probability that a normally distributed random variable will lie within $z = 2$ standard deviations of its mean.

Solution   The probability that we seek is the shaded area shown in Figure 6.6. Since the area between the mean 0 and $z = 2.0$ is exactly the same as the area between the mean and $z = -2.0$, we need find only the area between the mean and $z = 2$ standard deviations to the right of the mean. This area is given in Table 3, Appendix E, as .4772. Therefore, the probability P that a normally distributed random variable will lie within two standard deviations of its mean is

$$P = 2(.4772) = .9544$$

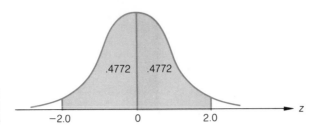

FIGURE 6.6
Standard Normal
Distribution: Example 6.4

EXAMPLE 6.5   Find the probability that a normally distributed random variable x will lie more than $z = 2$ standard deviations above its mean.

Solution   The probability we seek is the shaded area shown in Figure 6.7. The total area under a standard normal curve is 1; half the area lies to the left of the mean, half to the right. Consequently, the probability P that x will lie more than 2 standard deviations above the mean is equal to .5 less the area A, i.e.,

$$P = .5 - A$$

The area A corresponding to $z = 2.0$ is .4772. Therefore,

$$P = .5 - .4772 = .0228$$

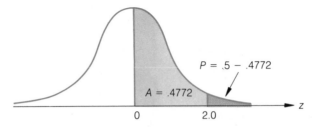

FIGURE 6.7
Standard Normal
Distribution: Example 6.5

EXAMPLE 6.6   Find the area under the normal curve between $z = 1.2$ and $z = 1.6$.

Solution   The area A that we seek lies to the right of the mean because both z-values are positive. It will appear as the shaded area shown in Figure 6.8. Let A_1 represent the area between $z = 0$ and $z = 1.2$, and A_2 represent the area between $z = 0$ and $z = 1.6$.

Then the area A that we desire is

$$A = A_2 - A_1$$

From Table 3, Appendix E, we obtain:

$$A_1 = .3849$$
$$A_2 = .4452$$

Then

$$A = A_2 - A_1$$
$$= .4452 - .3849$$
$$= .0603$$

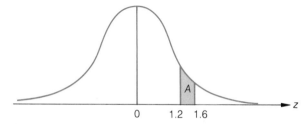

FIGURE 6.8
Standard Normal
Distribution: Example 6.6

EXAMPLE 6.7   Find the value of z such that the area to the right of z is .10.

Solution   The z-value that we seek appears as shown in Figure 6.9. Note that we show an area to the right of z equal to .10. Since the total area to the right of the mean $z = 0$ is equal to .5, the area between the mean 0 and the unknown z-value is $.5 - .1 = .4$ (as shown in the figure). Consequently, to find z, we must look in Table 3, Appendix E, for the z-value that corresponds to an area equal to .4.

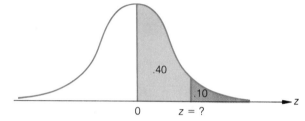

FIGURE 6.9
Standard Normal
Distribution: Example 6.7

The area .4000 does not appear in Table 3. The closest values are .3997, corresponding to $z = 1.28$, and .4015, corresponding to $z = 1.29$. Since the area .3997 is closer to .4000 than is .4015, we will choose $z = 1.28$ as our answer.

EXAMPLE 6.8   Teleconferences, electronic mail, and word processors are among the tools that can reduce the length of business meetings. A recent survey indicated that the percentage reduction, x, in time spent by business professionals in meetings due to automated office equipment is approximately normally distributed with mean equal to 15% and standard deviation equal to 4%. What proportion of all business professionals with access to automated office equipment have reduced their time in meetings by more than 22%?

Solution   The proportion P of business professionals who have reduced their time in meetings by more than $x = 22\%$ is shown (shaded) in Figure 6.10(a). The next step is to find the z-value corresponding to $x = 22\%$. Substituting $x = 22$, $\mu = 15$, and $\sigma = 4$ into the formula for z, we obtain

$$z = \frac{x - \mu}{\sigma} = \frac{22 - 15}{4} = \frac{7}{4} = 1.75$$

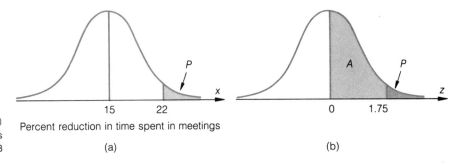

FIGURE 6.10
Normal Curve Sketches
for Example 6.8

Percent reduction in time spent in meetings

(a)   (b)

Then, the area P to the right of $x = 22$ in Figure 6.10(a) is the same as the area to the right of $z = 1.75$ in Figure 6.10(b). Since half (.5) of the area under the z-distribution lies to the right of $z = 0$, it follows that

$$P = .5 - A$$

where A is the area shown in Figure 6.10(b), an area that corresponds to $z = 1.75$. This area, given in Table 3, is $A = .4599$. Therefore, the proportion of business professionals who have reduced their time in meetings by more than 22% through the use of automated office equipment is

$$P = .5 - A$$
$$= .5 - .4599$$
$$= .0401$$

Therefore, 4.01% of business professionals have reduced their time in meetings by more than 22% through the use of automated office equipment.

EXAMPLE 6.9   Refer to Example 6.8. What is the probability that new automated office equipment will reduce a professional's time in meetings by no more than 16%?

Solution   The probability P that new automated office equipment will reduce time in meetings by no more than 16% (i.e., by 16% or less) is the shaded area in Figure 6.11(a). The z-value corresponding to $x = 16$ (shown in Figure 6.11(b)) is

$$z = \frac{x - \mu}{\sigma} = \frac{16 - 15}{4} = \frac{1}{4} = .25$$

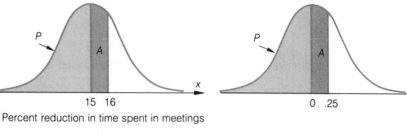

FIGURE 6.11
Normal Curve Sketches
for Example 6.9

Percent reduction in time spent in meetings

(a)   (b)

Since the area to the left of $z = 0$ is equal to .5, the probability that x is less than or equal to 16 (the shaded area in Figure 6.11(b)) is

   $P = .5 + A$

where A is the tabulated area corresponding to $z = .25$. This value, given in Table 3, Appendix E, is $A = .0987$. Then, the probability that new automated office equipment will reduce a professional's time in meetings by no more than 16% is

   $P = .5 + A = .5 + .0987 = .5987$

EXAMPLE 6.10   Recently, the federal government passed a law which enables banks to offer interest-on-checking-account programs. This interest-checking plan allows customers to earn 5¼% interest on the money that is normally kept in checking accounts. (Previously, interest could be earned only on savings account deposits.)

   A national bank, serving the metropolitan area of Atlanta, Georgia, determined that the interest earned by its customers after one year of the interest-checking plan was approximately normally distributed with a mean of $270 and a standard deviation of $110. What proportion of the bank's customers earned between $138 and $300 on the interest-checking plan last year?

Solution   The proportion P of the bank's customers who earned between $x = 138$ dollars and $x = 300$ dollars is the shaded area in Figure 6.12(a). Before we can compute this area, we need to determine the z-values which correspond to $x = 138$ and $x = 300$. Substituting $\mu = 270$ and $\sigma = 110$ into the formula for z, we compute the z-value for $x = 138$ as

$$z = \frac{x - \mu}{\sigma} = \frac{138 - 270}{110} = \frac{-132}{110} = -1.2$$

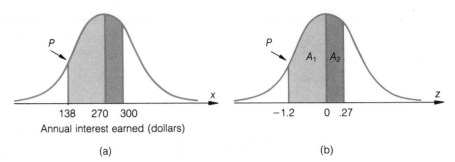

FIGURE 6.12
Normal Curve Areas for
Example 6.10

Annual interest earned (dollars)

(a)   (b)

The corresponding z-value for $x = 300$ (rounded to the nearest hundredth) is

$$z = \frac{x - \mu}{\sigma} = \frac{300 - 270}{110} = \frac{30}{110} = .27$$

Figure 6.12(b) shows these z-values along with P. From this figure, we see that

$$P = A_1 + A_2$$

where A_1 is the area corresponding to $z = -1.2$, and A_2 is the area corresponding to $z = .27$. These values, given in Table 3, Appendix E, are $A_1 = .3849$ and $A_2 = .1064$. Thus,

$$P = A_1 + A_2 = .3849 + .1064 = .4913$$

So 49.13% of the bank's customers earned between $138 and $300 interest from the interest-checking plan last year.

EXAMPLE 6.11   Refer to Example 6.10. Only 10% of the bank's customers earned more than x dollars of annual interest on checking last year. Find x.

Solution   In this example, we are not requested to compute a probability or area under the normal relative frequency distribution, but instead we are asked to find a particular value of the normal random variable x, the annual interest on checking. We need to determine the annual checking interest that divides the top 10% of the annual checking interests from the remainder, that is, the value of the normal random variable x, say x_0, for which the area under the normal curve to the right of x_0 is $P = .10$. We call P the *tail probability associated with* x_0. This value x_0, along with its tail probability, is shown in Figure 6.13(a).

Notice that we have placed x_0 in the upper tail of the normal curve, i.e., to the right of the mean of 270. Our choice of the location of x_0 is not arbitrary, but depends upon the value of P. In order for the area under the curve to the right of x_0 to be $P = .10$, x_0 must lie above 270. To see this more clearly, try placing x_0 below (to the left of) 270. Now (mentally) shade in the corresponding tail probability P, i.e., the area to the right of x_0. You can see that this shaded area cannot possibly equal .10—it is too large (.50 or greater). Thus x_0 must lie to the right of 270. The first step, then, in solving problems of this type is to determine the location of x_0 in relation to the mean μ. The corresponding z-value for x_0, say z_0, is shown in Figure 6.13(b). Note that for $\mu = 270$ and $\sigma = 110$, we have the relation

$$z_0 = \frac{x_0 - \mu}{\sigma} = \frac{x_0 - 270}{110}$$

or the equivalent relation

$$x_0 = \mu + z_0(\sigma) = 270 + z_0(\sigma)$$

You can see from this relationship that if we can determine z_0, then we will be able to compute x_0. Thus, our next step is to find z_0.

Recall how Table 3, Appendix E, is constructed. For each particular value of the standard normal random variable z, the table gives the area under the curve between 0 and z. In order to find z_0 then, we must first determine the corresponding area between 0 and z_0. From Figure 6.13(b), it is easy to see that the area between 0 and z_0, say A, is the difference between .5 and the tail probability, i.e.,

$$A = .5 - P = .5 - .1 = .4$$

We now know that the z-value which we seek corresponds to the area $A = .4000$ in the table.

The next step is to locate $A = .4000$ in Table 3, Appendix E. Searching among the areas given in the body of the table, we see that the value closest to .4000 is .3997. The z-value corresponding to the area .3997 is 1.28. Thus, we take

$$z_0 = 1.28$$

The final step is to use this value of z_0 to determine x_0. Since $z_0 = 1.28$ is the corresponding z-value for x_0, then by definition we say that x_0 falls a distance of 1.28 standard deviations away from $\mu = 270$. Further, from Figure 6.13(a), x_0 falls a distance of 1.28 standard deviations above (to the right of) $\mu = 270$. For $\mu = 270$ and $\sigma = 110$, we compute x_0 as follows:

$$x_0 = \mu + z_0(\sigma) = 270 + (1.28)(110) = 270 + 140.8 = 410.8$$

Thus, our answer is $410.80; that is, only 10% of the bank's customers earned over $410.80 in interest on checking last year.

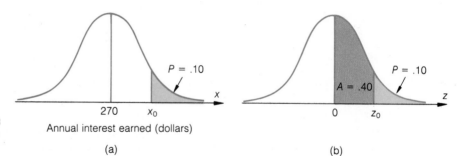

FIGURE 6.13
Normal Curve Areas for
Example 6.11

To help in solving problems of this type throughout the remainder of the chapter, we outline in the box the steps leading to the solutions.

THE DETERMINATION OF A PARTICULAR VALUE OF THE NORMAL RANDOM VARIABLE GIVEN AN ASSOCIATED TAIL PROBABILITY

1. Graph the relative frequency distribution of the normal random variable x. Shade the tail probability P and locate the corresponding value x_0 on the graph. Remember that x_0 will be to the right or left of the mean μ depending upon the value of P.
2. Graph the corresponding relative frequency distribution of the standard normal random variable z. Locate the z-value corresponding to x_0, say z_0, and shade the area corresponding to P.
3. Compute the area A associated with z_0 as follows:

$$A = .5 - P$$

4. Use the area A, i.e., the area between 0 and z_0, to find z_0 in Table 3, Appendix E. (If you cannot find the exact value of A in the table, use the closest value.) Note that z_0 will be negative if you place x_0 to the left of the mean in step 1.
5. Compute x_0 as follows:

$$x_0 = \mu + z_0(\sigma)$$

EXAMPLE 6.12   Many experts believe that the answer to the current energy crisis may lie in the field of synthetic fuels—the conversion of coal, shale oil, and tar sands to liquid fuel. The federal government is currently planning for synthetic fuel plants around the country to produce an average of 50,000 barrels of fuel per day by the turn of the century.

Let us suppose that by the year 2000 the daily production of a particular synthetic fuel plant will have a mean of 50,000 barrels and a standard deviation of 8,000 barrels. Further, let us assume that the daily production at the plant is approximately normally distributed. The federal government has allocated $81 billion to be used to aid synthetic fuel producers in meeting the projected demand. However, this aid, in the form of loan and price guarantees, will not be provided to any synthetic fuel plant which produces less than a specified number of barrels on 33% of the days. On 33% of the days, this particular plant's production is less than what amount?

Solution   We are asked to find the number of barrels which the plant's daily production falls below on 33% of the days. That is, we must determine the value x_0 of the normal random variable x, daily production (in barrels), for which the area under the curve to the left of this value x_0 is $P = .33$. We will find x_0 by following the steps given in the box above.

The first two steps are completed by drawing figures similar to those shown in Figure 6.14. In Figure 6.14(a), x_0 is shown in relation to $\mu = 50,000$ and the tail

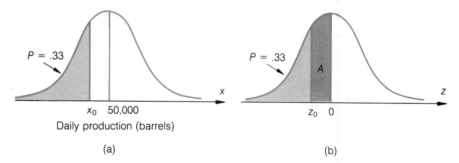

FIGURE 6.14
Normal Curve Areas for
Example 6.12

x_0 50,000
Daily production (barrels)

(a)

z_0 0

(b)

probability $P = .33$ (the shaded area). Notice that x_0 must lie to the left of 50,000. You can justify this by recognizing that if x_0 is located to the right of 50,000, the corresponding tail probability P (the area under the curve to the left of x_0) cannot possibly equal .33. Location of the corresponding z-value for x_0 is shown in Figure 6.14(b), as is $P = .33$. The third step is to compute the area A (see Figure 6.14(b)) which is associated with z_0 in Table 3, Appendix E. For this example, we have

$$A = .5 - P = .5 - .33 = .17$$

Searching for $A = .1700$ in the appropriate portion of the table, we see that the corresponding z-value is .44. Since z_0 lies to the left of 0, it is negative; thus, we have $z_0 = -.44$. This completes step 4. Our interpretation of this value is that the number we seek, x_0, falls a distance of .44 standard deviation below (to the left of) the mean $\mu = 50,000$.

Finally, we compute x_0 as follows:

$$x_0 = \mu + z_0(\sigma)$$
$$= 50,000 + (-.44)(8,000)$$
$$= 50,000 - 3,520 = 46,480$$

We conclude then, that the synthetic fuel plant's daily production will fall below 46,480 barrels on 33% of the days. By checking 46,480 against the figure specified by the federal government, we could determine whether the plant is eligible for loan and price guarantees.

The preceding examples should help you to understand the use of the table of areas under the normal curve. The practical applications of this information to inference making will become apparent in the following chapters.

EXERCISES **6.1** Find the area under the standard normal curve:
  a. Between $z = 0$ and $z = 1.2$ b. Between $z = 0$ and $z = 1.49$
  c. Between $z = -.48$ and $z = 0$ d. Between $z = -1.37$ and $z = 0$
  e. For values of z larger than 1.33
Show the respective area and the corresponding z-values on a sketch of the normal curve for each part of the exercise.

6.2 Find the area under the standard normal curve:
a.   Between $z = 0$ and $z = 1.96$ b.   Between $z = -1.96$ and $z = 0$
c.   Between $z = -1.96$ and $z = 1.96$ d.   For values of z larger than .55
e.   For values of z less than -1.24
Show the areas and corresponding values of z on a sketch of the normal curve for each part of the exercise.

6.3 Find the area under the standard normal curve:
a.   For values of z less than -1.32 b.   For values of z larger than 0
c.   For values of z less than 1.35   d.   For values of z larger than -1.32
e.   For values of z between $z = -1.33$ and $z = 1.33$
Show the areas and corresponding values of z on a sketch of the normal curve for each part of the exercise.

6.4 Find the area under the standard normal curve:
a.   Between $z = 1.21$ and $z = 1.94$ b.   For values of z larger than 2.33
c.   For values of z less than -2.33 d.   Between $z = -1.50$ and $z = 1.79$
Show the areas and corresponding values of z on a sketch of the normal curve for each part of the exercise.

6.5 Find the z-value (to two decimal places) that corresponds to a tabulated area, Table 3, Appendix E, equal to:
a.   .1000   b.   .3200   c.   .4000   d.   .4500   e.   .4750
Show the area and corresponding value of z on a sketch of the normal curve for each part of the exercise.

6.6 Find the z-value (to two decimal places) that corresponds to a tabulated area, Table 3, Appendix E, equal to:
a.   .3700   b.   .4900   c.   .2500   d.   .3000   e.   .3413
Show the area and corresponding value of z on a sketch of the normal curve for each part of the exercise.

6.7 Find the value of z (to two decimal places), Table 3, Appendix E, that cuts off an area in the upper tail of the standard normal curve equal to:
a.   .025   b.   .05   c.   .005   d.   .01   e.   .10
Show the area and corresponding value of z on a sketch of the normal curve for each part of the exercise.

6.8 Suppose that a normal random variable x has mean $\mu = 20.0$ and standard deviation $\sigma = 4.0$. Find the z-score corresponding to:
a. $x = 23.0$ b. $x = 16.0$ c. $x = 13.5$ d. $x = 28.0$ e. $x = 12.0$
Locate x and μ on a sketch of the normal curve. Check to make sure that the sign and magnitude of your z-score agree with your sketch.

6.9 Find a value z_0 such that the probability that z is larger than z_0 is:
a.   .2266   b.   .0721   c.   .0344   d.   .3520   e.   .1611
Show the area and the value of z_0 on a sketch of the normal curve for each part of the exercise.

6.10 Find the approximate value for z_0 such that the probability that z is larger than z_0 is:

a. $P = .10$ **b.** $P = .15$ **c.** $P = .20$ **d.** $P = .25$

Locate z_0 and the corresponding probability P on a sketch of the normal curve for each part of the exercise.

6.11 Find the approximate value for z_0 such that the probability that z is less than z_0 is:

a. $P = .10$ **b.** $P = .15$ **c.** $P = .30$ **d.** $P = .50$

Locate z_0 and the corresponding probability P on a sketch of the normal curve for each part of the exercise.

6.12 Experience has shown that the advertising revenue of a weekly professional newsletter is normally distributed with a mean of $7,800 per week and a standard deviation of $620. Find the probability that the advertising revenue in any given week is:

a. Less than $7,000 **b.** More than $8,000 **c.** More than $9,000

Locate μ and the desired probability on a sketch of the normal curve for each part of the exercise.

6.13 Suppose that the distribution of monthly rents for 2-bedroom apartments in a region is approximately normally distributed with mean $\mu = \$390$ and standard deviation $\sigma = \$35$.

a. What proportion of the apartments rent for more than $450?

b. What proportion of the apartments rent for less than $350?

c. What proportion of the apartments rent for less than $400?

Locate μ and the desired probability on a sketch of the normal curve for each part of the exercise.

6.14 Bond ratings and bond interest rates depend upon the current level of the cost of borrowing and the credit ratings of the respective cities. Returns on a class of municipal tax-free bonds currently are normally distributed with a mean of 9% and a standard deviation of .4%. A city's bonds are rated within this class. Find the probability that the city will have to pay:

a. More than 9% **b.** More than 9.5% **c.** Less than 8.5%

Locate μ and the desired probability on a sketch of the normal curve for each part of the exercise.

6.15 Suppose that experience has shown that the percentage annual appreciation x in residential property values is approximately normally distributed with a mean equal to the annual housing inflation rate and a standard deviation equal to 6%. [*Note:* A negative appreciation in the value of a house would be depreciation.] Suppose also that the annual housing inflation rate for a year is 10%. What percentage of all residential properties will depreciate in value? Locate μ and the desired probability on a sketch of the normal curve.

6.16 Refer to Exercise 6.15. What percentage of residential properties will appreciate more than 15%? Locate μ and the desired probability on a sketch of the normal curve.

6.17   A television cable company receives numerous phone calls throughout the day from customers reporting service troubles and from would-be subscribers to the cable network. Most of these callers are put "on hold" until a company operator is free to help them. The company has determined that the length of time that a caller is on hold is normally distributed with a mean of 3.1 minutes and a standard deviation of .9 minutes. Company experts have decided that if as many as 5% of the callers are put on hold for 4.8 minutes or longer, more operators should be hired. What proportion of the company's callers are put on hold for at least 4.8 minutes? Should the company hire more operators? Show the pertinent quantities on a sketch of the normal curve.

6.18   Refer to Exercise 6.17. At this company, 5% of the callers are put on hold for a period longer than what length of time? Show the pertinent quantities on a sketch of the normal curve.

6.19   Refer to Exercise 6.13. The monthly rents of 20% of the 2-bedroom apartments in the region fall below what value? Show the pertinent quantities on a sketch of the normal curve.

6.3 **Summary**

This chapter introduced an important probability model for continuous random variables—the normal distribution. Since the normal distribution is a model for a population relative frequency distribution, it follows that the total area under the curve is equal to 1, and areas under the curve correspond to the probabilities of drawing observations that fall within particular intervals.

You will learn in Chapter 7 why we expect many population relative frequency distributions to be approximately normally distributed. You will also begin to develop, in Chapter 7 and following chapters, an understanding of how areas under the normal curve will be used to assess the uncertainty associated with sample inferences.

KEY WORDS	
Probabilistic model	z-Score: $z = \dfrac{x - \mu}{\sigma}$
Normal distribution	Standard normal distribution
Normal curve	

SUPPLEMENTARY EXERCISES

6.20   Find the area under the normal curve:

a.   Between $z = .73$ and $z = 1.55$ **b.**   Between $z = -1.44$ and $z = -.49$

c.   Between $z = -1.03$ and $z = 2.00$ **d.**   For values of z less than 1.59

e.   For values of z greater than $-.77$

Show the respective areas and corresponding z-values on sketches of the normal curve.

6.21 Find the approximate value for z_0 such that the probability that z is larger than z_0 is:

a. .5   b. .12   c. .45   d. .25

Locate z_0 and the corresponding probability P on a sketch of the normal curve for each part of the exercise.

6.22 Find the approximate value for z_0 such that the probability that z is less than z_0 is:

a. .05   b. .025   c. .16   d. .22

Locate z_0 and the corresponding probability P on a sketch of the normal curve for each part of the exercise.

6.23 The length of collect telephone calls accepted by the business office of a large brokerage firm is normally distributed with a mean of 8.5 minutes and a standard deviation of 2.2 minutes. If a single collect call is selected at random, compute the probability that:

a. The call will be between 5 and 6 minutes in length.

b. The call will be 10 minutes or more in length.

c. The call will be 5 minutes or less in length.

Locate μ and the desired probability on a sketch of the normal curve for each part of the exercise.

6.24 A food processor packages instant orange juice in small jars. The weights of the filled jars are approximately normally distributed with a mean of 10.82 ounces and a standard deviation of .30 ounces.

a. Find the probability that a randomly selected jar of instant orange juice will exceed 10.2 ounces in weight.

b. Suppose that the Food and Drug Administration sets the minimum weight of the jars at 10 ounces. Jars with weights below the allowable minimum must be removed from the supermarket shelf. What proportion of the jars should we expect to be removed from the supermarket shelf?

c. Two percent of the packaged jars are below what weight?

For each part of the exercise, show the pertinent quantities on a sketch of the normal curve.

6.25 The average life of a certain steel-belted radial tire is advertised as 60,000 miles. Assume that the life of the tires is normally distributed with a standard deviation of 2,500 miles. (The "life" of a tire is defined as the number of miles the tire is driven before blowing out.)

a. Find the probability that a randomly selected steel-belted radial tire will have a life of 61,800 miles or less.

b. Find the probability that a randomly selected steel-belted radial tire will have a life between 62,000 miles and 66,000 miles.

c. In order to avoid a tire blowout, the company manufacturing the tires will warn purchasers to replace each tire after it has been used for a given number of miles. What should the replacement time (in miles) be so that only 1% of the tires will blow out?

For each part of the exercise, show the pertinent quantities on a sketch of the normal curve.

6.26   The bid prices on a parcel of real estate are expected to be normally distributed with mean $\mu = \$130,000$ and standard deviation $\sigma = \$10,000$. If a single bid is randomly selected from all those received, what is the probability that:

a.   It will exceed $150,000?

b.   It will be less than $120,000?

c.   It will be less than $140,000?

Locate μ and the desired probability on a sketch of the normal curve for each part of the exercise.

6.27   The difference between the actual and the scheduled arrival time for your local commuter train is normally distributed with a mean of 5 minutes (i.e., on the average, it is 5 minutes late) and a standard deviation of 11 minutes. On a given day, what is the probability that:

a.   The train will be late?

b.   The train will be early?

c.   The train will be more than 5 minutes late?

d.   The train will be at least 10 minutes late?

Locate μ and the desired probability on a sketch of the normal curve for each part of the exercise.

6.28   Refer to Exercise 6.27. The management of the commuter line would like to adjust the scheduled arrival time so that the commuter line appears to be operating more efficiently. To do this, they would like to adjust the scheduled time of arrival so that only 10% of the trains would arrive late, i.e., later than the scheduled time. How many minutes should they add to the current scheduled time in order to accomplish this goal? Show the pertinent quantities on a sketch of the normal curve.

CASE STUDY 6.1
Comparing
Reality with the
Normal Curve

You may wish to compare a relative frequency distribution of data with a normal curve to decide whether the normal curve provides an adequate model for the population relative frequency distribution. In this case study we shall graph the normal curve for various values of μ and σ and then apply this knowledge in Case Study 6.2.

The mathematical equation of a standard normal curve is

$$f(z) = \frac{e^{-z^2/2}}{\sqrt{2\pi}}$$

where

$$e = 2.7183$$

$$\pi = 3.1416$$

and

$$z = \frac{x - \mu}{\sigma}$$

The values of $f(z)$ for $z = 0$, .4, .8, 1.2, 1.6, 2.0, 2.4, and 2.8 are shown in the accompanying table. We do not show values of $f(z)$ for negative values of z because the normal distribution is symmetric about the mean, $z = 0$. Therefore, $f(-z) = f(z)$. For example, $f(-.4) = f(.4)$.

z	$f(z)$
0	.3989
.4	.3683
.8	.2897
1.2	.1942
1.6	.1109
2.0	.0540
2.4	.0224
2.8	.0079

a. Graph the standard normal curve $f(z)$, i.e., plot the points corresponding to z and $f(z)$ for $z = -2.8, -2.4, \ldots, -.4, 0, .4, \ldots, 2.4, 2.8$. Then sketch a smooth curve through the points. To graph any other normal curve, say $f(x)$, which has a mean μ and standard deviation σ, you find the x-value corresponding to a z-value and then read $f(x) = f(z)$ from the table. For example, if $\mu = 10$ and $\sigma = 2$, then the x-value corresponding to $z = .4$ is found by solving the equation

$$z = \frac{x - \mu}{\sigma}$$

Substituting for z, μ, and σ yields

$$.4 = \frac{x - 10}{2} \quad \text{or} \quad x = 10.8$$

The value of $f(x)$ corresponding to $x = 10.8$ would be the same as $f(z)$ for $z = .4$, i.e., $f(x) = .3683$. To plot this normal curve, you would repeat this process for the z-values given in the table, plot the points x and $f(x)$, and sketch a smooth curve through these points.

b. Graph the normal curve with $\mu = 10$, $\sigma = 2$. Then sketch a similar curve with $\mu = 10$, $\sigma = 4$.

CASE STUDY 6.2

A Random Walk Down Wall Street*

In his interesting and readable book *A Random Walk Down Wall Street,** Burton G. Malkiel devotes Chapter 6 to "Technical Analysis and the Random-Walk Theory." In brief, this chapter discusses the theory employed by stock market technical analysts to forecast the upward or downward movement of specific stocks or the market as a whole.

Technical analysts, or **chartists** as they are called, believe that "knowledge of a stock's past behavior can help predict its probable future behavior." According to

---

*B. G. Malkiel, *A random walk down Wall Street*. New York: Norton, 1975.

Malkiel, chartists strongly favor stocks that have made an upward move, and they advocate selling stocks that have moved downward in price. Similarly, when the stock market averages have shown strength and moved upward, they forecast further upward movement in the market averages. Malkiel clearly has little faith in the forecasts of chartists: He states, "On close examination, technicians are often seen with holes in their shoes and frayed shirt collars. I, personally, have never known a successful technician, but I have seen wrecks of several unsuccessful ones. (This is, of course, in terms of following their own technical advice. Commissions from urging customers to act on their recommendations are very lucrative.)" In brief, Malkiel does not agree that knowledge of a stock's past performance can be used to predict its future behavior.

A theory that is the antithesis of that held by chartists is known as the *random-walk theory*. According to this theory, the price movement of a stock (or the stock market) today is completely independent of its movement in the past: the price will rise or fall today by a random amount. A sequence of these random increases or decreases is known as a *random walk*. Note that this theory does not rule out the possibility of long-term trends, say a long-term upward trend in stock prices fueled by increased earnings, dividends, etc. It simply states that the *daily* change in price is independent of the changes that have occurred in the past.

To support his contention, Malkiel generated the stock price chart for several fictitious stocks by tossing a coin to decide whether a stock would move up (a head) or down (a tail) by a fixed amount, say ½ dollar, on a given day. This procedure was repeated for a large number of days. The movement of this fictitious stock was plotted, thus revealing its random walk. We performed an equivalent coin-tossing experiment in Chapter 4. Our fictitious stock charts are shown in Figure 4.2 (pp. 100–101). You can see how the price seems to surge upward and downward in these "charts" (suggesting short-term trends), although the coin tossings were independent.

One way that we can refine the random-walk theory is to postulate the probability distribution of the daily price change in a stock (or the daily change in a market average). The most common assumption is that the change (even though stock prices change by discrete amounts) has a distribution that is approximately normal. To examine this theory, we have listed in Appendix C the daily change in the Standard & Poor's Stock Index for each market day during the period 1975 to 1979. The relative frequency distribution for these changes, shown in Figure 6.15, possesses a mean equal to $.03 and a standard deviation equal to $.72. Does this distribution differ markedly from a normal distribution with $\mu = .03$ and $\sigma = .72$?

Statistical tests are available to detect distributional departures from normality but they are beyond the scope of this text. Nevertheless, we can get an indication of the answer by fitting a normal curve to the data, using the method described in Case Study 6.1. Assign values to the daily change x, calculate the corresponding z-value, and then read the value of $f(x) = f(z)$ in the table, Case Study 6.1. Plot these points and sketch a smooth normal curve, $f(x)$, superimposed over the relative frequency distribution, Figure 6.15. Compare the two distributions. Does it appear that the daily change in the Standard & Poor's Stock Index possesses a distribution that is approximately normal?

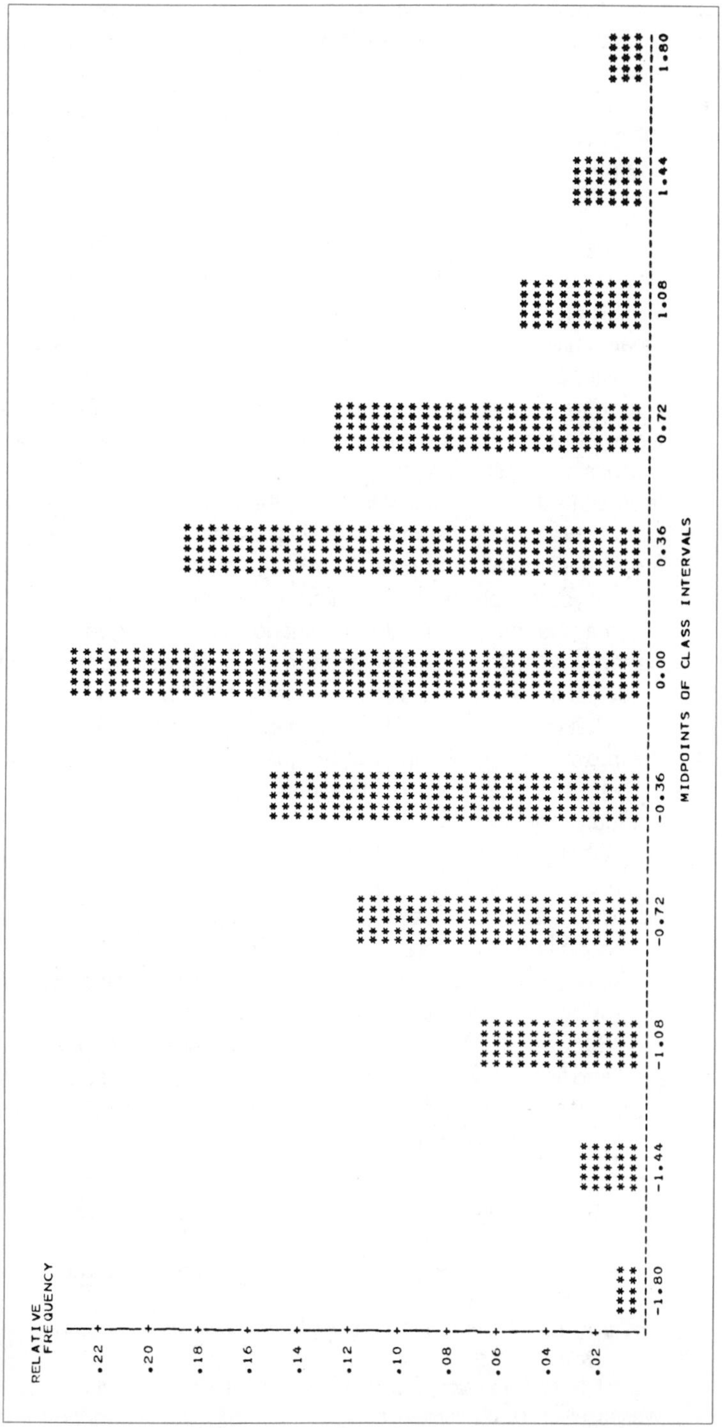

FIGURE 6.15   Distribution of Changes in Standard & Poor's Index from January 2, 1975 through December 31, 1979

CASE STUDY 6.3
**Interpreting
Those Wonderful
EPA Mileage
Estimates**

One common ploy of advertisements for new automobiles is to list the EPA (Environ-mental Protection Agency) estimated miles per gallon (mpg) for the make of car being advertised. A recent advertisement in a national magazine boasts that the 1981 Dodge Aries-K wagon is "America's highest mileage 6-passenger wagon." The EPA estimated miles per gallon for this model is listed as 24 mpg. However, footnoted in fine print is the statement:

> Use EPA estimated mpg for comparison only. Your mileage may vary depending on speed, weather, and trip length. Actual highway mileage will probably be less.

How should the observant reader, in view of the footnote, interpret the 24-mpg figure? The EPA tests cars under conditions (weather, brand of gasoline, speed, terrain, etc.) ideally suited for maximum mileage performance. Nevertheless, even under identical conditions it is unreasonable (and impractical) to assume that all Dodge Aries-K wagons tested will obtain the same gas mileage. If the EPA tested 50 Aries-K wagons, we would expect to observe 50 different mpg's. Conceivably, if all Dodge Aries-K wagons were tested under "ideal conditions," we would obtain a set of numbers which represents the population. Most likely then, the 24-mpg figure is the average miles per gallon obtained by the sample of wagons tested. The EPA uses this sample average mpg to estimate the population average mpg of all Dodge Aries-K wagons.

If you are an owner of (or are considering buying) a new Dodge Aries-K wagon, you may be interested in the likelihood that the wagon you own (or purchase) will perform "as advertised." The answer, of course, requires knowledge of the probability model for the continuous random variable Miles per gallon of Dodge Aries-K wagons.

Let us assume the EPA estimated mpg for this type of car is accurate, i.e., that the true mean mpg obtained under "ideal" conditions for all Dodge Aries-K wagons is, in fact, 24. Also, suppose that the distribution of mpg's is approximately normal with a standard deviation of 2.

a. What proportion of all Dodge Aries-K wagons tested under "ideal" conditions will obtain at least 29 mpg?

b. What is the probability that a Dodge Aries-K wagon, tested under "ideal" conditions, will obtain less than 20 mpg?

c. Fifteen percent of all Dodge Aries-K wagons tested will obtain an mpg rating above a particular value. Find this value.

d. Suppose that you test your new Dodge Aries-K wagon under "ideal" conditions and find that your car obtains 18 mpg. Does this result imply that you have bought a "lemon," or is it more likely that the EPA estimated mpg figure of 24 is too high? [*Hint:* Use your answer to part b.]

REFERENCES   Hogg, R. V., & Craig, A. T. *Introduction to mathematical statistics.* 4th ed. New York: Macmillan, 1978. Chapters 1 and 3.

Johnson, R., & Siskin, B. *Elementary statistics for business.* North Scituate, Mass.: Duxbury, 1980. Chapter 7.

McClave, J. T., & Benson, P. G. *Statistics for business and economics.* 2d ed. San Francisco: Dellen, 1982.

Malkiel, B. G. *A random walk down Wall Street.* New York: Norton, 1975. Chapter 6.

Wonnacott, T. H., & Wonnacott, R. J. *Introductory statistics for business and economics.* New York: Wiley, 1972. Chapter 4.

Seven

Sampling and Sampling Distributions

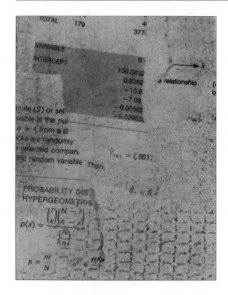

Do you think it advisable to buy that piece of timberland described in Case Study 3.3? Knowing the mean and standard deviation of the weights of the logs produced from a sample of 117 trees, how can we estimate the total weight of all logs that could be produced by the property? And, what is the reliability of this estimate? The behavior of sample statistics, described by their probability distributions, is the topic of Chapter 7.

Contents:

7.1 Why the Method of Sampling Is Important

We now return to the objective of statistics, namely, the use of sample information to infer the nature of a population. Predicting your company's annual sales from its sales records of the last ten years, the annual return on an investment from the results of a number of similar investments, or an evening's winnings at blackjack based upon your previous (successful and unsuccessful) treks to the casino are all examples of sample inferences, and each involves an element of uncertainty. In this chapter we discuss a technique for measuring the uncertainty associated with sample inferences.

Suppose that we wish to make an inference about the mean, or average, value in 1978 of *all* residential properties in the mid-sized Florida city discussed in earlier chapters. (We will assume that the 1978 value of a piece of property is the amount it did sell for, or would have sold for, in 1978.) In order to completely characterize this phenomenon, we would need the actual 1978 sale price, or the price for which the property would have sold, for each piece of residential property in the city. This complete listing of property values constitutes the population of interest to us, and we are particularly interested in the parameter μ, the mean of the population. Unfortunately, in this and in most practical situations, the entire population of property values is unavailable to us. However, we do have available (in Appendix A) a subset or *sample* of 2,862 pieces of data from the target population. But in order to use this sample to infer the characteristics of the population, the sample must be representative of the population about which inferences are to be made; i.e., the sample must possess characteristics similar to those which would be observed in the entire population, if it were available. In Example 1.2 (p. 5), we explained why this sample of 2,862 sale price values may not be characteristic of the much larger (and partly conceptual) population of all residential property values for 1978.

EXAMPLE 7.1   Suppose that an investor is interested in purchasing some undeveloped land which has been divided into 1,000 parcels. Now, unknown to the investor, suppose that the population relative frequency distribution for the percent increase in value for each parcel over the previous year appears as in Figure 7.1. (We emphasize that this example is for illustration only. In actual practice, the entire population of 1,000 values may not be easily accessible.) Now, assume that the seller provides the potential investor with the relative frequency distributions for each of two samples of 50 parcels (Figures 7.2(a) and 7.2(b)) selected from the 1,000 properties at this location.

Compare the distributions of percent increase in value for the two samples. Which appears to better characterize the phenomenon of percent increase in value for the population?

Solution   You can see that the two samples lead to quite different conclusions about the same population from which they were both selected. From Figure 7.2(b), 20% of the sample parcels increased in value by at least 50%, whereas from Figure 7.2(a), only 2% of the sample parcels had such a large increase in value. This may be compared to the

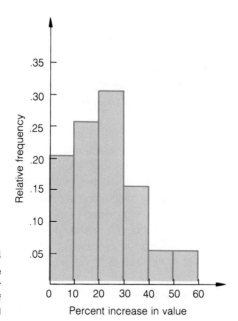

FIGURE 7.1

Percent Increase in Value
over Previous Year for
1,000 Parcels of
Undeveloped Land

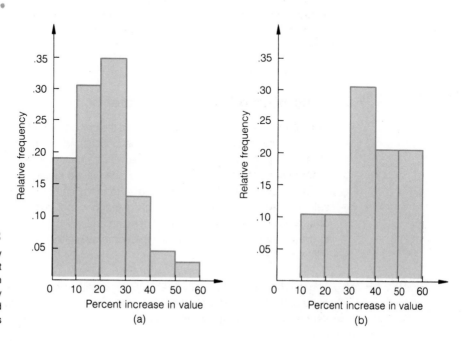

FIGURE 7.2

Relative Frequency
Distributions of Percent
Increase in Value for Each
of Two Samples of Fifty
Parcels of Land Selected
from 1,000 Parcels

relative frequency distribution for the population, Figure 7.1, in which we observe that 5% of all the properties increased by at least 50% in value. In addition, note that none of the properties in the second sample, Figure 7.2(b), increased by less than 10% in value, whereas 18% of the sample parcels, Figure 7.2(a), had an increase in value of less than 10%. This value from the first sample, Figure 7.2(a), compares favorably with the 20% of the increases in value for the entire population, Figure 7.1, which were less than 10%.

To rephrase the question posed in the example, we could ask: Which of the two samples is more representative of, or characteristic of, the phenomenon of percent increase in value for all 1,000 parcels of land? Clearly, the information provided by the first sample, Figure 7.2(a), gives a better picture of the actual population phenomenon; its relative frequency distribution is more similar to that for the entire population, Figure 7.1, than is the one provided by the second sample, Figure 7.2(b). Thus, if the investor were to rely upon information from the second sample (Figure 7.2(b)) only, he may have a distorted, or *biased,* impression of the true situation with respect to percent increase in value of all land parcels.

How is it possible that two samples from the same population can provide (apparently) contradictory information about the population? The key issue is the method by which the samples are obtained. The examples in this section demonstrate that great care must be taken in order to select a sample which will give an unbiased picture of the population about which inferences are to be made. One way to cope with this problem is to use random sampling. Random sampling will eliminate the possibility of bias in selecting a sample and, in addition, it will provide a probabilistic basis for evaluating the reliability of an inference. We will have more to say about random sampling in Section 7.2.

7.2 Obtaining a Random Sample

In the previous section, we demonstrated the importance of obtaining a sample which exhibits characteristics similar to those possessed by the population from which it came, the population about which we wish to make inferences. The selection of a random sample from the population is one way to satisfy this requirement. You will recall, Section 4.6, that we defined a random sample of n observations as one selected from a population in such a manner that each possible collection of n observations has the same chance of being chosen. In this section we will explain how to draw a random sample, and will then employ random sampling in the sections that follow.

EXAMPLE 7.2   The purchasing agent of a city can purchase stationery and office supplies from any of eight companies. If the purchasing agent decides to utilize three suppliers in a given year and wishes to avoid accusations of bias in their selection, the sample of three suppliers should be selected at random from among the eight.

a. How many different samples of 3 suppliers can be chosen from among the 8?

b. List them.

c. State the criterion which must be satisfied in order that the sample selected be random.

Solution a. In this example, the population of interest consists of 8 suppliers (call them A, B, C, D, E, F, G, H) from which we wish to select a sample of size $n = 3$. You will recall (Chapter 4) that the number of different samples of $n = 3$ elements that can be selected from a population of $N = 8$ elements is

$$C_n^N = \frac{N!}{n!(N-n)!} = \frac{8!}{3!5!} = \frac{8 \cdot 7 \cdot 6 \cdot 5 \cdot 4 \cdot 3 \cdot 2 \cdot 1}{(3 \cdot 2 \cdot 1)(5 \cdot 4 \cdot 3 \cdot 2 \cdot 1)} = 56$$

b. The following is a listing of these 56 different samples:

A,B,C	A,C,F	A,E,G	B,C,G	B,E,H	C,E,F	D,E,H
A,B,D	A,C,G	A,E,H	B,C,H	B,F,G	C,E,G	D,F,G
A,B,E	A,C,H	A,F,G	B,D,E	B,F,H	C,E,H	D,F,H
A,B,F	A,D,E	A,F,H	B,D,F	B,G,H	C,F,G	D,G,H
A,B,G	A,D,F	A,G,H	B,D,G	C,D,E	C,F,H	E,F,G
A,B,H	A,D,G	B,C,D	B,D,H	C,D,F	C,G,H	E,F,H
A,C,D	A,D,H	B,C,E	B,E,F	C,D,G	D,E,F	E,G,H
A,C,E	A,E,F	B,C,F	B,E,G	C,D,H	D,E,G	F,G,H

c. Each sample must have the same chance of being selected in order to ensure that we have a random sample. Since there are 56 possible samples of size $n = 3$, each must have a probability equal to $\frac{1}{56}$ of being selected by the sampling procedure.

What procedures may one use to generate a random sample? If the population is not too large, each observation may be recorded on a piece of paper and placed in a suitable container. After the collection of papers is thoroughly mixed, the researcher can remove n pieces of paper from the container; the elements named on these n pieces of paper would be the ones to be included in the sample. This simple method could be easily implemented by the purchasing agent of Example 7.2: Each of the eight suppliers would be listed on a separate piece of paper and placed in a container for thorough mixing. The purchasing agent would then select three of the pieces of paper and contact the three suppliers named on the chosen papers. This method has its drawbacks, however: (1) It is not feasible when the population consists of a large number of observations; and (2) Since it is very difficult to achieve a thorough mixing, the procedure provides only an approximation to random sampling. A more practical method of generating a random sample, and one that may be used with large populations, is the use of a table of random numbers (Table 9, Appendix E). The details are summarized in the box on p. 188.

USING A TABLE OF RANDOM NUMBERS TO GENERATE A RANDOM SAMPLE OF SIZE n FROM A POPULATION OF N ELEMENTS

Step 1. Label the elements in the population from 1 to N.

Step 2. Begin at an arbitrary starting point in a table of random numbers (Table 9, Appendix E). The starting point may be obtained, for example, by closing your eyes and placing a pencil point haphazardly at an entry in the table.

Step 3. Record this number and then proceed in some direction (up or down, left or right, or diagonally), recording each number to identify the corresponding population element to be included in the sample. Continue in this manner until n elements have been selected. [*Note:* Use the necessary number of digits from the random numbers to accommodate the numbering of the elements in step 1.]

EXAMPLE 7.3   Refer to Example 7.2. Use the portion of Table 9, Appendix E, reproduced in Table 7.1 to select a random sample of three suppliers for the purchasing agent.

TABLE 7.1
Reproduction of a Portion
of Table 9, Appendix E

ROW \ COLUMN	1	2	3	4	5	6
1	10480	15011	01536	02011	81647	91646
2	22368	46573	25595	85393	30995	89198
3	24130	48360	22527	97265	76393	64809
4	42167	93093	06243	61680	07856	16376
5	37570	39975	81837	16656	06121	91782
6	77921	06907	11008	42751	27756	53498
7	99562	72905	56420	69994	98872	31016
8	96301	91977	05463	07972	18876	20922

Solution   Step 1.   We first number the $N = 8$ suppliers from 1 to 8. For example, supplier *A* may be assigned the number 1, supplier *B*, the number 2, and so on. (This initial labelling is arbitrary; we are preserving the alphabetical ordering merely for convenience.)

Step 2.   Let us begin in Column 4, Row 2 of the table. The random number entry given there is 85393. Since we need only a single digit to identify the elements in our population, we choose element number 8 (supplier *H*) for the sample.

Step 3.   We will now proceed down Column 4, recording random numbers until we have $n = 3$ elements identified for the sample. The next entry in the column is 9; since we have no element numbered 9, we skip this entry and continue to move downward in the column. The next two entries are 6 and 1. Thus, the purchasing agent would select suppliers numbered 8, 6, and 1; i.e., suppliers *H, F,* and *A*.

A sample selected according to the procedure described above would eliminate the possibility of a biased selection. Every sample of three suppliers would have an equal probability of being selected.

EXAMPLE 7.4 Use the portion of Table 9, Appendix E, that is reproduced in Table 7.1 to select a random sample of size $n = 5$ from the 2,862 observations on appraised improvements values in Appendix A.

Solution **Step 1.** The observations have already been numbered from 0001 to 2,862 in our listing of the data, Appendix A. This labelling implies that we will obtain random numbers of four digits from the table.

Step 2. Let us begin in Row 3, Column 1, and proceed horizontally to the right across the rows. The first element selected is numbered 2413.

Step 3. The next four elements to be included in the sample are those numbered 0483, 6022 (skip), 5279 (skip), 7265 (skip), 7639 (skip), 3648 (skip), 0942 (proceeding to Row 4), 1679, 3093 (skip), and 0624.

The random numbers and the associated observations on appraised improvements values are shown in Table 7.2.

TABLE 7.2
Random Sample of $n = 5$ Observations on Appraised Improvements Values from Appendix A

RANDOM NUMBER OBTAINED	APPRAISED IMPROVEMENTS VALUE FOR CORRESPONDING POPULATION ELEMENT
2,413	$22,120
483	20,280
942	22,270
1,679	20,810
624	42,680

Note in Example 7.4 that, for this sample of $n = 5$ observations on appraised improvements values, the mean is

$$\bar{x} = \frac{\Sigma x}{n} = \frac{22,120 + 20,280 + 22,270 + 20,810 + 42,680}{5} = \$25,632$$

whereas the mean for all 2,862 observations is $24,638. In the next section, we will discuss how to judge the performance of a statistic computed from a random sample.

EXERCISES **7.1** Use Table 9, Appendix E, to generate a random sample of $n = 15$ observations on ratio of sale price to total appraised value from Appendix A.

7.2 A homeowner wishes to list his residential property for sale with the Multiple Listing Service (MLS) in the county. Since there are seven real estate agencies in the county which are affiliated with MLS, the homeowner has decided to randomly select three of them, and to personally interview a sales representative from each of the three selected agencies. Then he will decide with which of the three agencies the property will be listed.

a. How many different samples of three real estate agencies may be selected by the homeowner?

b. List them.

c. State the criterion which must be satisfied in order that the sample selected be random.

7.3   Many opinion surveys are conducted by mail. In this sampling procedure, a random sample of persons is selected from among a list of people who are supposed to constitute a target population (purchasers of a product, etc.). Each is sent a questionnaire and is requested to complete and return the questionnaire to the pollster. Why might this type of survey yield a sample that would produce biased inferences?

7.4   One of the most infamous examples of improper sampling was conducted in 1936 by the *Literary Digest* to determine the winner of the Landon—Roosevelt presidential election. The poll, which predicted Landon to be the winner, was conducted by sending ballots to a random sample of persons selected from among the names listed in the telephone directories of that year. In the actual election, Landon won in Maine and Vermont but lost in the remaining forty-six states. The *Literary Digest's* erroneous forecast is believed to be the major reason for its eventual failure.

What was the cause of the *Digest's* erroneous forecast; i.e., why might the sampling procedure described above yield a sample of people whose opinions might be biased in favor of Landon?

7.5   Use Table 9, Appendix E, to generate a random sample of $n = 20$ supermarket A customer service times from Appendix D. Suppose that you were to construct a relative frequency distribution for the 20 customer service times. Do you believe that the relative frequency distribution for the "population" of 500 supermarket A customer service times will possess a shape similar to the relative frequency distribution you constructed? If so, will the sample produce reliable inferences about the population?

7.6   A file clerk is assigned the task of selecting a random sample of 26 company accounts (from a total of 5,000) to be audited. The clerk is considering two sampling methods:

Method A.   Organize the 5,000 company accounts in alphabetical order (according to the first letter of the client's last name), then randomly select one account card for each of the 26 letters of the alphabet.

Method B.   Assign each company account a four-digit number from 0001 to 5000. From a table of random numbers, choose 26 four-digit numbers (in the range of 0001−5000) and match the numbers with the corresponding company account.

Which of the two methods would you recommend to the file clerk? Which sampling method could possibly yield a biased sample?

7.3 Sampling Distributions

In the previous section, we learned how to generate a random sample from a population of interest, the ultimate goal being to use information from the sample to make an inference about the nature of the population. In many situations, the objective will be to estimate a numerical characteristic of the population (called a *parameter*), using information from the sample. To illustrate, in Example 7.4, we computed $\bar{x} = \$25,632$, the mean appraised improvements value for a random sample of $n = 5$ observations from the data on the appraised improvements values in Appendix A; that is, we used the sample information to compute a *statistic,* namely, the sample mean, $\bar{x}$.

DEFINITION 7.1

A numerical descriptive measure of a population is called a *parameter.*

DEFINITION 7.2

A quantity computed from the observations in a sample is called a *statistic.*

You may have observed that the value of a population parameter (for example, the mean μ) is constant (although it is usually unknown to us); its value does not vary from sample to sample. However, the value of a sample statistic (for example, the sample mean, $\bar{x}$) is highly dependent upon the particular sample which is selected. If, in Example 7.4, we had begun at a different point in the random number table, we would have obtained a different random sample of five observations, and thus a different value of $\bar{x}$.

Since statistics vary from sample to sample, any inferences based on them will necessarily be subject to some uncertainty. How, then, do we judge the reliability of a sample statistic as a tool in making an inference about the corresponding population parameter? Fortunately, the uncertainty of a statistic generally has characteristic properties which are known to us, and which are reflected in its *sampling distribution.*

DEFINITION 7.3

The *sampling distribution* of a sample statistic (based on n observations) is the relative frequency distribution of the values of the statistic generated by taking repeated random samples of size n and computing the value of the statistic for each sample.

Knowledge of the sampling distribution of a particular statistic provides us with information about its performance over the long run.

We will illustrate the notion of a sampling distribution with an example, in which our interest focuses on the values of all residential properties which were *sold* during 1978 in the mid-sized Florida city described previously. In particular, we wish to estimate the mean sale price of all such properties. Then, the target population consists of the 2,862 observations on sale price contained in Appendix A. (We note again that the researcher is the one who defines the population. Depending on how the target population is defined, the data in Appendix A could represent only a sample, as described in Example 1.2. In this case, however, the 2,862 observations constitute the entire population, since we are interested only in those properties which were sold in 1978, and data on *all* 1978 residential property sales are available in Appendix A. In addition, although the true value of μ, the mean of these 2,862 observations, is already known to us (Example 3.10), this example will serve to illustrate the concepts.)

EXAMPLE 7.5 Describe the generation of the sampling distribution of $\bar{x}$, the mean of a random sample of $n = 5$ observations from the population of 2,862 sale price values in Appendix A.

Solution The sampling distribution for the statistic $\bar{x}$, based on a random sample of $n = 5$ measurements, would be generated in this manner: Select a random sample of 5 measurements from the population of 2,862 observations on sale price in Appendix A; compute and record the value of $\bar{x}$ for this sample. Now return these 5 measurements to the population and repeat the procedure; i.e., draw another random sample of $n = 5$ measurements and record the value of $\bar{x}$ for this sample. Return these measurements and repeat the process. If this sampling procedure could be repeated an infinite number of times, the infinite number of values of $\bar{x}$ so obtained could be summarized in a relative frequency distribution, called the *sampling distribution* of $\bar{x}$.

This task, which may seem impractical if not impossible, is not performed in actual practice. Instead, the sampling distribution of a statistic is obtained by applying mathematical theory or computer simulation, as illustrated in the next example.

EXAMPLE 7.6 Use computer simulation to find the approximate sampling distribution of $\bar{x}$, the mean of a random sample of $n = 5$ observations from the population of 2,862 sale prices in Appendix A.

Solution We obtained 100 computer-generated random samples of size $n = 5$ from the target population. The first ten of these samples are presented in Table 7.3.

For example, the first computer-generated sample contained the following measurements:

27,500	21,500	72,000	23,000	69,900

SAMPLE	MEASUREMENTS (IN DOLLARS)				
1	27,500	21,500	72,000	23,000	69,900
2	16,000	36,400	24,200	53,800	56,500
3	11,500	28,800	60,000	38,000	66,000
4	32,900	22,900	38,600	26,900	25,500
5	35,500	23,000	21,800	52,500	33,600
6	30,000	37,300	37,300	44,000	65,600
7	65,800	38,500	28,000	32,900	18,300
8	84,900	34,900	44,300	37,900	63,000
9	39,000	63,000	39,800	82,000	52,600
10	38,500	40,000	37,000	36,500	35,600

The corresponding value of the sample mean is

$$\bar{x} = \frac{\Sigma x}{n} = \frac{27,500 + 21,500 + 72,000 + 23,000 + 69,900}{5} = \$42,780$$

For each sample of five observations, the sample mean $\bar{x}$ was computed. The 100 values of $\bar{x}$ are summarized in the relative frequency distribution, Figure 7.3.

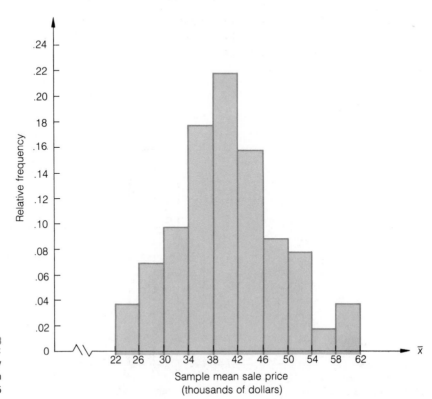

FIGURE 7.3
Sampling Distribution of $\bar{x}$:
Relative Frequency
Distribution of $\bar{x}$ Based on
100 Samples of Size $n = 5$

Let us compare the relative frequency distribution for $\bar{x}$, Figure 7.3, with the relative frequency distribution for the population, Figure 3.7 (p. 61). Note that the values of $\bar{x}$, Figure 7.3, tend to cluster around the population mean, $\mu = \$42,040$; also, the values of the sample mean are less spread out (that is, they have less variation) than the population values shown in Figure 3.7. These two observations are borne out by comparing the means and standard deviations of the two sets of observations, as shown in Table 7.4.

TABLE 7.4
Comparison of the
Population Distribution
and the Approximate
Sampling Distribution of $\bar{x}$,
Based on 100 Samples of
Size $n = 5$

	MEAN	STANDARD DEVIATION
Population of 2,862 sale prices (Figure 3.7)	$\mu = \$42,040$	$\sigma = \$28,322$
100 values of $\bar{x}$ based on samples of size $n = 5$ (Figure 7.3)	$\$42,663$	$\$15,038$

EXAMPLE 7.7   Refer to Example 7.6. Simulate the sampling distribution of $\bar{x}$ for samples of size $n = 20$ from the population of 2,862 sale price observations. Compare the result with the sampling distribution of $\bar{x}$, based on samples of size $n = 5$, obtained in Example 7.6.

Solution   We obtained 100 computer-generated random samples of size $n = 20$ from the target population. A relative frequency distribution for the 100 corresponding values of $\bar{x}$ is shown in Figure 7.4.

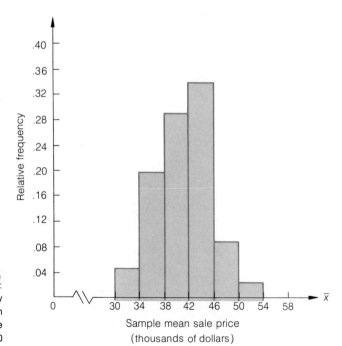

FIGURE 7.4
Sampling Distribution of $\bar{x}$:
Relative Frequency
Distribution of $\bar{x}$ Based on
100 Samples of Size
$n = 20$

Sample mean sale price
(thousands of dollars)

It can be seen that, as with the sampling distribution based on samples of size $n = 5$, the values of $\bar{x}$ tend to center about the population mean. However, a visual inspection shows that the variation of the $\bar{x}$-values about their mean, Figure 7.4, is less than the variation in the values of $\bar{x}$ based on samples of size $n = 5$, Figure 7.3. The mean and standard deviation for these 100 values of $\bar{x}$ are shown in Table 7.5 for comparison with previous results.

TABLE 7.5

	MEAN	STANDARD DEVIATION
Population of 2,862 sale prices (Figure 3.7)	$\mu = \$42{,}040$	$\sigma = \$28{,}322$
100 values of $\bar{x}$ based on samples of size $n = 5$ (Figure 7.3)	$\$42{,}663$	$\$15{,}038$
100 values of $\bar{x}$ based on samples of size $n = 20$ (Figure 7.4)	$\$41{,}365$	$\$ 4{,}980$

From Table 7.5 we observe that, as the sample size increases, there is less variation in the sampling distribution of $\bar{x}$; that is, the values of $\bar{x}$ tend to cluster more closely about the population mean as n gets larger. This intuitively appealing result will be stated formally in the next section.

EXERCISES

7.7 Suppose it is desired to assess the talents of residential property appraisers in the mid-sized Florida city in 1978. One method would be to consider the population of ratios of sale price to total appraised value for all residential properties sold during 1978; the data appear in Appendix A.

a. Which parameter of the target population may be of particular interest? What value would you expect this parameter to assume? [*Hint:* Consider the cases in which (i) the sale price for a piece of property is equal to the total appraised value; (ii) the sale price exceeds the total appraised value, etc.]

b. Use Table 9, Appendix E, to generate 50 random samples of size $n = 10$ from the target population. (Alternatively, each class member may generate several random samples and the results for the entire class can be pooled.) Construct the approximate sampling distribution of the sample mean, $\bar{x}$. Compare with the population relative frequency distribution shown in Figure 3.10 (p. 65).

7.8 Refer to Exercise 7.7. We have reason to expect that the population relative frequency distribution for ratio of sale price to total appraised value would be markedly skewed to the right since no such value can be less than zero, most values would presumably be near one and, occasionally, very large values would be observed. Now, recalling from Section 3.4 that the mean is sensitive to very large observations, one could argue that the population median ratio would provide more information than would the mean about the abilities of property appraisers.

Suppose that an investigator has proposed two different statistics (call them *A* and *B*) for estimating the population median. In an attempt to judge which of the statistics is more suitable, you simulated the approximate sampling distributions for each of the statistics, based on random samples of size $n = 10$. Your results were as shown in Figure 7.5. Comment on the two sampling distributions. Which of the statistics, A or B, would you recommend for use? (In the next section, we will discuss desirable properties of a sampling distribution.)

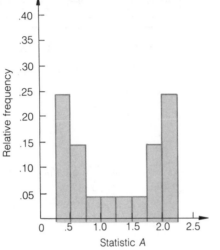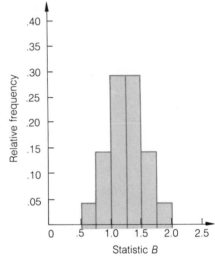

FIGURE 7.5
Approximate Sampling
Distributions of Two
Statistics

7.9 Use computer simulation or Table 9, Appendix E, to obtain 30 random samples of size $n = 5$ from the "population" of 500 supermarket B customer service times in Appendix D. (Again, each class member could generate several random samples and the results could be pooled.)

a. Calculate $\bar{x}$ for each of the 30 samples. Construct a relative frequency distribution for the 30 sample means.
b. Compute the average of the 30 sample means.
c. Compute the standard deviation of the 30 sample means.
d. Locate the average of the 30 sample means, part b, on the relative frequency distribution. This value could be used as an estimate for μ, the mean of the entire population of 500 supermarket B customer service times.

7.10 Repeat parts a, b, c, and d of Exercise 7.9 but use random samples of size $n = 10$. Compare the relative frequency distribution with that of Exercise 7.9(a). Do the values of $\bar{x}$ generated from samples of size $n = 10$ tend to cluster more closely about μ?

7.11 Describe the generation of the sampling distribution of $\bar{x}$, the mean daily price change of a random sample of $n = 15$ observations from the population of Standard & Poor's Stock Index daily changes, 1975–1979, in Appendix C.

7.4 The Sampling Distribution of $\bar{x}$; the Central Limit Theorem

Estimating the mean sale price for all residential properties sold during 1978 in a specific Florida city, or the average increase in value over the previous year for parcels of land in a certain development, or the mean value per acre of property zoned for industrial use in a particular area, are all examples of practical problems in which the goal is to make an inference about the mean, μ, of some target population. In previous sections, we have indicated that the sample mean $\bar{x}$ is often used as a tool for making an inference about the corresponding population parameter μ, and we have shown how to approximate its sampling distribution. The following theorem, of fundamental importance in statistics, provides information about the actual sampling distribution of $\bar{x}$:

THE CENTRAL LIMIT THEOREM

If the sample size is sufficiently large, then the mean $\bar{x}$ of a random sample from a population has a sampling distribution which is approximately normal, regardless of the shape of the relative frequency distribution of the target population. As the sample size increases, the better will be the normal approximation to the sampling distribution.

The sampling distribution of $\bar{x}$, in addition to being approximately normal, has other known characteristics which are summarized in the accompanying box.

PROPERTIES OF THE SAMPLING DISTRIBUTION OF $\bar{x}$

If $\bar{x}$ is the mean of a random sample of size n from a population with mean μ and standard deviation σ, then:

1. The sampling distribution of $\bar{x}$ has a mean which is equal to the mean of the population from which the sample was selected. That is, if we let $\mu_{\bar{x}}$ denote the mean of the sampling distribution of $\bar{x}$, then

   $$\mu_{\bar{x}} = \mu$$

2. The sampling distribution of $\bar{x}$ has a standard deviation which is equal to the standard deviation of the population from which the sample was selected, divided by the square root of the sample size. That is, if we let $\sigma_{\bar{x}}$ denote the standard deviation of the sampling distribution of $\bar{x}$, then

   $$\sigma_{\bar{x}} = \frac{\sigma}{\sqrt{n}}$$

EXAMPLE 7.8   Discuss the Central Limit Theorem and the two properties of the sampling distribution of $\bar{x}$, making reference to the empirical evidence obtained in Examples 7.6 and 7.7. Recall that, in Examples 7.6 and 7.7, we obtained repeated random samples of sizes $n = 5$ and $n = 20$ from the population of sale prices for all residential properties sold in the city during 1978. For this target population, we know the values of the parameters μ and σ:

Population mean: $\mu = \$42,040$

Population standard deviation: $\sigma = \$28,322$

Solution   In Figures 7.3 and 7.4, we noted that the values of $\bar{x}$ tended to cluster about the population mean, $\mu = \$42,040$. This is guaranteed by property 1, which implies that, in the long run, the average of *all* values of $\bar{x}$ which would be generated in infinite repeated sampling would be equal to μ.

We also observed, from Table 7.5, that the standard deviation of the sampling distribution of $\bar{x}$ decreased as the sample size increased from $n = 5$ to $n = 20$. Property 2 quantifies the decrease and relates it to the sample size. As an example, note that for our approximate (simulated) sampling distribution based on samples of size $n = 5$, we obtained a standard deviation of \$15,038, whereas property 2 tells us that, for the actual sampling distribution of $\bar{x}$, the standard deviation is equal to

$$\sigma_{\bar{x}} = \frac{\sigma}{\sqrt{n}} = \frac{\$28,322}{\sqrt{5}} = \$12,666$$

Similarly, for samples of size $n = 20$, the sampling distribution of $\bar{x}$ actually has a standard deviation of

$$\sigma_{\bar{x}} = \frac{\sigma}{\sqrt{n}} = \frac{\$28,322}{\sqrt{20}} = \$6,333$$

The value we obtained by simulation was \$4,980.

Finally, the Central Limit Theorem guarantees an approximately normal distribution for $\bar{x}$, regardless of the shape of the original population. In our examples, the population from which the samples were selected is seen in Figure 3.7 (p. 61) to be highly skewed to the right. Note from Figures 7.3 and 7.4 that, although the sampling distribution of $\bar{x}$ tends to be mound-shaped in each case, the normal approximation improved when the sample size was increased from $n = 5$ (Figure 7.3) to $n = 20$ (Figure 7.4).

EXAMPLE 7.9   Three relative frequency distributions which provide reasonably accurate probability models for certain business phenomena are the *normal distribution* (which we discussed in Chapter 6), the *uniform distribution,* and the *exponential distribution.* Their vastly different shapes are shown in Figure 7.6(a). Simulate the sampling distributions

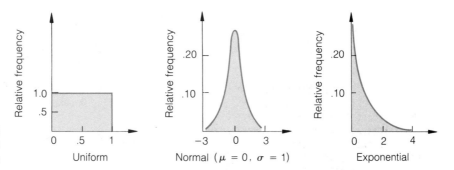

FIGURE 7.6(a)
Three Population Relative
Frequency Distributions

of x̄ by drawing 1,000 samples of $n = 5$ observations from populations that possess the relative frequency distributions shown in Figure 7.6(a). Repeat the procedure for $n = 10, 15, 25$, and 100. Does the Central Limit Theorem appear to provide adequate information about the shapes of the sampling distributions of x̄?

Solution   We obtained 1,000 computer-generated random samples of size $n = 5$ from each of the three populations. Relative frequency distributions for the 1,000 values of x̄ obtained from each of the populations are shown in Figure 7.6(b) on p. 200. Note their shapes for this small n.

The relative frequency distributions of x̄ for $n = 10, 15, 25$, and 100, also simulated by computer, are shown in Figures 7.6(c), 7.6(d), 7.6(e), and 7.6(f), respectively. Note that the values of x̄ tend to cluster about the mean of the probability distribution from which the sample was taken, and that as n increases, there is less variation in the sampling distribution. You can also see that as the sample size increases, the shape of the sampling distribution of x̄ tends toward the shape of the normal distribution (symmetric and mound-shaped), regardless of the shape of the relative frequency distribution of the sampled population. The results of our computer simulations thus offer visual verification of the Central Limit Theorem and the other properties of the sampling distribution of x̄ given in the box. (It is interesting to note that when sampling from a normal population, the sampling distribution of x̄ is approximately normal for all values of n simulated in this example. In fact, it can be theoretically shown that when the relative frequency distribution of the target population is normal, the sample mean will have a normal sampling distribution, regardless of the sample size.)

EXAMPLE 7.10   A consumer magazine recently reported that for families residing in the northeast, the distribution of the weekly (per capita) expenditure for food consumed away from home has an average of $3.28 and a standard deviation of $1.12. In order to check this claim, an economist randomly samples 100 families residing in the northeast and monitors their expenditures for food consumed away from home for one week.

a.   Assuming the consumer magazine's claim is true, describe the sampling distribution of the mean weekly (per capita) expenditure for food purchased away from home for a random sample of 100 families residing in the northeast.

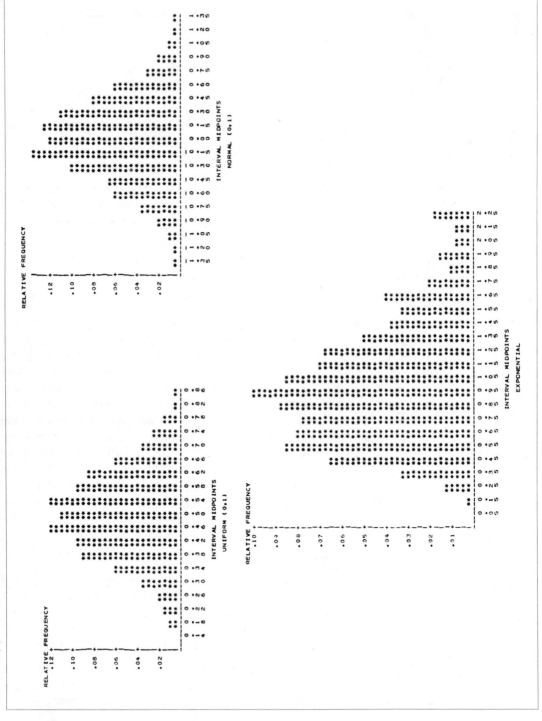

FIGURE 7.6(b) Relative Frequency Distribution of a Random Sample of 1,000 Sample Means ($n = 5$)

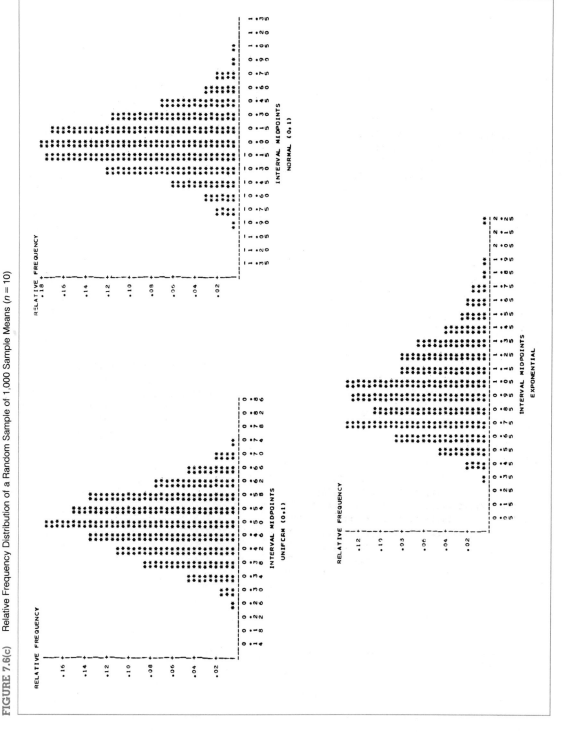

FIGURE 7.6(c)   Relative Frequency Distribution of a Random Sample of 1,000 Sample Means (n = 10)

FIGURE 7.6(d) Relative Frequency Distribution of a Random Sample of 1,000 Sample Means ($n = 15$)

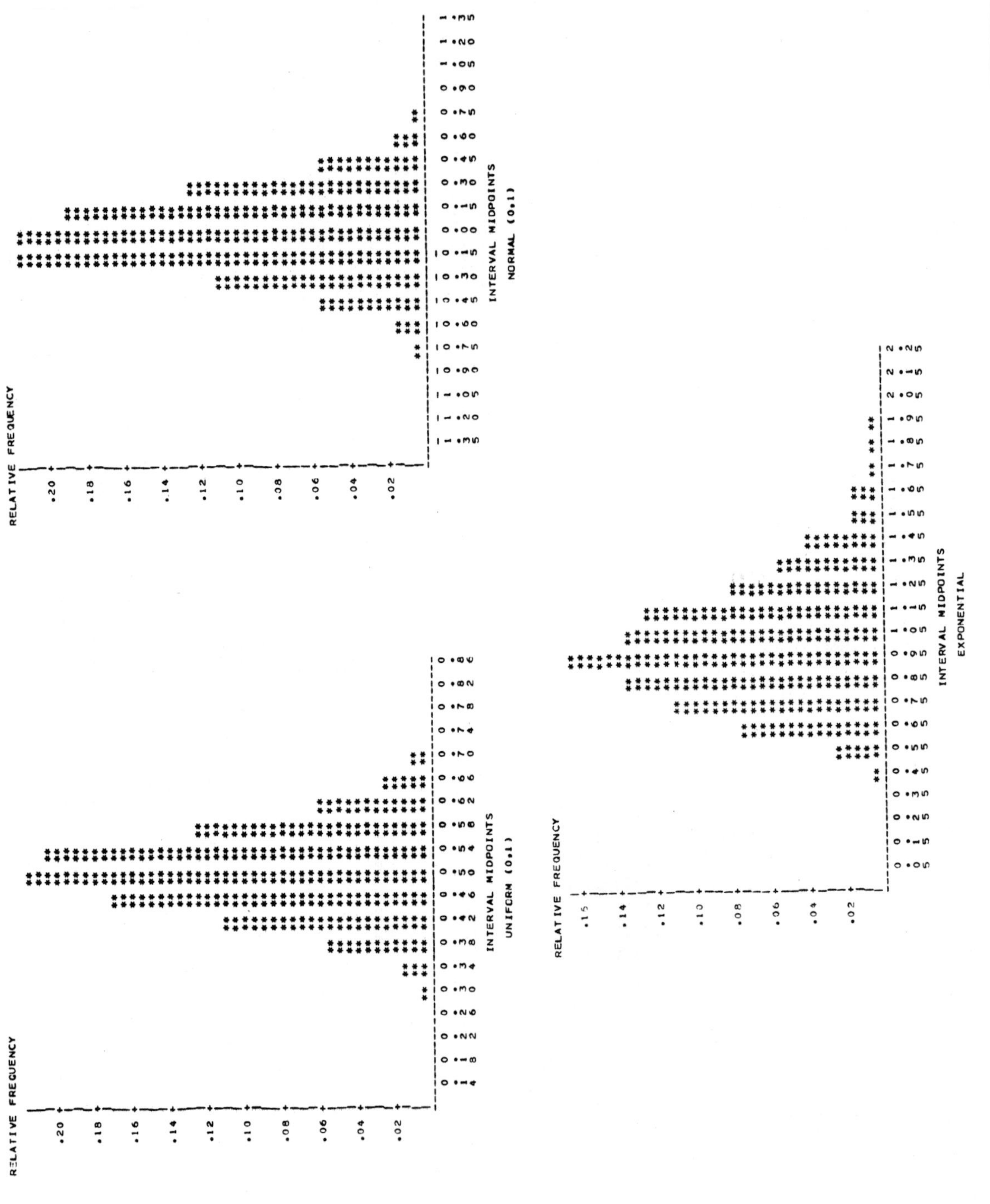

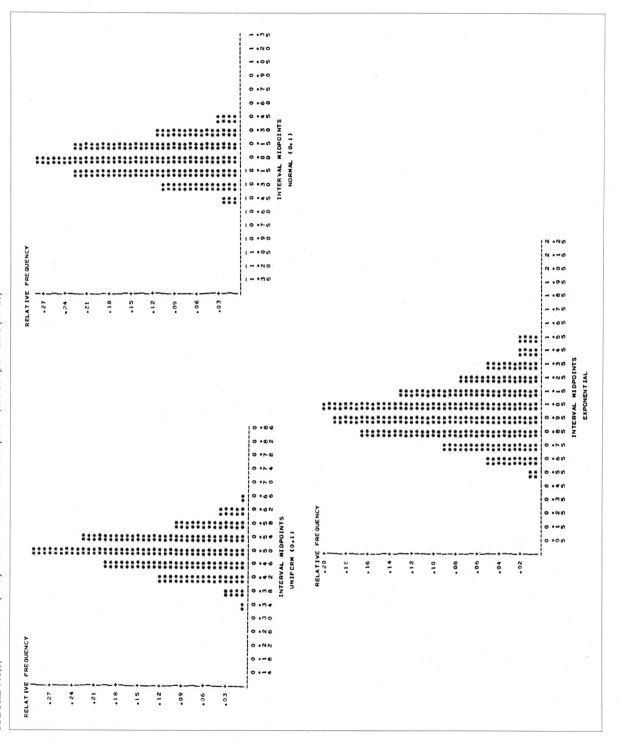

FIGURE 7.6(e)   Relative Frequency Distribution of a Random Sample of 1,000 Sample Means ($n = 25$)

FIGURE 7.6(f)   Relative Frequency Distribution of a Random Sample of 1,000 Sample Means ($n = 100$)

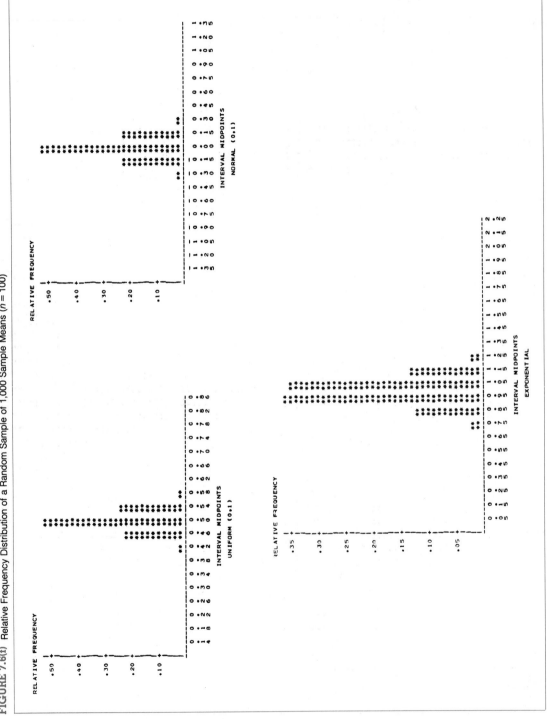

b. Assuming the consumer magazine's claim is true, what is the probability that the sample mean weekly (per capita) expenditure for food purchased away from home will be at least $3.60?

Solution **a.** Although we have no information about the shape of the relative frequency distribution of the weekly (per capita) expenditures for food purchased away from home for families residing in the area, we apply the Central Limit Theorem to conclude that the sampling distribution of the sample mean weekly (per capita) expenditure, based on 100 observations, is approximately normally distributed. In addition, the mean, $\mu_{\bar{x}}$, and the standard deviation, $\sigma_{\bar{x}}$, of the sampling distribution are given by

$$\mu_{\bar{x}} = \mu = \$3.28$$

and

$$\sigma_{\bar{x}} = \frac{\sigma}{\sqrt{n}} = \frac{1.12}{\sqrt{100}} = .112$$

assuming that the consumer magazine's reported values of μ and σ are correct.

b. If the consumer magazine's claim is true, then $P(\bar{x} \geq 3.60)$, the probability of observing a mean weekly (per capita) expenditure of $3.60 or more in the sample of 100 observations, is equal to the shaded area shown in Figure 7.7.

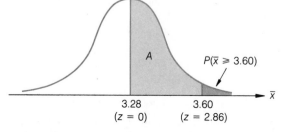

FIGURE 7.7
Sampling Distribution of x̄
in Example 7.10

A

$P(\bar{x} \geq 3.60)$

3.28   3.60
$(z = 0)$ $(z = 2.86)$

Since the sampling distribution is approximately normal, with mean and standard deviation as obtained in part a, we can compute the desired area by obtaining the z-score for $\bar{x} = 3.60$:

$$z = \frac{\bar{x} - \mu_{\bar{x}}}{\sigma_{\bar{x}}} = \frac{3.60 - 3.28}{.112} = 2.86$$

Thus, $P(\bar{x} \geq 3.60) = P(z \geq 2.86)$, and this probability (area) may be found using Table 3, Appendix E, and the methods of Chapter 6:

$$P(\bar{x} \geq 3.60) = P(z \geq 2.86)$$
$$= .5 - A \quad \text{(see Figure 7.7)}$$
$$= .5 - .4979$$
$$= .0021$$

The probability that we would obtain a sample mean weekly (per capita) expenditure for food purchased away from home of $3.60 or greater is only .0021, if the consumer magazine's claim is valid. If the 100 randomly selected families spend (per capita) an average of $3.60 or more on food while away from home during the week, the economist would have strong evidence that the consumer magazine's claim is false, because such a large sample mean is very unlikely to occur if the claim is true.

In practical terms, the Central Limit Theorem and the two properties of the sampling distribution of $\bar{x}$ assure us that the sample mean $\bar{x}$ is a reasonable statistic to use in making inferences about the population mean μ, and they allow us to compute a measure of the reliability of inferences made about μ. (This topic will be treated more thoroughly in Chapter 8.)

As was noted earlier, we will not be required to obtain sampling distributions by simulation or by mathematical arguments. Rather, for all the statistics to be used in this course, the sampling distribution and its properties (which are a matter of record) will be presented as the need arises.

EXERCISES   **7.12**   Suppose we select a random sample of 40 recently issued building permits for improvements to existing residential structures, and record the value, x, of each permit. Prior experience has shown that, in a particular county, the relative frequency distribution for the value of such building permits has a mean of $\mu = \$8,000$ and a standard deviation of $\sigma = \$1,500$.

a.   Describe the sampling distribution of $\bar{x}$, the mean value of a sample of 40 building permits.

b.   What is the probability that the mean value of the permits in the sample will be less than $7,500?

c.   What is the probability that the mean value of the permits in the sample will be between $7,500 and $8,500?

7.13   The manufacturer of a new instant-picture camera claims that its product has "the world's fastest-developing color film by far." Extensive laboratory testing has shown that the relative frequency distribution for the time it takes the new instant camera to begin to reveal the image after shooting has a mean of 9.8 seconds and a standard deviation of 0.55 seconds. Suppose that 50 of these cameras are randomly selected from the production line and tested. The time until the image is first revealed, x, is recorded for each.

a.   Describe the sampling distribution of $\bar{x}$, the mean time it takes the sample of 50 cameras to begin to reveal the image.

b.   Find the probability that the mean time until the image is first revealed for the 50 sampled cameras is greater than 9.70 seconds.

c.   If the mean and standard deviation of the population relative frequency distribution for the times until the cameras begin to reveal the image are correct, would you expect to observe a value of $\bar{x}$ below 9.55 seconds? Explain.

7.14   Refer to Exercise 7.13. Describe the changes in the sampling distribution of $\bar{x}$ if the sample size were:

a. Decreased from $n = 50$ to $n = 20$

b. Increased from $n = 50$ to $n = 100$

7.15 For weeks before the 1980 presidential election, public opinion pollsters were nearly unanimous in agreeing that the race between the then-incumbent President Carter and challenger Ronald Reagan was "too close to call." Reagan, of course, won comfortably. One possible explanation for the inaccurate projections is the following: Most of the private firms which conduct public opinion polls did not survey intensively right up until election time due to the high cost of interviewing voters.

Suppose that data from major national surveys (surveys which contact at least 1,500 people) for the past five years indicate that the relative frequency distribution of the cost of conducting a public opinion poll has a mean of $22,500 and a standard deviation of $6,000.

a. The financial records for thirty major national surveys conducted during the past five years are randomly selected, and $\bar{x}$, the sample mean cost of the polls, is computed. Describe the sampling distribution of $\bar{x}$.

b. What is the probability that $\bar{x}$, the mean cost of the thirty surveys, will be between $20,000 and $25,000?

7.16 Refer to Exercise 7.15. Suppose that the financial records for 60 major national surveys conducted during the past five years are randomly selected, and $\bar{x}$ computed.

a. How will $P(20,000 < \bar{x} < 25,000)$ for $n = 60$ compare to the probability you computed in Exercise 7.15(b)? Do not compute the probability—base your answer on your mental images of the sampling distributions of $\bar{x}$ for $n = 30$ and $n = 60$.

b. Compute $P(20,000 < \bar{x} < 25,000)$ when $n = 60$. Was your answer to part a correct?

7.17 Research conducted by a tobacco company indicates that the relative frequency distribution of the tar content of their newly developed low-tar cigarette has a mean, μ, equal to 3.9 milligrams of tar per cigarette and a standard deviation, σ, equal to 1.0 milligram. Suppose that a sample of 100 low-tar cigarettes is randomly selected from a day's production and the tar content measured in each.

a. Find the probability that the mean tar content of the sample is greater than 4.15 milligrams, i.e., compute $P(\bar{x} > 4.15)$. Assume that the tobacco company's claim is true.

b. Suppose that the sample mean is computed to be $\bar{x} = 4.18$ milligrams. Based upon the probability of part a, do you think the tobacco company may have understated the true value of μ?

c. Refer to part b. If the tobacco company's figures are correct, give a plausible explanation for the observed value of $\bar{x} = 4.18$ milligrams.

7.5 Summary

The objective of most statistical investigations is to make an inference about a population parameter. Since we often base inferences upon information contained in a sample from the target population, it is essential that the sample be properly selected. A procedure for obtaining a random sample, using a table of random numbers, was described in this chapter.

After the sample has been selected, we compute a statistic which contains information about the target parameter. The sampling distribution of the statistic characterizes the relative frequency distribution of values of the statistic over an infinitely large number of samples.

The Central Limit Theorem provides information about the sampling distribution of the sample mean, $\bar{x}$. In particular, the sampling distribution will be approximately normal if the sample size is sufficiently large.

KEY WORDS

Population	Parameter
Sample	Statistic
Biased	Sampling distribution
Random sample	Computer simulation
Table of random numbers	Central Limit Theorem

SUPPLEMENTARY EXERCISES

7.18   The owners of a chain of coin-operated beverage machines operating in South Florida will contract with two wholesalers to supply the 8-ounce paper cups used in the machines. A total of six wholesalers of paper cups are available for selection.

a.   How many different samples of two wholesalers can be chosen from among the six?

b.   List the different samples.

c.   Using Table 9, Appendix E, randomly select the two wholesalers who will be contracted to supply the beverage machines with 8-ounce paper cups.

7.19   Before each year's Christmas shopping rush, a New York City department store sends Amount Due notices to each of its 10,000 customers who possess charge accounts. Last year's records revealed that the relative frequency distribution of the amount owed by the 10,000 customers had a mean of $170 and a standard deviation of $90. Suppose that a clerk at the store randomly selected 36 customers' charge accounts during the pre-Christmas period and recorded the amount owed on each account.

a.   Describe the sampling distribution of $\bar{x}$, the mean amount owed for the 36 charge accounts sampled.

b.   Find the probability that the mean amount owed for the 36 charge accounts falls between $190 and $200.

c.   Find the probability that the mean amount owed for the 36 charge accounts is less than $160.

7.20   A local realty company advertises in the college newspaper that the average age of a home buyer at the purchase of the first home is 29.5 years, and the standard deviation is 2.4 years. Suppose a private mortgage-lending institution decides to check the claim, based on an examination of the ages of 50 randomly selected first-home buyers in the area.

a. Assuming the realty company's claim is true, describe the sampling distribution of the mean age for a sample of 50 first-home buyers.

b. Assuming the realty company's claim is true, what is the probability that the sample mean age will be 30.5 years or greater?

c. Suppose that the mortgage-lending institution computes a sample mean age of 31.2 years. Is this sufficient evidence to contradict the realty company's claim? Explain. [*Hint:* Use your answer to part b.]

7.21 Every ten years the U.S. population census provides essential information about our nation and its people. The basic constitutional purpose of the census is to apportion the membership of the House of Representatives among the states. However, the census has many other important uses. For example, private business uses the census for plant location and marketing.

The 1980 census included questions on age, sex, race, marital status, family relationship, and income; this census was mailed to every household in the U.S. In some cities, however, a series of questions was added for a 5% sample of the city's households. That is, each of a random sample of the city's households was mailed a census form which included additional questions. Suppose that the city contained 100,000 households and, of these, 5,000 were selected and mailed the longer census form.

a. If you worked for the Bureau of the Census and were assigned the task of selecting a random sample of 5,000 of the city's households, describe how you would proceed. [*Hint:* Utilize Table 9, Appendix E.]

b. Suppose that one of the additional questions on the long form of the census concerned energy consumption. The city used this sample information to project the average energy consumption for the city's 100,000 households. Explain why it is important that the sample of 5,000 households be random.

7.22 Five hundred applicants are vying for three equivalent positions at a steel factory. The company has been able to narrow the field to six equally qualified applicants, three of whom are minority candidates.

a. How many different samples of three applicants can be selected from the six?

b. List the different samples.

c. If the three applicants who are chosen are selected at random from this final group of six, would you expect them to be the three minority candidates?

d. Use Table 9, Appendix E, to randomly select the three applicants who will be awarded positions at the steel factory. How many minority candidates are included in your selection?

7.23 Suppose that the amount of heating oil used annually by households in a particular state has a relative frequency distribution with a mean of 200 gallons and a standard deviation of 40 gallons. The monthly utility bills for a random sample of 100 households in the state are examined and the amount of heating oil used annually by each is recorded.

a. Describe the sampling distribution of $\bar{x}$, the mean amount of heating oil used annually by the 100 randomly selected households.

b. Compute $P(\bar{x} < 196)$.

c. Compute $P(\bar{x} > 190)$.

d. Compute the probability that $\bar{x}$ falls within 1 gallon of the true mean of 200, i.e., compute $P(199 < \bar{x} < 201)$.

7.24 As part of a company's quality control program, it is common practice to monitor the quality characteristics of a product. For example, the amount of alkali in soap might be monitored by randomly selecting from the production process and analyzing $n = 30$ test quantities twice each day. If the mean, $\bar{x}$, of the sample falls within specified control limits, the process is deemed to be in control. If $\bar{x}$ is outside the limits, the monitor flashes a warning signal and suggests that something is wrong with the process. Suppose that the upper and lower control limits are located, respectively, $3\sigma_{\bar{x}}$ above and below μ, the true mean amount of alkali in the soap.

a. For the soap process, experience has shown that $\mu = 2\%$ and $\sigma = 1\%$. Specify the upper and lower control limits for the process. [*Hint:* Calculate $\mu - 3\sigma_{\bar{x}}$ and $\mu + 3\sigma_{\bar{x}}$.]

b. If the process is in control, what is the probability that $\bar{x}$ falls outside the control limits? Use the fact that the probability that $\bar{x}$ falls outside the control limits is given by

$$1 - P(\text{the process is in control}) = 1 - P(\mu - 3\sigma_{\bar{x}} < \bar{x} < \mu + 3\sigma_{\bar{x}})$$

7.25 A telephone company has determined that during non-holidays the number of phone calls which pass through the main branch office each hour has a relative frequency distribution with a mean, μ, of 80,000 and a standard deviation, σ, of 35,000.

a. Describe the shape of the sampling distribution of $\bar{x}$, the mean number of incoming phone calls per hour for a random sample of 60 non-holiday hours.

b. What is the mean of the sampling distribution, part a?

c. What is the standard deviation of the sampling distribution, part a?

d. Find the probability that $\bar{x}$, the mean number of incoming phone calls per hour for a random sample of 60 non-holiday hours, will be larger than 91,970.

e. Suppose that the telephone company wishes to determine whether the true mean number of incoming calls per hour during holidays is the same as for non-holidays. To accomplish this, the company randomly selects 60 hours during a holiday period, monitors the incoming phone calls each hour, and computes $\bar{x}$, the sample mean number of incoming phone calls. If the sample mean is computed to be $\bar{x} = 91,970$ calls per hour, do you believe that the true mean for holidays is $\mu = 80,000$ (the same as for non-holidays)? Assume that σ for holidays is 35,000 calls per hour. [*Hint:* If in fact $\mu = 80,000$ for holidays, the sampling distribution of $\bar{x}$ for holidays is identical to the sampling distribution, parts a, b, and c. Thus, the probability, part d, may be used to infer whether $\bar{x} = 91,970$ is a rare event.]

7.26 A manufacturer of photocopy machines buys back many of their photocopiers from businesses which are clearing their old inventory. Thus, the depreciation time of the photocopiers, i.e., the time until the resale value of the photocopiers diminishes, is of importance to the company. Suppose that, unknown to the company, the depreciation time of their copy machines has a relative frequency distribution with a true mean of 45 months and a standard deviation of 10 months.

a. What is the probability that a sample of 25 photocopiers sold to various businesses will have a mean depreciation time between 40 and 44 months?

b. What is the probability that the sample mean will be less than 42 months?

c. Suppose the sample represents the depreciation times of 25 photocopiers sold to businesses during a period when the U.S. economy was in a deep recession. Why might the sample information be biased?

7.27 The Chamber of Commerce of a certain city publishes a brochure which contains housing information for new-home buyers. The brochure states that the average cost of new homes built within the city's limits is $72,750. Believing this figure is too low, a local real estate appraiser will obtain the records of sale for 49 randomly selected new homes built in the city and compute $\bar{x}$, the mean sale price of the sample.

a. Suggest a method which will produce a random sample of 49 new homes built within the city limits.

b. Assuming that the relative frequency distribution of all new-home costs in the city has a standard deviation of $44,030, find the probability that the mean cost of a random sample of 49 new homes is larger than $91,650 (i.e., compute $P(\bar{x} > 91,650)$).

c. Suppose that the appraiser computes $\bar{x} = $91,650$ for the sampled homes. What could you infer about the figure quoted in the Chamber of Commerce's brochure? Does it appear that the true mean cost of new homes built within the city's limits is greater than $72,750? [*Hint:* Use your answer to part b.]

7.28 Let $\bar{x}_{25}$ represent the mean of a random sample of size 25 obtained from a population with mean $\mu = 17$ and standard deviation $\sigma = 10$. Similarly, let $\bar{x}_{100}$ represent the mean of a random sample of size 100 selected from the same population.

a. Describe the sampling distribution of $\bar{x}_{25}$.

b. Describe the sampling distribution of $\bar{x}_{100}$.

c. Which of the probabilities, $P(15 < \bar{x}_{25} < 19)$ or $P(15 < \bar{x}_{100} < 19)$, would you expect to be the larger?

d. Calculate the two probabilities, part c. Was your answer to part c correct?

7.29 One of the monitoring methods the Environmental Protection Agency (EPA) uses to determine whether sewage treatment plants are conforming to standards is to take thirty-six 1-liter specimens from the plant's discharge during the period of investigation. Chemical methods are applied to determine the percentage of sewage in each specimen. If the sample data provide evidence to indicate that the true mean percentage of sewage exceeds a limit set by the EPA, the treatment plant must undergo mandatory repair and retooling. At one particular plant, the mean sewage discharge limit has been set at 15%. This plant is suspected of being in violation of the EPA standard.

a. Unknown to the EPA, the relative frequency distribution of sewage percentages in 1-liter specimens at the plant in question has a mean, μ, of 15.7% and a standard deviation, σ, of 2.0%. Thus, the plant is in violation of the EPA standard. What is the probability that the EPA will obtain a sample of thirty-six 1-liter specimens with a mean less than 15%, even though the plant is violating the sewage discharge limit?

b. Suppose that the EPA computes $\bar{x} = 14.95\%$. Does this result lead you to believe that the sample of thirty-six 1-liter specimens obtained by the EPA was not random, but biased in favor of the sewage treatment plant? Explain. [*Hint:* Use your answer to part a.]

7.30 This year a large insurance firm began a program of compensating its salespeople for sick days not used. The firm decided to pay each salesperson a bonus for every unused sick day. In previous years, the number of sick days used per salesperson per year had a relative frequency distribution with a mean of 9.2 and a standard deviation of 1.8. To determine whether the compensation program has effectively reduced the mean number of sick days used, the firm randomly sampled 81 salespeople and recorded the number of sick days used by each at the year's end.

a. Assuming that the compensation program was not effective in reducing the average number of sick days used, find the probability that the 81 randomly selected salespeople produce a sample mean less than 8.76 days. [*Hint:* If the compensation program was not effective, then the mean and standard deviation of the relative frequency distribution of number of sick days used per salesperson this year is the same as in previous years, i.e., $\mu = 9.2$ and $\sigma = 1.8$.]

b. If the sample mean is computed to be $\bar{x} = 8.76$ days, is there sufficient evidence to conclude that the compensation program was effective, i.e., that the true mean number of sick days used per salesperson this year is less than 9.2, the mean for previous years?

7.31 A large freight elevator can transport a maximum of 9,800 pounds (4.9 tons). Suppose that a load of cargo containing 49 boxes needs to be transported via the elevator. Experience has shown that the weights of boxes for this type of cargo have a relative frequency distribution with $\mu = 205$ pounds and $\sigma = 14$ pounds. Given this information, what is the probability that all 49 boxes can be safely loaded onto the freight elevator and transported? [*Hint:* In order for all 49 boxes to be safely loaded onto the freight elevator, the total weight of the 49 boxes must not exceed the maximum of 9,800 pounds. This implies that $\bar{x}$, the average weight of the 49 boxes, must not exceed $9,800 \div 49 = 200$ pounds. Thus, the desired probability can be found by computing $P(\bar{x} < 200)$.]

CASE STUDY 7.1
Pollsters Blast
ABC-TV's Survey

The ABC-TV poll of television viewers following the Carter–Reagan presidential debate produced cries of protest from professional pollsters. The cause of the pollsters' concern is described in the following article (Gainesville *Sun*, October 31, 1980):

> Some leading pollsters, recalling damage done to their industry by a Literary Digest survey that predicted Franklin D. Roosevelt would lose in 1936, are denouncing an ABC telephone survey taken after this week's presidential debate.
>
> "No credence at all should be given to the figures," said Dr. George Gallup Sr., whose surveys are among the nation's best known samples of public opinion.

In the ABC survey, nearly three-quarters of a million "votes" were cast by telephone Tuesday night during a 100 minute-period following the nationally televised debate between President Carter and Republican challenger Ronald Reagan.

Callers were given two numbers—one for Carter, the other for Reagan—to automatically register their opinion on who gained the most in the debate. Some 477,815 callers dialed the Reagan number; 243,554 dialed for Carter.

While he discounted the survey's likely impact on next Tuesday's election, White House spokesman Jody Powell called it "sort of a shame" that an unscientific survey with "no credibility" got a lot of attention.

Gallup, commenting Wednesday, derided the method as discredited and having "all the faults of the Literary Digest procedures of 1936, in which postcard ballots were sent to people who had car registrations and were listed in the telephone books, which biased the sample toward people with higher income levels."

That survey, a Waterloo for the soon-to-be defunct magazine and the darkest hour of the then-young polling industry, predicted Republican Alf Landon would whip Roosevelt.

Landon took Maine and Vermont and their eight electoral votes. The rest, 46 states and 523 electoral votes, went to Roosevelt in the most one-sided election of modern times.

ABC stressed that its survey was not scientific or statistically valid. Roone Arledge, the network's president for news, defended it, however, as providing "an early indication of what people generally thought about who came off better."

"I see it as comparable to reporting early election returns on election day. They don't prove anything, but there is an interest in them," said Arledge. He added that ABC was doing a separate scientific poll of reaction to the debate.

Albert Cantril, president of the National Council for Public Opinion Research, an association of 16 major pollers, said that despite ABC's disclaimers of the survey's reliability, "Getting 700,000 responses conveys a false impression of reliability, simply by the numbers."

He said that ABC's vigorous disclaimers "raises the question of why they did it at all."

ABC's scientific polling is done by Louis Harris Associates, which said it had nothing to do with the telephone survey.

Explain why the sample of opinions collected by the ABC-TV survey could have produced a biased forecast of the debate "winner."

CASE STUDY 7.2
The Role of Patient Waiting Time

F. A. Sloan and J. H. Lorant, in their article, "The Role of Patient Waiting Time: Evidence from Physicians' Practices" (*Journal of Business,* October 1977), report on the advantages and disadvantages of the time patients spend waiting in physicians' offices before they receive health care services. They write:

Past studies by economists have considered waiting time to be fully unproductive in the provision of a particular service; their conceptual discussions have emphasized the dead-weight loss associated with a queue [i.e., a line waiting for services]. By contrast, operations researchers, especially in health care applications, have assessed productive aspects of waiting. The latter type of study is based on the premise that increasing patient waiting time is likely to reduce idle time of doctors and their staffs. The queue in the office serves at least three roles. First, with patients waiting, the pace of the physicians' practice is less likely to be disturbed by late patient arrivals. If a patient arrives late for his appointment, the physician can draw from the queue of waiting patients. Second, given unanticipated variability in visit lengths (and visit complexity), the physician may use waiting patients to fill up unexpected idle moments in his schedule and that of staff when other patients are receiving X rays and the like. Finally, even if all patients were punctual and there were no variability in visit lengths, the patient may use waiting time to complete forms and/or undress prior to the medical examination. Were patient waiting to be reduced to an absolute minimum, the physician and/or his staff might have to wait for these tasks to be completed.

By maintaining queues, say Sloan and Lorant, patient demand for the physicians' services is reduced due to the higher patient (opportunity) time price. (For example, some patients will be reluctant to give up their opportunity to earn income during this possibly long waiting-time period.) It is up to physicians, then, to "determine the optimal mean wait in their practices by balancing the efficiency of their operations against patient demand considerations."

As part of a study to determine the relationship between the time patients wait in the physician's office and certain demand and cost factors, Sloan and Lorant obtained data on the typical patient waiting times for 4,500 physicians in the five largest specialties—general practice, general surgery, internal medicine, obstetrics/gynecology, and pediatrics. They reported a mean waiting time of 24.7 minutes and a standard deviation of 19.3 minutes. Sloan and Lorant note that the 4,500 observations in the data set represent estimates of waiting time based on recall by the physician. They warn that these "estimates may be biased downward because physicians may tend to underestimate the amount of time their patients wait."

For the purposes of this case study, let us assume that the 4,500 observations in the data set represent the *actual* waiting times of all patients who visited a particular pediatrician last year. Suppose also that the relative frequency distribution of the 4,500 patient waiting times has a mean $\mu = 24.7$ minutes and a standard deviation $\sigma = 19.3$ minutes, and that these figures are unavailable to the pediatrician.

In order to determine whether the "optimal" mean waiting time for his practice has been attained, the pediatrician has one of his staff monitor the waiting times for 100 randomly selected patients during the year. The sample average waiting time, $\bar{x}$, is computed. Applying the Central Limit Theorem, we know that the sampling distribution of $\bar{x}$ has a shape which is approximately normal. Also, the mean of the sampling distribution, $\mu_{\bar{x}}$, is

$$\mu_{\bar{x}} = \mu = 24.7 \text{ minutes}$$

and the standard deviation of the sampling distribution, $\sigma_{\bar{x}}$, is

$$\sigma_{\bar{x}} = \frac{\sigma}{\sqrt{n}} = \frac{19.3}{\sqrt{100}} = \frac{19.3}{10} = 1.93 \text{ minutes}$$

From experience, the pediatrician has learned that maximum operational efficiency for his practice is attained when the mean patient waiting time is $\mu = 22$ minutes. We, of course, having access to the records of all 4,500 patients, know that $\mu = 24.7$ and that, if the pediatrician is correct, his practice is not operating at maximum efficiency. But since this fact is unknown to the pediatrician, he will utilize the following decision-making procedure: If the sample mean waiting time, $\bar{x}$, of the randomly selected patients falls between 19 minutes and 25 minutes, the pediatrician will assume that μ is approximately 22 minutes and that his practice is operating close to maximum efficiency. If $\bar{x}$ falls outside the interval $(19, 25)$, the current patient appointment policy will be restructured.

a. Use the sampling distribution of $\bar{x}$ to find the probability that $\bar{x}$ falls between 19 minutes and 25 minutes.

b. The probability that you computed in part a is also the probability that the pediatrician will make the wrong decision and assume that the optimal mean waiting time has been nearly attained. If this probability is even as large as .15 to .20, the pediatrician is taking an unnecessary risk. Based on this probability, would you recommend that the pediatrician revise his strategy? (In Chapters 9 and 10 we will discuss a statistically valid decision-making process called a *test of hypothesis*.)

CASE STUDY 7.3
Estimating the Total Weight of Short-Leaf Pine Trees

Throughout this chapter, we have demonstrated that the sample mean $\bar{x}$ provides a useful estimate of the population mean μ. In this case study, we will show how to use the quantity $\bar{x}$ to obtain an estimate of a population total for a finite population.

Refer to Case Study 1.2 (p. 13). Suppose that a prospective investor desires an estimate of the total weight of short-leaf pine trees on the 40-acre tract of land located in western Arkansas. The population of interest to the investor, then, is the collection of weights of all trees on the property, and the target parameter is the sum of these weights, i.e., the total weight of the trees. How can we use the sample information provided by Table 1.1 to estimate the total weight? The first step is to determine the (approximate) number of trees on the entire 40-acre tract. Recall that the weights of the sample of 117 trees were obtained by "cruising" twenty ⅕-acre plots, a total of four acres. Since these four acres represent ¹⁄₁₀ of the total area of the 40-acre tract of land, it is reasonable to assume that the total number of trees, N, on the entire 40-acre property is approximately 10 times the number of trees on the sampled four acres, i.e., $N \approx 10(117) = 1,170$ trees. For the purposes of this case study, we will assume that the total number of trees on the entire tract is in fact 1,170.

Now consider the following relationship between a population total and a population mean μ:

Population total $= N\mu$

where N is the total number of observations in the (finite) population. Since the value of μ is usually unknown, so too is the population total. To estimate a population total, we simply substitute our best estimate of μ, namely $\bar{x}$, into the equation. Thus, an estimate of a population total is given as:

Estimated population total $= N\bar{x}$

where $\bar{x}$ is the mean of a sample of n elements selected at random from the population of N elements. Applying this to the case at hand, we obtain an estimate of the total weight of trees on the 40-acre tract of land:

Estimated total weight $= N\bar{x} = (1,170)\bar{x}$

where $\bar{x}$ is the mean weight of the sample of $n = 117$ trees selected from the entire population of $N = 1,170$ trees.

a. In Case Study 3.3 (p. 91), you computed $\bar{x}$, the mean weight of the sample of 117 short-leaf pine trees. Use this value to estimate the total weight of trees on the entire 40-acre tract of land.

b. Since $N\bar{x}$ is a sample statistic, it possesses a sampling distribution. Explain how you could generate (by computer) the sampling distribution of $N\bar{x}$.

c. From the properties of the sampling distribution of $\bar{x}$, it can be shown (proof omitted) that the sampling distribution of $N\bar{x}$ is approximately normal for large n, with a mean of $N\mu$ and a standard deviation of $N\sigma/\sqrt{n}$. Compute an estimate of the standard deviation of the sampling distribution of the estimated total weight of short-leaf pine trees. [*Hint:* Use $Ns/\sqrt{n}$ as an estimate of $N\sigma/\sqrt{n}$, where s is the sample standard deviation that you calculated for Case Study 3.3.]

d. Find the probability that your estimate of the total weight of short-leaf pine trees on the 40-acre tract, $N\bar{x}$, falls within 100,000 pounds of the true total weight. [*Hint:* Compute $P(N\mu - 100,000 < N\bar{x} < N\mu + 100,000)$, using the properties of the sampling distribution of $N\bar{x}$ given in part c and Table 3, Appendix E.]

REFERENCES   Hogg, R. V., & Craig, A. T. *Introduction to mathematical statistics.* 4th ed. New York: Macmillan, 1978. Chapter 4.

Neter, J., Wasserman, W., & Whitmore, G. A. *Fundamental statistics for business and economics.* 4th ed. Boston: Allyn and Bacon, 1973. Chapters 9, 10, and 11.

"Pollsters Blast ABC-TV's Survey." Gainesville *Sun*, October 31, 1980.

Sloan, F. A., & Lorant, J. H. "The role of patient waiting time: Evidence from physicians' practices." *Journal of Business*, October 1977, *50*, 486–507.

Summers, G., Peters, W., & Armstrong, C. *Basic statistics in business and economics.* 3d ed. Belmont, Ca.: Wadsworth, 1981. Chapter 7.

Eight

Estimation of Means and Proportions

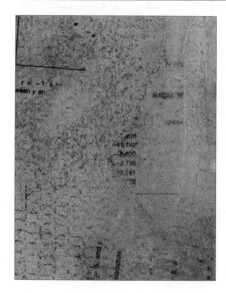

The newly formed *Florida Independent Professional,* a monthly newspaper for accountants, engineers, physicians, lawyers, and other professionals, mailed the newspaper free of charge to 166,000 professionals in the state. Management wished to conduct a survey of a sample selected from the 166,000 recipients of the newspaper to examine their attitudes and to estimate the proportion of all professionals in the state who were favorably impressed by the *Professional*'s content. How many of the 166,000 recipients of the paper should be sampled? How does the sample size affect the accuracy of the estimate? In this chapter you will learn how sample size and other factors affect the behavior of sample statistics.

Contents:

8.1 Introduction

In preceding chapters we learned that populations are characterized by numerical descriptive measures (parameters), and that inferences about parameter values are based on statistics computed from the information in a sample selected from the population of interest. In this chapter, we will demonstrate how to estimate population means or proportions, and how to estimate the difference between two population means or proportions. We will also be able to assess the reliability of our estimates, based on knowledge of the sampling distributions of the statistics being used.

EXAMPLE 8.1 Suppose we are interested in estimating the average sale price of all residential properties sold during 1978 in the Florida city described in Chapter 1. (Recall that the target population consists of the 2,862 observations on sale price in Appendix A. Although we already know the value of the population mean, this example will be continued to illustrate the concepts involved in estimation.) How could one estimate the parameter of interest in this situation?

Solution An intuitively appealing estimate of a population mean, μ, is the sample mean, $\bar{x}$, computed from a random sample of n observations from the target population. Assume, for example, that we obtain a random sample of size $n = 30$ from the sale price measurements in Appendix A, and then compute the sample mean and find its value to be $\bar{x} = \$43,560$. This value of $\bar{x}$ provides a **point estimate** of the population mean.

DEFINITION 8.1

A **point estimate** of a parameter is a statistic, a single value computed from observations in a sample, that is used to estimate the value of the target parameter.

How reliable is a point estimate for a parameter? In order to be truly practical and meaningful, an inference concerning a parameter (in this case, estimation of the value of μ) must consist not only of a point estimate, but also must be accompanied by a measure of the reliability of the estimate; that is, we need to be able to state how close our estimate is likely to be to the true value of the population parameter. This can be done by using the characteristics of the sampling distribution of the statistic which was used to obtain the point estimate; the procedure will be illustrated in the next section.

8.2 Estimation of a Population Mean: Large-Sample Case

Recall from Section 7.4 that, for sufficiently large sample sizes, the sampling distribution of the sample mean, $\bar{x}$, is approximately normal, as indicated in Figure 8.1.

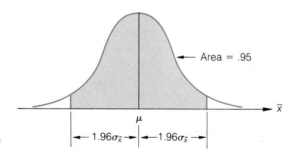

FIGURE 8.1
Sampling Distribution of $\bar{x}$

EXAMPLE 8.2   Suppose we plan to take a sample of $n = 30$ measurements from the population of sale prices in Appendix A and construct the interval

$$\bar{x} \pm 1.96\sigma_{\bar{x}} = \bar{x} \pm 1.96\left(\frac{\sigma}{\sqrt{n}}\right)$$

where σ is the population standard deviation of the 2,862 sale price values. In other words, we will construct an interval 1.96 standard deviations around the sample mean, $\bar{x}$. What can we say about how likely it is that this interval will contain the true value of the population mean, μ?

Solution   We arrive at a solution by the following three-step process:

Step 1.   First note that the area beneath the sampling distribution of $\bar{x}$ between $\mu - 1.96\sigma_{\bar{x}}$ and $\mu + 1.96\sigma_{\bar{x}}$ is approximately .95. (This area, shaded in Figure 8.1, is obtained from Table 3, Appendix E.) This implies that before the sample of 30 measurements is drawn, the probability that $\bar{x}$ will fall in the interval $\mu \pm 1.96\sigma_{\bar{x}}$ is .95.

Step 2.   If in fact the sample yields a value of $\bar{x}$ that falls within the interval $\mu \pm 1.96\sigma_{\bar{x}}$, then it is also true that the interval $\bar{x} \pm 1.96\sigma_{\bar{x}}$ will contain μ. This point is demonstrated in Figure 8.2. For a particular value of $\bar{x}$ (shown with an arrow) which falls within the interval $\mu \pm 1.96\sigma_{\bar{x}}$, a distance of $1.96\sigma_{\bar{x}}$ is drawn both to the left and to the right of $\bar{x}$. You can see that the value of μ must fall between $\bar{x} \pm 1.96\sigma_{\bar{x}}$.

Step 3.   Steps 1 and 2 combined imply that, before the sample is drawn, the probability that the interval $\bar{x} \pm 1.96\sigma_{\bar{x}}$ will enclose μ is approximately .95.

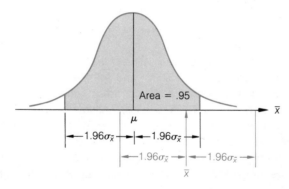

FIGURE 8.2
Sampling Distribution of $\bar{x}$,
Example 8.2

The interval $\bar{x} \pm 1.96\sigma_{\bar{x}} = \bar{x} \pm 1.96(\sigma/\sqrt{n})$ is called a large-sample 95% *confidence interval* for the population mean μ. The term *large-sample* refers to the sample being of such a size that we can apply the Central Limit Theorem to determine the form of the sampling distribution of $\bar{x}$. Although it is arbitrary, the conventional rule of thumb is that a sample size of $n \geq 30$ is required to employ large-sample confidence interval procedures.

DEFINITION 8.2

A *confidence interval* for a parameter is an interval of numbers within which we expect the true value of the population parameter to be contained. The endpoints of the interval are computed based on sample information.

EXAMPLE 8.3   Suppose that a random sample of 30 observations from the population of sale prices yielded the following sample statistics:

$$\bar{x} = \$43,560$$
$$s = \$17,435$$

Construct a 95% confidence interval for μ, the population mean sale price, based on this sample information.

Solution   A 95% confidence interval for μ, based on a sample of size $n = 30$, is given by

$$\bar{x} \pm 1.96\sigma_{\bar{x}} = \bar{x} \pm 1.96\left(\frac{\sigma}{\sqrt{n}}\right)$$

$$= 43,560 \pm 1.96\left(\frac{\sigma}{\sqrt{30}}\right)$$

In most practical applications, the value of the population standard deviation, σ, will be unknown. However, for large samples ($n \geq 30$), the sample standard deviation, s, provides a good approximation to σ, and may be used in the formula. Then the confidence interval becomes

$$43,560 \pm 1.96\frac{17,435}{\sqrt{30}} = 43,560 \pm 6,239$$

or (37,321, 49,799). Hence, we estimate that the population mean sale price falls within the interval between \$37,321 and \$49,799.

How much confidence do we have that μ, the true population mean sale price, lies within the interval (\$37,321, \$49,799)? Although we cannot be certain whether the sample interval contains μ (unless we calculate the true value of μ for all 2,862 observations), we can be reasonably sure that it does. This confidence is based on the interpretation of the confidence interval procedure: If we were to select repeated random samples of size $n = 30$ sale prices, and form a 1.96 standard deviation interval around $\bar{x}$ for each sample, then approximately 95% of the intervals so constructed would contain μ. Thus, we are 95% confident that the particular interval ($37,321, $49,799) contains μ, and this is our measure of the reliability of the point estimate $\bar{x}$.

EXAMPLE 8.4   To illustrate the classical interpretation of a confidence interval, we generated 40 random samples, each of size $n = 30$, from the population of sale prices in Appendix A. For each sample, the sample mean and standard deviation are presented in Table 8.1. We then constructed the 95% confidence interval for μ, using the information from each sample. Interpret the results, which are shown in Table 8.2 (p. 222).

Solution   For the target population of 2,862 sale prices, we have previously obtained the population mean value, $\mu = \$42,040$. In the 40 repetitions of the confidence interval procedure described above, note that only 2 of the intervals (those based on samples 13 and 19) do not contain the value of μ, whereas the remaining 38 of the 40 intervals (or 95% of the intervals) do contain the true value of μ.

   Keep in mind that, in actual practice, you would not know the true value of μ and you would not perform this repeated sampling; rather you would select a single random sample and construct the associated 95% confidence interval. The one confidence interval you form may or may not contain μ, but you can be fairly sure it does because of your confidence in the statistical procedure, the basis for which was illustrated in this example.

TABLE 8.1

SAMPLE	MEAN	STANDARD DEVIATION	SAMPLE	MEAN	STANDARD DEVIATION
1	39983.3	22129.9	21	50501.7	37621.3
2	38000.0	18024.2	22	49026.7	67388.7
3	44041.8	26976.1	23	38446.7	17341.5
4	45316.7	17983.0	24	37651.7	18241.6
5	37483.3	13556.8	25	42000.0	15938.4
6	37411.7	18572.8	26	41020.0	14006.3
7	51405.0	69778.7	27	38142.0	15074.1
8	37293.3	15332.3	28	40353.3	15455.8
9	40885.3	16989.1	29	46561.0	25622.7
10	38393.3	12804.6	30	48783.3	42795.2
11	39345.6	12806.8	31	38321.7	12525.3
12	44713.3	21075.6	32	37996.7	12064.9
13	51828.3	20695.8	33	40980.0	14703.3
14	36900.0	15372.5	34	41433.3	17168.5
15	46753.3	21253.3	35	37231.7	15194.4
16	41300.0	18257.9	36	41636.0	17058.7
17	37563.3	21338.1	37	43316.7	20257.2
18	40856.7	19441.9	38	38173.3	11380.3
19	34463.3	11622.1	39	42780.0	14949.9
20	41815.0	18906.2	40	37015.7	17274.2

TABLE 8.2

SAMPLE	CORRESPONDING 95% CONFIDENCE INTERVAL FOR μ	SAMPLE	CORRESPONDING 95% CONFIDENCE INTERVAL FOR μ
1	(32064.3, 47902.4)	21	(37039.1, 63964.3)
2	(31550.1, 44449.9)	22	(24911.9, 73141.4)
3	(34388.6, 53695.1)	23	(32241.1, 44652.2)
4	(38881.5, 51751.8)	24	(31124.0, 44179.3)
5	(32632.1, 42334.6)	25	(36296.5, 47703.5)
6	(30765.5, 44057.8)	26	(36007.9, 46032.1)
7	(26435.0, 76375.0)	27	(32747.8, 43536.2)
8	(31806.7, 42779.9)	28	(34822.5, 45884.1)
9	(34805.9, 46964.8)	29	(37392.0, 55730.0)
10	(33811.3, 42975.4)	30	(33469.3, 64097.4)
11	(34762.8, 43928.4)	31	(33839.6, 42803.8)
12	(37171.5, 52255.1)	32	(33679.3, 42314.0)
13	(44422.4, 59234.2)	33	(35718.5, 46241.5)
14	(31399.0, 42401.0)	34	(35289.7, 47577.0)
15	(39147.9, 54358.7)	35	(31794.4, 42668.9)
16	(34766.5, 47833.5)	36	(35531.6, 47740.4)
17	(29927.6, 45199.1)	37	(36067.7, 50565.6)
18	(33899.5, 47813.9)	38	(34100.9, 42245.7)
19	(30304.4, 38622.2)	39	(37430.3, 48129.7)
20	(35049.5, 48580.5)	40	(30834.2, 43197.1)

Suppose you wish to construct an interval which you believe will contain μ with some degree of confidence other than 95%; that is, you want to choose a confidence coefficient other than .95.

DEFINITION 8.3

The *confidence coefficient* is the proportion of times that a confidence interval encloses the true value of the population parameter if the confidence interval procedure is used repeatedly a very large number of times.

The first step in learning how to construct a confidence interval with any desired confidence coefficient is to notice from Figure 8.1 that, for a 95% confidence interval, the confidence coefficient of .95 is equal to the total area under the sampling distribution, less .05 of the area which is divided equally between the two tails of the distribution. Thus, each of the tails has an area of .025. Secondly, consider that the tabulated value of z from Table 3, Appendix E, which cuts off an area of .025 in the right tail of the standard normal distribution is 1.96 (see Figure 8.3). The value $z = 1.96$ is also the distance, in terms of standard deviations, that $\bar{x}$ is from the upper endpoint of the 95% confidence interval. Thus, this z-value provides the key to constructing a confidence interval with any desired confidence coefficient.

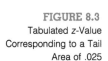

FIGURE 8.3
Tabulated z-Value
Corresponding to a Tail
Area of .025

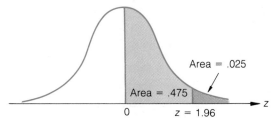

By assigning a confidence coefficient other than .95 to the confidence interval, we change the area under the sampling distribution between the endpoints of the interval, which in turn changes the tail area associated with z. In general, we have:

DEFINITION 8.4

$z_{\alpha/2}$ is defined to be the z-value such that an area of $\alpha/2$ lies to its right (see Figure 8.4).

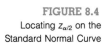

FIGURE 8.4
Locating $z_{\alpha/2}$ on the
Standard Normal Curve

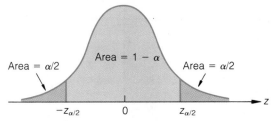

Now, if an area of $\alpha/2$ lies beyond $z_{\alpha/2}$ in the right tail of the distribution, then an area of $\alpha/2$ lies to the left of $-z_{\alpha/2}$ in the left tail (Figure 8.4) because of the symmetry of the distribution. The remaining area, $(1 - \alpha)$, is equal to the confidence coefficient; i.e., the probability that $\bar{x}$ falls within $z_{\alpha/2}$ standard deviations of μ is $(1 - \alpha)$. Thus, a large-sample confidence interval for μ, with confidence coefficient equal to $(1 - \alpha)$, is given by

$$\bar{x} \pm z_{\alpha/2}\sigma_{\bar{x}}$$

EXAMPLE 8.5 In published works which employ confidence interval techniques, a very common confidence coefficient is .90. Determine the value of $z_{\alpha/2}$ which would be used in constructing a 90% confidence interval for a population mean based on large samples.

Solution For a confidence coefficient of .90, we have

$$1 - \alpha = .90$$
$$\alpha = .10$$
$$\alpha/2 = .05$$

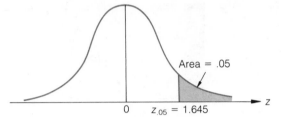

FIGURE 8.5
Location of $z_{\alpha/2}$ for
Example 8.5

and we need to obtain the value $z_{\alpha/2} = z_{.05}$ which locates an area of .05 in the upper tail of the standard normal distribution. Since the total area to the right of 0 is .50, $z_{.05}$ will be the value such that the area between 0 and $z_{.05}$ will be $.50 - .05 = .45$. From the body of Table 3, Appendix E, we find $z_{.05} = 1.645$ (see Figure 8.5). We conclude that a large-sample 90% confidence interval for a population mean is given by

$$\bar{x} \pm 1.645\sigma_{\bar{x}}$$

In Table 8.3, we present the values of $z_{\alpha/2}$ for the most commonly used confidence coefficients.

TABLE 8.3
Commonly Used
Confidence Coefficients

CONFIDENCE COEFFICIENT $1 - \alpha$	$\alpha/2$	$z_{\alpha/2}$
.90	.05	1.645
.95	.025	1.96
.98	.01	2.33
.99	.005	2.58

A summary of the large-sample confidence interval procedure for estimating a population mean appears in the accompanying box.

LARGE-SAMPLE $(1 - \alpha)$ 100% CONFIDENCE INTERVAL FOR A POPULATION MEAN, μ

$$\bar{x} \pm z_{\alpha/2}\sigma_{\bar{x}} = \bar{x} \pm z_{\alpha/2}\frac{\sigma}{\sqrt{n}}$$

where $z_{\alpha/2}$ is the z-value which locates an area of $\alpha/2$ to its right, σ is the standard deviation of the population from which the sample was selected, n is the sample size, and $\bar{x}$ is the value of the sample mean.
[*Note:* When the value of σ is unknown (as will usually be the case), the sample standard deviation s may be used to approximate σ in the formula for the confidence interval.]

EXAMPLE 8.6   Based on the set of all residential properties which were sold during 1978 in the Florida city, we wish to assess the collective ability of the city's real estate appraisers. A random sample of $n = 50$ observations from the population of values of ratio of sale price to total appraised value, Appendix A, produced the following statistics:

$$\bar{x} = 1.586$$

$$s = .462$$

Estimate μ, the mean ratio of sale price to total appraised value for all properties sold in 1978, using a 99% confidence interval. Interpret the interval in terms of the problem.

Solution   The general form of a large-sample 99% confidence interval for μ is

$$\bar{x} \pm 2.58 \frac{\sigma}{\sqrt{n}}$$

We will substitute the value of s for σ to obtain

$$1.586 \pm 2.58 \frac{.462}{\sqrt{50}} = 1.586 \pm .169$$

or (1.417, 1.755).

We can be 99% confident that the interval (1.417, 1.755) encloses the true mean ratio of sale price to total appraised value for all residential properties sold in the mid-sized Florida city in 1978. Since all the values in the interval exceed 1, we conclude that there was a general tendency for the sale price of a property in 1978 to exceed its total appraised value. Further investigation would be required to relate this phenomenon to the skills of the appraisers in this city.

EXAMPLE 8.7   Refer to Example 8.6.

a.   Using the sample information provided in Example 8.6, construct a 95% confidence interval for the mean ratio of sale price to total appraised value for properties sold in 1978 in this Florida city.

b.   For a fixed sample size, how does the width of the confidence interval relate to the confidence coefficient?

Solution   a.   The form of a large-sample 95% confidence interval for a population mean μ is

$$\bar{x} \pm 1.96 \frac{\sigma}{\sqrt{n}} \approx \bar{x} \pm 1.96 \frac{s}{\sqrt{n}}$$

$$= 1.586 \pm 1.96 \frac{.462}{\sqrt{50}}$$

$$= 1.586 \pm .128$$

or (1.458, 1.714).

b.   The 99% confidence interval for μ was determined in Example 8.6 to be (1.417, 1.755). The 95% confidence interval, obtained in part a and based on the same sample information, is narrower than the 99% confidence interval. This will hold true in general, as noted in the box at the top of the next page.

RELATION OF WIDTH OF CONFIDENCE INTERVAL TO THE CONFIDENCE COEFFICIENT

For a given sample size, the width of the confidence interval for a parameter increases as the confidence coefficient increases. Intuitively, the interval must become wider for us to have greater assurance (confidence) that it contains the true parameter value.

EXAMPLE 8.8   Refer to Example 8.6.

a.   Assume that the given values of the statistics $\bar{x}$ and s were based on a sample of size $n = 100$ instead of a sample of size $n = 50$. Construct a 99% confidence interval for μ, the population mean ratio of sale price to total appraised value.

b.   For a fixed confidence coefficient, how does the width of the confidence interval relate to the sample size?

Solution   a.   Substitution of the values of the sample statistics into the general formula for a 99% confidence interval for μ yields

$$\bar{x} \pm 2.58 \frac{\sigma}{\sqrt{n}} \approx 1.586 \pm 2.58 \frac{.462}{\sqrt{100}}$$

$$= 1.586 \pm .119$$

or (1.467, 1.705).

b.   The 99% confidence interval based on a sample of size $n = 100$, part a, is narrower than the 99% confidence interval constructed from a sample of size $n = 50$, Example 8.6. This will also hold true in general, as noted in the box.

RELATION OF WIDTH OF CONFIDENCE INTERVAL TO THE SAMPLE SIZE

For a fixed confidence coefficient, the width of the confidence interval decreases as the sample size increases. In other words, larger samples generally provide more information about the target population than do smaller samples.

In this section, we have introduced the concepts of point and interval estimation for the population mean, μ, based on large samples. The general theory appropriate for the estimation of μ also carries over to the estimation of other population parameters. Hence, in subsequent sections, we will present only the point estimate, its sampling distribution, the general form of a confidence interval for the parameter of interest, and any assumptions required for the validity of the procedure.

EXERCISES   **8.1** In a large-sample confidence interval for a population mean, what does the confidence coefficient represent?

8.2 Use Table 3, Appendix E, to determine the value of $z_{\alpha/2}$ which would be used to construct a large-sample confidence interval for μ, for each of the following confidence coefficients:

   a. .85   **b.** .95   **c.** .975

8.3 Give a precise interpretation of the statement, "We are 95% confident that the interval estimate contains μ."

8.4 Legislators in a certain state wish to investigate the amount of revenue lost in taxes on federal government-owned properties, which are not subject to state or local taxes. A random sample of 36 records for government-owned properties throughout the state indicated that, at current tax rates, the amount which would be assessed annually to each property had a mean of $\bar{x} = \$3,412$ and a standard deviation of $s = \$580$. Estimate the mean annual tax which would be assessed on a government property in this state, using a 98% confidence interval.

8.5 Refer to Exercise 8.4. What steps could you take to reduce the width of the confidence interval for the population mean?

8.6 You are interested in purchasing a new automobile which is designed to run most efficiently when fueled by gasohol. Before you decide whether or not to buy this model, you desire an estimate of the mean highway mileage obtained by the car. Information pertaining to highway mileages for 35 randomly selected gasohol-fueled models tested by the EPA is summarized as follows:

     $\bar{x} = 37.1$ miles per gallon

     $s = 1.4$ miles per gallon

Construct a 95% confidence interval for the mean highway gasohol mileage obtained by all cars of this model. Interpret the interval.

8.7 By law, a manufacturer of a food product is required to list Food and Drug Administration (FDA) estimates of the contents of the packaged product. Suppose that the FDA wished to estimate the mean sugar content (by weight) in a 16-ounce box of corn flakes. The FDA randomly selected 100 boxes of corn flakes and measured the sugar content in each, with the following results: $\bar{x} = 3.2$ ounces, $s = .5$ ounces.

   a. Estimate the true mean sugar content in the 16-ounce boxes of corn flakes cereal with a 90% confidence interval.

   b. Interpret the interval, part a.

   c. How could the FDA reduce the width of the confidence interval in part a? Are there any drawbacks to reducing the interval width? Explain.

8.8 Refer to the data given in Appendix D. The manager of supermarket B, which uses automated checkers, desires an estimate of the average customer service time at the supermarket. Select a random sample of 30 checkout service times and use this information to construct a 99% confidence interval for the true average customer service time at supermarket B. Interpret your interval.

8.9 As part of a Department of Energy survey, 240 American families were randomly selected and interviewed concerning the amount of money they spent last year on home heating oil or gas. The survey results indicated that the amount spent by the 240 families had an average of $425 and a standard deviation of $130.

a. Give a point estimate for the true mean amount spent, per family, last year on home heating oil or gas.

b. Use the sample information to construct a 97% confidence interval for the true mean amount of money, per family, spent last year on home heating oil or gas.

c. What is the confidence coefficient for the interval, part b? Interpret this value.

d. Based upon your interval, part b, would you expect the true mean annual expenditure per family on home heating oil or gas to fall below $400?

8.3 Estimation of a Population Mean: Small-Sample Case

In the previous section, we discussed estimation of a population mean based on large samples (samples of size 30 or greater). However, time or cost limitations may often restrict the number of sample observations which may be obtained, so that the estimation procedures of Section 8.2 would not be applicable.

With small samples, the following two problems arise:

1. Since the Central Limit Theorem applies only to large samples, we are not able to assume that the sampling distribution of $\bar{x}$ is approximately normal. For small samples, the sampling distribution of $\bar{x}$ depends on the particular form of the relative frequency distribution of the population being sampled.

2. The sample standard deviation s may not be a satisfactory approximation to the population standard deviation σ if the sample size is small.

Fortunately, we may proceed with estimation techniques based on small samples if we can make the following assumption:

ASSUMPTION REQUIRED FOR ESTIMATION OF μ BASED ON SMALL SAMPLES ($n < 30$)

The population from which the sample is selected has an approximate normal distribution.

If this assumption is valid, then we may again use $\bar{x}$ as a point estimate for μ, and the general form of a small-sample confidence interval for μ is as shown in the box at the top of the next page.

Upon comparing this to the large-sample confidence interval for μ, you will observe that the sample standard deviation s replaces the population standard deviation σ. Also, the sampling distribution upon which the confidence interval is based is no longer normal, but is known as a *Student's t distribution*. Consequently,

---

SMALL-SAMPLE CONFIDENCE INTERVAL FOR μ

$$\bar{x} \pm t_{\alpha/2} \frac{s}{\sqrt{n}}$$

where the distribution of t is based on $(n-1)$ degrees of freedom.

---

we must replace the value of $z_{\alpha/2}$ used in a large-sample confidence interval by a value obtained from the t distribution.

The t distribution is very much like the z distribution. In particular, both are symmetric, mound-shaped, and have a mean of zero. However, the distribution of t depends on a quantity called its **degrees of freedom (df),** which is equal to $(n-1)$ when estimating a population mean based on a small sample of size n. Intuitively, we can think of the number of degrees of freedom as the amount of information available for estimating, in addition to μ, the unknown quantity σ^2. Table 4, Appendix E, a portion of which is reproduced in Figure 8.6, gives the value of t_α which locates an area of α in the upper tail of the t distribution for various values of α and for degrees of freedom ranging from 1 to 29.

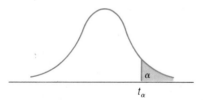

DEGREES OF FREEDOM	$t_{.100}$	$t_{.050}$	$t_{.025}$	$t_{.010}$	$t_{.005}$
1	3.078	6.314	12.706	31.821	63.657
2	1.886	2.920	4.303	6.965	9.925
3	1.638	2.353	3.182	4.541	5.841
4	1.533	2.132	2.776	3.747	4.604
5	1.476	2.015	2.571	3.365	4.032
6	1.440	1.943	2.447	3.143	3.707
7	1.415	1.895	2.365	2.998	3.499
8	1.397	1.860	2.306	2.896	3.355
9	1.383	1.833	2.262	2.821	3.250
10	1.372	1.812	2.228	2.764	3.169
11	1.363	1.796	2.201	2.718	3.106
12	1.356	1.782	2.179	2.681	3.055
13	1.350	1.771	2.160	2.650	3.012
14	1.345	1.761	2.145	2.624	2.977
15	1.341	1.753	2.131	2.602	2.947

FIGURE 8.6
Reproduction of a Portion
of Table 4, Appendix E

EXAMPLE 8.9   Use Table 4, Appendix E, to determine the *t*-value which would be used in constructing a 95% confidence interval for μ based on a sample of size $n = 14$.

Solution   For a confidence coefficient of .95, we have

$$1 - \alpha = .95$$
$$\alpha = .05$$
$$\alpha/2 = .025$$

We thus require the value of $t_{.025}$ for a *t* distribution based on $n - 1 = 14 - 1 = 13$
degrees of freedom. Now, in Table 4, at the intersection of the column labelled $t_{.025}$
and the row corresponding to df $= 13$, we find the entry 2.160 (see Figure 8.7). Hence,
a 95% confidence interval for μ, based on a sample of 14 observations, would be
given by

$$\bar{x} \pm 2.160 \frac{s}{\sqrt{14}}$$

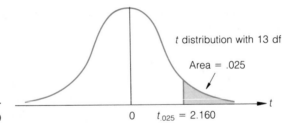

FIGURE 8.7
Location of $t_{.025}$ for
Example 8.9

At this point, the reasoning for the arbitrary cutoff point of $n = 30$ for dis-
tinguishing between large and small samples may be better understood. Observe that
the values in the last row of Table 4 (corresponding to df $=$ infinity) are the values from
the standard normal *z* distribution. This phenomenon occurs because, as the sample
size increases, the *t* distribution becomes more and more like the *z* distribution. By the
time *n* reaches 30, i.e., df $= 29$, there is very little difference between tabulated values
of *t* and *z*.

EXAMPLE 8.10   The Chamber of Commerce of a large city is interested in monthly rental rates of
3-bedroom, 2-bath apartments in the area. The managers of six apartment complexes
submitted the following monthly rental rates for their 3-bedroom, 2-bath units:

$340, $405, $260, $500, $380, $390

a.   Construct a 90% confidence interval for μ, the average monthly rental rate of a
3-bedroom, 2-bath apartment in this area.
b.   State the assumption(s) required for the validity of the procedure you used in
part a.

Solution   **a.**   It is first required to compute the values of the sample mean and standard deviation:

$$\bar{x} = \frac{\Sigma x}{n} = \frac{340 + 405 + 260 + 500 + 380 + 390}{6} = 379.17$$

$$s = \sqrt{\frac{\Sigma x^2 - (\Sigma x)^2/n}{n-1}}$$

$$= \sqrt{\frac{(340)^2 + (405)^2 + (260)^2 + (500)^2 + (380)^2 + (390)^2 - (2{,}275)^2/6}{5}}$$

$$= \sqrt{\frac{893{,}725 - 862{,}604.17}{5}} = \sqrt{6{,}224.1667} = 78.89$$

A small-sample 90% confidence interval for μ will be based on $t_{\alpha/2} = t_{.05}$, where the distribution of t has $n - 1 = 6 - 1 = 5$ df. From Table 4, we obtain the value

$$t_{.05} = 2.015$$

Substitution of these values into the general form for a 90% confidence interval yields:

$$\bar{x} \pm t_{.05}\frac{s}{\sqrt{n}} = 379.17 \pm 2.015\frac{78.89}{\sqrt{6}}$$

$$= 379.17 \pm 64.90$$

or (314.27, 444.07).

We are 90% confident that the interval \$314.27 to \$444.07 encloses the true average rental rate for a 3-bedroom, 2-bath apartment in this area. If we were to employ this estimation procedure for repeated random samples, then 90% of the intervals constructed in this manner would contain the true value of μ.

b.   The procedure requires the assumption that the relative frequency distribution of the prices for all 3-bedroom, 2-bath apartments in the area is approximately normal.

EXAMPLE 8.11   Rising interest rates on loans to new automobile purchasers are pushing potential customers out of the market. Suppose that it is desired to estimate the average interest rate charged for a 48-month loan to new car buyers in Michigan last year. The 48-month loan statements for a random sample of $n = 20$ new car buyers in Michigan were selected, and the interest rate charged was recorded for each. The following summary statistics were computed:

$$\bar{x} = 16.05\%$$

$$s = 1.25\%$$

Estimate μ, the average interest rate charged for a 48-month loan last year to new car buyers in Michigan, with a 95% confidence interval.

Solution Since we must base our estimation procedure on a small sample ($n = 20$), it is necessary to assume that the population of interest rates charged on 48-month loans to new car buyers in Michigan last year has a relative frequency distribution which is approximately normal.

The desired confidence interval is based on a t distribution with $n - 1 = 20 - 1 = 19$ degrees of freedom; we obtain the value of $t_{\alpha/2} = t_{.025} = 2.093$ from Table 4, Appendix E. Then we have

$$\bar{x} \pm t_{.025}\frac{s}{\sqrt{n}} = 16.05 \pm 2.093\frac{1.25}{\sqrt{20}}$$

$$= 16.05 \pm .585$$

or (15.465%, 16.635%).

Thus, we are reasonably confident that the interval from 15.465% to 16.635% contains the true average interest rate charged on a 48-month new car loan in Michigan last year.

EXERCISES **8.10** Use Table 4, Appendix E, to determine the values of $t_{\alpha/2}$ which would be used in the construction of a confidence interval for a population mean for each of the following combinations of confidence coefficient and sample size:

a. Confidence coefficient .99, $n = 18$
b. Confidence coefficient .95, $n = 10$
c. Confidence coefficient .90, $n = 15$

8.11 Give two reasons why the interval estimation procedure of Section 8.2 may not be applicable when the sample size is small, i.e., when $n < 30$.

8.12 A major utilities firm is currently working with the U.S. Department of Energy in developing an electric car. A prototype, which needs absolutely no gasoline, has already been developed. Tests on a random sample of $n = 8$ of these prototype electric cars produced the following statistics on maximum speed attained:

$\bar{x} = 54.8$ miles per hour

$s = 10.3$ miles per hour

a. Estimate the average maximum speed of all prototype electric cars manufactured by this utilities firm, using a 99% confidence interval.
b. What assumption is required for the confidence interval procedure of part a to be valid?

8.13 A branch office of a company must periodically make shipments to a certain branch office in another state. In order to estimate the mean delivery time of shipments between the two offices, five randomly selected shipments are monitored and the delivery time is recorded for each. The results are:

$\bar{x} = 14.71$ hours

$s = .87$ hours

a. Construct a 90% confidence interval for the true mean delivery time for all shipments between the two branch offices.

b. How would the width of the interval change if the sample size were increased from $n = 5$ to $n = 20$?

c. What assumption is required for the confidence interval procedure of part a to be valid?

8.14 A random sample of 25 families living in a particular housing district yielded the following summary statistics on annual income:

$\bar{x} = \$31,000$

$s = \$4,500$

a. Provide a 95% confidence interval for the average annual income for all families within the housing district. Interpret your result.

b. What assumption is required for the confidence interval procedure of part a to be valid?

8.15 How are the t distribution and z distribution similar? How are they different?

8.16 One of the problems encountered by fresh fruit growers is spoilage of the fruit during transport to market. Each day during the harvest, a Florida citrus grower transports 100 bushels of fruit by truck to the nearest market to be sold. In order to estimate the mean number of bushels of fruit per truckload lost to spoilage, the citrus grower randomly selects 6 departing truckloads (each carrying 100 bushels of fresh fruit) and counts the number of bushels of spoiled fruit in each at the end of the trip. Suppose that these 6 sample measurements produce a mean of 10.1 bushels and a standard deviation of 2.8 bushels.

a. State the assumption, in the words of the problem, which is required for a small-sample confidence interval technique to be valid.

b. Construct a 98% confidence interval for the true mean number of bushels of spoiled fruit per truckload.

c. Interpret the interval, part b.

8.17 Designer jeans (Jordache, Calvin Klein, Brittania, Sassoon, etc.) became best-selling items despite their high retail price. The jeans were very marketable because they were designed to fit both males and females and came to represent a symbol of status among the younger generation. In order to estimate the mean retail price of designer jeans, a buyer for a major clothing chain sampled 19 retailers in the New York City area and recorded the selling price of the particular brand of designer jeans sold by each. The following information was obtained:

$\bar{x} = \$41.75$

$s = \$ 5.50$

a. Form a 95% confidence interval for the true mean retail price of designer jeans in the New York City area.

b. What assumption is required for the interval estimation procedure, part a, to be valid?

c. Should the buyer for the major clothing chain use the interval to infer the value of the mean price of designer jeans at retail outlets across the entire U.S.? Explain.

8.4 Estimation of a Population Proportion: Large-Sample Case

We will now consider the method for estimating the proportion of elements in a population which have a certain characteristic. For example, a realtor would be interested in the proportion of condominium units located in South Florida which were furnished prior to their sale at auction; a mortgage lending institution would be interested in estimating the proportion of its customers who will default on their loans; or a supplier of heating oil might be interested in the proportion of homes in its service area heated by natural gas. How would you estimate a population proportion p (e.g., the proportion of condominium units which were furnished prior to sale), based on information contained in a sample from the population?

EXAMPLE 8.12   A local realty agency is interested in estimating the proportion of its clients who have previously owned a home or condominium. A random sample of 300 recent clients showed that 180 were previous owners of a home or condominium. Estimate the true proportion p of all the firm's clients who are previous owners of a residence.

Solution   A logical candidate for a point estimate of the population proportion p is the proportion of observations in the sample which have the characteristic of interest; we will call this sample proportion $\hat{p}$ (read "p hat"). In this example, the sample proportion of previous owners is given by

$$\hat{p} = \frac{\text{Number of clients in sample who were previous owners}}{\text{Total number of clients in the sample}}$$

$$= \frac{180}{300} = .60$$

That is, 60% of the clients in the sample previously owned a residence; the value $\hat{p} = .60$ serves as our point estimate of the population proportion, p.

To assess the reliability of the point estimate $\hat{p}$, we need to know its sampling distribution. This information may be derived by an application of the Central Limit Theorem (details are omitted here). Properties of the sampling distribution of $\hat{p}$ (Figure 8.8) are given in the box.

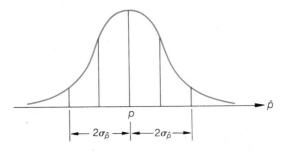

FIGURE 8.8
Sampling Distribution of $\hat{p}$

SAMPLING DISTRIBUTION OF $\hat{p}$

For sufficiently large samples, the sampling distribution of $\hat{p}$ is approximately normal, with

Mean $\mu_{\hat{p}} = p$

and

Standard deviation $\sigma_{\hat{p}} = \sqrt{\dfrac{pq}{n}}$

where $q = 1 - p$.

A large-sample confidence interval for p may be constructed by using a procedure which is analogous to that used for estimating a population mean.

LARGE-SAMPLE $(1 - \alpha)$ 100% CONFIDENCE INTERVAL FOR A POPULATION PROPORTION, p

$$\hat{p} \pm z_{\alpha/2}\sigma_{\hat{p}} \approx \hat{p} \pm z_{\alpha/2}\sqrt{\frac{\hat{p}\hat{q}}{n}}$$

where $\hat{p}$ is the sample proportion of observations with the characteristic of interest, and $\hat{q} = 1 - \hat{p}$.
[*Note:* We have substituted the sample values $\hat{p}$ and $\hat{q}$ for the corresponding population values required for $\sigma_{\hat{p}}$. This approximation is valid for large sample sizes.]

As a rule of thumb, the condition of a "sufficiently large" sample size will be satisfied if the interval $\hat{p} \pm 2\sigma_{\hat{p}}$ does not contain 0 or 1.

EXAMPLE 8.13   Refer to Example 8.12. Construct a 95% confidence interval for p, the population proportion of the realty agency's clients who have previously owned a home or condominium.

Solution   For a confidence coefficient of .95, we have $1 - \alpha = .95$; $\alpha = .05$; $\alpha/2 = .025$; and the required z-value is $z_{.025} = 1.96$. In Example 8.12, we obtained $\hat{p} = {}^{180}/_{300} = .60$. Thus, $\hat{q} = 1 - .60 = .40$. Substitution of these values into the general formula for a confidence interval yields

$$\hat{p} \pm z_{\alpha/2}\sqrt{\frac{\hat{p}\hat{q}}{n}} = .60 \pm 1.96\sqrt{\frac{(.60)(.40)}{300}}$$

$$= .60 \pm .06$$

or (.54, .66).

We are 95% confident that the interval from .54 to .66 contains the true proportion of the agency's clients who have previously owned their residence. That is, in repeated construction of 95% confidence intervals, 95% of all samples would produce confidence intervals that enclose p.

EXAMPLE 8.14 Each winter the struggle between the natural gas and oil industries to supply heating fuel to American homes increases. Recently, the American Gas Association (AGA) has undertaken a multimillion-dollar advertising campaign in the hopes of persuading the owners of homes heated with oil that gas is "the most efficient way to heat" (*Time*, December 1, 1980). Suppose that the AGA is interested in estimating the proportion of homes in the Northern states (where oil usage is heavy) which are heated by gas. A random sample of 80 Northern homes indicated that 42 were heated by gas and 38 were heated by oil or other fuels. Estimate p, the proportion of all Northern homes heated by gas, using a 90% confidence interval.

Solution The sample proportion of homes which are heated by gas is

$$\hat{p} = \frac{\text{Number of homes in sample which are heated by gas}}{\text{Number of homes in sample}}$$

$$= \frac{42}{80} = .525$$

Thus, $\hat{q} = 1 - .525 = .475$.

The 90% confidence interval is then

$$\hat{p} \pm z_{.05}\sqrt{\frac{\hat{p}\hat{q}}{n}} = .525 \pm 1.645\sqrt{\frac{(.525)(.475)}{80}}$$

$$= .525 \pm .092$$

or (.433, .617).

We are 90% confident that the interval from .433 to .617 encloses the true proportion of Northern homes which are heated by gas. If we repeatedly selected random samples of $n = 80$ Northern homes and constructed a 90% confidence interval based on each sample, then we would expect 90% of the confidence intervals constructed to contain p.

It should be noted that small-sample procedures are available for the estimation of a population proportion, p. The details are not included in our discussion, however, because most surveys in actual practice use samples that are large enough to employ the procedure of this section.

EXERCISES **8.18** A mortgage lending institution is interested in estimating p, the proportion of their customers who default within the first three years after receiving a loan. The records for a random sample of 100 people who received loans in 1978 were obtained; it was determined that 12 of these people defaulted on their loans in the following three years.

a. Construct a 95% confidence interval for the true proportion of this institution's loan recipients who default within three years.
b. Interpret the interval in terms of the problem.
c. How would the width of the confidence interval in part a change if the confidence coefficient were increased from .95 to .99?

8.19   Potential advertisers value television's well-known Nielsen ratings as a barometer of a TV show's popularity among viewers. The Nielsen rating of a certain TV program is an estimate of the proportion of viewers, expressed as a percentage, who tune their sets to the program on a given night. In a random selection of 165 families who regularly watch television, a Nielsen survey indicated that 101 of the families were tuned to a certain TV program on the night of its premiere. Estimate the true proportion of all TV-viewing families who watched the premiere. Use a 90% confidence interval.

8.20   As part of its normal audit procedure, a bank randomly selects 30 customer checking accounts and mails a statement of the balance showing in the bank's records to each customer. The customer is asked to compare his or her own statement of the balance with the bank's statement. If the statements disagree, the customer is requested to return to the bank a form describing the differences. If the statements agree, no reply is necessary. In last month's audit, 9 of the 30 customers mailed in the forms, i.e., 9 of the 30 received balance statements which disagreed with their own records. Estimate the true proportion of the bank's checking account customers who had balance statements which disagreed with the bank's records last month. Use a 98% confidence interval.

8.21   One piece of information of great interest to an individual who wishes to contract for the services of a home builder is the proportion of the builder's construction projects which are completed on or before the target date. The records for a random sample of 60 recent construction projects for a particular contractor indicated that 27 of the projects were completed on time and 33 extended beyond the estimated completion date.
a. Estimate p, the proportion of this builder's projects which are completed by the target date, using a 95% confidence interval.
b. Explain how the width of the interval constructed in part a could be decreased.

8.22   As part of the employee interview process at a large corporation, all applicants are required to take a written exam, scored from 0 to 700. Only those applicants who score above 500 on the exam are further considered for possible employment. Suppose that the company wishes to estimate the proportion of its applicants who score above 500 on the test. Exam results are obtained from the company's files for a random selection of 200 applicants. If 48 of the 200 applicants scored above 500 on the exam, find a 99% confidence interval for the true proportion of the company's applicants who score above 500. Interpret the interval.

8.23   The jobless figure compiled by the U.S. Bureau of the Census showed that in January 1981, 7.4% of the labor force was unemployed. However, some critics believe that this figure underestimates actual unemployment since so-called "discouraged workers," those who have given up hope of finding a job, are sometimes not counted as part of the labor force by the Bureau. Suppose that in a random sample of 1,000 members of the labor force, some of whom are discouraged workers, 86 are found to be unemployed.

a. Give a point estimate for the unemployment rate when discouraged workers are included.

b. Construct a 92% confidence interval for the true unemployment rate when discouraged workers are included.

c. Based upon your interval, part b, does it appear that the figure reported by the Census Bureau is actually an underestimate of the true unemployment rate when discouraged workers are included?

8.5   Estimation of the Difference between Two Population Means: Large-Sample Case

In Section 8.2, we learned how to estimate the parameter μ based on a large sample from a single population. We now proceed to a technique for using the information in two samples to estimate the difference between two population means. For example, we may wish to compare the mean 1978 sale prices for residential properties in neighborhoods D and E, or the mean gasoline consumptions that may be expected this year for drivers in two areas of the country, or the mean sales per customer for salesmen and saleswomen at a steel company. The technique to be presented is a straightforward extension of that used for large-sample estimation of a single population mean.

EXAMPLE 8.15   It is desired to estimate the difference between the mean sale prices for all residential properties sold during 1978 in neighborhoods D and E of the mid-sized Florida city. The following information is available:

1. A random sample of 30 sale prices for neighborhood D produced a sample mean of \$42,356 and a standard deviation of \$8,572.

2. A random sample of 40 sale prices for neighborhood E produced a sample mean of \$36,491 and a standard deviation of \$4,264.

Calculate a point estimate for the difference between mean sale prices for the two neighborhoods.

Solution   We will let the subscript 1 refer to neighborhood D and the subscript 2 to neighborhood E, and we will also define the following notation:

μ_1 = The population mean sale price of all neighborhood D residential properties sold in 1978

μ_2 = The population mean sale price of all neighborhood E residential properties sold in 1978

Similarly, let $\bar{x}_1$ and $\bar{x}_2$ denote the respective sample means; s_1 and s_2, the respective sample standard deviations; and n_1 and n_2, the respective sample sizes. The given information may be summarized as in Table 8.4.

TABLE 8.4

Summary of Information
for Example 8.15

	NEIGHBORHOOD D	NEIGHBORHOOD E
SAMPLE SIZE	$n_1 = 30$	$n_2 = 40$
SAMPLE MEAN	$\bar{x}_1 = \$42{,}356$	$\bar{x}_2 = \$36{,}491$
SAMPLE STANDARD DEVIATION	$s_1 = \$8{,}572$	$s_2 = \$4{,}264$

Now, to estimate $(\mu_1 - \mu_2)$, it seems logical to use the difference between the sample means

$$(\bar{x}_1 - \bar{x}_2) = (\$42{,}356 - \$36{,}491) = \$5{,}865$$

as our point estimate of the difference between the population means. The properties of the point estimate $(\bar{x}_1 - \bar{x}_2)$ are summarized by its sampling distribution, shown in the accompanying box (see also Figure 8.9).

SAMPLING DISTRIBUTION OF $(\bar{x}_1 - \bar{x}_2)$

For sufficiently large sample sizes (say, $n_1 \geq 30$ and $n_2 \geq 30$), the sampling distribution of $(\bar{x}_1 - \bar{x}_2)$, based on independent random samples from two populations, is approximately normal, with

Mean $\mu_{(\bar{x}_1 - \bar{x}_2)} = (\mu_1 - \mu_2)$

Standard deviation $\sigma_{(\bar{x}_1 - \bar{x}_2)} = \sqrt{\dfrac{\sigma_1^2}{n_1} + \dfrac{\sigma_2^2}{n_2}}$

where σ_1^2 and σ_2^2 are the variances of the two populations from which the samples were selected.

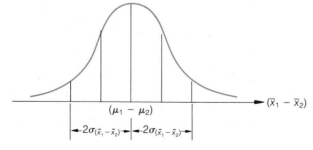

FIGURE 8.9

Sampling Distribution of
$(\bar{x}_1 - \bar{x}_2)$

As was the case with large-sample estimation of a single population mean, the requirement of "large" sample sizes enables us to apply the Central Limit Theorem to obtain the sampling distribution of $(\bar{x}_1 - \bar{x}_2)$; it also justifies the use of s_1^2 and s_2^2 as approximations to the respective population variances, σ_1^2 and σ_2^2.

The procedure for forming a confidence interval for $(\mu_1 - \mu_2)$ appears in the accompanying box.

LARGE-SAMPLE $(1 - \alpha)$ 100% CONFIDENCE INTERVAL FOR $(\mu_1 - \mu_2)$

$$(\bar{x}_1 - \bar{x}_2) \pm z_{\alpha/2}\sigma_{(\bar{x}_1 - \bar{x}_2)} = (\bar{x}_1 - \bar{x}_2) \pm z_{\alpha/2} \sqrt{\frac{\sigma_1^2}{n_1} + \frac{\sigma_2^2}{n_2}}$$

$$\approx (\bar{x}_1 - \bar{x}_2) \pm z_{\alpha/2} \sqrt{\frac{s_1^2}{n_1} + \frac{s_2^2}{n_2}}$$

[*Note:* We have employed the sample variances s_1^2 and s_2^2 as approximations to the corresponding population parameters.]

The assumptions upon which the above procedure is based are the following:

ASSUMPTIONS REQUIRED FOR LARGE-SAMPLE ESTIMATION OF $(\mu_1 - \mu_2)$

1. The two random samples are selected in an *independent* manner from the target populations. That is, the choice of elements in one sample does not affect, and is not affected by, the choice of elements in the other sample.
2. The sample sizes n_1 and n_2 are sufficiently large. (We recommend $n_1 \geq 30$ and $n_2 \geq 30$.)

EXAMPLE 8.16   Refer to Example 8.15. Construct a 95% confidence interval for $(\mu_1 - \mu_2)$, the difference between the mean sale prices for all residential properties in neighborhoods D and E which were sold during 1978. Interpret the interval.

Solution   The general form of a 95% confidence interval for $(\mu_1 - \mu_2)$, based on large samples from the target populations, is given by

$$(\bar{x}_1 - \bar{x}_2) \pm z_{.025} \sqrt{\frac{\sigma_1^2}{n_1} + \frac{\sigma_2^2}{n_2}}$$

Recall that $z_{.025} = 1.96$ and use the information in Table 8.4 to make the following substitutions to obtain the desired confidence interval:

$$(42,356 - 36,491) \pm 1.96 \sqrt{\frac{\sigma_1^2}{30} + \frac{\sigma_2^2}{40}}$$

$$\approx (42,356 - 36,491) \pm 1.96 \sqrt{\frac{(8,572)^2}{30} + \frac{(4,264)^2}{40}}$$

$$= 5,865 \pm 3,340$$

or ($2,525, $9,205).

The use of this method of estimation produces confidence intervals which will enclose $(\mu_1 - \mu_2)$, the difference between population means, 95% of the time. Hence, we can be reasonably confident that the mean sale price of neighborhood D homes in 1978 was between $2,525 and $9,205 higher than the mean sale price of neighborhood E homes during this period.

EXAMPLE 8.17 The personnel manager for a large steel company suspects a difference between the mean amounts of work time lost due to sickness for blue-collar and white-collar workers at the plant. She randomly samples the records of 45 blue-collar workers and 38 white-collar workers and records the number of days lost due to sickness within the past year. Summary statistics were computed, with the results shown in Table 8.5. Estimate $(\mu_1 - \mu_2)$, the difference between the population mean days lost to sickness for blue-collar and white-collar workers at the steel company last year, using a 90% confidence interval.

TABLE 8.5
Comparison of Lost Sick Days, Example 8.17

	BLUE COLLAR	WHITE COLLAR
SAMPLE SIZE	$n_1 = 45$	$n_2 = 38$
SAMPLE MEAN	$\bar{x}_1 = 10.4$	$\bar{x}_2 = 7.8$
SAMPLE STANDARD DEVIATION	$s_1 = 12.8$	$s_2 = 5.5$

Solution The general form of a large-sample 90% confidence interval for $(\mu_1 - \mu_2)$ is

$$(\bar{x}_1 - \bar{x}_2) \pm z_{.05} \sqrt{\frac{\sigma_1^2}{n_1} + \frac{\sigma_2^2}{n_2}}$$

Substitution of the sample variances, s_1^2 and s_2^2, for the corresponding population values, σ_1^2 and σ_2^2, together with $z_{.05} = 1.645$ and the statistics provided in Table 8.5, yields the approximate 90% confidence interval

$$(10.4 - 7.8) \pm 1.645 \sqrt{\frac{(12.8)^2}{45} + \frac{(5.5)^2}{38}} = 2.6 \pm 3.47$$

or $(-.87, 6.07)$.

Thus, we estimate that the difference between the mean days lost to sickness for the two groups of workers falls in the interval $-.87$ to 6.07. In other words, we estimate that μ_2, the mean days lost to sickness for white-collar workers, could be larger than μ_1, the mean days lost to sickness for blue-collar workers, by as much as .87, or it could be less than μ_1 by as much as 6.07. Since the interval contains the value zero, we are unable to conclude that there is a real difference between the mean numbers of sick days lost by the two groups. If, in fact, such a difference exists, we would have to increase the sample sizes to be able to detect it. This would reduce the width of the confidence interval and provide more information about the phenomenon under investigation.

EXERCISES **8.24** In the age of rapidly rising housing costs, comparisons are often made of the mean costs of new homes in different areas of the country. Recent random samples of the purchase prices for 100 new single-family dwellings in California and 80 such dwellings in Maine were obtained. A summary of the results is shown in Table 8.6. Estimate the difference between the mean costs of new single-family homes in California and those in Maine, using a 95% confidence interval. Interpret the interval.

TABLE 8.6
Comparison of Housing
Costs, Exercise 8.24
(Thousands of Dollars)

CALIFORNIA	MAINE
$n_1 = 100$	$n_2 = 80$
$\bar{x}_1 = 94.8$	$\bar{x}_2 = 73.4$
$s_1 = 12.75$	$s_2 = 16.8$

8.25 Every six months, Management Centre Europe (MCE), a Brussels-based consulting firm, measures living costs in 16 European cities for comparison with the cost of living in New York City. As a yardstick, MCE uses the dollar value of a group of 101 common items randomly selected from among foods, clothing, taxi rides, etc. In one survey, MCE wished to compare the costs of items in Stockholm, Sweden, to the costs in New York. MCE randomly selected 101 items and recorded their costs (in dollars) in Stockholm and in New York. The data are summarized in Table 8.7.

TABLE 8.7
Dollar Value of Common
Items, Exercise 8.25

STOCKHOLM	NEW YORK
$n_1 = 101$	$n_2 = 101$
$\bar{x}_1 = \$526$	$\bar{x}_2 = \$312$
$s_1 = \$214$	$s_2 = \$170$

a. Construct a 99% confidence interval for the difference between the mean costs of the common items in Stockholm and New York.
b. Interpret the interval.
c. Explain how MCE could decrease the width of the interval obtained in part a.

8.26 A distributor of coffee vending machines knows from experience that the mean number of cups of coffee a machine will sell per day varies according to the location of the machine. Thus, the distributor wishes to choose the location which maximizes daily profit. At a newly opened textile plant, two machines are placed on an experimental basis in what the distributor believes to be two different optimum locations. The machines are observed for 31 days (one month), and the number of cups of coffee sold per day for each machine is recorded. A summary of the data is given in Table 8.8.

TABLE 8.8
Coffee Machine Sales,
Exercise 8.26

LOCATION 1	LOCATION 2
$n_1 = 31$	$n_2 = 31$
$\bar{x}_1 = 50.6$	$\bar{x}_2 = 42.2$
$s_1 = 8.3$	$s_2 = 2.5$

a. Use the information provided in the table to find a 98% confidence interval for the difference between the mean numbers of cups sold per day at the two locations.
b. Based on the interval, part a, can the distributor conclude that either location is better than the other? [*Hint:* Is the value zero included in the interval?]

8.27 A restaurant specializing in all-natural foods has experienced a reduction in daily sales during the past year. The manager of the restaurant hopes to offset these losses by instituting a new advertising campaign. On an experimental basis, the campaign is begun, and the daily sales of the restaurant are recorded for 40 operating days. This information is to be compared with data on daily sales compiled before the campaign was initiated. The results are shown in Table 8.9.

TABLE 8.9
Comparison of Daily
Sales, Exercise 8.27

BEFORE CAMPAIGN	DURING CAMPAIGN
$n_1 = 50$	$n_2 = 40$
$\bar{x}_1 = \$487$	$\bar{x}_2 = \$548$
$s_1 = \$23$	$s_2 = \$31$

a. Give a point estimate for the difference between the mean daily sales before and after the advertising campaign.
b. Construct a 93% confidence interval for the difference between the means, part a.
c. What assumptions are necessary for the validity of the interval estimation procedure?
d. Suppose that the new advertising campaign will cost the restaurant $50 per day to run. Thus, the manager must decide whether the new campaign will increase mean daily sales over and above the cost of the campaign. Based on the interval, part b, should the manager adopt the new advertising campaign on a full-time basis? [*Hint:* The manager will adopt the campaign only if there is evidence that μ_2, the mean daily sales during the campaign, is greater than μ_1, the mean daily sales before the campaign, by an amount greater than $50, i.e., if $(\mu_1 - \mu_2) < -\$50.$]

8.28 An experiment was conducted to determine whether the productivity of assembly line workers is affected when the workers are allowed to operate without formal supervision. Two groups of 120 workers at a large factory were randomly and independently selected to take part in the study. For two weeks, one group worked under formal supervision, while the second group was allowed to operate without formal supervision. Table 8.10 shows summary statistics on the productivity per worker (i.e., the number of items produced per worker) for the two groups during this period.

TABLE 8.10
Productivity per Worker
(Number of Items),
Exercise 8.28

FORMAL SUPERVISION	NO FORMAL SUPERVISION
$n_1 = 120$	$n_2 = 120$
$\bar{x}_1 = 85.3$	$\bar{x}_2 = 89.9$
$s_1 = 6.2$	$s_2 = 18.1$

a. Use a 90% confidence interval to estimate the difference between mean pro-
    ductivities per worker for the two groups.
b. Interpret the interval, part a. Is there evidence of a difference between the mean
    productivities of workers under the two types of supervision?

8.6 Estimation of the Difference between Two Population Means: Small-Sample Case

This section presents a method for estimating the difference between two population
means, based on small samples from each population. As was the case with estimating a single population mean from information in a small sample, specific assumptions about the relative frequency distribution of the two populations must be made, as
indicated in the box.

**ASSUMPTIONS REQUIRED FOR SMALL-SAMPLE ESTIMATION
OF $(\mu_1 - \mu_2)$**

1. The populations from which the samples are selected both have relative
    frequency distributions which are approximately normal.
2. The variances σ_1^2 and σ_2^2 of the two populations are equal.
3. The random samples are selected in an independent manner from the two
    populations.

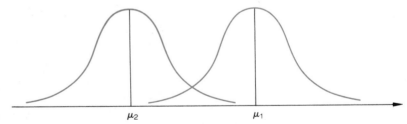

FIGURE 8.10

Assumptions Required for
Small-Sample Estimation
of $(\mu_1 - \mu_2)$: Normal
Distributions with Equal
Variances

Figure 8.10 illustrates the form of the population distributions implied by assumptions 1 and 2. Observe that both populations have relative frequency distributions which are approximately normal. Although the means of the two populations
may differ, we require the variances σ_1^2 and σ_2^2, which measure the spreads of the two
distributions, to be equal.

When the above assumptions are satisfied, we may use the following procedure
to construct a confidence interval for $(\mu_1 - \mu_2)$, based on small samples (say, $n_1 < 30$
and $n_2 < 30$) from the respective populations.

SMALL-SAMPLE $(1 - \alpha)$ 100% CONFIDENCE INTERVAL FOR $(\mu_1 - \mu_2)$

$$(\bar{x}_1 - \bar{x}_2) \pm t_{\alpha/2} \sqrt{s_p^2 \left(\frac{1}{n_1} + \frac{1}{n_2} \right)}$$

where

$$s_p^2 = \frac{(n_1 - 1)s_1^2 + (n_2 - 1)s_2^2}{n_1 + n_2 - 2}$$

and the value of $t_{\alpha/2}$ is based on $(n_1 + n_2 - 2)$ degrees of freedom.

Since we assume that the two populations have equal variances (i.e., $\sigma_1^2 = \sigma_2^2 = \sigma^2$), we construct an estimate of σ^2 which is based on the information contained in both samples. This **pooled estimate** is denoted by s_p^2 and is computed as shown in the box.

EXAMPLE 8.18   Table 8.11 shows summary statistics for random samples selected from two normal populations which are assumed to have the same variance. Estimate this common variance.

TABLE 8.11
Summary Information,
Example 8.18

DATA FROM POPULATION 1	DATA FROM POPULATION 2
$n_1 = 12$	$n_2 = 17$
$\bar{x}_1 = 10.6$	$\bar{x}_2 = 9.5$
$s_1 = 2.4$	$s_2 = 4.7$

Solution   We have made the following assumptions:

1a.   Population 1 has a relative frequency distribution which is normal, with mean μ_1 and variance σ^2.

1b.   Population 2 has a relative frequency distribution which is normal, with mean μ_2 and variance σ^2.

In order to estimate the variance, σ^2, common to both populations, we pool the information available from both samples and compute

$$s_p^2 = \frac{(n_1 - 1)s_1^2 + (n_2 - 1)s_2^2}{n_1 + n_2 - 2}$$

$$= \frac{(12 - 1)(2.4)^2 + (17 - 1)(4.7)^2}{12 + 17 - 2}$$

$$= \frac{11(5.76) + 16(22.09)}{27} = \frac{416.8}{27} = 15.44$$

Our pooled estimate of the common population variance is 15.44.

EXAMPLE 8.19   Refer to Example 8.18. Use the information provided in Table 8.11 to construct a 95% confidence interval for $(\mu_1 - \mu_2)$.

Solution   In order to properly apply the small-sample confidence interval procedure for $(\mu_1 - \mu_2)$, it is necessary to make the assumptions 1a and 1b in Example 8.18. In addition, we assume that the samples were randomly and independently selected from the two populations.

     The 95% confidence interval for $(\mu_1 - \mu_2)$ will be based on the value of $t_{.025}$, where t has $n_1 + n_2 - 2 = 12 + 17 - 2 = 27$ degrees of freedom. From Table 4, Appendix E, we obtain $t_{.025} = 2.052$. We are now ready to substitute the appropriate quantities into the general formula.

$$(\bar{x}_1 - \bar{x}_2) \pm t_{.025} \sqrt{s_p^2\left(\frac{1}{n_1} + \frac{1}{n_2}\right)}$$

$$= (10.6 - 9.5) \pm 2.052 \sqrt{15.44\left(\frac{1}{12} + \frac{1}{17}\right)}$$

$$= 1.1 \pm 3.0$$

or $(-1.9, 4.1)$.

     We estimate the difference $(\mu_1 - \mu_2)$ to fall in the interval from -1.9 to 4.1. In other words, we estimate the mean for population 1 to be anywhere from 1.9 less than to 4.1 greater than the mean for population 2.

EXAMPLE 8.20   A state insurance commissioner is interested in comparing the mean annual premium for homeowners' insurance policies in his state (A) to the average annual premium in a bordering state (B). (For purposes of comparison, we will restrict attention to policies for brick dwellings of approximately 1,500 square feet which are located within a fire district.) The relevant information, based on random samples of homeowners' policies in each of the two states, is provided in Table 8.12.

TABLE 8.12
Insurance Premiums,
Example 8.20

STATE A	STATE B
$n_1 = 8$	$n_2 = 13$
$\bar{x}_1 = \$420$	$\bar{x}_2 = \$380$
$s_1 = \$35$	$s_2 = \$32$

a.   Construct a 98% confidence interval for the true difference between mean annual premiums for such homeowners' policies in states A and B.

b.   What assumptions are required for the validity of the procedure you used in part a?

Solution **a.** The first step is to compute the pooled estimate of variance:

$$s_p^2 = \frac{(n_1 - 1)s_1^2 + (n_2 - 1)s_2^2}{n_1 + n_2 - 2}$$

$$= \frac{(8 - 1)(35)^2 + (13 - 1)(32)^2}{8 + 13 - 2}$$

$$= \frac{20{,}863}{19} = 1{,}098$$

Then, the 98% confidence interval for $(\mu_1 - \mu_2)$, the difference between the mean annual premiums for states A and B is

$$(\bar{x}_1 - \bar{x}_2) \pm t_{.01} \sqrt{s_p^2 \left(\frac{1}{n_1} + \frac{1}{n_2} \right)}$$

where the value of t is based on $(n_1 + n_2 - 2) = 19$ degrees of freedom. Thus, we have

$$(420 - 380) \pm 2.539 \sqrt{1{,}098 \left(\frac{1}{8} + \frac{1}{13} \right)}$$

$$= 40 \pm 37.8$$

or (2.2, 77.8). We can be 98% confident that the mean annual premium in state A exceeds the mean annual premium in state B by an amount which lies in the interval between $2.20 and $77.80.

b. The following assumptions must be satisfied:

1. The relative frequency distribution for the annual cost of homeowners' policies is approximately normal for both states.
2. The variance in the annual premiums is the same for both states.
3. The samples are randomly and independently selected from the two target populations.

EXERCISES **8.29** To use the t statistic in a confidence interval for the difference between the means of two populations, what assumptions must be made about the two populations? About the two samples?

8.30 Refer to Exercise 8.24. Suppose that time restrictions would have prevented the selection of such large samples, and that purchase prices could be obtained for random samples of only 10 single-family dwellings in each state. Assume that the sample means and standard deviations based on these samples of size $n_1 = n_2 = 10$ remain as shown in Table 8.6.

a. Construct a 95% confidence interval for the difference between the mean costs of new single-family homes in California and those in Maine. Compare the result with the 95% confidence interval you obtained in Exercise 8.24.

b. What assumptions do you need to make for the validity of the procedure used in part a? Do they seem reasonable?

8.31

a. Use a table of random numbers and the data in Appendix D to generate random samples of size $n_1 = n_2 = 6$ from the customer checkout service times for super-markets A and B. Compute the mean and standard deviation for each sample.

b. Use the information from part a to construct a 90% confidence interval for the difference between the mean customer checkout service times at supermarkets A and B. Interpret the interval.

c. State the assumptions necessary for the estimation procedure you used in part b to be valid.

d. State how you could construct a confidence interval with a smaller width than the interval you constructed in part b.

8.32 Whom would you trust to charge the fairer price for automobile service and labor, gas station mechanics or mechanics employed by car dealers? Data collected on the hourly labor rates of mechanics working at gas stations and at car dealerships in the city of Detroit are summarized in Table 8.13. Estimate the difference between the mean hourly labor rates of Detroit auto mechanics employed at gas stations and at car dealerships, using a 95% confidence interval. Interpret the interval. State any assumptions that are needed to make the interval estimate valid. [*Hint:* Recall that as df increases, *t*-values and *z*-values are nearly identical.]

TABLE 8.13
Hourly Labor Rates,
Exercise 8.32

	GAS STATIONS	CAR DEALERS
SAMPLE SIZE	20	15
MEAN ($)	26.75	30.50
STANDARD DEVIATION ($)	5.17	2.76

8.33 General Foods and Procter & Gamble, the nation's two largest roasters of coffee beans, have recently slashed their wholesale prices for ground coffee. Sup-pose that you decide to investigate the prices of the two brands of coffee at various supermarkets in your city. You randomly select five supermarkets and check the price per pound of General Foods' ground coffee at each. You then select another random sample of five supermarkets, independent of the first sample, and check the price per pound of Procter & Gamble's ground coffee at each of these. A summary of the results is given in Table 8.14.

TABLE 8.14
Price per Pound of
Ground Coffee,
Exercise 8.33

GENERAL FOODS	PROCTER & GAMBLE
$n_1 = 5$	$n_2 = 5$
$\bar{x}_1 = \$2.88$	$\bar{x}_2 = \$2.96$
$s_1 = \$.17$	$s_2 = \$.12$

a. Construct a 98% confidence interval for the difference between the true average prices per pound of General Foods' and Procter & Gamble's ground coffee at the supermarkets in your city. Interpret the interval.

b. What assumptions are necessary for the procedure you used in part a to be valid?

8.34   Two alloys, A and B, are used in the manufacture of steel bars. Suppose that a steel producer wishes to compare the two alloys on the basis of average load capacity, where the load capacity of a steel bar is defined as the maximum load (weight) it can support without breaking. Steel bars containing alloy A and steel bars containing alloy B were randomly selected and tested for load capacity. The results are summarized in Table 8.15.

TABLE 8.15

Load Capacities of Steel Bars (in Tons), Exercise 8.34

ALLOY A	ALLOY B
$n_1 = 11$	$n_2 = 17$
$\bar{x}_1 = 43.7$	$\bar{x}_2 = 48.5$
$s_1^2 = 24.4$	$s_2^2 = 19.9$

a.   Find a 99% confidence interval for the difference between the true average loading capacities for the two alloys.

b.   For the interval, part a, to be valid, what assumptions must be satisfied?

c.   Interpret the interval, part a. Can you conclude with reasonable confidence that the average load capacities for the two alloys are different?

8.7   Estimation of the Difference between Two Population Proportions: Large-Sample Case

This section extends the method of Section 8.4 to the case in which we wish to estimate the difference between two population proportions. For example, one may be interested in comparing the proportions of married and unmarried mortgage loan recipients who default, or the proportions of homes in two states that are heated by natural gas, or the proportions of U.S. and Japanese firms that employ industrial robots, etc.

EXAMPLE 8.21   A land developer in a popular retirement area in the Southeast is interested in the housing preferences of the area's citizens. In particular, he would like to estimate the difference between the proportions of senior citizens and those under 65 who would prefer condominium or multiple-family housing to single-family dwellings. He commissioned a survey of 200 senior citizens and 200 people under the age of 65; the respondents were asked whether they would prefer multiple-family living accommodations or single-family dwellings. The results of the survey are reported in Table 8.16.

TABLE 8.16

Housing Preferences, Example 8.21

	SENIOR CITIZENS	CITIZENS UNDER AGE 65
NUMBER SURVEYED	$n_1 = 200$	$n_2 = 200$
NUMBER IN SAMPLE WHO PREFER MULTIPLE-FAMILY ACCOMMODATIONS	146	118

Construct a point estimate for the difference between the proportions of senior citizens and those under age 65 who prefer multiple-family housing.

Solution Let us define

$p_1 =$ The population proportion of senior citizens in this region who prefer multiple-family housing

and

$p_2 =$ The population proportion of citizens under age 65 who prefer such living accommodations

As a point estimate of $(p_1 - p_2)$, we will use the difference between the corresponding sample proportions, $(\hat{p}_1 - \hat{p}_2)$, where

$$\hat{p}_1 = \frac{\text{Number of surveyed senior citizens who prefer multiple-family housing}}{\text{Number of senior citizens surveyed}}$$

$$= \frac{146}{200} = .73$$

and

$$\hat{p}_2 = \frac{\text{Number of surveyed citizens under 65 who prefer multiple-family housing}}{\text{Number of citizens under 65 surveyed}}$$

$$= \frac{118}{200} = .59$$

Thus, the point estimate of $(p_1 - p_2)$ is

$$(\hat{p}_1 - \hat{p}_2) = .73 - .59 = .14$$

To judge the reliability of our point estimate $(\hat{p}_1 - \hat{p}_2)$, we need to know the characteristics of its performance in repeated independent sampling from two populations. This information is provided by the sampling distribution of $(\hat{p}_1 - \hat{p}_2)$, shown in the box and illustrated in Figure 8.11.

SAMPLING DISTRIBUTION OF $(\hat{p}_1 - \hat{p}_2)$

For sufficiently large sample sizes, n_1 and n_2, the sampling distribution of $(\hat{p}_1 - \hat{p}_2)$, based on independent random samples from two populations, is approximately normal with

Mean $\mu_{(\hat{p}_1 - \hat{p}_2)} = (p_1 - p_2)$

and

Standard deviation $\sigma_{(\hat{p}_1 - \hat{p}_2)} = \sqrt{\dfrac{p_1 q_1}{n_1} + \dfrac{p_2 q_2}{n_2}}$

where $q_1 = 1 - p_1$ and $q_2 = 1 - p_2$.

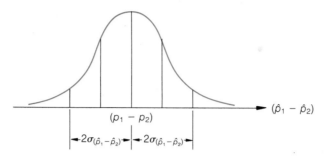

FIGURE 8.11
Sampling Distribution of
$(\hat{p}_1 - \hat{p}_2)$

It follows that a large-sample confidence interval for $(p_1 - p_2)$ may be obtained as shown in the box.

LARGE-SAMPLE $(1 - \alpha)$ 100% CONFIDENCE INTERVAL FOR $(p_1 - p_2)$

$$(\hat{p}_1 - \hat{p}_2) \pm z_{\alpha/2}\sigma_{(\hat{p}_1-\hat{p}_2)} \approx (\hat{p}_1 - \hat{p}_2) \pm z_{\alpha/2}\sqrt{\frac{\hat{p}_1\hat{q}_1}{n_1} + \frac{\hat{p}_2\hat{q}_2}{n_2}}$$

where $\hat{p}_1$ and $\hat{p}_2$ are the sample proportions of observations with the characteristic of interest.

(Note that we have followed the usual procedure of substituting the sample values $\hat{p}_1$, $\hat{q}_1$, $\hat{p}_2$, and $\hat{q}_2$ for the corresponding population values required for $\sigma_{(\hat{p}_1-\hat{p}_2)}$. The approximation is quite satisfactory for large sample sizes.)

EXAMPLE 8.22   Refer to Example 8.21. Estimate the difference between the proportions of senior citizens and those under 65 who prefer multiple-family dwellings to single-family units, using a 95% confidence interval.

Solution   For a confidence coefficient of .95, we will use $z_{.025} = 1.96$ in constructing the confidence interval. From Example 8.21, we have $n_1 = 200$, $n_2 = 200$, $\hat{p}_1 = .73$, and $\hat{p}_2 = .59$. Thus, $\hat{q}_1 = 1 - .73 = .27$, $\hat{q}_2 = 1 - .59 = .41$, and the approximate 95% confidence interval for $(p_1 - p_2)$ is given by

$$(\hat{p}_1 - \hat{p}_2) \pm z_{.025}\sqrt{\frac{\hat{p}_1\hat{q}_1}{n_1} + \frac{\hat{p}_2\hat{q}_2}{n_2}} = (.73 - .59) \pm 1.96\sqrt{\frac{(.73)(.27)}{200} + \frac{(.59)(.41)}{200}}$$

$$= .14 \pm .09$$

or (.05, .23). Thus, we estimate that the interval (.05, .23) encloses the difference $(p_1 - p_2)$ with 95% confidence. It appears that there are between 5% and 23% more senior citizens than younger people who prefer multiple-family housing accommodations to single-family units.

EXAMPLE 8.23   Refer to Example 8.14. Suppose the AGA would like to compare the proportion of homes heated by gas in the North with the corresponding proportion in the South. AGA selected a random sample of 60 homes located in the South and found that 34 of the homes use gas as a heating fuel. This information, together with that provided in Example 8.14, is summarized in Table 8.17. Construct a 90% confidence interval for the difference between the proportions of Northern homes and Southern homes which are heated by gas.

TABLE 8.17
Homes Heated by Gas,
Example 8.23

	NORTH	SOUTH
NUMBER OF HOMES SAMPLED	$n_1 = 80$	$n_2 = 60$
NUMBER OF SAMPLED HOMES WHICH ARE HEATED BY GAS	42	34

Solution   In Example 8.14 we obtained

$$\hat{p}_1 = .525, \qquad \hat{q}_1 = .475, \qquad n_1 = 80$$

Now, for Southern homes, $n_2 = 60$ and the sample proportion of homes heated by gas is

$$\hat{p}_2 = \frac{34}{60} = .567$$

Hence, $\hat{q}_2 = 1 - .567 = .433$.

The 90% confidence interval is then

$$(\hat{p}_1 - \hat{p}_2) \pm z_{.05} \sqrt{\frac{\hat{p}_1 \hat{q}_1}{n_1} + \frac{\hat{p}_2 \hat{q}_2}{n_2}}$$

$$= (.525 - .567) \pm 1.645 \sqrt{\frac{(.525)(.475)}{80} + \frac{(.567)(.433)}{60}}$$

$$= -.042 \pm .140$$

or $(-.182, .098)$.

The 90% confidence interval for $(p_1 - p_2)$ contains the value 0; thus, our samples have not indicated a real difference between the proportions of Northern homes and Southern homes which are heated by gas. The proportion of Northern homes heated by gas could be smaller than the corresponding proportion for Southern homes by as much as .182, or the proportion of Northern homes heated by gas could exceed the proportion for Southern homes by as much as .098.

Small-sample estimation procedures for $(p_1 - p_2)$ will not be discussed here for the reasons outlined at the end of Section 8.4.

EXERCISES   **8.35**   A group of consumer advocates wishes to compare the safety records of two electrical contractors. They have inspected residences wired by each of the contractors, and have recorded the number of residences which were electrically deficient and/or unsafe. The results are shown in Table 8.18. Construct a 95% confidence interval for the difference between the proportions of residences which are electrically deficient for the two contractors. Interpret the interval.

TABLE 8.18
Data on Electrical
Contractors, Exercise 8.35

	CONTRACTOR A	CONTRACTOR B
NUMBER OF RESIDENCES INSPECTED	$n_1 = 60$	$n_2 = 70$
NUMBER FOUND DEFICIENT	8	11

8.36   One of American industry's most fundamental problems—the stagnation in productivity—has economic experts seeking methods of "reindustrializing" the U.S. One possible answer to the productivity stagnation may be industrial robots (*Time*, December 8, 1980). An industrial robot has a control and memory system, often in the form of a minicomputer, which enables it to be programmed to carry out a number of work routines faster and more efficiently than a human. Since the Japanese now operate most of the robots in the world, it is decided to estimate the difference between the proportions of U.S. and Japanese firms which currently employ at least one industrial robot. Random samples of U.S. and Japanese firms were selected, and the number of firms employing at least one industrial robot recorded. The sample sizes and results are summarized in Table 8.19.

TABLE 8.19
Industrial Robot Study,
Exercise 8.36

	U.S.	JAPAN
NUMBER OF FIRMS SAMPLED	$n_1 = 75$	$n_2 = 50$
NUMBER OF SAMPLED FIRMS WHICH EMPLOY AT LEAST ONE INDUSTRIAL ROBOT	16	22

a.   Form a 99% confidence interval for the difference between the proportions of U.S. and Japanese firms which currently employ at least one industrial robot.

b.   Based on the interval in part a, which country has the higher proportion of firms which employ industrial robots?

c.   If the confidence coefficient were decreased to .95, would you expect the width of the interval to increase, decrease, or stay the same?

8.37   A new type of chicken feed, called Ration A, is now on the market. Ration A contains an unusually large amount of a certain feed ingredient which enables farmers to raise heavier chickens. However, farmers are warned that the new feed may be too strong and that the mortality rate for chickens on this special feed may be higher than that with the usual feed. One farmer wished to compare the mortality rate of chickens fed the new Ration A with the mortality rate of chickens fed the current best-selling feed, Ration B. The farmer fed the different feeds to two groups of 50 chickens each, for a one-week period. (Assume that all factors other than feed are the same for both groups.) Of those fed Ration A, 17 died within a week. Of those fed Ration B, 8 died within a week.

a. Assuming that all chicken deaths in the experiment are due to type of feed, find a 92% confidence interval for the difference between the true mortality rates for the two feeds.

b. Based on your interval, part a, can you conclude that there is a difference between the mortality rates for the two feeds? If so, which ration appears to kill the larger proportion of chickens?

8.38   The Environmental Protection Agency (EPA) wishes to compare the proportions of industrial plants which are in violation of government air pollution standards in two different industries: steel and utility. Independent random samples of 130 industrial plants are selected and monitored for each industry, and the number deemed by the EPA to be in violation of air pollution standards is recorded. This information is given in Table 8.20. Construct a 90% confidence interval for the difference between the true proportions of industrial plants violating air pollution standards in the two industries. Interpret the interval.

TABLE 8.20
Industrial Plants Violating
Air Pollution Standards,
Exercise 8.38

	STEEL	UTILITY
NUMBER OF PLANTS	130	130
NUMBER OF VIOLATIONS	8	12

8.39   Recently, the Florida Board of Regents proposed that courses offered at all state-supported universities or colleges be indexed under a common four-digit numbering system. In an attempt to determine faculty opinions regarding the common course-numbering system, the Board decided to survey opinions at the state's two largest universities: Florida State University (FSU) and the University of Florida (UF). At FSU, a random sample of 68 faculty yielded 16 in favor of the system and 52 opposed. At UF, a random sample of 103 faculty yielded 29 for the system and 74 against.

a. Establish a 95% confidence interval for the difference between the proportions of FSU and UF faculty who favor the common course-numbering system.

b. One member of the Florida Board of Regents has made the claim that there is no difference between the proportions of FSU and UF faculty who favor the system. Is this a reasonable claim? Explain.

c. How could the Board reduce the width of the confidence interval, part a?

8.8 Summary

This chapter presented the technique of estimation: using sample information to make an inference about the value of a population parameter, or the difference between two population parameters. In each instance, we presented the point estimate of the parameter of interest, its sampling distribution, the general form of a confidence interval, and any assumptions required for the validity of the procedure. These results are collected in Tables 8.21(a) and 8.21(b).

TABLE 8.21(a)

Summary of Estimation Procedures: One-Population Cases

PARAMETER	POINT ESTIMATE	SAMPLING DISTRIBUTION OF POINT ESTIMATE	$(1 - \alpha)$ 100% CONFIDENCE INTERVAL	ASSUMPTIONS
μ Population mean	$\bar{x}$ Sample mean	Approximately normal Mean μ Standard deviation $\sigma/\sqrt{n}$ where $\sigma =$ Standard deviation of sampled population	$\bar{x} \pm z_{\alpha/2}(\sigma/\sqrt{n})$ $\approx \bar{x} \pm z_{\alpha/2}(s/\sqrt{n})$	$n \geq 30$ (large sample)
μ Population mean	$\bar{x}$ Sample mean	t distribution with $(n-1)$ degrees of freedom	$\bar{x} \pm t_{\alpha/2}(s/\sqrt{n})$ where $t_{\alpha/2}$ is based on $(n-1)$ degrees of freedom	$n < 30$ (small sample) Relative frequency distribution of population is approximately normal
p Proportion of population with specified characteristic(s)	Sample proportion with specified characteristic(s): $\hat{p} = \dfrac{\text{Number in sample with characteristic}}{n}$ where $n =$ Number of observations sampled	Approximately normal Mean p Standard deviation $\sqrt{\dfrac{pq}{n}}$ where $q = 1 - p$	$\hat{p} \pm z_{\alpha/2}\sqrt{\dfrac{pq}{n}}$ $\approx \hat{p} \pm z_{\alpha/2}\sqrt{\dfrac{\hat{p}\hat{q}}{n}}$ where $\hat{q} = 1 - \hat{p}$	The interval $\hat{p} \pm 2\sqrt{\dfrac{\hat{p}\hat{q}}{n}}$ does not contain 0 or 1 (large sample)

TABLE 8.21(b)

Summary of Estimation Procedures: Two-Population Cases

PARAMETER	POINT ESTIMATE	SAMPLING DISTRIBUTION OF POINT ESTIMATE	$(1 - \alpha)$ 100% CONFIDENCE INTERVAL	ASSUMPTIONS
$(\mu_1 - \mu_2)$ Difference between population means	$(\bar{x}_1 - \bar{x}_2)$ Difference between sample means	Approximately normal Mean $(\mu_1 - \mu_2)$ Standard deviation $\sqrt{\dfrac{\sigma_1^2}{n_1} + \dfrac{\sigma_2^2}{n_2}}$ where σ_1^2 and σ_2^2 are the variances of the sampled populations	$(\bar{x}_1 - \bar{x}_2) \pm z_{\alpha/2}\sqrt{\dfrac{\sigma_1^2}{n_1} + \dfrac{\sigma_2^2}{n_2}}$ $\approx (\bar{x}_1 - \bar{x}_2) \pm z_{\alpha/2}\sqrt{\dfrac{s_1^2}{n_1} + \dfrac{s_2^2}{n_2}}$	$n_1 \geq 30$ (large samples) $n_2 \geq 30$ Samples are randomly and independently selected from the two populations
$(\mu_1 - \mu_2)$ Difference between population means	$(\bar{x}_1 - \bar{x}_2)$ Difference between sample means	t distribution with $(n_1 + n_2 - 2)$ degrees of freedom	$(\bar{x}_1 - \bar{x}_2) \pm t_{\alpha/2}\sqrt{s_p^2\left(\dfrac{1}{n_1} + \dfrac{1}{n_2}\right)}$ where $$s_p^2 = \frac{(n_1 - 1)s_1^2 + (n_2 - 1)s_2^2}{n_1 + n_2 - 2}$$ and $t_{\alpha/2}$ is based on $(n_1 + n_2 - 2)$ degrees of freedom	$n_1 < 30$ (small samples) $n_2 < 30$ 1. Relative frequency distributions of both populations are approximately normal 2. Variances of both populations are equal 3. Samples are randomly and independently selected from the two populations
$(p_1 - p_2)$ Difference between population proportions	$(\hat{p}_1 - \hat{p}_2)$ Difference between sample proportions	Approximately normal Mean $(p_1 - p_2)$ Standard deviation $\sqrt{\dfrac{p_1 q_1}{n_1} + \dfrac{p_2 q_2}{n_2}}$ where $q_1 = 1 - p_1$ and $q_2 = 1 - p_2$	$(\hat{p}_1 - \hat{p}_2) \pm z_{\alpha/2}\sqrt{\dfrac{p_1 q_1}{n_1} + \dfrac{p_2 q_2}{n_2}}$ $\approx (\hat{p}_1 - \hat{p}_2) \pm z_{\alpha/2}\sqrt{\dfrac{\hat{p}_1 \hat{q}_1}{n_1} + \dfrac{\hat{p}_2 \hat{q}_2}{n_2}}$ where $\hat{q}_1 = 1 - \hat{p}_1$ and $\hat{q}_2 = 1 - \hat{p}_2$	The intervals $\hat{p}_1 \pm 2\sqrt{\dfrac{\hat{p}_1 \hat{q}_1}{n_1}}$ and $\hat{p}_2 \pm 2\sqrt{\dfrac{\hat{p}_2 \hat{q}_2}{n_2}}$ do not contain 0 or 1

KEY WORDS

Point estimate
Confidence interval
Confidence coefficient
t distribution
Degrees of freedom
Proportion
Independent samples
Pooled estimate of variance

SUPPLEMENTARY EXERCISES

[*Note:* List the assumptions necessary to ensure the validity of the interval estimation procedures you use to work these exercises.]

8.40 List the assumptions necessary for each of the following inferential techniques:

a. Large-sample confidence interval for a population mean μ.
b. Small-sample confidence interval for a population mean μ.
c. Large-sample confidence interval for the difference $(\mu_1 - \mu_2)$ between population means.
d. Small-sample confidence interval for the difference $(\mu_1 - \mu_2)$ between population means.
e. Large-sample confidence interval for a population proportion p.
f. Large-sample confidence interval for the difference $(p_1 - p_2)$ between population proportions.

8.41 Suppose that a 95% confidence interval for μ is calculated to be (12.31, 19.55). Give a precise interpretation of the phrase, "We are 95% confident that the interval (12.31, 19.55) encloses the true value of μ."

8.42 A power corporation is considering building a floating nuclear power plant a few miles offshore of the Gulf of Mexico. Because there is concern about the possibility of a ship colliding with the floating (but anchored) plant, an estimate of the density of ship traffic in the area is needed. For each of 30 randomly selected days during the summer months of June, July, and August, the number of ships passing within 10 miles of the proposed power plant location was recorded. The sample had a mean of 7.5 ships and a standard deviation of 3.1 ships.

a. Using a 95% confidence interval, estimate the mean number of ships per day passing within 10 miles of the proposed power plant location during the summer months.
b. Ships were also monitored for a random sample of 30 days during the winter months of December, January, and February. This sample produced a mean of 3.8 and a standard deviation of 3.2. Use this additional information to construct a 95% confidence interval for the difference between the mean densities of ship traffic near the proposed power plant location in the summer and winter months.

8.43 Consumers reveal their lack of confidence in the economy in various ways, one of which is reduced spending and increased savings. Economists very often interpret an increase in the rate of consumer savings as a forewarning of a recessional trend in the economy. In one local community, a random sample of 200 savings accounts showed that the increase in savings account values over the past year had a mean of 8.5% and a standard deviation of 5.7%. Use this sample information to form a 99% confidence interval for the true mean increase in savings account values for depositors in the community over the past year. Interpret the interval.

8.44 Manufacturers of golf balls are continually improving the durability of their product. Suppose that a manufacturer wishes to compare the durability of its golf balls with that of a competitor's. Ten balls of each brand were randomly selected for the experiment. Each ball is put into a machine which consistently hits the ball with the same force that a typical golfer uses on the course. The number of hits required until the outer covering is cracked is recorded for each ball. The results of the durability test are presented in Table 8.22.

TABLE 8.22
Golf Ball Durability Data,
Exercise 8.44

	MANUFACTURER	COMPETITOR
NUMBER OF BALLS	10	10
AVERAGE NUMBER OF HITS UNTIL CRACKED	270.3	240.7
STANDARD DEVIATION	44.5	31.3

a. Construct a 98% confidence interval for the difference between the mean numbers of hits until cracking for the manufacturer's and competitor's golf balls.

b. Does the interval, part a, indicate that a difference in average durability exists between the two brands of golf balls? Explain.

c. If the respective sample sizes were increased to 100 golf balls each, do you think the width of the interval, part a, would increase or decrease? Explain.

8.45 A new recreation program is in the planning stages at a large corporation. The company's Board of Directors believes that participation in the recreation program will improve an employee's performance at work. Due to the high cost of the program, the board must determine whether enough employees would be willing to take part in the recreational activities. Suppose that in a random sample of 250 company employees, 82 indicated that they would regularly participate in the new recreational program. Estimate the true fraction of the company's employees who will regularly participate in the new program with a 90% confidence interval.

8.46 You are interested in purchasing a new clothes-drying machine from one of two companies, company A or company B. Before making your decision, you obtain information on the proportion of new dryers sold by each company which required repair during the first six months of use. Of 85 units randomly selected from those sold by company A last year, 3 required repair during the first six months. Of 190 units randomly selected from those sold by company B, 12 required repair during the first six months.

a. Establish a 99% confidence interval for the difference between the true proportions of dryers manufactured by the two companies which required repairs during the first six months of use.

b. Interpret the interval, part a. Is there evidence of a difference between the proportions of dryers manufactured by the two companies which need early repairs?

8.47 Chemical plants must be regulated to prevent poisoning of fish in nearby rivers or streams. One of the measurements made on fish to evaluate potential toxicity of chemicals is the total length reached by adults. If a river or stream is inhabited by an abundance of adult fish with total lengths less than the average adult length of their species, we have strong evidence that the river is being chemically contaminated. A chemical plant, under investigation for chlorine poisoning of a stream, has hired a biologist to estimate the mean length of fathead minnows (the main inhabitants of the stream) exposed to 20 micrograms of chlorine per liter of water. The biologist captures 11 newborn fish of this species from the stream and rears them in aquaria with this chlorine concentration. The length of each is measured after ten weeks maturation. The results are $\bar{x} = 27.5$ mm, $s = 2.6$ mm. Construct a 90% confidence interval for the true mean length of fathead minnows reared in chlorine-contaminated water. Interpret the interval.

8.48 Two preservatives, tested and determined safe for use in red meats, are to be compared for their effects on retarding spoilage. Fifteen cuts of fresh red meat are treated with preservative A and fifteen cuts of fresh red meat are treated with preservative B. The cuts are placed in a chilled container and the number of hours until spoilage begins recorded for each. The results are summarized in Table 8.23.

TABLE 8.23
Meat Spoilage Data,
Exercise 8.48

PRESERVATIVE A	PRESERVATIVE B
$n_1 = 15$	$n_2 = 15$
$\bar{x}_1 = 257.3$ hours	$\bar{x}_2 = 249.8$ hours
$s_1 = 12.8$ hours	$s_2 = 9.7$ hours

a. Estimate the difference between the true mean times until spoilage for the two preservatives using a 98% confidence interval.

b. Can you detect a real difference between mean times until spoilage for the two preservatives from the 98% confidence interval, part a? Explain.

c. Give two ways in which you could decrease the width of the interval, part a. Which of these do you recommend?

8.49 When food prices began their rapid increase in the early 1970's, some of the media began periodically to purchase a grocery basket full of food at supermarkets around the country. The same items were bought at each store so that the food prices could be compared. Suppose you, the consumer, wish to estimate the average price of a grocery basket of food in your home town. You purchase the specified items at twelve supermarkets selected at random from among those supermarkets in your home town. The mean and standard deviation of the costs at the twelve supermarkets are: $\bar{x} = \$47.17$, $s = \$5.88$.

a. Find a 95% confidence interval for the true average cost of a grocery basket of food in your home town.

b. Prior to your survey, a consumer report claimed that the average cost of a basket of food (specifying the same items you bought) purchased in your home town is $43. Based on your interval, part a, is the consumer report claim reasonable? Explain.

8.50 An economist is interested in comparing the proportions of eligible workers who are currently receiving unemployment compensation in the states of Pennsylvania and Ohio. Independent random samples of 50 eligible workers in each state are selected and interviewed. The economist found that 3 of the Pennsylvania workers interviewed and 7 of the Ohio workers interviewed are currently receiving unemployment compensation. Construct a 90% confidence interval for the difference between the proportions of eligible workers currently receiving unemployment compensation in the two states. Interpret the interval.

8.51 The *Wall Street Journal* (February 9, 1981) reported that Tyco Industries, Inc., the largest producer of electrical trains in the U.S., will begin to supplement its standard line of toy trains and racing cars with electrical trucks. Market research has convinced the corporation that "modern youngsters prefer the cab of an 18-wheeler to a coal car or caboose." This trend is reflected in Tyco's national advertising campaign slogan: "Some day your child may want to be a doctor. Right now, he wants to drive a truck." Suppose that one goal of Tyco's market research was to obtain an accurate estimate of the true proportion of children in the 6–10 year age group who would prefer playing with a toy truck rather than a toy train. Each of 1,000 youngsters was presented with a Tyco toy truck and a Tyco toy train, and the number who selected the toy truck was recorded. If 615 youngsters selected the toy truck, estimate the true proportion of children 6–10 years old who prefer toy trucks to toy trains with a 97% confidence interval. Interpret the interval.

8.52 A new type of band has been developed by a dental laboratory for children who wear braces. The bands are designed to be more comfortable and better looking, but some dental researchers fear that they are slower in realigning teeth than the old braces. The parents of children who require braces may then choose not to purchase the new bands in order to avoid paying for the dentist's costly services over a longer period of time. With this in mind, the dental researchers conducted an experiment to compare the mean wearing times necessary for the new bands and old braces to correct a specific type of misalignment. Two hundred children were randomly assigned, one hundred to each group. A summary of the data is shown in Table 8.24.

TABLE 8.24
Wearing Time of Braces
until Correction,
Exercise 8.52

OLD BRACES	NEW BANDS
$n_1 = 100$	$n_2 = 100$
$\bar{x}_1 = 412$ days	$\bar{x}_2 = 437$ days
$s_1 = 87$ days	$s_2 = 55$ days

a. Find a 99% confidence interval for the difference between the mean wearing times for the two types of braces.

b. Based on the interval, part a, can the dental researchers conclude that either type of band has a lower mean wearing time than the other?

8.53 A large-volume retailer of electrical appliances has placed an order for 7,000 electric blenders. However, the company will accept the shipment only if no more than 5% of the blenders are defective. To check the shipment, the company tests a random sample of 200 blenders and finds that 4 are defective.

a. Construct a 95% confidence interval for the true proportion of defective blenders in the entire shipment.

b. Can the retailer be confident that no more than 5% of the blenders in the entire shipment are defective? [*Hint:* Use the confidence interval, part a.]

8.54 Refer to the daily price changes of the Standard & Poor's Stock Index, Appendix C. Use a table of random numbers to randomly select 25 daily price changes from the period 1975–79. Construct a 90% confidence interval for μ, the mean daily change in price for the Standard & Poor's Stock Index, for the period 1975–79. Check to see whether the true value of μ (given in Case Study 6.2) lies within your interval.

8.55 A public utilities company is considering increasing the price of electricity during peak-load periods of the day (9:00 AM—4:00 PM) and reducing the price during off-peak periods. The company hopes that this revised pricing structure will force customers to conserve energy during the period when electrical consumption is the highest, and that it will eventually lead to an overall reduction in monthly consumption. To determine the effectiveness of the plan, the company randomly selected and notified 45 customers of the change in pricing policy, effective during the month of August. A random sample of 60 customers, independent of the first, was also selected, but these customers were billed under the regular pricing schedule during August. The total electric consumption (in kilowatt-hours) during the month was recorded for each. The data are summarized in Table 8.25. Estimate the difference between the true mean August electrical consumptions for the two groups of customers, using a 90% confidence interval. Interpret the interval. Is the revised pricing policy effective in reducing mean monthly electrical consumption?

TABLE 8.25

August Electrical Consumption (kilowatt-hours), Exercise 8.55

	REGULAR PRICING POLICY	REVISED POLICY
SAMPLE SIZE	60	45
MEAN CONSUMPTION	2,115	2,003
STANDARD DEVIATION	450	388

8.56 A large credit corporation desires an estimate of the average amount of money owed by its delinquent creditors, i.e., creditors who are more than one month behind in payment. The company samples 80 of their delinquent accounts and records the dollar amount overdue for each. These accounts produce the following sample statistics: $\bar{x} = \$371$, $s = \$66$. Choose a confidence coefficient and then give an interval estimate of the mean delinquency per account for all creditors who are more than one month behind in payment.

8.57 To help decide where to concentrate sales efforts, a manufacturer of campers wants to compare the potential market for its product in two geographical areas: the northeastern United States and the southwestern United States. The company randomly chooses 1,000 households in the Northeast and 1,000 households in the Southwest and determines whether each household plans to purchase or rent a camper within the next five years. Suppose 51 of the Northeastern households and 37 of the Southwestern households indicate that they will buy or rent a camper within five years.

a. Construct a 99% confidence interval for the difference between the true proportions of all households in the Northeast and in the Southwest who plan to purchase or rent a camper within five years.

b. Which area of the United States, the Northeast or Southwest, appears to have the larger proportion of households who plan to buy or rent a camper within five years?

8.58 In this age of escalating professional sports salaries, the salaries of players' agents have also increased tremendously. One agent, who represents both professional football and basketball players, desires to estimate the difference between the average annual salaries of National Football League (NFL) players' agents and National Basketball Association (NBA) players' agents. Independent random samples of $n_1 = 17$ NFL players' agents and $n_2 = 21$ NBA players' agents are selected and the annual salaries of each recorded. The data are summarized in Table 8.26.

TABLE 8.26
Player Agent Salaries,
Exercise 8.58

NFL	NBA
$n_1 = 17$	$n_2 = 21$
$\bar{x}_1 = \$187,330$	$\bar{x}_2 = \$100,440$
$s_1 = \$53,610$	$s_2 = \$32,720$

a. Estimate the difference between the true average annual salaries of NFL players' agents and NBA players' agents, using a 95% confidence interval.

b. A comment by an NFL team owner in a national publication reads as follows: "There is no significant difference between the salaries of NFL players' agents and NBA players' agents." Comment on this claim.

CASE STUDY 8.1
Self-Service
Gasoline
Stations: The
Likelihood of
Adoption

A major cost-saving innovation in the retail gasoline industry has been the introduction of self-serve retail outlets. The significant feature of these self-service stations is the elimination of pump operators; gasoline is, instead, pumped by the purchaser. In addition to saving labor costs, self-service facilitates greater gasoline consumption, which in the end results in lower retail gasoline prices for the consumer.

     In his article, "Self-Service Gasoline Stations: A Case Study of Competitive Innovation" (*Journal of Retailing*, 1978), Steven Globerman investigated the relationship between self-service adoption and Canadian oil company characteristics. In years prior to the publication of Globerman's paper, Canadian government officials had condemned as excessive the quantity of resources employed in the retail distribution of gasoline by the Canadian petroleum industry. Writes Globerman: "Specifically, it has been suggested that excess capacity and the resulting inefficiencies in gasoline retailing derive primarily from the fact that major oil companies use 'overbuilding' as a device to prevent entry [of independent dealers] at the retail level. The existence of too many unnecessary service stations and high rates of lessee turnover and business failures among independents are conditions which facilitate control of retailing by the [major oil companies]."

In order to rectify the condition of excess capacity, government officials had recommended that several structural changes be imposed on the Canadian petroleum industry, one of which would weaken or eliminate completely the system of tying retail outlets to large, integrated oil companies. This argument could be supported, says Globerman, if it is in fact true "that major oil companies have been slower than independents and off-brand companies to install self-service [outlets]. However, one should not be surprised to find that large, integrated oil companies were earlier users of self-serve outlets. There are strong theoretical arguments which suggest that 'dominant' firms can only maintain their market positions, in the long run, through the pursuance of consistent low-cost and low-price policies." Thus, the question of whether "large [Canadian oil] companies are quicker to adopt self-serve than are their smaller counterparts," writes Globerman, "could provide some important evidence on the arguments for imposing structural changes [in] the petroleum industry."

One of the objectives of Globerman's research was to obtain an estimate of the likelihood or probability of self-serve adoption for each Canadian oil company, based upon certain company characteristics. Globerman utilized a well-developed but fairly complex statistical technique called *multiple regression analysis.* (We will discuss the general details of this method of analysis in Chapter 13 and, specifically, Globerman's results in Case Study 13.2.) However, for the purposes of this case study, we will tackle the problem of obtaining the desired estimate by using the much simpler approach outlined in this chapter.

For his research, Globerman accumulated data on a number of firm-specific characteristics for twenty-four Canadian oil companies. This information included the number of these companies which were retailing gasoline in self-service outlets by May 1973. Let us simplify the problem by considering only this portion of the data. We will consider the target population for this case study to be the set of all Canadian oil companies, where each company is classified into one of two groups: those companies which were operating self-service outlets by May 1973, and those which were not. The information on the twenty-four companies, i.e., whether or not each of them was operating self-service outlets by May 1973, represents a sample of size $n = 24$ from the population.

α. Suppose that 16 of the 24 sampled companies were retailing gasoline in self-service outlets by the specified period. Give a point estimate of the true proportion of all Canadian oil companies which were operating self-service outlets by May 1973.

b. Using your answer to part a, construct a 98% confidence interval for the true proportion of all Canadian oil companies which were operating self-service outlets by May 1973.

c. Give two ways in which you could reduce the width of the interval in part b. Which of the two do you recommend?

CASE STUDY 8.2
Consumer
Attitudes toward
Automated
Supermarket
Checkers

In Chapter 1, Exercise 1.1, we introduced you to the data of Appendix D, the checkout times for 500 grocery shoppers at each of two supermarkets, supermarket A and supermarket B. Supermarket B, you will recall, employs automated checkers in contrast to the familiar manual checkers of supermarket A. After five years of experimentation and evaluation, these automated checkout systems, more formally known as Universal Product Code (UPC) symbol-scanning systems, are on the threshold of widespread use by retail food marketers. The system was originally developed (in 1972) to benefit both retailers and customers. Retailers who install scanning equipment can expect higher labor productivity in the form of faster checkouts and more efficient labor scheduling, labor savings from not price-marking individual items, and the accumulation of valuable marketing information by the scanner's microcomputer. The consumer who shops at a store with an automated checker is expected to benefit in four ways: (1) decreased checkout time; (2) increased accuracy; (3) a detailed receipt tape; and (4) lower prices as cost savings are passed on by retailers.

Pommer, Berkowitz, and Walton* conducted a study designed to elicit the true nature of consumer feelings on the benefits of the UPC scanning system. Questionnaires were distributed to a sample of shoppers at three different stores that employ automated checkers. (Two stores were located in Illinois, and the third was in Minnesota.) A total of 161 questionnaires were returned in readable form. The following is a brief description of some of the more important results of the survey:

1. In response to questions concerning the removal of prices from individual food items at scanning-equipped stores, 67% agreed that price removal would make it difficult to shop for the best buy, 51% agreed that price removal would allow store owners to raise prices without the consumer's knowledge, and 45% believed price removal would allow stores to take advantage of consumers.

2. The checkout service advantages of the scanning systems were recognized by the consumers sampled in that 78% believed that less time was spent waiting in line, 71% agreed that checkout service was better, and 62% wished to see automated checkers installed at other stores.

3. Only 17% of the sample indicated that the presence of scanning systems would influence their store-selection decisions, and even fewer, 15%, reported that this technological change caused them to shop more at a particular store.

4. Although 60% agreed with the statement that the scanner does not make mistakes, a full 50% of the sampled consumers still pay attention to automated checker accuracy.

---

*M. D. Pommer, E. N. Berkowitz, and J. R. Walton. "UPC scanning: An assessment of shopper response to technological change." *Journal of Retailing*, 1980, *56*, 25—44.

5. The detailed receipt tape was deemed both easy to understand (98% agreed) and helpful in verifying purchases (89% agreed).

The survey results of (2) indicate that a large majority of consumers believe that automated checking systems speed up the supermarket checkout process (at least for the three stores used in the survey). Let us use the data, Appendix D, to compare the mean checkout service times at the two supermarkets, A and B.

a. In Exercise 8.31, you constructed a 90% confidence interval for the difference between the mean checkout service times at the two supermarkets, based on samples of size $n_1 = n_2 = 6$. Does the interval provide evidence that the mean checkout service time at supermarket B (automated checkers) is less than the mean checkout service time at supermarket A (manual checkers)?

b. Now select independent random samples of size $n_1 = n_2 = 50$ from the checkout service time values for supermarkets A and B, Appendix D. Compute $\bar{x}$ and s for the two samples.

c. Use the sample information, part b, to construct a 90% confidence interval for the difference between the mean checkout service times at the two supermarkets. Compare this interval to the interval you found in Exercise 8.31. How have the increased sample sizes affected the width of the 90% confidence interval?

d. Does the interval, part c, provide evidence that the mean checkout service time at supermarket B is less than the mean checkout service time at supermarket A? Which interval, the interval of Exercise 8.31 or the interval of part c of this case study, would you recommend for making inferences concerning the difference between the mean checkout service times at the two supermarkets? Why?

CASE STUDY 8.3
Sample Surveys:
The Foot in the
Door and the
Door in the Face
Approach

Sample surveys often suffer from a lack of a suitable number of respondents; any inferences derived from surveys with low response rates could very well be biased. Many strategies have been devised for the purpose of increasing survey response rates. Although these compliance-gaining tactics originated in the nonbusiness behavioral sciences (social psychology, personality, etc.), much attention has recently been given to them in business and marketing literature. Marketing researchers are just beginning to investigate and understand how these behavioral influence techniques can be used successfully in a business setting.

Mowen and Cialdini* give brief descriptions of various manipulative strategies. The most popular of these among business and marketing researchers is the "foot-in-the-door" or, more simply, the "foot" principle. Mowen and Cialdini write: "In using this compliance-gaining tactic, a requester first makes a request so small that nearly anyone would comply, in effect getting a 'foot in the door.' After compliance with the first request occurs, a second, larger request is made—actually the one desired from the outset." For example, Hansen and Robinson** conducted an experiment in which a random group of subjects were contacted by phone and initially asked whether they

---

*J. C. Mowen and R. B. Cialdini. *Journal of Marketing Research*, May 1980, *17*, 253–258.

**R. A. Hansen and L. M. Robinson. *Journal of Marketing Research*, August 1980, *17*, 359–363.

had purchased a new car within the last three years. If they had, they were asked some basic questions on general perceptions toward automobile dealers, such as, "All car dealers overcharge on their repair work; do you agree or disagree?" After the brief (no longer than five minutes) "foot-in-the-door" interview, the subject was asked if he/she would be willing to participate in the mail portion of the survey (the desired, larger request). This "foot" technique has been shown to increase response rates in a number of business settings, typical of the one described above. The key to the success of the "foot" principle, say Hansen and Robinson, is that it allows the respondent to become involved in the subject area, which eventually leads to a greater degree of participation in the subsequent larger request.

A second strategy discussed by Mowen and Cialdini is labelled the "door-in-the-face" principle. In the "face" approach, "the [person administering the survey] begins with an initial request so large that nearly everyone refuses it (i.e., the door is slammed in his face). [After the first refusal,] the requester then retreats to a smaller favor—actually the one desired from the outset." The "face" principle is based upon the social rule of reciprocation that states, "One should make concessions to those who make concessions to oneself." Mowen and Cialdini explain: "The requester's movement from the initial, extreme favor to the second, more moderate one is seen by the [potential respondent] as a concession. To reciprocate this concession, the [respondent] must move from his or her initial position of noncompliance with the large request to a position of compliance with the smaller request." The key to the successful "face" approach is that the respondent perceive the original request as being legitimate, and that a concession was clearly made in the movement from the large to the small request.

An example of the "door-in-the-face" technique is given by Mowen and Cialdini. Subjects were approached by experimenters representing a fictitious corporation, the California Mutual Insurance Company. The experimenters' initial request went as follows:

> Hello, I'm doing a survey for the California Mutual Insurance Company. For each of the last twelve years, we have been on campus to gather survey information on safety in the home or dorm. The survey takes about one hour to administer. Would you be willing to take an hour, right now, to answer the questions?

After the subject declined to participate, the experimenter would make the second, smaller request:

> Oh, . . . well, look, one part of the survey is particularly important and is fairly short. It will take only fifteen minutes to administer. If you take fifteen minutes right now to complete this short survey, it would really help us out.

The "foot-in-the-door" and "door-in-the-face" strategies present an interesting contrast in sample survey designs. The "foot" approach uses an initial, small request to enhance the likelihood of compliance with a second, larger (desired) request; the "face" approach uses an initial, large request to increase the response rate on a second, smaller (desired) request. Suppose that we wish to compare the response rates of the "foot" and "face" techniques for a sample survey on insurance coverage in the home (similar to the experiment devised by Mowen and Cialdini). Two sample surveys are designed for our experiment, both intended to gather identical information on home insurance. However, one utilizes the "foot-in-the-door" principle, the other the "door-in-the-face" principle. The critical second request (i.e., the desired request) is the same in each. Suppose that we randomly and independently select two groups of subjects, 210 in the first group and 180 in the second. Each of the 210 subjects in the first group is interviewed using the "face" approach, while each of the 180 subjects in the second group is interviewed using the "foot" approach. We are interested in comparing the response rates (i.e., the proportions of subjects who agree to the critical second request) in each group.

a. What is the parameter of interest, in the words of the problem?

b. Suppose that 84 "face" subjects and 78 "foot" subjects responded affirmatively to the critical second request. Give a point estimate for the difference between the true response rates for the two groups.

c. Construct a 95% confidence interval for the difference between the response rates.

d. Interpret the interval, part c. Is there evidence of a difference between the response rates for the two groups of subjects?

REFERENCES

Globerman, S. "Self-service gasoline stations: A case study of competitive innovation." *Journal of Retailing,* 1978, *54,* 75–85.

Hansen, R. A., & Robinson, L. M. "Testing the effectiveness of alternative foot-in-the-door manipulations." *Journal of Marketing Research,* August 1980, *17,* 359–363.

McClave, J. T., & Benson, P. G. *Statistics for business and economics.* 2d ed. San Francisco: Dellen, 1982.

Mendenhall, W., & Reinmuth, J. E. *Statistics for management and economics.* 3d ed. North Scituate, Mass.: Duxbury, 1978. Chapters 8 and 9.

Mendenhall, W., Scheaffer, R., & Wackerly, D. *Mathematical statistics with applications.* 2d ed. Boston: Duxbury, 1981. Chapter 8.

Mowen, J. C., & Cialdini, R. B. "On implementing the door-in-the-face compliance technique in a business context." *Journal of Marketing Research,* May 1980, *17,* 253–258.

Pommer, M. D., Berkowitz, E. N., & Walton, J. R. "UPC scanning: An assessment of shopper response to technological change." *Journal of Retailing,* 1980, *56,* 25–44.

Nine

Collecting Evidence to Support a Theory: General Concepts of Hypothesis Testing

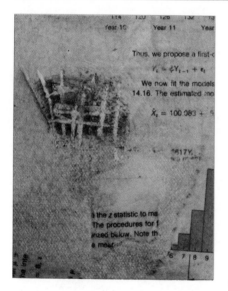

The famous *Schlitz versus Budweiser* confrontation (Mug-to-Mug) was viewed by sports enthusiasts across the country during the half-time break of the December 28, 1980, NFL–AFC wildcard football game between the Houston Oilers and the Oakland Raiders. According to Schlitz, 100 "loyal" Budweiser drinkers were selected to taste each of two unmarked mugs of beer, one Budweiser and the other Schlitz. Live, on television, 46 of the Budweiser drinkers chose the mug containing Schlitz. Ignoring the favorable publicity obtained from this live taste test, do the test results, 46 out of 100, suggest that Schlitz might carve a larger share of the market for itself? If all confirmed Budweiser drinkers were to conduct a similar nonlabelled taste test, would as many as 40% prefer Schlitz? In this chapter we will learn how sample data can be used to make decisions about population parameters, and we will examine the Mug-to-Mug confrontation in greater detail in Case Study 9.1.

Contents:

9.1 Introduction

In the next two chapters we turn our attention to another method of inference-making, called *hypothesis testing.* The procedures to be discussed are useful in situations where we are interested in making a decision about a parameter value, rather than obtaining an estimate of its value. For example, we may be interested in deciding whether the mean value per acre, μ, of land in a particular area exceeds a certain value, say, $8,000; whether the proportion of stockbrokers who believe that the Dow Jones Average will reach 1,000 by 1985 exceeds .5; whether the mean life of a product manufactured by industry A is less than the mean life of a similar product manufactured by industry B; or whether the proportion of blackjack games won by a professional card counter is larger than the proportion of games won by an experienced, but typical player; etc.

This chapter will treat the general concepts involved in hypothesis testing; specific applications will be demonstrated in Chapter 10.

9.2 Formulation of Hypotheses

When a researcher in any field sets out to test a new theory, he or she first formulates an *hypothesis,* or claim, which he or she believes to be true. For example, a real estate appraiser may claim that the mean appraised value of improvements for properties in neighborhood A is less than the mean appraised value of improvements for properties in neighborhood B. In statistical terms, the hypothesis that the researcher tries to establish is called the *alternative hypothesis,* or *research hypothesis.* To be paired with this alternative hypothesis, which the researcher believes is true, is the *null hypothesis,* which is the opposite of the alternative hypothesis. In this way, the null and alternative hypotheses, both stated in terms of the appropriate population parameters, describe two possible states of nature which cannot simultaneously be true. When the researcher begins to collect information about the phenomenon of interest, he or she generally tries to present evidence which lends support to the alternative hypothesis. As you will subsequently learn, we take an indirect approach to obtaining support for the alternative hypothesis. Instead of trying to show that the alternative hypothesis is true, we attempt to produce evidence to show that the null hypothesis (which may often be interpreted as "no change from the status quo") is false.

DEFINITION 9.1

A statistical *hypothesis* is a statement about the value of a population parameter.

DEFINITION 9.2

The hypothesis which we hope to disprove or reject is called the *null hypothesis,* denoted by H_0.

> **DEFINITION 9.3**
>
> The hypothesis for which we wish to gather supporting evidence is called the *alternative hypothesis,* denoted by H_a.

EXAMPLE 9.1 Formulate appropriate null and alternative hypotheses for testing the real estate appraiser's theory that the mean appraised value of improvements for properties in neighborhood A is less than the mean appraised value of improvements for properties in neighborhood B.

Solution The hypotheses must be stated in terms of a population parameter or parameters. We will thus define

μ_1 = The mean appraised value of improvements for all properties in neighborhood A

and

μ_2 = The mean appraised value of improvements for all properties in neighborhood B

The appraiser wishes to support the claim that μ_1 is less than μ_2; therefore, the null and alternative hypotheses, in terms of these parameters, are:

H_0: $(\mu_1 - \mu_2) = 0$ (i.e., $\mu_1 = \mu_2$; there is no difference between the mean appraised values of improvements for neighborhoods A and B)

H_a: $(\mu_1 - \mu_2) < 0$ (i.e., $\mu_1 < \mu_2$; the mean appraised value of improvements in neighborhood A is less than that for neighborhood B)

EXAMPLE 9.2 A producer of frozen grape juice believes that over one-fourth of all grape juice drinkers prefer its product. Specify the null and alternative hypotheses which would be used in testing the producer's theory.

Solution The producer wishes to make an inference about p, where p is the proportion of all grape juice drinkers who prefer its product. In particular, the producer wishes to collect evidence to support his claim that p exceeds .25; thus, the null and alternative hypotheses are:

H_0: $p = .25$

H_a: $p > .25$

Observe that the statement of H_0, in these examples and in general, is written with an equality ($=$) sign. In Example 9.2, you may have been tempted to write the null hypothesis as H_0: $p \le .25$. However, since the alternative of interest is that $p > .25$, then any evidence which would cause you to reject the null hypothesis H_0: $p = .25$ in favor of H_a: $p > .25$ would also cause you to reject H_0: $p = p'$, for any value of p' which is *less* than .25. In other words, H_0: $p = .25$ represents the worst possible case, from the researcher's point of view, if in fact the alternative hypothesis is *not* correct. Thus, for mathematical ease, we combine all possible situations for describing the opposite of H_a into one statement involving an equality.

EXAMPLE 9.3   Periodically, a metal lathe is checked to determine if it is producing machine bearings with a mean diameter of ½ inch. If the mean diameter of the bearings is larger or smaller than ½ inch, then the process is out of control and will need to be adjusted. Formulate the null and alternative hypotheses which could be used in testing whether the bearing production process is out of control.

Solution   We define the following parameter:

μ = The true mean diameter (in inches) of all bearings produced by the metal lathe

If either $\mu > ½$ or $\mu < ½$, then the metal lathe's production process is out of control. Since we wish to be able to detect either possibility, the null and alternative hypotheses would be:

H_0: $\mu = ½$ (i.e., the process is in control)

H_a: $\mu \neq ½$ (i.e., the process is out of control)

An alternative hypothesis may hypothesize a change from H_0 in a particular direction, or it may merely hypothesize a change without specifying a direction. In Examples 9.1 and 9.2, the researcher is interested in detecting departure from H_0 in a particular direction: interest focuses on whether the mean appraised value of improvements in neighborhood A is *less than* the mean in neighborhood B in Example 9.1; and whether the proportion of grape juice drinkers who prefer a particular product is *greater than* .25 in Example 9.2. These two tests are called *one-tailed tests.* In contrast, Example 9.3 illustrates a *two-tailed test* in which we are interested in whether the mean diameter of the machine bearings differs in either direction from ½ inch, i.e., whether the process is out of control.

DEFINITION 9.4

A *one-tailed test* of an hypothesis is one in which the alternative is directional, and includes either the symbol "<" or ">."

DEFINITION 9.5

A *two-tailed test* of an hypothesis is one in which the alternative does not specify departure from H_0 in a particular direction; such an alternative will be written with the symbol "$\neq$."

EXAMPLE 9.4   A large mail-order company has placed an order for 10,000 electric blenders with a supplier on condition that no more than 1% of the blenders will be defective. In order to check whether the shipment contains too many defectives, the company will test the null hypothesis

$$H_0: \quad p = .01$$

where p is the true proportion of defective electric blenders in the shipment of 10,000. Formulate the appropriate alternative hypothesis for the company.

Solution   The mail-order company is interested in detecting whether the true proportion of defectives in the shipment of 10,000 blenders is larger than 1%, for if it is the case that $p > .01$, then the supplier has violated the contractual agreement. Thus, the alternative hypothesis of interest to the company is

$$H_a: \quad p > .01$$

Note that the null hypothesis

$$H_0: \quad p = .01$$

actually represents all possible situations for which the supplier has met the contractual obligation that no more than 1% of the blenders are defective, i.e., $p \leq .01$. Since the alternative is directional, i.e., since the company is interested in detecting a departure from H_0 in the direction of p-values larger than .01, a one-tailed test is to be performed.

EXAMPLE 9.5   The economy of the state of Nevada depends heavily upon tourists, especially those who visit the city of Las Vegas. A state representative, wishing to determine whether there is a difference between the mean amounts of money spent by tourists visiting the state during the years 1980 and 1981, decides to test the null hypothesis

$$H_0: \quad (\mu_1 - \mu_2) = 0$$

where μ_1 and μ_2 represent the mean amounts of money tourists spent while in Nevada during 1980 and 1981, respectively. Specify the appropriate alternative hypothesis for this test.

Solution   The state representative is interested only in detecting whether there is a difference between the mean amounts spent by tourists in Nevada during 1980 and during 1981. If there is a difference, then $\mu_1 \neq \mu_2$ or, equivalently, the difference between means $(\mu_1 - \mu_2)$ differs from 0. Thus, the alternative hypothesis of interest to the representative is the two-tailed alternative $H_a: \quad (\mu_1 - \mu_2) \neq 0$.

EXERCISES   9.1   Explain the difference between an alternative hypothesis and a null hypothesis.

In Exercises 9.2–9.5, formulate the appropriate null and alternative hypotheses. Define all notation used.

9.2   A recent college graduate has been offered two similar positions, one in city A and one in city B. He is interested in whether the proportion of a family's income spent on housing in city A is less than the proportion spent on housing in city B.

9.3   It is desired to test whether the mean price of straight-leg jeans at all retail outlets in New York City is greater than $35.00 per pair.

9.4   The president of the alumni association at a particular university wishes to test whether there is a difference between the mean amounts donated to the school annually by those alumni who were graduated more than ten years ago and those alumni who were graduated within the past ten years.

9.5   Cannibalism among chickens is common when the birds are confined in small areas. A breeder and seller of live chickens wants to test whether the mortality rate of a certain breed of chickens is less than .04.

9.6   State whether the tests in Exercises 9.2–9.5 are one-tailed or two-tailed.

9.3   Conclusions and Consequences for an Hypothesis Test

The goal of any hypothesis-testing situation is to make a decision; in particular, we will decide whether to reject the null hypothesis, H_0, in favor of the alternative hypothesis, H_a. Although we would like to be able to make a correct decision always, we must remember that the decision will be based on sample information, and thus we are subject to make one of two types of error.

DEFINITION 9.6

A *Type I error* occurs if we reject a null hypothesis which is in fact true. The probability of committing a Type I error is usually denoted by α.

DEFINITION 9.7

A *Type II error* occurs if we fail to reject a null hypothesis which is in fact false. The probability of making a Type II error is usually denoted by β.

The alternative hypothesis can be either true or false; further, we will make a decision either to reject or not reject the null hypothesis. Thus, there are four possible situations which may arise in testing an hypothesis; these are summarized in Table 9.1.

Note that we risk a Type I error only if the null hypothesis is rejected, and we risk a Type II error only if the null hypothesis is not rejected. Thus, we may make no error, or we may make either a Type I error (with probability α), or a Type II error (with probability β), but not both. There is an intuitively appealing relationship between the probabilities for the two types of error: As α increases, β decreases; similarly, as β

TABLE 9.1
Conclusions and
Consequences for Testing
an Hypothesis

		TRUE STATE OF NATURE	
		H_a false	H_a true
DECISION	Do not reject H_0	Correct decision	Type II error
	Reject H_0	Type I error	Correct decision

increases, α decreases. The only way to reduce α and β simultaneously is to increase the amount of information available in the sample, i.e., to increase the sample size.

EXAMPLE 9.6   Refer to Example 9.3. Specify what Type I and Type II errors would represent, in terms of the problem.

Solution   A Type I error is that of incorrectly rejecting the null hypothesis. In our example, this would occur if we concluded that the process is out of control if in fact the process is in control, i.e., that the mean bearing diameter is different from ½ inch, if in fact the mean is equal to ½ inch. The consequence of making such an error would be that unnecessary time and effort would be expended to repair the metal lathe.

A Type II error, that of incorrectly failing to reject the null hypothesis, would occur if we concluded that the mean bearing diameter is equal to ½ inch, if in fact the mean differs from ½ inch. The practical significance of making a Type II error is that the metal lathe would not be repaired, when in fact the process is out of control.

Since the probability of making a Type I error is controlled by the researcher (how to do this will be explained in Section 9.4), it is often used as a measure of the reliability of the conclusion and thus has a special name.

DEFINITION 9.8

The probability, α, of making a Type I error is called the *level of significance* for an hypothesis test.

You may note that we have carefully avoided stating a decision in terms of "accept the null hypothesis H_0." Instead, if the sample does not provide enough evidence to support the alternative hypothesis H_a, we prefer a decision "not to reject H_0." This is because, if we were to "accept H_0," the reliability of the conclusion would be measured by β, the probability of a Type II error. However, the value of β is not constant, but depends on the specific alternative value of the parameter and is difficult to compute in most testing situations.

In summary, we recommend the following procedure for formulating hypotheses and stating conclusions: State the hypothesis you wish to support as the alternative hypothesis, H_a. The null hypothesis, H_0, will be the opposite of H_a and will contain an equality sign. Then, if the sample evidence supports the alternative hypothesis, you will reject the null hypothesis and will know that the probability of having made an incorrect decision (if in fact H_0 is true) is α, a quantity which you can manipulate to be as small as you wish. If the sample does not provide sufficient evidence to support the alternative, then conclude that the null hypothesis cannot be rejected on the basis of your sample. In this situation, you may wish to obtain a larger sample in order to collect more information about the phenomenon under study.

EXAMPLE 9.7   The logic used in hypothesis testing has often been likened to that used in the courtroom in which a defendant is on trial for committing a crime.

   a.   Formulate appropriate null and alternative hypotheses for judging the guilt or innocence of the defendant.
   b.   Interpret the Type I and Type II errors in this context.
   c.   If you were the defendant, would you want α to be small or large? Explain.

Solution   **a.**   Under our judicial system, a defendant is "innocent until proven guilty." That is, the burden of proof is *not* on the defendant to prove his or her innocence; rather, the court must collect sufficient evidence to support the claim that the defendant is guilty. Thus, the null and alternative hypotheses would be:

H_0:   The defendant is innocent.

H_a: The defendant is guilty.

   b.   The four possible outcomes are shown in Table 9.2.

TABLE 9.2
Conclusions and
Consequences,
Example 9.7

| | | TRUE STATE OF NATURE | |
		Defendant is innocent	Defendant is guilty
DECISION OF COURT	Defendant is innocent	Correct decision	Type II error
	Defendant is guilty	Type I error	Correct decision

A Type I error would be to conclude that the defendant is guilty, if in fact he or she is innocent; a Type II error would be to conclude that the defendant is innocent, if in fact he or she is guilty.

   c.   Most would agree that, in this example, the Type I error is by far the more serious. Thus, we would want α, the probability of committing a Type I error, to be very small indeed.

A convention that is generally observed when formulating the null and alternative hypotheses of any statistical test is to state H_0 so that the possible error of incorrectly rejecting H_0 (Type I error) is considered more serious than the possible error of incorrectly failing to reject H_0 (Type II error). In many cases, the decision as to which error, Type I or Type II, is more serious is admittedly not as clear-cut as that of Example 9.7; a little experience will help to minimize this potential difficulty.

EXERCISES **9.7** Refer to Exercise 9.2. Interpret the Type I and Type II errors in the context of the exercise. What would be the practical consequences of each for the college graduate?

9.8 Explain why each of the following statements is incorrect:
a. The probability that the null hypothesis is correct is equal to α.
b. If the null hypothesis is rejected, then the test proves that the alternative hypothesis is correct.
c. $\alpha + \beta = 1$ in all statistical tests of hypothesis.

9.9 Refer to Exercise 9.4. Specify what Type I and Type II errors would represent, in terms of the problem.

9.10 Why do we avoid stating a decision in terms of "accept the null hypothesis H_0"?

9.11 Over the last month, a large supermarket chain received many consumer complaints about the quantity of chips in 16-ounce bags of a particular brand of potato chips. Suspecting that the complaints were merely the result of the potato chips settling to the bottom of the bags during shipping, but wanting to be able to assure its customers they were getting their money's worth, the chain decided to test the following hypotheses concerning μ, the mean weight (in ounces) of a bag of potato chips in the next shipment of chips received from their largest supplier.

$$H_0: \quad \mu = 16$$
$$H_a: \quad \mu < 16$$

If there is evidence that $\mu < 16$, then the shipment would be refused and a complaint registered with the supplier.
a. What is a Type I error, in terms of the problem?
b. What is a Type II error, in terms of the problem?
c. Which type of error would the chain's customers view as more serious? Which type of error would the chain's supplier view as more serious?

9.4 Test Statistics and Rejection Regions

In this section we will describe how to arrive at a decision in an hypothesis-testing situation. Recall that when making any type of statistical inference (of which hypothesis testing is a special case), we collect information by obtaining a random sample from the population(s) of interest. In all our applications, we will assume that the appropriate sampling process has already been carried out.

EXAMPLE 9.8 Suppose we wish to test the hypotheses

$$H_0: \quad \mu = 80$$
$$H_a: \quad \mu < 80$$

What is the general format for carrying out a statistical test of hypothesis?

Solution   The first step is to obtain a random sample from the population of interest. The information provided by this sample, in the form of a sample statistic, will help us decide whether to reject the null hypothesis. The sample statistic upon which we base our decision is termed the ***test statistic.***

The second step, then, is to determine a test statistic which is reasonable in the context of a given hypothesis test. For this example, we are hypothesizing about the value of the population mean μ. Since our best guess at the value of μ is the sample mean $\bar{x}$ (see Section 8.2), it seems reasonable to use $\bar{x}$ as a test statistic. We will learn how to choose the test statistic for other hypothesis-testing situations in the examples that follow.

The third step is to specify the range of computed values of the test statistic for which the null hypothesis will be rejected. That is, what specific values of the test statistic will lead you to reject the null hypothesis in favor of the alternative hypothesis? These specific values are collectively known as the ***rejection region*** for the test. For this example, we would need to specify the values of $\bar{x}$ which would lead us to believe that H_a is true, i.e., that μ is less than 80. Again, we will learn how to find the appropriate rejection region in later examples.

DEFINITION 9.9

The ***test statistic*** is a sample statistic, computed from the information provided by the sample, upon which the decision concerning the null and alternative hypotheses is based.

DEFINITION 9.10

The ***rejection region*** is the set of computed values of the test statistic for which the null hypothesis will be rejected.

Once the rejection region has been specified, the fourth step is to use the data in the sample to compute the value of the test statistic. Finally, we make our decision by observing whether the computed value of the test statistic lies within the rejection region. If in fact the computed value falls within the rejection region, we will reject the null hypothesis; otherwise, we fail to reject the null hypothesis.

An outline of this hypothesis-testing procedure is given in the box on p. 279. Each step in this approach will be explained in greater detail as we proceed.

Recall that the null and alternative hypotheses will be stated in terms of specific population parameters. Thus, in step 2, we decide on a test statistic, to be computed from the sample, which will provide information about the target parameter.

OUTLINE FOR TESTING AN HYPOTHESIS

1. Obtain a random sample from the population(s) of interest. (In all our applications, we will assume that the appropriate sampling process has already been carried out.)
2. Determine a **test statistic** which is reasonable in the context of the given hypothesis test.
3. Specify the **rejection region,** the range of computed values of the test statistic for which the null hypothesis will be rejected.
4. Use the data in the sample to compute the value of the test statistic.
5. Observe whether the computed value of the test statistic lies within the rejection region. If so, reject the null hypothesis; otherwise, fail to reject the null hypothesis.

EXAMPLE 9.9 Refer to Example 9.2, in which the producer of frozen grape juice wishes to test

$$H_0: \quad p = .25$$
$$H_a: \quad p > .25$$

where p is the proportion of all grape juice drinkers who prefer the product. Suggest a test statistic which may be useful in deciding whether to reject H_0.

Solution Since the target parameter is a population proportion, p, it would be logical to use the sample proportion, $\hat{p}$, as a tool in the decision-making process. Recall from Section 8.4 that $\hat{p}$ is the point estimate of p used in the interval estimation procedure.

EXAMPLE 9.10 Refer to Example 9.1, in which we wish to test

$$H_0: \quad (\mu_1 - \mu_2) = 0$$
$$H_a: \quad (\mu_1 - \mu_2) < 0$$

where μ_1 and μ_2 are the population mean appraised values of improvements for all properties in neighborhoods A and B, respectively. Suggest an appropriate test statistic in the context of this problem.

Solution The parameter of interest is $(\mu_1 - \mu_2)$, the difference between two population means. Therefore, we will use $(\bar{x}_1 - \bar{x}_2)$, the difference between the corresponding sample means, as a basis for deciding whether to reject H_0. If the difference between the sample means, $(\bar{x}_1 - \bar{x}_2)$, falls greatly below the hypothesized value of $(\mu_1 - \mu_2) = 0$, then we have evidence that disagrees with our null hypothesis. In fact, it would support the alternative hypothesis that $(\mu_1 - \mu_2) < 0$. Again, we are using the point estimate of the target parameter as the test statistic in the hypothesis-testing approach.

> ### GUIDELINE FOR STEP 2 OF HYPOTHESIS TESTING
>
> In general, when the hypothesis test involves a specific population parameter, the test statistic to be used is the conventional *point estimate* of that parameter.

In step 3, we divide all possible values of the test statistic (or a standardized version of it) into two sets: the *rejection region* and its complement. If the computed value of the test statistic falls within the rejection region, we reject the null hypothesis. If the computed value of the test statistic does not fall within the rejection region, we fail to reject the null hypothesis.

EXAMPLE 9.11   Refer to Example 9.9. For the hypothesis test

$$H_0: \quad p = .25$$
$$H_a: \quad p > .25$$

indicate which decision you may make for each of the following values of the test statistic:

a. $\hat{p} = .78$ **b.** $\hat{p} = .10$ **c.** $\hat{p} = .29$

Solution   **a.**   If 78% of the grape juice drinkers in the sample preferred the frozen grape juice product, then much doubt is cast upon the null hypothesis. In other words, *if the null hypothesis were true* (i.e., if p is in fact equal to .25), then we would be very unlikely to observe a sample proportion $\hat{p}$ as large as .78. We would thus tend to reject the null hypothesis on the basis of information contained in this sample.

b.   Since the alternative of interest is $p > .25$, this value of the sample proportion, $\hat{p} = .10$, provides no support for H_a. Thus we would *not* reject H_0 in favor of H_a: $p > .25$, based on this sample.

c.   Does a sample value of $\hat{p} = .29$ cast sufficient doubt on the null hypothesis to warrant its rejection? Although the sample proportion $\hat{p} = .29$ is larger than the null hypothesized value of $p = .25$, is this due to chance variation, or does it provide strong enough evidence to conclude in favor of H_a? We think you will agree that the decision is not as clear-cut as in parts a and b, and that we need a more formal mechanism for deciding what to do in this situation.

We now illustrate how to determine a rejection region which takes into account such factors as the sample size and the maximum probability of a Type I error that you are willing to tolerate.

EXAMPLE 9.12   Refer to Example 9.9. Specify completely the form of the rejection region for a test of

$$H_0: \quad p = .25$$
$$H_a: \quad p > .25$$

at a significance level of $\alpha = .05$.

Solution We are interested in detecting a directional departure from H_0; in particular, we are interested in the alternative that p is **greater than** .25. Now, what values of the sample proportion $\hat{p}$ would cause us to reject H_0 in favor of H_a? Clearly, values of $\hat{p}$ which are "sufficiently greater" than .25 would cast doubt on the null hypothesis. But how do we decide whether a value, say $\hat{p} = .29$, is "sufficiently greater" than .25 to reject H_0? A convenient measure of the distance between $\hat{p}$ and .25 is the z-score, which "standardizes" the value of the test statistic $\hat{p}$:

$$z = \frac{\hat{p} - \mu_{\hat{p}}}{\sigma_{\hat{p}}} = \frac{\hat{p} - .25}{\sqrt{\dfrac{(.25)(.75)}{n}}}$$

(The z-score is obtained by using the values of $\mu_{\hat{p}}$ and $\sigma_{\hat{p}}$ which would be valid if the null hypothesis were true, i.e., if $p = .25$.) The z-score then gives us a measure of how many standard deviations the observed $\hat{p}$ is from what we would expect to observe *if H_0 were true.*

Now examine Figure 9.1 and observe that the chance of obtaining a value of $\hat{p}$ more than 1.645 standard deviations above .25 is only .05, *if in fact the true value of p is .25.* (We are assuming that the sample size is large enough to ensure that the sampling distribution of $\hat{p}$ is approximately normal.) Thus, if we observe a sample proportion which is more than 1.645 standard deviations above .25, then either H_0 is true and a relatively rare (with probability .05) event has occurred, *or H_a is true* and the population proportion exceeds .25. We would tend to favor the latter explanation for obtaining such a large value of $\hat{p}$, and would reject the null hypothesis.

In summary, our rejection region for this example consists of all values of z which are greater than 1.645 (i.e., all values of $\hat{p}$ which are more than 1.645 standard deviations above .25). The **critical value** 1.645 is shown in Figure 9.1. In this situation, the probability of a Type I error, that is, deciding in favor of H_a if in fact H_0 is true, is equal to $\alpha = .05$.

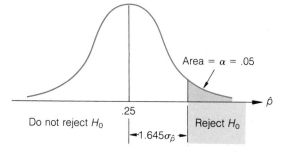

FIGURE 9.1
Location of Rejection
Region, Example 9.12

DEFINITION 9.11

In the specification of the rejection region for a particular test of hypothesis, the value at the boundary of the rejection region is called the **critical value**.

EXAMPLE 9.13   Refer to Example 9.8. Specify the form of the rejection region for a test of

$$H_0: \quad \mu = 80$$
$$H_a: \quad \mu < 80$$

at significance level $\alpha = .01$.

Solution   Here, we wish to be able to detect the directional alternative that μ is *less than* 80; in this case it is "sufficiently small" values of the test statistic $\bar{x}$ which would cast doubt on the null hypothesis. As in Example 9.12, we will standardize the value of the test statistic to obtain a measure of the distance between $\bar{x}$ and the null hypothesized value of 80:

$$z = \frac{(\bar{x} - \mu_{\bar{x}})}{\sigma_{\bar{x}}} = \frac{\bar{x} - 80}{\sigma/\sqrt{n}} \approx \frac{\bar{x} - 80}{s/\sqrt{n}}$$

This z-value tells us how many standard deviations the observed $\bar{x}$ is from what would be expected *if H_0 were true.* (Again, we have assumed that $n \geq 30$ so that the sampling distribution of $\bar{x}$ will be approximately normal. The appropriate modifications for small samples will be indicated in Chapter 10.)

Figure 9.2 shows us that, *if in fact the true value of μ is 80,* then the chance of observing a value of $\bar{x}$ more than 2.33 standard deviations below 80 is only .01. Thus, at significance level (probability of Type I error) equal to .01, we would reject the null hypothesis for all values of z which are less than -2.33, i.e., for all values of $\bar{x}$ which lie more than 2.33 standard deviations below 80.

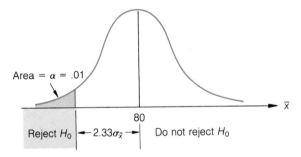

FIGURE 9.2
Location of Rejection
Region, Example 9.1^

EXAMPLE 9.14   Specify the form of the rejection region for a test of

$$H_0: \quad (\mu_1 - \mu_2) = 0$$
$$H_a: \quad (\mu_1 - \mu_2) \neq 0$$

where we are willing to tolerate a .05 chance of making a Type I error.

Solution   For this two-sided (nondirectional) alternative, we would reject the null hypothesis for "sufficiently small" *or* "sufficiently large" values of the test statistic, $(\bar{x}_1 - \bar{x}_2)$. We will standardize the value of $(\bar{x}_1 - \bar{x}_2)$, assuming $n_1 \geq 30$ and $n_2 \geq 30$, to obtain a measure of how far the observed difference $(\bar{x}_1 - \bar{x}_2)$ lies from zero, the value which would be expected *if H_0 were true:*

$$z = \frac{(\bar{x}_1 - \bar{x}_2) - \mu_{(\bar{x}_1 - \bar{x}_2)}}{\sigma_{(\bar{x}_1 - \bar{x}_2)}} = \frac{(\bar{x}_1 - \bar{x}_2) - 0}{\sqrt{\dfrac{\sigma_1^2}{n_1} + \dfrac{\sigma_2^2}{n_2}}} \approx \frac{(\bar{x}_1 - \bar{x}_2)}{\sqrt{\dfrac{s_1^2}{n_1} + \dfrac{s_2^2}{n_2}}}$$

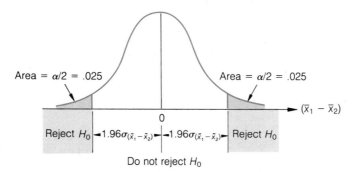

FIGURE 9.3
Location of Rejection
Region, Example 9.14

Now, from Figure 9.3, we note that the chance of observing a difference between the sample means, $(\bar{x}_1 - \bar{x}_2)$, more than 1.96 standard deviations below 0 *or* more than 1.96 standard deviations above 0, *if in fact H_0 is true,* is only $\alpha = .05$. Thus, the rejection region consists of two sets of values: We will reject H_0 if z is either less than -1.96 or greater than 1.96. For this rejection rule, the probability of a Type I error is .05.

The three previous examples all exhibit certain common characteristics regarding the rejection region, as indicated in the box on p. 284.

Steps 4 and 5 of the hypothesis-testing approach require the computation of a test statistic from the sample information. Then we determine if its standardized value lies within the rejection region in order to make a decision about whether to reject the null hypothesis.

EXAMPLE 9.15 Refer to Examples 9.9 and 9.12. Suppose that, in a random sample of $n = 30$ grape juice drinkers, 9 indicated that they prefer the frozen grape juice product. Perform a test of

$H_0: \quad p = .25$
$H_a: \quad p > .25$

at a significance level of $\alpha = .05$.

Solution In Example 9.12, we determined the following rejection rule for the given value of α and the alternative hypothesis of interest:

Reject H_0 if $z > 1.645$.

GUIDELINES FOR STEP 3 OF HYPOTHESIS TESTING

1. The value of α, the probability of a Type I error, is specified in advance by the researcher. It can be made as small or as large as desired; typical values are $\alpha = .01, .02, .05$, and $.10$. For a fixed sample size, the size of the rejection region decreases as the value of α decreases (see Figure 9.4). That is, for smaller values of α, more extreme departures of the test statistic from the null hypothesized parameter value are required to permit rejection of H_0.

2. The test statistic (i.e., the point estimate of the target parameter) is standardized to provide a measure of how great is its departure from the null hypothesized value of the parameter. The standardization is based on the sampling distribution of the point estimate, **assuming H_0 is true.** (It is through the standardization that the rejection rule takes into account the sample sizes.)

$$\text{Standardized test statistic} = \frac{\text{Point estimate} - \text{Hypothesized value}}{\text{Standard deviation of point estimate}}$$

3. The location of the rejection region depends upon whether the test is one-tailed or two-tailed, and upon the prespecified significance level, α.

   a. For a one-tailed test in which the symbol ">" occurs in H_a, the rejection region will consist of values in the upper tail of the sampling distribution of the standardized test statistic. The critical value is selected so that the area to its right is equal to α.

   b. For a one-tailed test in which the symbol "<" appears in H_a, the rejection region will consist of values in the lower tail of the sampling distribution of the standardized test statistic. The critical value is selected so that the area to its left is equal to α.

   c. For a two-tailed test, in which the symbol "$\neq$" occurs in H_a, the rejection region will consist of two sets of values. The critical values are selected so that the area in each tail of the sampling distribution of the standardized test statistic is equal to $\alpha/2$.

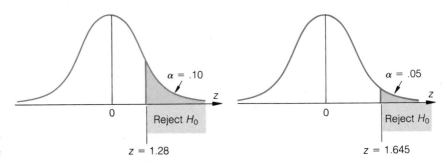

FIGURE 9.4
Size of the Upper-Tail
Rejection Region for
Different Values of α

Now, the test statistic is $\hat{p}$, the sample proportion of grape juice drinkers who prefer the frozen grape juice product, and

$$\hat{p} = \frac{9}{30} = .30$$

The test statistic is standardized, assuming H_0 is true:

$$z = \frac{\hat{p} - \mu_{\hat{p}}}{\sigma_{\hat{p}}} = \frac{\hat{p} - .25}{\sqrt{\frac{(.25)(.75)}{30}}} = \frac{.30 - .25}{\sqrt{\frac{(.25)(.75)}{30}}} = .63$$

This value does not lie within the rejection region (see Figure 9.5). We thus fail to reject H_0 and conclude there is insufficient evidence to support the producer's claim that over one-fourth of all grape juice drinkers prefer the frozen product. (Note that we do *not* conclude that H_0 is true; rather, we state that we have insufficient evidence to reject H_0.)

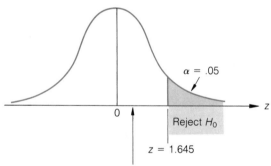

FIGURE 9.5
Location of Rejection
Region and Test Statistic,
Example 9.15

EXAMPLE 9.16 Refer to Example 9.14. Suppose that random samples of sizes $n_1 = 50$ and $n_2 = 80$ from the target populations yielded the information shown in Table 9.3. (Data may represent scores for males and females on a real estate brokers' examination.) Perform a test, at significance level .05, of

$$H_0: \quad (\mu_1 - \mu_2) = 0$$
$$H_a: \quad (\mu_1 - \mu_2) \neq 0$$

TABLE 9.3
Data for Example 9.16

DATA FROM POPULATION 1	DATA FROM POPULATION 2
$n_1 = 50$	$n_2 = 80$
$\bar{x}_1 = 79$	$\bar{x}_2 = 82$
$s_1 = 5$	$s_2 = 3$

Solution   In Example 9.14, we determined the form of the rejection region for this two-tailed test at significance level $\alpha = .05$:

Reject H_0 if $z < -1.96$ or if $z > 1.96$.

For a large-sample test about the difference between two means, the point estimate is $(\bar{x}_1 - \bar{x}_2)$, which is standardized as follows:

$$z = \frac{(\bar{x}_1 - \bar{x}_2) - \mu_{(\bar{x}_1 - \bar{x}_2)}}{\sigma_{(\bar{x}_1 - \bar{x}_2)}} \approx \frac{(\bar{x}_1 - \bar{x}_2) - 0}{\sqrt{\dfrac{s_1^2}{n_1} + \dfrac{s_2^2}{n_2}}} = \frac{79 - 82}{\sqrt{\dfrac{(5)^2}{50} + \dfrac{(3)^2}{80}}} = -3.8$$

This value lies within the rejection region shown in Figure 9.6; we therefore conclude that there is a significant difference between the means of the two populations (i.e., the mean scores for males and females on this brokers' examination are significantly different). We acknowledge that we may be making a Type I error, with probability $\alpha = .05$.

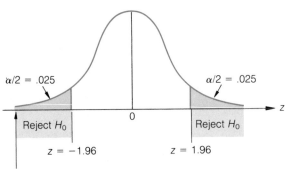

FIGURE 9.6
Location of Rejection
Region and Test Statistic,
Example 9.16

Observed value of test statistic
$z = -3.8$

In the sequel, we will not differentiate between the test statistic (point estimate) and its standardized value. We will employ the common usage, in which "test statistic" refers to the standardized value of the point estimate for the target parameter. Thus, in Example 9.16, the value of the **test statistic** was computed to be $z = -3.8$.

EXERCISES   **9.12**   Suppose it is desired to test

H_0: $\mu = 65$

H_a: $\mu \neq 65$

at significance level $\alpha = .02$. Specify the form of the rejection region. (You may assume that the sample size will be sufficient to guarantee the approximate normality of the sampling distribution of $\bar{x}$.)

9.13 Indicate the form of the rejection region for a test of

$H_0: (p_1 - p_2) = 0$

$H_a: (p_1 - p_2) > 0$

Assume that the sample sizes will be appropriate to apply the normal approximation to the sampling distribution of $(\hat{p}_1 - \hat{p}_2)$, and that the maximum tolerable probability of committing a Type I error is .05.

9.14 For each of the following rejection regions, determine the value of α, the probability of a Type I error:

a. $z < -1.96$ **b.** $z > 1.645$ **c.** $z < -2.58$ or $z > 2.58$

9.15 Assuming that the sample sizes will be appropriate to apply the normal approximation to the sampling distribution of $(\bar{x}_1 - \bar{x}_2)$, specify the form of the rejection region for a test of

$H_0: (\mu_1 - \mu_2) = 0$

$H_a: (\mu_1 - \mu_2) < 0$

at significance level:

a. $\alpha = .01$ **b.** $\alpha = .02$ **c.** $\alpha = .05$ **d.** $\alpha = .10$

Locate the rejection region, α, and the critical value on a sketch of the standard normal curve for each part of the exercise.

9.16 Refer to Exercise 9.11. The supermarket chain randomly samples $n = 50$ bags of potato chips from the shipment and measures the weight of the chips in each. The mean weight of the sample was determined to be $\bar{x} = 15.7$ ounces and the sample standard deviation was $s = .8$ ounce.

a. Calculate the appropriate (standardized) test statistic for this test.
b. Specify the form of the rejection region if the level of significance is $\alpha = .01$. Locate the rejection region, α, and the critical value on a sketch of the standard normal curve.
c. Use the results of parts a and b to make the proper conclusion in terms of the problem.

9.17 A manufacturer of typewriters wishes to determine if its business customers have a preference for one of two typewriter models: model A or model B. Let p represent the true proportion of its customers who prefer model A. If, in fact, the customers have no preference for either of the models, then $p = .5$. Thus, the manufacturer desires to test

$H_0: p = .5$

$H_a: p \neq .5$

a. Give the form of the rejection region if the manufacturer is willing to tolerate a Type I error probability of $\alpha = .05$. Locate the rejection region, α, and the critical value(s) on a sketch of the standard normal distribution. (Assume that the sample size will be sufficient to guarantee approximate normality of the sampling distribution of $\hat{p}$.)

b.   In a random sample of 75 of the manufacturer's business customers, 41 preferred the model A typewriter. Calculate the value of the appropriate test statistic.

c.   In terms of the problem, what is the proper conclusion for the manufacturer to make?

9.5 Summary

In this chapter, we have introduced the logic and general concepts involved in the statistical procedure of hypothesis testing. The techniques will be illustrated more fully with practical applications in Chapter 10.

KEY WORDS

Hypothesis testing	Type II error
Null hypothesis	Significance level
Alternative hypothesis	Rejection region
One-tailed test	Critical value
Two-tailed test	Test statistic
Type I error	

SUPPLEMENTARY EXERCISES

9.18   Explain the difference between the null hypothesis and the alternative hypothesis in a statistical test.

9.19   Define each of the following:
a.   Type I error   b.   Type II error
c. α d. β
e.   Critical value   f.   Level of significance
g.   One-tailed test   h.   Two-tailed test

9.20   What are the two possible conclusions in a statistical test of hypothesis?

9.21   In a test of hypothesis, is the size of the rejection region increased or decreased when α, the level of significance, is reduced?

9.22   When do you risk making a Type I error? A Type II error?

9.23   If the calculated value of the test statistic falls in the rejection region, we reject H_0 in favor of H_a. Does this prove that H_a is correct? Explain.

9.24   Specify the form of the rejection region for a two-tailed test of hypothesis conducted at significance level:
a. $\alpha = .01$ b. $\alpha = .02$ c. $\alpha = .04$

Locate the rejection region, α, and the critical values on a sketch of the standard normal curve for each part of the exercise. (Assume the sampling distribution of the test statistic is approximately normal.)

9.25 For each of the following rejection regions, determine the value of α, the probability of a Type I error:
a. $z > 2.576$ **b.** $z < -1.29$ **c.** $z < -1.645$ or $z > 1.645$
Locate the rejection region, α, and the critical value(s) on a sketch of the standard normal curve.

In Exercises 9.26–9.29, formulate the appropriate null and alternative hypotheses. Define all notation used.

9.26 A manufacturer of fishing line wishes to show that the mean breaking strength of a competitor's 22-pound line is really less than 22 pounds.

9.27 An auto insurance investigator wants to determine whether there is a difference between the proportions of claims made against insurance company A and insurance company B which are in excess of $200.

9.28 A college placement center will conduct an investigation to determine if the average starting salary for male graduates who seek jobs through the center is greater than the average starting salary for female graduates who seek jobs through the center.

9.29 A craps player who has experienced a long run of bad luck at the craps table wants to test whether the casino dice are "loaded," i.e., whether the proportion of "sevens" occurring in many tosses of the two dice is different from $\frac{1}{6}$ (if the dice are fair, the probability of tossing a "seven" is $\frac{1}{6}$).

9.30 Recently, Fiat Motors of North America, Inc., has been advertising its new 2-year, 24,000-mile warranty. The warranty covers the engine, transmission, and drive train of all new Fiat-made cars for up to two years or 24,000 miles, whichever comes first. However, one Fiat dealer believes the 2-year part of the warranty is unnecessary since μ, the true mean number of miles driven by Fiat owners in two years, is greater than 24,000 miles. Suppose that the dealer wishes to test

$$H_0: \quad \mu = 24,000$$
$$H_a: \quad \mu > 24,000$$

at a significance level of $\alpha = .01$.
a. Give the form of the rejection region for this test. Locate the rejection region, α, and the critical value on a sketch of the standard normal curve. (Assume the sample will be sufficient to guarantee normality of the test statistic.)
b. A random sample of 32 new Fiat owners produced the following statistics on number of miles driven after two years: $\bar{x} = 24,517$ and $s = 1,866$. Calculate the appropriate test statistic.
c. Make the appropriate conclusion in terms of the problem.
d. Describe a Type I error in terms of the problem.
e. Describe a Type II error in terms of the problem.

9.31   Refer to Exercise 9.29. In the next 100 tosses of the two dice at the craps table, 5 resulted in the outcome of "seven."

a.   Compute the test statistic appropriate for testing the hypothesis of Exercise 9.29.

b.   Set up the rejection region for the test if the craps player is willing to tolerate a Type I error probability of $\alpha = .10$. Locate the pertinent quantities on a sketch of the standard normal curve.

c.   Give a full conclusion in terms of the problem.

d.   What are the consequences of a Type I error for the craps player?

9.32   A consumer magazine is comparing the costs of portable air conditioners. Basically, two models dominate the U.S. market, an American-made model and a Japanese-made model. To determine whether a difference exists between the average retail prices of the two models, the magazine will test

$$H_0: \ (\mu_1 - \mu_2) = 0$$
$$H_a: \ (\mu_1 - \mu_2) \neq 0$$

where μ_1 is the average retail price of the American-made model and μ_2 is the average retail price of the Japanese-made model.

a.   If the test is performed at significance level $\alpha = .02$, specify the form of the rejection region. Locate the rejection region, α, and the critical values on a sketch of the standard normal curve. (Assume that the samples are sufficiently large to guarantee that the sampling distribution of $(\bar{x}_1 - \bar{x}_2)$ is approximately normal.)

b.   The consumer magazine randomly sampled $n_1 = 37$ appliance stores which sell the American-made model and $n_2 = 33$ appliance stores which sell the Japanese-made model and recorded the retail price of portable air conditioners at each. The results are given in the table. Use the sample data to calculate the appropriate test statistic.

AMERICAN-MADE MODEL	JAPANESE-MADE MODEL
$n_1 = 37$	$n_2 = 33$
$\bar{x}_1 = \$92.65$	$\bar{x}_2 = \$81.17$
$s_1 = \$14.07$	$s_2 = \$9.56$

c.   Can the consumer magazine conclude that a difference exists between the average retail prices of the two makes of portable air conditioners?

9.33   Refer to the data of Appendix D. Suppose that we wish to test the null hypothesis that μ_1, the average checkout service time of customers at supermarket A (manual checkers), is identical to μ_2, the average checkout service time of customers at supermarket B (automated checkers), i.e.,

$$H_0: \ (\mu_1 - \mu_2) = 0$$

against the alternative that the average at supermarket A is greater than the average at supermarket B, i.e.,

$$H_a: \ (\mu_1 - \mu_2) > 0$$

α.   Interpret Type I and Type II errors in the context of the problem.

b.   Which error has the more serious consequences for the manager of supermarket A? The manager of supermarket B?

CASE STUDY 9.1
Schlitz versus Budweiser— Mug to Mug

In a "bold gamble to revive depressed sales," the Joseph Schlitz Brewing Co. announced that it would broadcast on live television a taste test featuring 100 beer drinkers during half time of the December 28, 1980, National Football League AFC wildcard playoff game between the Houston Oilers and the Oakland Raiders.* During the live broadcast, Schlitz claimed that the 100 beer drinkers selected for the taste test were "loyal" drinkers of Budweiser, the industry's best-selling beer. Each of the participants was served two beers, one Schlitz and one Budweiser, in unlabelled ceramic mugs. Tasters were then told to make a choice by pulling an electronic switch left or right in the direction of the beer they preferred. (Prior to the test, the tasters were informed that one of the mugs contained their regular beer, Budweiser, and the other contained Schlitz, but the ordering was not revealed.) The percentage of the 100 "loyal" Budweiser drinkers who preferred Schlitz was then tabulated live, in front of millions of football fans. The newspaper report went on to say:

> One beer industry observer was quoted as calling the test "a giant roll of the dice" in Schlitz' effort to gain a bigger slice of the $8.5 billion beer industry, where consumption increased 25% from 1972 to 1979. Schlitz, a one-time brewery giant, has seen its sales tumble from 16 million barrels in 1974 to between 7 and 9 million barrels [in 1980]. However, Frank Sellinger, the newly appointed Chief Executive at Schlitz, disagrees that the move was a gamble: "Some people thought it was risky to do live TV taste tests. But it didn't take nerve, it just took confidence."

The results of the live TV taste test showed that 46 of the 100 "loyal" Budweiser beer drinkers preferred Schlitz. Schlitz, of course, labelled the outcome "an impressive showing" in a magazine advertisement following the test. For the purposes of this case study, let us suppose that market experts hired by Schlitz informed the company that the taste test would be successful in boosting sales if more than 40 of the 100 Budweiser drinkers selected Schlitz as their favorite. Since 46 tasters pulled the switch in the direction of Schlitz, the brewer called the outcome "impressive," and anxiously awaited sales of Schlitz beer to increase. However, do these sample results indicate that the true proportion of "loyal" Budweiser drinkers who prefer Schlitz is larger than 40%? We can obtain an answer to this question by applying the statistical methods outlined in this chapter.

α.   Set up the null and alternative hypotheses of a test to determine whether the true proportion of "loyal" Budweiser drinkers who prefer Schlitz over Budweiser in a similar taste test is larger than .40.

b.   For a significance level of $\alpha = .05$, specify the form of the rejection region. Locate the rejection region, α, and the critical value on a sketch of the standard normal curve.

---

*Orlando *Sentinel Star*, Thursday, December 11, 1980.

c. Use the results of the live taste test to determine the value of the appropriate test statistic.

d. What is the proper conclusion, in terms of the problem?

e. A valid test of hypothesis, of course, requires that the 100 tasters actually represent a random sample from the segment of the beer-drinking population who are truly "loyal" Budweiser drinkers. Discuss the problems with obtaining a truly random sample from the target population of "loyal" Budweiser drinkers. Do you think that it is possible to select such a sample? In what way(s) could Schlitz have selected the sample (either intentionally or unintentionally) in order to bias the results in their favor?

CASE STUDY 9.2
Drug Screening:
A Statistical
Decision Problem

Pharmaceutical companies are continually searching for new drugs. Charles W. Dunnett, in his essay,* "Drug Screening: The Never-Ending Search for New and Better Drugs," writes that "research chemists often know what types of chemical structures to look for to treat a particular disease, and the chemists can set about synthesizing compounds of the desired type. Sometimes, however, their knowledge may be vague, resulting in such a wide range of possibilities that many, many compounds have to be made and tested. In such a case, the search is very lengthy and requires years of effort by many people to develop a useful new drug." Testing these thousands of compounds for the few that might be effective is known in the pharmaceutical industry as *drug screening*. Because of the obvious impact on human health, drug screening requires highly organized, efficient testing methods, and "anything that improves the efficiency of the testing procedure," writes Dunnett, "increases the chance of discovering a new cure."

Drug-screening techniques have improved tremendously over the years, and one of the major contributors to this continual improvement is the discipline of statistics. In fact, Dunnett views the drug-screening procedure in its preliminary stage in terms of a statistical decision problem: "In drug screening, two actions are possible: (1) to 'reject' the drug, meaning to conclude that the tested drug has little or no effect, in which case it will be set aside and a new drug selected for screening; and (2) to 'accept' the drug provisionally, in which case it will be subjected to further, more refined experimentation." Since it is the goal of the researcher to find a drug which effects a cure, the null and alternative hypotheses in a statistical test would take the following form:

H_0: The drug is ineffective in treating a particular disease.

H_a: The drug is effective in treating a particular disease.

Dunnett comments on the possible errors associated with the drug-screening procedure: "To abandon a drug when in fact it is a useful one (a *false negative*) is clearly undesirable, yet there is always some risk in that. On the other hand, to go ahead with further, more expensive testing of a drug that is in fact useless (a *false positive*) wastes time and money that could have been spent on testing other compounds." Thus, to a

---

*From J. M. Tanur et al., eds. *Statistics: A guide to the unknown.* San Francisco: Holden-Day, 1978.

statistician, a false positive result corresponds to a Type I error (i.e., to reject H_0 if in fact H_0 is true), and a false negative result corresponds to a Type II error (i.e., to fail to reject H_0 if in fact H_0 is false).

For this case study, we will consider the following hypothetical drug-screening experiment: A drug developed by a pharmaceutical company for possible treatment of cancerous tumors is to be screened. An investigator implants cancer cells in 100 laboratory mice. From this group, 50 mice are randomly selected and treated with the drug. The remaining 50 are left untreated, and comprise what is known as the "control group." After a fixed length of time, the actual tumor weights of all the mice in the experiment are measured. If μ_1, the mean tumor weight of the treated mice, is significantly less than μ_2, the mean tumor weight of the control group, then the drug will be provisionally accepted and subjected to further testing; otherwise, the drug will be rejected.

a. Give the appropriate null and alternative hypotheses for the drug-screening test.
b. What are the Type I and Type II errors for this test? (Explain in terms of false positive and false negative results.)
c. Using a significance level of $\alpha = .05$, set up the rejection region for the test.
d. From the experimental results given in the table, calculate the required test statistic.

TREATED GROUP	CONTROL GROUP
$\bar{x}_1 = 1.23$ grams	$\bar{x}_2 = 1.77$ grams
$s_1 = .55$ grams	$s_2 = .21$ grams

e. Should the pharmaceutical company provisionally accept the drug and subject it to further testing?

CASE STUDY 9.3
The Marriage Tax: Double Trouble for Working Couples

Do married individuals face a heavier income tax burden than singles? For married couples where one spouse reports considerably less income than the other or no income at all, the answer is a definite "no." For example, a one-income couple filing jointly, with standard deductions on a $22,000 income, will pay $3,219 in taxes to the Internal Revenue Service (IRS).* In contrast, a single person earning the same amount has to pay $4,517, a difference of $1,298. And as a married couple's taxable income increases, so do the savings. For an earned income of $30,000, the married couple pays $1,724 less than a single person; for an earned income of $50,000, the married couple pays $3,289 less.

However, where both spouses report similar taxable incomes, marriage becomes a costly proposition, at least from a tax angle. For example, if both spouses earn $22,000 in taxable income, the IRS requires that they pay $11,086 in taxes. Compare this figure to the $9,034 that is due if the couple is unmarried but residing in the same home. And as the dual-income married couple's incomes rise, so too do the additional tax payments (over and above what single income earners would pay).

*The values reported in this case study are based on 1980 tax laws.

This "marriage penalty" has many couples thinking of ways to "beat" the tax system, and the following tax rule has enabled them to do so, at least until now: The IRS considers a person married for the entire year, even if that person marries on December 31, the last day of the year. Likewise, the IRS will consider a person unmarried for the entire year, even if that person divorces or obtains a legal separation on December 31. This latter interpretation has many dual-income couples divorcing each other in December and then remarrying in January to avoid paying extra taxes. However, the IRS recently issued a ruling that says it will disregard a divorce obtained solely to save taxes and require the couple to recalculate their taxes as if they had stayed married for the entire year.

Is there any relief in sight for the working married couple? Yes, if a bill suggested by Representative Barber B. Conable, Jr. (R-N.Y.) is passed. The bill aims to create a marriage-neutral system that would impose equal tax burdens on singles, married couples, and heads of households. However, the earliest the bill could go into effect is for the tax year of 1981.

In view of the existing tax laws, and the proposed new bill, let us consider the following statistical decision problem. We wish to determine if there is a difference between the proportions of one-income and dual-income married couples who favor passage of the new tax "equalizer" bill.

a.   What is the target parameter for this problem?

b.   Specify the appropriate null and alternative hypotheses for a statistical test to determine if a difference between the proportions exists.

c.   Independent random samples of $n_1 = 100$ single-income married couples and $n_2 = 100$ two-income married couples are surveyed. If 42 single-income earners and 74 dual-income earners favor passage of the new "equalizer" bill, calculate the appropriate test statistic. [*Hint:*   Utilize the mean and standard deviation of the sampling distribution of $(\hat{p}_1 - \hat{p}_2)$, discussed in Section 8.7.]

d.   Set up the rejection region if we are willing to tolerate a Type I error probability of $\alpha = .05$.

e.   Give the proper conclusion in terms of the problem.

REFERENCES   Daniel, W., & Terrell, J. *Business statistics: Basic concepts and methodology*. 2d ed. Boston: Houghton Mifflin, 1979. Chapter 7.

Johnson, R., & Siskin, B. *Elementary statistics for business*. North Scituate, Mass.: Duxbury, 1980. Chapter 9.

McClave, J. T., & Benson, P. G. *Statistics for business and economics*. 2d ed. San Francisco: Dellen, 1982.

Mendenhall, W. *Introduction to probability and statistics*. 5th ed. North Scituate, Mass.: Duxbury, 1979. Chapters 8 and 9.

Tanur, J. M., Mosteller, F., Kruskal, W. H., Link, R. F., Pieters, R. S., & Rising, G. R. *Statistics: A guide to the unknown*. San Francisco: Holden-Day, 1978.

Ten

Hypothesis Testing: Applications

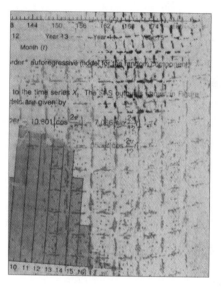

Is a motorcycle helmet law really effective in reducing fatal or serious head injuries? A sampling of hospital records in Michigan (which has a helmet law) revealed that 8 of 31 motorcyclists who received medical treatment suffered fatal or serious head injuries. In contrast, a similar sample of 55 cases in Illinois (which has no helmet law) indicated that 41 of the 55 received fatal or serious head injuries. Do the data imply a difference between the proportions of motorcycle accidents that result in serious head injuries for all motorcycle accidents that occur in the two states? We will learn how to answer this and similar questions in this chapter, and will examine the motorcycle accident data in Case Study 10.1.

Contents:

10.1   Introduction

In this chapter we will present applications of the hypothesis-testing logic developed in Chapter 9. The cases to be considered are those for which we developed estimation procedures in Chapter 8: large-sample test about μ; small-sample test about μ; large-sample test about p; large (independent) samples test about $(\mu_1 - \mu_2)$; small (independent) samples test about $(\mu_1 - \mu_2)$; and large (independent) samples test about $(p_1 - p_2)$.

Since the theory and reasoning involved are derived from the developments of Chapters 8 and 9, we will present only a summary of the hypothesis-testing procedure for one-tailed and two-tailed tests in each situation.

10.2   Hypothesis Test about a Population Mean: Large-Sample Case

Suppose that we wish to determine whether the mean level of billing per private customer per month for long-distance telephone calls is in excess of $30.00. That is, we will test

$$H_0: \quad \mu = 30$$

$$H_a: \quad \mu > 30$$

where

μ = Mean expenditure per private customer per month for long-distance telephone calls

We are conducting this study in an attempt to gather support for H_a; we hope that the sample data will lead to the rejection of H_0. Now, the point estimate of the population mean μ is the sample mean $\bar{x}$. Will the value of $\bar{x}$ which we obtain from our sample be large enough for us to safely conclude that μ is greater than 30? In order to answer this question, we need to perform each step of the hypothesis-testing procedure developed in Chapter 9. The box on p. 297 contains the elements of a large-sample hypothesis test about a population mean, μ.

In this large-sample case, only one assumption is required for the validity of the procedure:

ASSUMPTION REQUIRED

The sample size must be sufficiently large (say, $n \geq 30$) so that the sampling distribution of $\bar{x}$ is approximately normal and that s provides a good approximation to σ.

LARGE-SAMPLE TEST OF HYPOTHESIS ABOUT A POPULATION MEAN

a. One-tailed test

H_0: $\mu = \mu_0$

H_a: $\mu > \mu_0$

(or H_a: $\mu < \mu_0$)

Test statistic:

$$z = \frac{\bar{x} - \mu_0}{\sigma_{\bar{x}}} \approx \frac{\bar{x} - \mu_0}{s/\sqrt{n}}$$

Rejection region:

$z > z_\alpha$ (or $z < -z_\alpha$)

b. Two-tailed test

H_0: $\mu = \mu_0$

H_a: $\mu \neq \mu_0$

Test statistic:

$$z = \frac{\bar{x} - \mu_0}{\sigma_{\bar{x}}} \approx \frac{\bar{x} - \mu_0}{s/\sqrt{n}}$$

Rejection region:

$z < -z_{\alpha/2}$ or $z > z_{\alpha/2}$

where z_α is the z-value such that $P(z > z_\alpha) = \alpha$; and $z_{\alpha/2}$ is the z-value such that $P(z > z_{\alpha/2}) = \alpha/2$. [*Note:* μ_0 is our symbol for the particular numerical value specified for μ in the null hypothesis.]

EXAMPLE 10.1 The long-distance telephone charges during a given month for a random sample of $n = 37$ private customers were obtained from the billing files of a telephone company. The results are summarized below:

$\bar{x} = \$33.15$

$s = \$21.21$

Test the hypothesis that μ, the population mean monthly billing level for long-distance telephone calls, is equal to $\$30.00$ against the alternative that μ is larger than $\$30.00$, using a significance level of $\alpha = .05$.

Solution We have previously formulated the hypotheses as

H_0: $\mu = 30$

H_a: $\mu > 30$

Note that the sample size $n = 37$ is sufficiently large so that the sampling distribution of $\bar{x}$ is approximately normal and that s provides a good approximation to σ. Having satisfied the required assumption, we may proceed with a large-sample test about μ.

Using a significance level of $\alpha = .05$, we will reject the null hypothesis for this one-tailed test if

$z > z_\alpha = z_{.05}$

i.e., if $z > 1.645$. (This rejection region is shown in Figure 10.1.)

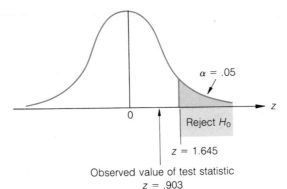

FIGURE 10.1
Rejection Region,
Example 10.1

Observed value of test statistic
z = .903

Computing the value of the test statistic, we obtain

$$z = \frac{\bar{x} - \mu_0}{s/\sqrt{n}} = \frac{33.15 - 30}{21.21/\sqrt{37}} = .903$$

Since this value does not fall within the rejection region (see Figure 10.1), we fail to reject H_0. We say that there is insufficient evidence (at $\alpha = .05$) to conclude that the mean billing level for long-distance calls per private customer during the given month is greater than $30.00. We would need to take a larger sample before we could detect whether $\mu > 30$, if in fact this were the case.

EXAMPLE 10.2   Consider the set of all residential properties which were sold during 1978 in the Florida city described in Chapter 1. If the sale price for a piece of property were approximately equal to its total appraised value, then μ, the mean value of the ratio of sale price to total appraised value for all such properties, would equal 1.0. A random sample of $n = 50$ observations from the population of values of this ratio, Appendix A, produced the following results:

$$\bar{x} = 1.534$$

$$s = .91$$

We wish to test the hypothesis that μ, the population mean ratio, is equal to 1.0 against the alternative that it is different from 1.0. Suppose that we also want a very small chance of rejecting H_0, if in fact μ is equal to 1.0. That is, it is important that we avoid making a Type I error. The hypothesis-testing procedure that we have developed gives us the advantage of choosing any significance level that we desire. Since the significance level, α, is also the probability of a Type I error, we will choose α very small. In general, researchers who consider a Type I error to have very serious practical consequences should perform the test at a very low α-value, say $\alpha = .01$. Other researchers may be willing to tolerate an α-value as high as .10 if a Type I error is not deemed a serious error to make in practice.

Test whether μ, the population mean ratio, is different from 1.0, using a significance level of $\alpha = .01$.

Solution We formulate the following hypotheses:

H_0: $\mu = 1.0$

H_a: $\mu \neq 1.0$

Since we wish to avoid making a Type I error, we choose a very small significance level of $\alpha = .01$. The sample size exceeds 30, thus we may proceed with the large-sample test about μ.

At significance level $\alpha = .01$, we will reject the null hypothesis for this two-tailed test if

$$z < -z_{\alpha/2} = -z_{.005} \quad \text{or if} \quad z > z_{\alpha/2} = z_{.005}$$

i.e., if $z < -2.58$ or if $z > 2.58$. (This rejection region is shown in Figure 10.2.)

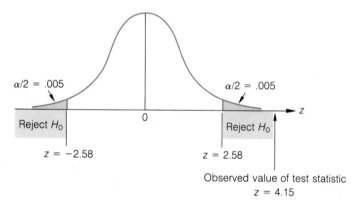

FIGURE 10.2
Rejection Region,
Example 10.2

The value of the test statistic is computed as follows:

$$z \approx \frac{\bar{x} - \mu_0}{s/\sqrt{n}} = \frac{1.534 - 1.0}{.91/\sqrt{50}} = 4.15$$

Since this value lies within the rejection region (see Figure 10.2), we reject H_0 and conclude that the mean ratio of sale price to total appraised value was significantly different from 1.0 for the residential properties sold in the city during 1978. If the null hypothesis is in fact true (i.e., if $\mu = 1.0$), then the probability that we have incorrectly rejected it is equal to $\alpha = .01$.

The practical implications of this result remain to be studied further. Perhaps there is a general tendency for the city's real estate appraisers to over-appraise or under-appraise a property's value. Alternatively, a tight housing market may tend to inflate the sale price for residential properties in the city. It is not always the case that a *statistically* significant result implies a *practically* significant result. The researcher must retain his or her objectivity and judge the practical significance using, among other criteria, his or her knowledge of the subject matter and the phenomenon under investigation.

EXAMPLE 10.3   Prior to the institution of a new safety program, the average number of on-the-job accidents per day at a factory was 4.5. To determine if the safety program has been effective in reducing the average number of accidents per day, a random sample of 30 days is taken after the institution of the new safety program and the number of accidents per day is recorded. The sample mean and standard deviation were computed as follows:

$$\bar{x} = 3.7$$

$$s = 1.3$$

a.   Is there sufficient evidence to conclude (at significance level .01) that the average number of on-the-job accidents per day at the factory has decreased since the institution of the safety program?

b.   What is the practical interpretation of the test statistic computed in part a?

Solution   a.   In order to determine whether the safety program was effective, we will conduct a large-sample test of

$$H_0: \quad \mu = 4.5 \text{ (i.e., no change in average number of on-the-job accidents per day)}$$

$$H_a: \quad \mu < 4.5 \text{ (i.e., average number of on-the-job accidents per day has decreased)}$$

where μ represents the mean number of on-the-job accidents per day at the factory after institution of the new safety program. For a significance level of $\alpha = .01$, we will reject the null hypothesis if

$$z < -z_{.01} = -2.33$$

(See Figure 10.3.) The computed value of the test statistic is

$$z \approx \frac{\bar{x} - \mu_0}{s/\sqrt{n}} = \frac{3.7 - 4.5}{1.3/\sqrt{30}} = -3.37$$

Since this value does fall within the rejection region (see Figure 10.3), there is sufficient evidence (at $\alpha = .01$) to conclude that the average number of on-the-job accidents per day at the factory has decreased since the institution of the safety program. It appears that the safety program was effective in reducing the average number of accidents per day.

b.   If the null hypothesis is true, $\mu = 4.5$. Recall that for large samples, the sampling distribution of $\bar{x}$ is approximately normal, with mean $\mu_{\bar{x}} = \mu$ and standard deviation $\sigma_{\bar{x}} = \sigma/\sqrt{n}$. Then the z-score for $\bar{x}$, under the assumption that H_0 is true, is given by

$$z = \frac{\bar{x} - 4.5}{\sigma/\sqrt{n}}$$

You can see that the test statistic computed in part a is simply the z-score for the sample mean $\bar{x}$, if in fact $\mu = 4.5$. A calculated z-score of -3.37 indicates that the

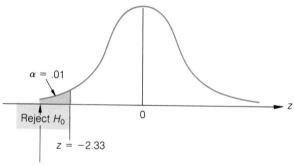

FIGURE 10.3
Rejection Region,
Example 10.3

$\alpha = .01$

Reject H_0

$z = -2.33$

0

z

Observed value of test statistic
$z = -3.37$

value of $\bar{x}$ computed from the sample falls a distance of 3.37 standard deviations below the hypothesized mean of $\mu = 4.5$. Of course, we would not expect to observe a z-score this extreme if in fact $\mu = 4.5$. Without benefit of a formal test of hypothesis, this fact alone indicates strongly that the true mean is less than 4.5.

EXERCISES [*Note:* In all the exercises for this chapter, you should carefully define any notation used, perform all steps of the relevant hypothesis test, state a conclusion in terms of the problem, and specify any assumptions required for the validity of the procedure.]

10.1 In the early 1970's, the average number of square feet of heated floor space for new homes built in a certain state was 1,600. A random sample of 30 new homes built in the state last year was selected, and the square footage for each was recorded. The sample mean and standard deviation were computed as follows:

$\bar{x} = 1,512$

$s = 250$

Is there sufficient evidence to conclude (at significance level $\alpha = .05$) that the average size of a new home in this state has decreased during the past decade?

10.2 To protect U.S. steel producers against competition from low-priced foreign imports, the government has adopted a trigger price mechanism. If steel imports enter this country at less than the minimum or trigger price (based on the cost of production in Japan, which has the world's most efficient steel factories), an investigation into the illegal dumping of cheap steel in the U.S. by foreign countries is launched. Last year, the average trigger price was set at $358.31 per ton. This year, a random sample of $n = 40$ days was selected, and the trigger price on each of the days was recorded. The data are summarized as follows:

$\bar{x} = \$390.88$

$s = \$106.19$

Does the sample evidence indicate that the mean trigger price during this year differs significantly from $358.31? Use a significance level of $\alpha = .10$.

10.3 The contents label on the back of a 16-ounce box of pre-sweetened cereal alleges that the mean sugar content (by weight) of all boxes of this brand is 3.0 ounces. The Food and Drug Administration (FDA) randomly sampled $n = 40$ boxes of this brand and measured the sugar content in each. The results are summarized as

$$\bar{x} = 3.2 \text{ ounces} \qquad s = .5 \text{ ounces}$$

Is this sufficient evidence (at $\alpha = .05$) for the FDA to claim that the true mean sugar content of 16-ounce boxes of this brand of cereal exceeds 3.0 ounces?

10.4 A recent "Fuel Gauge" report by the Automobile Association of America showed that the average price (per gallon) for all grades of gasoline selling at full-service pumps in Florida was \$1.429 (Gainesville *Sun*, February 27, 1981). Suppose that a Florida service station manager wants to compare the average price of gasoline in his state to the national average. A random sample of $n = 250$ full-service stations from various locations across the U.S. revealed the following summary statistics on price per gallon: $\bar{x} = \$1.475$, $s = \$.508$. Can the Florida service station manager conclude that the average price for all grades of gasoline selling at full-service pumps across the U.S. is higher than his statewide average of \$1.429? Test at $\alpha = .02$.

10.3 Hypothesis Test about a Population Mean: Small-Sample Case

An item of interest to a gold investor in the commodities market is the maximum price (per ounce) that gold futures will attain next year. One way of trying to project this ceiling price is to obtain the opinions of several gold experts. This sample of opinions can be used to make an inference about the mean projected ceiling price of gold futures, μ, of all gold market analysts. However, time and cost considerations would probably limit the sample of opinions to a small number. Consequently, the assumption required for a large-sample test of hypothesis about μ will be violated. We need, then, an hypothesis-testing procedure which is appropriate for use with small samples.

As we noticed in the development of estimation procedures, when we are making inferences based on small samples, more restrictive assumptions are required than when making inferences from large samples. In particular, the hypothesis test procedure requires the following assumption:

ASSUMPTION REQUIRED

The relative frequency distribution of the population from which the sample was selected is approximately normal.

An hypothesis test about a population mean, μ, based on a small sample ($n < 30$), consists of the following elements:

SMALL-SAMPLE TEST OF HYPOTHESIS ABOUT A POPULATION MEAN

a.   One-tailed test

H_0: $\mu = \mu_0$

H_a: $\mu > \mu_0$

(or H_a: $\mu < \mu_0$)

Test statistic:

$$t = \frac{\bar{x} - \mu_0}{s/\sqrt{n}}$$

Rejection region:

$t > t_\alpha$ (or $t < -t_\alpha$)

b.   Two-tailed test

H_0: $\mu = \mu_0$

H_a: $\mu \neq \mu_0$

Test statistic:

$$t = \frac{\bar{x} - \mu_0}{s/\sqrt{n}}$$

Rejection region:

$t < -t_{\alpha/2}$ or $t > t_{\alpha/2}$

where the distribution of t is based on $(n-1)$ degrees of freedom; t_α is the t-value such that $P(t > t_\alpha) = \alpha$; and $t_{\alpha/2}$ is the t-value such that $P(t > t_{\alpha/2}) = \alpha/2$.

EXAMPLE 10.4   What is the practical significance of the test statistic for a small-sample test of hypothesis about μ?

Solution   Notice that the test statistic given in the box is a t statistic and is calculated exactly as our approximation to the large-sample test statistic, z, given in Section 10.2. Therefore, just like z, the computed value of t will indicate the direction and approximate distance (in units of standard deviations) that the sample mean, $\bar{x}$, is from the hypothesized population mean, μ_0.

EXAMPLE 10.5   The building specifications in a certain city require that the sewer pipe used in residential areas has a mean breaking strength of more than 2,500 pounds per lineal foot. A manufacturer who would like to supply the city with sewer pipe has submitted a bid and provided the following additional information: An independent contractor randomly selected 7 sections of the manufacturer's pipe and tested each for breaking strength. The results (pounds per lineal foot) are shown below:

2,610	2,750	2,420	2,510	2,540	2,490	2,680

Do we have sufficient evidence to conclude that the manufacturer's sewer pipe meets the required specifications? Use a significance level of $\alpha = .10$.

Solution   The relevant hypothesis test has the following elements:

H_0: $\mu = 2,500$ (i.e., the manufacturer's pipe does not meet the city's specifications)

H_a: $\mu > 2,500$ (i.e., the pipe meets the specifications)

where μ represents the true mean breaking strength (in pounds per lineal foot) for all sewer pipe produced by this manufacturer.

This small-sample ($n = 7$) test requires the assumption that the relative frequency distribution of the population values of breaking strength for the manufacturer's pipe is approximately normal. Then the test will be based upon a t distribution with $(n - 1) = 6$ degrees of freedom. We will thus reject H_0 if

$$t > t_{.10} = 1.440$$

(See Figure 10.4.)

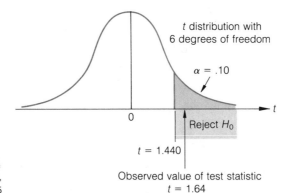

FIGURE 10.4
Rejection Region,
Example 10.5

In order to compute the value of the test statistic, we need to obtain the values of $\bar{x}$ and s:

$$\bar{x} = \frac{\Sigma x}{n} = \frac{2,610 + 2,750 + 2,420 + 2,510 + 2,540 + 2,490 + 2,680}{7}$$

$$= 2,571.43$$

$$s = \sqrt{\frac{\Sigma x^2 - (\Sigma x)^2/n}{n - 1}}$$

$$= \sqrt{\frac{(2,610)^2 + (2,750)^2 + (2,420)^2 + (2,510)^2 + (2,540)^2 + (2,490)^2 + (2,680)^2 - (18,000)^2/7}{6}}$$

$$= \sqrt{\frac{46,365,200 - 46,285,714}{6}} = 115.10$$

Substitution of these values yields the test statistic:

$$t = \frac{\bar{x} - \mu_0}{s/\sqrt{n}} = \frac{2,571.43 - 2,500}{115.10/\sqrt{7}} = 1.64$$

Since this value of t is larger than the critical value of 1.440 (see Figure 10.4), we reject H_0. There is sufficient evidence (at significance level .10) that the manufacturer's pipe meets the city's building specifications.

EXAMPLE 10.6 The off-campus housing office at a large university has published a guide which states that the average rent for a one-bedroom, one-bath apartment within three miles of campus is $175 per month. A student selected a random sample of $n = 16$ apartment complexes in the area and computed the following statistics based on the monthly rental rate information provided by the managers:

$$\bar{x} = \$205 \quad s = \$60$$

At the .05 significance level, does the sample evidence indicate that the guide needs to be updated to indicate higher rental rates?

Solution Define the parameter of interest:

μ = The true mean monthly rental rate for all one-bedroom, one-bath apartments within three miles of campus

We are interested in a test of

H_0: $\mu = 175$

H_a: $\mu > 175$

(The alternative which we wish to detect is that the housing guide needs to revise upward its value of the mean rental rate.)

Since we are restricted to a small sample, we must make the assumption that the monthly rental rates of one-bedroom, one-bath apartments within three miles of campus have a relative frequency distribution which is approximately normal. Under this assumption, the test statistic will have a t distribution with $(n - 1) = (16 - 1) = 15$ degrees of freedom. The rejection rule is then to reject the null hypothesis for values of t such that

$$t > t_{.05} = 1.753$$

(See Figure 10.5.)

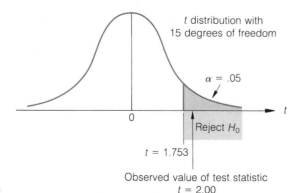

FIGURE 10.5
Rejection Region,
Example 10.6

The value of the test statistic is

$$t = \frac{\bar{x} - \mu_0}{s/\sqrt{n}} = \frac{205 - 175}{60/\sqrt{16}} = 2.0$$

The critical value of 1.753 is exceeded by the computed value of the test statistic, $t = 2.0$ (see Figure 10.5). We thus reject H_0 and conclude that the mean rental rate for one-bedroom, one-bath apartments is significantly greater than \$175; hence, the housing guide should be revised. If, in fact, the null hypothesis is true (i.e., if the housing guide is correct), the probability of our incorrectly rejecting it using this procedure is equal to $\alpha = .05$.

EXERCISES
10.5 Refer to Example 10.5. If you were the city building inspector, why might it be desirable from your viewpoint to use a smaller value of α, say, $\alpha = .01$, in conducting the test?

10.6 Recently, a new miniaturized component for use in desk-top calculators has been developed. These components greatly reduce the size of the calculators, but may not last long enough to be practical. It is known that the mean life length of the larger component used in a desk-top calculator manufactured by a successful firm is 500 hours. However, a random sample of 18 newly built miniaturized components yielded the following summary statistics on life length:

$\bar{x} = 482$ hours

$s = 59$ hours

Is there evidence, at significance level $\alpha = .01$, that the mean life length of the new miniaturized component is significantly less than the average of 500 hours for the larger components? What assumption is required for the hypothesis test to be valid?

10.7 The following is a random sample of size $n = 6$ salaries selected from the population of annual salaries for all business school deans employed by southern universities:

$46,000   \$39,500   \$46,500   \$54,000   \$62,000   \$54,700

Perform an hypothesis test to determine if the mean yearly salary of business school deans at southern universities exceeds \$50,000. Use a significance level of $\alpha = .05$. What assumption is required for the hypothesis test to be valid?

10.8 In any canning process, a manufacturer will lose money if the cans contain either more or less than is claimed on the label. Accordingly, canners pay close attention to the amount of their product being dispensed by the can-filling machines. Consider a company that produces a fast-drying rubber cement in 32-ounce aluminum cans. A quality control inspector is interested in testing whether the average number of ounces of rubber cement dispensed into the cans is really 32 ounces. Since inspection of the canning process requires that the dispensing machines be shut down, and shutdowns for any lengthy period of time cost the company thousands of dollars in lost revenues, the inspector is able to obtain a random sample of only 10 cans for testing. After measuring the weights of their contents, the inspector computes the following summary statistics:

$$\bar{x} = 31.55 \text{ ounces}$$

$$s = .48 \text{ ounces}$$

a. Does the sample evidence indicate that the dispensing machines are in need of adjustment? Test at significance level $\alpha = .05$.

b. What assumption is necessary for the hypothesis test, part a, to be valid?

10.9 In an effort to offset the Soviet Union's growing armored force, the United States Defense Department has selected a new Army tank designed by Chrysler Corp. The tank, called XM-1, can reach an average top speed of 45 miles per hour, a speed which the Defense Department believes is faster than the Soviets' fastest and most powerful tank, the T-72. The Defense Department would like to present evidence which supports this belief in order to justify the billions of dollars it must spend to mass-produce the XM-1. Suppose that a U.S. agent in the Soviet Union gained access to the top speeds of three of the T-72 tanks: 42, 46, and 41 miles per hour. Does the sample evidence indicate that the average top speed of the T-72 tanks is less than 45 miles per hour? Use a significance level of $\alpha = .10$. (Make any assumptions that are necessary for the hypothesis test to be valid.)

10.4 Hypothesis Test about a Population Proportion: Large-Sample Case

In this country, advertisements for automobiles have traditionally been directed towards males. However, according to researchers at the Ford Motor Co. (*Time*, October 27, 1980), women bought 39% of all new cars sold in the U.S. in 1979. Suppose that we wish to test the null hypothesis that the true proportion of new car buyers in 1980 who were female is equal to .39 (i.e., H_0: $p = .39$) against the alternative H_a: $p > .39$.

The procedure described in the box on p. 308 is used to test an hypothesis about a population proportion, p, based on a large sample from the target population.

In order to validly apply the procedure, the sample size must be sufficiently large to guarantee approximate normality of the sampling distribution of the sample proportion, $\hat{p}$:

ASSUMPTION REQUIRED

The interval $\hat{p} \pm 2\sqrt{\hat{p}\hat{q}/n}$ does not contain 0 or 1.

LARGE-SAMPLE TEST OF HYPOTHESIS ABOUT A POPULATION PROPORTION

a. One-tailed test

H_0: $p = p_0$

H_a: $p > p_0$

(or H_a: $p < p_0$)

Test statistic:

$$z = \frac{\hat{p} - p_0}{\sqrt{p_0 q_0 / n}}$$

Rejection region:

$z > z_\alpha$ (or $z < -z_\alpha$)

where $q_0 = 1 - p_0$

b. Two-tailed test

H_0: $p = p_0$

H_a: $p \neq p_0$

Test statistic:

$$z = \frac{\hat{p} - p_0}{\sqrt{p_0 q_0 / n}}$$

Rejection region:

$z < -z_{\alpha/2}$ or $z > z_{\alpha/2}$

EXAMPLE 10.7 Suppose that in a random sample of $n = 120$ new car buyers in 1980, 57 were women. Does this evidence indicate that the true proportion of new car buyers in 1980 who were women is significantly larger than .39, the 1979 proportion? Test at significance level $\alpha = .05$.

Solution We wish to perform a large-sample test about a population proportion, p. We define

H_0: $p = .39$ (i.e., no change from 1979 to 1980)

H_a: $p > .39$ (i.e., proportion of new car buyers who were women increased in 1980)

where p represents the true proportion of all new car buyers in 1980 who were women.

At significance level $\alpha = .05$, the rejection region for this one-tailed test consists of all values of z for which

$z > z_{.05} = 1.645$

(See Figure 10.6.)

The test statistic requires the calculation of the sample proportion, $\hat{p}$, of new car buyers who were women:

$$\hat{p} = \frac{\text{Number of sampled new car buyers who were women}}{\text{Number of new car buyers sampled}}$$

$$= 57/120 = .475$$

Noting that $q_0 = 1 - p_0 = 1 - .39 = .61$, we obtain the following value of the test statistic:

$$z = \frac{\hat{p} - p_0}{\sqrt{p_0 q_0 / n}} = \frac{.475 - .39}{\sqrt{(.39)(.61)/120}} = 1.91$$

This value of z lies within the rejection region (see Figure 10.6); we thus conclude that the proportion of new car buyers in 1980 who were women increased significantly from .39. The probability of our having made a Type I error (rejecting H_0 if, in fact, it is true) is $\alpha = .05$.

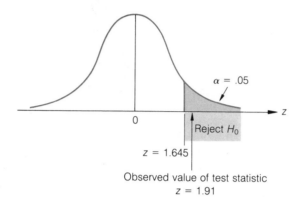

FIGURE 10.6
Rejection Region,
Example 10.7

$\alpha = .05$

0

Reject H_0

$z = 1.645$

Observed value of test statistic
$z = 1.91$

EXAMPLE 10.8   Refer to Example 8.14. Does the information given there provide evidence (at $\alpha = .01$) that the proportion of Northern homes which are heated by gas differs significantly from .5?

Solution   The parameter of interest is a population proportion, p. We define

$$H_0: \quad p = .5$$

$$H_a: \quad p \neq .5$$

where p is the true proportion of all Northern homes which are heated by gas. Note that we wish to be able to detect a departure in either direction from the null hypothesized value of $p = .5$; hence, the test is two-tailed.

At significance level $\alpha = .01$, the null hypothesis will be rejected if

$$z < -z_{.005} \quad \text{or} \quad z > z_{.005}$$

that is, H_0 will be rejected if

$$z < -2.58 \quad \text{or} \quad z > 2.58$$

This rejection region is shown in Figure 10.7 (p. 310). The sample proportion of Northern homes which are heated by gas is

$$\hat{p} = 42/80 = .525$$

Thus, the test statistic has the value

$$z = \frac{\hat{p} - p_0}{\sqrt{p_0 q_0/n}} = \frac{.525 - .5}{\sqrt{(.5)(.5)/80}} = .45$$

The null hypothesis cannot be rejected (at $\alpha = .01$), since the computed value of z does not lie within the rejection region (see Figure 10.7). There is insufficient

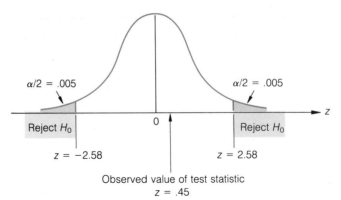

FIGURE 10.7

Rejection Region,
Example 10.8

evidence to support the hypothesis that the proportion of Northern homes heated by gas differs significantly from .5.

   Although small-sample procedures are available for testing hypotheses about a population proportion, the details are omitted from our discussion. It is our experience that they are of limited utility, since most surveys of binomial populations (e.g., opinion polls) performed in the real world use samples which are large enough to employ the techniques of this section.

EXERCISES   **10.10**   Past experience has shown that 10% of the recipients of loans from a particular mortgage-lending institution default within the first three years. The mortgage company has observed, however, that the proportion who default seems to be on the increase. If they can obtain evidence (at $\alpha = .02$) that the proportion of customers who default is now greater than .10, the company will review and revise its guidelines for granting mortgages. A random sample of 100 customers who received loans three years ago indicated that 16 have since defaulted. Test the hypothesis of interest to the mortgage company.

10.11   The Food Marketing Institute (FMI) was formed in 1977 to guard against forces outside the supermarket industry (including government) which impede the efficiency and productivity of the industry. With some 1,100 national members, FMI is the voice of 55% of the retail food business, including one-store operators, large food chains, and grocery wholesalers. However, in a random sample of $n = 40$ food retailers located in rural areas of the country, only 18 are registered members of FMI. Is there evidence, at $\alpha = .05$, that the true proportion of food retailers located in rural areas who are members of FMI is significantly less than the national proportion of .55?

10.12   A large manufacturer of frost-free refrigerators provides a particular model in one of three colors: white, yellow, or green. In a random selection of 700 refrigerators sold, 260 were green. Does this evidence indicate that buyers of this particular model refrigerator have a preference for green frost-free refrigerators, i.e., is the true proportion of customers who purchase green refrigerators larger than $\frac{1}{3}$? Use a significance level of $\alpha = .10$.

10.13   Usually, when trees grown in greenhouses are replanted in their natural habitat, there is only a 50% survival rate. However, a recent General Telephone and Electronics (GTE) advertisement claimed that trees grown in a particular environment ideal for plant growth have a 95% survival rate when replanted. These trees are grown inside a mountain in Idaho where the air temperature, carbon dioxide content, and humidity are all constant, and there are no major disease or insect problems. A key growth ingredient—light—is supplied by specially made GTE Sylvania Super-Metalarc lamps. These lights help the young trees develop a more fibrous root system which aids in the transplantation. Suppose that we wish to challenge GTE's claim, i.e., we wish to test whether the true proportion of all trees grown inside the Idaho mountain which survive when replanted in their natural habitat is less than .95. We randomly sample 50 of the trees grown in the controlled environment, replant the trees in their natural habitat, and observe that 46 of the trees survive. Perform the test at a level of significance of $\alpha = .01$.

10.5 Hypothesis Test about the Difference between Two Population Means: Large-Sample Case

General Foods and Procter & Gamble, the nation's two largest roasters of coffee beans, have recently slashed their wholesale prices for ground coffee. Suppose that a consumer group wishes to determine whether the mean price per pound, μ_1, of Procter & Gamble's ground coffee exceeds the mean price per pound, μ_2, of General Foods' ground coffee. That is, the consumer group will test the null hypothesis $H_0: (\mu_1 - \mu_2) = 0$ against the alternative $H_a: (\mu_1 - \mu_2) > 0$. The following large-sample procedure is applicable for testing an hypothesis about $(\mu_1 - \mu_2)$, the difference between two population means:

LARGE-SAMPLE TEST OF HYPOTHESIS ABOUT $(\mu_1 - \mu_2)$

a. One-tailed test

$H_0: (\mu_1 - \mu_2) = D_0$

$H_a: (\mu_1 - \mu_2) > D_0$

(or $H_a: (\mu_1 - \mu_2) < D_0$)

Test statistic:

$$z = \frac{(\bar{x}_1 - \bar{x}_2) - D_0}{\sigma_{(\bar{x}_1 - \bar{x}_2)}} \approx \frac{(\bar{x}_1 - \bar{x}_2) - D_0}{\sqrt{\dfrac{s_1^2}{n_1} + \dfrac{s_2^2}{n_2}}}$$

Rejection region:

$z > z_\alpha$ (or $z < -z_\alpha$)

b. Two-tailed test

$H_0: (\mu_1 - \mu_2) = D_0$

$H_a: (\mu_1 - \mu_2) \neq D_0$

Test statistic:

$$z = \frac{(\bar{x}_1 - \bar{x}_2) - D_0}{\sigma_{(\bar{x}_1 - \bar{x}_2)}} \approx \frac{(\bar{x}_1 - \bar{x}_2) - D_0}{\sqrt{\dfrac{s_1^2}{n_1} + \dfrac{s_2^2}{n_2}}}$$

Rejection region:

$z < -z_{\alpha/2}$ or $z > z_{\alpha/2}$

[*Note:* D_0 is our symbol for the particular numerical value specified for $(\mu_1 - \mu_2)$ in the null hypothesis. In many practical applications, we wish to hypothesize that there is no difference between the population means; in such cases, $D_0 = 0$.]

The following assumptions are required about the sample sizes and the sampling procedure:

ASSUMPTIONS REQUIRED

1. The sample sizes n_1 and n_2 are sufficiently large, say, $n_1 \geq 30$ and $n_2 \geq 30$.
2. The two samples are selected randomly and independently from the target populations.

EXAMPLE 10.9 A consumer group selected independent random samples of supermarkets located throughout the country for the purpose of comparing the retail prices per pound of General Foods and Procter & Gamble brands of ground coffee. The results of the investigation are summarized in Table 10.1. Does this evidence indicate that the mean retail price per pound of Procter & Gamble's ground coffee is significantly higher than the mean retail price per pound of General Foods' ground coffee? Use a significance level of $\alpha = .01$.

TABLE 10.1
Ground Coffee Prices,
Example 10.9

PROCTER & GAMBLE	GENERAL FOODS
$n_1 = 63$	$n_2 = 58$
$\bar{x}_1 = \$2.98$	$\bar{x}_2 = \$2.93$
$s_1 = \$.11$	$s_2 = \$.07$

Solution The consumer group wishes to test the hypotheses

H_0: $(\mu_1 - \mu_2) = 0$ (i.e., no difference in mean retail price)

H_a: $(\mu_1 - \mu_2) > 0$ (i.e., mean retail price per pound of Procter & Gamble brand is higher than that of the General Foods brand)

where

$\mu_1 =$ Mean retail price per pound of Procter & Gamble's ground coffee at all supermarkets

$\mu_2 =$ Mean retail price per pound of General Foods' ground coffee at all supermarkets

This one-tailed, large-sample test is based on a z statistic. Thus, we will reject H_0 if $z > z_\alpha = z_{.01}$. Since $z_{.01} = 2.33$, the rejection region, as shown in Figure 10.8, is given by

$z > 2.33$

We compute the test statistic as follows:

$$z \approx \frac{(\bar{x}_1 - \bar{x}_2) - D_0}{\sqrt{\frac{s_1^2}{n_1} + \frac{s_2^2}{n_2}}} = \frac{(2.98 - 2.93) - 0}{\sqrt{\frac{(.11)^2}{63} + \frac{(.07)^2}{58}}} = 3.01$$

Since this computed value of $z = 3.01$ lies in the rejection region (see Figure 10.8), there is sufficient evidence (at $\alpha = .01$) to conclude that the mean retail price per pound of Procter & Gamble brand ground coffee is significantly higher than the mean retail price per pound of General Foods brand ground coffee. The probability of our having committed a Type I error is $\alpha = .01$

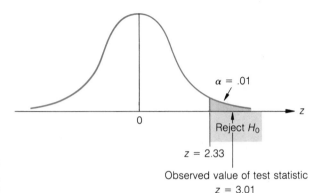

$\alpha = .01$

Reject H_0

$z = 2.33$

Observed value of test statistic
$z = 3.01$

FIGURE 10.8
Rejection Region,
Example 10.9

EXAMPLE 10.10   Neighborhoods D and E of the Florida city described in Chapter 1 have many similar characteristics. They both contain smaller, lower-priced homes, and are inhabited primarily by young people who are beginning their careers. However, a realtor in the city suspects there is a significant difference between the mean values of homes in the two neighborhoods. To test his claim, he selected independent random samples of the sale prices (during 1978) of homes in both neighborhoods, and summarized his results as shown in Table 10.2. Test the realtor's belief, using significance level $\alpha = .01$.

TABLE 10.2
Sale Price Data,
Example 10.10

NEIGHBORHOOD D	NEIGHBORHOOD E
$n_1 = 30$	$n_2 = 40$
$\bar{x}_1 = \$42,356$	$\bar{x}_2 = \$36,491$
$s_1 = \$8,572$	$s_2 = \$4,264$

Solution   The relevant hypothesis test consists of the elements

$$H_0: \ (\mu_1 - \mu_2) = 0$$

$$H_a: \ (\mu_1 - \mu_2) \neq 0$$

where μ_1 and μ_2 are the mean values (as characterized by the sale price) of the homes in neighborhoods D and E, respectively.

For this large-sample test, we will reject H_0 if $z < -z_{\alpha/2} = -z_{.005}$ or if $z > z_{\alpha/2} = z_{.005}$; in other words, the rejection region (see Figure 10.9) consists of the following sets of z-values:

$$z < -2.58 \quad \text{or} \quad z > 2.58$$

The test statistic is computed as follows:

$$z \approx \frac{(\bar{x}_1 - \bar{x}_2) - D_0}{\sqrt{\dfrac{s_1^2}{n_1} + \dfrac{s_2^2}{n_2}}} = \frac{(42,356 - 36,491) - 0}{\sqrt{\dfrac{(8,572)^2}{30} + \dfrac{(4,264)^2}{40}}} = 3.44$$

This z-value lies in the upper-tail rejection region (see Figure 10.9); there is sufficient evidence (at $\alpha = .01$) to support the realtor's claim of a significant difference between the mean values of homes in neighborhoods D and E.

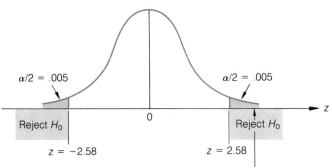

FIGURE 10.9
Rejection Region,
Example 10.10

EXERCISES   **10.14**   Refer to Exercise 8.24, in which the data, Table 10.3, relating to the costs of new homes (in thousands of dollars) in two areas of the country, were obtained. Does the sample information provide sufficient evidence (at $\alpha = .05$) that the mean cost of a new home in California is greater than the mean cost of a new home in Maine?

TABLE 10.3
Comparison of Housing
Costs, Exercise 10.14

CALIFORNIA	MAINE
$n_1 = 100$	$n_2 = 80$
$\bar{x}_1 = 94.8$	$\bar{x}_2 = 73.4$
$s_1 = 12.75$	$s_2 = 16.8$

10.15   A study was conducted to investigate the difference in the fees charged by land surveyors in two neighboring states. Independent random samples of the fees assessed to survey residential properties in the two states were obtained; the results are presented in Table 10.4. Can we conclude (at significance level .01) that there is a significant difference between the mean fees charged by land surveyors in the two states?

TABLE 10.4
Land Surveyor Fees,
Exercise 10.15

STATE A	STATE B
$n_1 = 50$	$n_2 = 50$
$\bar{x}_1 = \$85$	$\bar{x}_2 = \$92$
$s_1 = \$4$	$s_2 = \$10$

10.16   The Metro Atlanta Rapid Transit Authority (MARTA) has recently implemented a six-week bus driver training program designed to reduce tardiness of buses on regularly scheduled routes. In order to gauge the effectiveness of the training program, a study was conducted before and after the program was instituted. MARTA authorities were stationed at 30 randomly selected bus stops (involving 30 different buses) in the metro-Atlanta area before the program was implemented and observed tardiness (in minutes) of the scheduled bus arrivals. Similar data were collected at 35 randomly selected bus stops (involving 35 different buses) after the six-week training program. The results are summarized in Table 10.5. MARTA authorities are interested in determining if the mean tardiness of bus arrivals at metro-Atlanta bus stops has decreased significantly since the implementation of the training program. Perform a test of hypothesis for MARTA. Use a significance level of $\alpha = .02$.

TABLE 10.5
Bus Tardiness Times,
Exercise 10.16

BEFORE TRAINING PROGRAM	AFTER TRAINING PROGRAM
$n_1 = 30$	$n_2 = 35$
$\bar{x}_1 = 5.25$ minutes	$\bar{x}_2 = 2.37$ minutes
$s_1 = 1.88$ minutes	$s_2 = 1.45$ minutes

[*Note:*   The tardiness of a bus which arrived early or on time would be recorded as 0 minutes.]

10.17   A major oil company has developed a new gasoline additive that is designed to increase average gas mileage in subcompact cars. Before marketing the new additive, the company conducts the following experiment: One hundred subcompact cars are randomly selected and divided into two groups of 50 cars each. The gasoline additive is dispensed into the tanks of the cars in one group but not the other. The miles per gallon obtained by each car in the study is then recorded. The data are summarized in Table 10.6 on p. 316. Is there sufficient evidence for the oil company to claim that the average gas mileage obtained by subcompact cars with the additive is greater than the average gas mileage obtained by subcompact cars without the additive? Test at $\alpha = .10$.

TABLE 10.6
Gas Mileages,
Exercise 10.17

WITHOUT ADDITIVE	WITH ADDITIVE
$n_1 = 50$	$n_2 = 50$
$\bar{x}_1 = 28.4$ miles per gallon	$\bar{x}_2 = 32.1$ miles per gallon
$s_1 = 9.5$ miles per gallon	$s_2 = 10.7$ miles per gallon

10.6 Hypothesis Test about the Difference between Two Population Means: Small-Sample Case

The Environmental Protection Agency (EPA) often conducts studies designed to estimate highway and city gas mileages for automobiles (see Case Study 6.3). Suppose that the EPA is interested in comparing the mean highway mileages for cars using leaded and unleaded gasoline. That is, the EPA will test the hypothesis that μ_1, the mean highway mileage for cars using leaded gasoline, differs from μ_2, the mean highway mileage for cars using unleaded gasoline, i.e., $(\mu_1 - \mu_2) \neq 0$. However, the EPA is able to obtain independent random samples of only $n_1 = 11$ cars which use leaded gasoline and $n_2 = 10$ cars which require unleaded gasoline. When the sample sizes n_1 and n_2 are inadequate to permit use of the large-sample procedure of Section 10.5, the following modifications may be made to perform a small-sample test of an hypothesis about the difference between two population means:

SMALL-SAMPLE TEST OF HYPOTHESIS ABOUT $(\mu_1 - \mu_2)$

a. One-tailed test

H_0: $(\mu_1 - \mu_2) = D_0$

H_a: $(\mu_1 - \mu_2) > D_0$

(or H_a: $(\mu_1 - \mu_2) < D_0$)

Test statistic:

$$t = \frac{(\bar{x}_1 - \bar{x}_2) - D_0}{\sqrt{s_p^2 \left(\frac{1}{n_1} + \frac{1}{n_2} \right)}}$$

Rejection region:

$t > t_\alpha$ (or $t < -t_\alpha$)

b. Two-tailed test

H_0: $(\mu_1 - \mu_2) = D_0$

H_a: $(\mu_1 - \mu_2) \neq D_0$

Test statistic:

$$t = \frac{(\bar{x}_1 - \bar{x}_2) - D_0}{\sqrt{s_p^2 \left(\frac{1}{n_1} + \frac{1}{n_2} \right)}}$$

Rejection region:

$t < -t_{\alpha/2}$ or $t > t_{\alpha/2}$

where

$$s_p^2 = \frac{(n_1 - 1)s_1^2 + (n_2 - 1)s_2^2}{n_1 + n_2 - 2}$$

and the distribution of t is based on $(n_1 + n_2 - 2)$ degrees of freedom

---

The test procedure is based on the following assumptions, which are again more restrictive than in the large-sample case:

ASSUMPTIONS REQUIRED

1. The populations from which the samples are selected both have relative frequency distributions which are approximately normal.
2. The variances of the two populations are equal.
3. The random samples are selected in an independent manner from the two populations.

EXAMPLE 10.11   Each of the 21 cars (11 using leaded gas and 10 using unleaded gas) selected for the EPA study was tested and the number of miles per gallon (mpg) obtained by each recorded. The results are summarized in Table 10.7. Is there evidence (at $\alpha = .02$) that the mean number of miles per gallon obtained by all cars using leaded gasoline differs significantly from the mean number of miles per gallon obtained by all cars using unleaded gasoline?

TABLE 10.7
Gas Mileages, Example 10.11

LEADED	UNLEADED
$n_1 = 11$	$n_2 = 10$
$\bar{x}_1 = 17.2$ mpg	$\bar{x}_2 = 19.9$ mpg
$s_1 = 2.1$ mpg	$s_2 = 2.0$ mpg

Solution   The EPA desires to test the following hypotheses:

H_0: $(\mu_1 - \mu_2) = 0$ (i.e., no difference in mean mpg)

H_a: $(\mu_1 - \mu_2) \neq 0$ (i.e., mean mpg values for leaded and unleaded gas differ)

where

μ_1 = True mean mpg for cars using leaded gasoline

μ_2 = True mean mpg for cars using unleaded gasoline

Since the samples selected for the study are small ($n_1 = 11$, $n_2 = 10$), the following assumptions are required:

1. The populations of number of miles per gallon obtained by cars using leaded gasoline and cars using unleaded gasoline both have approximately normal distributions.
2. The variances of the populations of mpg values for the two types of gasoline are equal.
3. The samples were independently and randomly selected.

If these assumptions are valid, the test statistic will have a t distribution with $(n_1 + n_2 - 2) = (11 + 10 - 2) = 19$ degrees of freedom. Using a significance level of $\alpha = .02$, the rejection region is given by

$$t < -t_{.01} = -2.539 \quad \text{or} \quad t > t_{.01} = 2.539$$

(See Figure 10.10, p. 318.)

Since we have assumed that the two populations have equal variances (i.e., that $\sigma_1^2 = \sigma_2^2 = \sigma^2$), we need to compute an estimate of this common variance. Our pooled estimate is given by

$$s_p^2 = \frac{(n_1 - 1)s_1^2 + (n_2 - 1)s_2^2}{n_1 + n_2 - 2} = \frac{(11 - 1)(2.1)^2 + (10 - 1)(2.0)^2}{11 + 10 - 2} = 4.216$$

Using this pooled sample variance in the computation of the test statistic, we obtain

$$t = \frac{(\bar{x}_1 - \bar{x}_2) - D_0}{\sqrt{s_p^2\left(\frac{1}{n_1} + \frac{1}{n_2}\right)}} = \frac{(17.2 - 19.9) - 0}{\sqrt{4.216\left(\frac{1}{11} + \frac{1}{10}\right)}} = -3.01$$

Now the computed value of t falls within the rejection region (see Figure 10.10), thus we reject the null hypothesis (at $\alpha = .02$) and conclude that there is a significant difference between the mean number of miles per gallon obtained by cars using leaded gasoline and the mean number of miles per gallon obtained by cars using unleaded gasoline. The probability that we will incorrectly reject the null hypothesis (i.e., conclude that there is a difference in mean mpg if in fact there is no difference) is only .02.

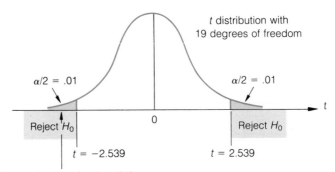

FIGURE 10.10
Rejection Region, Example 10.11

EXAMPLE 10.12 Two relatively new energy-saving concepts in home building are solar-powered homes and earth-sheltered homes. An individual is drawing up plans for a new home and wishes to compare his expected annual heating costs for the two types of innovation. Independent random samples of solar-powered homes (which receive 50% of their energy from the sun) and earth-sheltered homes yielded the summary data, Table 10.8, on annual heating costs. (You may assume the homes were comparable with respect to size, climatic conditions, etc.) Is there evidence (at $\alpha = .05$) that the mean annual cost of heating an earth-sheltered home is significantly less than the corresponding cost of heating a 50% solar-powered home?

TABLE 10.8		
Heating Costs, Example 10.12	SOLAR-POWERED	EARTH-SHELTERED
	$n_1 = 12$	$n_2 = 6$
	$\bar{x}_1 = \$285$	$\bar{x}_2 = \$234$
	$s_1 = \$55$	$s_2 = \$26$

Solution   Of interest to the potential home builder is a test of the hypotheses

$$H_0: \quad (\mu_1 - \mu_2) = 0$$

$$H_a: \quad (\mu_1 - \mu_2) > 0$$

where

$\mu_1 =$ True mean annual cost of heating a solar-powered home

$\mu_2 =$ True mean annual cost of heating an earth-sheltered home

Since we are restricted to small samples ($n_1 = 12$, $n_2 = 6$) from the target populations, we must make the following assumptions:

1. The populations of annual heating costs for both solar-powered and earth-sheltered homes have approximately normal distributions.
2. The variances of the populations of annual heating costs for the two types of homes are equal.
3. The samples were randomly and independently selected.

Under these assumptions, the test statistic will have a t distribution with $(n_1 + n_2 - 2) = (12 + 6 - 2) = 16$ degrees of freedom. Thus, at significance level $\alpha = .05$, the null hypothesis will be rejected if

$$t > t_{.05} = 1.746$$

This rejection region is shown in Figure 10.11.

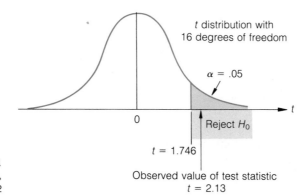

FIGURE 10.11
Rejection Region,
Example 10.12

We have assumed that the two populations have equal variances (i.e., that $\sigma_1^2 = \sigma_2^2 = \sigma^2$); our pooled estimate of this common variance is given by

$$s_p^2 = \frac{(n_1 - 1)s_1^2 + (n_2 - 1)s_2^2}{n_1 + n_2 - 2} = \frac{(12 - 1)(55)^2 + (6 - 1)(26)^2}{12 + 6 - 2} = 2{,}290.9$$

Now, the value of the test statistic may be computed as follows:

$$t = \frac{(\bar{x}_1 - \bar{x}_2) - D_0}{\sqrt{s_p^2\left(\frac{1}{n_1} + \frac{1}{n_2}\right)}} = \frac{(285 - 234) - 0}{\sqrt{2{,}290.9\left(\frac{1}{12} + \frac{1}{6}\right)}} = 2.13$$

The computed value of t exceeds the critical value of $t = 1.746$. We thus reject the null hypothesis (at significance level .05) and conclude that the mean annual cost of heating a solar-powered home exceeds the mean cost of heating an earth-sheltered home; i.e., the mean annual cost of heating an earth-sheltered home is significantly less than the cost of heating a solar-powered home.

We wish to note that the two-sample statistic used here (and in Section 8.6 for interval estimation) relies heavily upon the assumptions that the two target populations are (at least approximately) normally distributed and that their respective variances are equal. However, studies have shown that, when the sample sizes n_1 and n_2 are equal, the requirement of equal population variances can be relaxed somewhat. In other words, when $n_1 = n_2$, σ_1^2 and σ_2^2 can assume different values and the test statistic t will still be approximated by a t distribution with appropriate degrees of freedom.

EXERCISES   **10.18**   The main ingredient in a reputable car repair service is a good mechanic. However, many repair service owners in the city of Chicago are finding it difficult to hire good mechanics without charging exorbitant labor prices to the customer. Suppose that we wish to compare the hourly labor rates of mechanics working at gas stations and at car dealerships in Chicago. Independent random samples of 15 gas stations and 10 car dealerships are selected and the hourly labor rate of mechanics at each is recorded. The data are summarized in Table 10.9. Test to see whether there is a difference between the true mean hourly labor rates of mechanics working at gas stations and mechanics working at car dealerships in the city of Chicago. Use a significance level of $\alpha = .05$.

TABLE 10.9
Hourly Labor Rates,
Exercise 10.18

GAS STATIONS	CAR DEALERS
$n_1 = 15$	$n_2 = 10$
$\bar{x}_1 = \$25.77$	$\bar{x}_2 = \$32.50$
$s_1 = \$4.10$	$s_2 = \$5.60$

10.19   A local university has developed a special course on effective selling techniques which has been very popular with real estate agents, brokers, insurance agents, and others who generally are paid on a commission basis. Independent random samples of 11 insurance agents who had not taken the course and 8 who had taken it were selected; each agent was asked how many sales he or she had made during the past month. The results are presented in Table 10.10. Is there sufficient evidence, at significance level .05, to conclude that the mean number of monthly sales for agents who have taken the course exceeds the mean number of monthly sales for agents who have not taken the course?

TABLE 10.10
Sales Data,
Exercise 10.19

DID NOT TAKE COURSE	DID TAKE COURSE
$n_1 = 11$	$n_2 = 8$
$\bar{x}_1 = 10$	$\bar{x}_2 = 12$
$s_1 = 2.3$	$s_2 = 3.4$

10.20 An industrial plant wants to determine which of two types of fuel—gas or electric—will produce the most useful energy at the lowest cost. One measure of economical energy production, called the "plant investment per delivered quad," is calculated by taking the amount of money (in dollars) invested in the particular utility by the plant and dividing it by the amount of delivered energy (in quadrillion British thermal units). The smaller this ratio, the less an industrial plant pays for its delivered energy.

Random samples of eleven plants using electrical utilities and sixteen plants using gas utilities were taken, and the plant investment per quad was calculated for each. The resulting data are summarized in Table 10.11.

TABLE 10.11
Plant Investment/Quad
($ Billions), Exercise 10.20

ELECTRIC	GAS
$n_1 = 11$	$n_2 = 16$
$\bar{x}_1 = \$22.5$	$\bar{x}_2 = \$17.5$
$s_1 = \$4.18$	$s_2 = \$3.87$

a. Do these data provide sufficient evidence at the $\alpha = .01$ level of significance to indicate a difference between the average investments per quad for plants using gas and those using electrical utilities?

b. What assumptions are required for the hypothesis test, part a, to be valid?

10.21 Since certain preservatives may have an effect on the nutritional quality of the food into which they are introduced, food packaging plants must continually test their products. A preliminary experiment to determine the nutritional effect of a certain preservative used 24 guinea pigs. The guinea pigs were randomly split into two equal groups so that 12 guinea pigs received a diet without the preservative and 12 were fed a diet with the preservative. The data yielded the summary information shown in Table 10.12. Test whether guinea pigs on a diet with this preservative gain less weight, on the average, than those on a diet without this preservative. Use a significance level of $\alpha = .02$. (List any assumptions necessary for the validity of the test.)

TABLE 10.12
Weight Gains,
Exercise 10.21

WITHOUT PRESERVATIVE	WITH PRESERVATIVE
$n_1 = 12$	$n_2 = 12$
$\bar{x}_1 = 6.8$ grams	$\bar{x}_2 = 5.3$ grams
$s_1 = 1.5$ grams	$s_2 = 0.9$ grams

10.7 Hypothesis Test about the Difference between Two Proportions: Large-Sample Case

Suppose that we are interested in comparing the proportion of unmarried applicants who are approved for personal loans, p_1, with the proportion of married applicants who are approved for personal loans, p_2. Then the target parameter about which we will test an hypothesis is $(p_1 - p_2)$. The method for performing a large-sample test of hypothesis about the difference, $(p_1 - p_2)$, between two population proportions is outlined in the box.

LARGE-SAMPLE TEST OF HYPOTHESIS ABOUT $(p_1 - p_2)$

a. One-tailed test

H_0: $(p_1 - p_2) = D_0$

H_a: $(p_1 - p_2) > D_0$

(or H_a: $(p_1 - p_2) < D_0$)

Test statistic:

$$z = \frac{(\hat{p}_1 - \hat{p}_2) - D_0}{\sigma_{(\hat{p}_1 - \hat{p}_2)}}$$

$$\approx \frac{(\hat{p}_1 - \hat{p}_2) - D_0}{\sqrt{\dfrac{\hat{p}_1\hat{q}_1}{n_1} + \dfrac{\hat{p}_2\hat{q}_2}{n_2}}}$$

Rejection region:

$z > z_\alpha$ (or $z < -z_\alpha$)

where $\hat{q}_1 = 1 - \hat{p}_1$ and $\hat{q}_2 = 1 - \hat{p}_2$

b. Two-tailed test

H_0: $(p_1 - p_2) = D_0$

H_a: $(p_1 - p_2) \neq D_0$

Test statistic:

$$z = \frac{(\hat{p}_1 - \hat{p}_2) - D_0}{\sigma_{(\hat{p}_1 - \hat{p}_2)}}$$

$$\approx \frac{(\hat{p}_1 - \hat{p}_2) - D_0}{\sqrt{\dfrac{\hat{p}_1\hat{q}_1}{n_1} + \dfrac{\hat{p}_2\hat{q}_2}{n_2}}}$$

Rejection region:

$z < -z_{\alpha/2}$ or $z > z_{\alpha/2}$

The sample sizes n_1 and n_2 must be sufficiently large to ensure that the sampling distributions of $\hat{p}_1$ and $\hat{p}_2$, and hence of the difference $(\hat{p}_1 - \hat{p}_2)$, are approximately normal. [*Note:* If the sample sizes are not sufficiently large, p_1 and p_2 can be compared using the technique discussed in Chapter 14.]

ASSUMPTIONS REQUIRED

The intervals

$$\hat{p}_1 \pm 2\sqrt{\frac{\hat{p}_1\hat{q}_1}{n_1}} \quad \text{and} \quad \hat{p}_2 \pm 2\sqrt{\frac{\hat{p}_2\hat{q}_2}{n_2}}$$

do not contain 0 or 1.

EXAMPLE 10.13 Unmarried individuals in a particular state have voiced the complaint that they are being discriminated against with respect to the granting of credit. In particular, they claim that the proportion of unmarried applicants who are approved for personal loans is significantly lower than the corresponding proportion of married applicants. They present the summary data, Table 10.13, based on independent random samples of 100 married and 100 unmarried applicants for personal loans. (Assume that the credit histories for all individuals sampled are nearly identical.) Is the claim of discrimination against the unmarried individuals supported (at significance level $\alpha = .01$) by the sample information?

TABLE 10.13
Data on Credit
Discrimination,
Example 10.13

	UNMARRIED	MARRIED
NUMBER OF APPLICANTS SAMPLED	100	100
NUMBER OF SAMPLED APPLICANTS TO WHOM PERSONAL LOANS WERE GRANTED	59	68

Solution We wish to perform a test of

$$H_0: \quad (p_1 - p_2) = 0$$

$$H_a: \quad (p_1 - p_2) < 0$$

where

p_1 = The proportion of all unmarried applicants whose requests for personal loans are approved

p_2 = The proportion of all married applicants whose requests for personal loans are approved

For this large-sample, one-tailed test, the null hypothesis will be rejected if

$$z < -z_{.01} = -2.33$$

(See Figure 10.12.)

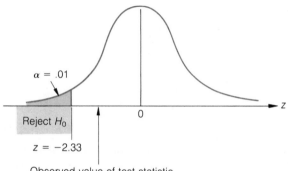

FIGURE 10.12
Rejection Region,
Example 10.13

$\alpha = .01$

Reject H_0

$z = -2.33$

Observed value of test statistic
$z = -1.33$

The sample proportions $\hat{p}_1$ and $\hat{p}_2$ are computed for substitution into the formula for the test statistic:

$\hat{p}_1$ = Sample proportion of unmarried applicants whose loans were approved

= 59/100 = .59

$\hat{p}_2$ = Sample proportion of married applicants whose loans were approved

= 68/100 = .68

hence,

$$\hat{q}_1 = 1 - \hat{p}_1 = 1 - .59 = .41$$
$$\hat{q}_2 = 1 - \hat{p}_2 = 1 - .68 = .32$$

Then the value of the test statistic is

$$z = \frac{(\hat{p}_1 - \hat{p}_2) - D_0}{\sqrt{\dfrac{\hat{p}_1 \hat{q}_1}{n_1} + \dfrac{\hat{p}_2 \hat{q}_2}{n_2}}} = \frac{(.59 - .68) - 0}{\sqrt{\dfrac{(.59)(.41)}{100} + \dfrac{(.68)(.32)}{100}}} = -1.33$$

This value is not less than the critical value of -2.33 (see Figure 10.12). Thus, at $\alpha = .01$, we fail to reject the null hypothesis; there is insufficient evidence to conclude that the proportion of unmarried applicants whose loans are approved is significantly less than the corresponding proportion for married applicants.

EXERCISES   **10.22**   Refer to Example 8.21, in which the results of a survey of the housing preferences of independent random samples of 200 senior citizens and 200 people under the age of 65 are reported. (The information is reproduced in Table 10.14.) Does the sample information indicate a significant difference between the proportions of senior citizens and those under 65 who prefer multiple-family housing? Perform an appropriate hypothesis test at significance level $\alpha = .05$.

TABLE 10.14
Housing Preferences,
Exercise 10.22

	SENIOR CITIZENS	CITIZENS UNDER AGE 65
NUMBER SURVEYED	200	200
NUMBER IN SAMPLE WHO PREFER MULTIPLE-FAMILY ACCOMMODATIONS	146	118

10.23   To market a new white wine, a winemaker decides to use two different advertising agencies, one operating in the East, one in the West. After the white wine has been on the market for eight months, independent random samples of wine drinkers are taken from each of the two regions and questioned concerning their white wine preference. The numbers favoring the new brand are shown in Table 10.15. Is

TABLE 10.15
Data on White Wine
Preference,
Exercise 10.23

	EAST	WEST
NUMBER OF WINE DRINKERS SAMPLED	516	438
NUMBER OF SAMPLED WINE DRINKERS WHO PREFER THE NEW WHITE WINE	18	23

there evidence that the proportion of wine drinkers in the West who prefer the new white wine is larger than the corresponding proportion of wine drinkers in the East? Test at significance level $\alpha = .02$.

10.24   A consumer agency claims that the proportion of defective new microwave ovens of brand Y is no larger than the proportion of defective new ovens of a much more expensive brand, brand Z. To test this claim, independent random samples of 64 new ovens of brand Y and 81 new ovens of brand Z were selected. In the brand Y group, 4 ovens were found to be defective; and in the brand Z group, 3 ovens were found to be defective. Is there sufficient evidence to reject the agency's claim, i.e., is the proportion of defective new brand Y ovens larger than the proportion of defective new brand Z ovens? Test at significance level $\alpha = .01$.

10.25   A large shipment of produce contains McIntosh and Red Delicious apples. To determine whether there is a difference between the percentages of nonmarketable fruit for the two varieties, random samples of 800 McIntosh apples and 800 Red Delicious apples were independently selected and the number of nonmarketable apples of each type were counted. It was found that 33 McIntosh and 58 Red Delicious apples from these samples were nonmarketable. Do these data provide sufficient evidence to indicate a difference between the percentages of nonmarketable McIntosh and Red Delicious apples in the entire shipment? Test at $\alpha = .10$.

10.8   Reporting Test Results: *p*-Values

The statistical hypothesis-testing technique which we have developed in Chapter 9 and in this chapter requires that we choose the significance level α (i.e., the maximum probability of a Type I error that we are willing to tolerate) prior to obtaining the data and computing the test statistic. By choosing α a priori, we in effect fix the rejection region of the test. Thus, no matter how large or how small the observed value of the test statistic, our decision regarding H_0 is clear-cut: reject H_0 (i.e., conclude that the test results are statistically significant) if the observed value of the test statistic falls into the rejection region; fail to reject H_0 otherwise (i.e., conclude that the test results are insignificant). This "fixed" significance level, α, then serves as a measure of the reliability of our inference. However, there is one drawback to a test conducted in this manner: a measure of the *degree* of significance of the test results is not readily available. That is, if in fact the value of the test statistic falls into the rejection region, we have no measure of the extent to which the data disagree with the null hypothesis, H_0.

EXAMPLE 10.14   A large-sample test of H_0: $\mu = 80$ versus H_a: $\mu > 80$ is to be conducted at a fixed significance level of $\alpha = .05$. Consider the following possible values of the computed test statistic:

$$z = 1.82 \qquad z = 5.66$$

a.   Which of the above values of the test statistic gives the stronger evidence for the rejection of H_0?

b.   How can we measure the extent of disagreement between the sample data and H_0 for each of the above values?

Solution   **a.**   The appropriate rejection region for this test, at $\alpha = .05$, is given by

$$z > z_{.05} = 1.645$$

Clearly, for either of the test statistic values given above, $z = 1.82$ or $z = 5.66$, we will reject H_0; hence, the result in each case is statistically significant. Recall, however, that the appropriate test statistic for a large-sample test concerning μ is simply the z-score for the observed sample mean, $\bar{x}$, calculated by using the hypothesized value of μ in H_0 (in this case, $\mu = 80$). The larger the z-score, the greater the distance (in units of standard deviations) that $\bar{x}$ is from the hypothesized value of $\mu = 80$. Thus, a z-score of 5.66 would present stronger evidence that the true mean is larger than 80 than would a z-score of 1.82. Our reasoning stems from our knowledge of the sampling distribution of $\bar{x}$; if in fact $\mu = 80$, we would certainly not expect to observe an $\bar{x}$ with a z-score as large as 5.66.

b.   One way of measuring the amount of disagreement between the observed data and the value of μ in the null hypothesis is to calculate the probability of observing a value of the test statistic equal to or greater than the actual computed value, if in fact H_0 were true. That is, if z_c is the computed value of the test statistic, calculate

$$P(z \geq z_c)$$

assuming the null hypothesis is true. This "disagreement" probability, or **p-value,** is calculated below for each of the computed test statistics, $z = 1.82$ and $z = 5.66$, using Table 3, Appendix E.

$$P(z \geq 1.82) = .5 - .4656 = .0344$$
$$P(z \geq 5.66) \approx .5 - .5 = 0$$

From our discussion in part a, you can see that the smaller the p-value, the greater the extent of disagreement between the data and the null hypothesis, i.e., the more significant the result.

In general, p-values are computed as follows:

MEASURING THE DISAGREEMENT BETWEEN THE DATA AND H_0: p-VALUES

Large-sample one-tailed test: p-value $= P(z \geq |z_c|)$

Large-sample two-tailed test: p-value $= 2 \cdot P(z \geq |z_c|)$

where z_c is the computed value of the test statistic.

Small-sample one-tailed test: p-value $= P(t \geq |t_c|)$

Small-sample two-tailed test: p-value $= 2 \cdot P(t \geq |t_c|)$

where t_c is the computed value of the test statistic.

[*Note:* $|z_c|$ and $|t_c|$ denote the *absolute values* of z_c and t_c and will always be positive.]

Notice that the p-value for a two-tailed test is twice the probability for the one-tailed test. This is because the disagreement between the data and H_0 can be in two directions.

When publishing the results of a statistical test of hypothesis in journals, case studies, reports, etc., many researchers make use of p-values. Instead of selecting α a priori and then conducting a test as outlined in this chapter, the researcher will compute and report the value of the appropriate test statistic and its associated p-value. It is left to the reader of the report to judge the significance of the result, i.e., the reader must determine whether to reject the null hypothesis in favor of the alternative, based upon the reported p-value. This p-value is often referred to as the **attained significance level** of the test. Usually, the null hypothesis will be rejected if the attained significance level is *less* than the fixed significance level, α, chosen by the reader. The inherent advantages of reporting test results in this manner are twofold: (1) each reader is permitted to select the maximum value of α that they would be willing to tolerate if they actually carried out a standard test of hypothesis in the manner outlined in this chapter; and (2) a measure of the degree of significance of the result (i.e., the p-value) is provided.

REPORTING TEST RESULTS AS p-VALUES: HOW TO DECIDE WHETHER TO REJECT H_0

1. Choose the maximum value of α that you are willing to tolerate.
2. If the attained significance level (p-value) of the test is less than the maximum value of α, then reject the null hypothesis.

EXAMPLE 10.15 Refer to Example 10.1. Compute the attained significance level of the test. Interpret this value.

Solution In this large-sample test concerning a population mean μ, the computed value of the test statistic was $z_c = .903$. Since the test is one-tailed, the associated p-value is given by

$$P(z \geq |z_c|) = P(z \geq .903)$$

$$\approx .5 - .3159 = .1841$$

Thus, the attained significance level of the test is approximately .184. In order to reject the null hypothesis H_0: $\mu > 30$, we would have to be willing to risk a Type I error probability, α, of at least .184. Most researchers would not be willing to take this risk and would deem the result insignificant (i.e., conclude that there is insufficient evidence to reject H_0).

EXAMPLE 10.16 Refer to Example 10.10.

a. Compute the attained significance level of the test.
b. Make the appropriate conclusion if you are willing to tolerate a Type I error probability of $\alpha = .01$.

Solution   **a.**   The computed test statistic for this large-sample test about $(\mu_1 - \mu_2)$ was given as $z_c = 3.44$. Since the test is two-tailed, the associated p-value is

$$2 \cdot P(z \geq |z_c|) = 2 \cdot P(z \geq |3.44|)$$
$$= 2 \cdot P(z \geq 3.44)$$
$$\approx 2(.5 - .4999) = 2(.0001) = .0002$$

Thus, the approximate attained significance level of the test is .0002.

b.   Since the attained significance level of .0002 is less than the maximum tolerable Type I error probability of $\alpha = .01$, we will reject H_0 and conclude that a significant difference exists between the mean values of homes in neighborhoods D and E. In fact, we could choose a Type I error probability as small as $\alpha = .0002$ and still have sufficient evidence to reject H_0. Thus, the result is highly significant.

EXAMPLE 10.17   Refer to Example 10.6. Compute the attained significance level of the test and interpret your result.

Solution   The computed test statistic for this small-sample test concerning μ was given as $t_c = 2.0$. Since the t-test is one-tailed, the associated p-value is found by calculating

$$P(t \geq |t_c|) = P(t \geq 2.0)$$

where the distribution of t is based on $(n - 1) = 15$ degrees of freedom. To find the p-value from the table of critical t-values provided in Table 4, Appendix E, search for the value 2.0 in the row corresponding to 15 df. You can see that 2.0 does not appear in this row but falls between the values 1.753 (in the $t_{.05}$ column) and 2.131 (in the $t_{.025}$ column). The p-value associated with 1.753 is .05, and the p-value associated with 2.131 is .025. Thus, the p-value associated with $t_c = 2.0$ is somewhere between .025 and .05. Since the exact p-value is unknown, we take the conservative approach and report the approximate p-value as the larger of the two endpoints, namely .05. This (approximate) p-value indicates that the null hypothesis H_0: $\mu = 175$ will be rejected in favor of H_a: $\mu > 175$ for any fixed significance level α larger than or equal to .05.

The above will be the usual procedure when computing a p-value from Table 4, Appendix E. That is, the exact value of the test statistic t_c will usually not appear in the row corresponding to the appropriate number of df. You will need to locate the tabled t-values between which t_c falls and determine the p-values associated with these tabled values (by noting the subscripts (α) in the respective column headings). Report the approximate attained significance level of the test as the larger of the two p-values.

Whether we conduct a test using p-values or the rejection region approach, our choice of a maximum tolerable Type I error probability becomes critical to the decision concerning H_0 and should not be hastily made. In either case, care should be taken to weigh the seriousness of committing a Type I error in the context of the problem.

EXERCISES   **10.26**   For a large-sample test of

$$H_0: \quad (\mu_1 - \mu_2) = 0$$
$$H_a: \quad (\mu_1 - \mu_2) > 0$$

compute the p-value associated with each of the following computed test statistic values:

a. $z_c = 1.96$ b. $z_c = 1.645$ c. $z_c = 2.67$ d. $z_c = 1.25$

10.27   For a large-sample test of

$$H_0: (p_1 - p_2) = 0$$

$$H_a: (p_1 - p_2) \neq 0$$

compute the p-value associated with each of the following computed test statistic values:

a. $z_c = -1.01$ b. $z_c = -2.37$ c. $z_c = 4.66$ d. $z_c = -1.45$

10.28   Refer to Exercise 10.1. Compute the attained significance level (p-value) of the test. Interpret the result.

10.29   Refer to Exercise 10.7. Compute the attained significance level (p-value) of the test. What is your decision regarding H_0 if you are willing to risk a maximum Type I error probability of only $\alpha = .01$?

10.30   Refer to Exercise 10.15. Compute the attained significance level (p-value) of the test. Compare to the fixed significance level, α, and make an appropriate conclusion.

10.31   Refer to Exercise 10.24. Compute the attained significance level (p-value) of the test. What is your decision regarding H_0 if you are willing to increase the probability of a Type I error to $\alpha = .10$?

10.9 Summary

In this chapter, we have summarized the procedures for testing hypotheses about various population parameters. As we noted with the estimation techniques of Chapter 8, fewer assumptions about the sampled populations are required when the sample sizes are large. We also wish to emphasize that *statistical* significance differs from *practical* significance, and the two must not be confused. A reasonable approach to hypothesis testing blends a valid application of the formal statistical procedures with the researcher's knowledge of the subject matter.

KEY WORDS

Statistical significance
Practical significance
Attained significance level
p-Value

SUPPLEMENTARY
EXERCISES

[*Note:* For each of these exercises, carefully define any notation used, perform all steps of the relevant hypothesis test, state a conclusion in terms of the problem, and specify any assumptions required for the validity of the procedure.]

10.32 Legislators in the state of New Jersey wish to compare the mean annual amount of tax paid on nongovernment-owned properties to the mean amount which would be assessed annually to government-owned properties in the state if they were subject to taxes. Independent random samples of $n_1 = 48$ nongovernment-owned properties and $n_2 = 36$ government-owned properties were selected for the study. The annual tax paid on each of the nongovernment-owned properties and the annual amount which would be assessed, at current tax rates, to each of the government-owned properties is recorded; the data are summarized in Table 10.16. Does the sample information provide sufficient evidence to conclude that the mean annual tax which would be paid on government-owned properties exceeds that paid on nongovernment-owned properties in New Jersey? Use a significance level of $\alpha = .05$.

TABLE 10.16
Property Tax Data,
Exercise 10.32

NONGOVERNMENT	GOVERNMENT
$n_1 = 48$	$n_2 = 36$
$\bar{x}_1 = \$3{,}074$	$\bar{x}_2 = \$3{,}412$
$s_1 = \$417$	$s_2 = \$580$

10.33 In order to stock their various departments with the type and style of goods that appeal to their potential group of customers, a downtown Los Angeles department store is interested in determining whether the average age of downtown Los Angeles shoppers is less than 35 years. A random sample of 20 downtown shoppers revealed the following summary statistics on their ages:

$$\bar{x} = 34.6 \text{ years}$$

$$s = 10.8 \text{ years}$$

Is there sufficient evidence to conclude that the average age of downtown Los Angeles shoppers is less than 35 years? Test at $\alpha = .10$.

10.34 As part of its energy conservation plan, the city of Portland, Oregon, has built an efficient new bus system. It is hoped that the new bus system will fight fuel waste by discouraging the use of automobiles. Suppose that the proportion of the city's residents who rode the old bus system regularly was known to be 14%. Three months after installation of the new bus system, a survey of 100 city residents indicated that 22 now ride the buses regularly. Is there evidence that the true proportion of the city's residents who ride the new bus system regularly is greater than .14? Test at $\alpha = .05$.

10.35 The rising price of oil has prompted Brazil to use alcohol, distilled mainly from its bumper crops of sugar cane, as a power source. Many of the automobiles traveling along Brazil's roads are powered by pure alcohol instead of gasoline. Suppose that it is desired to compare the proportion of cars powered by pure alcohol in Brazil to the proportion of cars powered by pure alcohol in the United States. Random samples of automobiles are selected independently in Brazil and the United States and the number using alcohol as a motor fuel (gasohol) determined. The data are shown in Table 10.17. Test (at significance level $\alpha = .01$) whether there is a significant difference between the proportion of Brazil's cars powered by alcohol and the corresponding proportion in the United States.

TABLE 10.17

Gasohol Data, Exercise 10.35

	BRAZIL	UNITED STATES
NUMBER OF AUTOMOBILES SAMPLED	70	108
NUMBER OF SAMPLED AUTOMOBILES WHICH ARE USING ALCOHOL AS A MOTOR FUEL	15	6

10.36 A Key West, Florida, condominium investor wishes to determine if a difference exists between the average yearly profits of small and large condominium developments presently operating in the state. Fifty small developments and sixty-five large developments in the state are randomly and independently selected, and last year's profits (or losses) are recorded for each. A summary of the data is given in Table 10.18. Test, at significance level $\alpha = .02$, whether a difference exists between the average yearly profits of small and large condominium developments in Florida.

TABLE 10.18

Yearly Profit ($ Thousands), Exercise 10.36

SMALL DEVELOPMENTS	LARGE DEVELOPMENTS
$n_1 = 50$	$n_2 = 65$
$\bar{x}_1 = 417$	$\bar{x}_2 = 588$
$s_1 = 225$	$s_2 = 317$

10.37 Suppose that Ford Motor Company is involved in a multimillion dollar court case concerning their LTD model luxury cars. To support their case, Ford needs to show that the mean dollar amount of damage done to an LTD as a result of a 35 mile per hour crash into the rear bumper of a parked car is less than $400. Ford test-crashed 32 of their LTDs into parked cars at 35 miles per hour and then had an independent claims adjuster appraise the dollar amount of damage done to each. The results are:

$$\bar{x} = \$366$$
$$s = \$54$$

Perform the appropriate test of hypothesis for Ford Motor Company. Base your conclusion on the attained significance level (p-value) of the test.

10.38 The manager of a fast-food hamburger chain is concerned with the unusually high proportion of crushed hamburger buns being delivered by a supplier. If the next shipment of 2,000 buns contains more than 10% which are crushed, the manager will return the entire shipment to the supplier. Because it is physically impossible to check every hamburger bun in such a large shipment, a random sample of 100 buns is selected for inspection. Based on this sample, the manager will decide whether to accept or reject the shipment. Suppose that on the next shipment, 14 of the 100 buns sampled were crushed. Is there sufficient evidence for the manager to reject the entire shipment, i.e., is the true proportion of crushed hamburger buns in the shipment larger than 10%? Test at $\alpha = .05$.

10.39   In order to compare the performances of two contract estimators, a large construction company obtained data on the difference between the actual cost of a job and the amount estimated for the job for random samples of 10 jobs by the first estimator and 16 jobs by the second estimator. The results are given in Table 10.19. Perform the comparison for the company, using $\alpha = .10$. [*Hint:* Test the null hypothesis H_0: $(\mu_1 - \mu_2) = 0$ against the alternative H_a: $(\mu_1 - \mu_2) \neq 0$, where μ_1 represents the mean difference between actual cost and amount estimated for jobs by Estimator 1, and μ_2 represents the mean difference between actual cost and amount estimated for jobs by Estimator 2.]

TABLE 10.19
Difference between the Actual Cost and Amount Estimated, Exercise 10.39

ESTIMATOR 1	ESTIMATOR 2
$n_1 = 10$	$n_2 = 16$
$\bar{x}_1 = \$-5,000$	$\bar{x}_2 = \$3,000$
$s_1 = \$10,000$	$s_2 = \$6,000$

10.40   A certain retailer believes that there is no difference between the reliabilities of his house brand of toasters and those of a name brand. In order to substantiate this belief, the retailer randomly sampled 36 toasters of his house brand and 40 of the name-brand toasters and checked each for defective workmanship. Of the house-brand toasters, 3 were found to be defective, and of the 40 name-brand toasters, 5 were found to be defective. Is there a difference between the true proportions of house-brand and name-brand toasters that are defective? Use a significance level of $\alpha = .10$.

10.41   A stereo manufacturer advertises that his top-of-the-line turntable has an average lifespan of more than 60 months. When asked by a consumer group to provide evidence which supports this claim, the manufacturer contacts 15 customers who have purchased this high-quality turntable, and asks each how long their turntable ran before needing replacement. From these 15 measurements, he computes an average lifespan of 61.7 months and a standard deviation of 12.6 months. Conduct a test to determine if the true average lifespan of the manufacturer's top-of-the-line turntable is greater than 60 months. Use a significance level of $\alpha = .01$.

10.42   In July 1977, the United States Congress was considering a bill that would make it illegal for an employer to force an employee to retire at age sixty-five. The bill was not passed, due basically to the lack of support from elderly and retired workers. Suppose that one Congressman believes that the majority of today's elderly and retired workers would have supported the bill. From a random sample of 300 workers who were asked to retire at age sixty-five, the Congressman found that 162 would have preferred to stay on the job. Is there evidence to support the Congressman's belief, i.e., is the true proportion of retired workers who would have preferred to stay on the job past age sixty-five larger than .50? Base your conclusion on the attained significance level (p-level) of the test.

10.43 To what extent, if any, can we influence local weather conditions? Some Texas farmers have hired a meteorologist to investigate the effectiveness of cloud seeding in the artificial production of rainfall. Two farming areas in Texas with similar past meteorological records were selected for the experiment. One is seeded regularly throughout the year, while the other is left unseeded. The monthly precipitation at the farms for the first six months of the year is monitored and the difference in precipitation between the seeded and unseeded areas recorded each month. These six measurements resulted in a sample mean of $\bar{x} = .18$ inches and a sample standard deviation of $s = .40$ inches. Using a significance level of $\alpha = .02$, test whether μ, the true mean difference between the average monthly precipitations in the seeded and unseeded farm areas, is greater than 0.

10.44 The advertising department of a major western Pennsylvania automobile dealership, which has branches in the cities of Pittsburgh and Erie, wished to determine whether advertising is really effective in influencing prospective customers. The dealership decided to heavily advertise its new diesel model car in the city of Pittsburgh for one week, while maintaining a low profile on the car in the city of Erie. One month after the campaign ended, 28 of the 215 cars sold by the dealer in Pittsburgh were diesels, while 2 of the 37 cars sold by the dealer in Erie were diesels. Do the results of the study indicate that the proportion of diesels sold in a city exposed to heavy advertising is higher than the proportion of diesels sold in a city where no advertising is planned? Base your decision on the attained significance level (p-value) of the test. Compare to your choice of a fixed significance level, α.

10.45 A breeder and seller of live hogs wishes to determine if there is a difference between the average weekly selling prices of hogs at two different Florida markets: Live Oak and Gainesville. The weekly selling prices at the two markets were obtained for independent random samples of $n_1 = 4$ and $n_2 = 5$ weeks. These results are summarized in Table 10.20. Conduct an hypothesis test to determine whether there is a difference between the average weekly selling prices of live hogs at the two Florida markets. Use a significance level of $\alpha = .05$.

TABLE 10.20
Selling Price of Live Hogs (¢ per Lb.), Exercise 10.45

LIVE OAK	GAINESVILLE
$n_1 = 4$	$n_2 = 5$
$\bar{x}_1 = 53.15$	$\bar{x}_2 = 54.20$
$s_1 = 3.57$	$s_2 = 3.32$

10.46 The amount of milk ordered daily at a large grocery store is very carefully monitored by the store owner. If not enough milk is ordered, the demand will not be met. If too much milk is ordered, there will be an excess supply and thus spoilage, costing the store money. Based on past experience, the store owner ordered, on the average, 1,000 gallons of milk per day to meet demand. However, the owner believes that the milk demand per day has changed. A check of the amount of milk (in gallons) purchased per day for a random sample of 50 days revealed the following summary information:

$$\bar{x} = 977 \text{ gallons}$$

$$s = 121 \text{ gallons}$$

Is there evidence that the average number of gallons of milk purchased per day is different from 1,000? Test at a significance level of $\alpha = .10$.

10.47   Last year's severe winter and late, cool spring played a major role in Wisconsin's small commercial apple crop production. The U.S. Department of Agriculture (USDA) will investigate the progress of this winter's crop. The USDA randomly selects 10 commercial orchards in the state and determines the number of pounds of McIntosh apples produced at each so far this year. A second random sample (independent of the first) of 20 commercial orchards is selected and the number of pounds of Red Delicious apples produced at each so far this year is recorded. (Each orchard selected contained 100 or more trees of bearing age.) The data are summarized in Table 10.21. At a level of significance of $\alpha = .05$, is there evidence of a difference between the average commercial productions so far this year of Wisconsin's two winter variety apples, McIntosh and Red Delicious?

TABLE 10.21
Wisconsin Apple Production (Thousands of Pounds), Exercise 10.47

McINTOSH	RED DELICIOUS
$n_1 = 10$	$n_2 = 20$
$\bar{x}_1 = 10.5$	$\bar{x}_2 = 9.7$
$s_1 = 4.1$	$s_2 = 6.6$

10.48   A new insecticide is advertised to kill more than 95% of roaches upon contact. In a laboratory test, the insecticide was applied to 400 roaches and, although all 400 eventually died, only 384 died immediately after contact. Is this sufficient evidence to support the advertised claim? Base your decision upon the computed p-value.

10.49   The following experiment was performed for a producer of 3-minute egg timers (i.e., timers that, if they are operating correctly, will track time for a period of 180 seconds). A random sample of 9 egg timers were timed in a vertical (upright) position, while a second random sample (independent of the first) of 9 egg timers were timed in a position 20 degrees from vertical. The results are given in Table 10.22. Conduct an hypothesis test to determine if there is a difference between the mean operating times of 3-minute egg timers in the two different positions. Test at $\alpha = .01$.

TABLE 10.22
Egg Timer Operation Times, Exercise 10.49

VERTICAL	20° FROM VERTICAL
$n_1 = 9$	$n_2 = 9$
$\bar{x}_1 = 187$ seconds	$\bar{x}_2 = 183$ seconds
$s_1 = 9$ seconds	$s_2 = 6$ seconds

10.50 An auditor for a hardware-store chain wished to compare the efficiencies of two different auditing techniques. A random sample of 30 store accounts were audited using technique 1 and a second random sample of 50 store accounts were audited using technique 2. The number of material (accounting) errors found in each store account was recorded. The data are summarized in Table 10.23. Is there evidence of a difference between the mean numbers of accounting errors detected by the two auditing techniques? Use $\alpha = .05$.

TABLE 10.23

Auditing Errors, Exercise 10.50

TECHNIQUE 1	TECHNIQUE 2
$n_1 = 30$	$n_2 = 50$
$\bar{x}_1 = 2.15$	$\bar{x}_2 = 1.98$
$s_1 = 1.36$	$s_2 = 1.40$

10.51 Most supermarket chains give each store manager a detailed plan showing exactly where each product belongs on each shelf. Since more products are picked up from shelves at eye level than from any others, the most profitable and fastest-moving items are placed at eye level to make them easy for shoppers to reach. Traditionally, the eye-level shelf has been slightly under 5 feet from the floor—just the right height for the average female shopper, 5-feet 4-inches tall. But nowadays, more men are shopping than ever before. Since the average male shopper is 5-feet 10-inches tall, how will this affect the eye-level shelf? To investigate this, a random sample of 100 supermarkets from across the country were selected and the height of the eye-level shelf (i.e., the shelf with the most popular products) was recorded for each. The results were:

$\bar{x} = 62$ inches

$s = 3$ inches

Is there evidence that the average height of the eye-level shelf at supermarkets is now higher than 60 inches from the floor (i.e., higher than the traditional height of 5 feet)? Base your decision on the attained significance level (p-value) of the test.

10.52 Many "solar" homes waste the sun's valuable energy. To be an efficient solar house, it must be specially designed to trap solar radiation and use it effectively. Basically, homes with energy-efficient solar heating systems can be categorized into two groups, *passive* solar heating systems and *active* solar heating systems. In a passive solar heating system, the house itself is a solar energy collector, while in an active solar heating system, elaborate mechanical equipment is used to convert the sun's rays into heat. Suppose that we wish to determine whether there is a difference between the proportions of passive solar and active solar heating systems which require less than 200 gallons of oil per year in fuel consumption. Independent random samples of 50 passive and 50 active solar-heated homes are selected and the number which required less than 200 gallons of oil last year is noted. The results are given in Table 10.24. Is there evidence of a difference between the proportions of passive and active solar-heated homes which required less than 200 gallons of oil in fuel consumption last year? Test at a level of significance of $\alpha = .02$.

	PASSIVE SOLAR	ACTIVE SOLAR
NUMBER OF HOMES	50	50
NUMBER WHICH REQUIRED LESS THAN 200 GALLONS OF OIL LAST YEAR	37	46

CASE STUDY 10.1
Motorcycle Accidents and Death Rates

In the past few years there has been a substantial increase in the number of motorcycles on the nation's highways. The *Statistical Bulletin* (April–June 1978) reports that "with motorcycle registrations exceeding five million in 1977, there is now, on the average, one motorcycle for every 43 persons in the United States. Increasing motorcycle use has been accompanied by a mounting death toll from motorcycle accidents." In 1976 there were 3,000 fatalities among motorcycle operators and their passengers, compared with the 2,043 motorcycle accident deaths in 1966. Writes the *Statistical Bulletin*:

> . . . When measured in terms of the number of miles driven, the hazards of motorcycling are even more pronounced. According to National Safety Council estimates, the death rate for motorcycle riders was about 13 deaths per million miles in 1976, compared with a rate of 3.3 for drivers, passengers, and pedestrians in all other motor vehicle accidents.
>
> Reflecting the strong appeal of motorcycles to younger people, nearly 80 percent of motorcycle accident fatalities occur among motorcyclists under 30 years of age. More than 90 percent of all fatalities are among males. . . . There is no doubt that inexperience and lack of skill are contributing factors to the relative higher fatality rates among motorcyclists.

Another major contributor to the high motorcycle fatality rate is that many motorcyclists fail to wear helmets. Studies have shown that the number of fatal or serious head injuries is significantly reduced when properly constructed and fitted protective headgear is worn. The *Statistical Bulletin* reported on a recent study conducted in Sacramento County, California, which determined that serious head injuries were 50% lower for those who wore helmets than for those who did not. At present, laws in 23 states and the District of Columbia require that helmets be worn by all motorcycle riders. However, 16 states require helmets only for motorcyclists under 18 years of age, one state for those only under age 17, and one state for those only under 16. This leaves 9 states with absolutely no motorcycle helmet requirements. These differing helmet laws are taken into consideration when state insurance companies assess the premium charged to motorcycle owners.

α. Suppose that an insurance company, with branch offices in Michigan (which has a helmet law) and Illinois (which has no helmet law), wishes to compare the proportions of motorcycle accidents in the two states last year which resulted in fatal or serious head injuries. What is the target parameter of interest to the insurance company?

b. An insurance agent, employed by the company to work mainly in the area of motorcycle insurance premiums, believes that the proportion of motorcycle accidents in Illinois which resulted in fatal or serious head injuries is over 50% higher than the corresponding proportion in Michigan. Set up the appropriate null and alternative hypotheses if the insurance company wishes to test this claim.

c. A random sample of 55 motorcyclists who received medical treatment in Illinois last year—as identified from police reports, death certificates, and the admission and emergency records of hospitals—showed that 41 received fatal or serious head injuries. In Michigan, 8 of the 31 sampled motorcycle accidents resulted in fatal or serious head injuries to the motorcyclist. Use this information to test the hypotheses of part b at significance level $\alpha = .05$.

CASE STUDY 10.2
Florida's "New
Look" Jury
System

Greetings, You are hereby requested to report for jury duty at 9 AM Monday in the courthouse. Please do not be upset about the inconvenience of being away from your job, sitting idle for several hours while attorneys plea bargain, and possibly reporting every day of the week for a trial that might be either postponed or cancelled.

With this facetious description of a jury summons, Frank Dorman, staff writer for the Gainesville *Sun,* began his article on Florida's jury selection system.* To most Floridians, the system is simply a waste of a lot of people's time that costs a lot of the taxpayers' money. Nevertheless, serving on jury duty is one of our most important civic responsibilities and should not be taken lightly.

Dorman reports that "serious attempts" at making "permanent improvements in the state's jury systems" have been underway since 1978. It was at that time that the Office of the (Florida) State Courts Administrator (OSCA) began a two-year, $300,000 pilot study of the new jury procedures in seven Florida counties. After the study, OSCA estimated that if all 67 Florida counties tried the new system, more than $500,000 in jury selection costs could be saved per year, a reduction of 50%. The study also indicates that the new system has markedly improved Floridians' outlook on jury service. Some of the highlights of the new juror system are:

1. Single-day juror empanelment (i.e., all judges use only one day to select jurors for trials during the week) which eliminates the need for having jurors continue to report to the court each day of the week and perhaps never being selected
2. 24-hour toll-free telephone call-in service which enables jurors to call the night prior to their service date to learn from a recorded message whether they should report the next day
3. The use of first class mail for summons distribution rather than registered mail or hand delivery
4. The use of computers to randomly choose venires, the large group (usually 100 or more) of people from which juries are selected

---

*Gainesville *Sun,* February 22, 1981.

a.   Jurors in Florida are paid $10 a day and 10¢ a mile for travel expenses. Under the old system, a jury trial in Alachua County involved an average juror cost of $600. With the new procedural changes described above, it is believed that the average juror cost will be less than 50% of the old cost, i.e., less than $300. Suppose that a random sample of 8 Alachua County jury trials operating under the new system had an average cost of $\bar{x} = \$292$ and a standard deviation of $s = \$83$. Test the hypothesis that the average juror cost under the new system in Alachua County is less than $300. Use a significance level of $\alpha = .05$.

b.   Suppose that OSCA wishes to determine if the average length of actual service on jury duty (in days) is less for jurors selected under the new system than under the old system. What are the null and alternative hypotheses of interest to OSCA?

c.   OSCA claims that only 7% of the "new system" jurors have unfavorable impressions of jury service. If a random sample of 250 jurors selected under the new system included 18 who had unfavorable impressions of jury service, test the OSCA claim. [*Hint:* Test H_0: $p = .07$ against H_a: $p > .07$, using a significance level of $\alpha = .05$.]

<table>
<tr><td>

CASE STUDY 10.3

Drug Prescriptions Linked to Medical Advertising

</td><td>

Have you ever purchased a product solely on the basis of an appealing advertisement? If you have, you are no exception, for almost all consumers have, at one time or another, been influenced by an eye-catching advertisement in a magazine, newspaper, or on television. Most well-planned advertising campaigns are successful because the advertiser (or manufacturer) of the product is able to correspond, on a one-to-one basis, with the consumer (or reader) through the media. With the majority of consumers' likes and dislikes already known in advance (through extensive market studies), the successful advertiser is able to conjure in the consumer's mind an appealing picture of the product being advertised.

</td></tr>
</table>

This approach to boosting a product's sales may not be so effective when the direct line between the advertiser and consumer is broken. For example, in the marketing of prescription drugs, the sales success of a certain product depends almost entirely upon the physician who writes the drug prescription. Although the consumer is the ultimate user of the product, it is the prescribing physician at whom medical (drug) advertisements are aimed. Harold Walton writes* that "those charged with responsibilities for advertising to physicians through the printed media rarely, if ever, expect a 'sales miracle.'" Medical advertisers do, however, "expect ongoing advertising to contribute to or to maintain a [physician's] awareness of a therapeutic message. His recollection . . . will be vivid and accurate enough for him to consider prescribing the advertised product at the appropriate time." Nevertheless, says Walton, almost all physicians "deny that advertising shapes their professional decisions." Physicians are very skeptical "about therapeutic concepts elaborated within a commercial frame," and this skepticism has many medical advertisers pursuing

---

*H. Walton. "Ad recognition and prescribing by physicians." *Journal of Advertising Research,* June 1980, *20,* 39–48. Reprinted from the *Journal of Advertising Research.* © Copyright 1980, by the Advertising Research Foundation.

their "programs with little enthusiasm, not fully convinced that medical advertising can deliver results. . . ."

Despite this outward negativity on the part of the physician, Walton conducted research for the purpose of showing that "advertising appearing in medical journals . . . has a positive effect on the prescribing behavior of physicians, an effect that is far from coincidental." A sample of 100 physicians involved in patient care was randomly selected from the circulation list of a medical journal which is among the most widely read and reaches approximately 90% of the physicians in private practice in the United States. Each physician was first asked to examine an ad for which all references to product name, generic name, company name, ingredients, and logo were blotted out, and then asked the question, "Have you seen this ad before?" After recording the response, the product in the ad was revealed and the physician was asked if he or she had prescribed or recommended the product in the month prior to the interview. The resulting data were then used in an hypothesis test to decide whether H_a: $(p_1 - p_2) > 0$ is true, that is, to determine if the proportion of physicians who prescribe a certain product is greater for those aware of the ad (p_1) than for those not aware of the ad (p_2). The results of the analysis for six such ads (i.e., six different products) are given in Table 10.25.

TABLE 10.25
Physicians' Responses to Ad Survey, Case Study 10.3

PRODUCT ADVERTISED		PHYSICIANS' RESPONSE	
		Ad Recalled	Ad Not Recalled
BRAND 1	Number in Sample	25	75
	Number Who Prescribed Product	17	30
BRAND 2	Number in Sample	46	54
	Number Who Prescribed Product	34	33
BRAND 3	Number in Sample	34	66
	Number Who Prescribed Product	1	2
BRAND 4	Number in Sample	40	60
	Number Who Prescribed Product	26	39
BRAND 5	Number in Sample	40	60
	Number Who Prescribed Product	7	0
BRAND 6	Number in Sample	34	66
	Number Who Prescribed Product	13	20

a. What assumptions are necessary for the hypothesis-testing procedure to be valid? Are they satisfied in each of the six cases (brands)?

b. For each case in which the assumptions are satisfied, compute the value of the appropriate test statistic.

c. Calculate the corresponding attained significance levels, i.e., *p*-values, for the computed test statistics, part b.

d. Based on the attained significance levels of the tests, for which of the products is the proportion of physicians who prescribe the product significantly greater for those aware of the ad than for those unaware of the ad (i.e., for which of the products does the sample evidence indicate that $(p_1 - p_2) > 0$)? Assume that you are willing to tolerate a Type I error probability of $\alpha = .05$ in each case.

REFERENCES   Daniel, W., & Terrell, J. *Business statistics: Basic concepts and methodology.* 2d ed. Boston: Houghton Mifflin, 1979. Chapter 7.

Dorman, F. " 'New look' in jury selection saving time and money." Gainesville *Sun,* February 22, 1981, 1a, 12a.

Johnson, R., & Siskin, B. *Elementary statistics for business.* North Scituate, Mass.: Duxbury, 1980. Chapters 10 and 11.

McClave, J. T., & Benson, P. G. *Statistics for business and economics.* 2d ed. San Francisco: Dellen, 1982.

Mendenhall, W. *Introduction to probability and statistics.* 5th ed. North Scituate, Mass.: Duxbury, 1979. Chapters 8 and 9.

Metropolitan Life Insurance Company. "Motorcycle accident fatalities." *Statistical Bulletin,* April–June 1978, 7–9.

Walton, H. "Ad recognition and prescribing by physicians." *Journal of Advertising Research,* June 1980, *20,* 39–48.

Eleven

Comparing More than Two Population Means: An Analysis of Variance

Are you better off buying your food at a grocery located in the inner city, one located in the suburbs, or one located in a rural area? And, if you priced the costs of a specific market basket of groceries at a sampling of groceries in each of the three locations, how would you decide whether the data indicate a difference between the mean prices at the three locations? In this chapter, we will consider the general problem of comparing more than two population means, and we will examine the comparison of mean market basket costs in greater detail in Case Study 11.1.

Contents:

11.1 Introduction

Many business firms which generate revenue from the sale of highly expensive equipment often pay their employees on a commission basis. A manufacturer and distributor of minicomputers which employs a large number of salespeople has three compensation plans available: (1) strict commission; (2) fixed salary; and (3) reduced fixed salary plus commission. Consider the problem of comparing the mean monthly sales of those salespeople strictly on commission, those with a fixed salary, and those with a reduced fixed salary plus commission. We can think of the totality of the monthly sales for all salespersons in a particular compensation group as constituting a population that characterizes the sales ability of salespeople in that compensation group. Thus, we wish to compare the mean monthly sales corresponding to the three (types of compensation) monthly sales populations.

The previous month's sales records for random samples of 7 salespeople on a strict commission, 7 with a fixed salary, and 6 on commission plus salary* were selected from the company's files. The data (in thousands of dollars) are recorded in Table 11.1. Scan the data. If the salespeople in each compensation group tend to be similar in ability and motivation, we would expect the mean monthly sales in the populations to be nearly equal. If the salespeople differ substantially in these characteristics, we would expect the population monthly sales means to be correspondingly different. Based on your scanning of the data, do you think that this sample information presents sufficient evidence to indicate a difference among the three population (compensation type) means?

TABLE 11.1
Monthly Sales for Three
Types of Compensation
(Thousands of Dollars)

COMMISSION	FIXED SALARY	COMMISSION PLUS SALARY
165	120	140
98	115	156
130	90	220
210	126	112
195	107	104
187	155	235
240	80	

We have explained in earlier sections that the reliability of inferences based upon intuition cannot be measured. Consequently, we will demonstrate a statistical procedure for deciding whether differences exist among two or more population means. The method we will use is known as *analysis of variance,* or *ANOVA.*

---

*One salesperson from the commission plus salary compensation group had to be eliminated because two of the minicomputer purchasers (whose sales were included in the salesperson's monthly sales total) had requested that the processing of their orders be held up pending further notification.

11.2 One-Way Analysis of Variance and the *F* Statistic

We learned an hypothesis-testing technique for comparing the means of two populations in Chapters 9 and 10. The null and alternative hypotheses in the analysis of variance test for comparing more than two population means take a familiar form.

EXAMPLE 11.1 Refer to the monthly sales-compensation type discussion in Section 11.1. State the null and alternative hypotheses for a test to determine whether there is a difference among the true mean monthly sales for the three types of compensation.

Solution Our objective is to determine whether differences exist among the three population (compensation type) monthly sales means. Consequently, we will select the null hypothesis "All three population means, μ_1, μ_2, μ_3, are equal." That is,

$$H_0: \quad \mu_1 = \mu_2 = \mu_3$$

where μ_1 is the mean monthly sales for those salespeople strictly on commission, μ_2 is the mean monthly sales for those with a fixed salary, and μ_3 is the mean monthly sales for those salespeople on a reduced salary plus commission.

The alternative hypothesis of interest is

$$H_a: \quad \text{At least two of the population means differ}$$

If the differences among the sample means are large enough to indicate differences among the corresponding population means, we will reject the null hypothesis H_0 in favor of the alternative hypothesis H_a; otherwise, we will fail to reject H_0 and conclude that there is insufficient evidence to indicate differences among the population means.

HYPOTHESES FOR A TEST OF *k* POPULATION MEANS

$H_0: \quad \mu_1 = \mu_2 = \cdots = \mu_k$

$H_a: \quad$ At least two population means differ

Experiments for the comparison of more than two population means can be designed using a variety of sampling schemes. However, in this chapter we shall consider only those experiments which use an *independent sampling design.*

DEFINITION 11.1

An *independent sampling design* is one in which independent random samples are drawn from each of the target populations.

When a test for the equality of more than two population means is conducted using the data obtained from an independent sampling design, the procedure is often referred to as a *one-way analysis of variance.* The prefix *one-way* is used because each of the sampling units is classified in only *one* direction. For example, for the monthly sales-compensation type problem of Section 11.1, each salesperson (sampling unit) included in the sample was classified only according to type of compensation received (commission, fixed salary, salary plus commission). In contrast, if the salespeople were also classified according to sex (male or female), then the classification would be *two-dimensional* and, under the appropriate sampling design, a subsequent test for equality of means would be called a *two-way* analysis of variance. Throughout this chapter, when we use the terminology *analysis of variance,* we are referring to a one-way analysis of variance, i.e., a technique for comparing more than two population means with an independent sampling design.

EXAMPLE 11.2   To see how the principle behind the analysis of variance method works, let us consider the following simple example. The means (μ_1 and μ_2) of two populations are to be compared using independent random samples of size 5 from each of the populations. The sample observations and the sample means are shown in Table 11.2.

TABLE 11.2
Data for Example 11.2a

SAMPLE FROM POPULATION 1	SAMPLE FROM POPULATION 2
6	5
−1	1
0	3
3	2
2	4
$\bar{x}_1 = 2$	$\bar{x}_2 = 3$

a. Do you think these data provide sufficient evidence to indicate a difference between the population means μ_1 and μ_2?

b. Now look at two more samples of $n_1 = n_2 = 5$ measurements from the populations, as shown in Table 11.3. Do these data appear to provide evidence of a difference between μ_1 and μ_2?

TABLE 11.3
Data for Example 11.2b

SAMPLE FROM POPULATION 1	SAMPLE FROM POPULATION 2
2	3
2	3
2	3
2	3
2	3
$\bar{x}_1 = 2$	$\bar{x}_2 = 3$

Solution   a.   One way to determine whether a difference exists between the population means μ_1 and μ_2 is to examine the spread (or variation) **between** the sample means $\bar{x}_1$ and $\bar{x}_2$, and to compare it to a measure of variability **within** the samples. The greater the difference in the variations, the greater will be the evidence to indicate a difference between μ_1 and μ_2.

You can see from the data of Table 11.2 that *the difference between the sample means is small in relation to the variability within the sample observations.* Thus, we think you will agree that the difference between $\bar{x}_1$ and $\bar{x}_2$ is not large enough to indicate a difference between μ_1 and μ_2.

b.   Notice that the difference between the sample means for the data of Table 11.3 is identical to the difference shown in Table 11.2. However, since there is now no variability within the sample observations, *the difference between the sample means is large in comparison with the variability within the sample observations.* Thus, the data appear to give clear evidence of a difference between μ_1 and μ_2.

We can apply this principle to the general problem of comparing k population means. If the *variability among the k sample means* is large in relation to the *variability within the k samples,* then there is evidence to indicate that a difference exists among the k population means. The term *analysis of variance* is thus quite descriptive of the procedure. We give and illustrate the use of the computational formulas for these two measures of variability in the following examples.

EXAMPLE 11.3   Refer to Example 11.1, and suppose the data of Table 11.1 represent random samples selected **independently** from the 3 compensation groups. Compute the test statistic appropriate for testing

H_0: $\mu_1 = \mu_2 = \mu_3$

H_a: At least two population means are different

where μ_1 is the true mean monthly sales for salespeople strictly on commission, μ_2 is the true mean monthly sales for those with a fixed salary, and μ_3 is the true mean monthly sales for those on a commission plus salary.

Solution   As stated in Example 11.2, the criterion for testing the equality of means involves a comparison of two measures of variability: (1) the variation among the k sample means; and (2) the variation within the k samples. The first step in obtaining a measure of the variation among the sample means is to compute a weighted sum of squares of deviations of the sample means $\bar{x}_1, \bar{x}_2, \ldots, \bar{x}_k$ about the overall mean. In analysis of variance, this quantity is often called the **sum of squares for treatments** (SST).* The second step is to divide SST by the quantity $(k - 1)$ to obtain the **mean square for**

---

*The term *treatment* evolves from agricultural experiments in which the analysis of variance technique first achieved importance. The sampling units (for example, fields, animals, etc.) in the experiment were "treated" in two or more different ways, and then a comparison of the means of the populations of measurements corresponding to the different treatments made.

treatments (MST). The mean square for treatments, MST, is then used to measure the variation among the k sample means.

When the data are given in the column form of Table 11.1, the computational formulas for SST and MST are simplified. Table 11.4 gives the column totals necessary for computing SST and MST in this example.

TABLE 11.4
Column Totals for Data of Table 11.1

COMMISSION	FIXED SALARY	COMMISSION PLUS SALARY
165	120	140
98	115	156
130	90	220
210	126	112
195	107	104
187	155	235
240	80	
$T_1 = 1{,}225$	$T_2 = 793$	$T_3 = 967$
$n_1 = 7$	$n_2 = 7$	$n_3 = 6$

Total of all observations = 2,985

STEPS IN COMPUTING A MEASURE OF THE VARIATION AMONG k SAMPLE MEANS

1. $\text{SST} = \dfrac{T_1^2}{n_1} + \dfrac{T_2^2}{n_2} + \cdots + \dfrac{T_k^2}{n_k} - \text{CM}$

    where T_i = Total of all observations in column i

    n_i = Number of observations in column i

    CM = Correction for the mean

    $= \dfrac{(\text{Total of all } n \text{ observations})^2}{n}$

    $n = n_1 + n_2 + \cdots + n_k$

2. $\text{MST} = \dfrac{\text{SST}}{k - 1}$

    where k = Number of means to be compared

To obtain a measure of the variation among the 3 sample means, $\bar{x}_1, \bar{x}_2, \bar{x}_3$, in this example, we first compute

$$\text{SST} = \frac{T_1^2}{n_1} + \frac{T_2^2}{n_2} + \frac{T_3^2}{n_3} - \text{CM}$$

$$= \frac{(1{,}225)^2}{7} + \frac{(793)^2}{7} + \frac{(967)^2}{6} - \frac{(\text{Total of all } n \text{ observations})^2}{n}$$

$$SST = 214{,}375 + 89{,}835.57 + 155{,}848.17 - \frac{(2{,}985)^2}{(7 + 7 + 6)}$$

$$= 460{,}058.74 - 445{,}511.25 = 14{,}547.49$$

Dividing SST by $(k - 1) = 2$, since we are comparing $k = 3$ means, we obtain

$$MST = \frac{SST}{k - 1} = \frac{14{,}547.49}{2} = 7{,}273.745$$

To determine how large the value of MST must be before we reject the null hypothesis H_0, we must compare its value, MST = 7,273.745, to the variability within the sample observations themselves. A measure of this within-sample variability, called the **mean square for error** (MSE), is obtained by first computing the **sum of squared errors** (SSE) and then dividing SSE by $(n - k)$.

It can be shown (proof omitted) that the SSE is the pooled sum of squares of deviations of the x-values about their respective sample means:

$$SSE = \sum_{i=1}^{n_1} (x_{1i} - \bar{x}_1)^2 + \sum_{i=1}^{n_2} (x_{2i} - \bar{x}_2)^2 + \cdots + \sum_{i=1}^{n_k} (x_{ki} - \bar{x}_k)^2$$

Thus, the MSE is a pooled measure of the variability within the k samples (an extension of the pooled estimator of σ^2 first discussed in Chapter 8).

STEPS IN COMPUTING A MEASURE OF THE WITHIN-SAMPLE VARIABILITY

1. SSE = SS(Total) − SST

    where   SS(Total) = Total sum of squares

    $\qquad\qquad\qquad$ = (Sum of squares of all observations) − CM

    $\qquad\quad$ SST = Sum of squares for treatments
    $\qquad\qquad\qquad$ (see formula in previous box)

    $\qquad\quad$ CM = Correction for mean
    $\qquad\qquad\qquad$ (see formula in previous box)

2. $MSE = \dfrac{SSE}{n - k}$

    where n = Total number of observations

    $\qquad\quad k$ = Number of means to be compared

To compute SSE and MSE for this example we need, in addition to the previously computed quantities CM = 445,511.25 and SST = 14,547.49,

$$SS(Total) = (\text{Sum of squares of all observations}) - CM$$

$$= (165)^2 + (98)^2 + (130)^2 + \cdots + (235)^2 - 445{,}511.25$$

$$= 492{,}819 - 445{,}511.25 = 47{,}307.75$$

Then

$$SSE = SS(\text{Total}) - SST$$
$$= 47{,}307.75 - 14{,}547.49 = 32{,}760.26$$

and

$$MSE = \frac{SSE}{n-k} = \frac{32{,}760.26}{(20-3)} = \frac{32{,}760.26}{17} = 1{,}927.07$$

Once we have computed measures of the two sources of variability—a measure of the variability due to differences among the sample means (MST = 7,273.745) and a measure of the variability due to within-sample differences among the observations (MSE = 1,927.07)—we are ready to form the test statistic appropriate for testing H_0: $\mu_1 = \mu_2 = \mu_3$. The statistic, called an **F statistic,** is simply the ratio of the mean squares:

$$F = \frac{MST}{MSE}$$

TEST STATISTIC FOR COMPARING k MEANS (INDEPENDENT RANDOM SAMPLES)

Test statistic: $F = \dfrac{MST}{MSE}$

where   MST = Mean square for treatments

$$= \frac{SST}{k-1}$$

MSE = Mean square for error

$$= \frac{SSE}{n-k}$$

n = Total number of observations

k = Number of means to be compared

The appropriate test statistic for this problem is then

$$F = \frac{MST}{MSE} = \frac{7{,}273.745}{1{,}927.07} = 3.77$$

Large values of the F statistic indicate that differences between the sample means are large, and therefore support the alternative hypothesis that the population means differ. We discuss the appropriate rejection region for the analysis of variance F test in Example 11.4. First, we summarize the steps necessary for the computation of the F statistic.

SUMMARY OF STEPS IN COMPUTING THE TEST STATISTIC FOR COMPARING k POPULATION MEANS

1. CM = Correction for mean

$$= \frac{(\text{Total of all observations})^2}{\text{Total number of observations}} = \frac{(\Sigma x_i)^2}{n}$$

2. SS(Total) = Total sum of squares

$$= (\text{Sum of squares of all observations}) - \text{CM}$$

$$= \Sigma x_i^2 - \text{CM}$$

3. SST = Sum of squares for treatments

$$= \left(\begin{array}{c} \text{Sum of squares of column totals} \\ \text{with each square divided by the} \\ \text{number of observations in that column} \end{array} \right) - \text{CM}$$

$$= \frac{T_1^2}{n_1} + \frac{T_2^2}{n_2} + \cdots + \frac{T_k^2}{n_k} - \text{CM}$$

4. SSE = Sum of squares for error

$$= \text{SS(Total)} - \text{SST}$$

5. MST = Mean square for treatments $= \dfrac{\text{SST}}{k-1}$

6. MSE = Mean square for error $= \dfrac{\text{SSE}}{n-k}$

7. F = Test statistic $= \dfrac{\text{MST}}{\text{MSE}}$

EXAMPLE 11.4   Refer to Example 11.3. Specify the rejection region for testing H_0: $\mu_1 = \mu_2 = \mu_3$ using a significance level of $\alpha = .05$. Is there evidence that the mean monthly sales differ among the three types of compensation?

Solution   Under certain conditions (see Section 11.5), the F statistic has a repeated sampling distribution known as the **F distribution.** The shape of the F distribution will depend upon two quantities: **numerator degrees of freedom** and **denominator degrees of freedom.** In a one-way analysis of variance procedure, the F distribution has $(k-1)$ numerator degrees of freedom and $(n-k)$ denominator degrees of freedom. Note that the numerator degrees of freedom, $(k-1)$, was divided into SST to obtain MST (the quantity which appears in the **numerator** of the F statistic). Similarly, the denominator degrees of freedom, $(n-k)$, was divided into SSE to obtain MSE (the quantity which appears in the **denominator** of the F statistic). An F distribution with 7 and 9 df (numerator and denominator df, respectively) is shown in Figure 11.1 (p.350). As you can see, the distribution is skewed to the right.

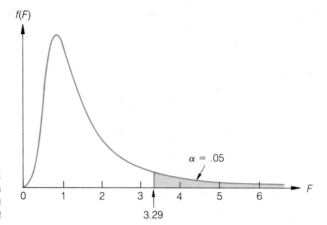

FIGURE 11.1
An F Distribution with
7 Numerator df and
9 Denominator df

In order to establish the rejection region for our test of hypothesis, we need to be able to find F values corresponding to the tail areas of this distribution. We need to find only upper-tail F-values, however, because we will reject H_0 if the value of the computed F statistic is too large. The upper-tail F-values can be found in Tables 5, 6, and 7 of Appendix E. Table 6, partially reproduced in Figure 11.2, gives F-values that correspond to $\alpha = .05$ upper-tail areas for different pairs of degrees of freedom. (Tables 5 and 7 give F-values that correspond to $\alpha = .10$ and $\alpha = .025$, respectively.) The columns of the table correspond to various numerator degrees of freedom, while the rows correspond to various denominator degrees of freedom. Thus, if the numerator degrees of freedom is 7 and the denominator degrees of freedom is 9, we look in the seventh column and ninth row to find the F-value

$$F_{.05} = 3.29$$

As shown in Figure 11.1, $\alpha = .05$ is the tail area to the right of 3.29 in the F distribution with 7 numerator df and 9 denominator df, i.e., the probability that the F statistic will exceed 3.29 is $\alpha = .05$.

Given this information on the F distribution, we are now able to find the rejection region for the analysis of variance F test.

REJECTION REGION FOR A TEST TO COMPARE k POPULATION MEANS

Rejection region: $F > F_\alpha$

where the distribution of F is based on $(k - 1)$ numerator df and $(n - k)$ denominator df, and F_α is the F-value such that $P(F > F_\alpha) = \alpha$

FIGURE 11.2 Reproduction of Part of Table 6, Appendix E: $\alpha = .05$

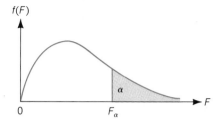

		NUMERATOR DEGREES OF FREEDOM							
ν_1 / ν_2	1	2	3	4	5	6	7	8	9
1	161.4	199.5	215.7	224.6	230.2	234.0	236.8	238.9	240.5
2	18.51	19.00	19.16	19.25	19.30	19.33	19.35	19.37	19.38
3	10.13	9.55	9.28	9.12	9.01	8.94	8.89	8.85	8.81
4	7.71	6.94	6.59	6.39	6.26	6.16	6.09	6.04	6.00
5	6.61	5.79	5.41	5.19	5.05	4.95	4.88	4.82	4.77
6	5.99	5.14	4.76	4.53	4.39	4.28	4.21	4.15	4.10
7	5.59	4.74	4.35	4.12	3.97	3.87	3.79	3.73	3.68
8	5.32	4.46	4.07	3.84	3.69	3.58	3.50	3.44	3.39
9	5.12	4.26	3.86	3.63	3.48	3.37	3.29	3.23	3.18
10	4.96	4.10	3.71	3.48	3.33	3.22	3.14	3.07	3.02
11	4.84	3.98	3.59	3.36	3.20	3.09	3.01	2.95	2.90
12	4.75	3.89	3.49	3.25	3.11	3.00	2.91	2.85	2.80
13	4.67	3.81	3.41	3.18	3.03	2.92	2.83	2.77	2.71
14	4.60	3.74	3.34	3.11	2.96	2.85	2.76	2.70	2.65

DENOMINATOR DEGREES OF FREEDOM

Since we are comparing $k = 3$ means in Example 11.3, the numerator degrees of freedom is $(k - 1) = (3 - 1) = 2$. There are $n = 20$ measurements in the combined samples, so the denominator degrees of freedom is $(n - k) = (20 - 3) = 17$. Using $\alpha = .05$, we will reject the null hypothesis that the three means are equal if

$$F > F_{.05}$$

where from Table 6, Appendix E, the F-value associated with 2 numerator df and 17 denominator df is $F_{.05} = 3.59$. This rejection region is shown in Figure 11.3 (p. 352). The next step is to compare the computed value, $F = 3.77$, of the test statistic (obtained in Example 11.3) with the tabulated value, $F_{.05} = 3.59$. Since this calculated value exceeds the tabulated value of F, it lies in the rejection region (see Figure 11.3). Consequently, we have sufficient evidence (at significance level $\alpha = .05$) to conclude that the true mean monthly sales differ for at least two of the three types of compensation. The chance that this procedure will result in a Type I error (conclude that there are differences when in fact no differences among the means exist) is, at most, $\alpha = .05$.

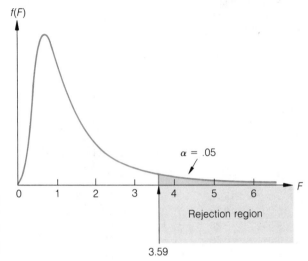

FIGURE 11.3
Rejection Region for
Example 11.4:
Numerator df = 2,
Denominator df = 17

The key elements in a test to compare more than two population means using independent random samples are summarized in the box.

TEST TO COMPARE k POPULATION MEANS FOR AN INDEPENDENT SAMPLING DESIGN

H_0: $\mu_1 = \mu_2 = \cdots = \mu_k$

H_a: At least two treatment means differ

Test statistic: $F = \dfrac{\text{MST}}{\text{MSE}}$

Rejection region: $F > F_\alpha$

where the distribution of F is based on $(k - 1)$ numerator df and $(n - k)$ denominator df, and F_α is the F-value such that $P(F > F_\alpha) = \alpha$

Assumptions: See Section 11.5.

EXERCISES   **11.1**   Find $F_{.05}$ for an F distribution with:
a.   Numerator df = 7, denominator df = 25
b.   Numerator df = 10, denominator df = 8
c.   Numerator df = 30, denominator df = 60
d.   Numerator df = 15, denominator df = 4
Show the location of $F_{.05}$ on a sketch of the F distribution for each part of the exercise.

11.2   Find F_α for an F distribution with 15 numerator df and 12 denominator df for the following values of α:
a. $\alpha = .025$ **b.** $\alpha = .05$ **c.** $\alpha = .10$
Show the location of F_α on a sketch of the F distribution for each part of the exercise.

11.3 Independent random samples were selected from three populations. The data are shown in Table 11.5.

TABLE 11.5
Data for Exercise 11.3

SAMPLE 1	SAMPLE 2	SAMPLE 3
2.1	4.4	1.1
3.3	2.6	0.2
0.2	3.0	2.0
	1.9	

a. Calculate MST for the data. What type of variability is measured by this quantity?
b. Calculate MSE for the data. What type of variability is measured by this quantity?
c. How many degrees of freedom are associated with MST?
d. How many degrees of freedom are associated with MSE?
e. Compute the test statistic appropriate for testing H_0: $\mu_1 = \mu_2 = \mu_3$ against the alternative that at least one population mean is different from the other two.
f. Specify the rejection region, using a significance level of $\alpha = .05$.
g. Make the proper conclusion, based on your answers to parts e and f.

11.4 Most new products are test marketed in several locations, frequently using different advertising techniques. A new type of bourbon, called California Brandy, is test marketed at each of four locations in the state, San Francisco, Los Angeles, San Diego, and Sacramento. The number of sales for the product at each city during each of 5 randomly selected days last month is recorded in Table 11.6.

TABLE 11.6
California Brandy Sales
(Bottles), Exercise 11.4

SAN FRANCISCO	LOS ANGELES	SAN DIEGO	SACRAMENTO
37	40	22	28
15	42	10	49
30	36	8	20
21	12	26	42
53	29	15	41

a. Assuming the samples were independently selected, specify the hypotheses for testing whether there is a difference among the mean daily sales of California Brandy in the four cities.
b. Calculate a measure of the variability among the four sample means (i.e., compute MST).
c. Calculate a measure of the within-sample variability (i.e., compute MSE).
d. Calculate the appropriate statistic for testing the hypothesis of part a.
e. How many degrees of freedom are associated with MST, the numerator of the *F* statistic?
f. How many degrees of freedom are associated with MSE, the denominator of the *F* statistic?
g. Using a significance level of $\alpha = .025$, specify the rejection region.
h. Is there evidence of a difference among the mean daily sales of California Brandy in the four cities?

11.5   As oil drilling costs rise at unprecedented rates, the task of measuring drilling performance becomes essential to a successful oil company. One method of lowering drilling costs is to increase drilling speed. Researchers at Cities Service Co. have developed a drill bit, called the PD-1, which they believe penetrates rock at a faster rate than any other bit on the market. It is decided to compare the speed of the PD-1 with the two fastest drill bits known, the IADC 1-2-6 and the IADC 5-1-7, at 12 drilling locations in Texas. Four drilling sites were randomly assigned to each bit, and the rate of penetration (RoP) in feet per hour (fph) was recorded after drilling 3,000 feet at each site. The data are given in Table 11.7. Based on this information, can Cities Service Co. conclude that the mean RoP differs for at least two of the three drill bits? Test at the $\alpha = .05$ level of significance.

TABLE 11.7
Rate of Penetration (fph),
Exercise 11.5

PD-1	IADC 1-2-6	IADC 5-1-7
35.2	25.8	14.7
30.1	29.7	28.9
37.6	26.6	23.3
34.3	30.1	16.2

11.6   A fast-food chain, specializing in Mexican food (tacos, burritos, etc.), is opening a new franchise in a university town. An important consideration in determining where the franchise will be located is traffic density. Five possible locations (each near a major intersection) are under consideration by the chain. To compare the density of traffic at the possible sites, company employees are placed at each of the five locations to count the number of cars passing each location daily for a period of 10 randomly selected days. (At location IV, the counter assigned to record traffic density became ill and could obtain data for only 8 of the days.) The results are listed in Table 11.8. Assuming the samples of days were independently selected, test for a difference in average daily traffic density among the five locations. Use a significance level of $\alpha = .10$.

TABLE 11.8
Traffic Density,
Exercise 11.6

		LOCATION		
I	II	III	IV	V
344	412	237	518	367
382	441	390	501	445
353	607	365	577	480
395	531	355	642	323
207	486	217	489	366
312	508	268	475	325
407	337	117	532	316
421	419	273	540	381
366	499	288		407
222	387	351		339

11.7   In U.S. business, two basic types of management attitudes prevail: Theory-X bosses believe that workers are basically lazy and untrustworthy, and Theory-Y managers hold that employees are hard-working, dependable individuals (*Time,*

March 2, 1981). Japanese firms take a third approach: Theory-Z companies emphasize long-range planning, consensus decision-making, and strong, mutual worker-employer loyalty. Suppose we wish to compare the hourly wage rates of workers at Theory-X, -Y, and -Z-style corporations. Independent random samples of six engineering firms of each managerial philosophy were selected, and the starting hourly wage rates for laborers at each recorded in Table 11.9. Is there evidence of a difference among the mean starting hourly wages of engineers at Theory-X, -Y, and -Z-style firms? Test at a significance level of $\alpha = .025$.

TABLE 11.9
Hourly Labor Rates
(Dollars), Exercise 11.7

MANAGERIAL ATTITUDE		
Theory X	Theory Y	Theory Z
5.20	6.25	5.50
5.20	6.80	5.75
6.10	6.87	4.60
6.00	7.10	5.36
5.75	6.30	5.85
5.60	6.35	5.90

11.3 Confidence Intervals for Means

An analysis of variance for an independent sampling design may include the construction of confidence intervals for a single mean or for the difference between two means. Because the independent sampling design involves the selection of independent random samples, we can find a confidence interval for a single mean using the method of Section 8.3 and for the difference between two population means using the method of Section 8.6. The only modification we will make in these two procedures is that we will use an estimate of σ^2 based on the information contained in all k samples, namely, the pooled measure of variability within the k samples; that is,

$$\text{MSE} = s^2 = \frac{\text{SSE}}{n - k}$$

Note that this estimate of σ^2 is based upon $(n - k)$ degrees of freedom and that it is the same quantity used in the denominator for the analysis of variance F test. The formulas for the confidence intervals of Chapter 8 are reproduced in the box.

CONFIDENCE INTERVALS FOR MEANS

Single population mean μ_i: $\bar{x}_i \pm t_{\alpha/2} \dfrac{s}{\sqrt{n_i}}$

Difference $(\mu_i - \mu_j)$ between two population means: $(\bar{x}_i - \bar{x}_j) \pm t_{\alpha/2} s \sqrt{\dfrac{1}{n_i} + \dfrac{1}{n_j}}$

where $s = \sqrt{\text{MSE}}$; the distribution of t is based on $(n - k)$ degrees of freedom (the denominator degrees of freedom in the ANOVA and the degrees of freedom associated with s^2); and $t_{\alpha/2}$ is the t-value such that $P(t > t_{\alpha/2}) = \alpha/2$

EXAMPLE 11.5 Refer to Example 11.3. Construct a 95% confidence interval for μ_2, the true mean monthly sales of all salespeople with a fixed salary.

Solution From Example 11.3,

$$MSE = 1{,}927.07$$

Then

$$s = \sqrt{MSE} = \sqrt{1{,}927.07} = 43.90$$

The sample mean monthly sales (in thousands of dollars) for those salespeople with a fixed salary is

$$\bar{x}_2 = \frac{T_2}{n_2} = \frac{793}{7} = 113.286$$

and the tabulated value, $t_{.025}$, for 17 df (the same as the denominator df in the ANOVA), is (from Table 4, Appendix E)

$$t_{.025} = 2.110$$

Therefore, a 95% confidence interval for μ_2, the mean monthly sales of all salespeople with a fixed salary, is

$$\bar{x}_2 \pm t_{\alpha/2} \frac{s}{\sqrt{n_2}} = 113.286 \pm 2.110 \frac{43.90}{\sqrt{7}}$$

$$= 113.286 \pm 35.010$$

or (78.276, 148.296). We say that the interval $78,276 to $148,296 encloses the true mean, μ_2, with 95% confidence.

EXAMPLE 11.6 Refer to Example 11.3. Find a 95% confidence interval for $(\mu_2 - \mu_1)$, the difference between mean monthly sales for those salespeople with a fixed salary and those strictly on a commission.

Solution The mean of the sample (in thousands of dollars) for salespeople strictly on commission is

$$\bar{x}_1 = \frac{T_1}{n_1} = \frac{1{,}225}{7} = 175.0$$

and from Example 11.5, $\bar{x}_2 = 113.286$. The tabulated t-value, $t_{.025}$, is the same as for Example 11.5, namely 2.110. Then the 95% confidence interval for $(\mu_2 - \mu_1)$ is

$$(\bar{x}_2 - \bar{x}_1) \pm t_{\alpha/2} s \sqrt{\frac{1}{n_2} + \frac{1}{n_1}} = (113.286 - 175.0) \pm (2.110)(43.90) \sqrt{\frac{1}{7} + \frac{1}{7}}$$

$$= -61.714 \pm 49.512$$

or $(-111.226, -12.202)$.

Since the interval includes only negative numbers, we can conclude, with 95% confidence, that the mean monthly sales of those salespeople strictly on commission

(μ_1) exceeds the mean monthly sales of those with a fixed salary (μ_2). The difference could be as large as \$111,226 or as small as \$12,202.

To obtain narrower confidence intervals than those constructed in Examples 11.5 and 11.6, we would have to select larger samples of salespeople from within each compensation group.

EXERCISES **11.8** Refer to Exercise 11.4 and the data of Table 11.6. Calculate a 99% confidence interval for ($\mu_3 - \mu_1$), the difference between mean daily sales of California Brandy in San Diego and San Francisco. Interpret the interval.

11.9 Refer to Exercise 11.5 and the data of Table 11.7.
a. Find a 95% confidence interval for μ_1, the mean RoP for the new PD-1 drill bit. Interpret the interval.
b. Find a 95% confidence interval for ($\mu_1 - \mu_2$), the difference between the mean RoPs for the PD-1 and the IADC 1-2-6 drill bits. Which of the two drill bits appears to have the faster mean RoP? Explain.

11.10 Refer to Exercise 11.6 and the data of Table 11.8.
a. Construct 90% confidence intervals for each of the five population means tested.
b. Based on your intervals, part a, does it appear that any of the locations has an average daily traffic density as large as 500 cars?

11.11 Refer to Exercise 11.7 and the data of Table 11.9.
a. Calculate 99% confidence intervals for each of the three differences, ($\mu_1 - \mu_2$), ($\mu_1 - \mu_3$), and ($\mu_2 - \mu_3$).
b. Based on your intervals, part a, which type of engineering firm appears to pay its employees a higher average starting hourly wage rate, Theory-X, Theory-Y, or Theory-Z-style firms? [*Hint:* Compare the means in a pairwise fashion. For example, first compare μ_1 to μ_2 by checking the interval for the difference ($\mu_1 - \mu_2$). If the interval indicates that μ_1 is greater than μ_2, then compare μ_1 to μ_3 by checking the interval for the difference ($\mu_1 - \mu_3$). If this interval indicates that μ_1 is greater than μ_3, then there is evidence that μ_1 is the largest of the three means, i.e., greater than both μ_2 and μ_3.]

11.4 An Example of a Computer Printout

As the sizes of the samples in the independent samples design are increased, the computations in an analysis of variance become tedious. This difficulty can easily be circumvented (if you have access to a computer) by using one of the many statistical computer packages designed to carry out a complete analysis of variance. In this section, we discuss the location and interpretation of the key ANOVA elements on a computer printout from one of the more popular computer packages, called the Statistical Analysis System (SAS). At your institution, other computer packages such as Biomed, Minitab, and SPSS may be installed. These packages also have ANOVA procedures available, and their respective printouts are similar to that of the SAS. Whichever computer package you have access to, you should be able to understand the ANOVA results after reading the discussion that follows.

The results of an analysis of variance are often summarized in tabular form. The general form of an *ANOVA table* for an independent samples design is shown in Table 11.10. *Source* refers to the source of variation (*Treatments* for the variability among the sample means, and *Error* for the within-sample variability), and for each source, **df** refers to the degrees of freedom, **SS** to the sum of squares, **MS** to the mean square, and **F** to the *F* statistic. Most computer packages present the analysis of variance results in the form of an ANOVA table.

TABLE 11.10
ANOVA Summary Table for an Independent Samples Design

SOURCE	df	SS	MS	F
Treatments	$k-1$	SST	MST	MST/MSE
Error	$n-k$	SSE	MSE	
Total	$n-1$	SS(Total)		

EXAMPLE 11.7 Consider the problem of comparing the mean 1978 sale prices of properties contained in the six neighborhoods (A, B, C, D, E, F) of the mid-Florida city discussed in Section 1.1. Many of these properties were not sold, so we will never know their sale prices, but we can still imagine that a sale price exists for each property in a neighborhood and that the totality of these prices constitutes a population that characterizes property values in that neighborhood. Thus, we wish to compare the mean sale prices corresponding to the six neighborhood sale price populations, i.e., we wish to test

$$H_0: \quad \mu_A = \mu_B = \mu_C = \mu_D = \mu_E = \mu_F$$

$$H_a: \quad \text{At least two means are different}$$

In order to perform the comparison, independent random samples of sale prices were selected from the actual sale prices for the six neighborhoods listed in Appendix B (see Table 11.11) and the data subjected to an analysis of variance using the SAS. A portion of the SAS printout is reproduced in Figure 11.4. Interpret these results.

TABLE 11.11
Sale Prices of Properties in the Six Neighborhoods

NBHD A	NBHD B	NBHD C	NBHD D	NBHD E	NBHD F
$69,900	$66,500	$30,500	$43,000	$47,700	$44,000
86,500	95,000	20,000	40,000	43,000	72,000
83,500	52,000	32,000	34,500	32,500	55,000
64,000	59,500	33,000	43,700	27,300	27,000
45,000	80,000	25,900	52,000	33,900	49,500
75,000	72,000	32,800	44,900	37,200	82,500
29,700	80,000	34,000	37,000	38,700	59,000
35,000	59,500	31,900	42,000	37,900	52,500
72,000	70,300	32,000	40,000	28,500	30,800
39,700	75,000	28,900	33,700	33,000	65,000

FIGURE 11.4
Portion of the SAS Printout
of the ANOVA,
Example 11.7

SOURCE	DF	SUM OF SQUARES	MEAN SQUARE	F VALUE	PR > F
MODEL	5	12161294833.3333430	2432258966.6666686	14.97	0.0001
ERROR	54	8771595000.0000000	162436944.4444444		
CORRECTED TOTAL	59	20932889833.3333430			

Solution   You can see from Figure 11.4 that the SAS printout presents the results in the form of an ANOVA table. The source of variation attributable to treatments, i.e., to the variability among the sample means for the six neighborhoods, is labelled MODEL, and the source of variation attributable to error, i.e., to the within-sample variability, is labelled ERROR. Their corresponding sums of squares and mean squares are:

$$SST = 12,161,294,833.3333430$$
$$SSE = 8,771,595,000.0000000$$
$$MST = 2,432,258,966.6666686$$
$$MSE = 162,436,944.4444444$$

The computed value of the test statistic, given under the column heading F VALUE, is

$$F = 14.97$$

To determine whether to reject the null hypothesis

$$H_0: \quad \mu_A = \mu_B = \cdots = \mu_F$$

in favor of the alternative

$$H_a: \quad \text{At least two population means are different}$$

we may consult Appendix E for tabulated values of the F distribution corresponding to an appropriately chosen significance level α. However, since the SAS printout gives the attained significance level (p-value) of the test, we will use this quantity to assist us in reaching a conclusion.

Under the column headed $PR > F$ is the attained significance level of the test. This value, .0001, implies that H_0 will be rejected at any chosen level of α larger than .0001. Thus, there is very strong evidence of a difference among the mean 1978 sale prices of residential properties in the six neighborhoods. The probability that this procedure will lead to a Type I error (conclude that there is a difference among the means when in fact they are all equal) is .0001.

EXERCISES   **11.12**   Refer to Exercise 11.4. Give the results of the ANOVA in the form of a summary table, Table 11.10.

11.13   Refer to Exercise 11.7. Give the results of the ANOVA in the form of a summary table, Table 11.10.

11.14   A drug company synthesized three new drugs that should alleviate pain due to ulcers. To determine whether the drugs will be absorbed by the stomach (and hence have a possibility of being effective), 24 pigs were randomly assigned, 8 to each drug, to receive oral doses. After a given amount of time, the concentration of the drug in the stomach lining of each pig was determined. The data are shown in Table 11.12. In order to determine if there is a difference among the mean concentrations for the three drugs, the data of Table 11.12 were subjected to an ANOVA using the SAS. A portion of the SAS printout is shown in Figure 11.5. Locate the key elements of the ANOVA on the printout and interpret their values. At a significance level of $\alpha = .025$, is there evidence of a difference among the mean concentrations for the three drugs after the fixed period of time?

TABLE 11.12
Drug Concentration
(Cubic Centimeters),
Exercise 11.14

	DRUG	
1	2	3
1.70	1.73	1.67
1.72	1.79	1.63
1.81	1.76	1.60
1.79	1.75	1.55
1.75	1.70	1.63
1.66	1.80	1.61
1.83	1.81	1.67
1.75	1.73	1.59

FIGURE 11.5
Output from the SAS for
the Drug Concentration
Data, Exercise 11.14

SOURCE	DF	SUM OF SQUARES	MEAN SQUARE	F VALUE	PR > F
MODEL	2	0.09923333	0.04961667	23.12	0.0001
ERROR	21	0.04506250	0.00214583		
CORRECTED TOTAL	23	0.14429583			

11.15   Before purchasing a $10,000 life insurance policy, a young executive wishes to determine if there are significant differences among the mean monthly premiums of four types of policies that he is considering: (1) individual convertible term, (2) individual renewable term, (3) group renewable term, and (4) government group insurance. For each of these policies he obtains price quotations from six randomly selected insurance companies (thus, 24 insurance companies, 6 for each type of policy, are included in the total sample). The data were analyzed for differences among the mean prices for the four policy types by using the ANOVA procedure of the SAS. The results are given in Figure 11.6.

a.   Locate the following quantities on the SAS printout and interpret their values: SST, SSE, MST, MSE, F.

b.   Are there significant differences among the mean monthly premiums of the four types of insurance policies?

FIGURE 11.6
SAS ANOVA Procedure,
Exercise 11.15

SOURCE	DF	SUM OF SQUARES	MEAN SQUARE	F VALUE	PR > F
MODEL	3	7.01500000	2.33833333	24.83	0.0001
ERROR	20	1.88333333	0.09416667		
CORRECTED TOTAL	23	8.89833333			

11.5 Assumptions: When the Analysis of Variance F Test Is Appropriate

Most of the statistical procedures which we have discussed throughout Chapters 8–10 require that certain assumptions be satisfied in order for their inferences to be valid. The assumptions necessary for a valid analysis of variance F test for comparing more than two population means are extensions of those assumptions required for comparing two means (Chapters 8–10). These assumptions, which must be satisfied regardless of the sample sizes employed in the sampling design, are summarized in the box.

ASSUMPTIONS FOR A TEST TO COMPARE
k POPULATION MEANS: INDEPENDENT SAMPLES DESIGN

1. All k population probability distributions are normal.
2. The k population variances are equal.

In most business applications the assumptions will not be satisfied exactly. However, the analysis of variance procedure is flexible in the sense that slight departures from the assumptions will not significantly affect the analysis or the validity of the resulting inferences.

11.6 Summary

This chapter presents an extension of the independent sampling experiment to allow for the comparison of more than two means. The independent sampling design uses independent random samples selected from each of k populations. The comparison of the population means is made by comparing the variation among the sample means, as measured by the mean square for treatments (MST), to the variation attributable to differences within the samples, as measured by the mean square for error (MSE). If the ratio of MST to MSE is large, we conclude that a difference exists between the means of at least two of the k populations.

We point out that there are various methods of collecting data and designing experiments for the purpose of comparing more than two population means; an independent sampling design is the simplest of these preconceived plans. If you would like to study other types of experimental designs and the ANOVA technique associated with each, consult the references at the end of this chapter.

KEY WORDS

Analysis of variance
Independent sampling design
Variability among the sample means
Within-sample variability
F distribution

KEY SYMBOLS

Analysis of variance: ANOVA
Sum of squares for treatments: SST
Sum of squared errors: SSE
Mean square for treatments: MST
Mean square for error: MSE
Ratio of mean squares: F

SUPPLEMENTARY EXERCISES

[*Note:* List the assumptions necessary to ensure the validity of the procedure you use to solve these problems.]

11.16 Suppose that you wish to compare the means of three treatments using independent random samples of size $n_1 = n_2 = n_3 = 15$.
a. How many degrees of freedom are associated with the numerator of the F statistic?
b. How many degrees of freedom are associated with the denominator of the F statistic?

11.17 Suppose that you wish to compare the means of eight treatments using independent random samples of size $n_1 = n_2 = \cdots = n_8 = 4$.
a. How many degrees of freedom are associated with the numerator of the F statistic?
b. How many degrees of freedom are associated with the denominator of the F statistic?

11.18 Complete the ANOVA summary table shown below.

SOURCE	df	SS	MS	F
Treatments	9		15.2	
Error	___	200.7		
Total	39			

11.19 Complete the ANOVA summary table shown below.

SOURCE	df	SS	MS	F
Treatments				
Error	16	32		
Total	17	60		

11.20 In hopes of attracting more riders, a city transit company plans to have express bus service from a suburban terminal to the downtown business district. These buses will travel along a major city street where there are numerous traffic lights that will affect travel time. The city decides to perform a study on the effect of four different plans (a special bus lane, traffic signal progression, etc.) on the travel times for the buses. Travel times (in minutes) are measured for several weekdays during a morning rush-hour trip while each plan is in effect. The results are recorded in Table 11.13.

TABLE 11.13
Bus Travel Times,
Exercise 11.20

	PLAN		
1	2	3	4
27	25	34	30
25	28	29	33
29	30	32	31
26	27	31	
	24	36	

a. Construct an ANOVA summary table for this experiment.
b. Is there evidence of a difference among the mean travel times for the four plans? Use $\alpha = .025$.
c. Form a 95% confidence interval for the difference between the mean travel times of buses under plan 1 (express lane) and plan 3 (a control—no special travel arrangements).

11.21 Great Britain has experimented with different 40-hour work weeks to maximize production and minimize expenses. A factory tested a 5-day week (8 hours per day), a 4-day week (10 hours per day), and a 3⅓-day week (12 hours per day). The weekly production results are shown in Table 11.14 on p. 364 (in thousands of dollars worth of items produced).

TABLE 11.14
Weekly Production,
Exercise 11.21

8-HOUR DAY	10-HOUR DAY	12-HOUR DAY
87	75	95
96	82	76
75	90	87
90	80	82
72	73	65
86	87	71

a. Construct an ANOVA summary table for this experiment.
b. Is there evidence of a difference among the mean weekly productivity levels for the three lengths of workdays? Test using a significance level of $\alpha = .10$.
c. Using a 90% confidence interval, estimate the mean weekly productivity level when 12-hour workdays are used.
d. Estimate the difference between mean weekly productivity levels for 8-hour workdays and 10-hour workdays, using a 90% confidence interval.

11.22 A plastics company hypothesizes that treatment, after casting, of a plastic used in optic lenses will improve wear. Six different treatments are to be tested. To determine whether any differences in mean wear exist among the treatments, 18 castings from a single formulation of the plastic were made, and 3 castings were randomly assigned to each of the treatments. Wear was determined by measuring the increase in "haze" after 200 cycles of abrasion (better wear being indicated by smaller increases). These results are shown in Table 11.15.

TABLE 11.15
Plastic "Haze"
Measurements,
Exercise 11.22

		TREATMENT			
A	B	C	D	E	F
13.29	15.15	9.54	10.00	8.73	14.86
12.07	11.95	11.47	12.45	9.75	15.03
11.97	14.75	11.26	12.38	8.01	11.18

a. Construct an ANOVA summary table for this experiment.
b. Is there evidence of a difference in mean wear among the six treatments? Test using $\alpha = .05$.
c. Estimate the difference between the mean haze increases for treatments B and E, using a 95% confidence interval.
d. Estimate the mean increase in haze for optic lenses receiving treatment A, using a 95% confidence interval.

11.23 A Japanese watchmaking firm manufactures three types of watches: digital, mechanical, and quartz analog. The firm conducted the following experiment to compare the performances of the watches. Five watches of each type were timed for a period of twenty-four hours and the time gains (or losses) were recorded for each. The data are recorded in Table 11.16. [*Note:* A negative gain denotes a loss in time.]

DIGITAL	MECHANICAL	QUARTZ ANALOG
0.10	1.33	0.01
0.08	−1.20	−0.12
0.22	−2.17	0.00
−0.67	0.03	0.45
0.91	−1.55	−0.28

a. Construct an ANOVA summary table for the experiment.

b. Is there evidence of a difference among the mean time gains for the three types of watches? Test using $\alpha = .025$.

c. Find a 90% confidence interval for the difference between the mean time gains for digital and quartz analog watches.

CASE STUDY 11.1
Where to Buy Your Food— Inner-City, Suburban, or Rural Grocery Stores?

Nowadays, a widely held belief is that grocery prices faced by the urban poor (i.e., residents of the inner city) are higher than grocery prices in suburban areas. Surprisingly, studies of price comparisons between the two areas have generally indicated the exact opposite —the price of a grocery basket of food in inner-city areas is decidedly lower than in suburban neighborhoods. However, an equally important question is the comparison of rural grocery prices to those of metropolitan areas. David M. Ambrose* expanded the previous studies to include the rural grocery store. He states:

> Rural areas add an entirely new dimension to the traditional grocery-pricing question. Rural populations have many of the characteristics and circumstances of inner city populations. Rural incomes are generally below national averages, as are inner city incomes, and therefore these persons may exhibit food-consumption patterns different from their suburban metropolitan counterparts because of income differences. Consumption patterns may be further altered by the presence of home produce and by specific ethnic groupings and cultural dietary patterns.
>
> The grocery-shopping alternatives of many people in rural areas are generally restricted to those retail food institutions present in the immediate community. Mobility is limited due to the relatively high cost of transportation to alternative retail food locations and the associated small cost savings which could be realized. Although the nature of the mobility restriction is different from the restrictions of the inner city resident, the resulting effect is the same—patronage of the groceries in the immediate locale.

Ambrose conducted the research in Omaha, Nebraska, a city frequently used as a test market because of its representative composition of racial, religious, and ethnic groupings, industrial concerns, and income levels and distribution. A total of 14 grocery stores were selected—6 inner-city, 5 suburban, and 3 rural stores—and all price information was collected on a Tuesday to avoid any possible variations which would occur because of weekly sale or pricing patterns. The market basket consisted of 54 food items which included cereal and bakery products, meat, poultry, fish, dairy products, fruits, vegetables, and other home foods. After collecting the data, a price index for the total market basket was computed for each of the 14 stores. (The price index for a store is simply the total price of the market basket at that store expressed as a percentage of the average price for all 14 stores. Thus, a price index greater than 100% indicates that the store's total market basket price exceeded the average, while a price index smaller than 100% indicates that the store's total market basket price fell below the average.)

"In examining the pricing indexes of the 14 stores in the study," states Ambrose, "there were distinct differences in the ranges of prices of the stores according to their location (inner city, suburban, or rural), as given in the figure." The figure Ambrose refers to is reproduced in Figure 11.7. It shows the minimum, maximum, and mean ($\bar{x}$) store index for each of the three locations. Based upon this figure and similar pricing index tables by product type, Ambrose concludes that "inner city residents have on the average grocery prices 2.3% below the general averaged market-basket price level . . . [and] in almost all product classifications . . . have a price advantage over patrons of suburban or rural stores. From this study, the evidence indicates that the inner city person is clearly the advantaged individual with respect to retail grocery stores. People in rural areas are on the extreme upper end of the price spectrum. The retail prices of groceries in rural areas are higher than the prices of inner city or suburban groceries. The rural population is at an absolute price disadvantage in groceries. At an index of 100.6, the prices in suburban groceries tend to constitute the average."

a. Visually inspect Figure 11.7. Do you think it is possible to determine whether differences among the mean price indices exist for the three store locations, based upon this figure alone? Why is a statistical test needed?

b. Set up the appropriate null and alternative hypotheses to determine if there is a difference among the mean price indices for a market basket in inner-city, suburban, and rural grocery stores.

c. If you had access to the 14 store price indices, what statistical procedure would you use to analyze the data?

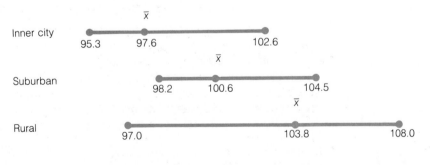

FIGURE 11.7
Comparison of Store
Index Means by Location

CASE STUDY 11.2
Identifying Management Potential: The In-Tray Exercise

R. W. T. Gill considered the role of the "in-tray" exercise in assessing the management potential of future administrators and executives.* The in-tray or in-basket exercise was developed 25 years ago as a training tool for officers in the U.S. Air Force. In describing how the technique works, Gill writes: "The in-tray is a simulation representing the typical contents of an executive's in-tray with a variety of everyday problems in a written form—letters, memoranda, notes, reports, and telephone messages—both expected and unexpected requiring decisions and action. [Trainees] are provided with instructions, information on the company, its organization and the role to be played, and the in-tray contents. There is a fixed time allowed, usually 1½ hours, during which they write letters, memoranda and notes on their decisions and actions as if they were really doing the job." After completing the tasks, the trainees' performances are assessed by one or more expert raters. However, "the utility of the in-tray exercise," says Gill, "rests on the logical assumption that it must be realistic. The 'content validity' of the in-tray exercise has to be established for a given situation, both in terms of perceived relevance, realism and representativeness and in terms of actual representativeness of items on which [trainees'] relative performance can be discriminated."

Ratings of overall in-tray performance are usually given on a scale of 1 (high performance) to 6 (low performance). This overall rating is based upon performance in the following areas: planning/organizing, communication/control, judgment/analysis, decision-making, work attitude, and output. Because of the difficulty of scoring performance in the in-tray exercise, the need for experienced, trained assessors or raters is evident. "Insufficient assessor training," writes Gill, "can lead to unreliable evaluations by assessors and thus lower exercise validity. A possible tendency to the mean must be checked, especially where assessors are inexperienced, overcautious, or overanxious." That is, the reliability of assessors' ratings should be determined before using the in-tray results as a measure of managerial effectiveness.

To investigate the phenomenon of rater reliability, Gill obtained data for 7 subjects who were given the in-tray test. The subjects, all candidates for a general management position in a manufacturing company in the British motor industry, were from a variety of backgrounds—engineering, finance, production, and marketing. Overall in-tray performance of each candidate was assessed by three different raters. The results are given in Table 11.17.

TABLE 11.17
Ratings of Candidates by Individual Assessors on Overall In-Tray Performance

CANDIDATE	RATER 1	RATER 2	RATER 3
A	4.5	4.5	5.0
B	2.5	4.5	4.5
C	5.0	3.0	4.0
D	4.0	4.5	4.5
E	1.5	2.0	4.5
F	3.5	4.5	4.5
G	4.0	4.0	4.0

*R. W. Gill. "The in-tray (in-basket) exercise as a measure of management potential." *Journal of Occupational Psychology,* 1979, *52,* 185–195.

a. One way to determine whether the overall in-tray ratings are reliable is to compare the mean performance scores assessed by the three raters. A difference among means most likely indicates that the raters are in disagreement on the candidates' overall performances. Visually inspect the data of Table 11.17. Do you think that the mean score assessed to the candidates differs among the three raters? What null hypothesis should you test?

Note that the three groups of 7 performance scores do not represent independent random samples selected from the respective populations. They are, in fact, dependent samples since each of the three raters judges the overall performance of all 7 candidates. (Truly independent samples would consist of a total of 21 *different* candidates, 7 judged by each rater.) Consequently, the assumptions necessary for a valid one-way ANOVA are not satisfied. However, you can see the obvious advantage of selecting the dependent samples. With this sampling method we are able to compare the raters' ability to score each individual candidate, something we could not have accomplished using an independent sampling design. The group of three scores for each candidate is called a **block,** and the resulting design is called a **randomized block design.** A randomized block design provides more information than an independent sampling design because it attempts to remove or block out an unwanted source of variability—in this case, the variability due to differences in the candidates' performances.

The ANOVA table for the data of Table 11.17 is provided in Table 11.18. Note that the ANOVA for a randomized block design requires some additional calculations.

TABLE 11.18
ANOVA Summary Table for the Randomized Block Design, Case Study 11.2

SOURCE	df	SS	MS	F
Raters	2	2.66667	1.3333	1.96
Blocks (candidates)	6	7.11905	1.1865	1.74
Error	12	8.16666	0.6805	
Total	20	17.95238		

b. Is there evidence of a difference among the mean performance scores assessed by the three raters? Use a significance level of $\alpha = .05$. [*Hint:* Compare the computed F-value corresponding to the source of variability "Raters" with the critical F-value associated with 2 numerator df and 12 denominator df tabulated in Table 6, Appendix D.]

[*Note:* If you are interested in learning more about randomized block experiments, consult the references at the end of this chapter.]

CASE STUDY 11.3
A Comparison of the Shopping Habits of Four Types of Grocery Shoppers

Classifying shoppers, particularly grocery shoppers, into various groups based upon certain market characteristics has long been a research tradition. Williams, Painter, and Nicholas ("A Policy-Oriented Typology of Grocery Shoppers." *Journal of Retailing,* 1978) present a grouping of grocery shoppers oriented toward store "policy" which not only offers insight into consumer behavior, but also provides suggestions for the choice of marketing tools to influence particular market segments."

Williams et al. derive their "policy-oriented" typology from a competition angle. They first identify the two most important areas in which grocery retailers compete for buyers: (1) pricing policies, and (2) customer service policies.

The price images customers maintain about different stores may be the one most important factor differentiating these stores. Also, customer service, defined here to include location and shopping convenience, is also a major dimension along which customers select stores to patronize. Given that store managers and marketing executives can design and implement strategy along at least these two dimensions, customers likewise maintain differing degrees of concern or interest in the pricing practices and customer service policies of the stores where they shop. Specifically, customers can be highly involved with the pricing or customer service practices or rather uninvolved or apathetic about these procedures.

By cross-classifying shoppers on the basis of either high or low involvement along both price and customer service dimensions, a typology of grocery shoppers results. The four groups identified by the authors (and shown in Table 11.19) are: (1) Involved shoppers, (2) Convenience shoppers, (3) Price shoppers, and (4) Apathetic shoppers.

TABLE 11.19
Grocery Shopping Orientations or Buying Styles

		STORE OR CHAIN'S PRICING PRACTICES	
		High Customer Involvement	Low Customer Involvement
STORE OR CHAIN'S CUSTOMER SERVICE PRACTICES	High Customer Involvement	Involved shopper	Convenience shopper
	Low Customer Involvement	Price shopper	Apathetic (uninvolved) shopper

Williams et al. point out that the four types of shoppers "actually represent rough groupings or aggregations of shoppers which in an empirical sense would only be expected to display a general or dominant orientation. Consequently within each shopper group a researcher would expect to find some diversity. The important question, however, is not whether some diversity exists [within the groups] but whether the aggregation process leads to a useful market segmentation." That is, if shoppers in each group are subjected to various marketing mix variables, will significant differences among the groups' responses exist? If so, a market segmentation strategy based upon this "policy-oriented" typology should be employed.

In order to investigate this phenomenon, Williams et al. gathered data from a representative sample of households located in metropolitan Salt Lake City during April and May of 1974. The principal grocery buyer in each household was interviewed, and the data collected included information on a respondent's favorite store, shopping habits, store loyalty, and various socioeconomic and demographic variables. The responses for a total of 298 households were deemed usable in the analysis.

The first phase of the study involved an empirical derivation of the four groups of grocery shoppers illustrated in Table 11.19. Using a statistical technique called *cluster analysis,* the authors were able to classify each of the 298 respondents into one of the four groups (clusterings): Apathetic shoppers (59 respondents), Convenience shoppers (125), Price shoppers (81), and Involved shoppers (33). For the purposes of this case study, we will assume that the data were obtained using an independent sampling design—random samples of $n_1 = 59$ Apathetic shoppers, $n_2 = 125$ Convenience shoppers, $n_3 = 81$ Price shoppers, and $n_4 = 33$ Involved shoppers, independently selected from among the four shopping groups.

For the second phase of the study, of particular interest in this case study, Williams et al. subjected the data to a one-way analysis of variance in order to detect significant differences among the mean responses to questions concerning socio-economic, demographic, and shopping habit variables. A listing of the variables, along with the sample mean responses* of the shoppers in each group, is given in Table 11.20. The extreme right column of the table gives the *F*-values, corresponding to a one-way analysis of variance test for equality of mean responses among the four groups for each of the five variables.

TABLE 11.20   Mean Response and *F*-Values for Socioeconomic and Demographic Variables

	MEAN RESPONSES				
SOCIOECONOMIC AND DEMOGRAPHIC VARIABLES	Apathetic Shoppers ($n_1 = 59$)	Convenience Shoppers ($n_2 = 125$)	Price Shoppers ($n_3 = 81$)	Involved Shoppers ($n_4 = 33$)	*F*-VALUE
1. Total weekly grocery* expenditure ($)	2.10	2.12	2.25	2.12	.95
2. Household size (number)	3.22	3.18	3.57	3.52	1.28
3. Age (years)	37.36	40.60	43.90	49.85	4.69
4. Income* ($)	3.98	3.94	4.16	4.06	.30
5. Life-cycle stage*	3.59	3.92	4.38	4.73	4.56

*Coded variables

The detection of significant differences among the mean responses (for a particular variable) for the four shopping groups could be of invaluable help to a grocery store manager or supermarket chain executive who is planning a market strategy. In summarizing their results, Williams et al. write:

> Each [of the four major types of shoppers identified in this research] represents a unique shopper orientation or buying style, and thus represents varying propensities for being influenced by different marketing methods. Store managers and supermarket chain store executives must consciously choose which group or groups of customers to satisfy and then implement a planned marketing program which has been especially designed for the target segment or segments the decision-maker has chosen.

*Some of the responses were coded for the convenience of the shopper who filled out the questionnaire. For example, weekly expenditures were coded 1 for expenditures under $20 per week, 2 for between $20 and $50, 3 for between $50 and $100, and 4 for expenditures greater than $100 per week.

a. Use the results of Table 11.20 to test the hypothesis of a difference among the true mean total weekly grocery expenditures for the four shopping groups. Use a significance level of $\alpha = .05$.

b. Repeat part a for the variables Household size, Age, Income, and Life-cycle stage.

c. What assumptions are necessary for the valid implementation of the one-way analysis of variance F test used in parts a and b?

REFERENCES

Ambrose, D. M. "Retail grocery pricing: Inner city, suburban, and rural comparisons." *Journal of Business,* January 1979, *52,* 95–101.

Barr, A., Goodnight, J., Sall, J., Blair, W., & Chilko, D. *SAS User's Guide.* 1979 ed. SAS Institute, P.O. Box 10066, Raleigh, N. C. 27605.

Gill, R. W. T. "The in-tray (in-basket) exercise as a measure of management potential." *Journal of Occupational Psychology,* 1979, *52,* 185–195.

McClave, J. T., & Benson, P. G. *Statistics for business and economics.* 2d ed. San Francisco: Dellen, 1982.

Mendenhall, W. *Introduction to linear models and the design and analysis of experiments.* Belmont, Ca.: Wadsworth, 1968. Chapter 8.

Scheffé, H. *The analysis of variance.* New York: Wiley, 1959.

Williams, R. H., Painter, J. J., & Nicholas, H. R. "A policy-oriented typology of grocery shoppers." *Journal of Retailing,* 1978, *54,* 27–41.

Twelve

Simple Linear Regression and Correlation

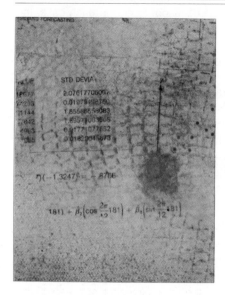

Are you a pill taker? If you are, some would contend that this behavior was learned in childhood, spawned by the flood of TV advertising for over-the-counter drugs. Are children's attitudes toward these drugs linked to the amount of TV advertising they receive? Does an increase in drug advertising imply an increase in child acceptance of over-the-counter drugs? And can you use the level of advertising to actually predict a level of acceptance? These and other questions concerning the relationship between two variables will be discussed in this chapter, and you will learn more about television, children, and drugs in Case Study 12.1.

Contents:

12.1 Introduction: Bivariate Relationships

The procedures discussed in the previous four chapters are most useful in cases where we are interested in testing hypotheses about or estimating the values of one or more population parameters based on random sampling. However, a more important concern may be the relationship between two different random variables, x and y, known as a *bivariate* relationship. For example, real estate appraisers, tax assessors, real estate investors, and home buyers will be interested in the relationship between the appraised value of a property, x, and its sale price, y; or, an automobile dealer may be interested in the bivariate relationship between the size of his sales force, x, and his yearly sales revenue, y; or, a concessions manager at a baseball park may be interested in the bivariate relationship between a game's total attendance, x, and the number of hot dogs purchased, y; etc. In each case, the object of this interest is not merely academic. The real estate investor wants to know whether the appraised value of a property is a good indicator of the property's actual selling price (if it were to be put on the market for sale); the auto dealer would like to know if the size of his sales force is a reliable predictor of his yearly sales revenue; and the concessions manager wishes to determine if total game attendance is a good indicator of the number of hot dogs which will be purchased at that game. How can we determine if one variable, x, is a reliable predictor of another variable, y? In order to answer this question, we must be able to model the bivariate relationship, that is, describe how the two variables, x and y, are related. In this chapter we present a method useful for modeling the (straight-line) relationship between two variables—a method called *simple linear regression analysis.*

12.2 Simple Linear Correlation

If two variables are related in such a way that the value of one is indicative of the value of the other, we sometimes say that the variables are *correlated.* For example, the claim is often made that the crime rate and the unemployment rate are "highly correlated." Another popular belief is that the GNP and the rate of inflation are "correlated." In the following example we show how to calculate a numerical descriptive measure of the correlation between two variables, x and y.

EXAMPLE 12.1   A firm wants to know the correlation between the size of its sales force and its yearly sales revenue. The records for the past 10 years were examined, and the results are listed in Table 12.1. Calculate a numerical descriptive measure of the correlation between size of sales force, x, and yearly sales revenue, y.

Solution   The first step in computing a measure of correlation between x and y for the $n = 10$ pairs of observations is to find the sums of the x-values (Σx) and y-values (Σy), the squares of the x-values (Σx^2), the squares of the y-values (Σy^2), and the cross products of the corresponding x- and y-values (Σxy). As an aid in finding these quantities, construct a "sums of squares" table of the type shown in Table 12.2. Notice that the quantities Σx, Σy, Σx^2, Σy^2, and Σxy appear in the bottom row of the table.

TABLE 12.1	YEAR	NUMBER OF SALESPEOPLE x	SALES y, hundred thousand dollars
Size of Sales Force–Sales Revenue Data, Example 12.1	1971	15	1.35
	1972	18	1.63
	1973	24	2.33
	1974	22	2.41
	1975	25	2.63
	1976	29	2.93
	1977	30	3.41
	1978	32	3.26
	1979	35	3.63
	1980	38	4.15

TABLE 12.2
Sums of Squares for Data of Table 12.1

	x	y	x^2	y^2	xy
	15	1.35	225	1.8225	20.25
	18	1.63	324	2.6569	29.34
	24	2.33	576	5.4289	55.92
	22	2.41	484	5.8081	53.02
	25	2.63	625	6.9169	65.75
	29	2.93	841	8.5849	84.97
	30	3.41	900	11.6281	102.30
	32	3.26	1,024	10.6276	104.32
	35	3.63	1,225	13.1769	127.05
	38	4.15	1,444	17.2225	157.70
TOTALS	$\Sigma x = 268$	$\Sigma y = 27.73$	$\Sigma x^2 = 7{,}668$	$\Sigma y^2 = 83.8733$	$\Sigma xy = 800.62$

The second step is to calculate the quantities SS_{xy}, SS_{xx}, and SS_{yy}, as shown below:

$$SS_{xy} = \Sigma xy - \frac{(\Sigma x)(\Sigma y)}{n} = 800.62 - \frac{(268)(27.73)}{10} = 57.456$$

$$SS_{xx} = \Sigma x^2 - \frac{(\Sigma x)^2}{n} = 7{,}668 - \frac{(268)^2}{10} = 485.6$$

$$SS_{yy} = \Sigma y^2 - \frac{(\Sigma y)^2}{n} = 83.8733 - \frac{(27.73)^2}{10} = 6.97801$$

Finally, compute the measure of correlation, denoted by the symbol r, as follows:

$$r = \frac{SS_{xy}}{\sqrt{SS_{xx}SS_{yy}}} = \frac{57.456}{\sqrt{(485.6)(6.97801)}} = \frac{57.486}{58.211} = .99$$

The formal name given to r is the *Pearson product moment coefficient of correlation,* and its formula is given in the box. It can be shown (proof omitted) that r is scaleless, i.e., it is not measured in dollars, pounds, etc., but always assumes a value between -1 and $+1$ regardless of the units of measurement of the variables x and y. In the examples that follow, we will learn that the correlation coefficient r is a measure of the strength of the linear relationship between x and y.

DEFINITION 12.1

The *Pearson product moment coefficient of correlation, r,* is computed as follows for a sample of n measurements on x and y:

$$r = \frac{SS_{xy}}{\sqrt{SS_{xx}SS_{yy}}}$$

where

$$SS_{xy} = \Sigma xy - \frac{(\Sigma x)(\Sigma y)}{n}$$

$$SS_{xx} = \Sigma x^2 - \frac{(\Sigma x)^2}{n}$$

$$SS_{yy} = \Sigma y^2 - \frac{(\Sigma y)^2}{n}$$

It is a measure of the strength of the linear relationship between two random variables x and y.

EXAMPLE 12.2

What are the implications of various possible values of the correlation coefficient r?

Solution

We have suggested that the coefficient of correlation r is a measure of the strength of the linear relationship between two variables. We can gain insight into this interpretation by observing the plots of typical sample data presented in Figure 12.1. These plots, called *scattergrams,* are constructed by plotting the pairs of sample observations (x, y) on a piece of graph paper (x-values on the horizontal axis and y-values on the vertical axis).

Consider first the scattergram in Figure 12.1(b). The correlation coefficient for this set of points is near zero. We can see that a value of r near or equal to zero implies little or no linear relationship between x and y. That is, as x increases (or decreases), there is no definite trend in the values of y. In contrast, Figure 12.1(a) shows that positive values of r imply a positive linear relationship between y and x, i.e., y tends to increase as x increases. Similarly, a negative value of r implies a negative linear relationship between y and x, i.e., y tends to decrease as x increases (see Figure 12.1(c)).

A perfect linear relationship exists when all the (x, y) points fall exactly along a straight line, as shown in Figures 12.1(d) and 12.1(e). We can see that a value of $r = +1$ implies a perfect positive linear relationship between y and x (Figure 12.1(d)), and a value of $r = -1$ implies a perfect negative linear relationship between y and x (Figure 12.1(e)).

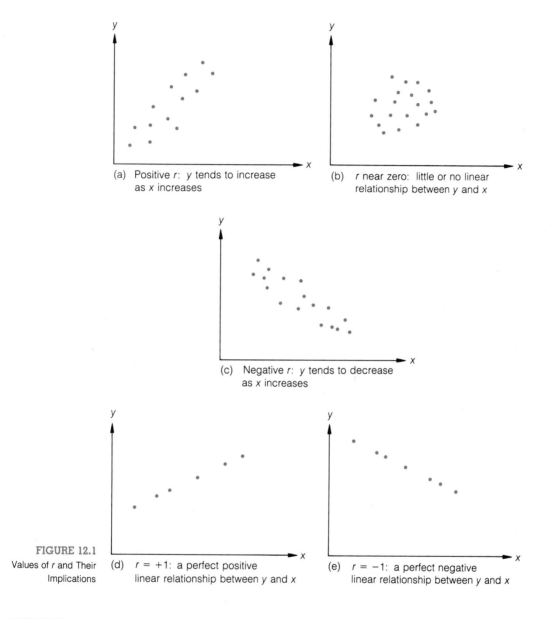

FIGURE 12.1
Values of r and Their
Implications

(a) Positive r: y tends to increase as x increases

(b) r near zero: little or no linear relationship between y and x

(c) Negative r: y tends to decrease as x increases

(d) r = +1: a perfect positive linear relationship between y and x

(e) r = −1: a perfect negative linear relationship between y and x

EXAMPLE 12.3   Interpret the value of r obtained for the size of sales force – sales revenue data of Table 12.1, Example 12.1.

Solution   From Example 12.1, the coefficient of correlation was calculated as $r = .99$. How should the firm interpret this large positive value of r? From our previous discussion, the implication is that a strong positive linear relationship between size of sales force and sales revenue exists over the past 10 years, i.e., the yearly sales revenue tends to increase as the size of the sales force increases, *for this sample of 10 years*. We can see this nearly perfect positive linear relationship clearly in the scattergram, Figure

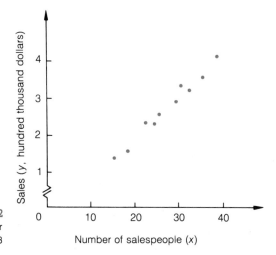

FIGURE 12.2
Scattergram for
Example 12.3

12.2, for the data of Table 12.1. However, the firm should not use this result to conclude that the optimum strategy for increasing sales is to hire a large number of new salespeople; it is incorrect to assume that there is a *causal relationship* between the two variables. In this example, there are probably many things that have contributed both to the increase in the size of the sales force and to the increase in sales revenue, e.g., an inflated economy, improvement in the firm's marketing sales strategies, a broadening of the products and services sold by the firm, etc. The only appropriate conclusion to be made by the firm based on the high positive correlation in the sample data is that a positive linear trend may exist between the size of the sales force, x, and the yearly sales, y.

WARNING

High correlation does not imply causality. If a large positive or negative value of the sample correlation coefficient r is observed, it is incorrect to conclude that a change in x causes a change in y. The only valid conclusion is that a linear trend *may* exist between x and y.

We pause here to remind you that the correlation coefficient r is defined as a measure of the linear correlation between x-values and y-values *in the sample;* thus, r is a sample statistic. Similarly, we define the *population correlation coefficient* to be a measure of the linear correlation for the population from which the sample of (x, y) data points was selected.* Our interpretation of the value of the population correlation

---

*The population correlation coefficient is often represented by the Greek letter ρ (rho).

coefficient is analogous to that of r: the population coefficient of correlation measures the strength of the linear relationship between x-values and y-values in the entire population.

EXAMPLE 12.4 Does linear correlation in a sample imply correlation in the population? That is, if the calculated value of r is nonzero, does this imply that the population correlation coefficient is nonzero?

Solution Sometimes, but not always. For example, we think you will agree that a sample correlation coefficient of $r = -.97$ provides strong evidence that the x-values and y-values in the population from which the sample was obtained are negatively linearly correlated. Likewise, a sample correlation coefficient of $r = .01$ indicates that little or no correlation between x and y exists in the population. Consider though, the value $r = .36$. Here the decision is not clear-cut. This sample value may be due to actual linear correlation in the population, or it may be due simply to random variation in the sample even though no linear correlation exists in the population. To help us decide, we employ the statistical decision-making tools of Chapters 9 and 10: an hypothesis test.

The null hypothesis which we wish to test is

H_0: There is no linear correlation between the variables x and y (i.e., the population correlation coefficient equals zero)

As our test statistic, we use the sample coefficient of correlation, r. The method outlined in Chapter 9 for determining the form of the rejection region requires that we choose an appropriate significance level α and then find the critical value based on the sampling distribution of the test statistic r. Like the distribution of the Student's t statistic, the sampling distribution of r under the null hypothesis is symmetric with a mean of 0. Table 10, Appendix E, gives critical values of r for various values of α and the sample size n. A portion of this table is reproduced in Table 12.3. Notice that the table is constructed similar to the table of critical t-values, Table 4, Appendix E. The critical value, r_α, has the same interpretation as t_α. That is, we define r_α to be the value such that $P(r > r_\alpha) = \alpha$. We illustrate the use of these critical values in the following example.

TABLE 12.3
Reproduction of a Portion of Table 10, Appendix E: Critical Values of the Sample Correlation Coefficient, r

SAMPLE SIZE n	$r_{.050}$	$r_{.025}$	$r_{.010}$	$r_{.005}$
3	.988	.970	.951	.988
4	.900	.950	.980	.900
5	.805	.878	.934	.959
6	.729	.811	.882	.917
7	.669	.754	.833	.875
8	.621	.707	.789	.834
9	.582	.666	.750	.798
10	.549	.632	.715	.765

EXAMPLE 12.5   **a.**   Test (at significance level $\alpha = .05$) for evidence of linear correlation between the variables x and y if the sample size (number of measurements in the sample) is $n = 8$ and the value of r computed from the sample is $r = -.83$.

b.   Test (at significance level $\alpha = .05$) for evidence that the variables x and y are positively correlated if the sample size is $n = 10$ and the value of r computed from the sample is $r = .37$.

Solution   **a.**   Since we are interested in detecting whether the variables x and y are linearly correlated (either positively or negatively), we wish to test the hypotheses

H_0:   The population correlation coefficient equals zero

H_a: The population correlation coefficient is nonzero

Hence, our test is two-sided and we must consider both large and small values of r as possible areas of rejection. For a two-tailed test conducted at significance level α, we will reject the null hypothesis of no linear correlation if the computed value of the test statistic r is either greater than $r_{\alpha/2}$ or less than $-r_{\alpha/2}$, i.e., our rejection region takes the form

$$r > r_{\alpha/2} \quad \text{or} \quad r < -r_{\alpha/2}$$

(This decision-making procedure is illustrated in Figure 12.3 for $\alpha = .05$.)

For $\alpha = .05$ and $n = 8$, the critical value of r obtained from Table 12.3 is .707 (the entry in the row corresponding to $n = 8$ and the column corresponding to $r_{\alpha/2} = r_{.025}$). Thus, we will reject H_0 if $r > .707$ or $r < -.707$. Since the computed value $r = -.83$ falls below the lower-tailed critical value of $-.707$, we reject H_0 and conclude (at the $\alpha = .05$ level of significance) that linear correlation exists between x and y. This procedure yields an $\alpha = .05$ chance of committing a Type I error, i.e., concluding that x and y are linearly correlated, if in fact no correlation exists.

b.   Now we want to determine whether the two variables x and y are positively correlated. That is, we wish to test

H_0:   The population coefficient of correlation equals zero

H_a: The population coefficient of correlation is positive (greater than zero)

This test is one-tailed (an upper-tailed test), and we will reject H_0 if the computed value of r is too large, specifically if $r > r_\alpha$, where r_α depends on the sample size n. From Table 12.3, the critical value corresponding to $n = 10$ is $r_\alpha = r_{.05} = .549$. Thus, our rejection region takes the form

$$r > r_{.05} = .549$$

Since the computed value $r = .37$ does not exceed .549, we fail to reject H_0. There is insufficient evidence (at $\alpha = .05$) to conclude that the variables x and y are positively correlated in the population.

A test for negative correlation between x and y, i.e., a test to determine whether the population correlation coefficient is negative (less than zero) is conducted similarly. Both the one-tailed and two-tailed tests for linear correlation in the population are summarized in the box.

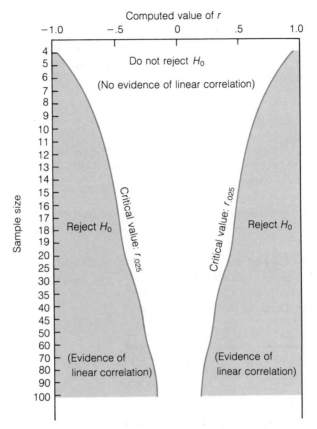

FIGURE 12.3
Rejection Region for Testing H_0: No linear correlation
Two-Tailed Test, $\alpha = .05$

TEST OF HYPOTHESIS FOR LINEAR CORRELATION

a. One-tailed test

H_0: There is no linear correlation between x and y

H_a: The variables x and y are positively correlated

(or H_a: The variables x and y are negatively correlated)

Test statistic: r

Rejection region:

$r > r_\alpha$ (or $r < -r_\alpha$)

b. Two-tailed test

H_0: There is no linear correlation between x and y

H_a: The variables x and y are linearly correlated

Test statistic: r

Rejection region:

$r > r_{\alpha/2}$ or $r < -r_{\alpha/2}$

where the distribution of r depends on the sample size n, and r_α and $r_{\alpha/2}$ are the critical values obtained from Table 10, Appendix E, such that

$$P(r > r_\alpha) = \alpha \quad \text{and} \quad P(r > r_{\alpha/2}) = \alpha/2$$

Recall that our ultimate objective is to predict the value of one variable, y, from the value of another variable, x. While the correlation coefficient r indicates the strength of the linear relationship between the variables, it does not tell us what the exact relationship is. In Section 12.3, we introduce a model which will enable us to make predictions.

EXERCISES 12.1 The number of buyers of new automobiles in a specific month, say, February, is likely to be correlated with the prime interest rate. Will this correlation be positive or negative? Explain.

12.2 Is the demand for a product, say, hamburgers, correlated with its price? If it is, would you expect the correlation to be positive or negative? Explain.

12.3 Give an example of two economic or business variables that are:
a. Positively correlated   b. Negatively correlated

12.4 Consider the five data points:

x	−1	0	1	2	3
y	−1	1	1	2.5	3.5

a. Construct a scattergram for the data. After examining the scattergram, do you think that x and y are correlated? If correlation is present, is it positive or negative?
b. Find the correlation coefficient r and interpret its value.
c. Do the data provide sufficient evidence to indicate that x and y are linearly correlated? Test using $\alpha = .05$.

12.5 Consider the seven data points:

x	−5	−3	−1	0	1	3	5
y	.8	1.1	2.5	3.1	5.0	4.7	6.2

a. Construct a scattergram for the data. After examining the scattergram, do you think that x and y are correlated? If correlation is present, is it positive or negative?
b. Find the correlation coefficient r and interpret its value.
c. Do the data provide sufficient evidence to indicate that x and y are linearly correlated? Test using $\alpha = .05$.

12.6 A company conducted a survey of its customers to investigate the relationship between the demand (in numbers of units per month) for the company's products and the price per unit. Five prices were selected for the study and two customers were randomly selected for each price and asked to estimate their monthly purchase rate. The data are shown in the table.

PRICE PER UNIT x, dollars	PURCHASE RATE y, units per month
450	32
450	36
475	34
475	28
500	26
500	23
525	25
525	17
550	12
550	16

a. Construct a scattergram for the data. After examining the scattergram, do you think that x and y are correlated? If correlation is present, is it positive or negative?

b. Find the correlation coefficient r and interpret its value.

c. Do the data provide sufficient evidence to indicate that x and y are linearly correlated? Test using $\alpha = .05$.

12.7 A savings and loan company conducted a study to determine the correlation between the number of weekly home loan applications and the current mortgage rate. Ten weeks were selected at random from among the 156 weeks of the past three years. The number of loan applications and the mortgage rate for each of the ten weeks are recorded in the table.

WEEK	NUMBER OF LOAN APPLICATIONS y	MORTGAGE RATE x, %
1	55	13.5
2	48	14.0
3	73	11.5
4	52	13.0
5	44	14.5
6	79	10.0
7	68	11.0
8	66	12.0
9	53	14.0
10	57	13.0

a.   Construct a scattergram for the data. After examining the scattergram, do you
     think that x and y are correlated? If correlation is present, is it positive or negative?
b.   Find the correlation coefficient r and interpret its value.
c.   Do the data provide sufficient evidence to indicate that x and y are linearly
     correlated? Test using $\alpha = .05$.

12.8   The manager of a clothing store decided to investigate the relationship between the number of sales clerks on duty and the amount (in hundreds of dollars) of
merchandise lost (called *shrinkage*) due to shoplifting or other causes. The dollar
volume lost due to shrinkage was recorded for each of twelve weeks. The number of
sales clerks was held constant within a given week but was varied from one week to
another. The data are shown in the table.

WEEK	SHRINKAGE y, hundreds of dollars	NUMBER OF SALES CLERKS x
1	20	20
2	23	21
3	18	22
4	17	23
5	17	24
6	12	25
7	17	25
8	26	20
9	21	22
10	11	24
11	10	26
12	4	28

a.   Would you expect the coefficient of correlation between shrinkage and number of
     sales clerks on duty to be positive or negative? Explain.
b.   Find the coefficient of correlation, r, and interpret its value.
c.   Do the data provide sufficient evidence to indicate a linear correlation between x
     and y? Test using $\alpha = .05$.

12.3 Straight-Line Probabilistic Models

Consider the sales data for neighborhood A given in Appendix B. Suppose that you
wish to model the relationship between the 1978 sale price of properties in the
neighborhood and the total appraised value of the properties.

EXAMPLE 12.6   Do you believe that an exact relationship exists between the two variables, Sale price
and Appraised value? That is, would it be possible to state the exact sale price of a

property in the neighborhood if you knew the total appraised value (land value plus improvements value) of the property?

Solution In reality, the answer is a very definite no! The sale price for any given property will depend not only on the total appraised value but also on such variables as the price set by the realtor, the strength of appeal of the property to a specific buyer, and the present state of the money and real estate markets. You can probably think of additional variables which play an important role in determining the sale price of a residential property. How can we construct a model, then, for two variables for which no exact relationship exists? We illustrate with an example.

EXAMPLE 12.7 Given in Table 12.4 are the total appraised property values and sale prices of a sample of five different properties located in neighborhood A, as obtained from Appendix B. Hypothesize a reasonable model for the relationship between sale price and total appraised property value.

TABLE 12.4
Sale Price–Appraised
Value Data, Example 12.7

PROPERTY	TOTAL APPRAISED PROPERTY VALUE x, dollars	SALE PRICE y, dollars
1	24,370	36,900
2	25,020	35,000
3	52,860	75,000
4	36,820	56,000
5	45,960	72,000

Solution Upon examination of the data, we see that y, the sale price in neighborhood A, is approximately one and one-half times x, the property's total appraised value. In Figure 12.4 we have plotted the actual sale prices against the respective total appraised property values in a scattergram. Notice that sale price appears to vary randomly about the straight line $y = 1.5x$. A reasonable model, then, is one which will allow for unexplained variation in sale prices caused by important variables not included in the model (such as those discussed in Example 12.6) or simply by random phenomena which cannot be modeled or explained. Models that account for this *random error* are called *probabilistic models.*

The probabilistic model relating the sale price y to the total appraised property value x is written

$y = 1.5x$ + Random error

We note that probabilistic models include two components: a *deterministic component* and a *random error component.* For this model, the deterministic component is $1.5x$. If y could always be determined exactly when x is known, then a deterministic relationship, such as $y = 1.5x$, would hold true. By including a random error component in our model, we allow for the random variation of sale prices shown in Figure 12.4 (p. 386).

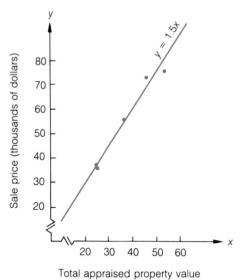

FIGURE 12.4
Scattergram of Sale Price
Versus Appraised Value,
Example 12.7

Total appraised property value
(thousands of dollars)

Probabilistic relationship: $y = 1.5x$ + Random error

GENERAL FORM OF PROBABILISTIC MODELS

y = Deterministic component + Random error

where y is the variable to be predicted.

Assumption: The mean value of the random error equals 0. This is equivalent to assuming that the mean value of y, $E(y)$, equals the deterministic component of the model, i.e.,

$$E(y) = \text{Deterministic component}$$

In this chapter, we consider only the simplest of probabilistic models—*the straight-line model*—which derives its name from the fact that the deterministic portion of the model graphs as a straight line. The elements of the straight-line model are summarized in the box at the top of the next page.

We use the Greek symbols, β_0 and β_1, to represent the y-intercept and the slope of the model, respectively. They are population parameters which will be known only if we have access to the entire population of (x, y) measurements. In the section that follows, we will use the sample data to estimate the slope (β_1) and the y-intercept (β_0) of the deterministic portion of our straight-line model.

THE STRAIGHT-LINE PROBABILISTIC MODEL

$$y = \beta_0 + \beta_1 x + \text{Random error}$$

where

y = Variable to be predicted, called the **dependent variable**

x = Variable to be used as a predictor of y, called the **independent variable**

$E(y) = \beta_0 + \beta_1 x$ is the deterministic portion of the model (the equation of a straight line)

β_0 (beta zero) = y-intercept of the line, i.e., the point at which the line intercepts or cuts through the y-axis (see Figure 12.5)

β_1 (beta one) = Slope of the line, i.e., amount of increase (or decrease) in the deterministic component of y for every 1 unit increase in x (see Figure 12.5)

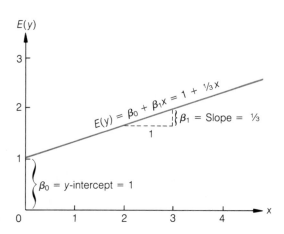

FIGURE 12.5
The Straight-Line Model

12.9 Suppose that y is exactly related to x by the equation

$$y = 1.5 + 2x$$

a. Find the value of y that corresponds to $x = 1$.
b. Find the value of y that corresponds to $x = 2$.
c. Plot the two (x, y) points found in parts a and b on graph paper and draw a line through the points. This line corresponds to the equation, $y = 1.5 + 2x$.
d. Find the value of y that corresponds to $x = 1.5$. Plot this point on the graph, part c, and confirm that it falls on the line that passes through the points found in parts a and b.

e.   Part d illustrates an important relationship between graphs and equations. All the points that satisfy the equation, $y = 1.5 + 2x$, possess a common property. What is it?

12.10   Refer to Exercise 12.9.
a.   Find the y-intercept for the line and interpret its value.
b.   Find the slope of the line and interpret its value.
c.   If you increase x by one unit, how much will y increase or decrease?
d.   If you decrease x by one unit, how much will y increase or decrease?
e.   What is the value of y when $x = 0$?

12.11   Answer the questions contained in Exercise 12.9, using the line, $y = 1.5 - 2x$.

12.12   Refer to Exercise 12.11.
a.   Find the y-intercept for the line and interpret its value.
b.   Find the slope of the line and interpret its value.
c.   If you increase x by one unit, how much will y increase or decrease?
d.   What is the value of y when $x = 0$?
e.   What do the two lines, Exercises 12.9 and 12.11, have in common? How do they differ?

12.13   Graph the lines corresponding to the following equations:
a. $y = 1 + 3x$ **b.** $y = 1 - 3x$
c. $y = -1 + (\frac{1}{2})x$ **d.** $y = -1 - 3x$
e. $y = 2 - (\frac{1}{2})x$ **f.** $y = -1.5 + x$
g. $y = 3x$ **h.** $y = -2x$

12.14   Give the values of β_0 and β_1 corresponding to each of the lines, Exercise 12.13.

12.4   How to Fit the Model: The Least Squares Approach

The following example illustrates the technique we will use to *fit* the straight-line model to the data, i.e., to estimate the slope and y-intercept of the line using information provided by the sample data.

EXAMPLE 12.8   We return to modeling the relationship between the sale price, y, and the total appraised value, x, of a property located in neighborhood A. (Recall that the sale price is the price that the property would sell for if it were to be placed on the retail market.) We have hypothesized the deterministic component of the probabilistic model as

$$E(y) = \beta_0 + \beta_1 x$$

If we were able to obtain the appraised value and sale price of every property in the neighborhood, i.e., the entire population of (x, y) measurements, then the values of the population parameters β_0 and β_1 could be determined exactly. Of course, we will never have access to the entire population of (x, y) measurements, since a great majority of the properties in the neighborhood will not be sold during the year. The problem, then, is to estimate the unknown population parameters based upon the information contained in a sample of (x, y) measurements. Suppose that we randomly sample five properties in the neighborhood that were sold during the past year. The sale prices and total appraised property values are given in Table 12.5. How can we best use the sample information to estimate the unknown y-intercept β_0 and the slope β_1?

TABLE 12.5

Sale Price–Appraised Value Data, Example 12.8

PROPERTY	TOTAL APPRAISED PROPERTY VALUE *x*, thousands of dollars	SALE PRICE *y*, thousands of dollars
1	20	20
2	30	50
3	40	70
4	50	100
5	60	110

Solution   Estimates of the unknown parameters β_0 and β_1 are obtained by finding the best-fitting straight-line through the sample data points of Table 12.5. (These points are plotted in Figure 12.6.) The procedure we will use to find the best fit is known as the ***method of least squares,*** and the best-fitting line, called the ***least squares line,*** is written

$$\hat{y} = \hat{\beta}_0 + \hat{\beta}_1 x$$

The first step in finding the least squares line is to construct a sums of squares table in order to find the sums of the x-values (Σx), y-values (Σy), the squares of the x-values (Σx^2), and the cross products of the corresponding x- and y-values (Σxy).

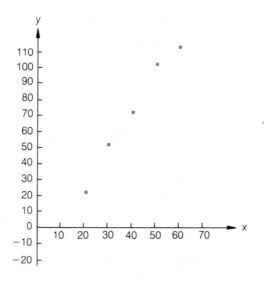

FIGURE 12.6

Scattergram of Sale Price–Appraised Value Data, Table 12.5

The sums of squares table for the sale price–appraised value data is given in Table 12.6.

TABLE 12.6
Sums of Squares for Data
of Table 12.5

x	y	x^2	xy
20	20	400	400
30	50	900	1,500
40	70	1,600	2,800
50	100	2,500	5,000
60	110	3,600	6,600
TOTALS $\Sigma x = 200$	$\Sigma y = 350$	$\Sigma x^2 = 9,000$	$\Sigma xy = 16,300$

The second step is to substitute the values of Σx, Σy, Σx^2, and Σxy into the formulas for SS_{xy} and SS_{xx} given in Section 12.2:

$$SS_{xy} = \Sigma xy - \frac{(\Sigma x)(\Sigma y)}{n} = 16,300 - \frac{(200)(350)}{5}$$

$$= 16,300 - 14,000 = 2,300$$

$$SS_{xx} = \Sigma x^2 - \frac{(\Sigma x)^2}{n} = 9,000 - \frac{(200)^2}{5}$$

$$= 9,000 - 8,000 = 1,000$$

Next, use these values of SS_{xy} and SS_{xx} to compute the estimate $\hat{\beta}_1$, as shown in the box:

SLOPE OF THE LEAST SQUARES LINE

$$\hat{\beta}_1 = \frac{SS_{xy}}{SS_{xx}}$$

Substituting, we find $\hat{\beta}_1$, the slope of the least squares line, to be

$$\hat{\beta}_1 = \frac{SS_{xy}}{SS_{xx}} = \frac{2,300}{1,000} = 2.3$$

Finally, calculate $\hat{\beta}_0$, the y-intercept of the least squares line, as follows:

---
y-INTERCEPT OF THE LEAST SQUARES LINE

$$\hat{\beta}_0 = \bar{y} - \hat{\beta}_1 \bar{x}$$

$$\hat{\beta}_0 = \bar{y} - \hat{\beta}_1 \bar{x} = \frac{\Sigma y}{5} - \hat{\beta}_1 \left(\frac{\Sigma x}{5} \right)$$

$$= \frac{350}{5} - (2.3)\left(\frac{200}{5} \right) = 70 - (2.3)(40) = 70 - 92 = -22$$

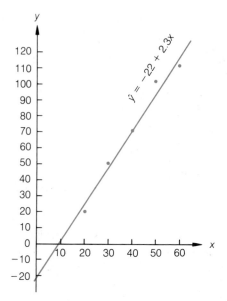

FIGURE 12.7
Least Squares Line,
Example 12.8

Therefore, $\hat{\beta}_0 = -22$, $\hat{\beta}_1 = 2.3$, and the least squares line is

$$\hat{y} = -22 + (2.3)x$$

A graph of this line is shown in Figure 12.7.

This four-step least squares procedure is summarized in the box.

**STEPS TO FOLLOW IN FITTING A LEAST SQUARES LINE
TO A SET OF DATA**

1. Construct a table (similar to Table 12.6) to find Σx, Σy, Σx^2, and Σxy.
2. Substitute the values into the formulas for SS_{xy} and SS_{xx}:

$$SS_{xy} = \Sigma xy - \frac{(\Sigma x)(\Sigma y)}{n}$$

$$SS_{xx} = \Sigma x^2 - \frac{(\Sigma x)^2}{n}$$

where n = sample size (number of pairs of observations).
3. Substitute the values into the formula for $\hat{\beta}_1$. Then find $\hat{\beta}_0$.

$$\hat{\beta}_1 = \frac{SS_{xy}}{SS_{xx}}$$

$$\hat{\beta}_0 = \bar{y} - \hat{\beta}_1\bar{x}$$

4. Use the computed values of $\hat{\beta}_0$ and $\hat{\beta}_1$ to form the equation of the least squares line, i.e.,

$$\hat{y} = \hat{\beta}_0 + \hat{\beta}_1 x$$

EXAMPLE 12.9 In what sense is the least squares line the "best-fitting" straight line to a set of data?

Solution In deciding whether a line provides a good fit to a set of data, we examine the vertical distances, or **deviations,** between the data points and the fitted line. (Since we are attempting to predict y, a measure of fit will involve the difference between the observed value y and the predicted value $\hat{y}$—a quantity which is represented by the vertical deviation between the data point and the fitted line.) The deviations for the least squares line

$$\hat{y} = -22 + 2.3x$$

are shown in Figure 12.8(a). Let us compare the deviations of the least squares line with the deviations of another fitted line (one fitted visually), given by the equation

$$\hat{y} = -10 + 2x$$

The deviations of the visually fitted line are shown in Figure 12.8(b). Notice first that some of the deviations are positive, some are negative, and that even though three of the five data points fall exactly on the visually fitted line, the individual deviations tend to be smaller for the least squares line than for the visually fitted line. Second, note that the sum of squares of deviations (SSE $= \Sigma(y - \hat{y})^2$) is smaller for the least squares line. (The values of SSE for the least squares and visually fitted lines are given at the bottom of Figures 12.8(a) and 12.8(b), respectively.) *In fact, it can be shown that there is one and only one line which will minimize the sum of squares of deviations of the points about the fitted line. It is the least squares line.*

FIGURE 12.8 Deviations about the Fitted Line, Example 12.9

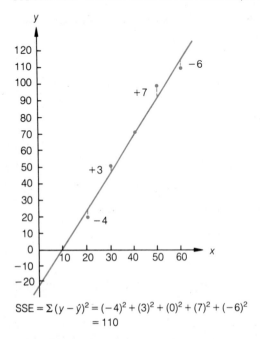

SSE $= \Sigma(y - \hat{y})^2 = (-4)^2 + (3)^2 + (0)^2 + (7)^2 + (-6)^2$
$= 110$

(a) Least squares line: $\hat{y} = -22 + 2.3x$

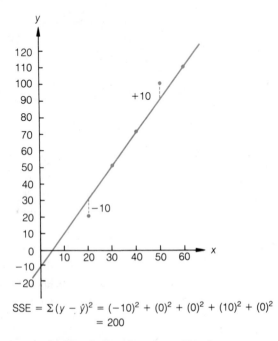

SSE $= \Sigma(y - \hat{y})^2 = (-10)^2 + (0)^2 + (0)^2 + (10)^2 + (0)^2$
$= 200$

(b) Visually fitted line: $\hat{y} = -10 + 2x$

**LEAST SQUARES CRITERION FOR FINDING
THE "BEST-FITTING" LINE**

Choose the line that minimizes the sum of squared deviations, SSE. This is called the *least squares line,* or alternatively, the *least squares prediction equation.*

The fact that the least squares line is the one that minimizes the sum of squares of deviations does not guarantee that it is the "best" line to fit the data. However, intuitively, it would seem that this is a desirable property for a good fitting line.* A second reason for liking the method of least squares is that we know the sampling distributions of the estimates of β_0 and β_1, something that would be unknown for lines fitted intuitively or visually. A third and final reason is that, under certain conditions, the least squares estimators of β_0 and β_1 will have smaller standard errors than other types of estimators.

EXAMPLE 12.10   A car dealer is interested in modeling the relationship between the number of cars sold by the firm each week and the number of salespeople who work on the showroom floor. The dealer believes that the relationship between the two variables can best be described by a straight line. The sample data shown in Table 12.7 were supplied by the car dealer.

TABLE 12.7
Car Sales Data, Example 12.10

WEEK	NUMBER OF CARS SOLD	NUMBER OF SALESPEOPLE ON DUTY
January 30	20	6
June 3	18	6
March 2	10	4
October 26	6	2
February 7	11	3

Use the method of least squares to estimate the *y*-intercept and slope of the line. According to the least squares line, approximately how many cars should the dealer expect to sell in a week if five salespeople are kept on the showroom floor each day?

---

*The sum of the deviations from the least squares line will also always equal 0. Since there are many other fitted lines which also have this property, we do not use this as a criterion for choosing the "best-fitting" line.

Solution The straight-line model describing the relationship between the average number of cars sold per week and number of salespeople on duty is

$$E(y) = \beta_0 + \beta_1 x$$

To use the method of least squares to estimate β_0 and β_1, we must first (step 1) make the preliminary computations shown in Table 12.8.

TABLE 12.8
Preliminary Computations,
Example 12.10

x	y	x^2	xy
6	20	36	120
6	18	36	108
4	10	16	40
2	6	4	12
3	11	9	33
TOTALS $\Sigma x = 21$	$\Sigma y = 65$	$\Sigma x^2 = 101$	$\Sigma xy = 313$

We now calculate (step 2)

$$SS_{xy} = 313 - \frac{(21)(65)}{5}$$

$$= 313 - 273 = 40$$

$$SS_{xx} = 101 - \frac{(21)^2}{5}$$

$$= 101 - 88.2 = 12.8$$

The slope of the least squares line is then (step 3)

$$\hat{\beta}_1 = \frac{SS_{xy}}{SS_{xx}} = \frac{40}{12.8} = 3.125$$

and the y-intercept is

$$\hat{\beta}_0 = \bar{y} - \hat{\beta}_1(\bar{x}) = \frac{65}{5} - (3.125)\frac{(21)}{5}$$

$$= 13 - 13.125 = -.125$$

The least squares line can then be written (step 4)

$$\hat{y} = -.125 + (3.125)x$$

To answer the second question, we need to obtain the predicted value for y, the number of cars sold in a week, if $x = 5$ salespeople are kept on the showroom floor each day. Substituting $x = 5$ into the least squares equation, we obtain

$$\hat{y} = -.125 + (3.125)(5)$$

$$= -.125 + 15.625 = 15.5$$

On the average then, the dealer can expect to sell approximately 15.5 cars per week if five salespeople are on the showroom floor each day. We will obtain a measure of reliability for a prediction such as this in Section 12.8.

EXERCISES   **12.15**   The data for Exercise 12.4 are reproduced below:

x	−1	0	1	2	3
y	−1	1	1	2.5	3.5

a. Construct a scattergram for the data.
b. Find the least squares prediction equation.
c. Graph the least squares line on the scattergram and visually confirm that it provides a good fit to the data points.

12.16   Consider the four data points:

x	1	1.5	1.9	2.5
y	3.1	2.2	1.0	.3

a. Construct a scattergram for the data.
b. Find the least squares prediction equation.
c. Graph the least squares line on the scattergram and visually confirm that it provides a good fit to the data points.

12.17   The data for Exercise 12.5 are reproduced below:

x	−5	−3	−1	0	1	3	5
y	.8	1.1	2.5	3.1	5.0	4.7	6.2

a. Construct a scattergram for the data.
b. Find the least squares prediction equation.
c. Graph the least squares line on the scattergram and visually confirm that it provides a good fit to the data points.

12.18   Consider the four data points:

x	−3.0	2.4	−1.1	2.0
y	2.7	.4	1.3	.5

α. Construct a scattergram for the data.
b. Find the least squares prediction equation.
c. Graph the least squares line on the scattergram and visually confirm that it provides a good fit to the data points.

12.19   The data for Exercise 12.6 are reproduced in the table.

PRICE PER UNIT x, dollars	PURCHASE RATE y, units per month
450	32
450	36
475	34
475	28
500	26
500	23
525	25
525	17
550	12
550	16

α. Construct a scattergram for the data.
b. Find the least squares prediction equation.
c. Graph the least squares line on the scattergram.
d. Use the least squares prediction equation to predict the purchase rate y when the price per unit is $x = \$480$. [*Note:* We will find a measure of the reliability of this prediction in Section 12.8.]

12.20   The data for Exercise 12.8 are reproduced in the table.

WEEK	SHRINKAGE y, hundreds of dollars	NUMBER OF SALES CLERKS x
1	20	20
2	23	21
3	18	22
4	17	23
5	17	24
6	12	25
7	17	25
8	26	20
9	21	22
10	11	24
11	10	26
12	4	28

    a.   Construct a scattergram for the data.

    b.   Find the least squares prediction equation.

    c.   Graph the least squares line on the scattergram.

    d.   Use the least squares prediction equation to estimate the mean weekly shrinkage y when $x = 23$ clerks are on duty. [*Note:* We will find a measure of reliability for this estimate in Section 12.8.]

12.5 Estimating σ^2

Is the sale price y of Example 12.8 really related to total appraised property value x, or is the linear relation that we seem to see a figment of our imagination? That is, could it be the case that x and y are completely unrelated, and that the apparent linear configuration of the data points in the scattergram, Figure 12.6, is due to random variation? We could obtain an answer to this question by testing for the existence of correlation in the population as outlined in Section 12.2. A second method, one which will also enable us to predict the value of y from a given x and attach a measure of reliability to our predictions, requires that we know how much y will vary for a given value of x. That is, we need to know the value of the quantity, called σ^2, which measures the variability of the y-values about the least squares line. Since the variance σ^2 will rarely be known, we will estimate its value using the sum of the squared deviations (sum of the squared errors, SSE) and the procedure shown in the box.

ESTIMATION OF σ^2, A MEASURE OF THE VARIABILITY OF THE y-VALUES ABOUT THE LEAST SQUARES LINE

An estimate of σ^2 is given by

$$s^2 = \frac{SSE}{(n-2)}$$

where

$$SSE = \Sigma (y - \hat{y})^2 = SS_{yy} - \hat{\beta}_1 SS_{xy}$$

$$SS_{yy} = \Sigma (y - \bar{y})^2 = \Sigma y^2 - \frac{(\Sigma y)^2}{n}$$

Warning: When performing these calculations, you may be tempted to round the calculated values of SS_{yy}, $\hat{\beta}_1$, and SS_{xy}. We recommend carrying at least six significant figures for each of these quantities to avoid substantial rounding errors in the calculation of SSE.

Note: The denominator of s^2 is termed *the number of degrees of freedom for error variance estimation.*

EXAMPLE 12.11   Refer to Example 12.8. Estimate the value of σ^2 for the data of Table 12.5.

Solution   According to the formulas given in the box, the first step is to compute SS_{yy}. We have

$$SS_{yy} = \Sigma y^2 - \frac{(\Sigma y)^2}{n}$$

$$= (20)^2 + (50)^2 + (70)^2 + (100)^2 + (110)^2 - \frac{(350)^2}{5}$$

$$= 29{,}900 - 24{,}500 = 5{,}400$$

Recall from Example 12.8 that $\hat{\beta}_1 = 2.3$ and $SS_{xy} = 2{,}300$. Thus, we compute

$$SSE = SS_{yy} - \hat{\beta}_1 SS_{xy}$$

$$= 5{,}400 - (2.3)(2{,}300) = 5{,}400 - 5{,}290 = 110$$

Notice that this value of SSE agrees with the value previously given in Figure 12.8(a). Our estimate of σ^2 is therefore

$$s^2 = \frac{SSE}{n-2} = \frac{110}{5-2} = \frac{110}{3} = 36.667$$

We could also compute the estimated standard deviation s by taking the square root of s^2. In this example, we have

$$s = \sqrt{s^2} = \sqrt{36.667} = 6.055$$

Since s measures the spread of the distribution of the y-values about the least squares line, we should not be surprised to find that most of the observations lie within $2s$ or $2(6.055) = 12.11$ of the least squares line. From Figure 12.9 we see that, for this

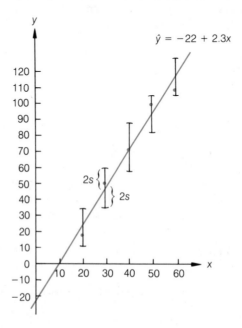

FIGURE 12.9
Observations within $2s$ of
the Least Squares Line

example, all five data points have y-values which lie within $2s$ of $\hat{y}$, the least squares predicted value.

12.6 Making Inferences about the Slope β_1

After fitting the model to the data and computing an estimate of σ^2, our next task is to statistically check the usefulness of the model. That is, use a statistical procedure (a test of hypothesis or confidence interval) to determine whether the least squares straight-line (linear) model is a reliable tool for predicting y for a given value of x.

EXAMPLE 12.12 Consider the probabilistic model

$$y = \beta_0 + \beta_1 x + \text{Random error}$$

How do we determine, statistically, whether this model is useful for prediction purposes, i.e., how could we test whether x provides useful information for the prediction of y?

Solution Suppose that x is **completely unrelated** to y. What could we say about the values of β_0 and β_1 in the probabilistic model if in fact x contributes no information for the prediction of y? We think you will agree that for y to be independent of x, the true slope of the line, β_1, must be equal to zero. Therefore, to test the null hypothesis that x contributes no information for the prediction of y against the alternative that these variables are linearly related with a slope differing from zero, we test

$$H_0: \quad \beta_1 = 0 \qquad H_a: \quad \beta_1 \neq 0$$

If the data support the alternative hypothesis, we will conclude that x does contribute information for the prediction of y using the straight-line model (although the true relationship between $E(y)$ and x could be more complex than a straight line). [*Note:* This test is equivalent to the test for correlation discussed in Section 12.2. If x and y are in fact linearly correlated, then the slope β_1 of the straight-line model will be different from 0.]

Using the hypothesis-testing techniques developed in Chapters 9 and 10, we set up the test for the predictive ability of the model as shown in the box at the top of the next page.

Inferences based upon this hypothesis test require certain assumptions about the random error term (see Section 12.10). However, the test statistic has a sampling distribution that remains relatively stable for minor departures from the assumptions. That is, our inferences remain valid for practical cases in which the assumptions are nearly, but not completely, satisfied.

We illustrate the test for determining whether the model is useful for predicting y from x with a practical example.

EXAMPLE 12.13 Let us return to the appraised value–sale price problem of Example 12.8. At significance level $\alpha = .05$, test the hypothesis that total appraised property value x

---

TEST OF HYPOTHESIS FOR DETERMINING WHETHER THE STRAIGHT-LINE MODEL IS USEFUL FOR PREDICTING y FROM x

a. One-tailed test

H_0: $\beta_1 = 0$

H_a: $\beta_1 > 0$

(or H_a: $\beta_1 < 0$)

Test statistic:

$$t = \frac{\hat{\beta}_1}{s/\sqrt{SS_{xx}}}$$

Rejection region:

$t > t_\alpha$ (or $t < -t_\alpha$)

b. Two-tailed test

H_0: $\beta_1 = 0$

H_a: $\beta_1 \neq 0$

Test statistic:

$$t = \frac{\hat{\beta}_1}{s/\sqrt{SS_{xx}}}$$

Rejection region:

$t < -t_{\alpha/2}$ or $t > t_{\alpha/2}$

where the distribution of t is based on $(n - 2)$ degrees of freedom, t_α is the t-value such that $P(t > t_\alpha) = \alpha$, and $t_{\alpha/2}$ is the t-value such that $P(t > t_{\alpha/2}) = \alpha/2$.

Assumptions: See Section 12.10

Note: The test statistic is derived from the sampling distribution of the least squares estimator of the slope, $\hat{\beta}_1$.

---

contributes useful information for the prediction of sale price y, i.e., test the predictive ability of the least squares straight-line model

$$\hat{y} = -22 + 2.3x$$

Solution   Testing the usefulness of the model requires testing the hypotheses

H_0: $\beta_1 = 0$

H_a: $\beta_1 \neq 0$

With $n = 5$ and $\alpha = .05$, the critical value based on $(5 - 2) = 3$ df is obtained from Table 4, Appendix E:

$$t_{\alpha/2} = t_{.025} = 3.182$$

Thus, we will reject H_0 if $t < -3.182$ or $t > 3.182$.

    In order to compute the test statistic, we need the values of $\hat{\beta}_1$, s, and SS_{xx}. In previous examples, we computed $\hat{\beta}_1 = 2.3$, $s = 6.055$, and $SS_{xx} = 1,000$. Hence, our test statistic is

$$t = \frac{\hat{\beta}_1}{s/\sqrt{SS_{xx}}} = \frac{2.3}{6.055/\sqrt{1,000}} = 12.01$$

Since this calculated t-value falls in the upper-tail rejection region (see Figure 12.10), we reject the null hypothesis and conclude that the slope β_1 is not zero. At the $\alpha = .05$

level of significance then, the sample data provide sufficient evidence to conclude that total appraised property value does contribute useful information for the prediction of sale price via the linear model.

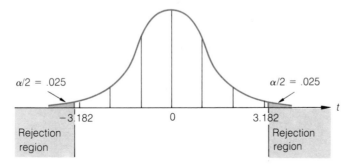

FIGURE 12.10
Rejection Region,
Example 12.13

$\alpha/2 = .025$ $\alpha/2 = .025$

-3.182 0 3.182 t

Rejection region   Rejection region

If the test statistic had not fallen in the rejection region, would we have concluded that $\beta_1 = 0$? The answer to this question is "no" (recall the discussion in Chapter 9). Rather, we acknowledge that additional data might indicate that β_1 differs from zero, or that a more complex relationship (other than a straight line) may exist between y and x. We may also wish to examine the attained significance level of the test.

EXAMPLE 12.14

A consumer investigator obtained the following least squares straight-line model relating the yearly food cost y for a family of four and annual income x:

$$\hat{y} = 467 + .26x$$

based on a sample of $n = 100$ families. In addition, the investigator computed the quantities $s = 1.1$ and $SS_{xx} = 26$. Compute the attained significance level (p-value) for a test to determine whether mean yearly food cost y increases as annual income x increases, i.e., whether the slope of the line, β_1, is positive. Interpret this value.

Solution

The consumer investigator wishes to test

$$H_0:\quad \beta_1 = 0$$

$$H_a:\quad \beta_1 > 0$$

To compute the attained significance level of the test we must first find the calculated value of the test statistic, t_c. Since $\hat{\beta}_1 = .26$, $s = 1.1$, and $SS_{xx} = 26$, we have

$$t_c = \frac{\hat{\beta}_1}{s/\sqrt{SS_{xx}}} = \frac{.26}{1.1/\sqrt{26}} = 1.21$$

From Section 10.8, the attained significance level or p-value is given by

$$P(t > t_c) = P(t > 1.21)$$

where the distribution of t is based on $(n-2) = (100-2) \doteq 98$ degrees of freedom. Since df is greater than 30, we can approximate the t distribution with the z distribution. Thus,

$$p\text{-value} = P(t > 1.21) \approx P(z > 1.21)$$

$$= .5 - .3869 = .1131$$

In order to conclude that the mean yearly food cost increases as annual income increases (i.e., $\beta_1 > 0$), the investigator would have to be willing to tolerate a Type I error probability, α, of .1131 or larger. Since it is very doubtful that the investigator would be willing to take this risk, we consider the sample result to be statistically insignificant.

In addition to testing whether the slope β_1 is zero, we may also be interested in estimating its value with a confidence interval.

EXAMPLE 12.15   Using the information supplied in Example 12.13, construct a 95% confidence interval for the slope β_1 in the straight-line model relating sale price to total appraised property value.

Solution   The methods of Chapter 8 are used to construct a confidence interval for β_1. The interval, derived from the sampling distribution of $\hat{\beta}_1$, is given in the box.

A $(1-\alpha)$ 100% CONFIDENCE INTERVAL FOR THE SLOPE β_1

$$\hat{\beta}_1 \pm t_{\alpha/2}\left(\frac{s}{\sqrt{SS_{xx}}}\right)$$

where the distribution of t is based on $(n-2)$ degrees of freedom and $t_{\alpha/2}$ is the value of t such that $P(t > t_{\alpha/2}) = \alpha/2$.

For a 95% confidence interval, $\alpha = .05$. Therefore we need to find the value of $t_{.025}$ based on $(n-2) = (5-2) = 3$ df. In Example 12.13, we found that $t_{.025} = 3.182$. Also we have $\hat{\beta}_1 = 2.3$, $s = 6.055$, and $SS_{xx} = 1,000$. Thus, a 95% confidence interval for the slope in the model relating sale price to total appraised property value is

$$\hat{\beta}_1 \pm (t_{.025})\frac{s}{\sqrt{SS_{xx}}} = 2.3 \pm (3.182)\frac{6.055}{\sqrt{1,000}} = 2.3 \pm .61$$

Our interval estimate of the slope parameter β_1 is then 1.69 to 2.91.

EXAMPLE 12.16   Interpret the interval estimate of β_1 derived in Example 12.15.

Solution   Since all the values in the interval (1.69, 2.91) are positive, we say that we are 95% confident that the slope β_1 is positive. That is, we are 95% confident that the mean sale price, $E(y)$, increases as total appraised property value, x, increases. In addition, we can say that for every 1 dollar increase in the appraised value x of the property, the increase in mean sale price $E(y)$ of the property could be as small as 1.69 dollars or as large as 2.91 dollars. However, the rather large width of the interval reflects the small number of data points (and, consequently, a lack of information) in the experiment. We would expect a narrower interval if the sample size were increased.

EXERCISES   **12.21**   The data for Exercise 12.4 are reproduced below.

x	−1	0	1	2	3
y	−1	1	1	2.5	3.5

a. Find SSE and s^2 for the data.
b. How many degrees of freedom are associated with s^2?
c. Test the null hypothesis that the slope β_1 of the line equals 0 against the alternative hypothesis that β_1 is not equal to 0. Use $\alpha = .10$.
d. Compute the approximate attained significance level of the test.
e. Find a 90% confidence interval for the slope β_1.

12.22   The data for Exercise 12.5 are reproduced below:

x	−5	−3	−1	0	1	3	5
y	.8	1.1	2.5	3.1	5.0	4.7	6.2

a. Find SSE and s^2 for the data.
b. How many degrees of freedom are associated with s^2?
c. Test the null hypothesis that the slope β_1 of the line equals 0 against the alternative hypothesis that β_1 is not equal to 0. Use $\alpha = .10$.
d. Compute the approximate attained significance level of the test.
e. Find a 90% confidence interval for the slope β_1.

12.23   The data for Exercise 12.6 are reproduced in the table.

PRICE PER UNIT x, dollars	PURCHASE RATE y, units per month
450	32
450	36
475	34
475	28
500	26
500	23
525	25
525	17
550	12
550	16

α. Find SSE and s^2 for the data.
b. How many degrees of freedom are associated with s^2?
c. Do the data provide sufficient evidence to indicate that price per unit x contributes information for the prediction of purchase rate y? Test using $\alpha = .05$.

12.24 The data for Exercise 12.8 are reproduced in the table.

WEEK	SHRINKAGE y, hundreds of dollars	NUMBER OF SALES CLERKS x
1	20	20
2	23	21
3	18	22
4	17	23
5	17	24
6	12	25
7	17	25
8	26	20
9	21	22
10	11	24
11	10	26
12	4	28

α. Find SSE and s^2 for the data.
b. How many degrees of freedom are associated with s^2?
c. Do the data provide sufficient evidence to indicate that the number x of sales clerks contributes information for the prediction of shrinkage y? Use $\alpha = .01$.

12.25 Buyers are often influenced by bulk-rate advertising of a particular product. For example, suppose you have a product that sells for 25¢. If it is advertised at 2 for 50¢, 3 for 75¢, or 4 for $1, some people may think they are getting a bargain. To test this theory, a store manager advertised an item for equal periods of time at five different bulk rates and observed the data listed in the table. Do the data provide sufficient evidence to indicate that mean sales increase as the number in the bulk increases? Use $\alpha = .05$. [*Hint:* Note that you wish to determine whether the slope β_1 is greater than 0. Therefore, you will want to conduct a one-tailed test of hypothesis.]

ADVERTISED NUMBER IN BULK x	VOLUME SOLD y
1	27
2	36
3	34
4	63
5	52

12.26 A large car rental agency sells its cars after using them for a year. Among the records kept for each car are mileage and maintenance costs for the year. To evaluate the performance of a particular car model in terms of maintenance costs, the agency wants to use a 95% confidence interval to estimate the mean increase in maintenance cost for each additional 1,000 miles driven. Assume the relationship between maintenance cost and miles driven is linear.

CAR	MILES DRIVEN x, thousands	MAINTENANCE COST y, dollars
1	54	326
2	27	159
3	29	202
4	32	200
5	28	181
6	36	217

a. Use the six data points in the table to find the least squares prediction equation.

b. Find SSE and s^2.

c. Find a 95% confidence interval for the mean increase in maintenance cost per additional 1,000 miles driven. [*Hint:* Find a 95% confidence interval for the slope β_1.]

12.7 How Well Does the Least Squares Line Fit the Data?

So far, we have discussed a numerical descriptive measure of the correlation between two variables and a method of evaluating the usefulness of the straight-line model. The correlation coefficient r measures the strength of the straight-line (linear) relationship between two variables x and y. An inference about the slope β_1 of a straight-line model (either an hypothesis test or confidence interval) leads to a determination of whether the independent variable x in the model contributes information for the prediction of the dependent variable y. In this section, we define an alternative numerical descriptive measure of how well the least squares line fits the sample data. This measure, called the **coefficient of determination,** is very useful for assessing how much the errors of prediction of y can be reduced by using the information provided by x.

EXAMPLE 12.17 Refer to the sale price–total appraised value examples. Suppose that you do not use x, total appraised property value, to predict y, sale price. If you have access to a sample of property sale prices only, what quantity would you use as the best predictor for any y-value?

Solution If we have no information on the relative frequency distribution of the y-values other than that provided by the sample, then $\bar{y}$, the sample average sale price, would be the best predictor for **any** y-value. Using $\bar{y}$ as our predictor, the sum of squared prediction errors would be Σ (actual y − predicted $y)^2 = \Sigma (y - \bar{y})^2$ which is the familiar quantity SS_{yy}. The magnitude of SS_{yy} is an indicator of how well $\bar{y}$ behaves as a predictor of y.

EXAMPLE 12.18   Refer to Example 12.17. Suppose now that you use the information on total appraised property value, x, to predict sale price, y. How do we measure the additional information provided by using the value of x in the least squares prediction equation rather than $\bar{y}$ to predict y?

Solution   If we use the information on x to predict y, the sum of squares of the deviations of the y-values about the predicted values obtained from the least squares equation $\hat{y} = \hat{\beta}_0 + \hat{\beta}_1 x$ is

$$SSE = \Sigma (y - \hat{y})^2$$

A convenient way of measuring how well the least squares equation performs as a predictor of y is to compute the reduction in the sum of squares of deviations that can be attributed to x, expressed as a proportion of SS_{yy}. This quantity, called the **coefficient of determination,** is

$$\frac{SS_{yy} - SSE}{SS_{yy}}$$

It can be shown that this proportion is equal to the square of the simple linear coefficient of correlation r.

DEFINITION 12.2

The **coefficient of determination** is

$$r^2 = \frac{SS_{yy} - SSE}{SS_{yy}} = 1 - \frac{SSE}{SS_{yy}}$$

It represents the proportion of the sum of squares of deviations of the y-values about their mean that can be attributed to a linear relationship between y and x. (It may also be computed as the square of the coefficient of correlation.)

Note that r^2 is always between 0 and 1 since r is between -1 and $+1$. Thus, $r^2 = .75$ means that 75% of the sum of squares of deviations of the y-values about their mean is attributable to the linear relationship between y and x. In other words, the error of prediction can be reduced by 75% when the least squares equation, rather than $\bar{y}$, is used to predict y.

EXAMPLE 12.19   Calculate the coefficient of determination for the appraised value–sale price data of Example 12.8 and interpret its value. (The data are repeated in Table 12.9 for convenience.)

TABLE 12.9

PROPERTY	APPRAISED VALUE x, thousands of dollars	SALE PRICE y, thousands of dollars
1	20	20
2	30	50
3	40	70
4	50	100
5	60	110

Solution   We will use the formula given in the box of Definition 12.2 to compute r^2. From previous calculations, $SS_{yy} = 5,400$ and $SSE = 110$. Therefore,

$$r^2 = \frac{SS_{yy} - SSE}{SS_{yy}} = \frac{5,400 - 110}{5,400} = \frac{5,290}{5,400} = .9796$$

We interpret this value as follows: The use of total appraised property value, x, to predict sale price, y, with the least squares line

$$\hat{y} = -22 + 2.3x$$

accounts for approximately 98% of the total sum of squares of deviations of the five sample sale prices about their mean. That is, we can reduce the total sum of squares of our prediction errors by nearly 98% by using the least squares equation $\hat{y} = -22 + 2.3x$, instead of $\bar{y}$, to predict y.

Since the two numerical descriptive measures r and r^2 are very closely related, there may be some confusion as to when each should be used. Our recommendations are as follows: If you are only interested in measuring the strength of the linear relationship between two variables x and y, use the coefficient of correlation r. However, if you wish to determine how well the least squares straight-line model fits the data, use the coefficient of determination r^2.

EXERCISES   **12.27**   Suppose you were to fit a straight line to model the relationship between the weekly demand y for hamburgers at a fast-food outlet and the price x per hamburger. Suppose also that the data were collected over a period during which the price per hamburger was set at several different values. The value of r^2 for the least squares prediction equation was computed to be .73. Interpret this value.

12.28   Refer to the data of Exercises 12.4, 12.15, and 12.21. Find the coefficient of determination r^2 and interpret its value.

12.29   Refer to the data of Exercises 12.5, 12.17, and 12.22. Find the coefficient of determination r^2 and interpret its value.

12.30   Refer to the data of Exercises 12.6, 12.19, and 12.23. Find the coefficient of determination r^2 and interpret its value.

12.31   Refer to the data of Exercises 12.8, 12.20, and 12.24. Find the coefficient of determination r^2 and interpret its value.

12.8   Using the Model for Estimation and Prediction

After we have statistically checked the usefulness of our straight-line model and are satisfied that x contributes information for the prediction of y, we are ready to accomplish our original objective—using the model for prediction, estimation, etc.

The most common uses of a probabilistic model for making inferences can be divided into two categories and are listed in the box.

USES OF THE PROBABILISTIC MODEL FOR MAKING INFERENCES

1.   Use the model for estimating the mean value of y, $E(y)$, for a specific value of x.
2.   Use the model for predicting a particular y-value for a given value of x.

In the first case, we wish to estimate the mean value of y for a very large number of experiments at a given x-value. For example, we may want to estimate the mean sale price for all neighborhood A properties which are appraised at \$30,000. In the second case, we wish to predict the outcome of a single experiment (predict an individual value of y) at the given x-value. For example, we may want to predict the sale price of a particular property located in neighborhood A which has been appraised at \$30,000.

We will use the least squares model

$$\hat{y} = \hat{\beta}_0 + \hat{\beta}_1 x$$

both to estimate the mean value of y, $E(y)$, and to predict a particular value of y for a given value of x.

EXAMPLE 12.20   Refer to Example 12.8. We found the least squares model relating sale price, y, to total appraised property value, x, to be

$$\hat{y} = -22 + (2.3)x$$

Give a point estimate for the mean sale price of all properties which have been appraised at \$30,000.

Solution   We need to find an estimate of $E(y)$. Using the least squares model, our estimate is simply $\hat{y}$. Then, when $x = 30$,

$$\hat{y} = -22 + (2.3)(30) = -22 + 69 = 47$$

Thus, the estimated mean sale price for all properties with appraised values of \$30,000 is \$47,000.

EXAMPLE 12.21   Refer to Example 12.20. Use the least squares model to predict the sale price of a particular property whose total appraised value is \$30,000.

Solution   Just as we may use $\hat{y}$ from the least squares model to estimate $E(y)$, we also use $\hat{y}$ to predict a particular value of y for a given value of x. Again, when $x = 30$, we obtain $\hat{y} = 47$. Thus, we predict that a property in neighborhood A appraised at $30,000 would be sold for $47,000.

Since the least squares model is used to obtain both the estimator of $E(y)$ and the predictor of y, how do the two model uses differ? The difference lies in the accuracies with which the estimate and the prediction are made. These accuracies are best measured by the repeated sampling errors of the least squares line when it is used as an estimator and predictor, respectively. These errors are given in the box.

SAMPLING ERRORS FOR THE ESTIMATOR OF THE MEAN OF y AND THE PREDICTOR OF AN INDIVIDUAL y

1. The standard deviation of the sampling distribution of the estimator $\hat{y}$ of the mean value of y at a fixed x is

$$\sigma_{\hat{y}} = \sigma \sqrt{\frac{1}{n} + \frac{(x - \bar{x})^2}{SS_{xx}}}$$

where σ is the square root of σ^2, the measure of variability discussed in Section 12.5.

2. The standard deviation of the prediction error for the predictor $\hat{y}$ of an individual y-value at a fixed x is

$$\sigma_{(y - \hat{y})} = \sigma \sqrt{1 + \frac{1}{n} + \frac{(x - \bar{x})^2}{SS_{xx}}}$$

where σ is the square root of σ^2, the measure of variability discussed in Section 12.5.

Since the true value of σ will rarely be known, we estimate σ by s. The sampling errors are then used in estimation and prediction intervals as shown in the box.

A $(1 - \alpha)$ 100% CONFIDENCE INTERVAL FOR THE MEAN VALUE OF y AT A FIXED x

$$\hat{y} \pm (t_{\alpha/2})s \sqrt{\frac{1}{n} + \frac{(x - \bar{x})^2}{SS_{xx}}}$$

A $(1 - \alpha)$ 100% PREDICTION INTERVAL FOR AN INDIVIDUAL y AT A FIXED x

$$\hat{y} \pm (t_{\alpha/2})s \sqrt{1 + \frac{1}{n} + \frac{(x - \bar{x})^2}{SS_{xx}}}$$

EXAMPLE 12.22   Find a 95% confidence interval for the mean sale price of properties located in neighborhood A which have been appraised at $30,000.

Solution   For a total appraised property value of $30,000, $x = 30$ and the confidence interval for the mean of y is

$$\hat{y} \pm (t_{\alpha/2})s \sqrt{\frac{1}{n} + \frac{(x - \bar{x})^2}{SS_{xx}}} = \hat{y} \pm (t_{.025})s \sqrt{\frac{1}{5} + \frac{(30 - \bar{x})^2}{SS_{xx}}}$$

where the distribution of t is based on $(n - 2) = 3$ degrees of freedom. Recall from previous examples that $\hat{y} = 47$, $s = 6.055$, $\bar{x} = 40$, and $SS_{xx} = 1,000$. From Table 4, Appendix E, $t_{.025} = 3.182$. Thus, we have

$$47 \pm (3.182)(6.055) \sqrt{\frac{1}{5} + \frac{(30 - 40)^2}{1,000}} = 47 \pm (3.182)(6.055)(.548)$$

$$= 47 \pm 10.55 = (36.45,\ 57.55)$$

Hence, the 95% confidence interval for the mean sale price of all neighborhood A properties appraised at $30,000 is $36,450 to $57,550. Note that the small sample size ($n = 5$ properties) is reflected in the large width of the confidence interval.

EXAMPLE 12.23   Using a 95% prediction interval, predict the sale price of a property located in neighborhood A if its total appraised value is $30,000.

Solution   For $x = 30$, the 95% prediction interval for y is computed as

$$\hat{y} \pm (t_{\alpha/2})s \sqrt{1 + \frac{1}{n} + \frac{(x - \bar{x})^2}{SS_{xx}}} = 47 \pm (3.182)(6.055) \sqrt{1 + \frac{1}{5} + \frac{(30 - 40)^2}{1,000}}$$

$$= 47 \pm (3.182)(6.055)(1.140)$$

$$= 47 \pm 21.97 = (25.03,\ 68.97)$$

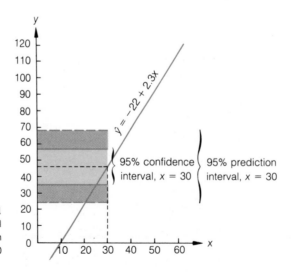

FIGURE 12.11
95% Confidence Interval
for $E(y)$ and Prediction
Interval for y when $x = 30$

Thus, we predict that the sale price for this particular property will fall within the interval from $25,030 to $68,970. Again, the large width of this interval can be attributed to the unusually small number of data points (only five) used to fit the least squares line. The width of the prediction interval could be reduced by using a larger number of data points.

In comparing the results of Examples 12.22 and 12.23, it is important to note that the prediction interval for an individual property sale price is wider than the corresponding confidence interval for the mean sale price (see Figure 12.11). By examining the formulas for the two intervals, you can see that this will always be true.

WARNING

Using the least squares prediction equation to estimate the mean value of y or to predict a particular value of y for values of x that fall **outside the range** of the values of x contained in your sample data may lead to errors of estimation or prediction that are much larger than expected. Although the least squares model may provide a very good fit to the data over the range of x-values contained in the sample, it could give a poor representation of the true model for values of x outside this region.

EXERCISES   **12.32**   The data for Exercises 12.4, 12.15, and 12.21 are reproduced below:

x	-1	0	1	2	3
y	-1	1	1	2.5	3.5

a. Estimate the mean value of y when x = 1, using a 90% confidence interval. Interpret the interval.
b. Suppose that you plan to observe the value of y for a particular experimental unit with x = 1. Find a 90% prediction interval for the value of y that you will observe. Interpret the interval.
c. Which of the two intervals, parts a and b, is wider?

12.33   The data for Exercises 12.5, 12.17, and 12.22 are reproduced below:

x	-5	-3	-1	0	1	3	5
y	.8	1.1	2.5	3.1	5.0	4.7	6.2

a. Estimate the mean value of y when x = −1, using a 90% confidence interval. Interpret the interval.

b. Suppose that you plan to observe the value of y for a particular experimental unit with $x = -1$. Find a 90% prediction interval for the value of y that you will observe. Interpret the interval.

c. Which of the two intervals, parts a and b, is wider?

12.34 In Exercise 12.20, you found the least squares prediction equation relating the shrinkage y (disappearing merchandise) per week at a clothing store to the number x of sales clerks and used it to estimate the mean weekly shrinkage when $x = 23$. The data are reproduced in the table.

WEEK	SHRINKAGE y, hundreds of dollars	NUMBER OF SALES CLERKS x
1	20	20
2	23	21
3	18	22
4	17	23
5	17	24
6	12	25
7	17	25
8	26	20
9	21	22
10	11	24
11	10	26
12	4	28

a. Find a 90% confidence interval for this mean and interpret it.
b. Suppose that you were to predict the shrinkage next week when $x = 23$ sales clerks will be on duty. Find a 90% prediction interval for this value of y and interpret it.

12.35 The data for Exercise 12.7 are reproduced in the table.

WEEK	NUMBER OF LOAN APPLICATIONS y	MORTGAGE RATE x, %
1	55	13.5
2	48	14.0
3	73	11.5
4	52	13.0
5	44	14.5
6	79	10.0
7	68	11.0
8	66	12.0
9	53	14.0
10	57	13.0

a. Find the least squares prediction equation relating the number y of weekly home loan applications at a savings and loan company to the mortgage rate x.

b. Find a 95% confidence interval for the mean number of loan applications per week when the mortgage rate is 14%. Interpret this interval.

c. Predict the number of applications you will observe next week if the mortgage rate is 14%. Use a 95% prediction interval. Interpret this interval.

12.9 Simple Linear Regression: An Example of a Computer Printout

In the previous sections we have presented the basic elements necessary to fit and use the straight-line regression model $E(y) = \beta_0 + \beta_1 x$. Throughout, we have illustrated the numerical techniques through an example relating sale price to total appraised value of a residential property. Even with a small number of measurements (five data points), the required computations, if performed without the aid of a pocket or desk calculator, can become tedious and cumbersome. Many institutions have installed computer packages which fit a straight-line regression model by the method of least squares. These packages enable the user to greatly decrease the burden of calculation. In this section, we locate, discuss, and interpret the elements of a simple linear regression on a computer printout.

We will again present output from the Statistical Analysis System (SAS), first introduced in Section 11.4. Since the linear regression output of the SAS is similar to that of most other package regression programs (such as Minitab and SPSS), you should have little trouble interpreting output from other packages. We relate all the examples in this section to the SAS output for the sale price–appraised value data in Table 12.5. A portion of the SAS printout is given in Figure 12.12. Again, we let y be the sale price of a residential property in the neighborhood and x the total appraised value of the property.

DEPENDENT VARIABLE: Y

SOURCE	DF	SUM OF SQUARES	MEAN SQUARE	F VALUE
MODEL	1	5290.00000000	5290.00000000	144.27
ERROR	3	110.00000000	36.66666667	PR > F
CORRECTED TOTAL	4	5400.00000000		0.0012

R-SQUARE	C.V.	STD DEV	Y MEAN
0.979630	8.6504	6.05530071	70.00000000

PARAMETER	ESTIMATE	T FOR H0: PARAMETER=0	PR > |T|	STD ERROR OF ESTIMATE
INTERCEPT	-22.00000000	-2.71	0.0733	8.12403840
X	2.30000000	12.01	0.0012	0.19148542

FIGURE 12.12
Portion of the SAS Printout for the Sale Price–Appraised Value Data

EXAMPLE 12.24   Locate on the SAS printout in Figure 12.12 the least squares estimates of the y-intercept β_0 and the slope β_1 for the straight-line model relating sale price to total appraised property value.

Solution   The least squares estimates of the y-intercept and slope are shaded in Figure 12.13. Note that the estimate of the y-intercept, i.e., $\hat{\beta}_0 = -22.0000$, and the estimate of the slope, i.e., $\hat{\beta}_1 = 2.3000$, given in the printout agree with our previous calculations made by hand. The least squares model relating sale price to total appraised value can thus be written

$$\hat{y} = -22 + 2.3x$$

FIGURE 12.13

SAS Printout with the
Least Squares Estimates
Shaded

DEPENDENT VARIABLE: Y

SOURCE	DF	SUM OF SQUARES	MEAN SQUARE	F VALUE
MODEL	1	5290.00000000	5290.00000000	144.27
ERROR	3	110.00000000	36.66666667	PR > F
CORRECTED TOTAL	4	5400.00000000		0.0012

R-SQUARE	C.V.	STD DEV	Y MEAN
0.979630	8.6504	6.05530071	70.00000000

PARAMETER	ESTIMATE	T FOR H0: PARAMETER=0	PR > |T|	STD ERROR OF ESTIMATE
INTERCEPT	-22.00000000	-2.71	0.0733	8.12403840
X	2.30000000	12.01	0.0012	0.19148542

EXAMPLE 12.25   Locate the SSE on the SAS printout in Figure 12.12. Also, find s^2 and s, the estimates of σ^2 and σ, respectively.

Solution   The SSE is found by locating the entry under the column heading SUM OF SQUARES in the row labelled ERROR. This quantity, shaded in Figure 12.14, is SSE = 110.0000.

FIGURE 12.14

SAS Printout with SSE, s^2,
and s Shaded

DEPENDENT VARIABLE: Y

SOURCE	DF	SUM OF SQUARES	MEAN SQUARE	F VALUE
MODEL	1	5290.00000000	5290.00000000	144.27
ERROR	3	110.00000000	36.66666667	PR > F
CORRECTED TOTAL	4	5400.00000000		0.0012

R-SQUARE	C.V.	STD DEV	Y MEAN
0.979630	8.6504	6.05530071	70.00000000

PARAMETER	ESTIMATE	T FOR H0: PARAMETER=0	PR > |T|	STD ERROR OF ESTIMATE
INTERCEPT	-22.00000000	-2.71	0.0733	8.12403840
X	2.30000000	12.01	0.0012	0.19148542

A check of our previous calculations confirms its validity. The estimate of σ^2 is given in the figure (shaded) as MEAN SQUARE for ERROR and is located to the immediate right of SSE. Thus, we have $s^2 = 36.6667$. The least squares estimate of σ, shaded in Figure 12.14 under the heading STD DEV, is $s = 6.0553$. Except for rounding errors, our computed values of s^2 and s agree with the figures given in the printout.

EXAMPLE 12.26   Use the SAS output to test the null hypothesis that x contributes no information for the prediction of y against the alternative hypothesis that x and y are linearly related.

Solution   We desire a test of the hypotheses

$$H_0: \quad \beta_1 = 0$$

$$H_a: \quad \beta_1 \neq 0$$

The value of the test statistic for this test is shaded in Figure 12.15 under the column heading T FOR H0: PARAMETER = 0 in the lower portion of the printout. The value shown here is $t = 12.01$, which agrees with our computed test statistic. To determine whether this value falls within the rejection region, check the shaded quantity to the immediate right under PR > |T|. This quantity is the attained significance level or p-value of the test. Generally, if the p-value is smaller than .05, there is evidence to reject the null hypothesis that the slope is zero in favor of the alternative hypothesis that the slope differs from zero. In this example, an attained significance level of .0012 indicates that total appraised property value x and sale price y are linearly related (a result consistent with the test conducted in Example 12.13).

DEPENDENT VARIABLE: Y

SOURCE	DF	SUM OF SQUARES	MEAN SQUARE	F VALUE
MODEL	1	5290.00000000	5290.00000000	144.27
ERROR	3	110.00000000	36.66666667	PR > F
CORRECTED TOTAL	4	5400.00000000		0.0012

R-SQUARE	C.V.	STD DEV	Y MEAN
0.979630	8.6504	6.05530071	70.00000000

PARAMETER	ESTIMATE	T FOR H0: PARAMETER=0	PR > |T|	STD ERROR OF ESTIMATE
INTERCEPT	-22.00000000	-2.71	0.0733	8.12403840
x	2.30000000	12.01	0.0012	0.19148542

FIGURE 12.15
SAS Printout with r^2 and Value of the Test Statistic Shaded

EXAMPLE 12.27   To determine how well the least squares straight-line model fits the data, find the value of the coefficient of determination r^2.

Solution   The value of r^2, shaded in Figure 12.15, is given as $r^2 = .979630$. The result that we computed in a previous example is accurate to four decimal places. We say, then, that by using the least squares equation, instead of $\bar{y}$, to predict y, we can reduce the total sum of squares of our prediction errors by approximately 98%. Notice that the coefficient of correlation r is not given in the SAS printout.

EXAMPLE 12.28   Construct a 95% confidence interval for $E(y)$, the mean sale price of all residential properties in the neighborhood that have a total appraised value of $30,000.

Solution   A portion of the SAS printout not previously shown is given in Figure 12.16. For $x = 30$ (i.e., total appraised property value of $30,000), we see that the least squares predicted value of y is $\hat{y} = 47$, and that a 95% confidence interval for the mean, $E(y)$, is 36.44484198 to 57.55515802. Thus, the mean sale price for properties appraised at $30,000 falls between $36,444.84 and $57,555.16, with 95% confidence. In Example 12.22, we computed the interval to be $36,450 to $57,550. The differences in the intervals are due to rounding error.

FIGURE 12.16
Portion of SAS Printout for
the Sale Price–Appraised
Value Data

X	PREDICTED VALUE	LOWER 95% CL FOR MEAN	UPPER 95% CL FOR MEAN
30	47.00000000	36.44484198	57.55515802

EXAMPLE 12.29   Find a 95% prediction interval for the sale price of an individual property appraised at $30,000.

Solution   The 95% prediction interval for an individual value of y with $x = 30$ is given in Figure 12.17 as (25.02768644, 68.97231356). We predict that the sale price for a particular property appraised at $30,000 will fall between $25,027.69 and $68,972.31. The difference between this result and the interval we computed in Example 12.23, $25,030 to $68,970, is again due to rounding error.

FIGURE 12.17
Portion of SAS Printout for
the Sale Price–Appraised
Value Data

X	PREDICTED VALUE	LOWER 95% CL INDIVIDUAL	UPPER 95% CL INDIVIDUAL
30	47.00000000	25.02768644	68.97231356

In Chapter 13 we will discuss the interpretation of those portions of the SAS printout which were not shaded or mentioned here. However, the important elements of a linear regression analysis have been located, and you should be able to use this example as a guide to interpreting linear regression computer printouts.

12.10 Assumptions Required for a Linear Regression Analysis

As with most statistical procedures, the validity of the confidence intervals, prediction intervals, and statistical tests associated with a simple linear regression analysis depend on certain assumptions being satisfied. These assumptions are made about the random error term in the straight-line probabilistic model.

ASSUMPTIONS REQUIRED FOR A LINEAR REGRESSION ANALYSIS

1. The mean of the probability distribution of the random error is 0. That is, for each setting of the independent variable x, the average of the errors over an infinitely long series of experiments is 0.
2. The variance of the probability distribution of the random error is constant for all settings of the independent variable x and is equal to σ^2, i.e., the variance of the random error is equal to σ^2 for all values of x.
3. The probability distribution of the random error is normal.
4. The errors associated with any two observations are independent. That is, the error associated with one value of y has no effect on the errors associated with other y-values.

Figure 12.18 shows a pictorial representation of the assumptions given in the box. For each value of x shown in the figure, the relative frequency distribution of the errors is normal with mean zero, and with a constant variance (all the distributions shown have the same amount of spread or variability) equal to σ^2.

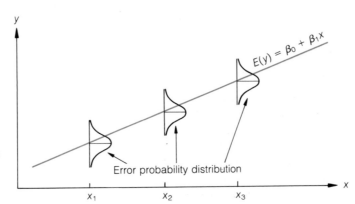

FIGURE 12.18
The Probability
Distribution of the
Random Error Component

In practice, you will never know whether your data satisfy the four assumptions listed above. Fortunately, the estimators and test statistics used in a simple linear regression have sampling distributions that remain relatively stable for minor departures from the assumptions.

12.11 Summary

In this chapter we introduced bivariate relationships and showed how to compute the coefficient of correlation, r, a measure of the strength of the linear relationship between two variables. We also introduced an extremely useful tool—the method of least squares—for fitting a straight-line model to a set of data. This procedure, along with associated statistical tests and estimations, is called a regression analysis.

After hypothesizing the straight-line probabilistic model

$$y = \beta_0 + \beta_1 x + \text{Random error}$$

perform the following steps:

1. Use the method of least squares to estimate the unknown parameters in the deterministic component, $\beta_0 + \beta_1 x$. You may obtain the estimates by either applying the computational formulas given in this chapter or, if you have access to a computer package, from a computer printout. The least squares estimates will yield a model $\hat{y} = \hat{\beta}_0 + \hat{\beta}_1 x$ with a sum of squared errors (SSE) that is smaller than that produced by any other straight-line model.

2. Check that the assumptions about the random error component (outlined in the box in Section 12.10) are satisfied. You should also determine s^2 (either by hand calculation or from a computer printout), an estimate of σ^2, the variance of the random error component.

3. Assess the usefulness of the hypothesized model, i.e., determine how well x performs as a predictor of y. Included here are making inferences about the slope β_1 and computing the coefficient of determination, r^2.

4. Finally, if you are satisfied with the model, use it to estimate the mean y-value, $E(y)$, for a given x-value and/or to predict an individual y-value for a specific x.

KEY WORDS

Bivariate relationships
Coefficient of correlation
Linear regression analysis
Method of least squares
Probabilistic models
Deterministic component
Random error component
Least squares line (prediction equation)
Coefficient of determination

KEY SYMBOLS

y-intercept of the line: β_0
Slope of the line: β_1
Coefficient of correlation: r
Coefficient of determination: r^2

SUPPLEMENTARY EXERCISES

12.36 Use the method of least squares to fit a straight line to the following six data points:

x	1	2	3	4	5	6
y	1	2	2	3	5	5

a. What are the least squares estimates of β_0 and β_1?
b. Plot the data points and graph the least squares line. Does the line pass through the data points?
c. Do the data provide sufficient evidence to indicate that x contributes information for the prediction of y? Test at $\alpha = .05$.

12.37 Refer to Exercise 12.36.
a. If y and x are linearly correlated, will the correlation be positive or negative? Explain.
b. Calculate the coefficient of correlation r. Interpret its value.
c. Calculate the coefficient of determination r^2 and interpret its value.
d. Based on the test, Exercise 12.36(c), can you conclude that y and x are linearly correlated? Explain.
e. Test for linear correlation between y and x, using the method of Section 12.2. Does your result agree with that of Exercise 12.36(c)?

12.38 Refer to Exercise 12.36.
a. Find a 90% confidence interval for the mean value of y when $x = 2$.
b. Find a 90% prediction interval for y when $x = 2$.
c. Interpret the intervals, parts a and b.

12.39 Use the method of least squares to fit a straight line to the following five data points:

x	-2	-1	0	1	2
y	4	3	3	1	-1

a. What are the least squares estimates of β_0 and β_1?
b. Plot the data points and graph the least squares line. Does the line pass through the data points?
c. Do the data provide sufficient evidence to indicate that x contributes information for the prediction of y? Test at $\alpha = .05$.

12.40 Refer to Exercise 12.39.
a. If y and x are linearly correlated, will the correlation be positive or negative? Explain.
b. Calculate the coefficient of correlation r. Interpret its value.
c. Calculate the coefficient of determination r^2 and interpret its value.

d. Based on the test, Exercise 12.39(c), can you conclude that y and x are linearly correlated? Explain.

e. Test for linear correlation between y and x, using the method of Section 12.2. Does your result agree with that of Exercise 12.39(c)?

12.41 Refer to Exercise 12.39.

a. Find a 90% confidence interval for the mean value of y when $x = 2$.

b. Find a 90% prediction interval for y when $x = 2$.

c. Interpret the intervals, parts a and b.

12.42 Use the method of least squares and the sample data in the table to model the relationship between the number of items produced by a particular manufacturing process and the total variable cost involved in production. Find the coefficient of determination and explain its significance in the context of this problem.

TOTAL OUTPUT y	TOTAL VARIABLE COST x, dollars
10	10
15	12
20	20
20	21
25	22
30	20
30	19

12.43 As a result of the increase in the number of suburban shopping centers, many center-city stores are suffering financially. A downtown department store thinks that increased advertising might help lure more shoppers into the area. To study the relationship between sales and advertising, records were obtained for several mid-year months during which the store varied advertising expenditures.

SALES y, thousands of dollars	ADVERTISING EXPENSE x, thousands of dollars
30	0.9
34	1.1
32	0.8
37	1.2
31	0.7

a. Estimate the coefficient of correlation between sales and advertising expenditures.

b. Do the data provide sufficient evidence to indicate a correlation between sales, y, and advertising expense, x?

12.44 A certain manufacturer evaluates the sales potential for a product in a new marketing area by selecting several stores within the area to sell the product on a trial basis for a 1-month period. The sales figures for the trial period are then used to project sales for the entire area. [*Note:* The same number of trial stores are used each time.]

TOTAL SALES DURING TRIAL PERIOD x, hundreds of dollars	TOTAL SALES FOR FIRST MONTH FOR ENTIRE AREA y, hundreds of dollars
16.8	48.2
14.0	46.8
18.3	54.3
22.1	59.7
14.9	48.3
23.2	67.5

a. Use the data in the table to develop a simple linear model for predicting first-month sales for the entire area based on sales during the trial period.
b. Plot the data and graph the line as a check on your calculations.
c. Do the data provide sufficient evidence to indicate that total sales during the trial period contribute information for predicting total sales during the first month?
d. Use a 90% prediction interval to predict total sales for the first month for the entire area if the trial sales equal $2,000.

12.45 The management of a manufacturing firm is considering the possibility of setting up its own market research department rather than continuing to use the services of a market research firm. The management wants to know what salary should be paid to a market researcher, based on years of experience. An independent consultant checks with several other firms in the area and obtains the information on market researchers shown in the table.

ANNUAL SALARY y, thousands of dollars	EXPERIENCE x, years
20.3	2
20.2	1.5
32.0	11
37.4	15
29.5	9
25.3	6

a. Fit a least squares line to the data.
b. Plot the data and graph the line as a check on your calculations.
c. Calculate r and r^2. Interpret these values.
d. Estimate the mean annual salary of market researchers with 8 years of experience. Use a 90% confidence interval.
e. Predict the salary of a market researcher with 7 years of experience, using a 90% prediction interval.

Concern has been expressed that Americans are becoming a nation of pill takers. Many critics contend that this behavior is learned in childhood and that it is encouraged by TV advertising for proprietary (advertised nonprescription or "over-the-counter") drugs.

This is how J. R. Rossiter and T. S. Robertson began their article* on children's attitudes toward drugs advertised on television. Despite this belief, lack of information on the potential relationship of TV drug advertising to children's attitudes caused the Federal Communications Commission (FCC) to deny a petition seeking to prohibit TV advertising for proprietary drugs until after 9:00 PM when fewer children would be in the audience. At present, proprietary drugs cannot be advertised on children's programs, but they can be advertised during adult and family programs which constitute 85% of children's viewing.

Previous studies have shown that "children's and teenagers' dispositions toward proprietary drugs are only weakly related to their exposure to TV drug advertising." One researcher "found correlations in the .07 to .22 range with children's exposure to TV drug advertising, with only about half of the correlations reaching the .05 level of significance." However, Rossiter and Robertson criticize these studies because they "focused on a limited set of proprietary drugs, including cold and stomachache remedies but excluding cough and headache remedies." Thus, in March 1977 the authors conducted their own study of the relationship between children's attitudes toward proprietary drugs and TV advertising. Their study included a sample of 668 children drawn from inner-city and suburban areas of Philadelphia. With permission from their respective parents, each child was asked to fill out a questionnaire of the type shown below:

*Sample
Questions*

Belief variable: (1) "When I have a cold, cold medicine can make me feel better."
    Scoring: 1 = strongly disagree to 4 = strongly agree.

Affect variable: (2) "When I have a cold, I like to take cold medicine."
    Scoring: 1 = strongly disagree to 4 = strongly agree.

Intention variable: (3) "When I have a cold, I want to take cold medicine."
    Scoring: 1 = never to 4 = always.

Request variable: (4) "When I have a cold, I ask my parents for cold medicines."
    Scoring: 1 = never to 4 = always.

Usage variable: (5) "Since school started in September, how many times have your parents given you cold medicines?"
    Scoring: 1 = never to 5 = five or more times.

TV drug advertising exposure variable: Number of proprietary drug commercials viewed per program.

Rossiter and Robertson calculated the Pearson product moment coefficient of correlation (*r*) of each of the five variables (Belief, Affect, Intention, Request, and

---

*J. R. Rossiter and T. S. Robertson. "Children's dispositions toward proprietary drugs and the role of television drug advertising." *Public Opinion Quarterly,* Fall 1980, 316–329. Reprinted by permission. Copyright 1980 by Elsevier North Holland, Inc.

Usage) with TV drug ad exposure. Results are given in the table for two subsamples of the 668 children: (1) $n = 132$ children from educationally "disadvantaged" families who receive little parental instruction about proprietary drugs and the way they are advertised; and (2) $n = 55$ children who are never allowed to take proprietary drugs without parental supervision. Does it appear that children's attitudes toward proprietary drugs are linearly related to TV drug advertising exposure? Use Table 12.3 to determine which, if any, of the sample correlations are large enough to indicate (at $\alpha = .05$) that linear correlation exists between TV drug ad exposure and the variable measured.

Correlation with TV Drug Advertising Exposure

VARIABLE	LOW PARENT EDUCATION ($n = 132$) r	NO SELF-ADMINISTRATION ($n = 55$) r
Belief	.06	.29
Affect	.13	.26
Intention	.44	.23
Request	.39	.34
Usage	.12	.23

CASE STUDY 12.2

The Relation of Corporate Presidents' Tenures to Size of the Board of Directors

How much influence does the board of directors have on the length of tenure of the chief executive of a large corporation? In his article "Board Size Variation and Rates of Succession in the Corporate Presidency" (*Journal of Business Research,* 1980),* Donald L. Helmich examines the possible relationship between the size of the board (i.e., the number of members on the board) and the tenure lengths of newly appointed corporate presidents.

"Periodic changes in leadership positions, whether it be in the chief executive office or in the board membership, are necessary for sustained organizational growth," offers Helmich. "Corporations are likely to be more successful if, from time to time, they add or delete board directors who represent varying geographical, social, and economic sectors of the corporate environment." Thus, board membership will vary in response to a changing organizational environment. "Since changes in corporate leaders are [also] necessary to reflect [these] changes in the environment, and since boards do become involved in selection of successors [to the chief executive], one may advance the following hypothesis: variations in an organization's board size at the time of succession of the chief executive are related to the tenures of newly appointed successors." The object of Helmich's research (simplified for the purposes of this case study) is to test this theory, i.e., that variation in the size of the membership of the board of directors is linearly related to the rate of replacement of the chief executive.

*D. L. Helmich. "Board size variation and rates of succession in the corporate presidency." *Journal of Business Research,* March 1980, *8,* 51–63. Reprinted by permission. Copyright 1980 by Elsevier North Holland, Inc.

The data for the analysis were obtained from a sample of 54 petrochemical companies engaged in the manufacture of petroleum derivatives, plastics, and chemical and allied products. (The petrochemical industry was chosen because of its reputation as a growth leader, the mounting evidence that it is adjusting more quickly than other industries to the demands of the environment, and the relatively homogeneous administrative process of selection, retention, and replacement of executives within the industry.) Obtained from each corporation were the chief executive office tenures during the period 1947–1977 and the number of directors serving on the board during each year of the 30-year period. Using this information, the following variables were measured on each of the 54 companies:

y = Average succession rate at the corporation (a measure of the rate of replacement of the chief executive)

x = Variation coefficient for corporation board size (a measure of the variability of board size adjusted for annual and long-term linear trends due to organizational growth or decline)

The linear relationship between the two variables, average rate of succession and variation in board size, may be explained by the probabilistic model

$y = \beta_0 + \beta_1 x + \text{Random error}$

Helmich subjected the 54 (x, y) data points to a (least squares) simple linear regression analysis. The slope of the least squares line was found to be $\hat{\beta}_1 = 0.254$, while a test of the null hypothesis H_0: $\beta_1 = 0$ resulted in an attained significance level (p-value) less than .05. Thus, Helmich concluded that "board size variation had a significant positive influence upon the rate of succession in the office of chief executive over the 30-year interval of study for the total sample of 54 companies. That is, the higher the variation in board size, the more rapid the change in leadership in the chief executive office."

Knowledge of the (apparent) positive linear relationship between variation in board size and rate of succession becomes important during the process of succession planning by directors in the corporate structure. However, what may be even more important is knowing whether this positive relationship is exhibited by profitable as well as unprofitable companies. As suggested by Helmich, "Advocating parallel changes in board size with concurrent changes in presidents would not make sense if this relationship were found to be a characteristic of unsuccessful rather than successful firms."

To examine this phenomenon, Helmich categorized each of the sampled companies into unsuccessful versus successful companies (based upon profit performance). The linear regression was then performed independently on each of the two groups ($n = 27$ observations in each group) of data. The results are summarized in Table 12.10.

α.   Is there evidence of a linear relationship between rate of succession and degree of board membership for those unsuccessful companies? If so, does the relationship appear to be positive, as suggested by the previous results?

UNSUCCESSFUL COMPANIES	SUCCESSFUL COMPANIES
$\hat{\beta}_1 = .603$	$\hat{\beta}_1 = -.230$
p-value $< .05$	p-value $< .05$

b. Answer part a for the group of successful companies.

[*Note:* Commenting on these contradictory results, Helmich suggests that "in planning for presidential succession, either (1) successful organizations exhibit a degree of rigidity in board membership size, increasing the likelihood that successions will be routinely treated and that frequent replacements of chief executive officers will occur, or (2) instability through membership size change in the board is reflected in infrequent changes of chief executive officers." In either case, "what is characteristic of the industry [as a whole], is not necessarily characteristic of relatively successful companies, and certainly relatively unsuccessful organizations might consider this aspect in planning for succession in the presidency."]

CASE STUDY 12.3
Evaluating the
Protein Efficiency
of a New Food
Product

One aspect of the preliminary evaluation of a new food product is determination of the nutritive quality of the product. This is often accomplished by feeding the food product to animals whose metabolic processes are very similar to our own. In a 1978 article,* Elizabeth Street and Mavis Carroll discussed such an evaluation of a new product developed by General Foods Corporation.

General Foods wished to compare the protein efficiency of two forms of a product (known by the pseudonym *H*), one solid and the other liquid. Because previous experience had shown that 28-day feeding of 10 to 15 rats on a diet gives a fairly reliable estimate of the diet's protein efficiency, General Foods conducted a rat-feeding study. Thirty male rats, all newly weaned, were used in the experiment. Ten rats were randomly assigned a diet of solid *H*, ten a diet of liquid *H*, and ten a standard (control) diet. During the feeding period, each rat was permitted to eat as much as it wished. At the end of the 28 days, the total protein intake *x* (in grams) and the weight gain *y* (in grams) were recorded for each of the 30 rats.

Using a computer program, General Foods fit a straight line to the 10 (x, y) data points for each diet by the method of least squares. The three least squares prediction equations were

Liquid *H:* $\hat{y} = 109.3 + 3.72x$

Solid *H:* $\hat{y} = 106.7 + 3.66x$

Control: $\hat{y} = 50.6 + 2.91x$

a. Graph the three lines on the same piece of graph paper. For a given increase in protein intake, which of the three diets resulted in the greatest increase in weight gain? [*Hint:* Which line has the greatest slope?]

---

*Elizabeth Street and Mavis B. Carroll. "Preliminary evaluation of a new food product." In *Statistics: A guide to the unknown.* Tanur et al., eds. San Francisco: Holden-Day, 1978.

b. Estimate the mean weight gain in rats with a 28-day protein intake of 40 grams for each of the three diets. Compare these values.

c. Predict the weight gain for a rat on each of the three diets if the rat's 28-day protein intake is 40 grams. Compare these values.

d. How would the width of a confidence interval for any of the estimates, part b, compare with the width of a prediction interval for the corresponding prediction, part c? Explain.

REFERENCES

Barr, A., Goodnight, J., Sall, J., Blair, W., & Chilko, D. *SAS user's guide.* 1979 ed. SAS Institute, P. O. Box 10066, Raleigh, N. C. 27605.

Draper, N., & Smith, H. *Applied regression analysis.* New York: Wiley, 1966. Chapter 1.

Helmich, D. L. "Board size variation and rates of succession in the corporate presidency." *Journal of Business Research,* March 1980, *8,* 51–63.

Johnson, R., & Siskin, B. *Elementary statistics for business.* North Scituate, Mass.: Duxbury, 1980. Chapters 15 and 16.

Mendenhall, W., & McClave, J. T. *A second course in business statistics: Regression analysis.* San Francisco: Dellen, 1981. Chapter 3.

Neter, J., & Wasserman, W. *Applied linear statistical models.* Homewood, Ill.: Richard Irwin, 1974. Chapters 2–6.

Rossiter, J. R., & Robertson, T. S. "Children's dispositions toward proprietary drugs and the role of television drug advertising." *Public Opinion Quarterly,* Fall 1980, 316–329.

Tanur, J. M., Mosteller, F., Kruskal, W. H., Link, R. F., Pieters, R. S., & Rising, G. R. *Statistics: A guide to the unknown.* San Francisco: Holden-Day, 1978.

Thirteen

Multiple Regression

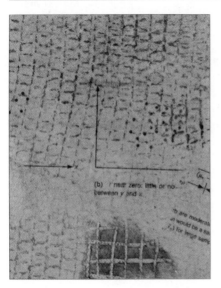

"Other than food and sex, nothing is quite as universally interesting as the size of our paychecks." So say N. L. Preston and E. R. Fiedler in an article that examines the relationship between the compensation of an economist and the economist's qualifications (see Case Study 13.1). In this chapter, we will extend the ideas of Chapter 12 and build a regression model to relate a variable y to two or more independent variables. We will see that Preston and Fiedler use this technique to develop a model for determining "fair compensation" for an economist.

Contents:

13.1 Introduction: Linear Statistical Models and Multiple Regression Analysis

Most practical applications of regression analysis require models that are more complex than the simple straight-line model. For example, a realistic probabilistic model for the number y of cars sold per week by a dealer would include more variables than the number x of salespeople who work on the showroom floor (discussed in Chapter 12): Additional variables such as season, current interest rate on bank loans, make and model of cars on the showroom floor, and rebates might also be related to weekly car sales. Thus, we would want to incorporate these and other potentially important independent variables into the model if we needed to make accurate predictions of the weekly car sales, y. This more complex probabilistic model relating y to these various independent variables, say $x_1, x_2, x_3, \ldots$, is called a *general linear statistical model,* or more simply, a *linear model.*

EXAMPLE 13.1   How does a general linear model differ from the following simple straight-line model?

$$y = \beta_0 + \beta_1 x + \text{Random error}$$

Solution   General linear models are more flexible than straight-line models in the sense that they may include more than one independent variable. A linear model for y, the number of cars sold per week, could be written

$$y = \beta_0 + \beta_1 x_1 + \beta_2 x_2 + \beta_3 x_3 + \text{Random error}$$

In addition to the independent variable x_1, the number of salespeople who work on the showroom floor, the model includes two other independent variables: the current interest rate on bank loans, x_2, and the dollar rebate offered to the car buyers, x_3. (Note how the data for fitting general linear models would be collected: For each experimental unit—in our example, a sales week—we measure the dependent variable y and record the current values of the independent variables x_1, x_2, and x_3.)

A general linear model may include some independent variables which appear at higher orders, e.g., terms such as x_1^2, $x_1 x_2$, x_3^3, etc. For example,

$$y = \beta_0 + \beta_1 x_1 + \beta_2 x_2 + \beta_3 x_1 x_2 + \beta_4 x_1^2 + \beta_5 x_2^2 + \text{Random error}$$

is a linear model. You may wonder why the model is referred to as a linear model if these higher order terms are present. The model is called linear because it represents a linear function of the unknown parameters, $\beta_0, \beta_1, \beta_2, \ldots$. That is, each term contains only one of the β parameters and each β is a coefficient of the remaining portion of the term. For example, the term $\beta_1 x_1 x_2^2$ satisfies this requirement, but the term $\beta_1 x_1^{\beta_2}$ does not because it contains two unknown parameters (β_1 and β_2) and, secondly, because β_2 appears as an exponent rather than a multiplicative coefficient.

This chapter will employ the method of least squares to fit a general linear model to a set of data. This process, along with the estimation and test procedures associated with it, is called a *multiple regression analysis.* Because the computations involved in a multiple regression analysis are very complex, most regression analyses are performed on a computer. In the following sections we will present an example of a multiple regression analysis and will examine and interpret the printouts for one of the standard multiple regression computer program packages.

13.2 The Quadratic Model

The formula for a general linear model is given in the box.

THE GENERAL LINEAR MODEL

$$y = \beta_0 + \beta_1 x_1 + \beta_2 x_2 + \cdots + \beta_k x_k + \text{Random error}$$

where y is the dependent variable (variable to be predicted) and $x_1, x_2, \ldots, x_k$ are the independent variables.

[*Note:* Remember that the symbols $x_1, x_2, \ldots, x_k$ may represent higher order terms. For example, x_1 might represent the current interest rate, x_2 might represent x_1^2, etc.]

$E(y) = \beta_0 + \beta_1 x_1 + \beta_2 x_2 + \cdots + \beta_k x_k$ is the deterministic portion of the model

β_0 is the y-intercept

β_i determines the contribution of the independent variable x_i

---

In this chapter we consider a special case of the general linear model, a case in which the model includes only two independent variables, one of which is a higher order term. The form of this model, called the **quadratic (or second-order) model,** is

$$y = \beta_0 + \beta_1 x + \beta_2 x^2 + \text{Random error}$$

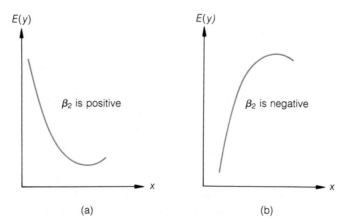

FIGURE 13.1
Graphs for Two Quadratic Models

Technically, the quadratic model includes only one independent variable, x, but we can think of the model as a general linear model in two independent variables with $x_1 = x$ and $x_2 = x^2$. The term involving x^2, called the **quadratic term,** enables us to hypothesize curvature in the graph of the response model relating y to x. Graphs of the quadratic model for two different values of β_2 are shown in Figure 13.1. When the curve opens upward (i.e., the curve "holds water"), the sign of β_2 is positive (see Figure 13.1(a)); when the curve opens downward (i.e., the curve "spills water"), the sign of β_2 is negative (see Figure 13.1(b)).

EXAMPLE 13.2   Refer to the real estate appraisal data, Appendix B. Suppose that a real estate investor wishes to model the relationship between the 1978 sale price of a property located in neighborhood F and the corresponding appraised improvements value of the property. A random sample of 10 properties in neighborhood F which were sold in 1978 was selected for the analysis. The resulting data (obtained from Appendix B) are given in Table 13.1.

TABLE 13.1
Sale Price–Appraised
Improvements Value for
10 Properties in
Neighborhood F

| SALE PRICE | APPRAISED IMPROVEMENTS |
y, dollars	x, dollars
22,500	13,140
27,000	15,890
31,900	18,700
33,000	20,730
29,000	16,510
46,600	24,180
51,500	26,150
54,700	35,870
55,000	40,100
54,900	43,460

a.   Construct a scattergram for the sale price–appraised improvements value data of Table 13.1.

b.   Hypothesize a probabilistic model relating sale price to appraised improvements value for all neighborhood F properties sold in 1978.

Solution   a.   A plot of the data of Table 13.1 is given in Figure 13.2. You can see that the 1978 sale price of neighborhood F properties appears to increase in a curvilinear manner with appraised improvements value.

b.   The apparent curvature in the graph relating appraised improvements values, x, to the 1978 sale price, y, provides some support for the inclusion of a quadratic term, x^2, in the response model. Thus, we think that the quadratic model

$$y = \beta_0 + \beta_1 x + \beta_2 x^2 + \text{Random error}$$

might yield a better prediction equation than one based on the straight-line model of Chapter 12. To determine if this model gives an adequate representation of the relationship between y and x, we follow the same steps that we applied in developing the straight-line model.

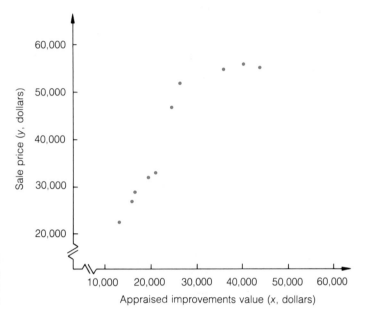

FIGURE 13.2
Scattergram of the Sale
Price–Appraised
Improvements Data

STEPS TO FOLLOW IN A MULTIPLE REGRESSION ANALYSIS

1. Hypothesize the form of the linear model.
2. Estimate the unknown parameters β_0, β_1, β_2, ...
3. Check whether the fitted model is useful for predicting y.
4. If we decide that the model is useful, use it to estimate the mean value of y or to predict a particular value of y for given values of the independent variables.

13.3 Fitting the Model

To fit a general linear model by the method of least squares, we choose the estimated model

$$\hat{y} = \hat{\beta}_0 + \hat{\beta}_1 x_1 + \hat{\beta}_2 x_2 + \cdots + \hat{\beta}_k x_k$$

that minimizes $\text{SSE} = \Sigma (y_i - \hat{y}_i)^2$. We will use the Statistical Analysis System (SAS), referred to in Chapters 11 and 12, to fit the linear model and to illustrate each of the remaining steps in a multiple regression analysis.

EXAMPLE 13.3   Refer to Example 13.2. Use the method of least squares to estimate the unknown parameters β_0, β_1, β_2 in the quadratic model relating sale price, y, to appraised improvements value, x, for properties located in neighborhood F.

Solution   Part of the output of the SAS multiple regression routine for the data of Table 13.1 is reproduced in Figure 13.3. The least squares estimates of the β parameters appear (shaded) in the column labelled ESTIMATE. You can see that $\hat{\beta}_0 = -26,391.07$, $\hat{\beta}_1 = 4.2624$, and $\hat{\beta}_2 = -.00005522$. Therefore, the equation that minimizes SSE for the data is

$$\hat{y} = -26,391.07 + 4.2624x - .00005522x^2$$

From Figure 13.4 we see that the graph of the quadratic regression model provides a good fit to the data of Table 13.1. We note here that the small value of $\hat{\beta}_2$ does *not* imply that the curvature is insignificant, since the numerical scale of $\hat{\beta}_2$ is dependent upon the scale of measurements. We will test the contribution of the quadratic coefficient in Section 13.4.

```
DEPENDENT VARIABLE: Y

SOURCE                   DF        SUM OF SQUARES            MEAN SQUARE         F VALUE

MODEL                    2      1484489413.91039800     742244706.95519900       84.40

ERROR                    7        61559586.08960193       8794226.58422885      PR > F

CORRECTED TOTAL          9      1546049000.00000000                             0.0001

R_SQUARE               C.V.                   STD DEV              Y MEAN

.960183               7.3024              2965.50612615       40610.00000000


                                               T FOR H0:      PR > |T|       STD ERROR OF
PARAMETER             ESTIMATE             PARAMETER=0                        ESTIMATE

INTERCEPT         -26391.06854166             -2.95          0.0214        8945.31427948
X                     4.26240155              6.03           0.0005           0.70732695
X*X               -5.5219285E-05             -4.48           0.0029           0.00001233
```

FIGURE 13.3
Output from the SAS for
the Sale Price–Appraised
Improvements Data

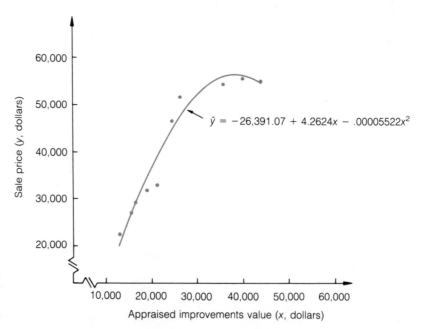

FIGURE 13.4
Least Squares Model for
the Sale Price–Appraised
Improvements Data

EXAMPLE 13.4   Locate the minimum value of SSE on the SAS printout reproduced in Figure 13.3. Also, obtain an estimate of σ^2, the variance of the random error term in the probabilistic model.

Solution   The minimum value of SSE, 61,559,586.09, is shaded in the row labelled ERROR under the column labelled SUM OF SQUARES in the printout shown in Figure 13.3. Recall from Section 12.5 that we can use this quantity to estimate σ^2. The estimator for the straight-line model was $s^2 = \text{SSE}/(n-2)$. Note that the denominator is $n -$ (Number of estimated β parameters) which, in the case of the straight-line model, is equal to $n - 2$. Since we must estimate one more parameter, β_2, for the quadratic model, $y = \beta_0 + \beta_1 x + \beta_2 x^2 +$ Random error, the estimator of σ^2 is $s^2 = \text{SSE}/(n-3)$. That is, the denominator becomes $(n-3)$ because there are now three β parameters in the model.

The numerical estimate of σ^2 for this example is

$$s^2 = \frac{\text{SSE}}{10-3} = \frac{61{,}559{,}586.09}{7}$$

$$= 8{,}794{,}226.584$$

Note that this estimate appears on the printout as the MEAN SQUARE for ERROR. Similarly, the standard deviation $s = 2{,}965.506$ appears in the column headed STD DEV (see Figure 13.3).

ESTIMATOR OF σ^2

$$s^2 = \frac{\text{SSE}}{n - (\text{Number of estimated } \beta \text{ parameters})}$$

where n is the number of data points.

The importance of the estimator of σ^2 is that we use its numerical value both to check the predictive ability of the model (Sections 13.4, 13.5, and 13.6) and to provide a measure of the reliability of predictions and estimates when the model is used for those purposes (Section 13.7).

13.4   Estimating and Testing Hypotheses about the β Parameters

Recall from our discussion in Chapter 12 of the straight-line model

$$y = \beta_0 + \beta_1 x + \text{Random error}$$

that β_1 has a practical interpretation. It is the mean change in y for every 1 unit increase in x. One method of determining whether the mean value of y changes as x

increases is to test the null hypothesis H_0: $\beta_1 = 0$.

Consider now the quadratic model

$$y = \beta_0 + \beta_1 x + \beta_2 x^2 + \text{Random error}$$

What is the practical interpretation of β_2? As noted earlier, β_2 measures the amount of curvature in the response curve (see Figure 13.1). Thus, one method of determining whether curvature exists in the population is to test the null hypothesis H_0: $\beta_2 = 0$. A test of hypothesis about β_2 is illustrated in the following example.

EXAMPLE 13.5   Refer to Example 13.3. Test the hypothesis that the quadratic term in the model contributes significantly to the prediction of sale price, y (i.e., test the null hypothesis H_0: $\beta_2 = 0$). Use $\alpha = .05$.

Solution   We require a test of the hypotheses

$$H_0: \beta_2 = 0 \quad \text{(No curvature in the response curve)}$$

$$H_a: \beta_2 \neq 0 \quad \text{(Curvature exists in the response curve)}$$

This test, a t test, is quite similar to the test of the slope of the simple straight-line model (Section 12.6). The details for a test about any β parameter in the general linear model are given in the box.

TEST ABOUT AN INDIVIDUAL PARAMETER COEFFICIENT IN THE GENERAL LINEAR MODEL (TWO-TAILED)

$$y = \beta_0 + \beta_1 x_1 + \beta_2 x_2 + \cdots + \beta_k x_k + \text{Random error}$$

$H_0: \beta_i = 0$

$H_a: \beta_i \neq 0$

Test statistic: $t = \dfrac{\hat{\beta}_i}{s_{\hat{\beta}_i}}$

Rejection region: $t > t_{\alpha/2}$ or $t < -t_{\alpha/2}$

where

$n = $ Number of observations

$s_{\hat{\beta}_i} = $ Estimated standard deviation of the repeated sampling distribution of $\hat{\beta}_i$

and the distribution of t is based on ($n -$ Number of β parameters in the model) degrees of freedom, and $t_{\alpha/2}$ is the t-value such that $P(t > t_{\alpha/2}) = \alpha/2$.

Assumptions: See Section 13.9.

We use the symbol $s_{\hat{\beta}_2}$ to represent the estimated standard deviation of $\hat{\beta}_2$. Since the formula for $s_{\hat{\beta}_2}$ is very complex, we will not present it here. However, this will not cause difficulty since the printouts for most computer packages list the estimated standard deviation $s_{\hat{\beta}_i}$ for each of the estimated model coefficients $\hat{\beta}_i$ in the linear model as well as the corresponding calculated t-values.

DEPENDENT VARIABLE: Y

SOURCE	DF	SUM OF SQUARES	MEAN SQUARE	F VALUE
MODEL	2	1484489413.91039800	742244706.95519900	84.40
ERROR	7	61559586.08960193	8794226.58422885	PR > F
CORRECTED TOTAL	9	1546049000.00000000		0.0001

R_SQUARE	C.V.	STD DEV	Y MEAN
.960183	7.3024	2965.50612615	40610.00000000

PARAMETER	ESTIMATE	T FOR H0: PARAMETER=0	PR > |T|	STD ERROR OF ESTIMATE
INTERCEPT	-26391.06854166	-2.95	0.0214	8945.31427948
X	4.26240155	6.03	0.0005	0.70732695
X*X	-5.5219285E-05	-4.48	0.0029	0.00001233

FIGURE 13.5
Output from the SAS

In order to test the null hypothesis that $\beta_2 = 0$, we again consult the SAS printout for the sale price–appraised improvements value example. From Figure 13.5, we see that the computed value of the test statistic corresponding to the test of H_0: $\beta_2 = 0$ (shaded under the column headed T FOR H0: PARAMETER = 0) is $t = -4.48$. The appropriate rejection region is obtained by consulting Table 4, Appendix E. For $\alpha = .05$ and $(n - 3) = 7$ degrees of freedom, we have $t_{\alpha/2} = t_{.025} = 2.365$. Note that the critical t-value used to specify the rejection region depends upon $n - 3$ degrees of freedom because the quadratic model contains three parameters (β_0, β_1, β_2). Then the rejection region (shown in Figure 13.6) is

$$t > 2.365 \quad \text{or} \quad t < -2.365$$

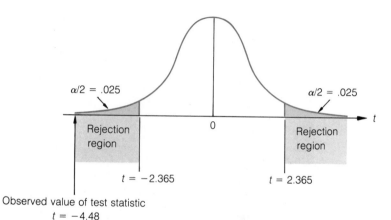

FIGURE 13.6
Rejection Region for Test about β_2

Since $t = -4.48$ falls into the lower tail of the rejection region, we conclude that the quadratic term $\beta_2 x^2$ makes an important contribution to the prediction model of 1978 sale price of properties located in neighborhood F.

This result could be obtained directly from the SAS printout, which lists the two-tailed attained significance levels (p-values) for each t-value under the column headed PR > |T|. The significance level .0029 corresponds to the quadratic term, and this implies that we would reject H_0: $\beta_2 = 0$ in favor of H_a: $\beta_2 \neq 0$ at any α level larger than .0029. Thus, there is very strong evidence of curvature in the response model relating sale price to appraised improvements value for properties located in neighborhood F.

EXAMPLE 13.6   Refer to Example 13.3. Form a 95% confidence interval for the parameter β_2 in the quadratic model.

Solution   A confidence interval for any β parameter in a general linear model is given in the box. From Figure 13.5, $\hat{\beta}_2 = -.00005522$. The estimated standard deviations of the model coefficients appear in the SAS printout under the column labelled STD ERROR OF ESTIMATE. The value, $s_{\hat{\beta}_2} = .00001233$, is shaded in Figure 13.5. Substituting the values of $\hat{\beta}_2$, $s_{\hat{\beta}_2}$, and $t_{.025} = 2.365$ (based on $n - 3 = 7$ degrees of freedom) into the formula for a confidence interval, we find the 95% confidence interval for β_2 to be

$$\hat{\beta}_2 \pm t_{\alpha/2} s_{\hat{\beta}_2} = -.00005522 \pm (2.365)(.00001233)$$

or $(-.00008438, -.00002606)$. This interval can be used to estimate the rate of curvature in mean sale price as appraised improvements value is increased. Note that all values in the interval are negative, reconfirming our test conclusion that β_2 is nonzero.

A $(1 - \alpha)$ 100% CONFIDENCE INTERVAL FOR AN INDIVIDUAL PARAMETER COEFFICIENT IN THE GENERAL LINEAR MODEL

$$\hat{\beta}_i \pm t_{\alpha/2} s_{\hat{\beta}_i}$$

where

n = Number of observations

$s_{\hat{\beta}_i}$ = Estimated standard deviation of the repeated sampling distribution of $\hat{\beta}_i$

and the distribution of t is based on (n − Number of β parameters in the model) degrees of freedom, and $t_{\alpha/2}$ is the t-value such that $P(t > t_{\alpha/2}) = \alpha/2$.

13.5 Measuring How Well the Model Fits the Data

Recall that the coefficient of determination, r^2, is a measure of how well a straight-line model fits a set of data (Chapter 12). To measure how well a general linear model (e.g., a quadratic model) fits a set of data, we compute the multiple regression equivalent of r^2, called the **multiple coefficient of determination**, and denoted by the symbol R^2.

DEFINITION 13.1

The **multiple coefficient of determination**, R^2, is defined as

$$R^2 = 1 - \frac{SSE}{SS_{yy}}$$

where $SSE = \Sigma (y_i - \hat{y}_i)^2$, $SS_{yy} = \Sigma (y_i - \overline{y})^2$, and $\hat{y}_i$ is the predicted value of y_i for the multiple regression model.

Just as for the simple linear model, R^2 represents the proportion of the sum of squares of deviations (SS_{yy}) of the y-values about $\overline{y}$ that can be attributed to the regression model. Thus, $R^2 = 0$ implies a complete lack of fit of the model to the data and $R^2 = 1$ implies a perfect fit, with the model passing through every data point. In general, the larger the value of R^2, the better the model fits the data.

EXAMPLE 13.7 Refer to Example 13.3. Locate the value of R^2 on the SAS printout and interpret its value. Does the quadratic model appear to provide a good fit to the 1978 sale price data for the neighborhood F properties?

Solution The SAS printout for the sale price–appraised improvements data is reproduced in Figure 13.7. The value of R^2 (shaded) is shown to be $R^2 = .960$. This very high value implies that, by using the independent variable Appraised improvements value in a

DEPENDENT VARIABLE: Y

SOURCE	DF	SUM OF SQUARES	MEAN SQUARE	F VALUE
MODEL	2	1484489413.91039800	742244706.95519900	84.40
ERROR	7	61559586.08960193	8794226.58422885	PR > F
CORRECTED TOTAL	9	1546049000.00000000		0.0001

R_SQUARE	C.V.	STD DEV	Y MEAN
.960183	7.3024	2965.5061 2615	40610.00000000

PARAMETER	ESTIMATE	T FOR H0: PARAMETER=0	PR > |T|	STD ERROR OF ESTIMATE
INTERCEPT	-26391.06854166	-2.95	0.0214	8945.31427948
X	4.26240155	6.03	0.0005	0.70732695
X*X	-5.5219285E-05	-4.48	0.0029	0.00001233

FIGURE 13.7
Output from the SAS

quadratic model instead of $\bar{y}$ to predict y, we can reduce the sum of squared prediction errors by 96%. Thus, this large value of R^2 indicates that the quadratic model provides a good fit to the $n = 10$ sample data points.

A large value of R^2 computed from the **sample** data does not necessarily mean that the model provides a good fit to all of the data points in the **population**. For example, a quadratic model which contains 3 parameters will provide a perfect fit to a sample of 3 data points and R^2 will equal 1. Likewise, you will always obtain a perfect fit $(R^2 = 1)$ to a set of n data points if your model contains exactly n parameters. Consequently, if you wish to use the value of R^2 as a measure of how useful the model will be for predicting y, it should be based on a sample that contains substantially more data points than the number of parameters in the model.

WARNING

In a multiple regression analysis, use the value of R^2 as a measure of how useful a linear model will be for predicting y only if the sample contains substantially more data points than the number of β parameters in the model.

We discuss a more formal method of checking the predictive ability of a general linear model, a statistical test of hypothesis, in the following section.

13.6 Testing Whether the Model Is Useful for Predicting y

A test of the utility of a general linear model, i.e., a test to determine whether the model is really useful for predicting y, involves testing all the β parameters in the model simultaneously. Conducting individual t tests on each β parameter in a model (Section 13.4) is generally not a good way to determine whether a model is contributing information for the prediction of y. Even if all the β parameters (except β_0) in the model are in fact equal to zero, $100(\alpha)\%$ of the time you will incorrectly reject the null hypothesis and conclude that some β parameter differs from zero. A better way to test the overall utility of a linear model is to conduct a test involving all the β parameters (except β_0). The null and alternative hypotheses for this test of model utility are given in the box.

HYPOTHESES FOR TESTING WHETHER A GENERAL LINEAR MODEL IS USEFUL FOR PREDICTING y

H_0: $\beta_1 = \beta_2 = \cdots = \beta_k = 0$

H_a: At least one of the β parameters in H_0 is nonzero

Practically speaking, this test for model utility is a comparison of the predictive ability of the estimated general linear model (which uses the predictor $\hat{y} = \hat{\beta}_0 + \hat{\beta}_1 x_1 + \hat{\beta}_2 x_2 + \cdots + \hat{\beta}_k x_k$) with a model that contains no x's (which uses the predictor $\hat{y} = \bar{y}$). If the test shows that at least one of the β's is nonzero, then the value of $\hat{y}$ obtained from the estimated linear model will, generally speaking, more accurately predict a future value of y than the sample mean $\bar{y}$. We illustrate a test of model utility in the following example.

EXAMPLE 13.8   Refer to Example 13.3. Test (using $\alpha = .05$) whether the quadratic model is useful for predicting y by testing the null hypothesis

$$H_0: \quad \beta_1 = \beta_2 = 0$$

Solution   The test statistic used in the test for model utility is an F statistic. The formula for computing the F statistic is given in the box. However, most computer regression analysis packages give this F-value. The F-value for the sale price example is shaded in the SAS computer printout shown in Figure 13.7. The value of the test statistic is $F = 84.40$. To determine whether this F-value is statistically significant, we read the value of the attained significance level given in the SAS printout. (For details on the appropriate rejection region, see Section 13.8.) The attained significance level for this test, .0001, is shaded in Figure 13.7 in the column headed PR > F. This implies that we would reject the null hypothesis for any α-value larger than .0001. Thus, we have strong evidence to reject H_0 and to conclude that at least one of the model coefficients, β_1 and β_2, is nonzero. Since the attained significance level is so small, there is ample evidence to indicate that $\hat{y} = \hat{\beta}_0 + \hat{\beta}_1 x + \hat{\beta}_2 x^2$ is useful for predicting the 1978 sale price of neighborhood F properties.

TEST STATISTIC FOR TESTING WHETHER A GENERAL LINEAR MODEL IS USEFUL FOR PREDICTING y

$$F = \frac{R^2/k}{(1 - R^2)/[n - (k + 1)]}$$

where

R^2 = Multiple coefficient of determination

n = Number of observations

k = Number of β parameters in the model (excluding β_0)

13.7 Using the Model for Estimation and Prediction

After checking the utility of the linear model and finding it to be useful for prediction and estimation, we are ready to use it for those purposes. Our methods for prediction and estimation using the quadratic or any general linear model are identical to those discussed for the simple straight-line model (Section 12.8). We will use the model to form a confidence interval for the mean $E(y)$ for a given value of x, or a prediction interval for a future value of y for a given x.

EXAMPLE 13.9 Refer to Example 13.3. Using the least squares quadratic model

$$\hat{y} = -26{,}391.07 + 4.2624x - .00005522x^2$$

estimate the mean 1978 sale price, $E(y)$, of a neighborhood F property with an appraised improvements value of $x = \$18{,}700$. Use a 95% confidence interval.

Solution Substituting $x = 18{,}700$ into the least squares prediction equation, the estimate of $E(y)$ is

$$\hat{y} = -26{,}391.07 + 4.2624(18{,}700) - .00005522(18{,}700)^2$$

$$= 34{,}006.21$$

To form a confidence interval for the mean, we need to know the standard deviation of the sampling distribution for the estimator $\hat{y}$. For general linear models, the form of this standard deviation is very complex. However, the SAS regression package allows us to obtain the confidence intervals for mean values of y at any given setting of the independent variables. This portion of the SAS output for the sale price example is shown in Figure 13.8. The 95% confidence interval for $E(y)$, the mean 1978 sale price

FIGURE 13.8
SAS Printout for Estimated
Mean and Corresponding
Confidence Interval for
$x = 18{,}700$

X	PREDICTED VALUE	LOWER 95% CL FOR MEAN	UPPER 95% CL FOR MEAN
18700	34006.20866573	31293.41293639	36719.00439507

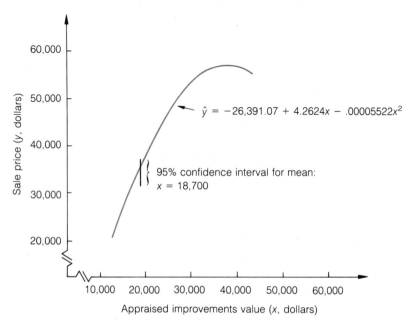

FIGURE 13.9
Confidence Interval for
Mean Sale Price

for all properties with an appraised improvements value of $x = \$18,700$, is shown to be $31,293.41 to $36,719.00 (see Figure 13.9).

EXAMPLE 13.10 Refer to Example 13.3. Construct a 95% prediction interval for y, the 1978 sale price of a particular neighborhood F property with an appraised improvements value of $x = \$18,700$.

Solution When $x = 18,700$, the predicted value for y is again $\hat{y} = 34,006.21$. However, the prediction interval for a particular value of y will be wider than the confidence interval for the mean value. This is reflected in the SAS printout shown in Figure 13.10. The prediction interval extends from $26,487.40 to $41,525.02 (see Figure 13.11).

FIGURE 13.10
SAS Printout for Predicted Value and Corresponding Prediction Interval for $x = 18,700$

X	PREDICTED VALUE	LOWER 95% CL INDIVIDUAL	UPPER 95% CL INDIVIDUAL
18700	34006.20866573	26487.40120860	41525.01612285

FIGURE 13.11
Prediction Interval for Sale Price

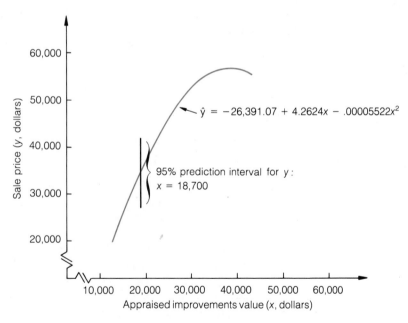

Just as in simple linear regression, it is dangerous to use the quadratic or any general linear prediction model for making predictions outside the region in which the sample data fall. (In our example, we would not use the estimated model to make estimates or predictions for properties with appraised improvements values less than $13,140 or greater than $43,460.) In general, the fitted model might not provide a good model for the relationship between the mean of y and the value of x when stretched over a wider range of x-values.

WARNING

Do not use the least squares model to predict a value of y outside the region in which the sample data fall, i.e., do not predict y for values of the independent variables $x_1, x_2, \ldots, x_k$ which are not within the range of the sample data.

13.8 Other Computer Printouts

We have highlighted the key elements of a multiple regression analysis as they appear on the SAS printout. However, there are a number of other different statistical program packages, such as Biomed, Minitab, and SPSS, to which you may have access at your computer center. The multiple regression computer programs for these packages may differ in programming methodology and in the appearance of their computer printouts, but all of them print sufficient information for conducting a multiple regression analysis. To illustrate, we compare the SAS regression analysis computer printout with the Minitab and SPSS printouts.

EXAMPLE 13.11   In Example 13.3, we used the SAS to fit the quadratic model

$$y = \beta_0 + \beta_1 x + \beta_2 x^2 + \text{Random error}$$

to $n = 10$ data points, where

   $y = 1978$ sale price of a residential property in neighborhood F

   $x = $ Appraised improvements value of the property

The Minitab and SPSS printouts for this example are given in Figure 13.12. (For convenience, we also reprint the SAS output originally given in Figure 13.3.) Compare the Minitab and SPSS printouts to the SAS.

Solution   In any multiple regression analysis, nine key elements are utilized. They are: (1) estimates of the β parameters; (2) the standard deviation, $s_{\hat{\beta}_i}$, of each least squares estimate $\hat{\beta}_i$; (3) computed values of t, the test statistics for testing H_0: $\beta_i = 0$; (4) attained significance levels of the t tests; (5) SSE; (6) s^2; (7) R^2; (8) computed value of the F statistic for testing whether the overall model is useful for predicting y; and (9) the attained significance level of the F test. With the aid of the arrows in Figure 13.12, you can see that all nine of these elements are located on the SAS printout (Figure 13.12(a)). However, some of these elements are missing on the Minitab (Figure 13.12(b)) and SPSS (Figure 13.12(c)) printouts.

   Although it gives the computed t-values for testing H_0: $\beta_i = 0$, the Minitab printout (Figure 13.12(b)) does not give the attained significance levels of the tests. Thus, in order to draw conclusions about the individual β parameters from the Minitab printout, we must compare the computed values of t with the critical values given in a t

FIGURE 13.12 Computer Printouts for Example 13.11

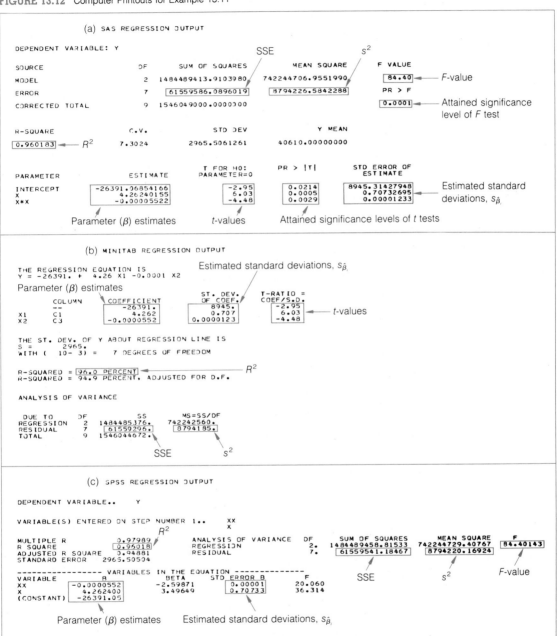

table (Table 4, Appendix E). Also, the Minitab printout does not give the F statistic for testing the overall utility of the model, i.e., testing the null hypothesis that all model parameters (except β_0) simultaneously equal zero. We show you how to obtain this F-value from the Minitab in an example that follows.

The elements missing on the SPSS printout (Figure 13.12(c)) also involve t and F tests. The SPSS does not print the computed t-values for testing the individual β parameters, nor does it give the corresponding attained significance levels. While the SPSS printout does report the value of the F statistic for testing whether the overall model is useful for predicting y, it fails to give the attained significance level of the F test. We learn how to obtain these elements missing from SPSS in the examples that follow.

For those elements of a multiple regression analysis which appear in all three printouts (SSE, s^2, R^2, etc.), you may have noticed the slight differences in their values. These differences are due to rounding errors inherent in the packaged programs.

EXAMPLE 13.12   How can we conduct tests about the individual model parameters, i.e., tests of H_0: $\beta_i = 0$, from the information provided by the SPSS printout, Figure 13.12(c)?

Solution   In contrast to the t tests of the SAS and Minitab packaged programs, SPSS conducts tests of H_0: $\beta_i = 0$ using an F statistic. The computed F-values are given in the SPSS printout in the column titled F in the bottom portion of the printout labelled VARIABLES IN THE EQUATION (see Figure 13.12(c)). It can be shown (proof omitted) that the square root of the F statistic appropriate for testing an individual β parameter in the model is equivalent to the absolute value of the familiar Student's t statistic, i.e.,

$$|t| = \sqrt{F}$$

For example, to conduct a test of H_0: $\beta_2 = 0$ using the SPSS printout, first locate the quantity $F = 20.060$ corresponding to the variable XX in Figure 13.12(c). Then compute

$$|t| = \sqrt{F} = \sqrt{20.060} = 4.48$$

To determine whether the actual computed t-value is positive or negative, observe the sign (positive or negative) of the corresponding parameter estimate, in this case, $\hat{\beta}_2$. The sign of the computed t-value will be identical to the sign of the parameter estimate. Since $\hat{\beta}_2$ is negative, the appropriate test statistic is $t = -4.48$. This computed value is then compared to the critical value of t, obtained from Table 4, Appendix E, as outlined in Section 13.4.

EXAMPLE 13.13   How can we compute the value of the F statistic for testing whether the overall model is useful for predicting y, using the information provided by the Minitab printout, Figure 13.12(b)?

Solution   In order to compute the value of the F statistic when using Minitab, we must use the formula given in Section 13.6,

$$F = \frac{R^2/k}{(1 - R^2)/[n - (k + 1)]}$$

Using the Minitab value $R^2 = .96$ from Figure 13.12(b), and the values $n = 10$ and $k = 2$, we have

$$F = \frac{.96/2}{(1 - .96)/[10 - (3)]} = \frac{.48}{(.04)/7} = 84.0$$

This value agrees with the values given in the SAS (Figure 13.12(a)) and SPSS (Figure 13.12(c)) printouts (except for rounding errors). We outline the method for finding the critical region for the test in Example 13.14.

EXAMPLE 13.14   The F statistic for testing whether the overall model is useful for predicting y, i.e., testing the null hypothesis that all model parameters (except β_0) equal zero, is shown in the SPSS printout and must be computed if Minitab is used. But in neither case is the attained significance level of the test given. Thus, if we use the SPSS or Minitab regression analysis package, we must compare the printed or computed F-value with those tabulated in the F tables, Tables 5, 6, and 7, Appendix E. What is the appropriate rejection region of the test?

Solution   The method for determining the appropriate critical value is given in the box. In Example 13.3, there are $n = 10$ data points and $k = 2$ parameters (β_1 and β_2) in the model other than β_0; hence, the critical value is based on an F distribution with $k = 2$ numerator degrees of freedom and $[10 - (2 + 1)] = 7$ denominator degrees of freedom. Using $\alpha = .05$, the critical value (obtained from Table 6) is $F_{.05} = 4.74$; thus, we will reject H_0 if

$$F > 4.74$$

Since the computed F-value given in the SPSS printout (Figure 13.12(c)) and computed from the Minitab (Figure 13.12(b)) falls within the rejection region, we reach the same conclusion that we reached in Section 13.6: Reject H_0 and conclude that at least one of the model parameters (β_1 and β_2) is nonzero; i.e., the model appears to be useful for predicting y, sale price.

We will not comment on the merits or drawbacks of the various computer program packages because you will have to use the package available at your computer center and you will have to become familiar with its output. As we have seen, most of the computer printouts are similar, and it is relatively easy to learn how to read one output after you have become familiar with another.

REJECTION REGION FOR A TEST OF WHETHER THE OVERALL MODEL IS USEFUL FOR PREDICTING y

H_0: $\beta_1 = \beta_2 = \cdots = \beta_k = 0$

Rejection region: $F > F_\alpha$

where the distribution of F depends on k numerator degrees of freedom and $[n - (k + 1)]$ denominator degrees of freedom, F_α is the value such that $P(F > F_\alpha) = \alpha$, and

   n = Number of observations

   k = Number of parameters in the model (excluding β_0)

13.9 Model Assumptions

In order for the statistical tests, confidence intervals, and prediction intervals of the preceding sections to be valid, certain assumptions must be satisfied. These assumptions, made about the random error term in the general linear model, follow the same general pattern as for the straight-line model. The assumptions are given in the box.

ASSUMPTIONS ABOUT THE RANDOM ERROR TERM IN THE GENERAL LINEAR MODEL

1. The mean of the probability distribution of the random error is 0.
2. The variance σ^2 of the probability distribution of the random error is constant for all settings of the independent variables in the model.
3. The probability distribution of the random error is normal.
4. The errors associated with any two observations are independent.

Various statistical techniques exist for checking the validity of these assumptions, and there are remedies to be applied when they appear invalid. But these are beyond the scope of this text. However, just as we stated in Chapter 12, these assumptions need not hold exactly in order for the results of a multiple regression analysis to be valid. In fact, in many practical business applications they will be adequately satisfied.

13.10 Summary

In this chapter we have discussed some of the methodology of multiple regression analysis. To illustrate the procedure, we utilized the quadratic model

$$y = \beta_0 + \beta_1 x + \beta_2 x^2 + \text{Random error}$$

to explain the curvilinear relationship between a dependent variable, y, and an independent variable, x. The quadratic model is just one type of linear model that can be fitted to a set of data using the method of least squares.

The steps employed in a multiple regression analysis (fitting, testing, and using the prediction equation) are identical to those employed in a simple linear regression analysis (Chapter 12):

1. The form of the probabilistic model is hypothesized (and the appropriate model assumptions are made).
2. The model coefficients are estimated using the method of least squares.
3. The utility of the model is checked.
4. If the model is deemed useful, it may be used to make estimates and to predict values of y to be observed in the future.

We stress that this is not intended to be a complete coverage of multiple regression analysis. Whole texts have been devoted to this topic. However, we have presented the core necessary for a basic understanding of multiple regression and general linear models. If you are interested in a more extensive coverage, you may wish to consult the references at the end of this chapter.

KEY WORDS

General linear model
Multiple regression analysis
Quadratic model
Multiple coefficient of determination: R^2
F test for determining whether the model is useful for predicting y

---

EXERCISES **13.1** Before accepting a job, a computer at a major university estimates the cost of running the job in order to see if the user's account contains enough money to cover the cost. As part of the job submission, the user must specify estimated values for two variables—Central processing unit (CPU) time and Lines printed. While the CPU time required and the lines printed do not account for the complete cost of the run, it is thought that knowledge of their values should allow a good prediction of job cost. The

FIGURE 13.13 Portion of the SAS Printout for Exercise 13.1

SOURCE	DF	SUM OF SQUARES	MEAN SQUARE	F VALUE	PR > F
MODEL	3	43.25090461	14.41696820	84.96	0.0001
ERROR	16	2.71515039	0.16969690		STD DEV
CORRECTED TOTAL	19	45.96605500		R-SQUARE	0.41194283
				0.940931	

PARAMETER	ESTIMATE	T FOR HO: PARAMETER = 0	PR > |T|	STD ERROR OF ESTIMATE
INTERCEPT	0.04564705	0.22	0.8313	0.21082636
X1	0.00078505	5.80	0.0001	0.00013537
X2	0.23737262	7.50	0.0001	0.03163301
X1 * X2	−0.00003809	−2.99	0.0086	0.00001273

X1	X2	PREDICTED VALUE	LOWER 95% CL FOR MEAN	UPPER 95% CL FOR MEAN
2000	42	8.38574865	7.32284845	9.44864885

following model is proposed to explain the relationship of lines printed and CPU time to job cost:

$$E(y) = \beta_0 + \beta_1 x_1 + \beta_2 x_2 + \beta_3 x_1 x_2$$

where

y = Job cost

x_1 = Lines printed

x_2 = CPU time (tenths of a second)

Records from twenty previous runs were used to fit this model. A portion of the SAS printout is shown in Figure 13.13.

a. Identify the least squares model that was fitted to the data.

b. What are the values of SSE and s^2 (estimate of σ^2) for the data?

c. What do we mean by the statement: This value of SSE (see part b) is minimum?

13.2 Refer to Exercise 13.1 and the portion of the SAS printout shown.

a. Is there evidence that the overall model is useful for predicting job cost? Test at $\alpha = .05$.

b. What assumptions are necessary for the validity of the test conducted in part a?

13.3 Refer to Exercise 13.1 and the portion of the SAS printout shown. Use a 95% confidence interval to estimate the mean cost of computer jobs that print 2,000 lines and require 4.2 seconds of CPU time.

13.4 Most companies institute rigorous safety programs in order to assure employee safety. Suppose that sixty reports of accidents over the last year at a company are randomly selected, and that the number of hours the employee had worked before the accident occurred, x, and the amount of time the employee lost from work, y, are recorded. A quadratic model is proposed to investigate a fatigue hypothesis that more serious accidents occur near the end of a day than near the beginning. Thus, the proposed model

$$E(y) = \beta_0 + \beta_1 x + \beta_2 x^2$$

was fitted to the data, and part of the computer printout appears in Figure 13.14.

FIGURE 13.14
Portion of the Computer Printout for Exercise 13.4

SOURCE	DF	SUM OF SQUARES	MEAN SQUARE	F VALUE
MODEL	2	112.110	56.055	1.28
ERROR	57	2496.201	43.793	R-SQUARE
TOTAL	59	2608.311		.0430

a. Do the data support the fatigue hypothesis? Use $\alpha = .05$ to test whether the proposed model is useful in predicting the lost work time, y.

b. Does the result of the test in part a necessarily mean that no fatigue factor exists? Explain. [*Hint:* The true model of the relationship between y and x may include higher order or other terms.]

13.5 Refer to Exercise 13.4. Suppose the company persists in using the quadratic model, despite its apparent lack of utility. The fitted model is

$$\hat{y} = 12.3 + .25x - .0033x^2$$

where $\hat{y}$ is the predicted time lost (days) and x is the number of hours worked prior to an accident.

a. Use the model to estimate the mean number of days missed by all employees who have an accident after 6 hours of work.

b. Suppose the 95% confidence interval for the estimated mean in part a is (1.35, 26.01). What is the interpretation of this interval? Does this interval reconfirm your conclusion about this model in Exercise 13.4?

13.6 A company that relies on door-to-door sales wants to determine the relationship, if any, between the proportion of customers who buy its product, y, and two independent variables: price, x_1 (in dollars), and years of experience of the salesperson, x_2. Twenty salespeople employed by the company are randomly assigned to sell the products, five to each of four prices ranging from $1.98 to $5.98. Each salesperson makes a sales presentation to thirty prospects, and the percentage of sales is recorded. The twenty observations (five salespeople for each of four prices) are used to fit the model

$$y = \beta_0 + \beta_1 x_1 + \beta_2 x_2 + \text{Random error}$$

The least squares model is

$$\hat{y} = -.30 - .010x_1 + .10x_2$$

with $s_{\hat{\beta}_1} = .0030$, $s_{\hat{\beta}_2} = .025$, and $R^2 = .86$.

a. Test the null hypothesis H_0: $\beta_1 = \beta_2 = 0$ to determine if the overall model is useful for predicting y. Use $\alpha = .05$.

b. Interpret the value of R^2.

c. Predict the percentage of customers who buy the company's product if the price of the product is $5 and the salesperson selling it door-to-door has 30 years of experience.

13.7 Mendenhall and McClave (1981) present a case study that involves fitting the linear model

$$E(y) = \beta_0 + \beta_1 x_1 + \beta_2 x_2$$

where

$$y = \text{Demand for a product}$$

$$x_1 = \text{Price of a product}$$

$$x_2 = \frac{1}{a}, \text{ where } a \text{ is the advertising expenditure employed to market the product}$$

The data and an SPSS computer printout for the regression analysis are shown in Table 13.2 and Figure 13.15, respectively.

TABLE 13.2
Annual Demand, Price, and Advertising Expenditures for Processed Grapefruit

OBSERVATION	y, million gallons	x_1, dollars per gallon	a, million dollars
1. 1972–1973	53.52	1.294	1.837
2. 1971–1972	51.34	1.344	1.053
3. 1970–1971	49.31	1.332	.905
4. 1969–1970	45.93	1.274	.462
5. 1968–1969	51.65	1.056	.576
6. 1967–1968	38.26	1.102	.260
7. 1966–1967	44.29	.930	.363

a. Write the least squares prediction equation.

b. Find R^2 on the computer printout, Figure 13.15, and interpret its value.

c. Do the data provide sufficient evidence to indicate that the overall model contributes information for the prediction of product demand? Explain.

d. Conduct tests about the individual β parameters, i.e., test H_0: $\beta_1 = 0$ and H_0: $\beta_2 = 0$. Use $\alpha = .05$ in each case. Do both the price, x_1, and advertising expenditure, x_2, contribute information for the prediction of product demand, y?

13.8 A supermarket chain conducted an experiment to investigate the effect of price p (in dollars) on the weekly demand y (in pounds) for a house brand of coffee. Eight supermarkets that had nearly equal past records of demand for the product were used in the experiment. Eight prices were randomly assigned to the stores and were advertised using the same procedures. The number of pounds of coffee sold during the following week was recorded for each of the stores and is shown in Table 13.3.

TABLE 13.3
Coffee Sales, Exercise 13.8

DEMAND y, pounds	PRICE p, dollars
1,120	3.00
999	3.10
932	3.20
884	3.30
807	3.40
760	3.50
701	3.60
688	3.70

a. Find the least squares prediction equation for fitting the model

$$E(y) = \beta_0 + \beta_1 x$$

to the data, letting $x = 1/p$. The Minitab computer printout for fitting this model to the data is shown in Figure 13.16 on p. 452.

FIGURE 13.15 SPSS Computer Printout for Exercise 13.7

```
DEPENDENT VARIABLE..   Y          ANNUAL DEMAND
VARIABLE(S) ENTERED ON STEP NUMBER  1..   X1     ANNUAL AVERAGE PRICE
                                          X2     RECIPROCAL OF A

MULTIPLE R          0.97937            ANALYSIS OF VARIANCE    DF      SUM OF SQUARES    MEAN SQUARE       F
R SQUARE            0.95917            REGRESSION              2.        162.26148        81.13074      45.98577
ADJUSTED R SQUARE   0.93876            RESIDUAL                4.          6.90683         1.72671
STANDARD ERROR      1.31404

------------ VARIABLES IN THE EQUATION ------------
VARIABLE          B          BETA      STD ERROR B        F
X1          -10.09196     -0.30553       4.51577        4.994
X2           -5.34766     -1.15883       0.02937       71.849
(CONSTANT)   69.75354

           OBSERVED      PREDICTED
SEQNUM         Y             Y           RESIDUAL
  1        53.52000      53.79047      -0.2704874
  2        51.34000      51.12367       0.2163125
  3        49.31000      50.41628      -1.106280
  4        45.93000      45.34926       0.5807204
  5        51.65000      49.83467       1.815310
  6        38.25000      38.11386       0.1461202
  7        44.29000      45.67168      -1.381695
```

```
THE REGRESSION EQUATION IS
Y = - 1180. + 6808. X

                                        ST. DEV.    T-RATIO =
            COLUMN      COEFFICIENT      OF COEF.    COEF/S.D.
            --             -1180.          108.        -10.96
   X        C3              6808.          358.         19.00

R-SQUARED = 98.4 PERCENT

ANALYSIS OF VARIANCE

   DUE TO       DF        SS         MS=SS/DF
   REGRESSION    1      157717.      157717.
   RESIDUAL      6        2622.         437.
   TOTAL         7      160339.
```

FIGURE 13.16
Minitab Printout for
Exercise 13.8

b. Do the data provide sufficient evidence to indicate that the model contributes information for the prediction of demand?

c. Find the value of the coefficient of determination and interpret its value.

CASE STUDY 13.1
Business Economists: Overworked and Underpaid?

Other than food and sex, nothing is quite as universally interesting as the size of our paychecks. Workers everywhere are preoccupied with the subject, and by the nature of their profession, this is no doubt especially true for economists. Why am I paid so little? Why does my friend in Chicago get a bigger salary for a less demanding job? Where does my boss get the crazy notion that my pay is so generous? And what can I do to justify a raise?

In an attempt to answer these questions, put forth in the introductory paragraph to their article,* Preston and Fiedler developed a model for determining "fair" compensation for an economist, based upon his or her contribution to a firm's total output. The authors use the method of multiple regression analysis to examine the relationship between an economist's pay and productivity. "Linear regression methods," they write, "are the mainstay of economic research, but all too frequently economists find themselves using such procedures for information about sales, new orders, or steel production when they are thinking about their own compensation and working conditions. This [research] uses the familiar statistical tools [i.e., multiple regression], applied to the NABE salary survey data, to isolate significant findings."

The NABE is the National Association of Business Economists, an organization which conducts periodic "salary characteristic" surveys of its members. These surveys provide a wealth of information that allows business economists to compare their own salaries with others in the profession. However, Preston and Fiedler point out that the survey's content allows salary comparisons only within single categories of classification. For example, "an NABE member can compare his salary with the average for his industry, the average for his level of education, and the average for his location. But he cannot make a comparison for all three characteristics simul-

---

*N. L. Preston and E. R. Fiedler, "Overworked and underpaid?" *Business Economics*, January 1980. Reprinted by permission of the National Association of Business Economists.

taneously. That is, he cannot find out how he stacks up against other NABE members who, e.g., have a Master's degree and work for a bank in New York City." To make the required comparisons, the authors conducted a multiple regression analysis on the data provided by the $n = 1,393$ responses to the 1978 NABE survey. The results are given below.

$$\hat{y} = 9.393 + .224x_1 + .019x_2 + .049x_3 + .190x_4 + .245x_5 - .180x_6$$
$$- .281x_7 - .266x_8 + .067x_9 + .078x_{10} + .122x_{11}$$

where

y = Natural logarithm of *total annual compensation* ($)

x_1 = Natural logarithm of *experience* (years)

x_2 = Number of *persons supervised*

x_3 = Level of *education* (no degree = 0, bachelor's = 4, master's = 6, all but Ph.D. = 8, Ph.D. = 10)

x_4 = *Sex* (male = 1, female = 0)

x_5 = Employed in *investments industry* (yes = 1, no = 0)

x_6 = Employed in *nonprofit research organization* (yes = 1, no = 0)

x_7 = Employed in *government* (yes = 1, no = 0)

x_8 = Employed by *academic institution* (yes = 1, no = 0)

x_9 = Located in *New York City* (yes = 1, no = 0)

x_{10} = *Economic advisor* (yes = 1, no = 0)

x_{11} = *General administration-economist* (yes = 1, no = 0)

Also, $R^2 = .54$ and all individual tests on the β coefficients are significant at $\alpha = .01$ (i.e., all tests have attained significance levels less than .01).

Preston and Fiedler illustrate the use of the least squares prediction equation for determining "fair" compensation for an economist with an example, shown in the box on p. 454.

a. Interpret the value of R^2.

b. Test whether the overall model is useful for predicting total compensation for business economists. Use a significance level of $\alpha = .05$. [*Hint:* Use the value of R^2 to calculate the F statistic.]

c. Predict the total compensation for a business economist with 6 years of experience, who supervises 25 other employees, has earned a Ph.D. degree, is female, is employed in government in Washington, D.C., and whose responsibilities are as economic advisor to the President.

We conclude this case study with some final remarks by Preston and Fiedler. "Every economist can use this regression to gauge where he or she stands competitively in the salary derby. Are you ahead of the pack, or behind? Plug your own characteristics into the equation and it will yield an estimate of your total compensation—a normative value of your services. If your actual salary is higher, you

USING THE REGRESSION EQUATION

For those not familiar with the process, here is an illustration of how to compare your compensation with the profession as a whole by plugging your own characteristics into the estimating equation. Our example is a business economist with 10 years of professional experience, who supervises 3 other employees, has earned a Master's degree, is male, is employed in banking in New York City, and whose responsibilities are in corporate planning.

y = Natural log of total compensation = Sum of the following:

Constant term		=		=	9.393
x_1	(experience)	=	.224 × natural log of 10		
			.224 × 2.3025	=	.516
x_2	(no. supervised)	=	.019 × 3	=	.057
x_3	(education)	=	.049 × 6	=	.294
x_4	(sex)	=	.190 × 1	=	.190
x_5	(securities and investments)	=	.245 × 0	=	0
x_6	(nonprofit res.)	=	−.180 × 0	=	0
x_7	(government)	=	−.281 × 0	=	0
x_8	(academic)	=	−.266 × 0	=	0
x_9	(New York City)	=	.067 × 1	=	.067
x_{10}	(economic advisor)	=	.078 × 0	=	0
x_{11}	(general administration- economist)	=	.122 × 0	=	0
				SUM =	10.517

Natural antilog of 10.517 = $36,938, which is the estimated total compensation for a business economist with this set of characteristics.

are a 'winner' in the derby! Alternatively, an actual pay level below the estimate would provide some justification for the feeling that you are overworked and underpaid. At the same time, however, it marks you a 'loser'! In the latter case you can . . . use the regression [equation] to demand higher pay from your boss! But if you're a winner, you may want to quickly discard this issue of *Business Economics* before your boss happens upon it!" (The authors' interpretation of the multiple regression results in terms of "winners" and "losers" is, of course, facetious. They note that the prediction equation is far from complete (refer to your answer to part a), for the model fails to include such unmeasurable factors as innate ability, communications skills, "horse sense," and just plain luck.)

CASE STUDY 13.2
Predicting the
Probability of
Self-Service
Gasoline
Adoption

Our discussion of a multiple regression analysis enables us to examine in greater detail S. Globerman's research on self-service gasoline stations (Case Study 8.1). Responding to allegations by Canadian government officials that major oil companies actively restrict price competition through a form of service station "overbuilding," Globerman (*Journal of Retailing,* Spring 1978) investigated the relationship between self-service adoption and oil company characteristics. Specifically, Globerman wished to obtain estimates of the probability of self-service adoption for Canadian oil companies, based upon certain profitability characteristics.

In general linear model terms, Globerman desired a prediction equation for the dependent variable y, the probability that an individual Canadian oil company will adopt the self-service concept. The set of independent variables seen by Globerman as factors likely to influence the adoption decision were the following:

$w_1 =$ Measure of the degree of price competition facing the oil company (weighted sum of percentage of total gallons sold by private-brand gasoline dealers)

$w_2 =$ Company size (total number of service stations operated by the company)

$w_3 =$ Percentage of total company stations which are operated by lessee-dealers

$w_4 =$ Percentage of total company stations located in Prince Edward Island and Nova Scotia

$w_5 =$ Refining facilities factor ($w_5 = 1$ if the company operates one or more refineries, $w_5 = 0$ otherwise)

The model first hypothesized by Globerman is given by

$$e^y = \alpha_0(w_1^{\alpha_1})(w_2^{\alpha_2})(w_3^{\alpha_3})(w_4^{\alpha_4})(w_5^{\alpha_5})(\text{Random error})$$

where the value of e (Euler's constant) is 2.71828. . . . Notice that this model is not in the form of a general linear model, since the independent variables ($w_1, w_2, \ldots, w_5$) are multiplied and the model coefficients ($\alpha_1, \alpha_2, \ldots, \alpha_5$) appear as powers of the independent variables. This type of model, referred to as a *multiplicative model,* is often hypothesized when analyzing business and economic data. Usually the independent variables in a multiplicative model are transformed to new variables which will improve the predictive ability of the model.

An appropriate transformation to use when the independent variables in the model are measured as percentages (as in this case study) is the natural logarithm transform. That is, new variables are obtained by taking the natural logarithms of the independent variables. Globerman defines these new variables as

$$x_1 = \ln(w_1)$$
$$x_2 = \ln(w_2)$$
$$\vdots \qquad \vdots$$
$$x_5 = \ln(w_5)$$

Notice the effect of the logarithm transform on the multiplicative model. If we take the logarithms of the terms on both sides of the equality sign in the model, we obtain

$$y \cdot \ln(e) = \ln(\alpha_0) + \alpha_1\ln(w_1) + \alpha_2\ln(w_2) + \alpha_3\ln(w_3)$$
$$+ \alpha_4\ln(w_4) + \alpha_5\ln(w_5) + \text{Random error}$$

Using the fact that $\ln(e) = 1$, and letting

$$\beta_0 = \ln(\alpha_0)$$
$$\beta_1 = \ln(\alpha_1)$$
$$\vdots \qquad \vdots$$
$$\beta_5 = \ln(\alpha_5)$$

we can rewrite the model with the transformed independent variables as

$$y = \beta_0 + \beta_1 x_1 + \beta_2 x_2 + \beta_3 x_3 + \beta_4 x_4 + \beta_5 x_5 + \text{Random error}$$

Does this model look familiar? The transformation has enabled us to write the multiplicative model as a linear model with $k = 5$ independent variables. It is this linear model which Globerman ultimately hypothesizes to explain the relationship between the dependent variable y and the (transformed) independent variables $x_1, x_2, \ldots, x_5$.

The values of the five independent variables were measured in May 1972, for each of the 24 Canadian oil companies included in the study. One year later (May 1973), the dependent variable y for each company was measured as follows:

$$y = \begin{cases} 1 & \text{if the company operated self-service stations by May 1973} \\ 0 & \text{otherwise} \end{cases}$$

The $n = 24$ data points were then subjected to a multiple regression analysis in order to obtain the least squares prediction equation

$$\hat{y} = \hat{\beta}_0 + \hat{\beta}_1 x_1 + \hat{\beta}_2 x_2 + \hat{\beta}_3 x_3 + \hat{\beta}_4 x_4 + \hat{\beta}_5 x_5$$

Globerman notes that the predicted value, $\hat{y}$, for an individual company can be interpreted as the probability that the company will have been operating self-service outlets by May 1973. The results of the analysis are given in Table 13.4. Interpret these results.

TABLE 13.4
Multiple Regression Results for Data on Self-Service Gasoline

ESTIMATE OF MODEL PARAMETER ($\hat{\beta}_i$)	TEST STATISTIC FOR H_0: $\beta_i = 0$	SIGNIFICANCE LEVEL (p-VALUE)
$\hat{\beta}_0 = -.584$	—	—
$\hat{\beta}_1 = 1.781$	$t = 1.64$	$p > .05$
$\hat{\beta}_2 = .616$	$t = 4.30$	$p < .01$
$\hat{\beta}_3 = -.347$	$t = -2.76$	$p < .01$
$\hat{\beta}_4 = -.365$	$t = -.138$	$p > .05$
$\hat{\beta}_5 = -.097$	$t = -.48$	$p > .05$

Multiple coefficient of determination: $R^2 = .612$
Test statistic for test of model utility: $F = 5.68$ ($p < .01$)

CASE STUDY 13.3
Factors that
Influence
Frequency of
Industrial Sales
Calls

One of the most critical elements influencing a firm's costs and revenues is the personal selling effort of the firm's sales representatives. Since the salesperson is often the company's major channel of communication with the (potential) customer, each and every sales call takes on added importance. Those calls that result in a customer purchase contribute to the company's incoming revenue, while those needed calls that are not made, or calls that are not successful, result in a forfeiture of company revenue. Thus, every sales call, whether successful or not, represents substantial direct and indirect expenses to the firm.

Rosann L. Spiro and William D. Perreault, Jr. ("Factors Influencing Sales Call Frequency of Industrial Salespersons." *Journal of Business Research,* January 1978)* considered the "problem of [how] sales representatives [allocate] their time in deciding which customers or prospects to call on and how frequently [they] make those calls." Specifically, Spiro and Perreault investigated the "relationship between the call frequency of salespersons and select characteristics of the [industrial] market, the customer, and the salesperson-customer interaction." They suggest that the following factors may "influence sales call behavior, and more generally, the salesperson-customer interaction":

x_1 = *Time in territory* (the number of months a salesperson has been in his or her current territory)

x_2 = *Rebuy customer* (a measure of how often the salesperson encounters customers who regularly rebuy from the company)

x_3 = *Important purchase decision* (a measure of how major or minor the buying decision is for the customers' firms)

x_4 = *Role consensus* (a measure of how differently the customers react than is expected by the salesperson)

x_5 = *Product shortages* (a measure of the degree of shortages of the selling product)

x_6 = *Competition* (a measure of the degree of competition facing the salesperson's firm)

x_7 = *Customer disposition* (a measure of the overall satisfaction customers have with the products and services of the salesperson's firm)

x_8 = *Congeniality* (a measure of the degree of friendship, trust, and respect the customer affords the salesperson)

x_9 = *Important customer* (a measure of the relative importance of the customer to the salesperson's firm)

α. Write the general linear model relating y, the sales call frequency (number of calls per year), to the nine independent variables indicated above. (Include only first-order terms.)

b. Data for the study were collected from questionnaires distributed to 83 salespersons who worked for different member firms of the Associated Equipment
Distributors. Responses to questions pertaining to the nine independent variables and sales call frequency (appropriately transformed using natural logarithms) were then subjected to a multiple regression analysis routine using the
SAS package. A portion of the results appear in Figure 13.17. Interpret the
results. Which of the independent variables would you recommend for further
examination as factors which influence sales call frequency?

```
DEPENDENT VARIABLE: Y (SALES CALLS)

SOURCE                      DF        SUM OF SQUARES      MEAN SQUARE        F VALUE

MODEL                        9             4.66              0.518            4.96

ERROR                       73             7.61              0.104          PR > F

CORRECTED TOTAL             82            12.27                               0.001


R-SQUARE           C.V.                STD DEV           Y MEAN

0.3844              *                    *                 *



                                        T FOR H0:       PR > |T|      STD ERROR OF
PARAMETER                  ESTIMATE    PARAMETER=0                       ESTIMATE

INTERCEPT                      *            *               *               *
X1 (TIME IN TERRITORY)      0.134          *             0.165             *
X2 (REBUY CUSTOMER)         0.042          *             0.678             *
X3 (IMPORTANT DECISION)     0.294          *             0.005             *
X4 (ROLE CONCENSUS)         0.284          *             0.006             *
X5 (PRODUCT SHORTAGE)       0.130          *             0.194             *
X6 (COMPETITION)            0.143          *             0.151             *
X7 (DISPOSITION)           -0.263          *             0.013             *
X8 (CONGENIALITY)          -0.065          *             0.556             *
X9 (IMPORTANT CUSTOMER)     0.418          *             0.000             *
```

FIGURE 13.17

A Portion of the SAS
Printout for the Sales Call
Frequency Multiple
Regression

REFERENCES   Barr, A., Goodnight, J., Sall, J., Blair, W., & Chilko, D. *SAS user's guide.* 1979 ed. SAS Institute,
P. O. Box 10066, Raleigh, N. C. 27605.

Globerman, S. "Self-service gasoline stations: A case study of competitive innovation." *Journal
of Retailing,* Spring 1978, *54,* 75–85.

Mendenhall, W., & McClave, J. T. *A second course in business statistics: Regression analysis.*
San Francisco: Dellen, 1981. Chapter 4.

Neter, J., & Wasserman, W. *Applied linear statistical models.* Homewood, Ill.: Richard Irwin,
1974. Chapter 7.

Preston, N. L., & Fiedler, E. R. "Overworked and underpaid?" *Business Economics,* January
1980, *15,* 9–15.

Ryan, T. A., Joiner, B. L., & Ryan, B. F. *Minitab student handbook.* North Scituate, Mass.:
Duxbury, 1979.

Spiro, R. L., & Perreault, W. D., Jr. "Factors influencing sales call frequency of industrial
salespersons." *Journal of Business Research,* January 1978, *6,* 1–15.

Fourteen

Opinion Polls and the Chi-Square Distribution

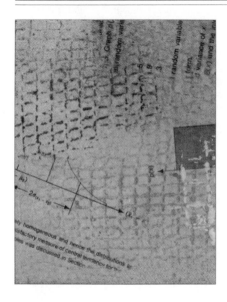

If you shop for groceries, are you an apathetic shopper, a convenience shopper, an involved shopper, or a price shopper? But, more important to a grocery chain is whether the type of store that you select for shopping, i.e., the perceived price level of the store, depends upon your shopping type. To answer this question, we need to be able to test for a dependence between two qualitative variables, Type of store and Type of shopper. In this chapter we will show you how to conduct this test, and we will deal more thoroughly with the grocery shopping problem in Case Study 14.3.

Contents:

14.1 A *Wall Street Journal*–Gallup Survey

Opinion polls that yield one of two responses (yes or no, favor or do not favor, etc.) for each person polled can be analyzed using the binomial probability distribution of Chapter 5. Polls that allow for more than two categories for a response are much more common, and these must be analyzed using a different method.

As an example of the latter, we will examine one portion of the results of a *Wall Street Journal*–Gallup survey of the opinions of 782 chief executives of U.S. corporations.* The 782 chief executives represent combined samples of 282 selected from among the country's largest firms, 300 from among medium-sized firms, and 200 from among the several million small companies in the United States.

One question in particular caught the eye of Frank Allen, staff reporter for the *Wall Street Journal:* "How many people in your company are capable of doing your job as chief executive?" Allen writes,*

> Speculation about likely heirs to the top jobs in corporate America may be mostly academic. Two-thirds of the chief executives of the largest U.S companies say they already have a clear idea who their successors will be. Half of the chief executives say they believe their top subordinates share that knowledge. But the smaller the company, the less certain the chief executive is likely to be about a successor. And the smaller the company, the shorter the list of prospects the incumbent chief considers capable of doing his job.

The data used to support Allen's observations are the percentages of the 782 chief executives' responses that fell into one of the categories shown in Table 14.1.

TABLE 14.1

Data Presented in the *Wall Street Journal* (November 18, 1980)

SUITABLE SUCCESSORS
Q. How many people in your company are capable of doing your job as chief executive?

	Large firms	Medium firms	Small firms
One person	6%	10%	22%
Two	14	27	30
Three	24	26	18
Four or five	30	21	8
Six or more	22	11	4
Don't know	4	5	18

To simplify our discussion, we will examine only one aspect of the data. It does appear, as Allen suggests, that the distribution of the percentages of responses in the categories corresponding to the "number of persons in your company capable of doing your job" does depend on the size of the company; in particular, it appears that the chief executives of larger companies think they have more people capable of

---

Wall Street Journal, November 18, 1980. Reprinted by permission. © Dow Jones & Company, Inc. 1980. All rights reserved.

doing their job than do the chief executives of small companies. The question is, of course, whether this informal inference is reliable. Remember, the executives included in the study are a sample of only 782 from among the roughly 3.5 million company chief executives in the United States. Do these sample results reflect actual differences in these percentages among large, medium, and small firms in the entire population of firms, or are the differences in the distributions of percentages shown in Table 14.1 due to sample variation? To answer this question, we will test the null hypothesis that the distributions of percentages are identical for large, medium, and small firms. If we are able to reject this hypothesis, we will be able to conclude that the differences seen in Table 14.1 are not due to chance.

14.2 The Chi-Square Statistic

The data of Table 14.1 represent the sample percentages of responses for the 782 randomly selected chief executives. If there is evidence of a significant difference in the distributions of these sample percentages from one size firm to another, we will conclude that the distributions of the true percentages for all chief executives at large, medium, and small firms are different. However, we cannot rely on these sample percentages alone to provide us with the information necessary to carry out a test of hypothesis. Recall from Chapter 8 that the reliability of a sample proportion as an estimator of a population proportion depends upon the size of the sample selected. The number of chief executives (282 from large firms, 300 from medium firms, and 200 from small firms) selected for the *Wall Street Journal*–Gallup survey is not indicated in Table 14.1. In order to attach a measure of reliability to our inference, we will need to present and analyze the data in a form which reflects the size of the sample selected. This requires converting the percentages of Table 14.1 into the observed number of responses in each category. A count of the categorical responses is given in Table 14.2. (In most analyses of this type, the data will be reported in the form of Table 14.2, called a **contingency table**. When the data are presented as counts, you will not need to convert percentages into observed numbers in each of the categories.) Notice that we have computed the total number of responses in each row and column category. These row and column totals become important when we are ready to calculate the value of the appropriate test statistic.

TABLE 14.2

Count of Responses to the *WSJ*–Gallup Survey of 782 Chief Executives

| | | SIZE OF FIRM | | | TOTALS |
		Large	Medium	Small	
	One	17	30	44	91
NUMBER CAPABLE OF DOING YOUR JOB	Two	39	81	60	180
	Three	68	78	36	182
	Four or five	85	63	16	164
	Six or more	62	33	8	103
	Don't know	11	15	36	62
TOTALS		282	300	200	782

EXAMPLE 14.1   Let us suppose that the distributions of percentages of responses in the categories corresponding to "number capable of doing your job" are identical for chief executives from large, medium, and small firms, i.e., the distribution of percentages is *independent* of size of firm. In particular, let us focus on the observed counts in the first row of the table, i.e, those responses corresponding to "one" capable successor to chief executive. How can we determine whether these observed counts contradict our assumption of identical distributions of percentages for large, medium, and small firms?

Solution   One method of detecting a difference in the distributions of percentages of responses in the category "one" is to compare the observed number of responses in each of the three cells *corresponding to size of firm* to the number of responses we would expect to see if, in fact, the percentages were identical. The larger the deviations between the observed numbers and their respective expected numbers, the more evidence there is that the true percentages are different.

The expected number of responses in the cells, i.e., the expected cell counts, although unknown, can be estimated using the row and column totals of the contingency table. An estimate of the expected number of responses for any cell in the table is computed by multiplying the row total and column total corresponding to the row and column in which the cell is located, and then dividing this product by the total sample size (which appears in the lower right-hand corner of the table). For example, the estimated number of responses for the cell in the upper left-hand corner of the table, denoted e_1, is

$$e_1 = \frac{(91)(282)}{782} = 32.816$$

Thus, if there is no difference in the distributions of percentages of responses for large, medium, and small firms, we would expect to observe approximately 33 chief executives from large firms who believe that only one person is capable of doing his or her job. Similarly, the estimated expected number of responses for the cells in the first row corresponding to medium and small firms are, respectively,

$$e_2 = \frac{(91)(300)}{782} = 34.910$$

and

$$e_3 = \frac{(91)(200)}{782} = 23.274$$

Compare these expected counts with the observed counts in the table.

In Example 14.2, we will compute a statistic which will help us determine if the differences between the observed cell counts and expected cell counts are large enough for us to conclude that the distributions of percentages are different.

In the box at the top of the next page we give the general formula for computing an estimate of the expected number of responses in any cell of the table.

GENERAL FORMULA FOR COMPUTING EXPECTED CELL COUNTS

$$e_i = \frac{(R_i)(C_i)}{n}$$

where

e_i = Estimated expected count for cell i

R_i = Row total corresponding to the row in which cell i appears

C_i = Column total corresponding to the column in which cell i appears

n = Sample size

EXAMPLE 14.2

What is the appropriate test statistic in a test of hypothesis to determine whether the distributions of percentages of responses in the categories corresponding to "number capable of doing your job" differ for chief executives from large, medium, or small firms?

Solution

From Example 14.1, we learned that the differences between the observed number of responses in the cells of Table 14.2 and their respective expected number of responses are used to detect differences in the response percentages. How should this information be combined into a single statistic? Let o_i denote the observed number of responses in cell i and e_i denote the (estimated) expected number of responses in cell i. Then the appropriate statistic which measures the disagreement between the data and the assumption that the distributions of percentages are identical is denoted by the symbol χ^2 and is computed as

$$\chi^2 = \frac{(o_1 - e_1)^2}{e_1} + \frac{(o_2 - e_2)^2}{e_2} + \cdots + \frac{(o_k - e_k)^2}{e_k}$$

where k is the number of cells in the table (i.e., the number of possible categories into which the responses may be classified). For the data of Table 14.2, we have 6 row

---

HOW TO COMPUTE THE χ^2 STATISTIC IN A TEST FOR DIFFERENCES OF PERCENTAGES OF CATEGORICAL RESPONSES

1. Compute the (estimated) expected cell counts, $e_1, e_2, \ldots, e_k$, for each of the k cells of the table.
2. Compute the differences $o_1 - e_1, o_2 - e_2, \ldots, o_k - e_k$ for each of the k cells of the table, where o_i denotes the observed number of responses in cell i.
3. Compute the χ^2 test statistic as follows:

$$\chi^2 = \frac{(o_1 - e_1)^2}{e_1} + \frac{(o_2 - e_2)^2}{e_2} + \cdots + \frac{(o_k - e_k)^2}{e_k}$$

categories (number capable of doing your job) and 3 column categories (size of firm); hence, $k = (6)(3) = 18$ cells for which we need to compute the expected counts. These expected cell counts and the observed cell counts are then substituted into the formula, and the χ^2 statistic is computed, as described in the box on p. 463.

Under the assumption that the distributions of percentages of categorical responses are identical, the χ^2 statistic has a sampling distribution which is approximately a **chi-square (χ^2) distribution.** The chi-square probability distribution, like the t distribution, is characterized by a quantity, called the **degrees of freedom associated with the distribution.** Several chi-square probability distributions with different degrees of freedom are shown in Figure 14.1.

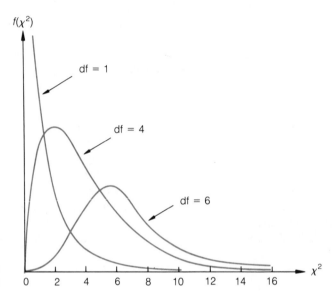

FIGURE 14.1
Several Chi-Square
Probability Distributions

Throughout this chapter, we will use the words *chi-square* and the Greek symbol χ^2 interchangeably. Tabulated values of the χ^2 distribution are given in Table 8, Appendix E; part of this table is shown in Figure 14.2. Entries in the table give an upper-tail value of χ^2, call it χ_α^2, such that $P(\chi^2 > \chi_\alpha^2) = \alpha$.

EXAMPLE 14.3   Find the tabulated value of χ^2 corresponding to 2 degrees of freedom which cuts off an upper-tail area of .05.

Solution   The value of χ^2 which we seek appears (shaded) in the partial reproduction of Table 8, Appendix E, given in Figure 14.2. The columns of the table identify the value of α associated with the tabulated value χ_α^2 and the rows correspond to the degrees of freedom. For this example, we have df = 2 and $\alpha = .05$. Thus, the tabulated value of χ^2 corresponding to 2 degrees of freedom is

$$\chi_{.05}^2 = 5.99147$$

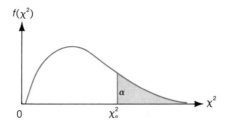

DEGREES OF FREEDOM	$\chi^2_{.100}$	$\chi^2_{.050}$	$\chi^2_{.025}$	$\chi^2_{.010}$	$\chi^2_{.005}$
1	2.70554	3.84146	5.02389	6.63490	7.87944
2	4.60517	5.99147	7.37776	9.21034	10.5966
3	6.25139	7.81473	9.34840	11.3449	12.8381
4	7.77944	9.48773	11.1433	13.2767	14.8602
5	9.23635	11.0705	12.8325	15.0863	16.7496
6	10.6446	12.5916	14.4494	16.8119	18.5476
7	12.0170	14.0671	16.0128	18.4753	20.2777
8	13.3616	15.5073	17.5346	20.0902	21.9550
9	14.6837	16.9190	19.0228	21.6660	23.5893
10	15.9871	18.3070	20.4831	23.2093	25.1882
11	17.2750	19.6751	21.9200	24.7250	26.7569
12	18.5494	21.0261	23.3367	26.2170	28.2995
13	19.8119	22.3621	24.7356	27.6883	29.8194
14	21.0642	23.6848	26.1190	29.1413	31.3193
15	22.3072	24.9958	27.4884	30.5779	32.8013
16	23.5418	26.2962	28.8454	31.9999	34.2672
17	24.7690	27.5871	30.1910	33.4087	35.7185
18	25.9894	28.8693	31.5264	34.8053	37.1564
19	27.2036	30.1435	32.8523	36.1908	38.5822

FIGURE 14.2
Reproduction of Part of
Table 8, Appendix E

We use the tabulated values of χ^2 given in Table 8, Appendix E, to locate the appropriate rejection region for the test of hypothesis which we carry out in the following section.

EXERCISES 14.1 A company conducted a survey to determine whether the proportion of employees favoring a new pension plan depends upon whether workers hold production, clerical, or management jobs. Four hundred employees were randomly selected for the survey. A summary of their responses is shown in Table 14.3.

TABLE 14.3
Employee Responses,
Exercise 14.1

	EMPLOYMENT CATEGORY			TOTALS
	Production	Clerical	Management	
Favor new plan	169	76	26	271
Do not favor new plan	87	35	7	129
TOTALS	256	111	33	400

a. Calculate the percentages of employees in favor of the new pension plan for each of the employee categories.
b. Do these percentages suggest a difference in the proportions for the three employment categories?
c. Why is a statistical test useful in answering part b?
[*Note:* You do not need to convert the response counts of Table 14.3 to percentages in order to carry out the statistical test referred to in part c. However, the calculations, part a, become necessary when additional analysis is required. See Section 14.3.]

14.2 Refer to the data in Exercise 14.1.
a. Calculate the number of employees that you would expect to fall in each of the six cells of the contingency table if, in fact, the percentages who favor the new plan in each employment category are identical.
b. Find the difference between the observed and the (estimated) expected number for each of the six cells.
c. Calculate the value of the chi-square statistic for the contingency table.

14.3 A survey was conducted to determine whether a relationship exists between a new college business graduate's expectations of acquiring rewarding employment and the graduate's college business major. Three hundred graduates were randomly selected for the survey. A summary of their responses is shown in Table 14.4.

TABLE 14.4
Graduates' Expectations,
Exercise 14.3

	COLLEGE MAJOR				TOTALS
	Accounting	Economics	Finance	Management	
High expectations for employment	34	45	43	48	170
Modest expectations for employment	18	27	31	20	96
Poor expectations for employment or no opinion	10	6	10	8	34
TOTALS	$\overline{62}$	$\overline{78}$	$\overline{84}$	$\overline{76}$	$\overline{300}$

a. Calculate the percentage of Accounting graduates in each of the three employment expectation response categories. Calculate these percentages for Economics, Finance, and Management graduates.
b. Do the distributions of percentages for the four college majors appear to differ?
c. Why is a statistical test useful in answering part b?

14.4 Refer to the data in Exercise 14.3.
a. Calculate the number of graduates that you would expect to fall in each of the twelve cells of the contingency table if, in fact, the distributions of percentages for the four college majors are identical.
b. Find the difference between the observed and the (estimated) expected number for each of the twelve cells.
c. Calculate the value of the chi-square statistic for the contingency table.

14.5   For each of the following combinations of α and degrees of freedom (df), find the value of chi-square, χ_α^2, that places an area α in the upper tail of the chi-square distribution. Sketch the chi-square distribution showing the locations of α and χ_α^2.

a. $\alpha = .05$,   df $= 7$
b. $\alpha = .10$,   df $= 16$
c. $\alpha = .01$,   df $= 10$
d. $\alpha = .025$,   df $= 8$
e. $\alpha = .005$,   df $= 5$

14.6   Find the value of α that corresponds to:
a.   A value $\chi^2 = 20.4831$, based on df $= 10$
b.   A value $\chi^2 = 13.2767$, based on df $= 4$
c.   A value $\chi^2 = 26.2962$, based on df $= 16$

14.3   Analysis of the *Wall Street Journal*–Gallup Data

Do the results of the *Wall Street Journal*–Gallup survey reflect actual differences in the distributions of percentages of responses in the categories corresponding to the "number of persons in your company capable of doing your job" among the population of roughly 3.5 million chief executives of large, medium, and small firms in the United States? We will answer this question by performing a complete test of hypothesis on the data of Table 14.2.

EXAMPLE 14.4   Set up the appropriate null and alternative hypotheses for the test.

Solution   We have already stated the null hypothesis in Section 14.1. For convenience, we restate it here:

> H_0:   The distributions of percentages of responses in the categories corresponding to "number of persons in your company capable of doing your job" are identical for chief executives of large, medium, and small firms. Equivalently, we are hypothesizing that the distribution of percentages for one direction of classification (Number capable of doing your job) in Table 14.2 is *independent* of the second direction of classification (Size of firm).

The alternative hypothesis can then be phrased:

> H_a: The distributions of percentages of responses in the categories corresponding to "number of persons in your company capable of doing your job" differ for chief executives of large, medium, and small firms. That is, the distribution *depends* on the size of the firm.

The null and alternative hypotheses for the statistical tests which we have discussed previously were given in terms of values of a target parameter or the differences between two target parameters. Since in the *WSJ*–Gallup survey there are many more parameters to consider (18 in fact, one proportion for each cell in Table 14.2), it is more convenient to write H_0 and H_a as above.

EXAMPLE 14.5   Use the data of Table 14.2 to compute the χ^2 test statistic.

Solution   The first step in the calculation of the test statistic is to compute the (estimated) expected count, e_i, in each cell of the table. In Example 14.1, we gave the formula for finding expected counts and illustrated its use by computing the expected number of responses in each of the three cells in the top row of Table 14.2. Using the formula

$$e_i = \frac{(R_i)(C_i)}{n}$$

we computed the expected counts for the remaining 15 cells. These values are given in parentheses with the observed counts in Table 14.5.

Once these (estimated) expected cell frequencies have been computed, we substitute their values into the formula for the χ^2 statistic given in the box following Example 14.2 in Section 14.2.

TABLE 14.5

Observed and Estimated Expected (in Parentheses) Counts for the WSJ–Gallup Survey

| | SIZE OF FIRM | | |
	Large	Medium	Small
One	17	30	44
	(32.816)	(34.910)	(23.274)
Two	39	81	60
	(64.910)	(69.054)	(46.036)
Three	68	78	36
	(65.632)	(69.821)	(46.547)
Four or five	85	63	16
	(59.141)	(62.916)	(41.944)
Six or more	62	33	8
	(37.143)	(39.514)	(26.343)
Don't know	11	15	36
	(22.358)	(23.785)	(15.857)

The computed χ^2 test statistic is

$$\chi^2 = \frac{(o_1 - e_1)^2}{e_1} + \frac{(o_2 - e_2)^2}{e_2} + \cdots + \frac{(o_{18} - e_{18})^2}{e_{18}}$$

$$= \frac{(17 - 32.816)^2}{32.816} + \frac{(30 - 34.910)^2}{34.910} + \cdots + \frac{(36 - 15.857)^2}{15.857}$$

$$= 139.28$$

Is the value 139.28 large enough for us to conclude that the distributions of percentages are different? We answer this question in the following example.

EXAMPLE 14.6   Specify the rejection region for the test and make the proper conclusion. Use a significance level of $\alpha = .05$.

Solution   If the computed value of the χ^2 statistic is "too large," there is evidence to reject H_0 and conclude that the differences in the distributions of percentages of responses exhibited by the data in Table 14.2 are due not to sampling variation but to actual differences in the populations. To determine how large χ^2 must be before it is too large to be attributed to chance, we make use of the fact that, under certain conditions (see Section 14.4), the sampling distribution of χ^2 is approximately a chi-square probability distribution if the null hypothesis is true. For a significance level of $\alpha = .05$, we need to find the tabulated value of $\chi^2_{.05}$ in Table 8, Appendix E. If our computed test statistic is larger than this critical value, i.e., if

$$\chi^2 > \chi^2_{.05}$$

then we will reject the null hypothesis. However, we noted in Section 14.2 that the tabulated values of χ^2 in Table 8, Appendix E, depend upon degrees of freedom. In analyses of data reported in the form of Table 14.2, the appropriate degrees of freedom will be $(r-1)(c-1)$, where r is the number of rows and c is the number of columns in the table.

For the *Wall Street Journal*–Gallup survey data, we have $r = 6$ rows and $c = 3$ columns; hence, the appropriate number of degrees of freedom for χ^2 is

$$df = (r-1)(c-1) = (5)(2) = 10$$

The tabulated value of $\chi^2_{.05}$ corresponding to 10 df is 18.3070; thus, the rejection region (shaded in Figure 14.3) is

$$\chi^2 > 18.3070$$

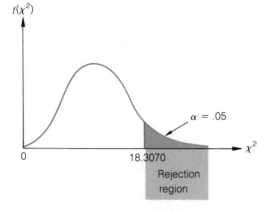

FIGURE 14.3
Rejection Region for the
WSJ–Gallup Survey
Example

Since the computed $\chi^2 = 139.28$ exceeds the critical value 18.3070, we reject the null hypothesis in favor of the alternative. At significance level $\alpha = .05$, the data of Table 14.2 support *Wall Street Journal* reporter Frank Allen's contention that the distributions of the percentages of responses in the categories corresponding to the "number of persons in your company capable of doing your job" are different among chief executives from large, medium, and small firms.

The elements of a χ^2 test for differences in the distributions of percentages of responses from opinion polls, sample surveys, etc., are summarized in the box.

GENERAL FORM OF A CHI-SQUARE TEST FOR INDEPENDENCE OF TWO DIRECTIONS OF CLASSIFICATION

H_0: The two directions of classification in the contingency table are independent

H_a: The two directions of classification in the contingency table are dependent

Test statistic: $\chi^2 = \sum_{i=1}^{k} \frac{(o_i - e_i)^2}{e_i}$

where

$k =$ Number of cells (rc) in the table consisting of r rows and c columns

$o_i =$ Observed number of responses in cell i

$e_i =$ Estimated expected number of responses in cell i

Rejection region: $\chi^2 > \chi_\alpha^2$

where χ_α^2 is the tabulated value of the chi-square distribution based on $(r - 1)(c - 1)$ degrees of freedom such that $P(\chi^2 > \chi_\alpha^2) = \alpha$.

Assumptions: See Section 14.4.

The data of Table 14.2 could also be used to obtain an estimate of the percentage of responses in a specific category of the population or to test hypotheses about the value of a particular percentage. The techniques are identical to those of Chapters 8, 9, and 10 where we considered large-sample inferences about binomial proportions. We illustrate with two examples.

EXAMPLE 14.7 Use the data of Table 14.2 to estimate the proportion of chief executives at all large firms who believe that only one subordinate is capable of doing their job. Use a 95% confidence interval.

Solution Note that the data in Table 14.2 represent three independent random samples of chief executives—one from large firms, one from medium firms, and one from small firms. We will restrict our attention to the sample of 282 chief executives selected from large firms.

Let the true proportion of chief executives of all large firms who believe that only one subordinate in their firm is qualified for the job be denoted by p. Since we are now interested in only one population proportion, we may treat the data of Table 14.2 as binomial data. We can think of the response of a chief executive of a large firm as being classified into one of only two categories: (1) one suitable successor; or (2) none or more than one suitable successor. The proportion p then represents the probability of success in a binomial experiment consisting of $n = 282$ trials (i.e., interviews of 282 chief executives of large firms), where a "success" is defined as observing a "one suitable successor" response.

Following the procedure of Chapter 8, a 95% confidence interval for p is given by

$$\hat{p} \pm 1.96 \sqrt{\frac{\hat{p}\hat{q}}{n}}$$

where $\hat{p}$ is the sample proportion of successes in n trials, and $\hat{q} = 1 - \hat{p}$. From Table 14.2, the number of "successes" (i.e., the number of "one suitable successor" responses) is 17. Thus, our estimate is

$$\hat{p} = \frac{\text{Number of successes in the sample}}{n} = \frac{17}{282} = .060$$

Substituting $\hat{p} = .060$, $\hat{q} = .940$, and $n = 282$ into the confidence interval for p, we obtain

$$\hat{p} \pm 1.96 \sqrt{\frac{\hat{p}\hat{q}}{n}} = .060 \pm 1.96 \sqrt{\frac{(.060)(.940)}{282}}$$
$$= .060 \pm (1.96)(.01414)$$
$$= .060 \pm .0277$$
$$= (.0323, .0877)$$

We estimate, with 95% confidence, that the percentage of chief executives of all large firms who believe that only one of their subordinates is capable of doing their job falls between 3.23% and 8.77%.

EXAMPLE 14.8   Refer to Table 14.2. Test to determine whether the proportion of chief executives at all large firms who believe that "six or more" subordinates are capable of doing their job is larger than the corresponding proportion at all medium-sized firms. Use $\alpha = .01$.

Solution   Let p_l and p_m represent the true proportions of chief executives at large and medium-sized firms, respectively, who believe that "six or more" in their company are capable of doing their job. To determine whether p_l is larger than p_m, we test the hypotheses:

H_0: $(p_l - p_m) = 0$

H_a: $(p_l - p_m) > 0$

Again, we recognize that the portion of the data of Table 14.2 which we are interested in may be treated as data from two independent binomial experiments; consequently, the procedure outlined in Chapters 9 and 10 for testing the difference between binomial proportions may be applied. The appropriate test statistic is given by

$$z = \frac{(\hat{p}_l - \hat{p}_m) - 0}{\sqrt{\dfrac{\hat{p}_l \hat{q}_l}{n_l} + \dfrac{\hat{p}_m \hat{q}_m}{n_m}}}$$

We need to obtain the estimates $\hat{p}_l$ and $\hat{p}_m$ from Table 14.2.

Consider first the sample of 282 chief executives selected from large firms. We can think of their responses as being classified into one of two categories: (1) six or more suitable successors; or (2) fewer than six suitable successors. The proportion p_l then represents the probability of success in a binomial experiment consisting of $n_l = 282$ trials, where "success" is defined as observing a "six or more" response. The sample proportion of successes used to estimate p_l is obtained from Table 14.2 as follows:

$$\hat{p}_l = \frac{\text{Number of "six or more" responses}}{282}$$

$$= \frac{62}{282} = .220$$

Similarly, p_m is the probability of success in a binomial experiment consisting of $n_m = 300$ trials and is estimated by

$$\hat{p}_m = \frac{\text{Number of "six or more" responses in the sample of 300 chief executives at medium-sized firms}}{300}$$

$$= \frac{33}{300} = .110$$

Substituting these values into the test statistic, we have

$$z = \frac{(\hat{p}_l - \hat{p}_m) - 0}{\sqrt{\dfrac{\hat{p}_l \hat{q}_l}{n_l} + \dfrac{\hat{p}_m \hat{q}_m}{n_m}}} = \frac{.22 - .11}{\sqrt{\dfrac{(.22)(.78)}{282} + \dfrac{(.11)(.89)}{300}}}$$

$$= \frac{.11}{.03} = 3.598$$

The rejection region for this test is given by

$$z > z_\alpha$$

For $\alpha = .01$, $z_\alpha = z_{.01} = 2.33$ (from Table 3, Appendix E). Since the computed value $z = 3.598$ exceeds the critical value 2.33, we reject the null hypothesis and conclude, at $\alpha = .01$, that the proportion of chief executives who believe that six or more in their company are capable of doing their job is greater for those at large firms than for those at medium-sized firms.

We conclude this section with another example of a χ^2 test for differences between the distributions of percentages of categorical responses.

EXAMPLE 14.9 In the past few years, many U.S. farmers have gone on strike to protest that the current prices of farm products, chiefly grains, are less than the cost of production. A common, though controversial, goal of many of the strikes is to induce farmers to reduce production, thereby reducing surpluses and boosting prices. Suppose that a survey of 100 randomly selected U.S. farmers was conducted to determine whether a relationship exists between a farmer's decision to participate in a strike and the farmer's opinion concerning the necessity for a 50% cutback in production. Use the survey results, Table 14.6, to determine if the distributions of percentages of responses corresponding to farmers' opinions about the production cutback are different for those farmers who participate and those who do not participate in the strike. Test at significance level $\alpha = .05$.

TABLE 14.6
Farmer Opinion Poll

| | | PARTICIPATION IN STRIKE | | TOTALS |
		Yes	No	
50% CUTBACK IN PRODUCTION	Favor	20	8	28
	Undecided	37	2	39
	Opposed	22	11	33
TOTALS		79	21	100

Solution Notice that the only difference between the structure of the farmer opinion poll and that of the *WSJ*–Gallup survey is that there are no restrictions on the row or column totals in Table 14.6. In the *WSJ*–Gallup survey, the column totals, i.e., the number of chief executives of large, medium, and small firms, were all determined before the experiment was conducted. (The pollsters predetermined that of the 782 chief executives to be sampled, 282 would be from large firms, 300 from medium-sized firms, and 200 from small firms.) In contrast, the column totals of Table 14.6 were not known until after the farmer opinion poll was conducted. Fortunately, this fact does not affect the analysis. We proceed, then, with the test of hypothesis outlined in the box following Example 14.6 (p. 470).

The null and alternative hypotheses we wish to test are

H_0: The distributions of percentages of responses corresponding to opinion on the cutback in production are identical for striking and nonstriking farmers (i.e., the two directions of classification "participation in strike" and "position on production cutback" are independent).

H_a: The distributions of percentages of responses corresponding to opinion on the cutback in production are different for striking and nonstriking farmers (i.e., the two directions of classification "participation in strike" and "position on production cutback" are dependent).

From the box, we have

Test statistic: $\quad \chi^2 = \sum_{i=1}^{k} \frac{(o_i - e_i)^2}{e_i}$

Rejection region: For $\alpha = .05$ and $(r-1)(c-1) = (3-1)(2-1) = 2$ df, we will reject H_0 if $\chi^2 > \chi^2_{.05}$, where $\chi^2_{.05} = 5.99147$.

The first step in the computation of the test statistic is to calculate the (estimated) expected cell frequencies, $e_i = R_i C_i / n$, according to the box. Proceeding as in Example 14.1, we obtain

$$e_1 = \frac{R_1 C_1}{n} = \frac{(28)(79)}{100} = 22.12$$

$$e_2 = \frac{R_2 C_2}{n} = \frac{(28)(21)}{100} = 5.88$$

and so forth. The observed numbers of responses and the expected counts (in parentheses) are shown in Table 14.7. Substituting the values of Table 14.7 into the expression for χ^2, we obtain

$$\chi^2 = \frac{(20 - 22.12)^2}{22.12} + \frac{(8 - 5.88)^2}{5.88} + \cdots + \frac{(11 - 6.93)^2}{6.93} = 9.915$$

Since the computed value $\chi^2 = 9.915$ exceeds the critical value of 5.99147 and thus falls in the rejection region, we have sufficient evidence, at $\alpha = .05$, to conclude that the distributions of percentages of responses corresponding to farmers' opinions about a 50% cutback in production are different for striking and nonstriking farmers.

TABLE 14.7

Observed and Expected (in Parentheses) Counts for the Farmer Poll

		PARTICIPATION IN STRIKE	
		Yes	No
	Favor	20	8
		(22.12)	(5.88)
50% CUTBACK IN PRODUCTION	Undecided	37	2
		(30.81)	(8.19)
	Opposed	22	11
		(26.07)	(6.93)

EXAMPLE 14.10 Refer to Example 14.9. Find the approximate attained significance level of the test. Interpret your result.

Solution The computed value of the χ^2 test statistic in Exercise 14.9 was found to be $\chi^2_c = 9.915$. Since the null hypothesis of independence will be rejected for large values of χ^2, the attained significance level of the test is given by the probability

$$P(\chi^2 > \chi^2_c) = P(\chi^2 > 9.915)$$

The distribution of the χ^2 statistic in this example is based on 2 df; hence, to find the attained significance level or p-value for the test, we need to search for the value 9.915 in the row corresponding to 2 df in Table 8, Appendix E. This computed value falls between 9.21034, the critical value in the $\chi^2_{.010}$ column, and 10.5966, the critical value in the $\chi^2_{.005}$ column. Thus, the attained significance level of the test falls between the p-values .005 and .01. By convention, we report the larger of these two p-values, namely .01, as the approximate attained significance level of the test. Our interpretation of this value is that we will reject the null hypothesis of independence for any fixed significance level α larger than or equal to .01.

EXERCISES

14.7 Give the degrees of freedom for a test of independence of the two directions of classification in a contingency table with:
a. $r = 2$ rows and $c = 2$ columns
b. $r = 4$ rows and $c = 2$ columns
c. $r = 3$ rows and $c = 3$ columns
d. $r = 3$ rows and $c = 4$ columns

14.8 The results of the employee pension survey, Exercise 14.1, are reproduced in Table 14.8.

OPINION	EMPLOYMENT CATEGORY			TOTALS
	Production	Clerical	Management	
Favor new plan	169	76	26	271
Do not favor new plan	87	35	7	129
TOTALS	256	111	33	400

a. State the null and alternative hypotheses of interest to the company.
b. How many degrees of freedom will the chi-square statistic for this contingency table possess?
c. Use the chi-square statistic to test the hypotheses specified in part a. Use $\alpha = .10$. Do the data provide sufficient evidence to indicate that employees' attitudes toward the new pension plan depend upon their employment category?

14.9 Find the approximate attained significance level for the test in part c of Exercise 14.8. Interpret its value.

14.10 The results of the college business graduate survey, Exercise 14.3, are reproduced in Table 14.9 at the top of p. 476.

a. State the null and alternative hypotheses involved in a test to determine whether the distributions of responses differ among the four types of majors.
b. How many degrees of freedom will the chi-square statistic for this contingency table possess?
c. Use the chi-square statistic to test the hypotheses, part a. Use $\alpha = .05$. Do the data provide sufficient evidence to indicate differences in the patterns of response for the four types of majors?

	COLLEGE MAJOR				TOTALS
	Accounting	Economics	Finance	Management	
High expectations for employment	34	45	43	48	170
Modest expectations for employment	18	27	31	20	96
Poor expectations for employment or no opinion	10	6	10	8	34
TOTALS	62	78	84	76	300

14.11 Find the approximate attained significance level for the test in part c of Exercise 14.10. Interpret its value.

14.12 Refer to Exercise 14.1. Estimate the proportion of all employees who favor the new pension plan. Use a 90% confidence interval and interpret your result. [*Hint:* See Section 8.4.]

14.13 Refer to Exercise 14.1. Do the data provide sufficient evidence to indicate a difference in preference for the new pension plan between production and clerical employees? Test using $\alpha = .10$. [*Hint:* See Section 10.7.]

14.14 Find the attained significance level for the test in Exercise 14.13. Interpret its value.

14.4 Assumptions: Situations for Which the Chi-Square Test Is Appropriate

We have discussed one method of analyzing data from opinion polls, sample surveys, experiments, etc., which allow for more than two categories for a response. However, as with most statistical procedures, the chi-square test for distributional differences in response percentages will be valid only when certain assumptions are satisfied. These assumptions will be met if the underlying probability distribution of the response data has the properties outlined in the box at the top of the next page.

Note that the properties in the box closely resemble those of a binomial experiment. (In fact, when $k = 2$, these are the properties of a binomial experiment.) This underlying probability distribution of the response data is simply an extension of the binomial distribution to include more than two possible outcomes.

Because it is widely used, the chi-square test is also one of the most abused statistical procedures. The user should always be certain that the experiment satisfies the boxed assumptions before proceeding with the test. *In addition, the chi-square test should be avoided when the estimated expected cell counts are small, for it is in this instance that the chi-square probability distribution gives a poor approximation to the sampling distribution of the χ^2 statistic.* As a rule of thumb, an estimated expected

PROPERTIES OF THE UNDERLYING DISTRIBUTION OF RESPONSE DATA
FROM OPINION POLLS

(ASSUMPTIONS: CHI-SQUARE TEST FOR INDEPENDENCE OF TWO
DIRECTIONS OF CLASSIFICATION)

1. The experiment consists of n identical trials.
2. There are k possible outcomes to each trial.
3. The probabilities of the k outcomes, denoted by $p_1, p_2, \ldots, p_k$, remain the same from trial to trial, where $p_1 + p_2 + \cdots + p_k = 1$.
4. The trials are independent.

cell count of at least five will mean that the chi-square distribution can be used to determine an approximate critical value to specify the rejection region.

ADDITIONAL ASSUMPTION FOR THE VALID USE OF THE
CHI-SQUARE TEST

5. The (estimated) expected number of responses for each of the k cells should be at least five.

14.5 Summary

Opinion polls which allow for more than two categories for a response can be analyzed using the technique outlined in this chapter, namely, the chi-square test for independence of two directions of classification. The appropriate test statistic, called the χ^2 statistic, has a sampling distribution which is (approximately) a chi-square probability distribution and measures the amount of disagreement between the observed number of responses and the expected number of responses in each category.

Caution should be exercised to avoid misuse of the χ^2 procedure. The underlying distribution of the response data should have the properties outlined in the box of Section 14.4. Also, the estimated number of responses in any cell should not be too small.

KEY WORDS

Observed cell counts	Chi-square probability distribution
Expected cell counts	Contingency table
Chi-square statistic: χ^2	Independence of two directions of classification

SUPPLEMENTARY
EXERCISES

14.15 For each of the following combinations of α and degrees of freedom (df), find the value of chi-square, χ_α^2, that places an area α in the upper tail of the chi-square distribution. Sketch the chi-square distribution, showing the location of α and χ_α^2 for each part of the exercise.

a. $\alpha = .025$,   df = 8
b. $\alpha = .05$,   df = 5
c. $\alpha = .05$,   df = 10
d. $\alpha = .10$,   df = 3
e. $\alpha = .01$,   df = 2

14.16 Find the values of $\chi_{.10}^2$, $\chi_{.05}^2$, $\chi_{.025}^2$, $\chi_{.01}^2$, and $\chi_{.005}^2$ for df = 2. Draw a rough sketch of a chi-square distribution with 2 df and locate the values of χ^2 along the horizontal axis.

14.17 A bank conducted a survey to compare the attitudes of young married customers (those having recently opened their first bank account) with the attitudes of older, established customers to their new automated teller system. Two hundred customers were randomly selected from each of these categories and asked whether they preferred the automated teller system to the personal service obtained at the bank. A summary of the customers' responses is shown in Table 14.10.

TABLE 14.10
Bank Customers'
Responses,
Exercise 14.17

	NEW CUSTOMER	ESTABLISHED CUSTOMER	TOTALS
Favor the automatic teller	87	65	152
Favor personal service	113	135	248
TOTALS	200	200	400

a.   Do the data provide sufficient evidence to indicate a difference between the proportions of new and established customers who favor use of the automatic teller? Test using $\alpha = .05$. Interpret the results of the test.
b.   Conduct this same test using the method of Section 10.7. Compare your result to that obtained in part a.
c.   When analyzing a contingency table, can you always use the method of Section 10.7 instead of the chi-square test? Explain.

14.18 An insurance company that sells hospitalization policies wants to know whether there is a relationship between the amount of hospitalization coverage a person has and the length of stay in the hospital. Records are selected at random at a large hospital by hospital personnel, and the information on length of stay and hospitalization coverage is given to the insurance company. The results are summarized in Table 14.11. Can you conclude that there is a relationship between length of stay and hospitalization coverage? Use $\alpha = .01$.

TABLE 14.11
Hospital Survey,
Exercise 14.18

		LENGTH OF STAY IN HOSPITAL (DAYS)			
		5 or under	6-10	11-15	Over 15
HOSPITALIZATION COVERAGE OF COSTS	Under 25%	26	30	6	5
	26-50%	21	30	11	7
	51-75%	25	25	45	9
	Over 75%	11	32	17	11

14.19 Several life insurance firms have policies geared toward college students. To get more information about this group of young adults, a major insurance firm interviewed college students to find out the type of life insurance preferred, if any. Table 14.12 presents the results of a survey of 1,600 students.

TABLE 14.12
Student Insurance Survey,
Exercise 14.19

	PREFERENCES		
	Term insurance	Whole-life insurance	No insurance
FEMALES	116	27	676
MALES	215	33	533

a. Is there evidence that the life insurance preference of students depends on sex? Test using $\alpha = .05$.

b. Using a 95% confidence interval, estimate the proportion of female students who prefer no life insurance.

14.20 Along with the technological age comes the problem of workers being replaced by machines. A labor management organization wants to study the problem of workers displaced by automation within three industries. Case reports for 100 workers whose loss of job is directly attributable to technological advances are selected within each industry. For each worker selected, it is determined whether he or she was given another job within the same company, found a job with another company in the same industry, found a job in a new industry, or has been unemployed for longer than 6 months. The results are given in Table 14.13. Does the plight of workers displaced by automation depend on the industry? Test using $\alpha = .01$.

TABLE 14.13
Current Status of Workers
Displaced by Automation,
Exercise 14.20

		SAME COMPANY	NEW COMPANY (SAME INDUSTRY)	NEW INDUSTRY	UNEMPLOYED
INDUSTRY	A	62	11	20	7
	B	45	8	38	9
	C	68	19	8	5

14.21 Refer to Exercise 14.20. Estimate the difference between the proportions of displaced workers who find work in another industry for industries A and C. Use a 95% confidence interval.

14.22   Refer to Exercise 14.20. Find the approximate attained significance level of the test and interpret its value.

CASE STUDY 14.1
Tough-Minded
Corporate
Managers: A
Wall Street
***Journal*–Gallup**
Survey

Speculation about likely heirs to the chief executives of U. S. firms was but one of the items covered by the *Wall Street Journal*–Gallup survey introduced in this chapter. Another area of questioning, the topic of this case study, is the subject of tough-minded managers. *Wall Street Journal* staff reporter Frank Allen writes,*

> Many corporate managers are adopting tougher styles for dealing with their subordinates. Often, their approach amounts to this: Reward good performers, don't reward poor performers, and don't apologize for expecting employees to work hard for the company. Compared with attitudes a few years ago, most chief executives of large and medium-sized U. S. companies believe their managers are more likely now to give big raises to their best performers and small raises or none at all to poor performers. These managers also are more likely to fire incompetent workers. But such tough-mindedness apparently isn't as prevalent in small companies.

Again, Allen bases these observations on the findings of the survey of 782 chief executives (282 from large firms, 300 from medium-sized firms, and 200 from small firms). Two questions put to the corporate bosses in this portion of the study were: "Compared with a few years ago, how likely are managers in the company you head to fire an incompetent worker?" and "Compared with a few years ago, how likely are your managers to give no raises or small raises to poor performers?" The 782 responses were classified by size of firm and degree of increasing tough-mindedness. The numbers of responses in each category (converted from percentages) are given in Tables 14.14 and 14.15.

TABLE 14.14   Q: Compared with a few years ago, how likely are managers in the company you head to fire an incompetent worker?

	SIZE OF FIRM			TOTALS
	Large	Medium	Small	
More likely	166	144	78	388
Less likely	71	114	100	285
No change	39	39	16	94
Don't know	6	3	6	15
TOTALS	282	300	200	782

α.   Using the procedure outlined in this chapter, analyze the data given in Table 14.14. Is there evidence that the distributions of percentages of responses corresponding to the categories "likelihood of firing an incompetent worker" differ among chief executives at large, medium, and small firms? Use $\alpha = .01$.

Wall Street Journal, November 21, 1980. Reprinted by permission. © Dow Jones & Company, Inc. 1980. All rights reserved.

TABLE 14.15   Q: Compared with a few years ago, how likely are your managers
to give no raises or small raises to poor performers?

	SIZE OF FIRM			TOTALS
	Large	Medium	Small	
More likely	195	177	104	476
Less likely	45	72	60	177
No change	34	33	20	87
Don't know	8	18	16	42
TOTALS	282	300	200	782

b. Do the data of Table 14.15 indicate that the two directions of classification "size of firm" and "likelihood of raises to poor performers" are dependent? Test at $\alpha = .05$.

c. Because the χ^2 test for independence is a highly abused statistical tool, we reemphasize that, in practice, the user should always check to see that the required assumptions are satisfied *before* applying the test. For the data of Tables 14.14 and 14.15, carefully check to see that each of the assumptions in the box of Section 14.4 is satisfied.

CASE STUDY 14.2
Testing the
Effectiveness of
an Antiviral
Drug

Vira-A is one of the few existing antiviral drugs on the market. Manufactured by Warner-Lambert Co., it is used primarily to treat herpes virus infections of the eye and brain in adults. However, the *Wall Street Journal* (October 8, 1980) reports that Warner-Lambert will seek approval from the Food and Drug Administration (FDA) to use the drug in treating a rare, but usually fatal, infant illness.

Warner-Lambert claims that Vira-A is useful in treating babies suffering from herpes simplex virus infection. The illness, often transmitted from an infected mother, can leave surviving infants with permanent brain damage. In one portion of a study conducted in 18 health centers throughout the country, the drug was given to 24 babies suffering from the disease. Included in the study was a control group of 19 infected babies who were left untreated. The number of infants surviving the illness in each group is given in Table 14.16.

TABLE 14.16

	SURVIVORS	DEATHS	TOTALS
Treated Group (Drug)	15	9	24
Control Group (No Drug)	5	14	19
TOTALS	20	23	43

a. Use a χ^2 test (if appropriate) to determine whether the distributions of the percentages of survivors and deaths are different for infected babies treated with the drug and those left untreated.

b. You can perform the identical analysis of part a by comparing the binomial proportions p_1 and p_2 using the techniques of Chapter 10, where p_1 is the true survival rate of infected babies treated with the drug, and p_2 is the true survival rate of infected babies who are left untreated. Test the hypothesis that p_1 is larger than p_2, using a significance level of $\alpha = .05$.

c. Based *only* on the results of the survivor-rate study shown in this case study, would you back Warner-Lambert's claim that the drug Vira-A is useful in treating babies suffering from herpes simplex virus infection?

CASE STUDY 14.3
Where Grocery Shoppers Shop— High-, Medium-, or Low-Priced Stores

Refer to the case study on the typology of grocery shoppers, Case Study 11.3. Williams et al. (*Journal of Retailing,* Spring 1978) developed the typology based on customers' involvement with either the price policies or customer service policies of retail food stores. The four types of shoppers are identified as (1) Apathetic shoppers, (2) Convenience shoppers, (3) Involved shoppers, and (4) Price shoppers.

In addition to the research outlined in Case Study 11.3, Williams et al. also investigated the stores and chains where members of each of the four groups shopped. The analysis necessitated that the stores included in the study (10 primary stores or chain supermarkets) be classified into various categories. Since the price level of grocery stores is one attribute which can be used to differentiate among stores, Williams et al. classified each of the ten stores as either high-, medium-, or low-priced. This classification was accomplished with the help of experts and shoppers, who were asked to evaluate each of the stores on the basis of their perception of the prices charged. Since there were differences in how the experts and shoppers ranked the stores, the combined rankings were used. (The combined rank of a store was simply the rank—high, medium, or low—provided by the majority of sources.)

After the ten stores were classified on price level, counts were made to determine what percentage of each grocery shopper group shopped in either high-priced, medium-priced, low-priced, or nonclassifiable stores. The results are shown in Table 14.17.

TABLE 14.17
Count of Group Respondents Shopping at High-, Medium-, Low- and Nonclassifiable-Priced Stores

		GROCERY SHOPPER GROUP				TOTALS
		Apathetic	Convenience	Price	Involved	
STORE PRICE LEVEL	High	17	38	13	6	74
	Medium	19	55	35	19	128
	Low	14	12	20	3	49
	Nonclassifiable	9	20	13	5	47
	TOTALS	59	125	81	33	298

Is there sufficient evidence to indicate that the two classifications "grocery shopper group" and "store price level" are dependent, i.e., are the distributions of percentages of responses corresponding to the "store price level" categories different among the four shopper groups? Use $\alpha = .05$.

REFERENCES

Allen, F. "Bosses getting tougher on firings and raises." *Wall Street Journal,* November 21, 1980, 31.

Allen, F. "Many bosses already have decided who successors will be and why." *Wall Street Journal,* November 18, 1980, 37.

Cochran, W. G., "The χ^2 test of goodness of fit." *Annals of Mathematical Statistics,* 1952, *23,* 315–345.

Johnson, R., & Siskin, B. *Elementary statistics for business.* North Scituate, Mass.: Duxbury, 1980, Chapter 12.

Siegel, S. *Nonparametric statistics for the behavioral sciences.* New York: McGraw-Hill, 1956. Chapter 9.

Summers, G., Peters, W., & Armstrong, C. *Basic statistics in business and economics.* 3d ed. Belmont, Ca.: Wadsworth, 1981. Chapter 12.

"Warner-Lambert finds antiviral drug useful." *Wall Street Journal,* October 8, 1980, 27.

Williams, R. H., Painter, J. J., & Nicholas, H. R. "A policy-oriented typology of grocery shoppers." *Journal of Retailing,* Spring 1978, *54,* 27–41.

Fifteen

Index Numbers and Time Series

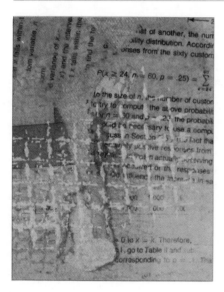

Is romance dead, or just very expensive? According to market strategist Raymond F. DeVoe, it is the latter. DeVoe bases his opinion on a comparison of today's cost of a first date, courtship, and honeymoon with prices and lifestyles in the mid-1950's. Among the items priced were a bottle of Dom Perignon champagne, a carriage ride through New York's Central Park, lunch at an intimate Italian restaurant, the tip to the violinists, and a ticket to the ballet. Can you measure the change in today's overall "cost of loving" relative to 1955 with one summary number? And if so, how should you compute this number? In this chapter we introduce various techniques that are useful in analyzing data that are collected sequentially over time and show how to calculate a measure of the degree of relative change in the time series data. We present the results of DeVoe's "cost of loving" comparison in Case Study 15.2.

Contents:

15.1 Introduction: Index Numbers and Time Series

You often hear from a television newscaster or read in your daily newspaper statements like these: "The Consumer Price Index rose to 174.8 in May, an increase of 2.3 over the previous month;" "The Dow Jones Industrial Average closed at 990 today in heavy trading;" "Inflation rate expected to reach 12% by this time next year;" or, "Chrysler Corporation reports annual net loss of $1 million." Each of these numerical variables—Consumer Price Index (CPI), Dow Jones Average (DJA), inflation rate, and annual profit (or loss) of a firm—characterizes a particular business or economic phenomenon. However, they are all similar in that each is observed sequentially on a regular chronological basis, either daily, monthly, or yearly. Business data that are collected sequentially over time are called *time series.*

DEFINITION 15.1

Numerical data that are calculated, measured, or observed sequentially on a regular chronological basis are called *time series.*

The values of a time series may be plotted on the *y*-axis, with time on the *x*-axis, to provide an easily understood summary of the past and present values of the series. We illustrate this graphical descriptive technique with an example.

EXAMPLE 15.1 The data of Table 15.1 represent the annual oil production of the 13-nation Organization of Petroleum Exporting Countries (OPEC) cartel expressed as a percentage of world total for the years 1973–1980. Identify the time series variable and plot its values.

TABLE 15.1
OPEC Oil Production as a
Percentage of World
Total, Example 15.1

YEAR	OPEC PRODUCTION % of world total
1973	67.8
1974	67.9
1975	65.6
1976	68.0
1977	66.5
1978	64.3
1979	63.2
1980	59.8

Source: *Time*, March 9, 1981.

Solution The time series variable, i.e., the variable that is measured or observed yearly over the time period 1973–1980, is OPEC oil production as a percentage of world total. A

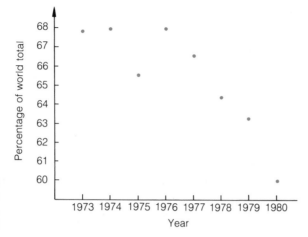

FIGURE 15.1

Graph of OPEC's World Share of Oil Production, 1973–1980

graph of the time series, with OPEC oil production on the *y*-axis and time (years) on the *x*-axis is shown in Figure 15.1.

Very often, time series phenomena are characterized by *index numbers.* Index numbers are used to measure how much a variable changes over time, relative to a *base period.* For example, we may be interested in comparing OPEC's share of world oil production in 1980 with the cartel's share in the base year of 1975 (a year during which OPEC oil prices skyrocketed). An index number will allow us to make this comparison.

DEFINITION 15.2

An *index number* is a number that measures the relative change in a variable over time. Index numbers are often used to characterize time series phenomena.

Index numbers may be computed from a single time series variable (e.g., world share of oil production), or they may be a composite of several time series variables. For example, an index familiar to everyone is the Consumer Price Index (CPI). The CPI, compiled monthly by the U.S. Bureau of Labor, measures overall price changes of a variety of consumer goods (including food, clothing, television equipment, housing, and transportation) relative to the base year of 1967. The CPI combines the prices of approximately 400 items into a single index which is often used to gauge the increase in the cost of living. Two other important business indices which combine or aggregate several variables are the Dow Jones Average (DJA) and the Wholesale Price Index.

In the three sections that follow, we will learn how to compute an index number and how index numbers are used to describe time series phenomena.

15.2 Simple Index Numbers

Suppose that an investor in silver futures wishes to investigate the trend in silver prices for the years 1960–1979. Particularly, the investor desires a measure of how much the price of silver has changed during this period. From our previous discussion, we know that a useful tool for measuring change in a variable over a period of time is an index number. Index numbers based on a single time series variable, such as the price of silver, are called *simple index numbers.* We illustrate the steps necessary for calculating a simple index number in Example 15.2.

EXAMPLE 15.2   The price of silver (dollars per ounce) is shown in Table 15.2 for the years 1960–1979. Calculate the simple index number for the price of silver for this period.

TABLE 15.2
Silver Prices (Dollars per Ounce), Example 15.2

YEAR	PRICE	YEAR	PRICE
1960	$0.914	1970	$1.771
1961	0.924	1971	1.546
1962	1.085	1972	1.684
1963	1.279	1973	2.558
1964	1.293	1974	4.708
1965	1.293	1975	4.419
1966	1.293	1976	4.353
1967	1.550	1977	4.623
1968	2.145	1978	5.401
1969	1.791	1979	11.109

Solution   The first step in calculating an index number is to select the *base period,* i.e., the time period (month, year, etc.), upon which the index is to be based. In this example, since the price of silver is measured each year, we will choose a particular year as a base period. The base period is selected with some purpose in mind since all comparisons in the price of silver will be made relative to the price in the base year. Usually, an economist will choose a year during which price levels are "normal," i.e., undisturbed by unusual or extenuating factors (defining price normality is a complex, if not impossible, problem). Many current business and economic indices, like the CPI, use 1967 as a base period, and for this example, we will also.

After selecting the base period, the next step is to compare the value of the time series variable at two different times, the time being indexed, say t, and the base period, say t_0. In our example, $t_0 = 1967$; thus, we will compare the price of silver in year t with the price of silver in 1967. In general, index numbers are expressed as percentages. We shall use the percentage

$$\frac{\text{Price of silver in year } t}{\text{Price of silver in base year 1967}}(100)$$

as a *simple index* of the price of silver at year t. This percentage will then be computed for all years from 1960 through 1979.

Let us start with the year $t = 1960$. To compute the silver price index for 1960, say, I_{1960}, first form the ratio

$$\frac{\text{Price of silver in 1960}}{\text{Price of silver in 1967}} = \frac{0.914}{1.550} = .59$$

Expressing this ratio as a percentage, we have

$$I_{1960} = \frac{\text{Price of silver in 1960}}{\text{Price of silver in 1967}}(100) = \frac{0.914}{1.550}(100) = 59.0$$

Thus, the silver price index for the year 1960 is 59%.

Similarly, the price index for the year $t = 1961$ is

$$I_{1961} = \frac{\text{Price of silver in 1961}}{\text{Price of silver in 1967}}(100) = \frac{0.924}{1.550}(100) = (0.596)(100) = 59.6$$

Notice that the silver price index for the base year $t_0 = 1967$ is

$$I_{1967} = \frac{\text{Price of silver in 1967}}{\text{Price of silver in 1967}}(100) = \frac{1.550}{1.550}(100) = 100$$

It will always be true that *the index number for the base period will equal 100%.*

STEPS IN CALCULATING A SIMPLE INDEX NUMBER FOR A TIME SERIES

1. Select the base period, i.e., the time t_0 upon which the index is to be based.
2. Letting Y_t represent the value of the time series variable at time t, compute the ratio

$$\frac{Y_t}{Y_{t_0}}$$

3. The simple index I_t for the time series variable at time t is the ratio in step 2 expressed as a percentage, i.e.,

$$I_t = \frac{Y_t}{Y_{t_0}}(100)$$

4. Repeat steps 2 and 3 for each value Y_t of the time series.

The complete silver price index for 1960–1979 is shown in Table 15.3 at the top of p. 490.

EXAMPLE 15.3   Refer to Exercise 15.2. Graph and interpret the complete silver price index for the period 1960–1979.

Solution   The index numbers of Table 15.3 reflect relative price changes in silver from the base year of 1967. Since the indices are percentages, they represent the percent change in

TABLE 15.3
Simple Index for Silver
Prices, Example 15.2

YEAR	INDEX	YEAR	INDEX
1960	59.0	1970	114.3
1961	59.6	1971	99.7
1962	70.0	1972	108.6
1963	82.5	1973	165.0
1964	83.4	1974	303.7
1965	83.4	1975	285.1
1966	83.4	1976	280.8
1967	100.0	1977	298.3
1968	138.4	1978	348.5
1969	115.5	1979	716.7

silver price relative to the base year of 1967. For example, the index for 1960 is 59.0. Thus we say that the price of silver in 1960 was 59% of the price in the base year 1967. Or, equivalently, the 1960 price was 41% *less* than the 1967 price. Now consider the 1976 silver price index of 280.8. This value implies that the price of silver in 1976 was 280.8% of the price in 1967, i.e., the price of silver increased 180.8% relative to the base year of 1967. The remaining index values are interpreted similarly.

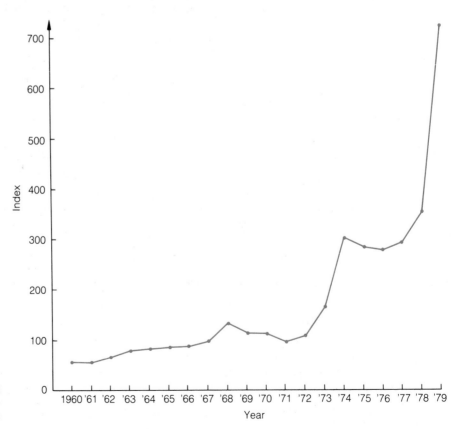

FIGURE 15.2
Graph of Silver Price
Index, Example 15.3

The graph of the silver price index for 1960–1979 is shown in Figure 15.2. Notice that the plot makes it easy to identify the highly inflationary period beginning in 1973 and the extreme jump in silver prices in 1979. This is one of the primary values of simple indices—they make price fluctuations and trends easier to identify and compare.

As previously stated, simple index numbers will always be based on a single time series variable. However, business and economic time series analysts are frequently more interested in examining index numbers for a composite of several variables, like a combination of wholesale prices of manufactured goods. We show how to calculate a *composite index number* in Sections 15.3 and 15.4.

EXERCISES   **15.1**   The Consumer Price Index for the years 1970–1980 (using 1967 as a base period) is shown in the table.

YEAR	CPI	YEAR	CPI
1970	116.3	1976	170.5
1971	121.3	1977	181.5
1972	125.3	1978	195.4
1973	133.3	1979	217.4
1974	147.7	1980	246.8
1975	161.2		

a.   Graph the time series.
b.   Interpret the 1979 CPI value of 217.4. Locate this point on the graph, part a.

15.2   A stock you are interested in buying has had the yearly closing prices shown in the table between 1970 and 1981. Using 1972 as the base period, calculate the simple index for this stock's yearly closing price from 1970–1981. Graph and interpret the index.

YEAR	STOCK PRICE	YEAR	STOCK PRICE
1970	$60.12	1976	$79.66
1971	55.50	1977	68.71
1972	62.00	1978	52.80
1973	68.37	1979	58.44
1974	72.50	1980	73.00
1975	77.13	1981	82.89

15.3   The table at the top of p. 492 lists the average first-of-the-month retail price (excluding taxes) of gasoline for a sample of 55 cities in the United States for each month during the period January 1978 through August 1980.

Retail Gasoline Prices (Cents Per Gallon)

	1978	1979	1980
JANUARY	51.15	68.42	112.70
FEBRUARY	51.06	70.05	119.10
MARCH	51.02	73.25	122.60
APRIL	51.22	77.25	122.90
MAY	51.74	81.41	123.40
JUNE	52.44	87.82	123.60
JULY	53.30	93.09	123.50
AUGUST	53.30	96.84	123.30
SEPTEMBER	54.53	99.03	
OCTOBER	54.69	99.77	
NOVEMBER	55.38	101.10	
DECEMBER	56.37	107.00	

Source: *Standard & Poor's Trade and Securities Statistics* (Annual), New York, Standard & Poor Corp.

a. The retail price of gasoline in January 1973 was 25.31 cents per gallon. Using January 1973 as the base period, calculate and plot the simple index for monthly retail gasoline prices between January 1978 and August 1980.

b. Interpret the value of the index you obtained for July 1980.

15.4 Using the data in the table and 1975 as the base year, compute the simple index for U.S. beer production during the period 1973–1979. Interpret the index values.

YEAR	U.S. BEER PRODUCTION Millions of barrels
1973	148.6
1974	156.2
1975	160.6
1976	163.5
1977	170.5
1978	179.0
1979	183.8

Source: *Standard & Poor's Trade and Securities Statistics* (Annual), New York, Standard & Poor Corp.

15.3 Simple Composite Index Numbers

Index numbers computed from a combination of several time series variables or commodities are called *composite index numbers*. The construction of a composite index requires choosing a method of combining the commodities that compose the index. The simplest method of combining these time series variables is to sum them. A composite index based upon this sum is called a *simple composite index.*

EXAMPLE 15.4 The annual expenditures for new plant and equipment (in billions of dollars) of all manufacturing and mining, transportation, and other United States enterprises for the period 1973–1979 are given in Table 15.4. Calculate the simple composite index for total annual expenditures for new plant and equipment in the United States, using the base period $t_0 = 1975$. Interpret the index.

TABLE 15.4

Annual Expenditures for New Plant and Equipment (Billions of Dollars), Example 15.4

YEAR	MANUFACTURING AND MINING	TRANSPORTATION	ALL OTHER*	TOTAL
1973	40,750	6,030	52,960	99,740
1974	49,190	6,660	56,560	112,410
1975	51,740	7,570	53,470	112,780
1976	56,480	7,450	56,570	120,500
1977	64,660	6,930	64,210	135,800
1978	72,400	8,050	73,370	153,820
1979	84,480	10,120	82,480	177,080

*Includes electrical and gas utilities, trade, service, finance, communications, and construction.

Solution To compute a simple composite index, we first need to sum the values of the respective time series variables—in this example, the sum of the annual expenditures for new plant and equipment for manufacturing and mining, transportation, and other United States enterprises. The sum of these annual expenditures is shown in the column labelled TOTAL in Table 15.4. It is this column of numbers which is used to compute the simple composite index.

Letting Y_t represent the total annual expenditures during year t, the simple composite index (using 1975 as a base) is

$$I_{1973} = \frac{Y_{1973}}{Y_{1975}}(100) = \frac{99,740}{112,780}(100) = 88.4$$

$$I_{1974} = \frac{Y_{1974}}{Y_{1975}}(100) = \frac{112,410}{112,780}(100) = 99.7$$

and so forth. The complete simple composite index for total annual expenditures for new plant and equipment during 1973–1979 is given in Table 15.5.

TABLE 15.5

Simple Composite Index for Total Annual Expenditures for New Plant and Equipment, Example 15.4

YEAR	INDEX
1973	88.4
1974	99.7
1975	100.0
1976	106.8
1977	120.4
1978	136.4
1979	157.0

Our interpretation of the simple composite index is identical to that of the simple index. For example, the 1978 index value of 136.4 represents a 36.4% increase (relative to the base year of 1975) in total annual expenditures for new plant and equipment in the United States.

STEPS IN CALCULATING A SIMPLE COMPOSITE INDEX NUMBER FOR A TIME SERIES

1. Select the base period, i.e., the time t_0 upon which the index is to be based.
2. If the index consists of k time series variables with respective values, Q_{1t}, $Q_{2t}, \ldots, Q_{kt}$ at time t, calculate

   Y_t = Sum of the time series variables at time t

   $= \Sigma Q_{it} = Q_{1t} + Q_{2t} + \cdots + Q_{kt}$

   Y_{t_0} = Sum of the time series variables at time t_0

   $= \Sigma Q_{it_0} = Q_{1t_0} + Q_{2t_0} + \cdots + Q_{kt_0}$

3. Calculate the index,

   $$I_t = \frac{Y_t}{Y_{t_0}}(100)$$

4. Repeat steps 2 and 3 for each value Y_t of the composite time series.

EXERCISES   **15.5**   The Gross National Product (GNP) is the sum of several components. One of these is personal consumption expenditures, which is itself the sum of durable goods, nondurable goods, and services. The amounts spent on durable goods, nondurable goods, and services in the United States for the period 1967–1980 are given in the table.

Personal Consumption Expenditures (Billions of Dollars)

YEAR	DURABLE GOODS	NONDURABLE GOODS	SERVICES
1967	69.6	211.6	208.1
1968	80.0	230.4	225.6
1969	85.5	247.0	247.2
1970	84.9	264.7	269.1
1971	97.1	277.7	293.4
1972	111.2	299.3	322.4
1973	122.9	334.4	351.3
1974	121.9	375.7	388.3
1975	131.7	409.1	432.4
1976	156.5	440.4	482.8
1977	178.8	481.2	549.8
1978	200.3	530.6	619.8
1979	212.3	602.2	696.3
1980	211.6	674.3	785.3

Source: *Survey of Current Business*, U.S. Department of Commerce, Bureau of Economic Analysis.

a. Using 1967 as a base period, construct a simple composite index for personal consumption for the years 1967 through 1980.

b. Graph the entire simple composite index, part a.

c. Interpret the value of the index for 1979.

15.6 The prices of coffee, gasoline, and sugar for the first ten months of 1980 are shown in the table. Using May 1980 as the base period, compute the simple composite price index of the three items for January through October 1980. Interpet your results.

MONTH 1980	PRICE OF COFFEE Per pound	PRICE OF GASOLINE Per gallon	PRICE OF SUGAR Per pound
January	$1.87	$1.13	$.27
February	1.84	1.19	.35
March	2.06	1.23	.31
April	1.94	1.23	.32
May	2.02	1.23	.42
June	2.02	1.24	.44
July	1.81	1.24	.40
August	1.78	1.23	.44
September	1.88	1.22	.47
October	1.90	1.22	.55

Source: *Standard & Poor's Trade and Securities Statistics,* New York, Standard & Poor Corp., January 1981.

15.7 Using 1972 as a base period, calculate the simple composite retail sales index for the years 1970–1978 from the data provided in the table. Interpret the index.

U.S. Retail Sales (Billions of Dollars)

YEAR	CATALOG/SHOWROOMS	DISCOUNT HOUSES*	DEPARTMENT STORES
1970	1.03	22.5	38.3
1971	1.22	25.6	42.8
1972	1.50	28.2	47.2
1973	2.00	31.5	51.5
1974	2.45	34.4	54.1
1975	3.00	38.0	57.4
1976	3.81	44.0	62.9
1977	4.68	47.0	71.5
1978	5.58	50.0	75.6

*Includes food

Source: *Journal of Marketing,* Summer 1979. Published by the American Marketing Association.

15.8 The number of transactions per quarter at a New York City bank are recorded for the years 1979 and 1980 in the table at the top of p. 496. Using Quarter I, 1979 as the base period, construct a simple composite index for the quarterly number of transactions at the New York City bank from 1979 to 1980. Graph the quarterly index and interpret your results.

Bank Transactions (Thousands)

| YEAR | QUARTER | WITHDRAWALS | | DEPOSITS | |
		Savings	Checking	Savings	Checking
1979	I	41.2	561.8	86.7	392.1
	II	50.8	490.0	71.1	424.0
	III	33.9	733.7	75.3	630.5
	IV	27.5	811.9	66.5	557.6
1980	I	20.8	852.5	70.9	610.4
	II	32.0	814.0	89.2	731.1
	III	39.4	966.1	107.5	500.3
	IV	18.5	1,045.5	93.4	872.2

15.4 Weighted Composite Index Numbers

Although it is easy to compute, a simple composite index has a major drawback. Time series variables with large values exert a greater influence on the index than those with smaller values. For example, with a simple composite price index, commodities with high prices tend to dominate the index more than those with low prices. The index therefore depends on the quantity of each commodity that is included. A more meaningful measure of composite time series is the *weighted composite index.* The time series values are weighted before being summed, where the weights are multipliers chosen to reflect the relative importance of each value.

In order to calculate a weighted composite index, we first need to decide on the appropriate weighting factors. That is, we need to determine how much weight to attach to each variable in the composite before summing their values. These weights should reflect the relative importance of each time series variable. Typically, the weight assigned to a commodity in a composite price index is the quantity of the item consumed. The calculations necessary for constructing a weighted composite price index using this weighting scheme are given in the following example.

EXAMPLE 15.5   Consider the information on the prices of dairy products for the years 1976–1980, as provided in Table 15.6. Using 1976 as a base period, calculate a weighted composite price index for the dairy products if the weights are the total quantities of the products consumed in 1976.

TABLE 15.6
Dairy Prices (Dollars),
Example 15.5

| YEAR | AVERAGE PRICE PER UNIT | | |
	Cheese, pounds	Milk, gallons	Butter, pounds
1976	$1.45	$1.60	$.70
1977	1.49	1.61	.80
1978	1.55	1.67	.83
1979	1.63	1.72	.91
1980	1.75	1.80	1.03

TOTAL QUANTITY CONSUMED (billions)

1976	2.6	47.6	3.1

Solution   The first step in calculating a weighted composite price index is to multiply the commodity prices at time t by the corresponding weights. In this example, we need to multiply the average price per unit of cheese, milk, and butter for each year by the corresponding quantity of the commodity consumed during 1976. The three products are then summed to give the value of the composite time series which is to be indexed. These preliminary calculations are shown in Table 15.7.

TABLE 15.7

Preliminary Calculations for Weighted Composite Index, Example 15.5

| YEAR | WEIGHTED PRICE = (PRICE) × (QUANTITY) | | | SUM OF WEIGHTED PRICES (VALUE TO BE INDEXED) |
	Cheese	Milk	Butter	
1976	(1.45)(2.6) = 3.77	(1.60)(47.6) = 76.16	(.70)(3.1) = 2.17	3.77 + 76.16 + 2.17 = 82.10
1977	(1.49)(2.6) = 3.87	(1.61)(47.6) = 76.64	(.80)(3.1) = 2.48	3.87 + 76.64 + 2.48 = 82.99
1978	(1.55)(2.6) = 4.03	(1.67)(47.6) = 79.49	(.83)(3.1) = 2.57	4.03 + 79.49 + 2.57 = 86.09
1979	(1.63)(2.6) = 4.24	(1.72)(47.6) = 81.87	(.91)(3.1) = 2.82	4.24 + 81.87 + 2.82 = 88.93
1980	(1.75)(2.6) = 4.55	(1.80)(47.6) = 85.68	(1.03)(3.1) = 3.19	4.55 + 85.68 + 3.19 = 93.42

After computing the weighted sums (the rightmost column of Table 15.7), the index is calculated in the usual manner. Letting Y_t represent the weighted sum in year t, we have (using 1976 as the base):

$$I_{1976} = \frac{Y_{1976}}{Y_{1976}}(100) = \frac{82.10}{82.10}(100) = 100$$

$$I_{1977} = \frac{Y_{1977}}{Y_{1976}}(100) = \frac{82.99}{82.10}(100) = 101.1$$

$$I_{1978} = \frac{Y_{1978}}{Y_{1976}}(100) = \frac{86.09}{82.10}(100) = 104.9$$

and so forth. The complete weighted composite dairy products price index is given in Table 15.8.

TABLE 15.8

Weighted Composite Index for Dairy (Cheese, Milk, Butter) Prices, Example 15.5

YEAR	INDEX
1976	100.0
1977	101.1
1978	104.9
1979	108.3
1980	113.8

Notice from Table 15.7 that the quantity of milk consumed in 1976 is much greater than the quantity consumed for either of the other two dairy products. By using consumption as a weighting factor, we have attached greater importance to milk price changes in our composite index of dairy prices. In effect, we are saying that the price of milk affects the consumer more heavily than either cheese or butter prices (based on total consumption) and we wish our composite price index to reflect this.

Again, our interpretation of the index numbers in Table 15.8 is analogous with those of the previous sections. For example, the 1980 index of 113.8 indicates that, using 1976 consumption as a weighting factor, the composite price of the three dairy products (milk, cheese, and butter) is 13.8% higher than the composite price in the base year of 1976.

STEPS IN CALCULATING A WEIGHTED COMPOSITE INDEX NUMBER FOR A TIME SERIES

1. Select the base period, i.e., the time t_0 upon which the index is to be based.
2. Choose the weights to be attached to each of the time series variables in the composite. (The weights should reflect the relative importance of each variable. For a price index, the weights are usually the quantities consumed of the respective variables.)
3. If the index consists of k time series variables with respective values Q_{1t}, $Q_{2t}, \ldots, Q_{kt}$ at time t, and the respective weights are denoted by W_1, W_2, $\ldots, W_k$, then calculate

   Y_t = Weighted sum of the time series variables at time t

   $$= \Sigma W_i Q_{it} = W_1 Q_{1t} + W_2 Q_{2t} + \cdots + W_k Q_{kt}$$

   Y_{t_0} = Weighted sum of the time series variables at time t_0

   $$= \Sigma W_i Q_{it_0} = W_1 Q_{1t_0} + W_2 Q_{2t_0} + \cdots + W_k Q_{kt_0}$$

4. Calculate the index,

   $$I_t = \frac{Y_t}{Y_{t_0}}(100)$$

5. Repeat steps 3 and 4 for each value Y_t in the composite time series.

Note that a composite index which uses the original base period weights for the calculations, as in Example 15.5, is called a *Laspeyres index.* A second method of computing a weighted composite index, called a *Paasche index,* uses weights computed for the period at which the index is being calculated. Still a third method employs weights for a "neutral" period, i.e., a period which is neither the base period nor the period being indexed. We will not detail the specifics of the calculations for the latter two composite indices but will refer you to the references at the end of this chapter.

We conclude this section with a warning. There is little doubt that index numbers provide useful descriptive summaries of the degree of relative change in business and economic activity. However, there is a danger of using index numbers for more than they are intended. For example, the Consumer Price Index (CPI) measures how prices of a market basket of goods, *purchased by moderate-income, urban Americans,* have changed. But the CPI is frequently used to gauge the cost of living for *all* Americans. While the CPI does reflect the cost of living to some degree, *all* Americans certainly do not purchase the same goods in the same quantities as urban Americans with moderate incomes. Thus, using the CPI to measure the cost of living of, say, low-income, inner-city families would be improper.

WARNING

Do *not* use index numbers for more than they are intended. In particular, it is inappropriate to generalize the results of an index or use a single index to predict future business or economic events.

EXERCISES   **15.9**   The accompanying table contains the average wholesale prices of three grain products for the period 1975–1979. Using 1975 as the base, construct a yearly weighted composite price index for the grain products if the weights are total production of the items in 1975. Interpret the index.

Average Wholesale Price (Dollars per Bushel)

YEAR	CORN	OATS	WHEAT
1975	2.88	1.67	4.84
1976	2.56	1.74	3.87
1977	2.22	1.34	2.88
1978	2.39	1.37	3.33
1979	2.42	1.57	3.73

TOTAL PRODUCTION (millions of bushels)

1975	5,797.0	657.6	2,135.0

Source: *Survey of Current Business,* U.S. Department of Commerce, Bureau of Economic Analysis.

15.10   Consider the information on the annual amount of life insurance in force in the United States, as provided in the table at the top of p. 500. Calculate a weighted composite index for total life insurance in force for the years 1972–1978 with 1972 as the base period and number of life insurance purchases in 1972 as a weighting factor. Interpret your results.

Life Insurance in Force in the U.S. (Billions of Dollars)

YEAR	ORDINARY POLICIES	GROUP CERTIFICATES	INDUSTRIAL POLICIES
1972	853.9	640.7	40.0
1973	928.2	708.3	40.6
1974	1,009.0	827.0	39.4
1975	1,083.4	904.7	39.4
1976	1,177.7	1,002.6	39.2
1977	1,289.3	1,115.0	39.0
1978	1,425.1	1,244.0	38.1

TOTAL NUMBER OF PURCHASES (millions)

1972	11.8	6.7	8.1

Source: *Life Insurance Fact Book,* 1979. Published by the American Council of Life Insurance.

15.11 From the information provided in the table, construct a weighted composite index (using 1975 as the base year) for U.S. gasoline sales revenue during the period 1975–1979. Use as weights the amount of 1975 gasoline sales to residential, commercial, industrial, and other customers, respectively.

Revenue from Gasoline Sales to Customers (Millions of Dollars)

YEAR	RESIDENTIAL	COMMERCIAL	INDUSTRIAL	OTHER
1975	8,445	3,303	6,745	608
1976	10,076	4,103	8,615	840
1977	11,541	4,980	11,385	397
1978	12,939	5,696	13,065	451
1979	14,769	6,609	17,495	506

TOTAL GASOLINE SALES (trillion BTU's)

1975	4,991	2,387	6,837	648

Source: *Survey of Current Business,* U.S. Department of Commerce, Bureau of Economic Analysis.

15.5 Time Series Components

Researchers often approach the problem of describing the nature of a time series by identifying four kinds of change, or variation, in the time series values. These four components are commonly known as: (1) *Secular trend;* (2) *Cyclical fluctuation;* (3) *Seasonal variation;* and (4) *Irregular (or residual) variation.*

EXAMPLE 15.6 What do each of the four time series components attempt to explain?

Solution The four components of a time series are most easily identified and explained pictorially. Figure 15.3 shows four typical time series plots, each of which identifies one of the four kinds of change.

Figure 15.3(a) shows a *secular trend* in the time series values. The secular component describes the tendency of the value of the variable to increase or decrease over a long period of time. Thus, this type of change or variation is also known as the *long-term trend.* In Figure 15.3(a), the long-term trend is of an increasing nature. However, this does not imply that the time series has always moved upward from month to month and year to year. You can see that the series fluctuates, but that the trend has been an increasing one over that period of time.

The *cyclical fluctuation* in a time series, as shown in Figure 15.3(b), is the wavelike or oscillating pattern (up and down fluctuations) about the secular trend that is attributable to business and economic conditions at the time. These wavelike fluctuations are sometimes called *business cycles.* During a period of general economic expansion, the business cycle lies above the secular trend, while during a recession, when business activity is likely to slump, the cycle lies below the secular trend. You can see that the cyclical fluctuation does not follow any definite trend, but moves rather unpredictably.

The *seasonal variation* in a time series describes the fluctuations that recur during specific portions of each year (e.g., monthly or seasonally). In Figure 15.3(c), you can see that the pattern of change in the time series within a year tends to be repeated from year to year.

The final component, the *irregular (or residual) variation,* is what remains after the secular, cyclical, and seasonal components have been removed. This component is not systematic and may be attributable to unpredictable influences such as wars, hurricanes, presidential assassination, and randomness of human actions. Figure 15.3(d) illustrates the characteristics of irregular variation.

FIGURE 15.3   Illustrating the Four Components of a Time Series, Example 15.6

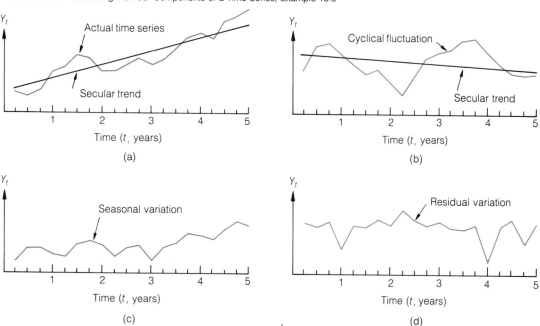

Various descriptive and inferential techniques are available for identifying and characterizing time series components. Since one goal of a business analyst is to detect the secular or long-term trend for purposes of projecting into the future, we present two methods of identifying the secular component of a time series in Sections 15.6 and 15.7.

15.6 Detecting a Long-Term Trend: Moving Average Method

One of the most popular techniques for identifying and characterizing time series components is the *moving average method.* A moving average, M_t, at time t is formed by averaging the time series values over adjacent time periods. Moving averages aid in identifying the secular trend of a time series because the averaging tends to modify the effect of short-term (cyclical or seasonal) variation. That is, a plot of the moving averages yields a "smooth" time series curve which clearly depicts the long-term trend. We illustrate with an example.

EXAMPLE 15.7   The quarterly power loads for a utility company located in a southern part of the United States are given in Table 15.9, with a graph in Figure 15.4. Use the moving average method to identify the long-term trend of the quarterly power load time series.

TABLE 15.9
Quarterly Power Loads, Example 15.7

YEAR	QUARTER	TIME t	POWER LOAD Y_t, megawatts
1977	I	1	103.5
	II	2	94.7
	III	3	118.6
	IV	4	109.3
1978	I	5	126.1
	II	6	116.0
	III	7	141.2
	IV	8	131.6
1979	I	9	144.5
	II	10	137.1
	III	11	159.0
	IV	12	149.5
1980	I	13	166.1
	II	14	152.5
	III	15	178.2
	IV	16	169.0

Solution   Figure 15.4 shows the pronounced seasonal variation, i.e., the fluctuation that recurs from year to year, in the quarterly time series. The quarterly power loads tend to be highest in the summer months (quarter III) with another smaller peak in the winter months (quarter I), and lowest during the spring and fall (quarters II and IV). In order to clearly identify the long-term trend of the series, we need to average, or "smooth out,"

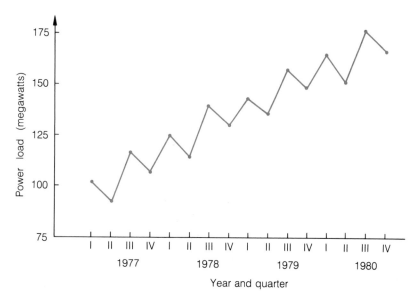

FIGURE 15.4
Graph of Quarterly Power
Loads, Table 15.9

these seasonal fluctuations. We will apply the moving average method for this purpose.

The first step in calculating a moving average for quarterly data is to sum the observed time series values Y_t—in this example, quarterly power loads—for the four quarters during the initial year 1977. Summing the values from Table 15.9, we have

$$Y_1 + Y_2 + Y_3 + Y_4 = 103.5 + 94.7 + 118.6 + 109.3$$
$$= 426.1$$

This sum is called a **4 point moving total,** which we denote by the symbol S_t. It is customary to use a subscript t to represent the time period at the midpoint of the four quarters in the total. Since for this sum, the midpoint is between $t = 2$ and $t = 3$, we will use the conventional procedure of "dropping it down one line" to $t = 3$. Thus, our first 4 point moving total is $S_3 = 426.1$.

We find the next moving total by eliminating the first quantity in the sum, $Y_1 = 103.5$, and adding the next value in the time series sequence, $Y_5 = 126.1$. This enables us to keep four quarters in the total of adjacent time periods. Thus, we have

$$S_4 = Y_2 + Y_3 + Y_4 + Y_5 = 94.7 + 118.6 + 109.3 + 126.1 = 448.7$$

Continuing this process of "moving" the 4 point total over the time series until we have included the last value, we find

$$S_5 = Y_3 + Y_4 + Y_5 + Y_6 \quad = 118.6 + 109.3 + 126.1 + 116.0 = 470.0$$

$$S_6 = Y_4 + Y_5 + Y_6 + Y_7 \quad = 109.3 + 126.1 + 116.0 + 141.2 = 492.6$$

$$\vdots \qquad\qquad \vdots \qquad\qquad \vdots \qquad\qquad \vdots$$

$$S_{15} = Y_{13} + Y_{14} + Y_{15} + Y_{16} = 166.1 + 152.5 + 178.2 + 169.0 = 665.8$$

The complete set of 4 point moving totals is given in the appropriate column of Table 15.10. Notice that three data points will be "lost" in forming the moving totals.

YEAR	QUARTER	TIME t	POWER LOAD Y_t	4 POINT MOVING TOTAL S_t	4 POINT MOVING AVERAGE M_t
1977	I	1	103.5	—	—
	II	2	94.7	—	—
	III	3	118.6	426.1	106.5
	IV	4	109.3	448.7	112.2
1978	I	5	126.1	470.0	117.5
	II	6	116.0	492.6	123.2
	III	7	141.2	514.9	128.7
	IV	8	131.6	533.3	133.3
1979	I	9	144.5	554.4	138.6
	II	10	137.1	572.2	143.1
	III	11	159.0	590.1	147.5
	IV	12	149.5	611.7	152.9
1980	I	13	166.1	627.1	156.8
	II	14	152.5	646.3	161.6
	III	15	178.2	665.8	166.5
	IV	16	169.0	—	—

After calculating the 4 point moving totals, the second step is to determine the *4 point moving average*, denoted by M_t, by dividing each of the moving totals by 4. For example, the first three values of the 4 point moving average for the quarterly power load data are:

$$M_3 = \frac{Y_1 + Y_2 + Y_3 + Y_4}{4} = \frac{S_3}{4} = \frac{426.1}{4} = 106.5$$

$$M_4 = \frac{Y_2 + Y_3 + Y_4 + Y_5}{4} = \frac{S_4}{4} = \frac{448.7}{4} = 112.2$$

$$M_5 = \frac{Y_3 + Y_4 + Y_5 + Y_6}{4} = \frac{S_5}{4} = \frac{470.0}{4} = 117.5$$

All of the 4 point moving averages are given in the appropriate column of Table 15.10.

We have graphed both the original power load time series and the 4 point moving average in Figure 15.5. Notice that the moving average has "smoothed" the time series, i.e., the averaging has modified the effects of the short-term or seasonal variation. The plot of the 4 point moving average clearly depicts the secular (long-term) trend component of the time series.

In addition to identifying a long-term trend, moving averages provide us with a measure of the seasonal effects in a time series. In this example, the difference between the observed power load Y_t and the 4 point moving average M_t for each

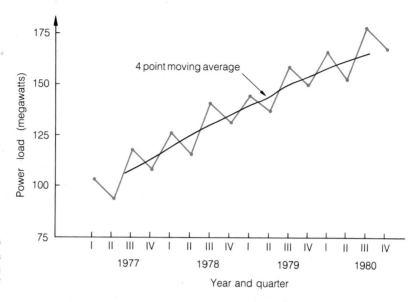

FIGURE 15.5
Quarterly Power Loads
and 4 Point Moving
Average, Example 15.7

DETECTING A LONG-TERM TREND: THE MOVING AVERAGE METHOD (MOVING AVERAGES FOR QUARTERLY DATA)

1. Calculate a 4 point moving total, S_t, by summing the time series values over 4 adjacent time periods. For example, if Y_t denotes the value of the series at time t, then find

$$S_3 = Y_1 + Y_2 + Y_3 + Y_4$$
$$S_4 = Y_2 + Y_3 + Y_4 + Y_5$$
$$S_5 = Y_3 + Y_4 + Y_5 + Y_6$$

and so on.

2. Compute the 4 point moving average, M_t, by dividing the corresponding moving total by 4, i.e.,

$$M_3 = \frac{Y_1 + Y_2 + Y_3 + Y_4}{4} = \frac{S_3}{4}$$

$$M_4 = \frac{Y_2 + Y_3 + Y_4 + Y_5}{4} = \frac{S_4}{4}$$

$$M_5 = \frac{Y_3 + Y_4 + Y_5 + Y_6}{4} = \frac{S_5}{4}$$

and so on.

3. Graph the moving average M_t on the y-axis with time t on the x-axis. This plot should reveal a "smooth" curve which identifies the long-term trend of the time series.

quarter indicates the size and direction of the seasonal effect for that quarter. The pronounced seasonal effect shown in Figure 15.4 (primarily attributable to temperature differences) is clearly indicated by the positive and negative differences between Y_t and M_t. In quarters I and III, the difference $(Y_t - M_t)$ is always positive, while in quarters II and IV, the difference $(Y_t - M_t)$ is always negative.

Note that the moving average method is not restricted to 4 points. For example, you may wish to calculate a 7 point moving average for daily data, a 12 point moving average for monthly data, or a 5 point moving average for yearly data. Although the choice of the number of points is arbitrary, you should search for the number that yields a smooth series, but is not so large that many points at the end of the series are "lost."

In addition to moving averages, there are several other methods of smoothing a time series to identify the various long-term and short-term effects. Consult the references at the end of the chapter if you desire information on these procedures. In the following section, we employ a familiar technique—simple linear regression—to detect long-term series trends.

EXERCISES   **15.12**   The quarterly number of new housing starts in the United States from Winter 1977 through Spring 1980 are recorded in the accompanying table.

YEAR	QUARTER	HOUSING STARTS Thousands of dwellings
1977	I	367.4
	II	581.1
	III	561.5
	IV	477.1
1978	I	292.3
	II	511.3
	III	459.8
	IV	387.0
1979	I	297.0
	II	523.2
	III	434.6
	IV	351.1
1980	I	218.7
	II	291.1

Source: *Standard & Poor's Trade and Securities Statistics* (Annual), New York, Standard & Poor Corp.

a.   Plot the quarterly time series. Can you detect a long-term trend? Can you detect any seasonal variation?

b. Calculate the 4 point moving average for the quarterly housing starts.
c. Graph the 4 point moving average on the same set of axes you used for part a. Is the long-term trend more evident? What effects has the moving average method removed or "smoothed"?

15.13   Standard & Poor's 500 Stock Composite Average (S&P 500) is a stock market index. Like the Dow Jones Industrial Average (DJA), it is an indicator of stock market activity. The accompanying table contains end-of-quarter values of the S&P 500 for the years 1972 through 1979.

YEAR	QUARTER	S&P 500	YEAR	QUARTER	S&P 500
1972	I	107.20	1976	I	102.77
	II	107.14		II	104.28
	III	110.55		III	105.24
	IV	118.06		IV	107.46
1973	I	111.52	1977	I	98.42
	II	104.26		II	100.48
	III	108.43		III	96.53
	IV	97.55		IV	95.10
1974	I	93.98	1978	I	89.21
	II	86.00		II	95.53
	III	63.54		III	102.54
	IV	68.56		IV	96.11
1975	I	83.36	1979	I	101.59
	II	95.19		II	102.91
	III	83.87		III	109.32
	IV	98.19		IV	107.94

Source: *Standard & Poor's Trade and Securities Statistics* (Annual), New York, Standard & Poor Corp.

a. Calculate a 4 point moving average for the quarterly stock market index.
b. Plot the quarterly index and the 4 point moving average on the same graph. Can you identify the secular trend of the time series? Can you identify any seasonal variations about the secular trend?

15.14   Calculate a 3 point moving average for the gold price time series recorded in the table. Plot the gold prices and the 3 point moving average on the same graph. Can you detect the long-term trend and any cyclical patterns in the time series? [*Hint:*   In order to construct a 3 point moving average, follow the instructions given in the box of Section 15.6, but use "3 points" instead of "4 points." Since the number of points is odd, you will not need to "drop" the moving total S_t and moving average M_t "down one line." The subscript t actually does represent the time period at the midpoint of the 3 values in the total or average.]

YEAR	PRICE OF GOLD Dollars per troy ounce
1970	36.41
1971	41.25
1972	58.61
1973	97.81
1974	159.70
1975	161.40
1976	124.80
1977	148.30
1978	193.50
1979	307.80
1980	606.01

Source: *Standard & Poor's Trade and Securities Statistics* (Annual), New York, Standard & Poor Corp.

15.15 The Federal Reserve Board (FRB) Index of Quarterly Output (with base year 1967) is an industrial production index that is often used as a leading indicator of business activity. Using the values of this index for 1965–1980 given in the table, calculate and graph:

a. A 3 point moving average
b. A 5 point moving average
c. A 7 point moving average
d. Which moving average clearly depicts the long-term trend of the index?
e. For the moving average chosen in part d, examine the difference between Y_t, the index at time t, and M_t, the moving average. Note that the larger the difference $(Y_t - M_t)$, the greater the cyclical effect at time t. Do there appear to be any cyclical effects?

YEAR	FRB INDEX	YEAR	FRB INDEX
1965	89.2	1973	125.6
1966	97.9	1974	124.8
1967	100.0	1975	117.8
1968	105.7	1976	129.8
1969	110.7	1977	138.2
1970	106.6	1978	146.1
1971	106.8	1979	152.2
1972	115.2	1980	138.8

Source: *Survey of Current Business*, U.S. Department of Commerce, Bureau of Economic Analysis.

15.7 Detecting a Long-Term Trend: Method of Least Squares

An alternative way of describing the long-term trend of a time series is to fit a line to the sample data, using the method of least squares discussed in Chapter 12. That is, if a plot of the sample data reveals a linear trend, we may hypothesize that the secular component of the time series can be explained by the straight-line model

$$E(Y_t) = \beta_0 + \beta_1 t$$

where Y_t is the time series value at time t.

EXAMPLE 15.8 Refer to the data on the quarterly power loads, Table 15.9. Since the graph of the data, Figure 15.4, reveals a linearly increasing long-term trend, the straight-line model

$$E(Y_t) = \beta_0 + \beta_1 t$$

seems plausible for the secular trend. Use the data of Table 15.9 to fit the model by the method of least squares. Plot the least squares line. Is the straight-line model appropriate for describing the long-term trend?

Solution The SAS printout of the simple linear regression for the data of Table 15.9 is given in Figure 15.6. The printout identifies the least squares estimates of the y-intercept β_0 and slope β_1 as

$$\hat{\beta}_0 = 95.6625$$
$$\hat{\beta}_1 = 4.8993$$

Thus, the least squares line which explains the secular trend for the quarterly power load is

$$\hat{Y}_t = \hat{\beta}_0 + \hat{\beta}_1 t = 95.6625 + 4.8993t$$

A graph of the power load data and the least squares line is shown in Figure 15.7 (p. 510). You can see that the power loads fluctuate about the line (seasonal variation), but the overall long-term trend is clearly depicted.

The fact that the least squares line provides a good description of the secular trend is supported by the information given in the SAS printout, Figure 15.6. A test of H_0: $\beta_1 = 0$ is highly significant (p-value = .0001) and $r^2 = .894$.

```
DEPENDENT VARIABLE: Y (POWER LOAD)

SOURCE                    DF      SUM OF SQUARES        MEAN SQUARE       F VALUE

MODEL                      1       8160.95018382      8160.95018382       118.21

ERROR                     14        966.55919118        69.03994223       PR > F

CORRECTED TOTAL           15       9127.50937500                          0.0001


R-SQUARE            C.V.                STD DEV              Y MEAN

0.894105          6.0515              8.30902775          137.30625000
```

FIGURE 15.6
SAS Printout for Least Squares Fit (Straight Line) to Y_t = Power Load, Example 15.8

```
                                        T FOR H0:     PR > |T|       STD ERROR OF
PARAMETER            ESTIMATE        PARAMETER=0                      ESTIMATE

INTERCEPT          ¯95.66250000          21.95          0.0001        4.35729091
T                    4.89926471          10.87          0.0001        0.45062030
```

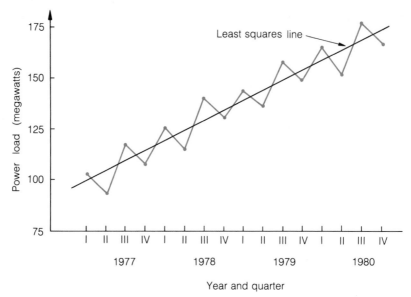

FIGURE 15.7
Plot of Quarterly Power
Loads and Least Squares
Line, Example 15.8

In addition to identifying the secular (long-term) trend of a time series, the method of least squares, like the moving average method, can be used to describe the cyclical or seasonal (short-term) fluctuations. This is accomplished by comparing the observed time series value, Y_t, to the least squares predicted value, $\hat{Y}_t$. The ratio of the two values gives a relative measure of the short-term variation in the series at time t. The mathematical details for computing this measure, often called the **percent of trend,** can be obtained from the references at the end of this chapter.

The least squares method of identifying the secular trend in a time series is not limited to fitting a straight line to the data. Many time series possess a long-term trend best described by curves. For these time series, the quadratic or other curvilinear multiple regression models described in Chapter 13 more adequately describe the change in the variable over a long period of time. Once we have selected a model to identify the secular trend and have developed the trend equation, we can use it to predict future values of the time series. [*Caution:*   There is always a risk in using the least squares model for prediction outside the experimental range of the independent variables—a problem which will occur when predicting the future. We discuss the risks associated with predicting future values of time series in greater detail in Section 15.8.]

EXERCISES   **15.16**   In the table shown at the top of the next page, a farmers' marketing cooperative recorded the volume of wheat harvested by its members for the period 1971–1980. The cooperative is interested in detecting the long-term linear trend of the wheat harvest.

a.   Graph the wheat harvest time series.

b.   Propose a model for the long-term linear trend of the time series.

YEAR	TIME t	WHEAT HARVESTED BY COOPERATIVE MEMBERS Y_t, thousands of bushels
1971	1	75
1972	2	78
1973	3	82
1974	4	82
1975	5	84
1976	6	85
1977	7	87
1978	8	91
1979	9	92
1980	10	92

c. Fit the model, using the method of least squares. Plot the least squares line on the graph of part a. Can you identify the long-term trend?

d. How well does the linear model describe the long-term trend? [*Hint:* Check the value of r^2.]

15.17 A realtor working in a large city wishes to identify the secular trend in the weekly number of one-family houses sold by her firm. For the past 15 weeks she has collected data on her firm's home sales, as shown in the table.

WEEK t	HOMES SOLD Y_t	WEEK t	HOMES SOLD Y_t	WEEK t	HOMES SOLD Y_t
1	59	6	137	11	88
2	73	7	106	12	75
3	70	8	122	13	62
4	82	9	93	14	44
5	115	10	86	15	45

a. Plot the time series. Is there visual evidence of a quadratic trend?

b. The realtor hypothesizes the model $E(Y_t) = \beta_0 + \beta_1 t + \beta_2 t^2$ for the secular trend of the weekly time series. Fit the model to the data, using the method of least squares (see Chapter 13).

c. Plot the least squares model on the graph of part a. How well does the quadratic model describe the secular trend?

15.18 Information on intercity passenger traffic since 1940 is given in the table at the top of p. 512. The data are recorded as percentages of total passenger-miles traveled.

a. Let Y_t be the percentage of total passenger-miles at time t for a particular mode of transportation. Consider the linear model $E(Y_t) = \beta_0 + \beta_1 t$. Which modes of transportation do you think have a secular trend adequately represented by this model?

YEAR	TIME	RAILROADS	BUSES	AIR CARRIERS	INLAND WATERWAYS
1940	1	67.1	26.5	2.8	3.6
1945	2	74.3	21.4	2.7	1.6
1950	3	46.3	37.7	14.3	1.7
1955	4	36.5	32.4	28.9	2.2
1960	5	28.6	25.7	42.1	3.6
1965	6	17.9	24.2	54.7	3.2
1970	7	7.3	16.9	73.1	2.7
1975	8	5.8	14.2	77.7	2.3

Source: Interstate Commerce Commission, Civil Aeronautics Board.

b. Fit the model in part a to the data for each mode of transportation, using the method of least squares.

c. Plot the data and the least squares model for each mode of transportation. Which models adequately describe the secular trend of percentage of total passenger-miles traveled? Does this agree with your answer to part a?

15.8 Predicting the Future: Forecasting

In many practical applications of time series to business problems, the objective is to *forecast* (predict) some *future value or values* of the series. For example, a firm may be interested in forecasting its sales revenue for each of the next 5 years; an investor may want to use past and present values of the DJA to forecast its value 6 months from now; or a community wishing to avoid a critical water shortage may want to forecast its water usage for the next 12 months. Since an inaccurate forecast may have dire consequences to the firm, investor, or community in the examples above, some measure of the forecast's reliability is required.

EXAMPLE 15.9 In Sections 15.6 and 15.7, we considered two methods for detecting the long-term trend in a time series: the moving average method and the method of least squares. Suppose the utility company in Example 15.7 wishes to forecast its quarterly power loads for the next year based upon the secular trend identified by these methods. The company will make its forecast in one of the following ways:

1. Graphically extend the 4 point moving average of the power loads depicted in Figure 15.5 into the future time periods, $t = 17, 18, 19, 20$, to obtain the predicted power loads for quarters I, II, III, and IV of 1981.

2. Use the least squares line of Figure 15.7,

$$\hat{Y}_t = 95.6625 + 4.8993t$$

to predict quarterly power loads for $t = 17, 18, 19,$ and 20 (quarters I, II, III, and IV of 1981) with 95% prediction intervals.

Which of the two forecasting methods would you recommend the utility company use? Why?

Solution First, consider the forecast obtained by a graphical extension of the 4 point moving average of the power loads into future time periods. From your knowledge of inferential statistics (Chapters 8–14), do you think that the utility company can assess the reliability of this forecast? The reliability of a forecast obtained by graphically projecting a moving average into future time periods is *unknown,* which makes its use for decision-making purposes very risky! In contrast, the 95% prediction intervals obtained from the least squares linear regression (see Section 12.8) do provide the utility company with a measure of the reliability of the forecasts. The forecasts of quarterly power loads and the corresponding 95% prediction intervals are shown in Figure 15.8, a portion of the SAS printout not previously shown. For example, for $t = 17$ (quarter I, 1981), we have

$$\hat{Y}_{17} = 178.95$$

with the corresponding 95% prediction interval (158.8, 199.1). Thus, the utility company can forecast, with 95% confidence, the power load for quarter I of 1981 to fall between 158.8 megawatts and 199.1 megawatts.

FIGURE 15.8
SAS Printout for Power
Load Forecasts,
Example 15.9

T	PREDICTED VALUE	LOWER 95% CL INDIVIDUAL	UPPER 95% CL INDIVIDUAL
17	178.95000000	158.82721041	199.07278959
18	183.84926471	163.31294992	204.38557949
19	188.74852941	167.76229673	209.73476210
20	193.64779412	172.17753856	215.11804967

Example 15.9 illustrates an important point. To assess the reliability of forecasts, we must first construct a time series model. However, there are some problems associated with forecasting time series using the least squares straight-line model. These are discussed in the following example.

EXAMPLE 15.10 Refer to Example 15.9. What are the problems associated with forecasting quarterly power loads using a least squares straight-line model?

Solution There are basically three problems associated with using the least squares line as a forecasting tool. First, we are using the least squares prediction equation to forecast values outside the region of observation of the independent variable, t. For example, in Example 15.9, we are forecasting for values of t between 17 and 20 (the four quarters of 1981), even though the observed power loads are for t-values between 1 and 16. We noted with warning boxes in both Chapters 12 and 13 that it is risky to use a least squares regression model for prediction outside the range of the observed data because some unusual change, economic or political, may make the model inappropriate for predicting future events. Because forecasting always involves predictions about future values of a time series, we must keep the risk in mind and recognize the dangers of this type of prediction.

The second problem involves the choice of the appropriate time series model. Although the straight-line model may adequately describe the long-term trend of the quarterly power loads, we have not built any seasonal or cyclical effects into the model. This omission could possibly lead to large forecasting errors because the model does not anticipate seasonal variation due to quarterly temperature differences. Fortunately, the forecaster often has more control over this second problem. Various models have been developed for describing the cyclical and seasonal fluctuations, as well as the secular trend of a time series. These time series models are often written as follows:

$$Y_t = \text{(Secular trend)} + \text{(Cyclical effect)} + \text{(Seasonal effect)}$$
$$+ \text{(Residual variation, i.e., Random error)}$$

Each of the components of the model may include more than a single term and often include trigonometric terms. For example,

$$\text{(Secular trend)} = \beta_0 + \beta_1 t + \beta_2 t^2$$

and

$$\text{(Seasonal effect)} = \beta_3 \cos\left(\frac{2\pi}{12}t\right) + \beta_4 \sin\left(\frac{2\pi}{12}t\right)$$

Thus, time series models can become quite complex. In practice, these models have proven to be reliable business forecasting tools. (Because of its complexity, time series modeling is beyond the scope of this text. The interested reader should consult the references at the end of this chapter.)

The third, and final problem associated with using the least squares straight-line model (or any other least squares model) for predicting future time series values lies with the standard assumptions made about the random error component of the regression model (Section 12.10). We assume that the errors have mean zero, constant variance, normal probability distributions, and are *independent.* The latter assumption is often violated in time series models which exhibit short-term trends. As an illustration, refer to the plot of the power load data, Figure 15.7. Notice that the power loads for the winter and summer months (quarters I and III) lie above the least squares trend line, while the power loads for the spring and fall months (quarters II and IV) fall below the line, for each year shown. Since the variation in the power loads is systematic, the implication is that the errors are correlated. Violation of this standard regression assumption could lead to unreliable forecasts.

Time series models have also been developed specifically for the purpose of making forecasts when the errors are known to be correlated. These models include an *autoregressive term* for the correlated errors that result from cyclical, seasonal, or other short-term effects. This autoregressive term is often incorporated into the residual component of the time series model, i.e.,

$$\text{(Residual variation)} = \text{Autoregressive (correlated) errors}$$

Again, because of their complexity, we omit a discussion of autocorrelated errors and autoregressive time series models in this text (see the references at the end of this chapter). However, we point out that these models are powerful time series forecasting tools.

The purpose of this final section has been twofold. First, we wished to warn you of the danger in using graphical techniques for forecasting purposes. These procedures lack a measure of reliability for the forecasts and, consequently, should be used with care. Secondly, we wished to introduce you to time series modeling, a useful and powerful tool for business forecasting. The successful construction of time series models requires much experience, and like regression modeling, entire texts are devoted to the subject.

WARNING

Many oversimplified forecasting methods have been proposed. They usually consist of graphical extensions of a secular trend or seasonal pattern to future time periods. There are usually no measures of reliability for these forecasts, and thus the risk associated with making decisions based on them cannot be assessed. These forecasting techniques should be used with care.

EXERCISES

15.19 Use the least squares straight-line model fit in Exercise 15.16 to forecast the volume of wheat harvested in 1981 by the members of the farmers' marketing cooperative. If you have access to a linear regression computer routine, obtain a 95% prediction interval. What are the dangers associated with this type of forecast?

15.20 Use the least squares quadratic model fit in Exercise 15.17 to forecast the number of one-family houses sold by the realtor's firm during week 17. If you have access to a multiple regression computer routine, obtain a 90% prediction interval. Comment on the reliability of this forecast.

15.21 Refer to your answer to part c of Exercise 15.18. Use these least squares prediction equations to forecast the percentage of total passenger-miles to be traveled for the respective modes of transportation in 1985. If you have access to a linear regression computer routine, obtain 95% prediction intervals. What are the risks associated with this forecast procedure?

15.9 Summary

Many practical business problems require analysis of data that are collected sequentially over time. Various methods are available for describing time series. These methods usually require the calculation of index numbers—simple, simple composite, or weighted composite index numbers—which characterize a time series phenomenon by measuring how much the time series variable changes over time.

Other descriptive techniques attempt to identify the four components of a time series—secular trend, cyclical fluctuation, seasonal variation, and irregular variation. These include the moving average method and the method of least squares.

Probabilistic time series models are used to predict future values of a time series. The reliability of these forecasts can be assessed by constructing prediction intervals about the forecast value.

The business forecaster should be careful to distinguish between graphical and inferential time series techniques. If a graphical technique is used to project future values of the series, no assessment of forecast reliability is possible.

KEY WORDS

Time series	Seasonal variation
Index numbers	Irregular variation
Simple index	Moving average method
Simple composite index	Method of least squares
Weighted composite index	Forecasting
Secular trend	Time series models
Cyclical fluctuation	

SUPPLEMENTARY EXERCISES

15.22   List and describe the four components of a time series.

15.23   Why is the choice of the base period important when computing an index?

15.24   What is the difference between a simple composite index and a weighted composite index?

15.25   What are the problems with forecasting time series using a graphical method?

15.26   What are the problems with forecasting time series using a least squares model?

15.27   The United States Balance of International Payments is an indicator of the country's status in the world economy. A table of its values from 1965 to 1979 is given here.

Balance on Goods and Services (Millions of Dollars)

YEAR	BALANCE	YEAR	BALANCE	YEAR	BALANCE
1965	7,140	1970	2,966	1975	16,316
1966	4,552	1971	−237	1976	9,603
1967	4,380	1972	−5,930	1977	−9,464
1968	1,620	1973	4,177	1978	−9,204
1969	1,020	1974	3,574	1979	4,878

Source: *Survey of Current Business,* U.S. Department of Commerce, Bureau of Economic Analysis.

a. Calculate and graph a simple international payments index, using 1970 as a base year.

b. Do the four negative values of the index have a meaningful interpretation? Explain.

15.28 Refer to Exercise 15.27. Calculate a 3 point moving average for the United States Balance of International Payments and graph it. Is there any apparent secular trend?

15.29 The number of business failures in the United States is given in the table by type of firm for the years 1975–1979. Using 1975 as the base period, construct a simple composite industrial and commercial failures index. Interpret the index.

Industrial and Commercial Failures

YEAR	COMMERCIAL SERVICE	CONSTRUCTION	MANUFACTURING AND MINING	RETAIL TRADE	WHOLESALE TRADE
1975	1,637	2,262	1,645	4,799	1,089
1976	1,331	1,770	1,360	4,139	1,028
1977	1,041	1,463	1,122	3,406	887
1978	773	1,204	1,013	2,889	740
1979	930	1,378	1,165	3,183	908

Source: *Survey of Current Business*, U.S. Department of Commerce, Bureau of Economic Analysis.

15.30 The average monthly retail prices of cotton and wool were recorded for a one-year period beginning November 1979 and ending October 1980. This monthly time series appears in the table.

Cotton and Wool Retail Prices (Cents per Pound)

YEAR	MONTH	COTTON	WOOL	YEAR	MONTH	COTTON	WOOL
1979	November	61.0	2.33	1980	May	59.6	2.25
	December	59.9	2.33		June	56.3	2.33
1980	January	59.8	2.38		July	72.4	2.45
	February	62.9	2.53		August	74.0	2.51
	March	60.9	2.56		September	82.3	2.53
	April	58.5	2.31		October	75.3	2.53

Source: *Survey of Current Business*, U.S. Department of Commerce, Bureau of Economic Analysis.

a. Calculate a simple composite price index for the textile products using January 1980 as the base period. Plot the index values.

b. Consumption figures for the two products in the base period of January 1980 are as follows: COTTON 241 million pounds; WOOL 8.5 million pounds. Using consumption as a weighting factor and January 1980 as a base, compute a weighted composite price index for the products.

c. Plot the weighted composite index on the same graph as the simple composite index. Compare the two indices. Which index do you think better characterizes the increase in price of the textile products? Explain.

15.31 The accompanying table lists the yearly outlays for the Federal Space Program (in millions of dollars) from 1960 through 1979.

YEAR	OUTLAY	YEAR	OUTLAY
1960	888	1970	5453
1961	1468	1971	4999
1962	2387	1972	4772
1963	4079	1973	4719
1964	5900	1974	4854
1965	6854	1975	4891
1966	7689	1976	5314
1967	7208	1977	5983
1968	6647	1978	6484
1969	6331	1979	7374

Source: *Statistical Abstract of the United States,* U.S. Department of Commerce, Bureau of the Census, 1979.

a. Plot the time series.
b. Calculate moving averages for 3 points, 5 points, and 7 points. Plot each moving average series on the same graph. Which moving average best characterizes the long-term trend of outlays for the Space Program?
c. Graphically extend the moving average you chose in part b to forecast the outlay for the Space Program in 1982. Comment on the reliability of this forecast. Is there a better forecasting method available? Explain.

15.32 The data of Exercise 15.4 are reproduced in the table. Suppose you are interested in forecasting U.S. beer production in 1980. Since a plot of the time series Y_t reveals a linearly increasing trend, you hypothesize the model

$$E(Y_t) = \beta_0 + \beta_1 t$$

for the secular trend.

YEAR	TIME t	U.S. BEER PRODUCTION Y_t, millions of barrels
1973	1	148.6
1974	2	156.2
1975	3	160.6
1976	4	163.5
1977	5	170.5
1978	6	179.0
1979	7	183.8

a. Fit the model to the data using the method of least squares.
b. Plot the least squares model from part a and extend the line to forecast Y_{1980}, the U.S. beer production (in millions of barrels) in 1980. How reliable do you think this forecast is?

c. If you have access to a linear regression computer routine, obtain a 95% prediction interval for Y_{1980}, the U.S. beer production in 1980. Why is this forecast preferred to that of part b?

15.33 The accompanying table lists total monthly retail sales in the United States for the period, January 1976 through September 1980. Calculate and plot a 12 point moving average for the total retail sales time series. Can you detect the secular trend? Does there appear to be a seasonal pattern?

Total Retail Sales (Billions of Dollars)

	1976	1977	1978	1979	1980
JANUARY	46.79	48.83	53.21	61.87	69.45
FEBRUARY	45.08	48.85	53.61	60.65	69.73
MARCH	51.28	57.20	64.76	72.19	74.94
APRIL	53.31	58.63	63.83	70.54	74.21
MAY	53.30	58.89	67.95	74.78	78.22
JUNE	54.40	60.03	69.05	74.81	76.44
JULY	55.19	59.84	66.56	72.08	78.94
AUGUST	53.62	60.70	69.10	77.80	80.79
SEPTEMBER	52.13	58.34	66.22	72.63	76.54
OCTOBER	54.73	60.84	68.62	76.39	
NOVEMBER	55.36	61.98	71.30	78.91	
DECEMBER	67.31	74.22	84.60	91.46	

Source: *Standard & Poor's Trade and Securities Statistics* (Annual), New York, Standard & Poor Corp.

15.34 Commercial banks, finance companies, credit unions, and retail outlets are the principal issuers of consumer installment credit. Since commercial banks and credit unions typically offer lower interest rates, they are referred to as *primary lenders.* Finance companies and retail outlets are referred to as *secondary lenders.* Data on the consumer installment credit market share of primary and secondary lenders are given in the table.

Consumer Installment Credit Market Share, by Holder

YEAR	TIME	PRIMARY LENDERS			SECONDARY LENDERS		
	t	Commercial banks	Credit unions	Total	Finance companies	Retail outlets	Total
1945	0	30.2%	4.1%	34.3%	36.9%	27.9%	64.8%
1950	5	39.4	4.0	43.4	36.1	19.7	55.8
1955	10	36.7	5.8	42.5	40.9	15.5	56.4
1960	15	38.9	9.2	48.1	35.4	14.7	50.1
1965	20	40.6	10.3	50.9	34.0	13.7	47.7
1966	21	40.4	10.6	51.0	33.6	13.9	47.5
1967	22	40.4	11.1	51.5	33.0	14.1	47.1
1968	23	41.1	11.3	52.4	32.4	13.8	46.2
1969	24	41.1	11.8	52.9	32.3	13.4	45.7
1970	25	41.4	12.4	53.8	30.8	13.9	44.7

Source: *Journal of Consumer Affairs*, Winter 1973.

α.   Use the method of least squares to model the secular trend in the total market share of primary lenders. [*Hint:* Consider a quadratic model.]

b.   Plot the least squares model on a scattergram of the data.

c.   Use your least squares model to forecast the market share of primary lenders for the years 1985 and 1990 ($t = 40$ and $t = 45$). If you have access to a multiple regression computer routine, obtain 95% prediction intervals. Discuss some of the pitfalls of this forecasting technique.

15.35   The monthly number of mortgage applications for new home construction processed by the Federal Housing Administration (FHA) for the period 1978–1980 is recorded in the table.

FHA Net Applications (Thousands)

	1978	1979	1980
JANUARY	7.2	9.4	8.2
FEBRUARY	7.2	8.3	8.9
MARCH	10.4	12.7	9.9
APRIL	11.0	12.2	10.0
MAY	12.0	15.2	12.3
JUNE	9.7	11.6	10.9
JULY	10.9	11.5	15.4
AUGUST	11.1	13.4	15.6
SEPTEMBER	8.6	11.3	16.5
OCTOBER	11.6	12.3	12.9
NOVEMBER	11.1	10.0	9.6
DECEMBER	8.0	5.9	—

Source: *Survey of Current Business*, U.S. Department of Commerce, Bureau of Economic Analysis.

α.   Graph the monthly time series.

b.   Construct a simple index for the monthly number of mortgage applications using January 1979 as the base period. Interpret the index.

c.   Calculate a 12 point moving average for the monthly time series. Plot the 12 point moving average on the graph, part a. Can you identify the long-term trend of the series? Is any seasonal component evident?

d.   What technique would you use to forecast FHA mortgage applications for the first six months of 1981?

15.36   One indicator of industrial activity is new plant and equipment expenditures. (We discussed a simple composite index of new plant and equipment expenditures for the years 1973–1979 in Example 15.4.) Quarterly figures for new plant and equipment expenditures from 1977 to 1980 are given in the table.

α.   Calculate a 4 point moving average for the quarterly expenditures.

b.   Plot the time series values and the 4 point moving average on the same graph. Describe the secular trend revealed by your graph. Can you detect any seasonal variation in the quarterly time series?

YEAR	TIME	QUARTER	EXPENDITURES
		t	Y_t, trillions of dollars
1977	1	I	29.20
	2	II	33.72
	3	III	34.82
	4	IV	38.06
1978	5	I	32.35
	6	II	37.89
	7	III	38.67
	8	IV	44.91
1979	9	I	37.41
	10	II	43.69
	11	III	44.68
	12	IV	51.30
1980	13	I	42.82
	14	II	48.81
	15	III	47.66
	16	IV	53.21

Source: *Survey of Current Business*, U.S. Department of Commerce, Bureau of Economic Analysis.

15.37 The number of accidental deaths in the United States for each month of 1977 and 1978 is recorded in the table. The National Safety Council would like to model Y_t, total deaths per month, as a function of time, t, for forecasting purposes. Since the number of accidental deaths seems to peak during the summer months and decline during the winter months, the following seasonal model (with trigonometric terms) is proposed:

$$E(Y_t) = \beta_0 + \beta_1 t + \beta_2\left(\cos\frac{2\pi}{12}t\right) + \beta_3\left(\sin\frac{2\pi}{12}t\right)$$

	MONTH	TIME	TOTAL DEATHS		MONTH	TIME	TOTAL DEATHS
		t	Y_t			t	Y_t
1977	January	1	7,792	1978	January	13	7,600
	February	2	6,957		February	14	6,800
	March	3	7,726		March	15	7,550
	April	4	8,106		April	16	7,950
	May	5	8,890		May	17	9,000
	June	6	9,299		June	18	9,600
	July	7	10,625		July	19	10,500
	August	8	9,302		August	20	9,750
	September	9	8,314		September	21	9,000
	October	10	8,850		October	22	9,100
	November	11	8,265		November	23	8,800
	December	12	8,796		December	24	8,850

Source: National Safety Council.

a. If you have access to a multiple regression computer package, fit the proposed time series model to the data.
b. From the output, write the least squares prediction equation for Y_t.
c. Forecast Y_{61}, the number of accidental deaths during January 1982, with a 95% prediction interval.

CASE STUDY 15.1
Analyzing the Standard & Poor's Stock Index

Consider the daily closing prices (index) and daily changes of Standard & Poor's stock for the period 1975–1979 listed in Appendix C. Suppose that you wish to analyze the daily time series using the methods outlined in this chapter. (Because the data set is so voluminous, you will need access to a computer to carry out the computations required for this case study.)

a. Plot the daily closing prices. Can you identify the secular, seasonal, cyclical, and irregular components of the time series?
b. Use the moving average method to clearly identify the secular or long-term trend of the daily time series. [*Hint:* You will need to try several different numbers of "points" in order to obtain a smooth series. Begin by constructing a 7 point moving average.]
c. The moving average of part b will also help you to identify any seasonal or cyclical fluctuations. Compare the actual time series value, Y_t, to the moving average, M_t, by forming the ratio

$$\frac{Y_t}{M_t}(100)$$

for each value of t in the daily series. The larger this ratio, the greater the seasonal or cyclical variation.
d. Suppose you wish to forecast the daily Standard & Poor's stock index for January of 1980. Suggest a forecasting technique which provides a measure of reliability for the predictions.

CASE STUDY 15.2
The Cost of Loving, Cost of Living It Up, and Trivia Indices

Throughout this chapter we have made reference to the Consumer Price Index. Although the CPI is designed to measure change over time in the prices of a fixed market basket of goods and services bought by consumers to meet personal living needs, it is often used to measure the "pain" of inflation for the average American family. However, the Gainesville *Sun* (March 15, 1981) reported that one financial expert strongly objects to using the CPI in this manner. "If the CPI accurately measures inflation for an average American family, it's purely an accident," says Raymond F. DeVoe, Jr. DeVoe, writes the *Sun,* believes that "the index doesn't reflect changing lifestyles or spending patterns, nor does it cover a lot of products—some of them admittedly frivolous—that people spend money on." One version of the CPI is based on the 1972–73 spending habits of Americans, and, according to DeVoe, those habits have changed.

In an effort "to show how anachronistic the CPI was," DeVoe, who writes a weekly newsletter on the stockmarket for Bruns Nordeman Rea & Co., devised three indices of his own—the "Cost of Loving," the "Cost of Living It Up," and the "Trivia." The Cost of Loving Index compares today's cost of a first date, courtship, and honeymoon with 1955 prices and lifestyles. "Among the specifics of seduction," reports the *Sun,* "were: a bottle of Dom Perignon champagne, $12 in 1965 vs. $65 today; a carriage ride through Central Park, $10 vs. $40; lunch at an intimate Italian restaurant, $3.75 vs. $19.75 per person; and a ticket to the ballet, $3.60 vs. $20. The tip to the violinists, DeVoe estimates, would have to be $5 today, up from 50¢ in 1955." The Cost of Loving Index has risen 420% since 1955, compared to a 228% increase in the CPI during this same period.

DeVoe's Cost of Living It Up Index measures the price of products bought by what he calls "upwardly mobile" people "trying to demonstrate . . . that they're wealthy." This index includes items such as a Brooks Brothers suit ($165 in 1974 and $360 today); dinner for one at La Grenouille, one of New York's most expensive restaurants ($18.75 vs. $40); and an hour of tennis at the Wall Street Racquet Club ($15 vs. $40). Just as with the Cost of Loving, the Cost of Living It Up has risen faster than the CPI; from 1974 to 1980 the Cost of Living It Up Index rose 133.5%, while the CPI rose only 75%.

The *Sun's* account of how DeVoe created his first index, a Trivia Index, in 1971, is as follows: "He had a hangover and went out to seek relief with a milk shake. It cost him 75¢. He was astonished and set out to measure the little things that 'nibble away'—things like an ice cream cone or a shoe shine. From 1974 to 1980, alone, DeVoe said, the Trivia Index has risen by 120 percent."

DeVoe is the first to admit that his calculations are not very scientific and are often based "just on personal experience." Nevertheless, his Cost of Loving, Cost of Living It Up and Trivia Indices are quite interesting and informative.

Devise an index of your own, one that you feel would accurately reflect price changes of some economic phenomenon of interest to you (e.g., a "discomfort" index, a "leisure time" index, a "hassle" factor). Your index may be a simple, simple composite, or a weighted composite index.

CASE STUDY 15.3
Forecasting TV Ratings of New Programs

Practitioners working in the advertising industry, be they employed by advertising agencies, marketing departments of corporations, or television networks, have long been aware of the general economic impact of television ratings as well as the often personal impact television ratings can have on their own organizations and careers. Consequently, there has been considerable research performed by organizations within the advertising industry that attempts to identify and understand the variables influencing total television viewing so as to improve the ability of these organizations to make reasonably accurate predictions of future ratings.

The above quotation appeared in the introductory paragraph of an article on forecasting television ratings by Dennis Gensch and Paul Shaman.* Gensch and Shaman note that the research performed within the advertising industry "is usually viewed as proprietary, and there is little information available . . . on prediction of television ratings." The purpose of their paper is "to put into the public domain a predictive methodology based on the techniques of time-series analysis."

---

*D. Gensch and P. Shaman. "Predicting TV ratings." *Journal of Advertising Research,* August 1980, *20*, 85–91. Reprinted from the *Journal of Advertising Research* © Copyright 1980, by the Advertising Research Foundation.

The data considered for Gensch and Shaman's research consisted of estimates of total U.S. network television audience size as reported in the Nielsen Television Index for the period spanning November 7, 1966, to August 24, 1969 (a total of 1,022 days or 146 weeks). Since a plot of the time series "indicated a seasonal pattern containing a stretch of high viewing over the fall, winter, and early spring months that was of longer duration than the stretch of low viewing during the late spring and summer months," the following daily time series model was proposed:

$$Y_t = \beta_0 + \beta_1 t + \sum_{j=1}^{6} \left\{ \gamma_j \cos\left(\frac{2\pi j}{365} t\right) + \delta_j \sin\left(\frac{2\pi j}{365} t\right) \right\}$$

$$+ \sum_{j=7}^{9} \left\{ \gamma_j \cos\left[\frac{2\pi(j-6)}{7} t\right] + \delta_j \sin\left[\frac{2\pi(j-6)}{7} t\right] \right\} + \text{Random error}$$

where Y_t is the estimate of total network viewing on day t. The $(\beta_0 + \beta_1 t)$ term attempts to explain any long-term linear trend of the series, and the trigonometric terms measure the annual, seasonal, and weekly fluctuations. The model was fit to the data and R^2-values at each of the six prime-time viewing periods (7:30 PM, 8:00 PM, 8:30 PM, 9:00 PM, 9:30 PM, and 10:00 PM) were calculated. The results are given in the table.

R^2-Values Resulting
from Time Series Model

HOUR	R^2-VALUE
7:30	.9215
8:00	.9188
8:30	.9107
9:00	.9080
9:30	.8684
10:00	.7835

Interpret these R^2-values. (Gensch and Shaman note that the R^2-values are very high for the early prime-time hours (the peak viewing period) and tend to taper off during the late prime-time hours. They suggest that this decreasing R^2, in combination with a decrease in intensity of the annual component evident from plots of the time series, "indicates that the audience, presumably mostly adults, at later time periods is not as seasonal in its viewing pattern as the early-evening audience.")

Gensch and Shaman checked the adequacy of the trigonometric regression model using well known time series methods and found that the "model accounts for a high proportion of the variation of the daily and weekly data." Furthermore, "it produces very good estimates of the total network viewing by day of year and time of day [which] provide us with basic bench marks of total network viewing." Gensch and Shaman use these "bench-mark" estimates to forecast ratings of individual television programs (see the box).

LIST OF NEW PROGRAMS

SET	NEW PROGRAM	NETWORK	DAY OF WEEK	TIME SLOT	DATE OF INTRODUCTION
1	Coronet Blue	CBS	Monday	10:00–11:00	5/29/67
2	Away We Go	CBS	Saturday	7:30–8:30	6/3/67
3	Malibu U	ABC	Friday	8:30–9:00	7/21/67
4	Custer	ABC	Wednesday	7:30–8:30	9/6/67
5	The Second Hundred Years	ABC	Wednesday	8:30–9:00	9/6/67
6	Off to See the Wizard	ABC	Friday	7:30–8:30	9/8/67
7	Gentle Ben	CBS	Sunday	7:30–8:00	9/10/67
8	The Mothers-in-Law	NBC	Sunday	8:30–9:00	9/10/67
9	Maya	NBC	Saturday	7:30–8:30	9/16/67
10	Rowan & Martin's Laugh-In	NBC	Monday	8:00–9:00	1/22/68
11	Dream House	ABC	Wednesday	8:30–9:00	3/27/68
12	The Prisoner	CBS	Saturday	7:30–8:30	6/1/68
13	The Champions	NBC	Monday	8:00–9:00	6/10/68
14	Showcase '68	NBC	Tuesday	8:00–8:30	6/11/68
15	Julia	NBC	Tuesday	8:30–9:00	9/17/68
16	Adam 12	NBC	Saturday	7:30–8:00	9/21/68
17	The Ghost and Mrs. Muir	NBC	Saturday	8:30–9:00	9/21/68
18	This Is Tom Jones	ABC	Friday	7:30–8:30	2/7/69
19	The Generation Gap	ABC	Friday	8:30–9:00	2/7/69
20	Animal World	CBS	Thursday	7:30–8:00	5/1/69
21	The John Davidson Show	ABC	Friday	8:00–9:00	5/30/69

Since Gensch and Shaman's predictions do not take into account program content or quality, it was decided to compare their forecasts with those of an "expert" television rater. With the aid of the library research department at the National Broadcasting Company (NBC), they found a set of predictions made by Stuart Gray for 1965–1966 television programs. "Gray's predictions," they write, "reflect an expert's opinion of the viewing trends, wear-out factors, and competitive interactions of the various program sets." However, Gray's forecasts differ from Gensch and Shaman's in that Gray predicted the average rating of a television program for an entire three-month period (October, November, December), while Gensch and Shaman's predictions were daily. We would expect the distribution of the errors of prediction for an average to be less variable than for a simple daily prediction. Surprisingly, the time series forecasts compared reasonably well with the estimates based on Gray's expert opinion.

In conclusion, Gensch and Shaman write: "The purpose of presenting the experienced practitioner's predictions is not to declare that any particular statistical approach provides better predictions than an expert in the field. . . . Rather, the point of comparison is to emphasize that bench-mark estimates derived from time-series models that do not use expert opinion or content analysis do provide reasonable predictions. . . . [We] believe that when the [time series] methodology illustrated in this paper is supplemented with the practitioner's insights on demographics, wear-out factors, bridging situations, and program content, it will be possible to improve upon both the predictive [television rating] results illustrated in this paper and upon the accuracy of the current proprietary models of practitioners."

REFERENCES

Barr, A., Goodnight, J., Sall, J., Blair, W., & Chilko, D. *SAS user's guide.* 1979 ed. SAS Institute, P. O. Box 10066, Raleigh, N. C. 27605.

Box, G. E. P., & Jenkins, G. M. *Time series analysis, forecasting and control.* San Francisco: Holden-Day, 1970.

" 'Cost of loving' robs dates of romance." Gainesville *Sun,* March 15, 1981.

Daniel, W., & Terrell, J. *Business statistics: Basic concepts and methodology.* 2d ed. Boston: Houghton Mifflin, 1979. Chapter 13.

Gensch, D., & Shaman, P. "Predicting TV ratings." *Journal of Advertising Research,* August 1980, *20,* 85–91.

Levine, R. I. *Statistics for management.* Englewood Cliffs, N. J.: Prentice-Hall, 1978. Chapters 13 and 14.

Mendenhall, W., & McClave, J. T. *A second course in business statistics: Regression analysis.* San Francisco: Dellen, 1981. Chapter 15.

Summers, G., Peters, W., & Armstrong, C. *Basic statistics in business and economics.* 3d ed. Belmont, Ca.: Wadsworth, 1981. Chapters 16 and 17.

Sixteen

Elements of Decision Analysis

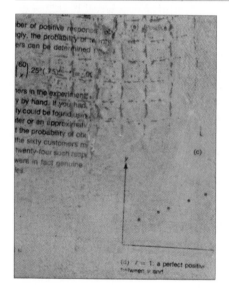

To drill or not to drill? That is the question. C. U. Ikoku writes about the decision-making problems that face the oil industry, decisions that must be made in the face of many uncertainties, an uncertain cost, an uncertain outcome (which may range from a dry hole, a moderate yield, to a high-producing well), and uncertain governmental regulatory action. Given a number of available actions and an array of possible outcomes, which should you choose? This chapter discusses the basic concepts of decision analysis. In addition, you will learn more about Dr. Ikoku and his oil exploration decision problems in Case Studies 16.1 and 16.2.

Contents:

16.1   Introduction: Decision-Making under Uncertainty

What do business managers, corporate chief executives, stock brokers, rock concert producers, advertisers, real estate investors, public relations directors, purchasing agents, and blackjack players have in common? Each, of course, is associated with some type of business (to some blackjack players, gambling *is* their business). However, we will focus on the fact that each of the above can be classified as a *decision-maker.* A chief executive may have the responsibility of determining whether his or her firm should expand its sales region to include the southwestern part of the United States; a stock broker may need to decide whether his or her client should buy silver futures in the commodities market or invest in American Telephone and Telegraph (AT&T) in the stock market; a rock concert producer might have to decide in May whether to hold a July concert outdoors in a stadium or indoors in a civic center; a blackjack player may need to determine whether to "hit" or "stay" with 15 points; etc.

How do these business analysts make their decisions? Many decisions in business are made intuitively, of course. However, when the decision to be made is a crucial one, one upon which a great deal depends (a firm's public image, a lifetime of savings, etc.), it is very helpful to have a systematic, logical decision-making procedure to follow. In this chapter, we consider a systematic approach to solving decision problems, called *decision analysis.* Decision analysis differs from the hypothesis-testing procedure of Chapters 9 and 10. In an hypothesis test, we made no attempt to assess the (monetary) gains or losses associated with falsely rejecting (Type I error) or falsely accepting (Type II error) the null hypothesis. But most business decisions depend upon how the decision-maker assesses the relative gains or losses associated with the possible courses of action. Decision analysis provides for such an assessment and, in addition, forces the decision-maker to consider carefully and logically all possible courses of action and the outcomes that could result from each.

Realistically, however, the chief executive, stock broker, rock concert producer, or blackjack player cannot expect to know with certainty the results that each alternative action will yield. That is, each must make a decision in the face of uncertainty, where chance and fate govern the outcome of an action. The branch of decision analysis that entails the selection of a course of action which leads to an outcome affected only by chance (and not by an opponent or competitor) is known as *decision-making under uncertainty.** In the remaining sections, we present the basic concepts of decision-making under uncertainty.

> **DEFINITION 16.1**
> *Decision-making under uncertainty* entails the selection of a course of action when we do not know with certainty the results that each alternative action will yield. Furthermore, we assume that the outcome of whatever course of action we select is affected only by chance and not by an opponent or competitor.

---

*This is in contrast to *decision-making under certainty,* where we know the result each alternative action will yield, and to *decision-making under conflict* where, although we do not know with certainty the result each alternative action will yield, the uncertainty is not due to fate or chance but to an opponent's or competitor's decision.

16.2 Elements Common to Decision Problems

Common to all decision problems involving uncertainty are four specific elements: (1) actions, (2) states of nature, (3) outcomes, and (4) the objective variable. We use the following example to illustrate these concepts.

EXAMPLE 16.1

A profit-motivated entrepreneur is committed to producing a July heavyweight championship boxing match in Cleveland, Ohio, featuring the current and charismatic World Boxing Association (WBA) heavyweight champion and the WBA's top-ranked contender (a native of Cleveland). The promoter has been unable to finalize plans, however, due to an indecision over whether to take a chance on it not raining and hold the fight in Cleveland's Municipal Stadium (80,000 seats outdoors), or play it safe and hold the fight in the Richfield Coliseum (25,000 seats indoors), located just outside Cleveland in suburban Richfield, Ohio. If Cleveland Stadium is chosen and the weather cooperates, an expected sellout crowd (no home television or radio broadcast) will net the promoter a profit of about $700,000 (ticket proceeds less costs, taxes, etc.). If it is raining on the night of the match, the majority of the fight fans are expected to stay away (50,000 seats are unprotected from rain), resulting in a loss of about $80,000 (unsold tickets, low concessions sales, etc.). However, if the Richfield Coliseum is chosen, a sellout is expected regardless of the weather, and the promoter will make a net profit of about $250,000. Identify the four elements of this decision problem.

Solution

We identify the four specific elements as follows:

First, a choice must be made between two possible courses of action—Rent the stadium or Rent the coliseum. We refer to these alternatives as **actions.** Actions, in general, comprise the set of alternatives the decision-maker has chosen to consider. The problem is to select one action from this set.

Second, it is uncertain which event will occur—Rain or No rain. We refer to these events as **states of nature,** chance events upon which the outcome of the decision-maker's chosen action depends.

Third, depending on which action is chosen and which state of nature occurs on the night of the championship bout, the decision-maker will receive either a financial reward or a penalty for the chosen action. The consequences of the decision problem are referred to as **outcomes,** which may be either positive or negative. In this example, if the action chosen by the promoter is Rent the stadium and the state of nature that occurs is Rain, the outcome that results is $-$80,000. That is, the action/state of nature combination, Rent the stadium/Rain, will cost the promoter $80,000. Similarly, the combination, Rent the stadium/No rain, will yield a profit of $700,000. The reward (or penalty) corresponding to each action/state of nature combination is called the **outcome** or **payoff.**

The final element of a decision problem, called the **objective variable,** is the quantity used to measure and express the outcomes. In this example, the promoter's motive—or objective—for producing the boxing match is net profit. Accordingly, we express the decision outcomes in terms of the objective variable Net profit (dollars). (If the objective had been to give as many people as possible an opportunity to see a live heavyweight championship bout, we would measure the outcomes of potential actions in terms of number of people attending the boxing match.)

Example 16.1 illustrates a theme that is common to all decision problems involving uncertainty. Both the set of actions to be considered and the choice of an action to implement are under the control of the decision-maker, but the state of nature is not. The decision-maker must choose a course of action prior to knowing which state of nature will occur and without being able to influence the random process generating the states of nature. Also, the list of states of nature in any decision problem (e.g., Rain, No rain) must be mutually exclusive (i.e., each state must be clearly identifiable as one and only one of the listed states—see Chapter 4) and collectively exhaustive (i.e., the list must include all possible states that can occur).

A summary of the four elements common to problems which entail decision-making under uncertainty is given in the box.

FOUR ELEMENTS COMMON TO DECISION PROBLEMS INVOLVING UNCERTAINTY

1. *Actions:* The set of two or more alternatives the decision-maker has chosen to consider. The decision-maker's problem is to choose one action from this set.
2. *States of nature:* The set of two or more mutually exclusive and collectively exhaustive chance events upon which the outcome of the decision-maker's chosen action depends.
3. *Outcomes:* The set of consequences resulting from all possible action/state of nature combinations.
4. *Objective variable:* The quantity used to measure and express the outcomes of a decision problem.

In the following two sections, we present two techniques for summarizing the elements of a decision problem.

EXERCISES   16.1   List and define the four primary elements of a decision problem under uncertainty.

16.2   The management of a bank is considering an application for a commercial loan of $10,000. If they decide to make the loan but the customer defaults, then the bank will lose the amount of the loan plus estimated lost profits of $3,000. On the other hand, if they decide to make the loan and the customer does not default, the bank will gain the interest on the loan, an amount of $1,500. If the bank fails to grant the loan, the net profit is $0. Identify the elements of this decision problem.

16.3   A record company has been sued by an independent songwriter for patent infringements. The company must decide whether to settle the suit out of court or proceed with the court case. An out of court settlement will cost the record company

$800,000 in royalty payments. If the company decides to go to court and if they win the case, they will have $50,000 in court costs. However, if the company loses the suit, damages (royalty payments) will be set at $2,000,000. Identify the elements of this decision problem.

16.4   The manager of a greeting card shop is preparing to place an order for hand-drawn Christmas cards. Each box purchased will cost the store $10 and will be sold at a retail price of $20. Because the cards will be designed with a message specific to this year, any boxes not sold by Christmas will have to be sold in the after-Christmas sale at the bargain basement price of $5 per box. The manager, who believes that between 1 and 5 boxes of these cards can be sold at the retail price, must determine how many boxes to order. Identify the elements of this decision problem.

16.5   An investor is considering an offer to buy a pizza restaurant near a university campus. If he buys the restaurant, there are three possible outcomes: a low demand for pizza (which yields a net loss of $125,000); a medium demand (net profit of $50,000); and a high demand (net profit of $200,000). If the investor does not buy, his net profit is $0. Identify the elements of this decision problem.

16.3   Illustrating a Decision Problem: The Payoff Table and Opportunity Loss Table

Decision analysts, when faced with a complex decision-making task, often employ a technique which summarizes the critical information in a decision problem. A convenient tool for summarizing the elements of a decision problem is the *payoff table,* as illustrated in Example 16.2.

EXAMPLE 16.2   Formulate a payoff table for the decision problem of Example 16.1.

Solution   In a payoff table, each of the set of possible actions the decision-maker has chosen to consider is associated with a row of the table. Each state of nature is associated with a column. The numbers in the table correspond to the outcomes or payoffs of the decision problem. The payoff table for the decision problem of Example 16.1 is given in Table 16.1.

TABLE 16.1

Payoff Table for the Boxing Promoter's Decision Problem, Example 16.2

		STATE OF NATURE	
		Rain	No rain
ACTION	Rent Cleveland Stadium	− $80,000	$700,000
	Rent Richfield Coliseum	$250,000	$250,000

You can see that the payoff table presents the alternative actions of the decision problem and their consequences in a condensed, but clear, manner. For example,

$700,000 is the outcome or payoff (net profit) that would result from the implementation of the action associated with the top row of the table (Rent Cleveland Stadium) and the occurrence of the state of nature associated with the right-hand column of the table (No rain). Similarly, −$80,000 is the payoff (net loss) resulting from the action Rent Cleveland Stadium in combination with the state of nature Rain.

EXAMPLE 16.3 Suppose that you have just inherited $100,000. You have an option of investing your $100,000 inheritance in a wildcat oil well for one year. If the well is drilled and it is dry, you will lose your entire inheritance. On the other hand, if the drilling strikes oil, you will end up with a total of $250,000 at the end of the year (a net gain of $150,000). However, as an alternative to the oil well investment, you may deposit your $100,000 inheritance in the bank for one year at 7% interest (a net gain of $7,000 at the end of the year).

a. Identify the four elements of this decision problem.

b. Formulate the payoff table for this problem.

Solution **a.** The set of alternatives, or **actions,** that you have chosen to consider are: Invest the $100,000 in the oil well and Deposit the $100,000 in the bank. The outcome of each action depends upon the chance events, or **states of nature:** Dry well and Strike oil. The action/state of nature combinations—Invest $100,000 in oil well/ Dry well, Invest $100,000 in oil well/Strike oil, Deposit $100,000 in bank/Dry well, and Deposit $100,000 in bank/Strike oil—represent the **outcomes** of the decision problem expressed in terms of the **objective variable,** net gain on investment after one year (dollars).

b. The payoff table for this decision problem is given in Table 16.2. Note that an outcome that results in a net loss is recorded as a negative payoff (see the outcome corresponding to Invest $100,000 in oil well/Dry well in the upper left-hand corner of Table 16.2). Also, the action Deposit $100,000 in bank will result in a net gain of $7,000 (7% of $100,000) whether the wildcat well strikes oil or not.

TABLE 16.2
Payoff Table for the Inheritance Decision Problem, Example 16.3

| | | STATE OF NATURE | |
		Dry well	Strike oil
ACTION	Invest $100,000 in oil well	−$100,000	$150,000
	Deposit $100,000 in bank	$7,000	$7,000

In both Examples 16.2 and 16.3, we expressed the outcomes of the decision problem in terms of the monetary reward that would be realized by the decision-maker. That is, the objective variable was Net profit for the boxing promoter and Net gain for you, the inheritor. In general, we will refer to outcomes that reflect the **actual** reward to the decision-maker in terms of the objective variable as **payoffs.** Alternatively, outcomes can be expressed in terms of **opportunities** for higher profits that the decision-maker has **lost** as a result of the action selected. For example, in the boxing match promotion example (Examples 16.1 and 16.2), if the weather is not rainy, a decision to hold the championship fight in the Richfield Coliseum will bring a profit of $250,000 and a decision to use Cleveland Stadium will bring a profit of $700,000. If, in fact, the coliseum were chosen, then by not choosing to rent the stadium, the promoter will have *lost the opportunity* to net an additional $450,000. We refer to this $450,000 as the *opportunity loss* associated with the action/state of nature combination, Rent Richfield Coliseum/No rain. We may then construct an *opportunity loss table,* similar to a payoff table, which gives the opportunity loss associated with each action/state of nature combination of a decision problem.

EXAMPLE 16.4

Refer to Example 16.2. Construct an opportunity loss table for the boxing promoter.

Solution

The first step in formulating an opportunity loss table is to construct a payoff table. The payoff table for the boxing promoter was given previously in Table 16.1. The entries in this payoff table will be used to compute the corresponding opportunity losses.

The second step is to determine the maximum payoff for each column of the payoff table (Table 16.1). That is, find the largest net profit that the promoter could receive for each possible state of nature. From Table 16.1, the maximum payoff under column 1 (Rain) is $250,000 and the maximum payoff under column 2 (No rain) is $700,000. These quantities are shown at the top of Table 16.3.

The third and final step is to compute the opportunity loss for each action/state of nature combination by subtracting each entry of the payoff table from the corresponding column's maximum payoff. That is, the promoter's opportunity loss is the difference between the payoff (net profit) the promoter receives for a chosen action and the maximum payoff that the promoter could have received for choosing the action yielding the highest payoff for the state of nature that occurred. For example, the opportunity loss associated with any payoff in column 1 is found by subtracting that payoff from the column's maximum payoff, $250,000. These opportunity loss calculations are shown in Table 16.3, and the resulting opportunity loss table is given in Table 16.4.

TABLE 16.3

Calculation of Opportunity Losses for the Boxing Promoter's Decision Problem, Example 16.4

		STATE OF NATURE (MAXIMUM PAYOFF)	
		Rain ($250,000)	No rain ($700,000)
	Rent Cleveland Stadium	$250,000	$700,000
		$-(-80,000)$	$-700,000$
		$330,000	0
ACTION			
	Rent Richfield Coliseum	$250,000	$700,000
		$-250,000$	$-250,000$
		0	$450,000

TABLE 16.4

Opportunity Loss Table for the Boxing Promoter's Decision Problem, Example 16.4

		STATE OF NATURE	
		Rain	No rain
ACTION	Rent Cleveland Stadium	$330,000	0
	Rent Richfield Coliseum	0	$450,000

Notice that none of the opportunity losses of Table 16.4 is less than zero, and that the opportunity loss associated with the maximum profit in each column is zero (see Table 16.1). These results are true in general for any opportunity loss table.

EXAMPLE 16.5

Refer to Example 16.3. Construct the opportunity loss table corresponding to the payoff table, Table 16.2.

Solution

For each column of the payoff table (Table 16.2), first find the maximum payoff. For column 1 (Dry well), the maximum payoff is $7,000; for column 2 (Strike oil), the maximum payoff is $150,000. The opportunity loss associated with each payoff of Table 16.2 is found by subtracting that payoff from the maximum payoff of the column in which it appears, as shown in Table 16.5. The resulting opportunity loss table is shown in Table 16.6.

TABLE 16.5

Calculation of Opportunity Losses for the Inheritance Decision Problem, Example 16.5

		STATE OF NATURE (MAXIMUM PAYOFF)	
		Dry well ($7,000)	Strike oil ($150,000)
ACTION	Invest $100,000 in oil well	$7,000	$150,000
		$-(-100,000)$	$-150,000$
		$107,000	0
	Deposit $100,000 in bank	$7,000	$150,000
		$-7,000$	$-7,000$
		0	$143,000

TABLE 16.6

Opportunity Loss Table for the Inheritance Decision Problem, Example 16.5

		STATE OF NATURE	
		Dry well	Strike oil
ACTION	Invest $100,000 in oil well	$107,000	0
	Deposit $100,000 in bank	0	$143,000

In Section 16.5 we will show that decision problems may be solved using outcomes expressed either as payoffs or as opportunity losses. We conclude this section with a summary of payoff tables (see Table 16.7) and opportunity loss tables (see box and Table 16.8).

TABLE 16.7

General Form of a Payoff Table

		STATE OF NATURE			
		S_1	S_2	$\cdots$	S_m
ACTION	a_1	P_{11}	P_{12}	$\cdots$	P_{1m}
	a_2	P_{21}	P_{22}	$\cdots$	P_{2m}
	.	.	.		.
	.	.	.		.
	.	.	.		.
	a_n	P_{n1}	P_{n2}	$\cdots$	P_{nm}

where

$S_1, S_2, \ldots, S_m$ denote all possible states of nature

$a_1, a_2, \ldots, a_n$ denote all actions being considered by the decision-maker

$P_{11}, P_{12}, \ldots, P_{nm}$ denote the payoffs (actual rewards) resulting from the action/state of nature combinations

OPPORTUNITY LOSS DETERMINATION

The *opportunity loss* is the difference between the payoff a decision-maker receives for a chosen action and the maximum that the decision-maker could have received for choosing the action yielding the highest payoff for the state of nature that occurred. Steps in calculating opportunity loss:

1. Construct a payoff table, as shown in Table 16.7.
2. Find the maximum payoff in each column of the payoff table.
3. The opportunity loss associated with any payoff in a column is found by subtracting that payoff from the maximum payoff in the column.

TABLE 16.8
General Form of an
Opportunity Loss Table

		STATE OF NATURE			
		S_1	S_2	$\cdots$	S_m
	a_1	L_{11}	L_{12}	$\cdots$	L_{1m}
	a_2	L_{21}	L_{22}	$\cdots$	L_{2m}
ACTION	.	.	.		.
	.	.	.		.
	.	.	.		.
	a_n	L_{n1}	L_{n2}	$\cdots$	L_{nm}

where

$S_1, S_2, \ldots, S_m$ denote all possible states of nature

$a_1, a_2, \ldots, a_n$ denote all actions being considered by the decision-maker

$L_{11}, L_{12}, \ldots, L_{nm}$ denote the opportunity losses resulting from the action/state of nature combinations

EXERCISES   **16.6**   The Research and Development Department of a major drug company has proposed an $8.5 million project to develop a new cancer-treating drug. If the proposal is adopted and the research is successful, the firm can expect to make $700 million in profit on the drug. However, if the research is unsuccessful in isolating the new drug, all research costs are lost. If the research proposal is rejected, the company will invest in surgical instruments for a guaranteed profit of $1 million.

a.   Formulate the payoff table for this problem.
b.   Construct the opportunity loss table.

16.7   A winery is considering marketing a new low-cost dinner wine. The introduction of the wine will cost $3 million in fixed and promotional costs per year. Each bottle sold will contribute $0.30 to profits. The management feels that sales could be 0.5 million, 10 million, 15 million, 20 million, or 25 million bottles per year.

α.   Formulate the payoff table for this problem.

b.   Construct the opportunity loss table.

16.8   The owner of a professional football team is contemplating limiting season ticket sales for the next season to 15,000 so that more tickets will be available on an individual game basis. (Last year, no limit was in effect.) The results of the limited season ticket sales will depend on the team's performance next year: if the team's record is poor, the owner will experience a profit loss of $150,000; if the team's record is mediocre, the owner will break even; and if the team has a good to excellent season, the owner will make a profit of $200,000. If the sale of season tickets is unlimited, the owner will lose $70,000 in a poor season, earn a profit of $20,000 with a mediocre team, and earn a profit of $95,000 with a successful team.

α.   Formulate the payoff table for this problem.

b.   Construct the opportunity loss table.

16.9   Refer to Exercise 16.2.

α.   Formulate the payoff table for this problem.

b.   Construct the opportunity loss table.

16.10   Refer to Exercise 16.3.

α.   Formulate the payoff table for this problem.

b.   Construct the opportunity loss table.

16.11   Refer to Exercise 16.4.

α.   Formulate the payoff table for this problem.

b.   Construct the opportunity loss table.

16.12   Refer to Exercise 16.5.

α.   Formulate the payoff table for this problem.

b.   Construct the opportunity loss table.

16.4   Illustrating a Decision Problem: The Decision Tree

The presentation of payoffs or opportunity losses in the form of a table is one method of illustrating a decision problem. An alternative technique, one which provides the same information as the payoff or opportunity loss table, but is often more convenient to use, is the *decision tree.* Each branch of a decision tree represents a path which leads to one of the possible outcomes or payoffs of the decision problem.

EXAMPLE 16.6   Refer to the boxing promoter's decision problem, Example 16.1. Give the decision tree which corresponds to the payoff table, Table 16.1.

Solution   The decision tree for this problem is displayed in Figure 16.1. Conceptually, the boxing promoter's move through time toward the outcome of the decision problem is represented by movement from left to right through the branches of the decision tree. The ☐ denotes a **decision fork** and signals that a decision must be made. At this position on the tree, the decision-maker must choose between the two actions, Rent Cleveland Stadium and Rent Richfield Coliseum. If the action Rent Cleveland Stadium is chosen, then from the decision fork we move along the upper branch of the tree. The ◯ denotes a **chance fork** and signals that the next branch of the tree the promoter will follow will be determined by the chance occurrence of a state of nature—in this example, Rain or No rain. From this position in the upper chance fork of Figure 16.1, rain on the night of the championship bout will lead the promoter to the payoff corresponding to the action/state of nature combination, Rent Cleveland Stadium/ Rain, i.e., −$80,000.

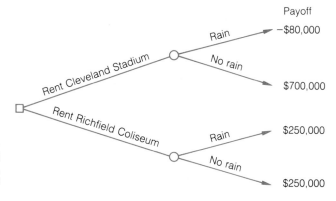

FIGURE 16.1
Decision Tree for Boxing
Match Decision Problem,
Example 16.6

Decision trees may also be used to depict opportunity losses.

EXAMPLE 16.7   Refer to Example 16.3. Give the decision tree corresponding to the opportunity loss table for the inheritance decision problem, Table 16.6.

Solution   The decision tree is shown in Figure 16.2 (p. 538). Again, the ☐ denotes a decision fork, signalling the decision-maker—in this case, you, the inheritor of $100,000—that a decision must be made: Invest $100,000 in oil well or Deposit $100,000 in bank. The chance fork ◯ warns that the outcome (opportunity loss) of the one-year investment is governed by the chance occurrence of a state of nature: Dry well or Strike oil.

The general form of a decision tree is shown in Figure 16.3 (p. 538).
Payoff tables, opportunity loss tables, and decision trees provide the decision-maker with a structured summary of the information in a decision problem. Whichever method you use to illustrate the problem, you will be able to use decision analysis to reach a decision.

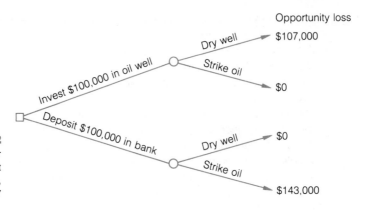

Opportunity loss

$107,000

$0

$0

$143,000

FIGURE 16.2
Decision Tree for
Inheritance Investment
Decision Problem,
Example 16.7

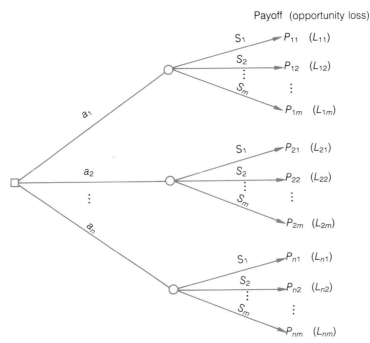

Payoff (opportunity loss)

FIGURE 16.3
General Form of a
Decision Tree

where

$S_1, S_2, \ldots, S_m$ denote all possible states of nature

$a_1, a_2, \ldots, a_n$ denote the actions being considered by the decision-maker

$P_{11}, P_{12}, \ldots, P_{nm}$ denote the payoffs resulting from the action/state of nature combinations

$L_{11}, L_{12}, \ldots, L_{nm}$ denote the opportunity losses resulting from the action/state of nature combinations

EXERCISES 16.13 The purchasing agent for an automobile manufacturer is concluding a purchase agreement with a supplier of preformed body pieces. The pieces will be purchased in lots of 500, and the cost of a lot is $15,000. Frequently, a body stamping has a defect called a burr. If a piece is found to have a burr, it can be filed off by the automobile manufacturer at a cost of $10 per piece. Past experience with this supplier has shown that the proportion of defects tends to be 5, 10, or 15%. The supplier now offers a guarantee that it will assume the costs for all defective body moldings greater than 50 in a production lot of 500. This guarantee may be purchased for a cost of $1,000 before the lot begins production. The purchasing agent is interested in determining whether the guarantee should be purchased. Draw the decision tree for this problem.

16.14 Local directory assistance at a telephone company is growing at an unprecedented rate of 20% per year. Attempts to discourage the rise in directory assistance contacts (including a required 7-digit telephone number) have not been successful. Thus, the company needs to decide on what is the most efficient and cost-effective method of handling their directory assistance volumes in the coming years. The telephone company recognizes that it has four viable options:

1. Continue the present manual directory assistance method at a cost of $1,500,000.
2. Study the feasibility of subcontracting directory assistance to another telephone company at a cost of $10,000. If the study is favorable, the subcontract option will be adopted at an additional cost of $670,000 (i.e., total cost of $680,000). If the study is unfavorable, the company will continue its present method at a cost of $1,500,000 (total cost of $1,510,000).
3. Study the feasibility of owning, operating, and supporting its own mechanized directory assistance system at a cost of $20,000. If the study is favorable, the system will be installed at an additional cost of $2,030,000 (total cost of $2,050,000). If the study is unfavorable, the company will continue its present method at a cost of $1,500,000 (total cost of $1,520,000).
4. Study the feasibility of contracting with a larger telephone company to develop, maintain, and operate a mechanized directory assistance system, but supply its own hardware, personnel, and circuits at a cost of $25,000. If the study is favorable, the company contract option will be adopted at an additional cost of $1,270,000 (total cost of $1,295,000). If the study is unfavorable, the company will continue its present method at a cost of $1,500,000 (total cost of $1,525,000).

Draw the decision tree for this problem.

16.15 Refer to Exercise 16.6. Draw the decision tree for this problem.

16.16 Refer to Exercise 16.7. Draw the decision tree for this problem.

16.17 Refer to Exercise 16.8. Draw the decision tree for this problem.

16.5 Using Expected Values to Solve Decision Problems

Now that we have shown you how to structure a decision problem by constructing a payoff table, opportunity loss table, or decision tree, we are ready to choose a rule for reaching a decision. Numerous decision rules have been proposed, but the one most commonly employed in decision analysis uses a payoff table and chooses the action that produces the *maximum expected payoff*. This rule, called the *expected payoff criterion,* requires that we assess the likelihood of occurrence of the states of nature associated with the problem. That is, to employ the expected payoff criterion, we need to assign probabilities to the chance events, the states of nature.

EXAMPLE 16.8   The probabilities which measure the likelihood of occurrence of the various states of nature in a decision problem may be unknown. In order to employ the expected payoff criterion to reach a decision, we will need to approximate these probabilities. How can these approximations be obtained?

Solution   Decision analysts approximate state of nature probabilities using one of the following:

1. Relative frequency information about the states
2. Judgmental (subjective) information about the states
3. A combination of relative frequency information and subjective information

In other words, decision analysts use any type of information that is available to assign probabilities to the states. For example, the boxing promoter of Example 16.1 could use historical weather data (relative frequency data) to assess the probabilities of Rain and No rain on the night of the championship fight. Or, referring to Example 16.3, you could rely on the advice of expert oil drillers (subjective information) to assess the likelihood of the wildcat well striking oil. Whichever method is used to determine probabilities for the states of nature, great care should be taken. Decision analyses based on poorly chosen probabilities often lead to inappropriate (and disastrous) actions. In the remaining examples and exercises of this chapter, we will assume that the probabilities of the various states of nature have been reliably assessed.

WARNING

Be extremely careful when assigning probabilities to the various states of nature in a decision problem. Decision rules based on poorly chosen probabilities could lead to inappropriate actions.

We now return to the decision rule based on maximum expected profit—the expected payoff criterion. We illustrate this technique with an example.

EXAMPLE 16.9   Refer to Example 16.1. The payoff table for the boxing promoter's decision problem is reproduced in Table 16.9. Suppose that the promoter, having access to past meteorological records for the Cleveland area, assessed the following probability distribution for the state of nature on the night of the fight:

STATE	P(State will occur)
Rain	.15
No rain	.85

Using the expected value criterion, what action will the promoter take?

TABLE 16.9
Payoff Table for the
Boxing Promoter's
Decision Problem,
Example 16.9

			STATE OF NATURE	
			S_1: Rain	S_2: No rain
ACTION	a_1:	Rent Cleveland Stadium	$-$ \$80,000	\$700,000
	a_2:	Rent Richfield Coliseum	\$250,000	\$250,000

Solution To understand how the expected payoff criterion is used to reach a decision, recall the definition of the expected value of a discrete random variable (Chapter 5). If x is a discrete random variable with probability distribution $p(x)$, then the expected (or mean) value of x, denoted by $E(x)$, is

$$E(x) = \Sigma \, x\, p(x)$$

In a decision problem, the random variable x is the payoff, and the probabilities associated with x are the same as those that describe the likelihood of occurrence of the states of nature. The first step, then, is to formulate probability distributions for each of the possible actions a decision-maker may choose to take.

Consider the action a_1: Rent Cleveland Stadium. If the promoter chooses to rent the stadium, the payoff will be either $-$ \$80,000 or \$700,000 (see row 1 of Table 16.9), with probabilities .15 (probability of Rain) and .85 (probability of No rain), respectively. Thus, the probability distribution for the payoff x if the promoter chooses action a_1 is

Action a_1

PAYOFF x	$p(x)$
$-$ \$80,000	.15
\$700,000	.85

Similarly, the probability distribution for the payoff x if the promoter chooses action a_2: Rent Richfield Coliseum is

Action a_2

PAYOFF x	$p(x)$
\$250,000	.15
\$250,000	.85

Once the payoff probability distributions for the actions have been determined, the next step is to compute the expected payoff, $E(x)$, for each action. The expected payoff of action a_1, denoted by the symbol $EP(a_1)$, is

$$EP(a_1) = \Sigma x p(x)$$
$$= (-\$80,000)(.15) + (\$700,000)(.85)$$
$$= \$583,000$$

and the expected payoff of action a_2, denoted by the symbol $EP(a_2)$, is

$$EP(a_2) = \Sigma x p(x)$$
$$= (\$250,000)(.15) + (\$250,000)(.85)$$
$$= \$250,000$$

These expected payoffs are summarized in Table 16.10.

TABLE 16.10
Expected Payoff Table for the Boxing Promoter's Decision Problem, Example 16.9

ACTION a_i	EXPECTED PAYOFF FOR ACTION a_i $EP(a_i)$
a_1: Rent Cleveland Stadium	$583,000
a_2: Rent Richfield Coliseum	$250,000

The expected values in Table 16.10 inform us that if we were faced with this decision problem a very large number of times and chose action a_1 each time, the mean or expected payoff would be $583,000 (assuming that the probabilities accurately reflect the likelihood of Rain and No rain). If we chose action a_2 each time, the mean or expected payoff would be $250,000. Using these interpretations, which action would you choose if you were the boxing promoter? According to the expected value criterion, you would choose action a_1 because it produces the largest expected payoff, namely $583,000. Thus, the promoter will choose to rent Cleveland Stadium and hold the heavyweight championship fight outdoors.

THE EXPECTED PAYOFF CRITERION

Choose the action that produces the largest expected payoff.

EXAMPLE 16.10 A beer producer with breweries and a distribution network located east of the Mississippi River is considering expanding its sales region to include the southwestern part of the United States. Due to refrigeration problems that would arise from having to transport its beer, a sales expansion to the southwest requires that the producer build a new brewery in Dallas, Texas. The problem is to determine how large a brewery to construct. It has been decided that the size should be based on the projected gross profits (profits before taxes) for the fifth year of operation for each of the three sizes of breweries under consideration. Recognizing that a new Dallas brewery cannot possibly obtain more than a 15% market share during the fifth year of operation, the payoff table shown in Table 16.11 was formulated by the firm's marketing department. Suppose that the marketing department also assessed the following distribution for the states of nature:

STATE (MARKET SHARE)	P(State will occur)
Less than 5%	.40
5–10%	.50
10–15%	.10

Use the expected payoff criterion to help the beer producer decide what size brewery to build.

TABLE 16.11
Payoff Table for the Brewer's Decision Problem, Example 16.10

		STATE OF NATURE (MARKET SHARE DURING 5TH YEAR OF OPERATION)		
		Less than 5%	5–10%	10–15%
ACTION	a_1: Small	$300,000	$350,000	$450,000
	a_2: Medium	$250,000	$700,000	$800,000
	a_3: Large	$200,000	$600,000	$1,000,000

Solution If we choose action a_1: Small (i.e., build a small brewery), the payoffs (projected gross profits) can be $300,000, $350,000, or $450,000, with probabilities .40, .50, and .10, respectively. Thus, the probability distribution for the payoff x if we choose action a_1 is

Action a_1

PAYOFF x	$p(x)$
$300,000	.40
$350,000	.50
$450,000	.10

and the expected payoff is

$$EP(a_1) = \Sigma\, x\, p(x)$$
$$= (\$300,000)(.4) + (\$350,000)(.5) + (\$450,000)(.1)$$
$$= \$340,000$$

Similarly, we find the probability distributions and expected payoffs for actions a_2 and a_3:

Action a_2

PAYOFF x	p(x)
$250,000	.40
$700,000	.50
$800,000	.10

$EP(a_2) = \Sigma x p(x)$

$= (\$250{,}000)(.4) + (\$700{,}000)(.5) + (\$800{,}000)(.1)$

$= \$530{,}000$

Action a_3

PAYOFF x	p(x)
$200,000	.40
$600,000	.50
$1,000,000	.10

$EP(a_3) = \Sigma x p(x)$

$= (\$200{,}000)(.4) + (\$600{,}000)(.5) + (\$1{,}000{,}000)(.1)$

$= \$480{,}000$

These expected (mean) payoffs are summarized in Table 16.12. Using the expected payoff criterion, we choose action a_2: Medium (i.e., construct a medium-sized brewery), since this strategy produces the largest expected payoff, namely $530,000.

TABLE 16.12
Expected Payoff Table for
the Brewer's Decision
Problem, Example 16.10

ACTION a_i: Brewery size	EXPECTED PAYOFF FOR ACTION a_i $EP(a_i)$
a_1: Small	$340,000
a_2: Medium	$530,000
a_3: Large	$480,000

SOLVING A DECISION PROBLEM USING THE EXPECTED PAYOFF CRITERION

1. Assign reasonable probabilities to each of the states of nature.
2. From the entries in a payoff table and the state of nature probabilities, specify the probability distribution $p(x)$ for the payoff x corresponding to each action a_i in the decision problem.
3. Compute the expected payoff of each action $EP(a_i)$, as follows:

   $EP(a_i) = \Sigma x \, p(x)$

4. Choose the action that produces the largest expected payoff.

An alternative to the expected payoff decision rule employs an opportunity loss table. The *expected opportunity loss criterion* requires that we find the expected opportunity loss for each action, and then choose the action that produces the *minimum expected opportunity loss.* It can be shown that the expected payoff criterion and the expected opportunity loss criterion are equivalent procedures, i.e., both criteria lead to the same decision.

THE EXPECTED OPPORTUNITY LOSS CRITERION

Choose the action that produces the smallest expected opportunity loss. (This will always lead to the same decision as the expected payoff criterion.)

We conclude this section with a note of caution. Maximizing the expected payoff (or minimizing the expected opportunity loss) does not consider risk. That is, a decision analyst who uses expected values to solve a decision problem fails to incorporate the fact that one action may be much riskier than any of the others. For example, the boxing promoter's decision, using the expected payoff criterion, is to rent the stadium, i.e., hold the championship fight outdoors. This action was selected because, in the long run, renting the stadium will lead to a larger expected profit. However, in the short run, this action is clearly much riskier than the alternative action of renting the coliseum and holding the fight indoors. If it rains on the night of the fight and the match is held outdoors, the promoter stands to lose $80,000, a risk he may not be willing to take! Various methods, such as *utility analysis,* attempt to incorporate risk into the decision problem. Although we do not discuss these decision-making techniques in this text, references are provided at the end of this chapter.

EXERCISES **16.18** Consider the accompanying payoff table (with the state of nature probabilities in parentheses).

		STATE OF NATURE		
		$S_1(.30)$	$S_2(.25)$	$S_3(.45)$
ACTION	α_1	−5	4	10
	α_2	0	8	−10

a. Use the expected payoff criterion to select the better action.
b. Convert the payoff table to an opportunity loss table and use the expected opportunity loss criterion to select the better action.
c. Do the results of parts a and b agree?

16.19 A speculator is considering three possible purchases: a large dairy farm, a condominium complex, and a small shopping center. The profit return from these investments depends on the course taken by the local economy during the next two years. The speculator has constructed the accompanying payoff table (with probabilities in parentheses). What is the speculator's decision using the expected payoff criterion?

		STATE OF NATURE		
		S_1: Local economy sags (.20)	S_2: No change in local economy (.50)	S_3: Local economy surges (.30)
ACTION	a_1: Buy large dairy farm	$20,000	$25,000	$30,000
	a_2: Buy condominium complex	$-15,000	$40,000	$80,000
	a_3: Buy small shopping center	$-30,000	$ 5,000	$100,000

16.20 A retail shoe company must decide whether to expand its present store or build an entirely new store in a different location. An important factor the company must consider is whether or not a new apartment complex will be constructed near the proposed location of the new store. Suppose that the shoe store company believes that there is a 60% chance that the new apartment complex will be constructed. This information, as well as estimates of the store's opportunity losses, is provided in the accompanying table. Using the expected opportunity loss criterion, what is the shoe company's decision?

		STATE OF NATURE	
		S_1: Complex built (.60)	S_2: Not built (.40)
ACTION	a_1: Expand present store	$30,000	$0
	a_2: Build new store	$0	$35,000

16.21 A large American minicomputer firm has an opportunity to enter the Japanese market. Management evaluated four possible means of marketing the computers against demand in the Japanese market, as shown in the accompanying payoff table. (Payoffs are in terms of net yearly profit, and state of nature probabilities are given in parentheses.) Find the optimal strategy, using the expected payoff criterion.

		STATE OF NATURE		
		S_1: Low demand (.15)	S_2: Medium demand (.60)	S_3: High demand (.25)
ACTION	a_1: Sell through company agents in Japan	$1,800,000	$4,000,000	$ 6,500,000
	a_2: Sell through brochures mailed to Japan	$ 500,000	$1,000,000	$ 2,000,000
	a_3: Hire Japanese sales force	$-1,700,000	$7,700,000	$15,400,000
	a_4: Build Japanese plant	$-6,300,000	$ 850,000	$25,000,000

16.22 A buyer for a New York City boutique must determine which fashion line in women's apparel to emphasize in her purchases. She must choose between expensive formal wear, leisure clothes, or functional work wear. The demand will depend on which line is featured in a major New York fashion show later this year. Although the featured fashion line is a carefully guarded secret, the buyer used subjective judgment to assign probabilities to each of the three possibilities. These possibilities (with probabilities in parentheses) and their respective payoffs (in dollars profit) are shown in the accompanying table.

		STATE OF NATURE (LINE FEATURED IN NY FASHION SHOW)		
		S_1: Formal (.4)	S_2: Leisure (.4)	S_3: Functional (.2)
	a_1: Formal	100,000	−30,000	30,000
ACTION	a_2: Leisure	−50,000	80,000	50,000
	a_3: Functional	−50,000	60,000	90,000

a. Find the optimal action, based on the expected payoff criterion.
b. Convert the payoff table into an opportunity loss table. Find the optimal action, based on the expected opportunity loss criterion.

16.23 Refer to Exercise 16.6. The drug company estimates that the probability of the proposed research being a success is .70. According to the expected payoff criterion, should the company adopt the cancer research proposal or invest in surgical instruments?

16.24 Refer to Exercise 16.4. The store manager for the greeting card shop has assessed the probabilities for the states of nature as shown in the table. According to the expected payoff criterion, how many boxes should the store manager order?

NUMBER OF BOXES THAT COULD BE SOLD AT RETAIL	PROBABILITY
1	.15
2	.20
3	.35
4	.25
5	.05

16.6 Other Decision Rules: Maximax, Maximin, and Minimax Criteria

The expected payoff (or opportunity loss) criterion requires that a probability distribution be assigned to the states of nature. However, if the likelihood of occurrence of these chance events is inaccurately assessed, the decision rule could possibly lead to an inappropriate action (see the warning box of the previous section). Thus, a decision-maker who is uncertain of the true (or even approximate) probability distribution of the states of nature may wish to apply an alternative decision rule. There are several criteria available that do not require the assignment of probabilities in order to reach a decision. Three common nonprobabilistic criteria are the *maximax, maximin, and minimax decision rules.* We describe these rules in the following examples.

EXAMPLE 16.11   Refer to the brewer's decision problem, Example 16.10. The payoff table is reproduced in Table 16.13. Use the *maximax rule* to determine the appropriate action.

TABLE 16.13
Payoff Table for the
Brewer's Decision
Problem, Example 16.11

| | | STATE OF NATURE (MARKET SHARE DURING 5TH YEAR OF OPERATION) | | |
		Less than 5%	5–10%	10–15%
	a_1: Small	$300,000	$350,000	$450,000
ACTION	a_2: Medium	$250,000	$700,000	$800,000
	a_3: Large	$200,000	$600,000	$1,000,000

Solution   To use the *maximax rule,* we determine the maximum payoff associated with each action and choose the action that corresponds to the *max*imum of these *max*imum payoffs (hence the name, *maximax*). The maximum of the maximum payoffs, of course, will be the largest payoff in the entire payoff table.

Applying the maximax criterion to the brewer's decision problem, we simply find the maximum payoff in the entire payoff table, Table 16.13. Since the largest payoff is $1,000,000, corresponding to action a_3:   Large, the maximax criterion leads to the decision to build a large brewery.

Note that the maximax criterion ignores all information in the payoff table except for the maximum value. That is, no other state of nature except that associated with the maximum payoff is considered, and the size of the difference between the maximum payoff and the other payoffs is ignored. The maximax decision is an optimistic one, since it is based on the hope that the most favorable state of nature will occur.

THE MAXIMAX DECISION RULE

Choose the action corresponding to the maximum payoff in the entire payoff table.

EXAMPLE 16.12   Refer to the brewer's decision problem, Example 16.10. Use the *maximin* rule to determine the appropriate action.

Solution   To use the *maximin rule,* we determine the minimum payoff associated with each action and select the action that corresponds to the *maxi*mum of these *min*imum payoffs.

From Table 16.13, the minimum payoffs for each action are:

ACTION	MINIMUM PAYOFF
a_1	$300,000
a_2	$250,000
a_3	$200,000

Since the maximum of these payoffs is $300,000, corresponding to action a_1, the maximin decision is to build a small brewery.

Note that the maximin criterion ignores all information except for the minimum payoffs corresponding to each action and, like the maximax criterion, the maximin rule ignores the size of the difference between the minimum payoffs and the other payoffs in the payoff table. The maximin criterion is pessimistic, since it is based on the assumption that the least favorable state of nature will occur.

THE MAXIMIN DECISION RULE

Determine the minimum payoff associated with each action, then choose the action corresponding to the maximum of the minimum payoffs.

The maximax and maximin decision rules are employed when the objective variable is in terms of payoffs or actual reward to the decision-maker. A decision rule which can be applied to opportunity loss tables is the *minimax rule.*

EXAMPLE 16.13   Refer to the inheritance decision problem, Example 16.3. The opportunity loss table for this problem is reproduced in Table 16.14. Use the *minimax rule* to determine the appropriate action.

TABLE 16.14
Opportunity Loss Table
for the Inheritance
Decision Problem,
Example 16.13

		STATE OF NATURE	
		Dry well	Strike oil
ACTION	a_1: Invest $100,000 in oil well	$107,000	$0
	a_2: Deposit $100,000 in bank	$0	$143,000

Solution   To use the *minimax rule,* we determine the maximum opportunity loss associated with each action and select the action that corresponds to the *mini*mum of these *max*imum opportunity losses.

From Table 16.14, the maximum opportunity loss for each action is:

ACTION	MAXIMUM OPPORTUNITY LOSS
a_1	$107,000
a_2	$143,000

Since the minimum of these maximum opportunity losses is $107,000, corresponding to action a_1, the minimax decision is to invest your $100,000 inheritance in the wildcat oil well.

In one sense, the minimax rule using opportunity loss is similar to the maximin rule for payoffs: both are pessimistic. That is, using the minimax criterion, the decision-maker expects the least favorable state of nature to occur and so selects the action that will give the minimum of the maximum opportunity losses. However, the rules differ in that the maximin rule maximizes the minimum payoff, while the minimax rule minimizes the maximum opportunity loss—different criteria that could possibly lead to different decisions.

THE MINIMAX RULE

Determine the maximum opportunity loss associated with each action, then choose the action corresponding to the minimum of these maximum opportunity losses.

Since much information in the payoff or opportunity loss table is ignored by the maximax, maximin, and minimax decision criteria, it is not surprising that they often lead to decisions that are intuitively unappealing. For example, the maximin criterion of Example 16.12 leads to the decision to build a small brewery, even though the slight loss that would be sustained if a larger brewery were built and less than 5% of the market were attained appears to be more than compensated for by the gain in profit which would be realized if a larger brewery were to be built and the market share were to reach between 5% and 15%. For this reason, most decision analysts prefer the expected payoff criterion to these nonprobabilistic criteria. The use of the maximax, maximin, or minimax rules is generally confined to decision problems for which the decision-maker is not willing to assign probabilities to the states of nature.

EXERCISES **16.25** Consider the payoff table at the top of the next page.
  a. Use the maximax decision criterion to select the optimal action.
  b. Use the maximin decision criterion to select the optimal action.
  c. Formulate the corresponding opportunity loss table.
  d. What is the minimax decision?

		STATE OF NATURE		
		S_1	S_2	S_3
ACTION	α_1	100	95	90
	α_2	50	75	90
	α_3	-25	25	110
	α_4	75	80	195

16.26 The accompanying payoff table is reproduced from Exercise 16.19.

		STATE OF NATURE		
		S_1: Local economy sags (.20)	S_2: No change in local economy (.50)	S_3: Local economy surges (.30)
ACTION	a_1: Buy large dairy farm	$20,000	$25,000	$30,000
	a_2: Buy condominium complex	-$15,000	$40,000	$80,000
	a_3: Buy small shopping center	-$30,000	$ 5,000	$100,000

a. Find the action selected by the maximax decision rule.
b. Find the action selected by the maximin decision rule.

16.27 The accompanying opportunity loss table is reproduced from Exercise 16.20. Find the action selected by the minimax decision rule.

		STATE OF NATURE	
		S_1: Complex built (.60)	S_2: Not built (.40)
ACTION	a_1: Expand present store	$30,000	$0
	a_2: Build new store	$0	$35,000

16.28 Refer to Exercise 16.8. Use the payoff and opportunity loss tables you constructed for the professional football team owner to find:
a. The action selected by the maximax criterion
b. The action selected by the maximin criterion
c. The action selected by the minimax criterion

16.7 Summary

Decision analysis prescribes a method for selecting an action when uncertainty exists concerning the outcome resulting from each action. The four elements common to this type of decision problem are: (1) actions, (2) states of nature, (3) outcomes, and (4) the objective variable. They can be summarized in a payoff table, opportunity loss table, or decision tree.

The expected payoff criterion (or expected opportunity loss criterion) uses the probability distribution assigned to the states of nature to select the action with the highest expected payoff (or lowest opportunity loss). However, this decision rule does not allow the decision-maker to express his or her attitude toward risk.

The maximax, maximin, and minimax rules represent three nonprobabilistic criteria for selecting an action. These rules are generally confined to decision problems for which reasonable probabilities cannot be assigned to the states of nature.

KEY WORDS

Decision-making under uncertainty	Decision tree
Actions	Expected payoff criterion
States of nature	Expected opportunity loss criterion
Outcomes	Maximax
Objective variable	Maximin
Payoff	Minimax
Opportunity loss	

SUPPLEMENTARY EXERCISE

16.29 Consider the accompanying payoff table with state of nature probabilities shown in parentheses.

		STATE OF NATURE		
		$S_1(.5)$	$S_2(.3)$	$S_3(.2)$
	α_1	12	77	−27
	α_2	24	2	12
ACTION	α_3	−20	41	80
	α_4	25	5	70
	α_5	40	50	10

a. Construct an opportunity loss table for this decision problem.
b. Calculate the expected payoff and the expected opportunity loss for each action, and verify that both criteria select the same action.
c. Find the maximax, maximin, and minimax decisions.

16.30 A doctor is involved in a $1 million malpractice suit. He can either settle out of court for $250,000 or go to court. If he goes to court and loses, he must pay $925,000 plus $75,000 in cour† costs. If he wins in court, the plaintiffs pay the court costs.
a. Identify the four elements of this decision problem.
b. Construct a payoff table for this decision problem.
c. Draw a decision tree for this problem.
d. The doctor's lawyer estimates the probability of winning in court to be .20. Use the expected payoff criterion to decide whether the doctor should settle or go to court.

e. Find the maximax decision.

f. Find the maximin decision.

g. Construct an opportunity loss table and determine which action is prescribed by the minimax criterion.

16.31 Two investment options are being considered by a realtor. Investment A involves multilevel housing and will bring a profit of $450,000 in 5 years. Investment B, which involves undeveloped property, will turn a profit of $100,000 over the same period. However, if rezoning of the latter property can be obtained, the profit will increase to $600,000, less costs of $20,000 in preparing and presenting the case to the zoning review board. The realtor assesses the probability of a successful appeal for rezoning at .65.

a. Identify the four elements of this decision problem.

b. Draw the decision tree for this problem.

c. Solve the decision problem, using the expected payoff criterion.

16.32 A common problem in business is the management of perishable inventories, that is, items that lose the major portion of their economic value after a given date due to either obsolescence or spoilage. For example, if a corner newsstand orders too many papers and cannot sell them all, the excess papers have little value. Hence, these types of problems are called *newsboy problems.* Newsboy problems are common in retailing situations such as the following: A buyer for a large department store is trying to decide how many of a new style of dress to order. Because of rapid changes in fashion, she does not wish to order too many dresses, but if she orders too few she will lose profits for her department. Each dress purchased will cost the store $30 and will sell for $50. Any dresses not sold at the end of the season will be sold at the annual half-price sale. The buyer feels that the department will sell between three and eight dozen dresses, with the probabilities shown in the table. If the dresses must be purchased in lots of one dozen, how many dozens should the buyer order?

DRESSES SOLD (DOZENS)	PROBABILITY
3	.05
4	.10
5	.35
6	.40
7	.05
8	.05

a. Identify the four elements of this decision problem.

b. Construct a payoff table for this problem.

c. Convert the payoff table into an opportunity loss table.

d. Select the optimal action according to the expected payoff criterion.

e. Verify that the expected opportunity loss criterion will select the same action as that identified in part d.

f. Find the action selected by the maximax criterion.

g.   Find the action selected by the maximin criterion.
h.   Find the action selected by the minimax criterion.

16.33   A producer of frozen orange juice is considering whether to sponsor a new children's television program shown on Saturday mornings. A year's sponsorship will cost the producer $100,000. If the producer sponsors the new program and viewer reaction is favorable (probability of .50), the producer's yearly orange juice sales will be $500,000; if viewer reaction is fair (probability of .30), yearly sales will be $250,000; and if viewer reaction is unfavorable (probability of .20), yearly sales will be $15,000. If the producer does not sponsor the children's television program, yearly sales will be $150,000. Should the producer sponsor the new children's television program?
a.   Identify the four elements of this decision problem.
b.   Illustrate the decision problem with either a payoff table, an opportunity loss table, or a decision tree.
c.   Based on expected values, what is the producer's decision?
d.   Use a nonprobabilistic criterion to find the optimal decision.

16.34   A political candidate is trying to decide whether to issue a last-minute campaign flyer which might be interpreted by some voters as representing "smear tactics" against his competitor. The candidate's pollster has informed him that the voters' reactions to the flyer will either be "favorable," "no reaction," or "unfavorable," with respective probabilities of .4, .3, and .3. If the flyer is issued and the reaction is "favorable," the candidate's standing in the latest opinion poll will increase 5 points; if the voters have "no reaction," the candidate's position in the poll will remain the same; and if the voter reaction is "unfavorable," the candidate will drop 7 points in the poll. If the candidate decides not to issue the flyer, his position in the poll will be unchanged.
a.   Identify the four elements of this decision problem.
b.   Construct a payoff table and find the optimal decision, using the expected payoff criterion.
c.   Find the maximax and maximin decisions.
d.   Construct an opportunity loss table and find the minimax decision.

CASE STUDY 16.1
Decision-Making
under
Uncertainty in
the Petroleum
Industry

Most decisions in the petroleum industry involve elements of risk and uncertainty, particularly in the area of oil exploration. When a decision is made to drill an exploratory oil well, company geologists and engineers are not able to measure or define specific values of factors contributing to overall profit (or loss) at the time of the decision. In addition, future events that could affect timing and/or size of projected cash flows from the prospective well (e.g., government price controls, cessation of oil imports from Iran) cannot be reliably predicted. These risks and uncertainties have decision-makers in the oil industry relying more and more on decision analysis techniques. Chi U. Ikoku, Associate Professor and Associate Director of Drilling Research at the University of Tulsa, writes:[*]

> Decision analysis methods provide new and much more comprehensive ways to evaluate and compare the degree of risk and uncertainty associated with each [oil] investment

---

[*]*World Oil*, September 1980.

choice. The net result is that the decision maker is given a clearer insight of potential profitability and the likelihoods of achieving various levels of profitability than older, less formal methods of investment analysis. Because of rising drilling costs, the need to search for petroleum in deeper horizons or in remote areas of the world, increasing government control, etc., most petroleum exploration decision makers are no longer satisfied to base decisions on experience, intuition, rules of thumb or similar approaches. Instead, they recognize that better ways to evaluate and compare drilling investment strategies are needed. Decision analysis is fulfilling this need.

Ikoku lists several distinct advantages that decision analysis has over the less formal oil drilling decision-making techniques used in the past:

1. Decision analysis forces the decision-maker to consider all possible alternatives and their corresponding outcomes.
2. Decision analysis provides an excellent way to evaluate the sensitivity of various oil drilling factors to overall profitability.
3. Decision analysis provides a means to compare the relative desirability of drilling prospects having varying degrees of risk and uncertainty.
4. Decision analysis is a convenient and unambiguous way to communicate judgments about risk and uncertainty.
5. Exceedingly complex oil investment options can be analyzed using decision analysis techniques.

The decision-making technique discussed by Ikoku in his *World Oil* article is the expected value criterion (see Section 16.5). This procedure requires that the decision-maker assess the probability of occurrence of each possible state of nature. "Assigning probabilities of occurrence to various outcomes of a petroleum venture," says Ikoku, "requires the cooperative judgement and skills of geologists, engineers, and geophysicists." Some of the types of risks that oil investors commonly encounter and consequently need to assess are: risk of an exploratory or development dry well; political risk; economic risk; risk relating to future oil and gas prices; risk of storm damage to offshore installations; risk that an oil discovery will not be large enough to recover initial exploratory costs; risk of at least a given number of oil discoveries in a multi-well drilling program; environmental risk; and risk of gambler's ruin. Because of certain characteristics which are unique to petroleum exploration, these state of nature probabilities cannot be determined exactly, and furthermore, their estimates often must be made on the basis of very little or no statistical data or experience. (Additional data can be obtained from additional wells, but, says Ikoku, "normally, delaying decisions until there is sufficient data upon which to base probability estimates cannot be afforded.") Thus, the decision-maker usually must rely on his or her subjective judgment or past success ratios in order to assess the state of nature probabilities.

As an illustration of how decision analysis may be applied to the petroleum industry, Ikoku presented the following example: A company is considering the purchase of 320 net acres in a proposed 640-acre oil unit. Three decision alternatives or actions are available to the company:

a_1: Participate in the unit (i.e., drill) with nonoperating 50% working interest

a_2: Farm out, but retain $\frac{1}{8}$ of $\frac{7}{8}$ overriding royalty interest

a_3: Be carried under penalty with a back-in privilege after recovery of 150% of investment by participating parties.

The possible outcomes or states of nature and their corresponding probabilities, based on detailed geological and engineering analyses of the prospect and surrounding wells, are given in Table 16.15. Since the company will base its decision on the objective variable Net profit, the projected net profits for the action/state of nature combinations were determined as shown in Table 16.16.

TABLE 16.15

STATE OF NATURE	PROBABILITY
S_1: Dry hole	.30
S_2: Unit produces 20,000 barrels	.25
S_3: Unit produces 40,000 barrels	.25
S_4: Unit produces 80,000 barrels	.10
S_5: Unit produces 100,000 barrels	.10

TABLE 16.16

ACTION/STATE	NET PROFIT
Drill/Dry hole	−$40,000
Drill/20,000 Bbls	$50,000
Drill/40,000 Bbls	$300,000
Drill/80,000 Bbls	$700,000
Drill/100,000 Bbls	$800,000
Farm out/Dry hole	$0
Farm out/20,000 Bbls	$12,000
Farm out/40,000 Bbls	$60,000
Farm out/80,000 Bbls	$120,000
Farm out/100,000 Bbls	$130,000
Back-in option/Dry hole	$0
Back-in option/20,000 Bbls	$12,000
Back-in option/40,000 Bbls	$145,000
Back-in option/80,000 Bbls	$400,000
Back-in option/100,000 Bbls	$500,000

a. Construct a payoff table for the oil investment decision problem.

b. Using the expected payoff criterion, which of the three alternative actions should the company accept?

c. What is the maximax decision? The maximin decision?

d. Construct an opportunity loss table for the oil investment decision problem and find the minimax decision.

CASE STUDY 16.2
Choosing the
Right Fork of a
Decision Tree

Chi U. Ikoku continues his *World Oil* article on decision analysis in the petroleum industry (see Case Study 16.1) with a discussion of decision trees and their importance in solving decision problems much more complex than the examples and exercises of Chapter 16. Nontrivial decision problems consist of not one but a sequence of major choices or decisions that must be made. Writes Ikoku: "In a complex decision problem involving a long sequence of alternatives, a formal procedure for decision analysis is necessary to array the alternatives so that economic ramifications of each are clearly delineated. This formal array also promotes effective internal communication. The decision tree analysis fits this criterion." To illustrate, Ikoku presented the following example of a drilling venture evaluation.

XYZ Enterprises has a nontransferable short-term option to drill on a certain plot of land. Two recent dry holes elsewhere have reduced XYZ's liquid assets to $130,000; and John Doe, president and principal stockholder, must decide whether XYZ should exercise its option (i.e., drill) or allow it to expire. Complicating the decision problem is the fact that Doe may pay to have a seismic test run in the next few days, and then, depending on the results, decide whether to drill. Thus, Doe has three possible alternatives or actions that he may take:

a_1: Drill immediately

a_2: Pay to have a seismic test run, then decide whether to drill

a_3: Let the option expire (i.e., do not pay for seismic test and do not drill)

XYZ can have the seismic test performed for a fee of $30,000 and the well can be drilled for $100,000. XYZ usually sells the rights of any oil discovered. A major oil company has promised to purchase all of the oil rights for $400,000.

The company geologist has examined the available geological data and states that there is a .55 probability that oil will be discovered if a well is sunk. Data on seismic test reliability indicate that if the results are favorable, the probability of finding oil will increase to .85; but if the results are unfavorable, it will fall to .10. The geologist has also computed that there is a .60 chance that the result will be favorable if a test is made.

What is the oil company's decision, using the expected payoff criterion?

This decision problem is structured in the form of a decision tree, as shown in Figure 16.4 on p. 558. As before, the □ denotes a decision fork and the ○ denotes a chance fork. Notice that the probabilities assigned to the states of nature, Strike oil, Do not strike oil (given in parentheses under the appropriate fork), vary according to whether the seismic test is run, and if run, whether the test is favorable. Also note that the objective variable in this decision problem is Net liquid assets (in dollars).

The expected payoff strategy as applied to decision trees which involve a sequence of choices to be made requires that the decision-maker work through the decision tree "backwards" (i.e., from right to left), computing at each chance fork ○ the corresponding expected payoff. Then at each decision fork □, choose the action with the maximum expected payoff (thereby eliminating all other alternatives at that particular fork from further consideration). Repeat the procedure until only a single action or branch remains. This is the optimal expected payoff strategy.

a. From Figure 16.4, compute the expected payoff for the action a_1: Drill immediately.

b. From Figure 16.4, compute the expected payoff for the action a_3: Do not run seismic test, do not drill.

c. The expected payoff for the action, a_2: Run seismic test, then decide whether to drill, is not computed as easily as for actions a_1 and a_3 since action a_2 involves

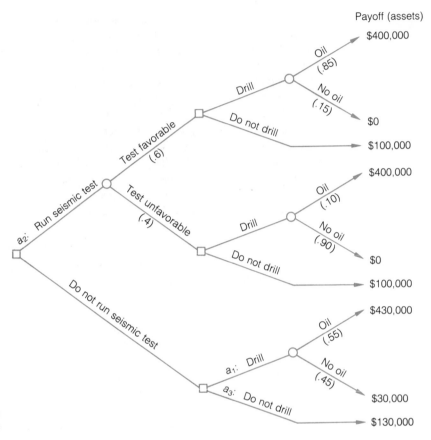

Payoff (assets)

FIGURE 16.4
Decision Tree for Drilling
Venture Example

two different chance forks—the fork corresponding to the result of the seismic test (Favorable or Unfavorable) and the fork corresponding to the result of drilling (Oil or No oil). The first step in computing the expected payoff for a_2 is to compute the expected payoff at each of the two rightmost chance forks in the Run seismic test branch of the tree. Place these expected values above the corresponding chance fork symbol ○ in Figure 16.4. (For example, the expected payoff for the top, rightmost fork is ($400,000)(.85) + ($0)(.15) = $340,000.)

d. The second step is to determine the optimal action at each decision fork □ in the Run seismic test branch by comparing the expected payoffs of the two actions Drill and Do not drill. Choose the action with the largest expected payoff and eliminate the alternative branch from further consideration. (For example, the optimal action corresponding to the top, rightmost decision fork □ is Drill, since the expected payoff for this action, namely $340,000, is larger than the expected payoff ($100,000) corresponding to the action Do not drill. Thus, we can eliminate the action Test favorable, Do not drill from further consideration.)

e. If you have performed the second step in part d correctly, there should remain only two "clear" paths or options available to the decision-maker in the upper portion of the tree: the Test favorable, Drill option and the Test unfavorable, Do not drill option. To compute the expected payoff for action a_2: Run seismic test, multiply the expected payoffs of these optimal actions by their corresponding state of nature (Favorable or Unfavorable) probabilities and sum these two values. [*Hint:* The correct expected payoff is ($340,000)(.6) + ($100,000)(.4) = $244,000.]

f. Now that you have computed the expected payoffs for each of the three actions, apply the expected payoff criterion in the usual manner, that is, choose the action with the maximum expected payoff. What is the oil company's decision?

CASE STUDY 16.3
The United Airlines Coupon Strategy

In late May 1979, employees at United Airlines ended their two-month strike. The walkout of ticket agents, flight attendants, mechanics, and other personnel had prevented the airline from flying passengers on its daily routes and had cost United millions of dollars in lost revenue. The strike settlement solved the immediate problem, but left United in a precarious position. Lester A. Digman explains:*

> Since most travelers make travel plans and arrangements some time before departure, it normally takes a period of time before an airline is operating at normal capacity after a strike or other shutdown. Thus, airlines typically experience a poor load factor during such periods, with some travelers having found a substitute favorite carrier in the meantime. United's problem was how to win back the air traveler as well as how to fill seats, perhaps with new travelers, during the period immediately after the strike.

United decided on a plan which would give each passenger a 50% discount coupon. That is, anyone taking a United flight during the first three weeks after the strike would receive a coupon good for half fare on a round trip between July 1 and December 15—a 5½-month period which includes both high-volume (July 4th, Labor Day, Thanksgiving) and low-volume travel times. United felt that this strategy would significantly reduce recovery time, i.e., the time it normally takes an airline to regain most or all of its passengers after a work stoppage, without turning away significant numbers of full-fare passengers during the high-volume travel periods.

United's coupon strategy had some interesting repercussions. "To make the idea administratively manageable," says Digman, "United passed out the coupons to every passenger on every flight, with no limitation that they be used by the recipient." This, of course, meant that the coupons were freely transferable, and a "white market" immediately developed, "with offers of $20 to $50 per coupon typical. . . . Tales of individuals, travel agents, and business people taking $30 short flights to get a coupon for use on later, more expensive flights became common." And "in an apparent spirit of competitive reaction," other airlines such as American Airlines and Pan Am duplicated United's plan. Furthermore, the National Aeronautics Board (NAB) grounded the DC-10 fleets of all airlines on June 6, 1979, until well into July. Nevertheless, United's coupon strategy appeared to be working, for even without its DC-10's (United operates 37 DC-10's which normally provide 22% of its capacity), the airline was near absolute capacity by the end of June. However, suggests Digman, "with the DC-10's [of all airlines] grounded, United could perhaps have achieved its

---

*Reprinted by permission of Lester A. Digman, "A decision analysis of the airline coupon strategy." *Interfaces*, *10*(2), April 1980. Copyright 1980 The Institute of Management Sciences.

goal of winning back passengers without the coupons, not to mention the impact of the gasoline shortage for motorists."

For the purposes of this case study, we will duplicate Digman's efforts and consider United's problem of winning back its customers in the form of a decision analysis problem. However, our approach will be much simpler than Digman's, in order that we may illustrate the important ideas presented in this chapter. The statement of the problem is as follows:

In an attempt to win back its pre-strike passengers without losing money, United Airlines is considering one of the following three actions:

a_1: Issue 50% discount coupons with no limitations on who may use the coupon
a_2: Issue 50% discount coupons, with use limited to the recipient
a_3: Do not issue discount coupons, and rely on the loyalty of its customers

If the discount coupons are distributed and used to fill otherwise empty seats (additional traffic), then United will have achieved its goal. However, if the coupons are used for travel that would have occurred anyway (normal traffic), then United will experience lost revenue. Based on studies of the strike recovery process at other airlines and the present economy of the airline industry, United has constructed the following payoff table, with June revenue (in $ millions) as the objective variable:

| | | STATE OF NATURE | |
		Normal traffic	Additional traffic
	Issue coupons, no limitations	−8.20	20.80
ACTION	Issue coupons with limitations	−3.70	15.50
	Do not issue coupons	10.50	10.50

United has assessed the probability of additional traffic being generated by the discount coupon as .70.

a. What is United's decision, using the expected payoff criterion?
b. What is United's decision, using the maximax criterion?
c. What is United's decision, using the maximin criterion?
d. What is United's decision, using the minimax criterion? [*Hint:* Construct an opportunity loss table.]

REFERENCES   Baird, B. F. *Introduction to decision analysis.* North Scituate, Mass.: Duxbury, 1978.
Brown, R. V., Kahr, A. S., & Peterson, C. *Decision analysis for the manager.* New York: Holt, Rinehart, and Winston, 1974.
Digman, L. A. "A decision analysis of the airline coupon strategy." *Interfaces,* April 1980, *10,* 97–101.
Ikoku, C. U. "Decision analysis: How to make risk evaluations." *World Oil,* September 1980, 71–74, 81.
McClave, J. T., & Benson, P. G. *Statistics for business and economics.* 2d ed. San Francisco: Dellen, 1982.
Summers, G., Peters, W., & Armstrong, C. *Basic statistics in business and economics.* 3d ed. Belmont, Ca.: Wadsworth, 1981. Chapters 18 and 19.

Appendix A

Data Set: Appraisals and Sale Prices for All 1978 Residential Property Sales in a Midsized Florida City

FIGURE A.1   Location of the City and Surrounding Areas

Location of sections within
a Range-Township block

6	5	4	3	2	1
7	8	9	10	11	12
18	17	16	15	14	13
19	20	21	22	23	24
30	29	28	27	26	25
31	32	33	34	35	36

T 8

T 9

T 10

THE
CITY

T 11

Township

R 17   R 18   R 19   R 20   R 21   R 22

Range

FIGURE A.2   The City and Adjacent Areas (City Is the Shaded Area)

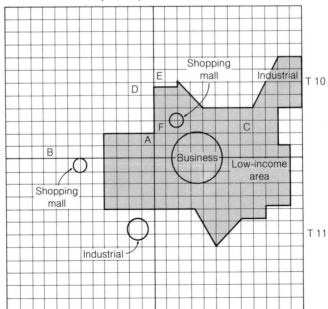

Shopping
mall

E   Industrial   T 10

D

F

A   C

B

Business   Low-income
area

Shopping
mall

Industrial

T 11

R 19   R 20

REAL ESTATE SALES FOR 1978
IN A MID-SIZED FLORIDA CITY

OBS	TOWNSHIP	RANGE	SECTION	LANDVAL	IMPROVAL	SALEPRIC	SALTOAPR
1	0	19	0	$1,500	$18,900	$32,500	1.59314
2	7	17	34	$720	$7,840	$25,000	2.92056
3	7	17	34	$360	$4,700	$13,000	2.56917
4	7	17	34	$480	$4,280	$12,000	2.52101
5	7	17	34	$2,650	$16,370	$40,000	2.10305
6	7	17	34	$1,800	$6,810	$17,500	2.03252
7	7	17	34	$1,200	$8,260	$19,000	2.00846
8	7	17	34	$1,200	$14,450	$30,000	1.91693
9	7	17	34	$1,200	$5,760	$13,000	1.86782
10	7	17	34	$1,680	$9,790	$21,000	1.83086
11	7	17	34	$1,200	$5,960	$12,700	1.77374
12	7	17	34	$960	$9,170	$18,000	1.77690
13	7	17	23	$11,510	$37,300	$79,900	1.63696
14	7	17	34	$960	$4,090	$8,000	1.58416
15	7	17	34	$1,440	$21,270	$35,000	1.54117
16	7	17	34	$1,200	$27,790	$43,000	1.48327
17	7	17	28	$4,800	$14,870	$28,000	1.42349
18	7	17	33	$240	$6,040	$9,000	1.43312
19	7	17	34	$960	$13,870	$21,000	1.41605
20	7	17	34	$600	$4,790	$7,500	1.39147
21	7	17	35	$2,400	$21,250	$32,500	1.37421
22	7	17	34	$1,200	$35,190	$50,000	1.37400
23	7	17	35	$2,580	$34,410	$50,000	1.35172
24	7	17	34	$800	$8,140	$12,000	1.34228
25	7	17	34	$2,000	$25,940	$36,500	1.30637
26	7	17	34	$2,280	$28,020	$38,500	1.27063
27	7	17	34	$600	$4,510	$6,000	1.17417
28	7	17	34	$840	$10,220	$11,600	1.04882
29	7	17	34	$2,000	$36,030	$38,700	1.01762
30	7	17	35	$1,500	$40,660	$39,900	0.94639
31	7	18	34	$850	$13,660	$75,000	5.16885
32	7	19	34	$800	$3,260	$6,000	1.47783
33	7	19	23	$5,000	$39,670	$112,500	2.51847
34	7	19	27	$1,150	$11,880	$17,500	1.34305
35	7	19	26	$3,080	$40,900	$84,000	1.90996
36	8	17	3	$1,200	$7,080	$47,000	5.67633
37	8	17	3	$3,140	$168,770	$770,000	4.47909
38	8	17	3	$670	$4,260	$20,500	4.15822
39	8	17	3	$1,200	$8,110	$35,000	3.75940
40	8	17	3	$1,250	$7,840	$29,500	3.24532
41	8	17	3	$750	$5,890	$19,900	2.99699
42	8	17	3	$3,960	$8,300	$35,000	2.85481
43	8	17	3	$960	$3,170	$10,000	2.42131
44	8	17	3	$1,000	$9,620	$24,000	2.25989
45	8	17	10	$1,050	$6,660	$17,600	2.28275
46	8	17	3	$1,330	$5,810	$16,000	2.24090
47	8	17	3	$1,000	$6,390	$16,500	2.23275
48	8	17	6	$3,000	$7,640	$22,300	2.09586
49	8	17	2	$2,400	$11,360	$26,000	1.88953
50	8	17	12	$780	$13,920	$26,500	1.80272
51	8	17	3	$960	$4,500	$9,000	1.64835
52	8	17	10	$1,200	$13,530	$22,000	1.49355
53	8	17	3	$1,000	$18,140	$27,900	1.45768
54	8	17	24	$7,930	$33,870	$60,000	1.4354
55	8	17	3	$1,000	$12,940	$19,500	1.3989
56	8	17	10	$1,400	$17,940	$26,700	1.3806
57	8	17	10	$1,200	$17,820	$25,500	1.3407
58	8	17	10	$1,200	$17,880	$25,500	1.3365
59	8	17	10	$1,200	$18,030	$25,500	1.3261
60	8	17	10	$1,200	$17,980	$25,500	1.3295
61	8	17	3	$820	$9,400	$13,500	1.3209
62	8	17	3	$800	$16,540	$22,500	1.2976
63	8	17	2	$1,350	$18,080	$24,500	1.2609
64	8	17	3	$1,320	$8,270	$11,000	1.1470
65	8	17	10	$1,200	$13,530	$17,000	1.1541
66	8	17	3	$1,320	$19,690	$24,000	1.1423
67	8	17	12	$680	$18,160	$21,500	1.1412
68	8	17	3	$1,000	$20,380	$24,000	1.1225
69	8	17	4	$1,400	$14,780	$15,800	0.9765
70	8	18	14	$400	$1,990	$25,000	10.4603
71	8	18	15	$3,120	$9,430	$57,000	4.5418
72	8	18	15	$1,600	$11,840	$38,800	2.8869
73	8	18	15	$780	$5,140	$15,000	2.5338
74	8	18	14	$6,060	$28,640	$82,500	2.3775
75	8	18	15	$1,300	$5,750	$17,000	2.4113
76	8	18	15	$1,900	$8,490	$24,000	2.3099
77	8	18	30	$1,860	$11,240	$40,000	3.0534
78	8	18	8	$9,280	$24,220	$70,000	2.0896
79	8	18	15	$1,600	$7,730	$18,600	1.9936
80	8	18	14	$4,030	$10,780	$28,000	1.8906

REAL ESTATE SALES FOR 1978
IN A MID-SIZED FLORIDA CITY (CONTINUED)

OBS	TOWNSHIP	RANGE	SECTION	LANDVAL	IMPROVAL	SALEPRIC	SALTOAPR
81	8	18	11	$290	$6,600	$12,500	1.8142
82	8	18	28	$500	$1,200	$3,100	1.8235
83	8	18	31	$5,590	$22,500	$50,000	1.7800
84	8	18	15	$3,600	$19,230	$38,500	1.6864
85	8	18	15	$1,200	$10,730	$20,000	1.6764
86	8	18	27	$2,000	$22,250	$39,900	1.6454
87	8	18	10	$300	$11,270	$18,500	1.5990
88	8	18	14	$1,600	$14,150	$25,000	1.5873
89	8	18	15	$1,480	$20,520	$35,000	1.5909
90	8	18	15	$1,080	$4,640	$8,900	1.5559
91	8	18	29	$1,750	$28,060	$45,700	1.5330
92	8	18	14	$1,060	$16,830	$27,000	1.5092
93	8	18	14	$4,350	$25,740	$45,000	1.4955
94	8	18	14	$1,580	$13,070	$22,000	1.5017
95	8	18	28	$5,890	$23,030	$43,000	1.4869
96	8	18	15	$1,260	$32,560	$50,000	1.4784
97	8	18	8	$1,200	$21,700	$33,250	1.4520
98	8	18	15	$2,000	$18,110	$29,000	1.4421
99	8	18	27	$1,800	$19,090	$30,000	1.4361
100	8	18	8	$1,200	$19,360	$29,000	1.4105
101	8	18	14	$2,740	$6,520	$13,000	1.4039
102	8	18	14	$1,400	$17,690	$27,000	1.4144
103	8	18	15	$840	$6,630	$10,500	1.4056
104	8	18	15	$1,600	$19,350	$29,500	1.4081
105	8	18	0	$10,260	$33,440	$143,300	3.2792
106	8	18	14	$1,110	$6,120	$10,000	1.3831
107	8	18	15	$9,800	$40,640	$70,000	1.38779
108	8	18	15	$740	$16,450	$23,500	1.36707
109	8	18	14	$1,730	$17,660	$25,700	1.32543
110	8	18	21	$1,200	$36,040	$50,000	1.34264
111	8	18	14	$1,400	$19,930	$28,100	1.31739
112	8	18	27	$4,550	$21,690	$34,000	1.29573
113	8	18	11	$5,290	$28,260	$43,000	1.28167
114	8	18	15	$1,010	$16,180	$22,000	1.27981
115	8	18	15	$1,180	$23,250	$31,000	1.26893
116	8	18	14	$4,700	$22,200	$33,500	1.24535
117	8	18	14	$4,300	$22,590	$33,800	1.25697
118	8	18	15	$1,010	$16,610	$22,030	1.25028
119	8	18	22	$1,720	$24,980	$32,800	1.22846
120	8	18	15	$1,010	$17,410	$22,500	1.22150
121	8	18	8	$1,200	$21,170	$26,900	1.20250
122	8	18	14	$1,170	$18,680	$24,000	1.20907
123	8	18	14	$500	$2,680	$3,800	1.19497
124	8	18	19	$2,340	$16,760	$22,500	1.17801
125	8	18	14	$1,600	$20,600	$25,000	1.12613
126	8	18	14	$4,350	$22,080	$29,500	1.11616
127	8	18	14	$4,600	$20,140	$26,200	1.05901
128	8	18	14	$600	$8,070	$8,850	1.02076
129	8	18	22	$1,640	$21,170	$23,000	1.00833
130	8	18	14	$4,600	$21,090	$25,200	0.98093
131	8	18	14	$18,300	$110,000	$120,000	0.93531
132	8	18	14	$1,000	$10,570	$9,900	0.85566
133	8	18	15	$1,350	$5,820	$6,000	0.83682
134	8	18	15	$1,440	$6,410	$6,500	0.82803
135	8	19	21	$960	$3,830	$22,500	4.69729
136	8	19	11	$2,000	$14,240	$40,300	2.48153
137	8	19	28	$4,800	$33,280	$68,900	1.80935
138	8	19	28	$2,660	$29,810	$58,000	1.78626
139	8	19	28	$4,800	$30,370	$59,900	1.70316
140	8	19	28	$2,240	$20,520	$38,700	1.70035
141	8	19	28	$4,800	$29,140	$55,900	1.64702
142	8	19	28	$2,660	$34,880	$61,000	1.62493
143	8	19	28	$2,100	$22,650	$39,800	1.60808
144	8	19	28	$2,870	$32,470	$56,300	1.59310
145	8	19	28	$2,100	$21,310	$36,900	1.57625
146	8	19	28	$2,870	$31,550	$53,500	1.55433
147	8	19	28	$2,950	$33,520	$56,500	1.54922
148	8	19	28	$2,800	$32,080	$53,900	1.54530
149	8	19	28	$2,170	$22,350	$37,900	1.54568
150	8	19	13	$9,490	$35,470	$68,000	1.51246
151	8	19	28	$2,870	$31,830	$52,500	1.51297
152	8	19	28	$2,660	$33,050	$53,000	1.48418
153	8	19	28	$3,190	$33,500	$55,200	1.50450
154	8	19	20	$2,880	$18,850	$31,900	1.46802
155	8	19	28	$2,170	$25,130	$40,100	1.46886
156	8	19	28	$6,700	$22,270	$41,800	1.44287
157	8	19	20	$3,600	$23,010	$37,900	1.42428
158	8	19	20	$3,600	$24,000	$37,500	1.35870
159	8	19	20	$3,600	$26,510	$40,000	1.32846
160	8	19	20	$3,600	$20,680	$31,500	1.2974

REAL ESTATE SALES FOR 1978
IN A MID-SIZED FLORIDA CITY (CONTINUED)

OBS	TOWNSHIP	RANGE	SECTION	LANDVAL	IMPROVAL	SALEPRIC	SALTOAPR
161	8	19	20	$3,600	$25,640	$36,900	1.2620
162	8	19	20	$3,600	$24,250	$35,000	1.2567
163	8	19	20	$3,600	$24,880	$35,200	1.2360
164	8	19	20	$3,600	$27,140	$37,000	1.2036
165	8	19	21	$3,500	$20,830	$25,100	1.0316
166	8	19	21	$1,910	$7,500	$9,150	0.9724
167	8	20	7	$200	$8,430	$25,500	2.9548
168	8	20	8	$6,310	$33,620	$55,500	1.3899
169	8	21	23	$600	$5,290	$18,200	3.0900
170	8	21	23	$1,000	$2,710	$11,000	2.9650
171	8	21	14	$900	$10,290	$29,500	2.6363
172	8	21	23	$980	$9,880	$23,800	2.1915
173	8	21	23	$1,000	$3,510	$9,000	1.9956
174	8	21	23	$1,000	$10,610	$23,000	1.9811
175	8	21	23	$1,330	$7,480	$15,000	1.7026
176	8	21	31	$4,440	$14,890	$30,100	1.5572
177	8	21	23	$800	$17,620	$28,000	1.5201
178	8	21	14	$600	$14,280	$20,000	1.3441
179	8	21	23	$500	$8,740	$11,500	1.2446
180	8	21	14	$13,500	$43,020	$67,500	1.1943
181	8	21	23	$1,000	$19,190	$23,500	1.1639
182	8	21	23	$1,200	$18,120	$18,500	0.9576
183	8	22	33	$1,000	$6,280	$22,500	3.0907
184	8	22	29	$390	$16,790	$43,500	2.5320
185	8	22	33	$830	$5,430	$13,500	2.1565
186	8	22	28	$5,860	$17,160	$46,400	2.0156
187	8	22	31	$3,300	$14,610	$31,000	1.7309
188	8	22	31	$2,650	$26,880	$35,000	1.1852
189	8	22	19	$2,500	$7,770	$11,500	1.1198
190	9	17	12	$7,250	$35,800	$60,500	1.4053
191	9	18	14	$9,500	$26,710	$529,000	14.6092
192	9	18	29	$1,000	$26,900	$100,000	3.5842
193	9	18	36	$16,000	$74,000	$175,000	1.9444
194	9	18	22	$5,000	$27,250	$61,500	1.9070
195	9	18	32	$1,600	$11,660	$25,000	1.8854
196	9	18	27	$6,540	$19,000	$45,900	1.7972
197	9	18	36	$9,230	$53,660	$110,000	1.7491
198	9	18	26	$7,290	$30,850	$63,000	1.6518
199	9	18	35	$2,500	$22,370	$40,000	1.6084
200	9	18	32	$11,520	$32,810	$67,300	1.5182
201	9	18	36	$8,740	$36,310	$67,500	1.4983
202	9	18	36	$8,000	$46,580	$82,000	1.5024
203	9	18	36	$8,740	$48,820	$81,000	1.4072
204	9	18	36	$10,500	$55,690	$91,200	1.3779
205	9	18	5	$140	$1,200	$1,500	1.1194
206	9	19	14	$2,500	$13,270	$91,000	5.7705
207	9	19	33	$5,500	$41,890	$110,000	2.3212
208	9	19	34	$2,500	$10,680	$28,500	2.1624
209	9	19	16	$2,000	$20,640	$48,000	2.1201
210	9	19	34	$2,500	$10,010	$26,000	2.0783
211	9	19	26	$2,500	$16,980	$39,900	2.0483
212	9	19	26	$24,800	$76,850	$208,000	2.0462
213	9	19	34	$2,500	$10,520	$26,000	1.99693
214	9	19	24	$3,630	$19,200	$44,500	1.94919
215	9	19	35	$5,250	$21,070	$51,500	1.95669
216	9	19	13	$4,300	$22,070	$50,000	1.89609
217	9	19	27	$2,870	$13,570	$31,000	1.88564
218	9	19	23	$3,600	$18,060	$39,500	1.82364
219	9	19	23	$3,600	$19,220	$41,500	1.81858
220	9	19	33	$9,070	$86,690	$175,000	1.82749
221	9	19	34	$3,000	$13,640	$30,500	1.83293
222	9	19	34	$3,500	$9,020	$22,900	1.82907
223	9	19	24	$3,490	$14,680	$32,500	1.78866
224	9	19	26	$4,750	$24,440	$51,900	1.77801
225	9	19	36	$9,500	$64,990	$133,000	1.78547
226	9	19	23	$3,600	$14,970	$32,500	1.75013
227	9	19	26	$4,070	$25,700	$52,000	1.74672
228	9	19	34	$2,500	$11,710	$25,000	1.75932
229	9	19	36	$5,600	$19,410	$44,000	1.75930
230	9	19	23	$3,500	$17,000	$35,500	1.73171
231	9	19	24	$3,450	$21,630	$43,000	1.71451
232	9	19	26	$4,800	$25,950	$53,000	1.72358
233	9	19	26	$4,800	$25,750	$53,000	1.73486
234	9	19	33	$12,600	$39,970	$90,000	1.71200
235	9	19	35	$6,500	$24,020	$52,700	1.72674
236	9	19	16	$6,000	$36,520	$72,000	1.69332
237	9	19	23	$8,370	$62,850	$120,000	1.68492
238	9	19	24	$3,490	$19,100	$38,000	1.68216
239	9	19	24	$3,490	$17,260	$35,500	1.71084
240	9	19	33	$5,500	$49,700	$94,000	1.70290

REAL ESTATE SALES FOR 1978
IN A MID-SIZED FLORIDA CITY (CONTINUED)

OBS	TOWNSHIP	RANGE	SECTION	LANDVAL	IMPROVAL	SALEPRIC	SALTOAPR
241	9	19	35	$5,100	$20,720	$43,900	1.70023
242	9	19	35	$5,000	$16,640	$37,000	1.70980
243	9	19	36	$5,600	$21,040	$45,000	1.68919
244	9	19	24	$3,500	$21,950	$42,500	1.66994
245	9	19	26	$4,100	$30,150	$57,500	1.67883
246	9	19	27	$2,340	$18,650	$35,000	1.66746
247	9	19	33	$5,500	$45,920	$86,000	1.67250
248	9	19	33	$7,000	$58,010	$109,000	1.67667
249	9	19	35	$6,200	$17,430	$39,500	1.67160
250	9	19	35	$5,000	$17,050	$36,500	1.65533
251	9	19	36	$8,600	$43,810	$88,000	1.67907
252	9	19	13	$4,300	$21,740	$42,500	1.63210
253	9	19	13	$4,770	$30,960	$58,500	1.63728
254	9	19	13	$3,990	$25,270	$48,200	1.64730
255	9	19	23	$4,200	$25,220	$47,900	1.62814
256	9	19	24	$3,490	$22,230	$42,000	1.63297
257	9	19	24	$5,400	$16,430	$35,900	1.64453
258	9	19	25	$4,450	$26,130	$50,000	1.63506
259	9	19	26	$4,200	$31,090	$57,500	1.62936
260	9	19	33	$5,500	$43,140	$80,000	1.64474
261	9	19	34	$3,000	$12,510	$25,500	1.64410
262	9	19	34	$3,000	$13,810	$27,500	1.63593
263	9	19	35	$6,500	$16,670	$38,100	1.64437
264	9	19	13	$4,300	$20,130	$39,500	1.61686
265	9	19	13	$5,500	$27,120	$52,600	1.61251
266	9	19	23	$3,600	$23,160	$43,000	1.60688
267	9	19	24	$3,400	$18,680	$35,800	1.62138
268	9	19	24	$3,590	$16,760	$33,000	1.62162
269	9	19	24	$3,590	$23,260	$43,000	1.60149
270	9	19	24	$3,600	$20,510	$39,000	1.61759
271	9	19	25	$5,210	$29,260	$56,000	1.62460
272	9	19	28	$7,350	$32,430	$64,000	1.60885
273	9	19	34	$5,500	$26,150	$51,500	1.62717
274	9	19	34	$4,000	$32,980	$59,500	1.60898
275	9	19	35	$6,000	$30,720	$59,000	1.60675
276	9	19	35	$5,000	$15,430	$32,900	1.61038
277	9	19	35	$5,000	$17,910	$37,000	1.61502
278	9	19	13	$4,000	$16,420	$32,500	1.59158
279	9	19	13	$3,990	$17,930	$34,600	1.57847
280	9	19	13	$3,990	$24,350	$45,300	1.59845
281	9	19	13	$3,990	$20,430	$38,500	1.57658
282	9	19	21	$7,200	$42,180	$77,900	1.57756
283	9	19	23	$5,000	$31,550	$58,000	1.58687
284	9	19	23	$3,600	$18,750	$35,500	1.58837
285	9	19	24	$3,570	$17,630	$33,700	1.58962
286	9	19	24	$3,490	$14,530	$28,500	1.58158
287	9	19	26	$9,400	$46,670	$88,500	1.57838
288	9	19	26	$4,100	$38,750	$68,000	1.58693
289	9	19	26	$4,200	$40,300	$70,700	1.58876
290	9	19	26	$4,200	$38,490	$68,000	1.59288
291	9	19	31	$5,320	$37,710	$68,000	1.58029
292	9	19	35	$5,100	$18,460	$37,300	1.58319
293	9	19	35	$5,900	$18,770	$39,100	1.58492
294	9	19	35	$5,900	$23,850	$46,900	1.57647
295	9	19	35	$5,000	$13,440	$29,500	1.59978
296	9	19	35	$7,000	$23,350	$48,000	1.58155
297	9	19	36	$8,600	$35,560	$69,900	1.58288
298	9	19	36	$5,600	$22,020	$44,000	1.59305
299	9	19	13	$900	$15,770	$25,900	1.55369
300	9	19	13	$5,600	$29,310	$55,000	1.57548
301	9	19	13	$3,950	$21,390	$39,900	1.57459
302	9	19	13	$3,990	$20,480	$38,500	1.57336
303	9	19	13	$4,300	$18,500	$35,500	1.55702
304	9	19	23	$5,000	$29,310	$53,800	1.56806
305	9	19	23	$3,810	$26,410	$47,000	1.55526
306	9	19	24	$5,000	$27,000	$49,900	1.55937
307	9	19	24	$3,490	$21,270	$38,500	1.55493
308	9	19	24	$3,440	$18,830	$34,900	1.56713
309	9	19	24	$3,420	$17,710	$33,000	1.56176
310	9	19	24	$3,500	$21,820	$39,800	1.57188
311	9	19	24	$3,970	$18,360	$34,900	1.56292
312	9	19	25	$4,100	$20,310	$38,000	1.55674
313	9	19	25	$4,100	$17,800	$34,300	1.56621
314	9	19	25	$4,180	$19,560	$36,900	1.55434
315	9	19	25	$4,100	$20,920	$39,000	1.55875
316	9	19	26	$8,000	$34,160	$65,500	1.55361
317	9	19	26	$4,800	$28,480	$51,900	1.55950
318	9	19	30	$5,000	$32,660	$58,500	1.55337
319	9	19	33	$9,360	$55,150	$101,500	1.57340
320	9	19	33	$6,000	$37,970	$68,500	1.55788

REAL ESTATE SALES FOR 1978
IN A MID-SIZED FLORIDA CITY (CONTINUED)

OBS	TOWNSHIP	RANGE	SECTION	LANDVAL	IMPROVAL	SALEPRIC	SALTOAPR
321	9	19	35	$6,500	$22,250	$45,000	1.56522
322	9	19	35	$5,100	$17,760	$35,600	1.55731
323	9	19	36	$6,260	$39,700	$72,000	1.56658
324	9	19	13	$4,500	$16,890	$33,000	1.54278
325	9	19	13	$4,300	$24,720	$45,000	1.55065
326	9	19	13	$3,910	$17,020	$32,100	1.53368
327	9	19	13	$3,990	$21,910	$39,900	1.54054
328	9	19	23	$4,000	$29,240	$50,900	1.53129
329	9	19	24	$6,100	$18,680	$37,900	1.52946
330	9	19	24	$3,440	$18,790	$34,300	1.54296
331	9	19	24	$3,900	$21,590	$39,400	1.54570
332	9	19	24	$3,800	$22,190	$40,000	1.53905
333	9	19	25	$3,600	$33,630	$57,000	1.53102
334	9	19	26	$6,280	$49,340	$85,000	1.52823
335	9	19	26	$5,550	$43,310	$75,000	1.53500
336	9	19	33	$5,200	$47,830	$82,000	1.54629
337	9	19	35	$7,400	$26,470	$52,500	1.55004
338	9	19	36	$6,040	$52,460	$90,000	1.53846
339	9	19	13	$4,300	$20,840	$37,900	1.50756
340	9	19	13	$5,400	$33,420	$59,200	1.52499
341	9	19	13	$4,100	$17,340	$32,400	1.51119
342	9	19	13	$4,100	$17,550	$32,900	1.51963
343	9	19	13	$3,910	$20,290	$36,500	1.50826
344	9	19	24	$3,690	$17,190	$31,500	1.50862
345	9	19	24	$6,400	$18,680	$37,900	1.51116
346	9	19	24	$6,000	$18,400	$36,900	1.51230
347	9	19	26	$5,850	$41,360	$71,500	1.51451
348	9	19	26	$5,600	$33,550	$59,000	1.50702
349	9	19	26	$6,300	$48,910	$83,200	1.50697
350	9	19	26	$4,100	$30,340	$52,500	1.52439
351	9	19	31	$5,540	$32,390	$57,500	1.51595
352	9	19	34	$2,500	$16,510	$29,000	1.52551
353	9	19	34	$8,060	$37,070	$68,900	1.52670
354	9	19	35	$6,000	$17,010	$35,000	1.52108
355	9	19	35	$5,100	$19,970	$38,000	1.51576
356	9	19	35	$5,800	$15,840	$33,000	1.52495
357	9	19	35	$5,880	$18,030	$36,000	1.50565
358	9	19	35	$5,000	$16,480	$32,600	1.51769
359	9	19	35	$5,500	$22,190	$41,800	1.50957
360	9	19	35	$5,500	$22,820	$42,900	1.51483
361	9	19	36	$7,500	$47,940	$83,500	1.50613
362	9	19	36	$6,050	$30,770	$56,000	1.52091
363	9	19	36	$5,800	$18,570	$36,900	1.51416
364	9	19	36	$6,270	$20,000	$40,000	1.52265
365	9	19	13	$4,820	$29,880	$51,900	1.49568
366	9	19	13	$4,300	$22,820	$40,800	1.50442
367	9	19	13	$4,370	$19,910	$36,400	1.49918
368	9	19	13	$3,990	$19,510	$35,000	1.48936
369	9	19	13	$3,990	$24,120	$41,800	1.48702
370	9	19	13	$4,200	$21,050	$37,700	1.49307
371	9	19	15	$7,250	$24,190	$46,700	1.48537
372	9	19	21	$7,000	$44,450	$76,500	1.48688
373	9	19	22	$980	$17,400	$27,500	1.49619
374	9	19	23	$4,100	$23,690	$41,300	1.48615
375	9	19	23	$4,200	$36,220	$60,000	1.48441
376	9	19	23	$1,000	$12,000	$19,300	1.48462
377	9	19	23	$5,200	$24,050	$43,900	1.50085
378	9	19	24	$2,400	$21,780	$36,000	1.48883
379	9	19	24	$2,900	$25,060	$41,500	1.48426
380	9	19	24	$3,490	$21,270	$37,000	1.49435
381	9	19	24	$6,000	$18,100	$36,000	1.49378
382	9	19	24	$6,000	$17,670	$35,100	1.48289
383	9	19	24	$6,000	$17,480	$35,000	1.49063
384	9	19	24	$4,370	$18,200	$33,500	1.48427
385	9	19	24	$3,440	$21,070	$36,800	1.50143
386	9	19	24	$3,420	$23,060	$39,700	1.49924
387	9	19	24	$3,500	$18,510	$32,900	1.49478
388	9	19	24	$3,550	$20,350	$35,900	1.50209
389	9	19	25	$6,600	$30,350	$55,000	1.48850
390	9	19	25	$4,450	$25,220	$44,000	1.48298
391	9	19	25	$4,200	$26,030	$45,000	1.48859
392	9	19	25	$4,800	$38,820	$65,000	1.49014
393	9	19	25	$5,840	$35,830	$62,500	1.49988
394	9	19	26	$6,220	$43,930	$75,000	1.49551
395	9	19	26	$5,500	$37,670	$64,900	1.50336
396	9	19	26	$6,000	$40,810	$69,500	1.48473
397	9	19	26	$4,100	$40,750	$67,000	1.49387
398	9	19	34	$7,200	$32,730	$59,500	1.49011
399	9	19	34	$8,100	$33,630	$62,000	1.48574
400	9	19	35	$5,000	$16,140	$31,500	1.49007

REAL ESTATE SALES FOR 1978
IN A MID-SIZED FLORIDA CITY (CONTINUED)

OBS	TOWNSHIP	RANGE	SECTION	LANDVAL	IMPROVAL	SALEPRIC	SALTOAPR
401	9	19	35	$5,000	$16,280	$32,000	1.50376
402	9	19	35	$8,000	$33,590	$62,000	1.49074
403	9	19	35	$5,500	$21,600	$40,200	1.48339
404	9	19	36	$5,600	$19,680	$37,500	1.48339
405	9	19	13	$4,300	$19,480	$34,900	1.46762
406	9	19	13	$4,500	$21,750	$38,500	1.46667
407	9	19	13	$4,300	$23,010	$39,900	1.46100
408	9	19	13	$4,300	$20,370	$36,500	1.47953
409	9	19	13	$4,200	$25,490	$43,500	1.46514
410	9	19	13	$3,910	$16,620	$30,000	1.46128
411	9	19	21	$3,600	$20,110	$35,000	1.47617
412	9	19	23	$5,060	$34,460	$58,300	1.47520
413	9	19	24	$2,900	$29,300	$47,500	1.47516
414	9	19	24	$4,040	$18,760	$33,500	1.46930
415	9	19	23	$3,630	$20,970	$36,000	1.46341
416	9	19	24	$6,000	$16,510	$33,200	1.47490
417	9	19	24	$6,300	$17,580	$35,100	1.46985
418	9	19	24	$4,000	$16,050	$29,500	1.47132
419	9	19	24	$4,280	$18,980	$34,000	1.46174
420	9	19	24	$4,800	$19,920	$36,500	1.47654
421	9	19	24	$3,900	$20,120	$35,200	1.46545
422	9	19	24	$3,450	$16,720	$29,800	1.47744
423	9	19	24	$3,420	$26,010	$43,500	1.47808
424	9	19	24	$3,500	$26,670	$44,500	1.47498
425	9	19	24	$3,420	$26,170	$43,500	1.47009
426	9	19	24	$4,070	$22,520	$38,900	1.46296
427	9	19	25	$4,100	$24,230	$41,500	1.46488
428	9	19	25	$4,450	$25,010	$43,300	1.46979
429	9	19	25	$4,000	$52,570	$83,500	1.47605
430	9	19	26	$5,610	$38,990	$66,000	1.47982
431	9	19	26	$5,550	$33,320	$57,500	1.47929
432	9	19	26	$6,000	$33,260	$58,000	1.47733
433	9	19	26	$5,550	$40,880	$68,000	1.46457
434	9	19	26	$4,290	$25,630	$43,900	1.46725
435	9	19	26	$9,500	$38,350	$70,500	1.47335
436	9	19	26	$9,500	$37,260	$69,000	1.47562
437	9	19	26	$9,600	$48,630	$86,000	1.47690
438	9	19	31	$5,320	$32,730	$56,000	1.47175
439	9	19	34	$3,000	$18,700	$31,900	1.47005
440	9	19	34	$7,700	$41,970	$72,700	1.46366
441	9	19	35	$6,500	$21,000	$40,500	1.47273
442	9	19	35	$8,000	$34,370	$62,800	1.48218
443	9	19	35	$5,250	$19,590	$36,500	1.46940
444	9	19	35	$5,500	$29,680	$52,000	1.47811
445	9	19	35	$5,500	$21,640	$39,800	1.46647
446	9	19	36	$6,500	$36,830	$64,000	1.47704
447	9	19	13	$5,270	$36,990	$61,000	1.44345
448	9	19	13	$5,500	$30,260	$52,000	1.45414
449	9	19	13	$4,600	$18,540	$33,700	1.45635
450	9	19	13	$4,100	$20,020	$34,900	1.44693
451	9	19	13	$4,400	$24,150	$41,500	1.45359
452	9	19	13	$4,000	$18,280	$32,500	1.45871
453	9	19	21	$7,000	$38,530	$65,600	1.44081
454	9	19	21	$7,000	$34,240	$60,000	1.45490
455	9	19	23	$4,000	$32,030	$51,900	1.44047
456	9	19	23	$7,600	$46,600	$78,900	1.45572
457	9	19	24	$2,400	$21,780	$34,900	1.44334
458	9	19	34	$6,200	$19,150	$36,600	1.44379
459	9	19	24	$4,280	$17,290	$31,500	1.46036
460	9	19	24	$3,460	$18,010	$31,100	1.44853
461	9	19	24	$3,440	$20,730	$35,000	1.44808
462	9	19	24	$3,440	$20,570	$34,900	1.45356
463	9	19	24	$3,600	$24,270	$40,400	1.44959
464	9	19	24	$3,500	$26,310	$43,200	1.44918
465	9	19	24	$3,970	$22,670	$38,500	1.44520
466	9	19	25	$4,450	$29,820	$50,000	1.45900
467	9	19	25	$3,600	$26,130	$43,000	1.44635
468	9	19	25	$7,700	$39,780	$68,800	1.44903
469	9	19	25	$5,600	$39,370	$65,000	1.44541
470	9	19	25	$6,400	$45,460	$75,000	1.44620
471	9	19	26	$5,720	$41,900	$69,000	1.44897
472	9	19	26	$5,500	$39,730	$65,600	1.45036
473	9	19	26	$5,550	$35,800	$59,600	1.44135
474	9	19	26	$4,360	$23,300	$40,000	1.44613
475	9	19	26	$9,400	$33,500	$62,000	1.44522
476	9	19	26	$9,400	$37,690	$68,200	1.44829
477	9	19	26	$4,100	$31,670	$51,800	1.44814
478	9	19	31	$5,130	$52,450	$83,500	1.45016
479	9	19	31	$5,130	$39,990	$65,100	1.44282
480	9	19	34	$2,850	$15,890	$27,000	1.44077

REAL ESTATE SALES FOR 1978
IN A MID-SIZED FLORIDA CITY (CONTINUED)

OBS	TOWNSHIP	RANGE	SECTION	LANDVAL	IMPROVAL	SALEPRIC	SALTOAPR
481	9	19	34	$7,000	$38,930	$66,900	1.45656
482	9	19	34	$8,140	$24,180	$46,600	1.44183
483	9	19	35	$5,100	$20,280	$37,000	1.45784
484	9	19	35	$5,100	$21,430	$38,300	1.44365
485	9	19	35	$6,000	$25,520	$46,000	1.45939
486	9	19	35	$6,000	$20,820	$39,000	1.45414
487	9	19	13	$4,300	$21,790	$37,500	1.43733
488	9	19	13	$4,300	$18,790	$32,900	1.42486
489	9	19	13	$4,300	$21,300	$36,500	1.42578
490	9	19	13	$4,500	$20,670	$36,000	1.43027
491	9	19	13	$900	$15,770	$23,900	1.43371
492	9	19	13	$4,000	$21,440	$36,500	1.43475
493	9	19	13	$4,600	$24,100	$41,000	1.42857
494	9	19	13	$4,300	$18,540	$32,500	1.42294
495	9	19	13	$4,300	$26,210	$43,500	1.42576
496	9	19	13	$3,990	$19,880	$33,900	1.42019
497	9	19	21	$6,800	$34,630	$59,500	1.43616
498	9	19	21	$6,800	$35,580	$61,000	1.43936
499	9	19	21	$6,800	$34,920	$59,900	1.43576
500	9	19	21	$7,000	$33,330	$58,000	1.43814
501	9	19	22	$980	$17,400	$26,200	1.42546
502	9	19	23	$4,200	$22,980	$38,900	1.43120
503	9	19	23	$3,810	$26,700	$43,500	1.42576
504	9	19	23	$3,790	$21,370	$36,000	1.43084
505	9	19	23	$3,790	$28,140	$45,900	1.43752
506	9	19	23	$4,100	$27,820	$45,500	1.42544
507	9	19	24	$6,000	$17,090	$33,000	1.42919
508	9	19	24	$5,000	$19,310	$34,700	1.42740
509	9	19	24	$4,100	$26,520	$43,500	1.42064
510	9	19	24	$3,500	$26,970	$43,800	1.43748
511	9	19	24	$4,100	$30,390	$49,000	1.42070
512	9	19	24	$3,970	$24,800	$41,000	1.42510
513	9	19	25	$4,800	$29,080	$48,500	1.43152
514	9	19	26	$9,500	$46,750	$80,500	1.43111
515	9	19	26	$9,600	$49,700	$84,800	1.43002
516	9	19	26	$4,300	$32,370	$52,500	1.43169
517	9	19	26	$4,100	$35,380	$56,500	1.43110
518	9	19	27	$3,000	$25,140	$40,500	1.43923
519	9	19	34	$8,100	$36,590	$64,000	1.43209
520	9	19	34	$8,630	$39,280	$68,300	1.42559
521	9	19	35	$7,500	$33,670	$59,000	1.43308
522	9	19	35	$5,100	$19,060	$34,500	1.42798
523	9	19	35	$5,000	$19,360	$35,000	1.43678
524	9	19	35	$5,500	$31,780	$53,000	1.42167
525	9	19	36	$7,300	$53,110	$86,500	1.43188
526	9	19	36	$7,170	$32,040	$56,300	1.43586
527	9	19	36	$8,450	$43,820	$74,500	1.42529
528	9	19	36	$8,600	$68,770	$110,000	1.42174
529	9	19	36	$5,500	$31,150	$52,200	1.42428
530	9	19	13	$4,300	$22,310	$37,500	1.40924
531	9	19	13	$4,960	$35,600	$57,000	1.40533
532	9	19	13	$4,210	$27,330	$44,500	1.41091
533	9	19	13	$5,400	$35,320	$57,000	1.39980
534	9	19	13	$4,100	$21,270	$36,000	1.41900
535	9	19	13	$4,300	$25,090	$41,200	1.40184
536	9	19	13	$4,300	$22,320	$37,300	1.40120
537	9	19	13	$3,910	$18,880	$32,300	1.41729
538	9	19	13	$3,910	$19,810	$33,500	1.41231
539	9	19	13	$3,910	$19,960	$33,700	1.41181
540	9	19	13	$3,990	$18,400	$31,500	1.40688
541	9	19	13	$3,930	$23,640	$39,000	1.41458
542	9	19	13	$3,930	$18,430	$31,300	1.39982
543	9	19	13	$3,990	$22,540	$37,500	1.41349
544	9	19	13	$3,990	$23,350	$38,500	1.40819
545	9	19	15	$10,500	$38,480	$69,000	1.40874
546	9	19	23	$3,900	$31,600	$49,900	1.40563
547	9	19	23	$4,100	$26,760	$43,500	1.40959
548	9	19	23	$7,600	$46,920	$77,200	1.41599
549	9	19	23	$7,840	$35,620	$61,000	1.40359
550	9	19	23	$7,840	$36,590	$62,700	1.41121
551	9	19	24	$6,000	$18,810	$35,000	1.41072
552	9	19	24	$6,000	$18,190	$34,100	1.40967
553	9	19	24	$6,000	$18,190	$34,300	1.41794
554	9	19	24	$6,000	$17,510	$33,300	1.41642
555	9	19	24	$6,000	$16,740	$32,100	1.41161
556	9	19	24	$6,100	$16,590	$32,200	1.41913
557	9	19	24	$6,500	$19,680	$36,900	1.40947
558	9	19	24	$3,570	$15,700	$27,300	1.41671
559	9	19	24	$3,610	$18,450	$31,200	1.41432
560	9	19	24	$4,100	$24,130	$39,750	1.40808

REAL ESTATE SALES FOR 1978
IN A MID-SIZED FLORIDA CITY (CONTINUED)

OBS	TOWNSHIP	RANGE	SECTION	LANDVAL	IMPROVAL	SALEPRIC	SALTOAPR
561	9	19	26	$5,470	$43,080	$68,300	1.40680
562	9	19	26	$11,000	$38,250	$69,200	1.40508
563	9	19	26	$4,100	$34,320	$54,200	1.41072
564	9	19	26	$4,100	$30,170	$48,000	1.40064
565	9	19	27	$4,200	$29,730	$48,000	1.41468
566	9	19	27	$6,000	$21,830	$39,000	1.40137
567	9	19	34	$8,250	$38,580	$66,000	1.40935
568	9	19	35	$5,300	$19,400	$34,900	1.41296
569	9	19	35	$5,100	$22,590	$39,200	1.41567
570	9	19	35	$6,000	$26,080	$45,000	1.40274
571	9	19	35	$5,500	$25,860	$44,500	1.41901
572	9	19	36	$7,680	$45,180	$75,000	1.41884
573	9	19	36	$7,040	$51,530	$82,500	1.40857
574	9	19	13	$4,400	$21,030	$35,500	1.39599
575	9	19	13	$5,160	$29,110	$47,500	1.38605
576	9	19	13	$4,740	$37,160	$58,200	1.38902
577	9	19	13	$3,850	$20,700	$34,000	1.38493
578	9	19	13	$4,300	$21,070	$35,400	1.39535
579	9	19	13	$4,200	$20,530	$34,500	1.39507
580	9	19	13	$4,300	$23,530	$38,900	1.39777
581	9	19	13	$3,910	$18,670	$31,600	1.39947
582	9	19	13	$3,990	$25,640	$41,300	1.39386
583	9	19	13	$3,950	$20,890	$34,500	1.38889
584	9	19	13	$3,990	$19,680	$33,000	1.39417
585	9	19	13	$3,990	$23,280	$38,000	1.39347
586	9	19	13	$3,990	$21,640	$35,500	1.38510
587	9	19	13	$4,300	$20,740	$34,900	1.39377
588	9	19	15	$10,500	$50,770	$85,400	1.39383
589	9	19	20	$4,070	$47,410	$72,000	1.39860
590	9	19	21	$6,900	$37,660	$61,800	1.38689
591	9	19	22	$980	$18,150	$26,700	1.39571
592	9	19	23	$4,200	$30,850	$48,500	1.38374
593	9	19	23	$3,600	$31,000	$48,000	1.38728
594	9	19	23	$4,100	$33,570	$52,700	1.39899
595	9	19	23	$4,200	$34,610	$54,000	1.39139
596	9	19	23	$5,180	$29,740	$48,500	1.38889
597	9	19	23	$4,000	$28,470	$45,000	1.38589
598	9	19	23	$3,900	$27,940	$44,000	1.38191
599	9	19	24	$2,900	$29,880	$45,500	1.38804
600	9	19	24	$6,000	$18,990	$34,900	1.39656
601	9	19	24	$6,200	$21,660	$38,700	1.38909
602	9	19	24	$6,500	$22,110	$39,500	1.38064
603	9	19	24	$6,000	$22,600	$40,000	1.39860
604	9	19	24	$6,000	$17,780	$33,185	1.39550
605	9	19	24	$6,000	$18,050	$33,300	1.38462
606	9	19	24	$6,200	$16,420	$31,600	1.39699
607	9	19	24	$7,150	$25,080	$45,000	1.39621
608	9	19	24	$3,500	$27,700	$43,200	1.38462
609	9	19	24	$3,610	$30,370	$47,100	1.38611
610	9	19	24	$3,420	$26,150	$41,200	1.39330
611	9	19	24	$3,970	$28,290	$44,900	1.39182
612	9	19	24	$3,750	$24,160	$38,600	1.38302
613	9	19	24	$3,630	$24,980	$40,000	1.39811
614	9	19	24	$3,800	$28,910	$45,700	1.39713
615	9	19	25	$7,000	$36,290	$59,800	1.38138
616	9	19	25	$5,750	$31,230	$51,500	1.39264
617	9	19	25	$5,850	$31,790	$52,500	1.39479
618	9	19	25	$4,000	$37,520	$58,000	1.39692
619	9	19	25	$5,720	$37,060	$59,500	1.39084
620	9	19	25	$5,620	$44,670	$70,000	1.39193
621	9	19	26	$6,500	$37,250	$60,500	1.38286
622	9	19	26	$5,980	$41,920	$67,000	1.39875
623	9	19	26	$5,550	$33,080	$53,900	1.39529
624	9	19	26	$9,500	$42,680	$73,000	1.39900
625	9	19	31	$5,090	$43,400	$67,000	1.38173
626	9	19	34	$3,000	$20,730	$33,000	1.39064
627	9	19	34	$3,000	$13,140	$22,500	1.39405
628	9	19	34	$4,000	$28,000	$44,500	1.39063
629	9	19	34	$4,000	$28,240	$44,500	1.38027
630	9	19	34	$8,250	$31,880	$55,500	1.38301
631	9	19	34	$8,250	$51,210	$82,500	1.38749
632	9	19	35	$5,100	$25,250	$41,900	1.38056
633	9	19	35	$6,100	$19,540	$35,450	1.38261
634	9	19	35	$6,000	$21,840	$38,800	1.39368
635	9	19	35	$7,100	$29,640	$51,100	1.39085
636	9	19	36	$7,170	$34,740	$58,000	1.38392
637	9	19	36	$5,600	$19,420	$35,000	1.39888
638	9	19	36	$6,160	$22,270	$39,700	1.39641
639	9	19	13	$4,300	$17,910	$30,600	1.37776
640	9	19	13	$4,300	$20,800	$34,600	1.37849

REAL ESTATE SALES FOR 1978
IN A MID-SIZED FLORIDA CITY (CONTINUED)

OBS	TOWNSHIP	RANGE	SECTION	LANDVAL	IMPROVAL	SALEPRIC	SALTOAPR
641	9	19	13	$3,600	$33,990	$51,300	1.36472
642	9	19	13	$3,810	$27,360	$43,000	1.37953
643	9	19	13	$4,600	$20,060	$34,000	1.37875
644	9	19	13	$4,300	$20,530	$34,000	1.36931
645	9	19	13	$4,300	$19,560	$32,500	1.36211
646	9	19	13	$4,300	$24,800	$40,100	1.37801
647	9	19	13	$4,400	$29,860	$46,900	1.36894
648	9	19	13	$4,300	$27,270	$43,000	1.36205
649	9	19	13	$3,910	$22,640	$36,200	1.36347
650	9	19	13	$3,910	$23,160	$37,300	1.37791
651	9	19	13	$3,910	$20,050	$33,000	1.37730
652	9	19	13	$3,910	$18,570	$30,900	1.37456
653	9	19	13	$4,120	$23,540	$38,000	1.37383
654	9	19	13	$3,990	$25,570	$40,500	1.37009
655	9	19	15	$7,100	$24,800	$43,900	1.37618
656	9	19	15	$10,500	$43,210	$74,000	1.37777
657	9	19	15	$10,500	$47,400	$79,900	1.37997
658	9	19	15	$10,500	$46,140	$77,500	1.36829
659	9	19	21	$6,800	$31,560	$52,900	1.37904
660	9	19	20	$6,900	$43,510	$69,000	1.36878
661	9	19	22	$980	$18,150	$26,300	1.37480
662	9	19	22	$980	$26,400	$37,500	1.36961
663	9	19	23	$4,100	$25,190	$40,000	1.36565
664	9	19	23	$3,810	$27,540	$42,800	1.36523
665	9	19	23	$3,810	$29,240	$45,500	1.37670
666	9	19	23	$3,810	$23,170	$37,000	1.37139
667	9	19	24	$2,300	$28,870	$43,000	1.37953
668	9	19	24	$6,800	$17,120	$32,600	1.36288
669	9	19	24	$7,000	$23,590	$41,700	1.36319
670	9	19	24	$6,000	$18,900	$34,100	1.36948
671	9	19	24	$6,000	$21,960	$38,200	1.36624
672	9	19	24	$6,000	$16,820	$31,430	1.37730
673	9	19	24	$6,000	$20,180	$36,100	1.37892
674	9	19	24	$6,000	$21,550	$37,900	1.37568
675	9	19	24	$5,400	$23,510	$39,600	1.36977
676	9	19	24	$6,000	$18,220	$33,000	1.36251
677	9	19	24	$6,600	$23,160	$41,000	1.37769
678	9	19	24	$5,800	$25,880	$43,600	1.37626
679	9	19	24	$4,300	$19,320	$32,400	1.37172
680	9	19	24	$3,500	$27,620	$42,900	1.37853
681	9	19	24	$3,500	$27,100	$41,900	1.36928
682	9	19	24	$3,420	$23,870	$37,500	1.37413
683	9	19	24	$4,000	$27,170	$42,600	1.36670
684	9	19	25	$6,400	$31,680	$52,500	1.37868
685	9	19	25	$5,750	$38,240	$60,000	1.36395
686	9	19	25	$8,750	$38,410	$64,800	1.37405
687	9	19	26	$4,100	$31,420	$49,000	1.37950
688	9	19	17	$6,200	$20,710	$37,000	1.37495
689	9	19	28	$7,500	$37,550	$61,900	1.37403
690	9	19	28	$7,000	$30,630	$51,500	1.36859
691	9	19	34	$4,200	$27,830	$44,000	1.37371
692	9	19	34	$9,500	$40,020	$67,500	1.36309
693	9	19	34	$8,250	$32,850	$56,000	1.36253
694	9	19	34	$8,700	$36,940	$62,400	1.36722
695	9	19	34	$8,480	$43,620	$71,500	1.37236
696	9	19	35	$7,500	$34,490	$57,200	1.36223
697	9	19	35	$5,820	$25,840	$43,600	1.37713
698	9	19	35	$5,100	$23,070	$38,600	1.37025
699	9	19	35	$7,150	$25,370	$44,300	1.36224
700	9	19	13	$4,300	$23,040	$37,000	1.35333
701	9	19	13	$4,400	$21,080	$34,500	1.35400
702	9	19	13	$900	$15,770	$22,500	1.34973
703	9	19	13	$5,290	$33,730	$52,500	1.34546
704	9	19	13	$5,510	$31,400	$49,900	1.35194
705	9	19	13	$5,510	$34,540	$54,000	1.34831
706	9	19	13	$5,160	$29,700	$47,000	1.34825
707	9	19	13	$4,100	$20,800	$33,500	1.34538
708	9	19	13	$4,400	$29,580	$46,000	1.35374
709	9	19	13	$4,400	$28,670	$44,900	1.35773
710	9	19	13	$4,400	$20,620	$34,000	1.35891
711	9	19	13	$4,300	$24,740	$39,300	1.35331
712	9	19	13	$3,910	$25,180	$39,200	1.34754
713	9	19	13	$3,930	$27,680	$42,500	1.34451
714	9	19	13	$3,930	$25,100	$39,000	1.34344
715	9	19	13	$3,930	$18,670	$30,500	1.34956
716	9	19	13	$3,990	$24,080	$37,900	1.35020
717	9	19	13	$3,990	$24,120	$37,800	1.34472
718	9	19	13	$3,990	$19,470	$31,600	1.34697
719	9	19	13	$3,990	$23,290	$37,000	1.35630
720	9	19	13	$3,990	$23,240	$36,600	1.34411

REAL ESTATE SALES FOR 1978
IN A MID-SIZED FLORIDA CITY (CONTINUED)

OBS	TOWNSHIP	RANGE	SECTION	LANDVAL	IMPROVAL	SALEPRIC	SALTOAPR
721	9	19	13	$3,990	$19,320	$31,400	1.34706
722	9	19	13	$3,950	$25,110	$39,400	1.35582
723	9	19	13	$3,950	$23,510	$37,200	1.35470
724	9	19	13	$3,990	$24,030	$38,000	1.35617
725	9	19	15	$6,900	$23,470	$41,000	1.35002
726	9	19	15	$10,500	$44,930	$74,500	1.34404
727	9	19	15	$10,500	$50,050	$82,000	1.35425
728	9	19	20	$4,070	$40,300	$60,000	1.35227
729	9	19	22	$980	$25,650	$36,000	1.35186
730	9	19	23	$4,510	$23,800	$38,500	1.35994
731	9	19	23	$4,200	$32,890	$50,000	1.34807
732	9	19	23	$4,200	$27,660	$43,300	1.35907
733	9	19	23	$3,500	$23,560	$36,500	1.34885
734	9	19	23	$4,830	$33,430	$52,000	1.35912
735	9	19	24	$2,300	$28,870	$42,000	1.34745
736	9	19	24	$6,000	$23,440	$39,900	1.35530
737	9	19	24	$6,100	$22,770	$39,000	1.35088
738	9	19	24	$3,500	$25,830	$39,500	1.34674
739	9	19	24	$3,500	$24,240	$37,500	1.35184
740	9	19	24	$3,440	$25,370	$38,700	1.34328
741	9	19	24	$3,670	$18,450	$29,900	1.35172
742	9	19	24	$3,870	$26,460	$40,800	1.34520
743	9	19	25	$4,620	$25,840	$41,000	1.34603
744	9	19	26	$6,280	$40,180	$63,200	1.36031
745	9	19	26	$4,400	$27,390	$43,000	1.35263
746	9	19	26	$9,400	$42,160	$70,000	1.35764
747	9	19	28	$7,000	$32,650	$53,900	1.35939
748	9	19	30	$8,160	$35,430	$59,000	1.35352
749	9	19	34	$3,200	$21,110	$33,000	1.35747
750	9	19	34	$5,700	$29,120	$47,000	1.34980
751	9	19	34	$5,700	$31,770	$51,000	1.36109
752	9	19	34	$8,140	$35,660	$59,500	1.35845
753	9	19	34	$8,630	$44,060	$71,000	1.34750
754	9	19	35	$7,800	$31,100	$52,900	1.35990
755	9	19	35	$7,500	$35,420	$57,800	1.34669
756	9	19	35	$7,500	$35,160	$57,900	1.35724
757	9	19	35	$5,100	$27,180	$43,700	1.35378
758	9	19	35	$6,000	$19,820	$35,000	1.35554
759	9	19	36	$7,200	$38,890	$62,000	1.34519
760	9	19	13	$4,300	$20,970	$33,900	1.34151
761	9	19	13	$4,960	$27,760	$43,500	1.32946
762	9	19	13	$5,270	$32,090	$49,900	1.33565
763	9	19	13	$4,300	$21,550	$34,500	1.33462
764	9	19	13	$3,990	$24,030	$37,500	1.33833
765	9	19	13	$3,930	$27,530	$42,000	1.33503
766	9	19	13	$3,930	$22,140	$34,600	1.32720
767	9	19	13	$3,930	$25,290	$39,000	1.33470
768	9	19	13	$4,120	$25,810	$39,900	1.33311
769	9	19	13	$3,990	$18,100	$29,500	1.33545
770	9	19	13	$3,990	$24,440	$38,100	1.34013
771	9	19	13	$3,990	$23,510	$36,560	1.32945
772	9	19	13	$5,500	$29,600	$46,900	1.33618
773	9	19	13	$5,300	$32,300	$50,000	1.32979
774	9	19	15	$7,100	$28,630	$47,900	1.34061
775	9	19	15	$7,200	$29,540	$48,900	1.33097
776	9	19	15	$10,500	$40,780	$68,100	1.32800
777	9	19	15	$10,500	$38,670	$65,900	1.34025
778	9	19	22	$980	$17,400	$24,500	1.33297
779	9	19	22	$980	$17,400	$24,500	1.33297
780	9	19	22	$980	$17,400	$24,500	1.33297
781	9	19	22	$980	$17,400	$24,500	1.33297
782	9	19	22	$980	$18,150	$25,500	1.33298
783	9	19	22	$980	$18,150	$25,500	1.33298
784	9	19	22	$980	$25,650	$35,450	1.33121
785	9	19	23	$4,400	$28,150	$43,700	1.34255
786	9	19	23	$3,810	$26,770	$41,000	1.34075
787	9	19	23	$4,000	$27,470	$42,000	1.33460
788	9	19	23	$3,790	$24,250	$37,500	1.33738
789	9	19	23	$4,830	$28,660	$44,900	1.34070
790	9	19	23	$3,810	$25,400	$39,000	1.33516
791	9	19	23	$3,900	$28,580	$43,500	1.33929
792	9	19	23	$4,100	$27,440	$42,000	1.33164
793	9	19	24	$3,690	$23,120	$36,000	1.34278
794	9	19	24	$3,570	$25,160	$38,500	1.34006
795	9	19	24	$6,000	$22,920	$38,500	1.33126
796	9	19	24	$6,000	$22,570	$38,000	1.33007
797	9	19	24	$6,100	$22,940	$38,900	1.33953
798	9	19	24	$6,100	$18,760	$33,100	1.33146
799	9	19	24	$5,900	$18,540	$32,500	1.32979
800	9	19	24	$3,570	$16,660	$27,000	1.33465

REAL ESTATE SALES FOR 1978
IN A MID-SIZED FLORIDA CITY (CONTINUED)

OBS	TOWNSHIP	RANGE	SECTION	LANDVAL	IMPROVAL	SALEPRIC	SALTOAPR
801	9	19	24	$3,420	$24,430	$37,000	1.32855
802	9	19	24	$4,100	$27,400	$42,000	1.33333
803	9	19	24	$4,070	$26,550	$40,800	1.33246
804	9	19	24	$3,970	$25,900	$40,000	1.33914
805	9	19	24	$4,100	$28,000	$43,000	1.33956
806	9	19	25	$4,620	$35,350	$53,000	1.32599
807	9	19	25	$5,210	$42,260	$63,500	1.33769
808	9	19	26	$5,550	$35,070	$54,000	1.32939
809	9	19	26	$5,550	$43,060	$64,900	1.33512
810	9	19	26	$6,280	$41,590	$64,000	1.33695
811	9	19	26	$6,250	$33,350	$52,500	1.32576
812	9	19	26	$4,300	$41,590	$61,600	1.34234
813	9	19	26	$4,620	$47,500	$69,900	1.34114
814	9	19	27	$4,200	$30,720	$46,500	1.33162
815	9	19	27	$6,200	$25,440	$42,000	1.32743
816	9	19	28	$7,500	$39,210	$62,000	1.32734
817	9	19	28	$7,550	$46,810	$72,700	1.33738
818	9	19	33	$6,000	$59,260	$87,000	1.33313
819	9	19	34	$4,000	$28,890	$43,900	1.33475
820	9	19	34	$7,150	$48,310	$74,000	1.33429
821	9	19	34	$7,500	$29,450	$49,500	1.33965
822	9	19	34	$8,250	$38,960	$62,600	1.32599
823	9	19	34	$8,100	$47,830	$75,000	1.34096
824	9	19	34	$7,500	$35,690	$58,000	1.34290
825	9	19	34	$9,780	$42,990	$70,000	1.32651
826	9	19	35	$8,000	$33,530	$55,500	1.33638
827	9	19	35	$7,500	$31,850	$52,500	1.33418
828	9	19	35	$5,000	$16,290	$28,500	1.33866
829	9	19	35	$7,200	$29,420	$48,900	1.33534
830	9	19	36	$7,360	$52,300	$80,000	1.34093
831	9	19	36	$7,200	$40,190	$63,000	1.32939
832	9	19	36	$9,600	$50,560	$80,000	1.32979
833	9	19	13	$5,400	$32,150	$49,500	1.31824
834	9	19	13	$5,520	$26,670	$42,500	1.32029
835	9	19	13	$5,500	$32,400	$50,000	1.31926
836	9	19	13	$4,000	$22,850	$35,400	1.31844
837	9	19	13	$4,300	$26,870	$41,000	1.31537
838	9	19	13	$3,930	$29,200	$43,900	1.32508
839	9	19	13	$3,930	$28,880	$43,000	1.31058
840	9	19	13	$3,930	$23,440	$36,000	1.31531
841	9	19	13	$3,990	$27,340	$41,100	1.31184
842	9	19	15	$7,200	$30,340	$49,300	1.31327
843	9	19	15	$10,500	$46,310	$75,000	1.32019
844	9	19	15	$10,500	$46,320	$75,000	1.31996
845	9	19	15	$10,500	$44,700	$73,000	1.32246
846	9	19	15	$10,500	$53,960	$84,900	1.31710
847	9	19	23	$3,600	$31,760	$46,500	1.31505
848	9	19	23	$3,600	$33,210	$48,500	1.31758
849	9	19	23	$4,830	$29,830	$45,500	1.31275
850	9	19	23	$4,600	$28,770	$43,800	1.31256
851	9	19	24	$2,200	$26,190	$37,500	1.32089
852	9	19	24	$3,570	$25,690	$38,700	1.32262
853	9	19	24	$6,400	$22,360	$37,900	1.31780
854	9	19	24	$7,000	$16,590	$30,900	1.30988
855	9	19	24	$6,800	$24,200	$40,900	1.31935
856	9	19	24	$6,000	$18,880	$32,700	1.31431
857	9	19	24	$6,000	$21,960	$36,700	1.31259
858	9	19	24	$6,000	$17,370	$30,900	1.32221
859	9	19	24	$6,000	$19,630	$33,600	1.31096
860	9	19	24	$3,420	$23,080	$34,900	1.31698
861	9	19	24	$4,000	$24,980	$38,000	1.31125
862	9	19	24	$3,500	$26,100	$38,800	1.31081
863	9	19	25	$5,980	$45,120	$67,500	1.32094
864	9	19	26	$5,610	$35,520	$54,000	1.31291
865	9	19	26	$5,770	$49,700	$73,500	1.32504
866	9	19	26	$4,360	$20,680	$33,000	1.31789
867	9	19	26	$4,000	$35,100	$51,500	1.31714
868	9	19	27	$6,200	$24,630	$40,500	1.31366
869	9	19	27	$6,200	$26,540	$43,000	1.31338
870	9	19	27	$6,000	$20,030	$34,100	1.31003
871	9	19	27	$6,300	$26,160	$42,900	1.32163
872	9	19	28	$7,500	$31,800	$52,000	1.32316
873	9	19	28	$7,500	$33,970	$54,900	1.32385
874	9	19	28	$7,000	$32,140	$51,800	1.32345
875	9	19	30	$8,160	$33,470	$54,700	1.31396
876	9	19	30	$7,820	$32,940	$53,500	1.31256
877	9	19	31	$5,320	$41,690	$61,500	1.30823
878	9	19	31	$4,550	$45,770	$66,000	1.31161
879	9	19	34	$2,500	$21,040	$30,800	1.30841
880	9	19	34	$7,000	$35,710	$56,500	1.32288

REAL ESTATE SALES FOR 1978
IN A MID-SIZED FLORIDA CITY (CONTINUED)

OBS	TOWNSHIP	RANGE	SECTION	LANDVAL	IMPROVAL	SALEPRIC	SALTOAPR
881	9	19	34	$8,630	$40,720	$65,000	1.31712
882	9	19	35	$6,000	$17,320	$30,900	1.32504
883	9	19	35	$6,000	$18,540	$32,500	1.32437
884	9	19	35	$6,300	$25,790	$42,000	1.30882
885	9	19	35	$5,000	$18,820	$31,300	1.31402
886	9	19	13	$4,300	$23,100	$35,500	1.29562
887	9	19	13	$5,280	$32,220	$48,500	1.29333
888	9	19	17	$5,520	$30,820	$47,500	1.30710
889	9	19	13	$5,510	$34,420	$51,900	1.29977
890	9	19	13	$5,380	$29,930	$46,000	1.30275
891	9	19	13	$4,740	$32,360	$48,000	1.29380
892	9	19	13	$5,400	$33,060	$49,900	1.29745
893	9	19	13	$4,600	$26,210	$39,900	1.29503
894	9	19	13	$4,200	$22,730	$34,870	1.29484
895	9	19	13	$3,930	$27,480	$41,000	1.30532
896	9	19	13	$4,370	$25,020	$38,000	1.29296
897	9	19	13	$3,990	$25,320	$37,900	1.29307
898	9	19	13	$3,990	$19,100	$29,900	1.29493
899	9	19	13	$3,950	$24,730	$37,500	1.30753
900	9	19	13	$3,960	$24,900	$37,700	1.30631
901	9	19	13	$3,990	$18,950	$29,900	1.30340
902	9	19	15	$7,000	$32,940	$52,000	1.30195
903	9	19	15	$10,500	$43,800	$71,000	1.30755
904	9	19	15	$10,500	$44,600	$72,000	1.30672
905	9	19	22	$980	$18,150	$25,000	1.30685
906	9	19	23	$4,400	$27,730	$42,000	1.30719
907	9	19	23	$4,000	$22,780	$35,000	1.30695
908	9	19	23	$4,000	$24,570	$37,000	1.29506
909	9	19	23	$4,100	$29,150	$43,000	1.29323
910	9	19	23	$4,610	$28,550	$42,900	1.29373
911	9	19	23	$3,810	$29,430	$43,000	1.29362
912	9	19	23	$4,830	$32,280	$48,300	1.30154
913	9	19	24	$6,500	$29,870	$47,000	1.29227
914	9	19	24	$2,900	$29,880	$42,500	1.29652
915	9	19	24	$6,000	$22,610	$37,200	1.30024
916	9	19	24	$6,400	$28,630	$45,600	1.30174
917	9	19	24	$6,000	$22,820	$37,600	1.30465
918	9	19	24	$6,000	$22,350	$36,800	1.29806
919	9	19	24	$6,000	$24,500	$39,500	1.29508
920	9	19	24	$6,000	$20,090	$33,900	1.29935
921	9	19	24	$6,100	$18,920	$32,400	1.29496
922	9	19	24	$5,400	$24,060	$38,500	1.30686
923	9	19	24	$3,610	$27,340	$40,000	1.29241
924	9	19	24	$3,500	$22,420	$33,500	1.29244
925	9	19	24	$3,440	$25,970	$38,000	1.29208
926	9	19	25	$7,800	$38,220	$59,500	1.29292
927	9	19	25	$6,600	$33,640	$52,500	1.30467
928	9	19	25	$5,210	$36,550	$54,000	1.29310
929	9	19	25	$5,700	$45,120	$66,000	1.29870
930	9	19	26	$4,300	$32,660	$48,000	1.29870
931	9	19	26	$9,300	$40,690	$64,900	1.29826
932	9	19	26	$5,000	$38,190	$56,000	1.29660
933	9	19	27	$6,200	$26,410	$42,300	1.29715
934	9	19	27	$6,200	$24,550	$40,000	1.30081
935	9	19	27	$6,200	$22,360	$37,000	1.29552
936	9	19	35	$7,800	$33,990	$54,000	1.29218
937	9	19	35	$7,500	$35,550	$56,000	1.30081
938	9	19	35	$7,500	$29,450	$47,900	1.29635
939	9	19	35	$5,100	$28,040	$43,000	1.29753
940	9	19	35	$6,000	$24,360	$39,500	1.30105
941	9	19	35	$6,000	$27,560	$43,800	1.30513
942	9	19	35	$6,000	$22,270	$36,600	1.29466
943	9	19	35	$7,000	$28,570	$46,500	1.30728
944	9	19	13	$4,400	$23,970	$36,500	1.28657
945	9	19	13	$5,520	$27,420	$42,000	1.27505
946	9	19	13	$5,270	$34,480	$51,000	1.28302
947	9	19	13	$4,100	$27,880	$41,000	1.28205
948	9	19	13	$4,000	$23,120	$35,000	1.29056
949	9	19	13	$5,000	$33,490	$49,500	1.28605
950	9	19	13	$4,400	$28,700	$42,500	1.28399
951	9	19	13	$3,910	$25,040	$37,000	1.27807
952	9	19	15	$7,000	$35,460	$54,500	1.28356
953	9	19	22	$980	$20,400	$27,400	1.28157
954	9	19	23	$4,200	$29,210	$42,700	1.27806
955	9	19	23	$4,700	$31,460	$46,500	1.28595
956	9	19	23	$7,600	$34,130	$53,300	1.27726
957	9	19	24	$2,300	$30,640	$42,500	1.29022
958	9	19	24	$2,300	$28,870	$40,000	1.28329
959	9	19	24	$2,900	$29,880	$42,000	1.28127
960	9	19	24	$2,900	$29,880	$42,000	1.28127

REAL ESTATE SALES FOR 1978
IN A MID-SIZED FLORIDA CITY (CONTINUED)

OBS	TOWNSHIP	RANGE	SECTION	LANDVAL	IMPROVAL	SALEPRIC	SALTOAPR
961	9	19	24	$5,000	$32,020	$47,200	1.27499
962	9	19	24	$6,000	$19,410	$32,800	1.29083
963	9	19	24	$4,800	$20,460	$32,500	1.28662
964	9	19	24	$3,500	$28,960	$41,500	1.27850
965	9	19	24	$3,500	$26,810	$39,000	1.28670
966	9	19	25	$6,600	$30,540	$47,900	1.28971
967	9	19	25	$4,180	$24,530	$36,900	1.28527
968	9	19	25	$5,460	$33,570	$49,900	1.27850
969	9	19	26	$5,550	$39,220	$57,500	1.28434
970	9	19	26	$5,750	$50,580	$72,500	1.28706
971	9	19	27	$6,200	$28,050	$44,000	1.28467
972	9	19	27	$6,300	$24,800	$40,000	1.28617
973	9	19	27	$6,300	$23,170	$38,000	1.28945
974	9	19	28	$7,000	$32,400	$50,400	1.27919
975	9	19	29	$5,000	$37,900	$55,000	1.28205
976	9	19	34	$6,700	$37,880	$57,000	1.27860
977	9	19	34	$7,150	$47,830	$70,500	1.28228
978	9	19	34	$6,500	$31,140	$48,000	1.27524
979	9	19	34	$7,440	$43,770	$66,000	1.28881
980	9	19	34	$8,030	$46,710	$70,000	1.27877
981	9	19	35	$7,260	$19,870	$35,000	1.29008
982	9	19	35	$6,600	$21,520	$35,900	1.27667
983	9	19	35	$5,100	$20,600	$33,000	1.28405
984	9	19	35	$5,700	$27,020	$42,000	1.28362
985	9	19	35	$6,420	$25,580	$41,000	1.28125
986	9	19	35	$8,000	$31,480	$50,500	1.27913
987	9	19	36	$7,260	$39,340	$60,000	1.28755
988	9	19	13	$5,180	$31,050	$46,000	1.26967
989	9	19	13	$5,290	$31,910	$47,000	1.26344
990	9	19	13	$3,850	$24,510	$35,800	1.26234
991	9	19	13	$4,300	$24,710	$36,900	1.27198
992	9	19	13	$4,300	$31,330	$45,000	1.26298
993	9	19	13	$4,300	$24,070	$36,000	1.26895
994	9	19	13	$4,300	$29,220	$42,500	1.26790
995	9	19	13	$4,300	$24,760	$37,000	1.27323
996	9	19	13	$3,990	$24,710	$36,500	1.27178
997	9	19	13	$3,990	$20,810	$31,400	1.26613
998	9	19	13	$3,990	$26,760	$39,100	1.27154
999	9	19	13	$3,990	$26,750	$39,000	1.26871
1000	9	19	13	$4,300	$24,890	$37,000	1.26756
1001	9	19	21	$7,000	$40,640	$60,000	1.25945
1002	9	19	23	$4,830	$30,100	$44,000	1.25966
1003	9	19	24	$2,400	$30,030	$41,100	1.26735
1004	9	19	24	$6,500	$32,170	$49,000	1.26713
1005	9	19	24	$2,900	$25,060	$35,500	1.26967
1006	9	19	24	$6,000	$23,740	$37,800	1.27102
1007	9	19	24	$6,000	$18,250	$30,900	1.27423
1008	9	19	24	$6,000	$19,170	$31,900	1.26738
1009	9	19	24	$6,000	$22,270	$35,900	1.26990
1010	9	19	24	$5,700	$23,530	$37,000	1.26582
1011	9	19	24	$3,510	$23,740	$34,500	1.26606
1012	9	19	24	$3,670	$23,710	$34,500	1.26004
1013	9	19	25	$6,400	$36,290	$54,000	1.26493
1014	9	19	26	$5,550	$40,500	$58,500	1.27036
1015	9	19	26	$4,680	$31,430	$45,500	1.26004
1016	9	19	27	$3,200	$40,180	$55,000	1.26787
1017	9	19	27	$6,200	$24,670	$38,900	1.26012
1018	9	19	27	$6,400	$26,550	$41,500	1.25948
1019	9	19	27	$6,400	$28,620	$44,500	1.27070
1020	9	19	28	$9,000	$37,890	$59,500	1.26893
1021	9	19	28	$7,200	$32,520	$50,000	1.25881
1022	9	19	35	$6,500	$28,100	$43,800	1.26590
1023	9	19	35	$5,400	$27,820	$42,250	1.27182
1024	9	19	35	$6,500	$22,610	$37,000	1.27104
1025	9	19	35	$5,850	$20,350	$33,000	1.25954
1026	9	19	35	$7,400	$32,050	$49,900	1.26489
1027	9	19	36	$7,200	$45,360	$66,900	1.27283
1028	9	19	13	$5,280	$40,570	$57,000	1.24318
1029	9	19	13	$4,200	$25,450	$37,100	1.25126
1030	9	19	13	$4,300	$27,840	$40,000	1.24456
1031	9	19	13	$4,300	$28,480	$40,900	1.24771
1032	9	19	13	$3,990	$24,890	$36,300	1.25693
1033	9	19	13	$3,910	$23,240	$34,000	1.25230
1034	9	19	13	$3,930	$27,930	$40,000	1.25549
1035	9	19	13	$3,990	$25,170	$36,500	1.25171
1036	9	19	13	$3,990	$25,610	$36,900	1.24662
1037	9	19	13	$3,990	$28,240	$40,200	1.24729
1038	9	19	13	$3,990	$25,710	$37,000	1.24579
1039	9	19	13	$3,990	$26,340	$38,000	1.25288
1040	9	19	15	$7,100	$27,330	$43,200	1.25472

REAL ESTATE SALES FOR 1978
IN A MID-SIZED FLORIDA CITY (CONTINUED)

OBS	TOWNSHIP	RANGE	SECTION	LANDVAL	IMPROVAL	SALEPRIC	SALTOAPR
1041	9	19	15	$10,500	$48,130	$73,400	1.25192
1042	9	19	20	$4,070	$47,130	$63,900	1.24805
1043	9	19	21	$6,800	$37,090	$55,000	1.25313
1044	9	19	22	$980	$18,150	$23,900	1.24935
1045	9	19	23	$4,550	$24,220	$36,000	1.25130
1046	9	19	23	$4,100	$26,880	$38,800	1.25242
1047	9	19	23	$4,500	$32,540	$46,500	1.25540
1048	9	19	23	$3,900	$25,700	$36,800	1.24324
1049	9	19	24	$2,200	$26,720	$36,000	1.24481
1050	9	19	24	$6,600	$23,370	$37,300	1.24458
1051	9	19	24	$6,100	$20,200	$32,800	1.24715
1052	9	19	24	$6,000	$22,630	$35,800	1.25044
1053	9	19	24	$4,280	$21,600	$32,500	1.25580
1054	9	19	24	$4,000	$30,320	$42,800	1.24709
1055	9	19	25	$4,510	$22,680	$34,000	1.25046
1056	9	19	27	$6,200	$22,970	$36,500	1.25129
1057	9	19	27	$6,200	$30,440	$46,000	1.25546
1058	9	19	27	$6,400	$27,350	$42,000	1.24444
1059	9	19	27	$6,500	$24,860	$39,300	1.25319
1060	9	19	28	$7,350	$41,040	$60,500	1.25026
1061	9	19	28	$7,000	$32,380	$49,500	1.25698
1062	9	19	34	$3,200	$24,840	$35,200	1.25535
1063	9	19	34	$8,060	$38,560	$58,000	1.24410
1064	9	19	35	$8,000	$67,490	$95,000	1.25844
1065	9	19	35	$7,200	$27,910	$44,000	1.25320
1066	9	19	36	$6,160	$17,550	$29,700	1.25264
1067	9	19	13	$4,300	$27,920	$40,000	1.24146
1068	9	19	22	$980	$28,650	$36,700	1.23861
1069	9	19	23	$3,600	$24,820	$35,000	1.23153
1070	9	19	23	$5,060	$29,330	$42,500	1.23582
1071	9	19	23	$3,900	$26,840	$38,000	1.23617
1072	9	19	23	$5,380	$24,080	$36,500	1.23897
1073	9	19	23	$7,600	$39,960	$58,900	1.23844
1074	9	19	23	$7,760	$40,140	$59,200	1.23591
1075	9	19	24	$6,100	$22,080	$34,900	1.23847
1076	9	19	24	$6,100	$23,650	$36,700	1.23361
1077	9	19	24	$5,800	$19,120	$30,700	1.23194
1078	9	19	26	$6,130	$35,140	$50,900	1.23334
1079	9	19	27	$2,040	$26,840	$35,500	1.22922
1080	9	19	28	$7,500	$43,630	$62,900	1.23020
1081	9	19	28	$7,500	$46,300	$66,500	1.23606
1082	9	19	34	$3,000	$24,290	$33,600	1.23122
1083	9	19	34	$5,700	$30,730	$44,800	1.22976
1084	9	19	34	$6,500	$31,230	$46,500	1.23244
1085	9	19	34	$6,960	$34,190	$51,000	1.23937
1086	9	19	34	$7,700	$40,590	$60,000	1.24249
1087	9	19	34	$8,140	$35,870	$54,700	1.24290
1088	9	19	35	$6,600	$23,330	$37,000	1.23622
1089	9	19	35	$7,500	$26,280	$41,500	1.22854
1090	9	19	35	$6,600	$27,090	$41,500	1.23182
1091	9	19	3	$4,000	$27,750	$38,900	1.22520
1092	9	19	13	$5,520	$32,540	$46,500	1.22176
1093	9	19	13	$5,000	$30,180	$42,900	1.21944
1094	9	19	13	$3,990	$23,030	$33,000	1.22132
1095	9	19	13	$3,990	$19,690	$29,000	1.22466
1096	9	19	15	$7,100	$33,400	$49,200	1.21481
1097	9	19	22	$980	$17,400	$22,500	1.22416
1098	9	19	23	$4,000	$30,260	$42,000	1.22592
1099	9	19	23	$3,500	$33,580	$45,000	1.21359
1100	9	19	23	$3,790	$25,240	$35,500	1.22287
1101	9	19	23	$3,810	$32,360	$44,000	1.21648
1102	9	19	23	$4,700	$23,780	$34,800	1.22191
1103	9	19	23	$3,810	$24,150	$34,000	1.21602
1104	9	19	23	$4,900	$34,320	$47,600	1.21367
1105	9	19	23	$5,210	$30,660	$44,000	1.22665
1106	9	19	24	$6,000	$19,500	$31,000	1.21569
1107	9	19	24	$6,000	$18,500	$30,000	1.22449
1108	9	19	24	$5,500	$21,630	$33,000	1.21637
1109	9	19	24	$3,990	$27,530	$38,500	1.22145
1110	9	19	24	$3,990	$30,230	$42,000	1.22735
1111	9	19	25	$5,460	$41,780	$57,300	1.21296
1112	9	19	26	$5,000	$46,510	$63,000	1.22306
1113	9	19	27	$6,000	$23,220	$35,800	1.22519
1114	9	19	28	$7,000	$30,880	$46,500	1.22756
1115	9	19	34	$8,250	$50,960	$72,000	1.21601
1116	9	19	35	$6,500	$27,250	$41,000	1.21481
1117	9	19	35	$7,000	$36,180	$52,500	1.21584
1118	9	19	35	$7,600	$28,370	$43,900	1.22046
1119	9	19	36	$8,320	$70,850	$97,000	1.22521
1120	9	19	13	$5,270	$34,420	$47,700	1.20181

REAL ESTATE SALES FOR 1978
IN A MID-SIZED FLORIDA CITY (CONTINUED)

OBS	TOWNSHIP	RANGE	SECTION	LANDVAL	IMPROVAL	SALEPRIC	SALTOAPR
1121	9	19	13	$3,990	$27,080	$37,500	1.20695
1122	9	19	15	$7,100	$29,180	$43,900	1.21003
1123	9	19	21	$6,800	$36,570	$52,500	1.21051
1124	9	19	22	$980	$26,400	$33,000	1.20526
1125	9	19	22	$980	$21,150	$26,600	1.20199
1126	9	19	23	$3,810	$27,890	$38,000	1.19874
1127	9	19	23	$5,060	$34,640	$48,000	1.20907
1128	9	19	24	$5,000	$41,580	$56,100	1.20438
1129	9	19	24	$6,000	$22,740	$34,700	1.20738
1130	9	19	24	$6,400	$23,470	$36,200	1.21192
1131	9	19	24	$6,500	$22,690	$35,000	1.19904
1132	9	19	24	$5,800	$21,120	$32,500	1.20728
1133	9	19	24	$5,500	$19,310	$30,000	1.20919
1134	9	19	24	$6,000	$23,140	$35,300	1.21139
1135	9	19	24	$4,000	$28,080	$38,500	1.20012
1136	9	19	27	$6,200	$26,790	$40,000	1.21249
1137	9	19	27	$6,200	$26,580	$39,500	1.20500
1138	9	19	27	$6,200	$25,270	$38,100	1.21068
1139	9	19	27	$6,300	$26,130	$38,900	1.19951
1140	9	19	28	$8,200	$41,310	$59,500	1.20178
1141	9	19	34	$6,500	$37,260	$53,000	1.21115
1142	9	19	34	$8,100	$47,710	$66,900	1.19871
1143	9	19	34	$8,630	$43,580	$63,000	1.20667
1144	9	19	35	$5,850	$27,450	$40,300	1.21021
1145	9	19	35	$5,500	$20,980	$32,000	1.20846
1146	9	19	35	$5,500	$26,980	$39,000	1.20074
1147	9	19	13	$4,400	$32,830	$44,500	1.19527
1148	9	19	15	$10,500	$56,560	$80,000	1.19296
1149	9	19	23	$4,200	$30,870	$42,000	1.19760
1150	9	19	24	$6,500	$44,450	$61,000	1.19725
1151	9	19	24	$6,000	$21,920	$33,200	1.18911
1152	9	19	24	$6,000	$22,500	$33,800	1.18596
1153	9	19	24	$4,100	$30,940	$41,500	1.18436
1154	9	19	25	$6,400	$35,640	$50,000	1.18934
1155	9	19	25	$6,600	$37,230	$52,000	1.18640
1156	9	19	25	$5,720	$41,250	$56,000	1.19225
1157	9	19	27	$6,200	$27,070	$39,800	1.19627
1158	9	19	27	$6,400	$26,500	$39,300	1.19453
1159	9	19	27	$6,400	$27,820	$41,000	1.19813
1160	9	19	28	$7,500	$32,430	$47,330	1.18532
1161	9	19	28	$7,500	$37,050	$53,000	1.18967
1162	9	19	34	$6,500	$37,800	$52,500	1.18510
1163	9	19	34	$7,500	$38,460	$55,000	1.19669
1164	9	19	34	$9,000	$42,740	$62,000	1.19830
1165	9	19	35	$5,700	$27,020	$39,000	1.19193
1166	9	19	35	$6,500	$39,420	$55,000	1.19774
1167	9	19	35	$5,500	$26,540	$38,000	1.18602
1168	9	19	35	$7,000	$32,670	$47,500	1.19738
1169	9	19	36	$9,300	$46,250	$66,500	1.19712
1170	9	19	13	$4,300	$24,040	$33,500	1.18207
1171	9	19	13	$3,910	$25,820	$34,800	1.17053
1172	9	19	13	$3,910	$24,080	$33,000	1.17899
1173	9	19	15	$10,500	$47,830	$69,000	1.18292
1174	9	19	23	$4,400	$24,120	$33,500	1.17461
1175	9	19	24	$5,000	$30,820	$42,200	1.17811
1176	9	19	24	$6,000	$22,920	$34,000	1.17566
1177	9	19	26	$5,550	$44,260	$58,500	1.17446
1178	9	19	27	$6,300	$26,500	$38,600	1.17683
1179	9	19	28	$7,500	$41,780	$57,700	1.17086
1180	9	19	28	$7,500	$42,160	$58,500	1.17801
1181	9	19	34	$8,250	$46,430	$64,000	1.17045
1182	9	19	35	$6,500	$26,750	$39,000	1.17293
1183	9	19	35	$5,500	$23,240	$34,000	1.18302
1184	9	19	36	$6,500	$40,950	$55,600	1.17176
1185	9	19	13	$5,400	$32,710	$44,500	1.16767
1186	9	19	19	$10,500	$42,910	$62,000	1.16083
1187	9	19	22	$980	$26,400	$32,000	1.16874
1188	9	19	24	$5,000	$37,880	$49,800	1.16138
1189	9	19	24	$3,500	$25,280	$33,500	1.16400
1190	9	19	25	$5,620	$42,650	$56,000	1.16014
1191	9	19	27	$6,200	$30,050	$42,000	1.15862
1192	9	19	28	$7,500	$42,630	$58,000	1.15699
1193	9	19	28	$6,800	$32,950	$46,000	1.15723
1194	9	19	34	$6,000	$28,170	$39,900	1.16769
1195	9	19	34	$4,000	$29,860	$39,500	1.16657
1196	9	19	34	$9,000	$41,710	$59,000	1.16348
1197	9	19	34	$7,730	$50,570	$68,000	1.16638
1198	9	19	34	$8,630	$48,040	$66,000	1.16464
1199	9	19	35	$6,000	$31,940	$44,000	1.15973
1200	9	19	35	$6,000	$24,980	$36,000	1.16204

REAL ESTATE SALES FOR 1978
IN A MID-SIZED FLORIDA CITY (CONTINUED)

OBS	TOWNSHIP	RANGE	SECTION	LANDVAL	IMPROVAL	SALEPRIC	SALTOAPR
1201	9	19	35	$7,000	$28,100	$40,900	1.16524
1202	9	19	13	$4,370	$28,110	$37,300	1.14840
1203	9	19	13	$5,500	$30,990	$41,900	1.14826
1204	9	19	15	$10,500	$50,570	$70,000	1.14623
1205	9	19	15	$10,500	$46,670	$66,000	1.15445
1206	9	19	23	$5,000	$29,900	$40,000	1.14613
1207	9	19	24	$6,500	$42,900	$56,900	1.15182
1208	9	19	27	$6,200	$27,760	$38,900	1.14547
1209	9	19	27	$6,200	$28,360	$39,800	1.15162
1210	9	19	28	$7,000	$38,340	$52,300	1.15351
1211	9	19	34	$6,700	$41,130	$55,000	1.14991
1212	9	19	13	$5,520	$37,790	$49,500	1.14292
1213	9	19	13	$3,990	$29,850	$38,500	1.13771
1214	9	19	23	$4,200	$27,530	$36,100	1.13772
1215	9	19	23	$3,500	$32,960	$41,600	1.14098
1216	9	19	23	$5,060	$28,440	$38,300	1.14328
1217	9	19	24	$6,500	$38,540	$51,000	1.13233
1218	9	19	25	$5,460	$43,010	$55,000	1.13472
1219	9	19	27	$2,040	$29,010	$35,500	1.14332
1220	9	19	34	$8,100	$40,100	$55,000	1.14108
1221	9	19	34	$9,780	$53,730	$72,000	1.13368
1222	9	19	35	$7,200	$32,180	$45,000	1.14271
1223	9	19	35	$8,000	$48,900	$65,000	1.14236
1224	9	19	13	$4,500	$25,640	$34,000	1.12807
1225	9	19	22	$980	$26,400	$30,700	1.12126
1226	9	19	25	$5,720	$44,440	$56,500	1.12640
1227	9	19	13	$4,300	$25,700	$33,300	1.11000
1228	9	19	20	$5,400	$55,460	$68,000	1.11732
1229	9	19	23	$3,500	$31,250	$38,500	1.10791
1230	9	19	24	$5,000	$38,090	$47,700	1.10699
1231	9	19	35	$7,000	$29,730	$40,900	1.11353
1232	9	19	15	$7,200	$32,810	$44,000	1.09973
1233	9	19	15	$10,500	$52,280	$68,800	1.09589
1234	9	19	23	$7,760	$40,890	$53,500	1.09969
1235	9	19	26	$6,200	$35,770	$46,000	1.09602
1236	9	19	34	$6,500	$43,460	$54,900	1.09888
1237	9	19	35	$7,000	$26,480	$37,000	1.10514
1238	9	19	25	$5,910	$42,610	$52,600	1.08409
1239	9	19	35	$5,500	$33,250	$42,300	1.09161
1240	9	19	35	$7,600	$33,180	$44,500	1.09122
1241	9	19	24	$6,100	$24,700	$32,900	1.06818
1242	9	19	35	$7,800	$39,340	$50,000	1.06067
1243	9	19	35	$7,000	$30,650	$39,900	1.05976
1244	9	19	34	$5,700	$32,080	$40,000	1.05876
1245	9	19	35	$5,100	$30,370	$37,500	1.05723
1246	9	19	35	$5,250	$19,360	$25,800	1.04835
1247	9	19	35	$6,000	$31,090	$38,500	1.03802
1248	9	19	27	$6,500	$29,900	$37,000	1.01648
1249	9	19	13	$4,300	$35,020	$39,900	1.01475
1250	9	19	24	$6,000	$27,780	$34,000	1.00651
1251	9	19	36	$8,200	$54,800	$63,000	1.00000
1252	9	19	30	$5,000	$51,010	$55,000	0.98197
1253	9	19	13	$4,300	$27,420	$30,900	0.97415
1254	9	19	26	$4,360	$24,780	$27,000	0.92656
1255	9	19	34	$5,800	$30,520	$29,600	0.81498
1256	9	20	29	$1,540	$3,410	$21,500	4.34343
1257	9	20	20	$4,000	$8,730	$48,900	3.84132
1258	9	20	29	$1,600	$5,370	$25,900	3.71593
1259	9	20	29	$1,000	$2,840	$14,000	3.64583
1260	9	20	29	$1,200	$4,500	$21,500	3.77193
1261	9	20	29	$1,600	$6,490	$26,800	3.31273
1262	9	20	32	$1,950	$4,740	$22,000	3.28849
1263	9	20	32	$1,060	$6,690	$25,000	3.22581
1264	9	20	30	$1,360	$5,640	$21,500	3.07143
1265	9	20	30	$1,210	$6,780	$24,500	3.06633
1266	9	20	12	$1,200	$6,660	$23,000	2.92621
1267	9	20	29	$1,200	$6,330	$22,500	2.98805
1268	9	20	32	$1,950	$5,190	$21,000	2.94118
1269	9	20	29	$1,600	$5,110	$19,000	2.83159
1270	9	20	30	$2,730	$6,040	$25,000	2.85063
1271	9	20	32	$2,250	$5,490	$22,000	2.84238
1272	9	20	32	$2,730	$14,530	$49,400	2.86211
1273	9	20	32	$1,500	$8,510	$28,900	2.88711
1274	9	20	33	$4,000	$15,710	$56,000	2.84120
1275	9	20	29	$1,500	$8,460	$28,000	2.81124
1276	9	20	20	$2,000	$4,790	$18,200	2.68041
1277	9	20	29	$1,150	$4,350	$15,000	2.72727
1278	9	20	29	$2,500	$11,950	$39,000	2.69896
1279	9	20	32	$1,800	$6,410	$22,000	2.67966
1280	9	20	33	$2,000	$7,340	$25,000	2.67666

REAL ESTATE SALES FOR 1978
IN A MID-SIZED FLORIDA CITY (CONTINUED)

OBS	TOWNSHIP	RANGE	SECTION	LANDVAL	IMPROVAL	SALEPRIC	SALTOAPR
1281	9	20	18	$2,500	$5,630	$21,550	2.65068
1282	9	20	29	$2,000	$9,700	$30,900	2.64103
1283	9	20	32	$2,630	$7,790	$26,900	2.58157
1284	9	20	32	$2,970	$12,340	$39,000	2.54735
1285	9	20	32	$1,620	$10,950	$32,000	2.54574
1286	9	20	32	$1,000	$8,970	$25,000	2.50752
1287	9	20	33	$2,000	$9,130	$27,600	2.47978
1288	9	20	29	$3,500	$11,090	$36,000	2.46744
1289	9	20	32	$1,950	$11,910	$34,000	2.45310
1290	9	20	33	$2,500	$13,300	$39,000	2.46835
1291	9	20	34	$600	$7,470	$19,500	2.41636
1292	9	20	20	$2,500	$9,280	$28,000	2.37691
1293	9	20	29	$2,100	$8,600	$25,400	2.37383
1294	9	20	30	$1,210	$6,130	$17,500	2.38420
1295	9	20	32	$2,250	$9,350	$27,500	2.37069
1296	9	20	32	$2,100	$9,670	$28,000	2.37893
1297	9	20	34	$1,140	$7,800	$21,500	2.40492
1298	9	20	31	$2,800	$9,280	$28,000	2.31788
1299	9	20	32	$1,060	$8,920	$23,000	2.30461
1300	9	20	33	$4,000	$22,750	$62,000	2.31776
1301	9	20	29	$2,700	$10,040	$28,800	2.26060
1302	9	20	32	$2,500	$10,200	$29,000	2.28346
1303	9	20	29	$2,400	$10,260	$28,500	2.25118
1304	9	20	33	$4,000	$13,630	$40,500	2.29722
1305	9	20	29	$3,500	$9,970	$30,000	2.22717
1306	9	20	33	$3,000	$14,020	$37,500	2.20329
1307	9	20	33	$3,080	$7,240	$22,800	2.20930
1308	9	20	27	$3,150	$15,000	$39,500	2.17631
1309	9	20	32	$2,460	$11,990	$31,200	2.15917
1310	9	20	33	$5,040	$13,230	$40,000	2.18938
1311	9	20	20	$4,500	$9,490	$29,700	2.12294
1312	9	20	32	$2,100	$12,410	$30,800	2.12267
1313	9	20	29	$2,100	$11,580	$28,500	2.08333
1314	9	20	29	$2,000	$12,040	$29,000	2.06553
1315	9	20	29	$2,640	$10,530	$27,500	2.08808
1316	9	20	30	$2,000	$14,220	$33,500	2.06535
1317	9	20	32	$1,000	$8,560	$20,000	2.09205
1318	9	20	33	$4,000	$31,870	$75,000	2.09088
1319	9	20	29	$2,100	$14,990	$35,000	2.04798
1320	9	20	29	$1,060	$14,820	$32,500	2.04660
1321	9	20	30	$11,000	$46,720	$118,500	2.05301
1322	9	20	32	$2,250	$15,220	$36,000	2.06068
1323	9	20	32	$2,410	$9,230	$24,000	2.06186
1324	9	20	33	$4,000	$8,580	$25,500	2.02703
1325	9	20	33	$4,320	$9,130	$27,500	2.04461
1326	9	20	29	$2,000	$16,490	$36,900	1.99567
1327	9	20	31	$5,060	$19,740	$50,000	2.01613
1328	9	20	32	$2,220	$15,330	$35,000	1.99430
1329	9	20	32	$2,190	$11,440	$27,500	2.01761
1330	9	20	29	$2,100	$15,490	$34,500	1.96134
1331	9	20	30	$1,580	$11,880	$26,500	1.96880
1332	9	20	31	$4,720	$33,500	$75,000	1.96232
1333	9	20	33	$3,600	$7,690	$22,000	1.94863
1334	9	20	28	$3,080	$11,430	$28,000	1.92970
1335	9	20	29	$2,300	$10,230	$24,200	1.93136
1336	9	20	30	$2,000	$12,040	$27,000	1.92308
1337	9	20	33	$4,000	$14,840	$36,600	1.94268
1338	9	20	33	$4,000	$8,510	$24,200	1.93445
1339	9	20	33	$4,320	$11,510	$30,300	1.91409
1340	9	20	34	$3,300	$13,580	$32,500	1.92536
1341	9	20	12	$1,200	$20,590	$41,000	1.88160
1342	9	20	29	$4,790	$34,900	$75,000	1.88964
1343	9	20	31	$5,170	$20,410	$48,000	1.87647
1344	9	20	34	$3,000	$12,440	$28,900	1.87176
1345	9	20	27	$3,360	$13,540	$31,300	1.85207
1346	9	20	28	$3,150	$12,060	$28,200	1.85404
1347	9	20	29	$2,300	$17,360	$36,300	1.84639
1348	9	20	29	$2,640	$13,360	$29,800	1.86250
1349	9	20	32	$2,970	$17,000	$36,700	1.83776
1350	9	20	33	$4,000	$13,150	$32,000	1.86589
1351	9	20	33	$4,000	$9,980	$26,000	1.85980
1352	9	20	33	$4,500	$10,370	$27,500	1.84936
1353	9	20	12	$1,000	$12,190	$23,800	1.80440
1354	9	20	20	$4,500	$14,800	$35,300	1.82902
1355	9	20	27	$4,200	$14,080	$33,000	1.80525
1356	9	20	28	$3,660	$12,580	$29,500	1.81650
1357	9	20	29	$1,440	$10,330	$21,500	1.82668
1358	9	20	30	$2,010	$12,210	$25,800	1.81435
1359	9	20	31	$5,000	$27,070	$58,000	1.80854
1360	9	20	33	$4,260	$11,960	$29,600	1.82491

REAL ESTATE SALES FOR 1978
IN A MID-SIZED FLORIDA CITY (CONTINUED)

OBS	TOWNSHIP	RANGE	SECTION	LANDVAL	IMPROVAL	SALEPRIC	SALTOAPR
1361	9	20	33	$4,320	$12,200	$30,000	1.81598
1362	9	20	34	$3,000	$12,740	$28,500	1.81067
1363	9	20	27	$5,400	$13,040	$33,000	1.78959
1364	9	20	28	$3,400	$14,580	$31,900	1.77419
1365	9	20	29	$2,410	$11,600	$25,000	1.78444
1366	9	20	31	$5,040	$32,590	$67,000	1.78049
1367	9	20	33	$3,570	$14,990	$33,000	1.77802
1368	9	20	27	$3,150	$15,100	$32,000	1.75342
1369	9	20	27	$4,200	$13,830	$31,500	1.74709
1370	9	20	28	$3,400	$15,330	$32,800	1.75120
1371	9	20	29	$1,200	$14,560	$27,900	1.77030
1372	9	20	30	$1,360	$12,770	$25,000	1.76929
1373	9	20	33	$4,100	$12,650	$29,500	1.76119
1374	9	20	33	$4,100	$15,990	$35,000	1.74216
1375	9	20	33	$4,310	$12,030	$28,500	1.74419
1376	9	20	33	$3,000	$12,800	$27,900	1.76582
1377	9	20	33	$3,190	$15,060	$32,200	1.76438
1378	9	20	33	$4,000	$12,550	$28,900	1.74622
1379	9	20	19	$3,760	$16,600	$35,200	1.72888
1380	9	20	28	$3,400	$13,430	$29,000	1.72311
1381	9	20	28	$3,400	$18,250	$37,500	1.73210
1382	9	20	28	$3,080	$13,470	$28,500	1.72205
1383	9	20	28	$3,460	$18,820	$38,400	1.72352
1384	9	20	31	$1,010	$33,580	$60,200	1.74039
1385	9	20	32	$2,450	$13,730	$28,000	1.73053
1386	9	20	33	$3,500	$13,130	$28,900	1.73782
1387	9	20	33	$3,570	$12,130	$27,200	1.73248
1388	9	20	34	$3,150	$16,880	$34,500	1.72242
1389	9	20	34	$3,700	$14,120	$30,700	1.72278
1390	9	20	28	$3,400	$13,720	$28,800	1.68224
1391	9	20	28	$3,400	$15,840	$32,500	1.68919
1392	9	20	28	$3,510	$14,210	$30,000	1.69300
1393	9	20	30	$1,360	$16,250	$30,000	1.70358
1394	9	20	30	$2,000	$18,540	$35,000	1.70399
1395	9	20	30	$2,000	$13,750	$26,800	1.70159
1396	9	20	33	$4,320	$25,370	$50,000	1.68407
1397	9	20	33	$4,100	$14,120	$30,900	1.69594
1398	9	20	33	$3,570	$15,410	$32,450	1.70969
1399	9	20	34	$3,570	$13,880	$29,800	1.70774
1400	9	20	34	$3,000	$12,570	$26,500	1.70199
1401	9	20	34	$3,600	$15,270	$31,900	1.69051
1402	9	20	20	$3,000	$12,520	$26,000	1.67526
1403	9	20	20	$3,500	$8,480	$20,000	1.66945
1404	9	20	27	$3,150	$16,000	$32,000	1.67102
1405	9	20	27	$3,150	$13,810	$28,500	1.68042
1406	9	20	27	$3,230	$17,540	$34,500	1.66105
1407	9	20	27	$3,150	$14,450	$29,500	1.67614
1408	9	20	28	$3,230	$14,660	$29,800	1.66574
1409	9	20	28	$3,460	$15,470	$31,550	1.66667
1410	9	20	28	$3,290	$13,710	$28,500	1.67647
1411	9	20	28	$3,540	$18,430	$36,800	1.67501
1412	9	20	29	$1,200	$10,500	$19,500	1.66667
1413	9	20	31	$6,960	$37,450	$73,700	1.65954
1414	9	20	31	$4,410	$29,960	$57,000	1.65842
1415	9	20	33	$3,230	$15,810	$31,500	1.65441
1416	9	20	34	$3,570	$17,670	$35,500	1.67137
1417	9	20	19	$3,700	$16,290	$33,000	1.65083
1418	9	20	27	$3,150	$14,990	$29,800	1.64278
1419	9	20	28	$3,650	$14,080	$28,900	1.63001
1420	9	20	28	$3,210	$17,670	$34,000	1.62835
1421	9	20	28	$3,800	$15,400	$31,500	1.64063
1422	9	20	30	$2,500	$21,420	$39,500	1.65134
1423	9	20	32	$2,970	$18,900	$36,000	1.64609
1424	9	20	32	$3,660	$15,400	$31,500	1.65268
1425	9	20	32	$10,500	$76,010	$142,800	1.65068
1426	9	20	33	$4,040	$14,020	$29,800	1.65006
1427	9	20	33	$4,300	$15,210	$31,900	1.63506
1428	9	20	33	$3,190	$14,200	$28,300	1.62737
1429	9	20	33	$3,190	$11,490	$24,000	1.63488
1430	9	20	33	$4,000	$15,080	$31,500	1.65094
1431	9	20	19	$4,500	$17,360	$35,500	1.62397
1432	9	20	19	$4,500	$17,660	$35,500	1.60199
1433	9	20	27	$3,800	$14,260	$29,000	1.60576
1434	9	20	27	$4,200	$12,820	$27,500	1.61575
1435	9	20	27	$3,150	$14,200	$28,000	1.61383
1436	9	20	28	$3,400	$19,200	$36,300	1.60619
1437	9	20	28	$3,230	$15,780	$30,600	1.60968
1438	9	20	28	$3,150	$23,340	$42,500	1.60438
1439	9	20	28	$3,540	$14,480	$29,000	1.60932
1440	9	20	30	$2,730	$17,780	$32,900	1.60410

REAL ESTATE SALES FOR 1978
IN A MID-SIZED FLORIDA CITY (CONTINUED)

OBS	TOWNSHIP	RANGE	SECTION	LANDVAL	IMPROVAL	SALEPRIC	SALTOAPR
1441	9	20	31	$850	$26,450	$44,000	1.61172
1442	9	20	31	$6,300	$22,750	$47,000	1.61790
1443	9	20	31	$3,910	$19,420	$37,500	1.60737
1444	9	20	31	$4,000	$20,020	$39,000	1.62365
1445	9	20	33	$4,260	$12,400	$27,000	1.62065
1446	9	20	33	$3,320	$15,200	$29,900	1.61447
1447	9	20	33	$3,190	$16,030	$31,000	1.61290
1448	9	20	33	$4,000	$12,870	$27,400	1.62418
1449	9	20	34	$3,570	$20,460	$38,500	1.60216
1450	9	20	34	$3,200	$17,490	$33,300	1.60947
1451	9	20	19	$4,500	$17,960	$35,500	1.58059
1452	9	20	19	$3,800	$16,800	$32,500	1.57767
1453	9	20	19	$3,500	$15,890	$30,900	1.59360
1454	9	20	27	$3,280	$18,000	$33,900	1.59305
1455	9	20	27	$3,230	$14,400	$28,000	1.58820
1456	9	20	27	$4,000	$18,910	$36,200	1.58010
1457	9	20	28	$3,400	$14,380	$28,200	1.58605
1458	9	20	28	$3,400	$13,150	$26,200	1.58308
1459	9	20	28	$3,400	$18,620	$35,000	1.58946
1460	9	20	28	$4,000	$20,550	$39,000	1.58859
1461	9	20	28	$3,460	$17,550	$33,500	1.59448
1462	9	20	28	$3,510	$13,870	$27,600	1.58803
1463	9	20	28	$3,660	$14,640	$29,000	1.58470
1464	9	20	29	$1,440	$17,110	$29,700	1.60108
1465	9	20	29	$1,440	$11,380	$20,400	1.59126
1466	9	20	31	$5,880	$27,660	$53,000	1.58020
1467	9	20	31	$6,900	$39,640	$73,500	1.57929
1468	9	20	32	$2,060	$16,450	$29,500	1.59373
1469	9	20	32	$2,970	$15,960	$30,000	1.58479
1470	9	20	32	$13,000	$27,790	$65,000	1.59353
1471	9	20	33	$4,600	$11,820	$25,900	1.57734
1472	9	20	33	$4,000	$14,700	$29,900	1.59893
1473	9	20	33	$4,000	$14,210	$28,700	1.57606
1474	9	20	34	$3,570	$15,560	$30,500	1.59435
1475	9	20	34	$3,000	$13,950	$27,000	1.59292
1476	9	20	19	$3,700	$16,590	$31,900	1.57220
1477	9	20	19	$4,500	$14,480	$29,500	1.55427
1478	9	20	27	$3,230	$14,710	$28,000	1.56076
1479	9	20	27	$4,300	$14,380	$29,400	1.57388
1480	9	20	27	$5,000	$38,660	$68,100	1.55978
1481	9	20	28	$3,400	$18,170	$33,500	1.55308
1482	9	20	28	$3,400	$14,540	$28,000	1.56076
1483	9	20	28	$3,460	$16,380	$31,000	1.56250
1484	9	20	28	$3,460	$19,590	$35,900	1.55748
1485	9	20	28	$3,150	$19,980	$36,400	1.57371
1486	9	20	28	$3,150	$20,070	$36,400	1.56761
1487	9	20	28	$3,300	$14,350	$27,700	1.56941
1488	9	20	28	$3,540	$15,850	$30,100	1.55235
1489	9	20	28	$3,660	$17,780	$33,500	1.56250
1490	9	20	29	$3,630	$27,630	$49,000	1.56750
1491	9	20	29	$3,680	$20,560	$37,800	1.55941
1492	9	20	31	$4,520	$29,110	$53,000	1.57597
1493	9	20	32	$1,250	$8,320	$15,000	1.56740
1494	9	20	33	$4,260	$12,510	$26,400	1.57424
1495	9	20	33	$2,000	$8,500	$16,300	1.55238
1496	9	20	33	$3,320	$13,020	$25,500	1.56059
1497	9	20	33	$4,000	$13,640	$27,400	1.55329
1498	9	20	33	$4,000	$15,080	$30,000	1.57233
1499	9	20	20	$10,500	$67,280	$120,000	1.54281
1500	9	20	27	$10,940	$83,470	$146,100	1.54751
1501	9	20	28	$4,300	$18,680	$35,500	1.54482
1502	9	20	28	$3,460	$13,980	$27,000	1.54817
1503	9	20	28	$3,150	$17,790	$32,000	1.52818
1504	9	20	28	$3,390	$14,350	$27,500	1.55017
1505	9	20	29	$3,000	$19,040	$34,000	1.54265
1506	9	20	31	$850	$28,160	$44,500	1.53395
1507	9	20	31	$4,000	$27,180	$48,000	1.53945
1508	9	20	32	$2,700	$19,170	$33,500	1.53178
1509	9	20	33	$4,100	$12,560	$25,500	1.53061
1510	9	20	33	$3,440	$17,880	$33,000	1.54784
1511	9	20	33	$4,000	$15,380	$29,700	1.53251
1512	9	20	34	$3,800	$21,660	$39,000	1.53181
1513	9	20	19	$3,600	$16,930	$30,900	1.50511
1514	9	20	27	$3,340	$18,450	$33,000	1.51446
1515	9	20	27	$4,200	$14,530	$28,500	1.52162
1516	9	20	27	$3,150	$13,500	$25,300	1.51952
1517	9	20	27	$3,230	$18,420	$32,900	1.51963
1518	9	20	28	$3,510	$14,360	$27,000	1.51091
1519	9	20	28	$3,540	$15,840	$29,500	1.52219
1520	9	20	31	$6,960	$37,450	$67,400	1.51768

REAL ESTATE SALES FOR 1978
IN A MID-SIZED FLORIDA CITY (CONTINUED)

OBS	TOWNSHIP	RANGE	SECTION	LANDVAL	IMPROVAL	SALEPRIC	SALTOAPR
1521	9	20	31	$4,410	$25,250	$44,800	1.51045
1522	9	20	33	$4,000	$21,560	$38,500	1.50626
1523	9	20	33	$4,000	$15,050	$29,000	1.52231
1524	9	20	34	$3,570	$16,930	$31,000	1.51220
1525	9	20	34	$3,200	$18,150	$32,500	1.52225
1526	9	20	19	$4,000	$18,160	$33,200	1.49819
1527	9	20	19	$4,500	$13,670	$27,000	1.48597
1528	9	20	19	$4,500	$17,400	$32,500	1.48402
1529	9	20	19	$5,000	$24,480	$44,000	1.49254
1530	9	20	20	$4,800	$17,620	$33,500	1.49420
1531	9	20	27	$4,200	$14,180	$27,400	1.49075
1532	9	20	27	$3,230	$16,910	$30,000	1.48957
1533	9	20	27	$4,000	$16,740	$30,800	1.48505
1534	9	20	27	$7,620	$54,330	$93,000	1.50121
1535	9	20	28	$3,400	$14,410	$26,500	1.48793
1536	9	20	28	$3,080	$17,540	$31,000	1.50339
1537	9	20	28	$3,080	$15,070	$27,000	1.48760
1538	9	20	28	$3,510	$19,820	$35,000	1.50021
1539	9	20	28	$3,460	$16,830	$30,500	1.50320
1540	9	20	28	$3,780	$15,830	$29,500	1.50433
1541	9	20	30	$1,360	$20,390	$32,500	1.49425
1542	9	20	30	$3,400	$8,990	$18,500	1.49314
1543	9	20	30	$4,000	$20,080	$36,000	1.49502
1544	9	20	33	$4,180	$12,880	$25,350	1.48593
1545	9	20	33	$4,260	$13,240	$26,000	1.48571
1546	9	20	33	$4,100	$14,610	$28,000	1.49653
1547	9	20	33	$2,000	$9,340	$17,000	1.49912
1548	9	20	33	$4,310	$12,260	$24,900	1.50272
1549	9	20	34	$3,570	$19,170	$34,000	1.49516
1550	9	20	34	$3,570	$15,720	$29,000	1.50337
1551	9	20	19	$3,600	$18,350	$32,500	1.48064
1552	9	20	19	$3,700	$22,160	$37,900	1.46558
1553	9	20	19	$4,500	$20,490	$36,700	1.46859
1554	9	20	20	$4,500	$17,320	$32,000	1.46654
1555	9	20	27	$3,190	$14,050	$25,500	1.47912
1556	9	20	28	$3,400	$15,530	$28,000	1.47913
1557	9	20	28	$3,510	$16,900	$30,000	1.46987
1558	9	20	28	$4,000	$15,730	$29,000	1.46984
1559	9	20	28	$3,460	$15,560	$28,000	1.47213
1560	9	20	28	$4,200	$20,680	$36,400	1.46302
1561	9	20	28	$3,360	$16,010	$28,500	1.47135
1562	9	20	30	$2,200	$17,740	$29,400	1.47442
1563	9	20	31	$1,010	$35,530	$54,000	1.47783
1564	9	20	32	$4,500	$24,210	$42,500	1.48032
1565	9	20	33	$2,040	$21,040	$34,000	1.47314
1566	9	20	33	$4,000	$19,120	$33,900	1.46626
1567	9	20	19	$3,700	$22,420	$37,900	1.45100
1568	9	20	19	$4,500	$15,390	$29,000	1.45802
1569	9	20	19	$4,500	$21,600	$38,000	1.45594
1570	9	20	19	$4,500	$14,640	$27,800	1.45246
1571	9	20	19	$4,500	$22,960	$39,900	1.45302
1572	9	20	19	$5,000	$22,230	$39,500	1.45061
1573	9	20	27	$3,230	$17,940	$30,600	1.44544
1574	9	20	27	$3,260	$16,160	$28,000	1.44181
1575	9	20	28	$4,300	$22,950	$39,400	1.44587
1576	9	20	28	$4,200	$19,800	$34,900	1.45417
1577	9	20	28	$3,600	$14,930	$27,000	1.45710
1578	9	20	28	$3,470	$17,160	$30,000	1.45419
1579	9	20	29	$2,000	$22,070	$35,100	1.45825
1580	9	20	31	$850	$27,590	$41,000	1.44163
1581	9	20	31	$6,800	$31,880	$56,500	1.46070
1582	9	20	31	$4,400	$30,130	$50,300	1.45670
1583	9	20	32	$1,650	$15,630	$25,000	1.44676
1584	9	20	33	$3,600	$7,360	$16,000	1.45985
1585	9	20	33	$3,190	$17,170	$29,500	1.44892
1586	9	20	33	$4,000	$15,290	$28,000	1.45153
1587	9	20	34	$3,720	$20,690	$35,500	1.45432
1588	9	20	34	$980	$12,140	$19,000	1.44817
1589	9	20	19	$3,800	$18,590	$32,000	1.42921
1590	9	20	19	$3,700	$23,790	$39,500	1.43689
1591	9	20	19	$3,500	$17,570	$30,000	1.42383
1592	9	20	19	$3,800	$23,760	$39,500	1.43324
1593	9	20	19	$3,700	$24,250	$39,900	1.42755
1594	9	20	27	$3,150	$14,460	$25,000	1.41965
1595	9	20	28	$3,080	$19,020	$31,500	1.42534
1596	9	20	28	$3,510	$18,630	$31,500	1.42276
1597	9	20	28	$3,780	$16,010	$28,200	1.42496
1598	9	20	28	$3,150	$16,010	$27,500	1.43528
1599	9	20	28	$3,470	$15,880	$27,500	1.42119
1600	9	20	29	$3,520	$15,290	$27,000	1.43541

REAL ESTATE SALES FOR 1978
IN A MID-SIZED FLORIDA CITY (CONTINUED)

OBS	TOWNSHIP	RANGE	SECTION	LANDVAL	IMPROVAL	SALEPRIC	SALTOAPR
1601	9	20	30	$3,000	$18,760	$30,900	1.42004
1602	9	20	30	$3,500	$20,760	$34,900	1.43858
1603	9	20	31	$6,900	$36,180	$61,500	1.42758
1604	9	20	32	$5,600	$27,270	$46,900	1.42683
1605	9	20	33	$3,500	$16,710	$28,900	1.42999
1606	9	20	33	$4,000	$25,390	$42,000	1.42906
1607	9	20	34	$3,570	$15,360	$27,000	1.42631
1608	9	20	34	$3,570	$16,310	$28,600	1.43863
1609	9	20	19	$3,600	$21,640	$35,800	1.41838
1610	9	20	19	$5,000	$19,850	$34,900	1.40443
1611	9	20	19	$4,500	$16,660	$30,000	1.41777
1612	9	20	19	$4,500	$18,940	$33,000	1.40785
1613	9	20	19	$4,500	$19,490	$33,600	1.40058
1614	9	20	19	$4,500	$17,040	$30,500	1.41597
1615	9	20	27	$3,440	$20,450	$33,600	1.40645
1616	9	20	27	$3,150	$13,810	$24,000	1.41509
1617	9	20	28	$4,000	$24,120	$39,700	1.41181
1618	9	20	28	$3,880	$26,600	$43,000	1.41076
1619	9	20	28	$3,780	$14,350	$25,400	1.40099
1620	9	20	28	$3,650	$15,850	$27,500	1.41026
1621	9	20	29	$1,980	$10,860	$18,000	1.40187
1622	9	20	30	$1,360	$19,330	$29,000	1.40164
1623	9	20	31	$850	$28,730	$41,500	1.40297
1624	9	20	31	$7,470	$45,880	$75,000	1.40581
1625	9	20	31	$6,480	$36,300	$60,500	1.41421
1626	9	20	31	$5,980	$29,150	$49,500	1.40905
1627	9	20	32	$2,550	$24,060	$37,300	1.40173
1628	9	20	33	$4,000	$14,130	$25,700	1.41754
1629	9	20	33	$3,230	$17,410	$29,000	1.40504
1630	9	20	33	$3,870	$16,770	$29,100	1.40988
1631	9	20	19	$3,600	$22,010	$35,700	1.39399
1632	9	20	19	$4,000	$20,770	$34,500	1.39281
1633	9	20	19	$5,000	$20,310	$35,300	1.39471
1634	9	20	19	$5,000	$21,540	$36,900	1.39035
1635	9	20	19	$2,500	$23,410	$36,100	1.39328
1636	9	20	28	$3,400	$16,070	$27,000	1.38675
1637	9	20	28	$3,510	$21,410	$34,800	1.39647
1638	9	20	28	$3,150	$16,020	$26,500	1.38237
1639	9	20	30	$3,000	$19,610	$31,500	1.39319
1640	9	20	30	$4,100	$30,980	$48,900	1.39396
1641	9	20	31	$4,530	$27,620	$44,900	1.39658
1642	9	20	33	$4,400	$15,740	$28,000	1.39027
1643	9	20	33	$4,100	$17,600	$30,000	1.38249
1644	9	20	34	$3,570	$18,010	$30,000	1.39018
1645	9	20	18	$1,200	$13,090	$19,600	1.37159
1646	9	20	19	$4,500	$26,430	$42,500	1.37407
1647	9	20	19	$4,500	$19,600	$33,000	1.36929
1648	9	20	19	$5,000	$24,440	$40,500	1.37568
1649	9	20	19	$4,100	$29,880	$46,500	1.36845
1650	9	20	20	$5,200	$28,690	$46,500	1.37209
1651	9	20	20	$4,500	$12,000	$22,700	1.37576
1652	9	20	27	$3,150	$22,400	$35,200	1.37769
1653	9	20	27	$3,780	$18,370	$30,500	1.37698
1654	9	20	28	$3,460	$16,860	$28,000	1.37795
1655	9	20	28	$3,290	$17,610	$28,700	1.37321
1656	9	20	28	$3,470	$15,260	$25,700	1.37213
1657	9	20	30	$2,500	$28,370	$42,300	1.37026
1658	9	20	30	$4,000	$21,580	$34,900	1.36435
1659	9	20	31	$6,000	$28,560	$47,500	1.37442
1660	9	20	31	$850	$29,300	$41,300	1.36982
1661	9	20	31	$6,960	$39,210	$63,500	1.37535
1662	9	20	33	$4,000	$19,630	$32,500	1.37537
1663	9	20	33	$4,100	$17,130	$29,000	1.36599
1664	9	20	33	$4,100	$14,170	$25,000	1.36836
1665	9	20	33	$4,390	$14,220	$25,500	1.37023
1666	9	20	33	$4,310	$16,400	$28,500	1.37615
1667	9	20	33	$3,700	$16,030	$27,000	1.36847
1668	9	20	34	$4,000	$22,830	$36,900	1.37533
1669	9	20	19	$5,000	$20,180	$33,900	1.34631
1670	9	20	19	$5,000	$22,000	$36,500	1.35185
1671	9	20	19	$5,000	$19,990	$34,000	1.36054
1672	9	20	28	$4,300	$16,740	$28,500	1.35456
1673	9	20	28	$3,470	$15,880	$26,000	1.34367
1674	9	20	28	$3,650	$15,840	$26,500	1.35967
1675	9	20	28	$3,540	$15,840	$26,100	1.34675
1676	9	20	28	$15,000	$95,990	$150,000	1.35147
1677	9	20	29	$3,000	$25,800	$39,000	1.35417
1678	9	20	29	$1,400	$9,020	$14,000	1.34357
1679	9	20	30	$1,360	$20,810	$29,900	1.34867
1680	9	20	30	$1,650	$20,090	$29,500	1.35695

REAL ESTATE SALES FOR 1978
IN A MID-SIZED FLORIDA CITY (CONTINUED)

OBS	TOWNSHIP	RANGE	SECTION	LANDVAL	IMPROVAL	SALEPRIC	SALTOAPR
1681	9	20	30	$4,000	$18,830	$31,000	1.35786
1682	9	20	31	$6,600	$29,580	$49,000	1.35434
1683	9	20	31	$6,720	$34,790	$56,500	1.36112
1684	9	20	33	$5,580	$17,800	$31,500	1.34731
1685	9	20	33	$4,320	$20,370	$33,500	1.35682
1686	9	20	34	$3,570	$23,960	$37,300	1.35489
1687	9	20	34	$3,200	$25,210	$38,500	1.35516
1688	9	20	19	$3,800	$20,940	$32,900	1.32983
1689	9	20	19	$5,000	$19,890	$33,000	1.32583
1690	9	20	19	$4,500	$25,380	$40,000	1.33869
1691	9	20	19	$4,500	$23,920	$38,000	1.33709
1692	9	20	19	$5,000	$23,170	$37,500	1.33120
1693	9	20	20	$5,300	$27,640	$44,000	1.33576
1694	9	20	27	$3,230	$17,490	$27,500	1.32722
1695	9	20	28	$4,200	$19,390	$31,500	1.33531
1696	9	20	28	$4,000	$19,330	$31,100	1.33305
1697	9	20	28	$3,780	$16,740	$27,500	1.34016
1698	9	20	28	$4,400	$14,350	$24,900	1.32800
1699	9	20	28	$4,000	$15,840	$26,500	1.33569
1700	9	20	29	$7,690	$101,660	$146,000	1.33516
1701	9	20	29	$1,200	$23,140	$32,300	1.32703
1702	9	20	30	$6,000	$27,490	$44,700	1.33473
1703	9	20	30	$3,000	$23,100	$34,900	1.33716
1704	9	20	31	$7,700	$49,100	$76,000	1.33803
1705	9	20	31	$4,530	$19,550	$32,000	1.32890
1706	9	20	31	$9,000	$53,140	$82,500	1.32765
1707	9	20	31	$5,580	$36,770	$56,500	1.33412
1708	9	20	32	$2,000	$19,370	$28,500	1.33365
1709	9	20	33	$4,180	$13,490	$23,600	1.33560
1710	9	20	33	$4,100	$22,280	$35,000	1.32676
1711	9	20	33	$3,570	$17,780	$28,300	1.32553
1712	9	20	34	$3,700	$15,860	$26,200	1.33947
1713	9	20	34	$3,150	$21,250	$32,500	1.33197
1714	9	20	19	$3,900	$19,420	$30,900	1.32504
1715	9	20	19	$5,000	$19,480	$32,200	1.31536
1716	9	20	19	$5,000	$20,820	$33,800	1.30906
1717	9	20	19	$5,000	$20,400	$33,500	1.31890
1718	9	20	19	$4,500	$21,430	$34,000	1.31122
1719	9	20	19	$5,000	$27,140	$42,500	1.32234
1720	9	20	19	$5,000	$28,590	$44,500	1.32480
1721	9	20	19	$5,000	$26,490	$41,200	1.30835
1722	9	20	19	$3,500	$15,890	$25,500	1.31511
1723	9	20	27	$3,400	$26,380	$39,000	1.30960
1724	9	20	28	$4,300	$16,880	$28,000	1.32200
1725	9	20	28	$3,880	$25,560	$38,900	1.32133
1726	9	20	30	$3,800	$21,060	$32,900	1.32341
1727	9	20	30	$3,500	$23,040	$35,000	1.31876
1728	9	20	31	$5,250	$33,520	$51,000	1.31545
1729	9	20	33	$4,160	$21,430	$33,500	1.30911
1730	9	20	33	$4,100	$17,720	$28,900	1.32447
1731	9	20	33	$4,000	$16,000	$26,300	1.31500
1732	9	20	19	$5,000	$22,640	$35,800	1.29522
1733	9	20	19	$5,000	$20,400	$33,000	1.29921
1734	9	20	19	$5,280	$23,880	$38,000	1.30316
1735	9	20	20	$5,200	$30,550	$46,500	1.30070
1736	9	20	20	$5,200	$30,550	$46,500	1.30070
1737	9	20	27	$4,000	$19,000	$30,000	1.30435
1738	9	20	29	$4,000	$28,920	$43,000	1.30620
1739	9	20	30	$3,000	$22,900	$33,500	1.29344
1740	9	20	30	$4,100	$23,620	$36,000	1.29870
1741	9	20	31	$6,800	$46,790	$70,000	1.30621
1742	9	20	31	$7,070	$34,670	$54,500	1.30570
1743	9	20	19	$4,500	$26,140	$39,500	1.28916
1744	9	20	19	$5,280	$25,440	$39,500	1.28581
1745	9	20	20	$5,200	$30,900	$46,500	1.28809
1746	9	20	28	$3,600	$18,540	$28,300	1.27823
1747	9	20	30	$4,000	$21,610	$32,800	1.28075
1748	9	20	31	$6,120	$36,460	$54,500	1.27994
1749	9	20	31	$1,010	$34,630	$45,800	1.28507
1750	9	20	31	$7,390	$35,380	$55,000	1.28595
1751	9	20	33	$4,800	$20,390	$32,300	1.28225
1752	9	20	18	$6,800	$29,880	$46,500	1.26772
1753	9	20	18	$6,800	$31,610	$48,500	1.26269
1754	9	20	19	$3,750	$25,610	$37,000	1.26022
1755	9	20	19	$5,000	$21,130	$33,200	1.27057
1756	9	20	19	$4,500	$24,530	$37,000	1.27454
1757	9	20	27	$4,000	$19,600	$30,000	1.27119
1758	9	20	28	$3,780	$21,210	$31,600	1.26451
1759	9	20	28	$3,570	$20,170	$30,000	1.26369
1760	9	20	30	$4,100	$31,650	$45,000	1.25874

REAL ESTATE SALES FOR 1978
IN A MID-SIZED FLORIDA CITY (CONTINUED)

OBS	TOWNSHIP	RANGE	SECTION	LANDVAL	IMPROVAL	SALEPRIC	SALTOAPR
1761	9	20	31	$6,350	$51,310	$73,000	1.26604
1762	9	20	33	$3,190	$24,410	$34,900	1.26449
1763	9	20	34	$3,400	$23,940	$34,500	1.26189
1764	9	20	34	$1,280	$17,180	$23,500	1.27302
1765	9	20	19	$5,000	$21,970	$33,700	1.24954
1766	9	20	20	$5,200	$30,970	$45,000	1.24412
1767	9	20	20	$5,200	$33,320	$48,000	1.24611
1768	9	20	28	$3,080	$18,600	$27,000	1.24539
1769	9	20	28	$4,000	$20,890	$31,100	1.24950
1770	9	20	31	$10,000	$43,340	$66,500	1.24672
1771	9	20	31	$5,450	$47,760	$66,500	1.24977
1772	9	20	33	$5,580	$27,680	$41,500	1.24775
1773	9	20	19	$5,000	$25,800	$38,000	1.23377
1774	9	20	20	$5,200	$31,210	$45,000	1.23592
1775	9	20	20	$5,100	$31,210	$45,000	1.23933
1776	9	20	27	$4,800	$16,340	$26,000	1.22990
1777	9	20	28	$3,230	$13,120	$20,100	1.22936
1778	9	20	28	$4,000	$19,960	$29,700	1.23957
1779	9	20	28	$4,300	$16,740	$25,900	1.23099
1780	9	20	30	$3,500	$24,330	$34,300	1.23248
1781	9	20	31	$7,390	$35,380	$53,000	1.23919
1782	9	20	31	$5,500	$40,710	$57,100	1.23566
1783	9	20	33	$4,100	$16,180	$25,000	1.23274
1784	9	20	33	$4,000	$20,310	$29,900	1.22995
1785	9	20	18	$6,800	$29,750	$44,500	1.21751
1786	9	20	19	$4,500	$23,820	$34,600	1.22175
1787	9	20	27	$3,150	$15,250	$22,500	1.22283
1788	9	20	32	$4,590	$34,270	$47,500	1.22234
1789	9	20	18	$10,000	$44,330	$65,500	1.20560
1790	9	20	19	$5,000	$26,450	$38,000	1.20827
1791	9	20	20	$5,200	$31,210	$44,000	1.20846
1792	9	20	20	$5,200	$31,210	$44,000	1.20846
1793	9	20	28	$3,230	$20,020	$28,000	1.20430
1794	9	20	31	$7,390	$36,540	$53,000	1.20646
1795	9	20	31	$5,500	$56,550	$75,000	1.20870
1796	9	20	33	$3,200	$20,570	$28,800	1.21161
1797	9	20	34	$3,570	$24,590	$33,900	1.20384
1798	9	20	31	$4,500	$34,190	$46,000	1.18894
1799	9	20	33	$4,000	$17,780	$26,000	1.19376
1800	9	20	19	$5,000	$21,880	$31,800	1.18304
1801	9	20	20	$5,300	$31,610	$43,500	1.17854
1802	9	20	28	$3,470	$15,850	$22,700	1.17495
1803	9	20	28	$3,230	$20,940	$28,500	1.17915
1804	9	20	33	$4,000	$23,090	$32,000	1.18125
1805	9	20	19	$5,500	$33,730	$45,500	1.15983
1806	9	20	20	$5,200	$31,780	$43,000	1.16279
1807	9	20	28	$4,100	$21,740	$30,000	1.16099
1808	9	20	31	$4,400	$29,810	$40,000	1.16925
1809	9	20	33	$4,000	$15,370	$22,500	1.16159
1810	9	20	12	$600	$5,480	$7,000	1.15132
1811	9	20	20	$5,200	$31,210	$42,000	1.15353
1812	9	20	30	$4,100	$23,990	$32,200	1.14632
1813	9	20	31	$9,680	$53,660	$72,500	1.14462
1814	9	20	19	$4,000	$23,830	$31,500	1.13187
1815	9	20	19	$5,000	$28,310	$37,600	1.12879
1816	9	20	31	$6,900	$43,520	$56,500	1.12059
1817	9	20	34	$1,200	$25,700	$30,000	1.11524
1818	9	20	31	$4,400	$35,580	$43,900	1.09805
1819	9	20	32	$5,310	$31,450	$40,400	1.09902
1820	9	20	20	$5,300	$35,140	$44,000	1.08803
1821	9	20	20	$4,400	$21,680	$28,200	1.08129
1822	9	20	33	$4,000	$21,190	$26,500	1.05200
1823	9	20	31	$4,730	$42,750	$48,500	1.02148
1824	9	20	28	$3,400	$16,350	$20,000	1.01266
1825	9	20	19	$5,000	$23,220	$27,000	0.95677
1826	9	20	33	$4,240	$25,160	$28,000	0.95238
1827	9	20	27	$4,200	$17,630	$20,500	0.93907
1828	9	20	20	$35,000	$259,250	$233,500	0.79354
1829	9	21	22	$400	$3,710	$20,000	4.86618
1830	9	21	35	$3,600	$7,270	$38,500	3.54186
1831	9	21	13	$4,750	$22,070	$54,000	2.01342
1832	9	21	32	$1,000	$29,760	$55,000	1.78804
1833	9	21	6	$2,200	$17,300	$30,900	1.58462
1834	9	21	31	$1,000	$17,640	$29,400	1.57725
1835	9	21	6	$1,300	$3,080	$4,500	1.02740
1836	9	21	6	$2,200	$22,060	$23,000	0.94806
1837	9	21	30	$450	$6,980	$7,000	0.94213
1838	9	22	13	$1,050	$3,810	$21,000	4.32099
1839	9	22	34	$4,880	$14,700	$125,000	6.38407
1840	9	22	13	$3,000	$9,480	$48,000	3.84615

REAL ESTATE SALES FOR 1978
IN A MID-SIZED FLORIDA CITY (CONTINUED)

OBS	TOWNSHIP	RANGE	SECTION	LANDVAL	IMPROVAL	SALEPRIC	SALTOAPR
1841	9	22	13	$1,500	$6,080	$24,400	3.21900
1842	9	22	7	$700	$6,060	$18,500	2.73669
1843	9	22	13	$900	$2,520	$9,000	2.63158
1844	9	22	4	$300	$10,520	$27,000	2.49538
1845	9	22	33	$1,000	$4,930	$15,000	2.52951
1846	9	22	13	$1,250	$6,160	$17,000	2.29420
1847	9	22	13	$1,000	$10,610	$26,500	2.28252
1848	9	22	15	$5,200	$29,070	$70,000	2.04260
1849	9	22	13	$1,660	$18,590	$37,500	1.85185
1850	9	22	13	$2,000	$5,280	$12,000	1.64835
1851	9	22	13	$6,000	$29,240	$55,700	1.58059
1852	9	22	13	$2,200	$20,170	$35,500	1.58695
1853	9	22	10	$5,000	$13,900	$27,000	1.42857
1854	9	22	10	$2,240	$15,590	$23,000	1.28996
1855	9	22	13	$1,540	$22,160	$29,000	1.22363
1856	9	22	13	$6,000	$23,270	$35,500	1.21285
1857	10	17	4	$700	$2,970	$21,000	5.72207
1858	10	17	4	$790	$3,770	$23,800	5.21930
1859	10	17	4	$1,080	$11,780	$41,500	3.22706
1860	10	17	4	$2,280	$14,190	$36,750	2.23133
1861	10	17	4	$1,140	$9,470	$19,500	1.83789
1862	10	17	4	$1,050	$9,810	$17,000	1.56538
1863	10	17	4	$2,500	$16,150	$28,200	1.51206
1864	10	17	4	$700	$16,780	$25,500	1.45881
1865	10	17	9	$1,500	$24,430	$36,900	1.42306
1866	10	17	4	$2,400	$16,750	$26,900	1.40470
1867	10	17	4	$1,200	$16,830	$24,500	1.35885
1868	10	17	4	$1,200	$17,170	$24,000	1.30648
1869	10	17	4	$2,500	$19,320	$28,000	1.28323
1870	10	17	4	$3,200	$17,930	$26,000	1.23048
1871	10	17	4	$860	$24,090	$31,000	1.24248
1872	10	17	9	$1,500	$28,840	$37,368	1.23164
1873	10	17	4	$3,200	$18,220	$26,000	1.21382
1874	10	17	4	$1,200	$22,140	$28,000	1.19966
1875	10	17	4	$3,300	$18,200	$25,800	1.20000
1876	10	17	4	$3,200	$18,220	$25,800	1.20448
1877	10	17	4	$3,200	$18,520	$25,800	1.18785
1878	10	17	4	$1,200	$17,880	$22,500	1.17925
1879	10	17	3	$2,400	$24,960	$31,900	1.16594
1880	10	17	4	$3,200	$19,460	$26,000	1.14740
1881	10	17	4	$3,000	$19,790	$25,800	1.13208
1882	10	17	4	$2,400	$17,130	$22,000	1.12647
1883	10	17	4	$3,000	$17,260	$22,800	1.12537
1884	10	17	4	$3,000	$17,460	$22,800	1.11437
1885	10	17	3	$2,400	$25,640	$30,500	1.08773
1886	10	17	4	$3,000	$22,820	$27,800	1.07668
1887	10	17	3	$750	$5,410	$6,500	1.05519
1888	10	17	4	$3,300	$25,370	$27,800	0.96965
1889	10	17	4	$2,400	$20,650	$21,900	0.95011
1890	10	18	3	$3,700	$13,480	$43,000	2.50291
1891	10	18	3	$4,320	$30,140	$68,000	1.97330
1892	10	18	28	$5,170	$11,940	$33,000	1.92870
1893	10	18	2	$6,000	$32,160	$70,600	1.85010
1894	10	18	20	$6,570	$25,010	$58,300	1.84611
1895	10	18	2	$4,200	$22,160	$39,900	1.51366
1896	10	18	12	$3,540	$29,410	$50,000	1.51745
1897	10	18	8	$4,970	$31,560	$53,500	1.46455
1898	10	18	6	$3,800	$30,290	$47,800	1.40217
1899	10	18	6	$3,800	$29,980	$47,800	1.41504
1900	10	18	2	$4,200	$21,750	$36,000	1.38728
1901	10	18	2	$4,200	$26,320	$42,400	1.38925
1902	10	18	6	$3,800	$36,310	$55,500	1.38369
1903	10	18	6	$3,800	$24,000	$38,900	1.39928
1904	10	18	36	$3,030	$21,780	$34,400	1.38654
1905	10	18	1	$4,500	$33,880	$52,500	1.36790
1906	10	18	1	$4,500	$30,690	$48,500	1.37823
1907	10	18	2	$6,000	$24,610	$41,800	1.36557
1908	10	18	21	$4,500	$23,790	$39,000	1.37858
1909	10	18	2	$6,000	$22,440	$38,500	1.35373
1910	10	18	36	$3,330	$24,120	$36,900	1.34426
1911	10	18	2	$6,300	$25,650	$42,900	1.34272
1912	10	18	2	$6,000	$28,870	$46,800	1.34213
1913	10	18	2	$4,700	$29,190	$45,500	1.34258
1914	10	18	2	$4,200	$29,020	$44,500	1.33955
1915	10	18	12	$4,510	$37,690	$56,500	1.33886
1916	10	18	2	$6,000	$24,940	$41,000	1.32515
1917	10	18	2	$6,000	$26,290	$42,300	1.31000
1918	10	18	12	$5,060	$33,050	$50,500	1.32511
1919	10	18	2	$6,000	$26,890	$43,000	1.30739
1920	10	18	2	$4,200	$25,880	$39,000	1.29654

REAL ESTATE SALES FOR 1978
IN A MID-SIZED FLORIDA CITY (CONTINUED)

OBS	TOWNSHIP	RANGE	SECTION	LANDVAL	IMPROVAL	SALEPRIC	SALTOAPR
1921	10	18	2	$4,700	$29,820	$45,000	1.30359
1922	10	18	2	$4,200	$31,630	$46,800	1.30617
1923	10	18	6	$4,000	$30,150	$44,300	1.29722
1924	10	18	36	$5,200	$20,420	$33,500	1.30757
1925	10	18	36	$3,300	$22,100	$32,900	1.29528
1926	10	18	2	$6,000	$25,940	$41,000	1.28366
1927	10	18	36	$3,030	$24,740	$35,500	1.27836
1928	10	18	2	$4,200	$30,580	$44,200	1.27085
1929	10	18	2	$21,000	$116,760	$175,000	1.27033
1930	10	18	2	$6,000	$22,800	$36,000	1.25000
1931	10	18	2	$4,200	$29,600	$42,000	1.24260
1932	10	18	13	$3,500	$38,150	$51,500	1.23649
1933	10	18	2	$4,200	$31,150	$43,000	1.21641
1934	10	18	21	$11,000	$33,810	$55,000	1.22740
1935	10	18	2	$4,200	$31,660	$43,200	1.20468
1936	10	18	36	$5,200	$24,570	$35,900	1.20591
1937	10	18	2	$6,000	$26,570	$38,900	1.19435
1938	10	18	5	$14,150	$28,710	$37,600	0.87727
1939	10	19	13	$1,500	$5,250	$23,500	3.48148
1940	10	19	1	$3,500	$10,590	$45,500	3.22924
1941	10	19	22	$1,500	$3,110	$14,500	3.14534
1942	10	19	22	$1,500	$6,500	$24,000	3.00000
1943	10	19	1	$2,800	$13,700	$44,300	2.68485
1944	10	19	11	$5,970	$35,480	$112,200	2.70688
1945	10	19	21	$2,500	$7,340	$26,500	2.69309
1946	10	19	0	$1,020	$8,870	$26,000	2.62892
1947	10	19	1	$2,600	$11,840	$37,500	2.59695
1948	10	19	6	$4,000	$18,100	$53,000	2.39819
1949	10	19	31	$2,500	$12,660	$36,500	2.40765
1950	10	19	29	$3,000	$7,910	$25,000	2.29148
1951	10	19	1	$3,500	$10,530	$31,000	2.20955
1952	10	19	0	$35,000	$85,370	$270,000	2.24308
1953	10	19	13	$1,000	$2,680	$8,000	2.17391
1954	10	19	21	$2,500	$5,690	$18,000	2.19780
1955	10	19	1	$3,040	$13,160	$34,500	2.12963
1956	10	19	1	$2,600	$13,310	$33,500	2.10559
1957	10	19	2	$3,570	$10,370	$29,000	2.08034
1958	10	19	8	$5,000	$25,770	$64,000	2.07995
1959	10	19	0	$3,000	$27,360	$63,400	2.08827
1960	10	19	2	$3,740	$14,480	$37,000	2.03074
1961	10	19	11	$1,200	$4,620	$12,000	2.06186
1962	10	19	11	$5,310	$49,790	$110,000	1.99637
1963	10	19	0	$5,600	$26,190	$64,000	2.01321
1964	10	19	0	$7,500	$50,180	$115,000	1.99376
1965	10	19	2	$4,030	$15,370	$37,900	1.95361
1966	10	19	7	$2,860	$25,590	$55,500	1.95079
1967	10	19	0	$3,000	$26,230	$57,500	1.96716
1968	10	19	1	$2,630	$19,650	$42,500	1.90754
1969	10	19	1	$4,000	$15,910	$38,600	1.93872
1970	10	19	2	$3,570	$12,830	$31,500	1.92073
1971	10	19	2	$3,500	$12,380	$30,500	1.92065
1972	10	19	2	$3,570	$15,730	$37,000	1.91710
1973	10	19	2	$3,570	$14,260	$34,000	1.90690
1974	10	19	21	$1,500	$15,100	$31,900	1.92169
1975	10	19	1	$2,630	$11,590	$27,000	1.89873
1976	10	19	2	$3,570	$12,640	$30,500	1.88155
1977	10	19	2	$3,570	$11,590	$28,600	1.88654
1978	10	19	2	$3,570	$16,230	$37,500	1.89394
1979	10	19	22	$800	$5,830	$12,500	1.88537
1980	10	19	0	$2,800	$18,960	$41,100	1.88879
1981	10	19	1	$3,800	$19,300	$42,500	1.83983
1982	10	19	1	$3,500	$19,220	$41,800	1.83979
1983	10	19	5	$6,200	$31,640	$70,300	1.85782
1984	10	19	2	$3,570	$16,430	$36,500	1.82500
1985	10	19	2	$3,830	$15,910	$36,200	1.83384
1986	10	19	2	$3,000	$15,910	$34,500	1.82443
1987	10	19	11	$15,660	$178,310	$350,000	1.80440
1988	10	19	21	$1,500	$12,850	$26,200	1.82578
1989	10	19	21	$2,500	$10,750	$24,000	1.81132
1990	10	19	0	$9,700	$50,830	$110,000	1.81728
1991	10	19	0	$6,300	$66,370	$132,000	1.81643
1992	10	19	2	$4,500	$14,190	$33,500	1.79240
1993	10	19	5	$5,900	$55,710	$110,000	1.78542
1994	10	19	1	$2,980	$16,250	$33,500	1.74207
1995	10	19	1	$4,800	$29,100	$60,000	1.76991
1996	10	19	2	$3,570	$14,360	$31,650	1.76520
1997	10	19	2	$3,830	$15,320	$33,500	1.74935
1998	10	19	7	$4,950	$23,430	$50,000	1.76180
1999	10	19	14	$4,500	$19,120	$41,500	1.75699
2000	10	19	2	$3,570	$15,870	$33,400	1.71811

REAL ESTATE SALES FOR 1978
IN A MID-SIZED FLORIDA CITY (CONTINUED)

OBS	TOWNSHIP	RANGE	SECTION	LANDVAL	IMPROVAL	SALEPRIC	SALTOAPR
2001	10	19	5	$5,500	$22,360	$48,200	1.73008
2002	10	19	21	$2,600	$7,820	$18,000	1.72745
2003	10	19	0	$6,000	$38,320	$76,800	1.73285
2004	10	19	0	$1,200	$13,780	$26,000	1.73565
2005	10	19	0	$6,000	$22,980	$49,900	1.72188
2006	10	19	1	$3,500	$22,780	$44,400	1.68950
2007	10	19	2	$3,570	$14,190	$30,000	1.68919
2008	10	19	2	$3,850	$15,690	$33,000	1.68884
2009	10	19	4	$450	$13,950	$24,500	1.70139
2010	10	19	1	$1,750	$21,580	$39,200	1.68024
2011	10	19	2	$3,570	$17,210	$34,800	1.67469
2012	10	19	2	$3,680	$19,070	$38,000	1.67033
2013	10	19	3	$5,500	$45,780	$85,000	1.65757
2014	10	19	5	$7,020	$40,790	$80,000	1.67329
2015	10	19	0	$8,000	$42,300	$84,000	1.66998
2016	10	19	0	$14,250	$223,680	$400,000	1.68117
2017	10	19	0	$9,600	$38,560	$80,000	1.66113
2018	10	19	1	$4,560	$14,310	$31,000	1.64282
2019	10	19	1	$15,000	$52,030	$110,000	1.64106
2020	10	19	2	$3,500	$13,260	$27,500	1.64081
2021	10	19	2	$3,570	$13,010	$27,000	1.62847
2022	10	19	2	$3,850	$15,750	$31,900	1.62755
2023	10	19	0	$10,200	$36,090	$75,400	1.62886
2024	10	19	0	$6,000	$34,700	$66,400	1.63145
2025	10	19	0	$2,140	$17,820	$32,500	1.62826
2026	10	19	3	$4,000	$27,050	$50,000	1.61031
2027	10	19	4	$450	$13,770	$22,900	1.61041
2028	10	19	4	$460	$14,120	$23,400	1.60494
2029	10	19	4	$460	$13,660	$22,900	1.62181
2030	10	19	0	$8,000	$35,800	$71,000	1.62100
2031	10	19	1	$6,200	$30,390	$58,000	1.58513
2032	10	19	4	$450	$14,050	$22,900	1.57931
2033	10	19	4	$460	$13,990	$22,900	1.58478
2034	10	19	4	$460	$14,010	$22,900	1.58258
2035	10	19	5	$5,000	$56,520	$97,500	1.58485
2036	10	19	5	$5,500	$34,430	$63,000	1.57776
2037	10	19	5	$6,200	$46,750	$84,500	1.59585
2038	10	19	5	$6,200	$35,270	$65,800	1.58669
2039	10	19	21	$2,500	$12,840	$24,500	1.59713
2040	10	19	0	$2,800	$23,810	$42,500	1.59714
2041	10	19	0	$1,500	$39,770	$66,000	1.59922
2042	10	19	1	$7,100	$30,660	$59,000	1.56250
2043	10	19	2	$3,680	$29,000	$51,000	1.56059
2044	10	19	4	$650	$20,360	$32,900	1.56592
2045	10	19	4	$510	$16,050	$26,000	1.57005
2046	10	19	4	$450	$13,930	$22,600	1.57163
2047	10	19	4	$460	$14,000	$22,500	1.55602
2048	10	19	4	$450	$13,950	$22,500	1.56250
2049	10	19	4	$460	$14,160	$22,900	1.56635
2050	10	19	5	$8,150	$44,030	$82,000	1.57148
2051	10	19	5	$7,020	$42,150	$77,000	1.56600
2052	10	19	5	$5,000	$41,990	$73,800	1.57055
2053	10	19	5	$5,500	$32,520	$59,500	1.56497
2054	10	19	0	$2,000	$21,110	$36,000	1.55777
2055	10	19	0	$2,500	$23,080	$39,900	1.55981
2056	10	19	0	$5,000	$26,960	$50,000	1.56446
2057	10	19	2	$3,850	$17,980	$33,700	1.54375
2058	10	19	2	$1,000	$19,690	$31,750	1.53456
2059	10	19	2	$3,680	$28,380	$49,000	1.52838
2060	10	19	2	$3,680	$24,210	$43,000	1.54177
2061	10	19	4	$660	$20,640	$32,900	1.54460
2062	10	19	4	$710	$21,450	$33,900	1.52978
2063	10	19	4	$520	$16,200	$25,900	1.54904
2064	10	19	4	$470	$14,450	$22,900	1.53485
2065	10	19	4	$460	$14,080	$22,500	1.54746
2066	10	19	5	$6,890	$39,310	$70,900	1.53463
2067	10	19	20	$6,800	$21,940	$44,300	1.54141
2068	10	19	0	$3,000	$23,910	$41,500	1.54218
2069	10	19	0	$1,500	$18,900	$31,500	1.54412
2070	10	19	1	$5,500	$21,690	$41,000	1.50791
2071	10	19	1	$7,450	$28,640	$55,000	1.52397
2072	10	19	1	$6,800	$75,050	$125,000	1.52718
2073	10	19	2	$3,490	$25,170	$43,700	1.52477
2074	10	19	2	$3,680	$32,400	$54,800	1.51885
2075	10	19	4	$650	$21,160	$32,900	1.50848
2076	10	19	4	$670	$21,060	$32,900	1.51404
2077	10	19	4	$670	$20,870	$32,900	1.52739
2078	10	19	4	$460	$14,710	$22,900	1.50956
2079	10	19	8	$6,000	$35,440	$62,400	1.50579
2080	10	19	17	$7,000	$56,780	$96,500	1.51301

REAL ESTATE SALES FOR 1978
IN A MID-SIZED FLORIDA CITY (CONTINUED)

OBS	TOWNSHIP	RANGE	SECTION	LANDVAL	IMPROVAL	SALEPRIC	SALTOAPR
2081	10	19	17	$7,500	$49,990	$87,500	1.52200
2082	10	19	0	$20,650	$66,770	$133,000	1.52139
2083	10	19	0	$2,000	$21,220	$35,000	1.50732
2084	10	19	0	$3,000	$28,450	$47,800	1.51987
2085	10	19	0	$14,000	$56,070	$105,900	1.51135
2086	10	19	0	$2,800	$20,960	$35,900	1.51094
2087	10	19	0	$1,500	$31,230	$50,000	1.52765
2088	10	19	1	$6,200	$20,700	$40,000	1.48699
2089	10	19	2	$3,570	$12,890	$24,500	1.48846
2090	10	19	2	$3,600	$24,900	$42,500	1.49123
2091	10	19	2	$3,680	$19,590	$35,000	1.50408
2092	10	19	4	$480	$14,850	$23,000	1.50033
2093	10	19	4	$700	$21,320	$32,900	1.49410
2094	10	19	4	$530	$16,590	$25,500	1.48949
2095	10	19	4	$460	$14,860	$22,900	1.49478
2096	10	19	4	$450	$13,880	$21,300	1.48639
2097	10	19	4	$460	$14,840	$22,900	1.49673
2098	10	19	5	$6,890	$39,670	$69,900	1.50129
2099	10	19	5	$6,890	$43,300	$74,500	1.48436
2100	10	19	6	$6,000	$28,530	$51,500	1.49146
2101	10	19	8	$5,800	$42,930	$72,600	1.48984
2102	10	19	0	$3,000	$29,890	$49,000	1.48981
2103	10	19	0	$2,500	$29,660	$48,000	1.49254
2104	10	19	0	$1,500	$35,390	$55,500	1.50447
2105	10	19	2	$1,370	$24,700	$38,100	1.46145
2106	10	19	2	$3,500	$30,310	$49,500	1.46406
2107	10	19	2	$3,680	$27,420	$46,000	1.47910
2108	10	19	2	$3,680	$25,240	$42,500	1.46957
2109	10	19	4	$540	$16,340	$24,900	1.47512
2110	10	19	4	$460	$14,130	$21,500	1.47361
2111	10	19	5	$7,200	$44,880	$76,900	1.47657
2112	10	19	5	$5,000	$44,220	$72,000	1.46282
2113	10	19	8	$5,900	$37,210	$63,110	1.46393
2114	10	19	0	$3,000	$32,580	$52,100	1.46431
2115	10	19	0	$1,500	$20,030	$31,800	1.47701
2116	10	19	0	$1,500	$31,650	$49,000	1.47813
2117	10	19	2	$3,570	$21,330	$36,100	1.44980
2118	10	19	2	$3,570	$16,750	$29,500	1.45177
2119	10	19	2	$3,600	$19,160	$33,000	1.44991
2120	10	19	2	$3,570	$21,460	$36,500	1.45825
2121	10	19	4	$820	$23,390	$35,000	1.44568
2122	10	19	4	$460	$13,980	$21,000	1.45429
2123	10	19	5	$5,880	$41,200	$68,000	1.44435
2124	10	19	5	$8,190	$57,350	$95,000	1.44950
2125	10	19	5	$7,020	$50,150	$83,200	1.45531
2126	10	19	5	$5,000	$39,990	$65,000	1.44477
2127	10	19	5	$5,800	$49,960	$80,800	1.44907
2128	10	19	8	$5,270	$36,710	$60,800	1.44831
2129	10	19	8	$5,600	$35,700	$60,000	1.45278
2130	10	19	8	$5,700	$35,770	$60,200	1.45165
2131	10	19	29	$5,000	$25,160	$43,500	1.44231
2132	10	19	0	$3,000	$25,020	$40,900	1.45967
2133	10	19	0	$1,500	$31,230	$47,500	1.45127
2134	10	19	1	$5,500	$48,920	$78,000	1.43330
2135	10	19	2	$3,740	$17,290	$30,200	1.43604
2136	10	19	2	$3,570	$17,440	$30,000	1.42789
2137	10	19	2	$4,800	$33,230	$54,500	1.43308
2138	10	19	2	$3,570	$26,080	$42,500	1.43339
2139	10	19	2	$3,500	$24,610	$40,000	1.42298
2140	10	19	3	$6,360	$33,550	$57,000	1.42821
2141	10	19	4	$790	$22,840	$33,900	1.43462
2142	10	19	4	$700	$21,360	$31,500	1.42792
2143	10	19	4	$460	$13,980	$20,600	1.42659
2144	10	19	5	$8,100	$35,450	$62,500	1.43513
2145	10	19	5	$8,050	$36,820	$64,500	1.43749
2146	10	19	5	$6,800	$39,660	$66,800	1.43780
2147	10	19	5	$7,020	$45,120	$74,600	1.43076
2148	10	19	5	$5,500	$34,890	$58,000	1.43600
2149	10	19	5	$5,700	$46,780	$75,000	1.42912
2150	10	19	6	$6,000	$33,710	$56,900	1.43289
2151	10	19	6	$6,000	$34,340	$57,500	1.42538
2152	10	19	6	$7,500	$28,730	$52,000	1.43527
2153	10	19	7	$3,200	$31,820	$49,900	1.42490
2154	10	19	8	$3,500	$27,380	$44,300	1.43459
2155	10	19	8	$6,000	$34,610	$58,000	1.42822
2156	10	19	17	$7,700	$39,740	$67,500	1.42285
2157	10	19	29	$5,000	$21,600	$38,000	1.42857
2158	10	19	0	$6,000	$35,280	$58,900	1.42684
2159	10	19	2	$3,740	$25,510	$41,000	1.40171
2160	10	19	2	$3,680	$31,570	$50,000	1.41844

REAL ESTATE SALES FOR 1978
IN A MID-SIZED FLORIDA CITY (CONTINUED)

OBS	TOWNSHIP	RANGE	SECTION	LANDVAL	IMPROVAL	SALEPRIC	SALTOAPR
2161	10	19	4	$780	$22,560	$32,900	1.40960
2162	10	19	4	$530	$16,590	$24,200	1.41355
2163	10	19	4	$780	$22,690	$32,900	1.40179
2164	10	19	4	$780	$22,660	$33,200	1.41638
2165	10	19	4	$510	$15,660	$22,900	1.41620
2166	10	19	4	$510	$15,640	$22,900	1.41796
2167	10	19	5	$8,100	$38,280	$65,000	1.40147
2168	10	19	5	$8,100	$38,310	$65,000	1.40056
2169	10	19	5	$7,200	$49,580	$80,000	1.40895
2170	10	19	6	$6,000	$35,620	$58,500	1.40557
2171	10	19	7	$4,800	$42,160	$66,180	1.40928
2172	10	19	21	$2,700	$15,040	$25,000	1.40924
2173	10	19	0	$2,450	$22,310	$35,000	1.41357
2174	10	19	0	$1,500	$24,850	$37,000	1.40417
2175	10	19	0	$1,500	$18,900	$28,750	1.40931
2176	10	19	0	$1,500	$28,100	$42,000	1.41892
2177	10	19	0	$1,500	$18,900	$28,800	1.41176
2178	10	19	0	$1,500	$32,350	$47,500	1.40325
2179	10	19	0	$1,500	$19,330	$29,500	1.41623
2180	10	19	1	$6,560	$33,750	$55,700	1.38179
2181	10	19	3	$3,400	$28,430	$44,500	1.39805
2182	10	19	4	$790	$22,840	$32,900	1.39230
2183	10	19	4	$790	$22,840	$32,900	1.39230
2184	10	19	4	$450	$13,950	$19,900	1.38194
2185	10	19	5	$5,500	$35,660	$57,000	1.38484
2186	10	19	5	$7,200	$40,600	$66,500	1.39121
2187	10	19	5	$5,800	$52,780	$81,700	1.39467
2188	10	19	5	$5,500	$37,460	$59,500	1.38501
2189	10	19	6	$6,000	$33,600	$55,000	1.38889
2190	10	19	6	$7,500	$29,270	$51,000	1.38700
2191	10	19	6	$7,750	$31,830	$55,000	1.38959
2192	10	19	8	$5,600	$22,910	$39,700	1.39249
2193	10	19	29	$2,190	$20,940	$32,000	1.38348
2194	10	19	29	$5,000	$21,220	$36,500	1.39207
2195	10	19	0	$9,500	$55,170	$90,000	1.39168
2196	10	19	0	$14,000	$61,910	$105,500	1.38980
2197	10	19	0	$1,500	$35,390	$51,000	1.38249
2198	10	19	0	$1,500	$24,850	$36,500	1.38520
2199	10	19	0	$1,500	$19,330	$29,000	1.39222
2200	10	19	0	$1,500	$19,330	$28,800	1.38262
2201	10	19	0	$1,500	$20,030	$30,000	1.39340
2202	10	19	1	$7,450	$27,430	$47,800	1.37041
2203	10	19	2	$3,570	$16,760	$28,000	1.37727
2204	10	19	2	$1,370	$24,700	$35,500	1.36172
2205	10	19	4	$810	$23,220	$32,900	1.36912
2206	10	19	4	$810	$23,170	$32,900	1.37198
2207	10	19	5	$8,200	$39,830	$65,500	1.36373
2208	10	19	5	$7,020	$53,440	$82,500	1.36454
2209	10	19	5	$5,000	$64,010	$95,000	1.37661
2210	10	19	6	$7,300	$33,080	$55,500	1.37444
2211	10	19	6	$7,300	$32,910	$55,000	1.36782
2212	10	19	11	$5,310	$92,480	$134,500	1.37540
2213	10	19	0	$6,980	$47,660	$75,000	1.37262
2214	10	19	0	$13,200	$74,010	$120,000	1.37599
2215	10	19	0	$1,500	$39,770	$56,400	1.36661
2216	10	19	0	$1,500	$27,770	$39,900	1.36317
2217	10	19	0	$1,500	$27,770	$40,000	1.36659
2218	10	19	0	$1,500	$31,230	$44,600	1.36266
2219	10	19	0	$1,500	$27,400	$39,500	1.36678
2220	10	19	0	$1,500	$19,330	$28,500	1.36822
2221	10	19	1	$7,450	$38,830	$63,000	1.36128
2222	10	19	4	$700	$21,590	$30,000	1.34590
2223	10	19	5	$9,500	$67,810	$105,000	1.35817
2224	10	19	5	$8,050	$36,020	$59,500	1.35012
2225	10	19	6	$5,000	$31,150	$49,000	1.35546
2226	10	19	6	$5,000	$29,320	$46,500	1.35490
2227	10	19	6	$7,500	$30,530	$51,500	1.35419
2228	10	19	6	$7,500	$32,080	$53,800	1.35927
2229	10	19	6	$7,500	$35,670	$58,500	1.35511
2230	10	19	8	$5,600	$24,990	$41,100	1.34358
2231	10	19	8	$5,700	$39,160	$61,000	1.35979
2232	10	19	8	$6,000	$44,310	$68,000	1.35162
2233	10	19	14	$4,500	$16,310	$28,000	1.34551
2234	10	19	20	$6,950	$28,780	$48,500	1.35740
2235	10	19	29	$5,000	$22,520	$37,000	1.34448
2236	10	19	0	$3,000	$31,010	$45,900	1.34960
2237	10	19	0	$1,500	$35,390	$50,000	1.35538
2238	10	19	0	$1,500	$25,550	$36,500	1.34935
2239	10	19	0	$1,500	$28,100	$40,000	1.35135
2240	10	19	1	$4,200	$25,920	$40,000	1.32802

REAL ESTATE SALES FOR 1978
IN A MID-SIZED FLORIDA CITY (CONTINUED)

OBS	TOWNSHIP	RANGE	SECTION	LANDVAL	IMPROVAL	SALEPRIC	SALTOAPR
2241	10	19	2	$3,970	$38,210	$56,000	1.32764
2242	10	19	2	$3,680	$34,550	$51,300	1.34188
2243	10	19	3	$3,400	$29,560	$43,900	1.33192
2244	10	19	4	$840	$25,160	$34,900	1.34231
2245	10	19	4	$520	$16,740	$22,900	1.32677
2246	10	19	4	$990	$28,810	$39,900	1.33893
2247	10	19	5	$8,050	$40,550	$64,800	1.33333
2248	10	19	5	$7,200	$38,620	$60,800	1.32693
2249	10	19	5	$7,920	$44,570	$70,000	1.33359
2250	10	19	7	$4,000	$36,430	$54,000	1.33564
2251	10	19	8	$5,600	$25,780	$41,700	1.32887
2252	10	19	8	$3,500	$31,860	$47,000	1.32919
2253	10	19	8	$5,750	$43,810	$66,000	1.33172
2254	10	19	17	$5,500	$43,740	$66,000	1.34037
2255	10	19	20	$6,950	$27,300	$45,500	1.32847
2256	10	19	20	$6,950	$27,260	$45,500	1.33002
2257	10	19	29	$2,000	$24,760	$35,900	1.34155
2258	10	19	0	$7,000	$30,400	$50,000	1.33690
2259	10	19	0	$3,000	$28,510	$42,300	1.34243
2260	10	19	0	$10,500	$29,050	$53,000	1.34008
2261	10	19	1	$5,500	$25,890	$41,500	1.32208
2262	10	19	2	$4,600	$35,950	$53,500	1.31936
2263	10	19	2	$3,500	$30,610	$44,900	1.31633
2264	10	19	3	$3,400	$28,840	$42,500	1.31824
2265	10	19	5	$5,700	$41,310	$62,000	1.31887
2266	10	19	6	$6,000	$33,380	$51,800	1.31539
2267	10	19	6	$5,000	$29,250	$45,000	1.31387
2268	10	19	6	$7,600	$32,570	$52,900	1.31690
2269	10	19	8	$5,600	$25,380	$40,900	1.32021
2270	10	19	8	$5,600	$26,720	$42,800	1.32426
2271	10	19	22	$2,000	$24,160	$34,400	1.31498
2272	10	19	29	$5,000	$20,980	$34,000	1.30870
2273	10	19	0	$6,000	$42,710	$64,500	1.32416
2274	10	19	0	$3,000	$36,510	$52,000	1.31612
2275	10	19	0	$3,000	$38,410	$54,200	1.30886
2276	10	19	0	$13,000	$54,720	$89,000	1.31424
2277	10	19	1	$6,560	$38,620	$58,900	1.30367
2278	10	19	2	$3,800	$31,830	$46,500	1.30508
2279	10	19	2	$3,500	$41,690	$58,500	1.29453
2280	10	19	4	$820	$23,750	$31,900	1.29833
2281	10	19	4	$800	$24,470	$32,900	1.30194
2282	10	19	5	$8,200	$47,780	$73,000	1.30404
2283	10	19	6	$6,000	$36,440	$54,900	1.29359
2284	10	19	6	$6,000	$39,700	$59,500	1.30197
2285	10	19	8	$5,600	$25,380	$40,500	1.30730
2286	10	19	8	$6,000	$30,160	$47,200	1.30531
2287	10	19	8	$5,400	$28,140	$43,500	1.29696
2288	10	19	8	$5,600	$46,280	$67,000	1.29144
2289	10	19	8	$6,000	$36,450	$54,900	1.29329
2290	10	19	14	$30,000	$74,190	$135,000	1.29571
2291	10	19	0	$6,000	$31,340	$48,500	1.29888
2292	10	19	0	$1,500	$27,770	$38,000	1.29826
2293	10	19	0	$1,500	$19,600	$27,500	1.30332
2294	10	19	2	$3,570	$22,940	$33,800	1.27499
2295	10	19	2	$3,300	$29,750	$42,500	1.28593
2296	10	19	2	$4,200	$43,370	$60,800	1.27812
2297	10	19	4	$910	$26,400	$34,900	1.27792
2298	10	19	5	$5,000	$35,710	$52,000	1.27733
2299	10	19	6	$6,000	$34,440	$52,000	1.28586
2300	10	19	6	$7,500	$30,860	$49,000	1.27737
2301	10	19	8	$5,600	$24,750	$39,000	1.28501
2302	10	19	8	$5,900	$28,530	$43,900	1.27505
2303	10	19	8	$5,600	$49,600	$71,200	1.28986
2304	10	19	8	$5,900	$43,610	$63,500	1.28257
2305	10	19	8	$6,150	$37,760	$56,600	1.28900
2306	10	19	11	$14,000	$76,240	$116,000	1.28546
2307	10	19	17	$5,500	$39,170	$57,400	1.28498
2308	10	19	20	$7,400	$28,680	$46,000	1.27494
2309	10	19	0	$9,500	$27,230	$47,000	1.27961
2310	10	19	0	$1,500	$39,770	$53,000	1.28423
2311	10	19	0	$1,500	$35,390	$47,500	1.28761
2312	10	19	2	$6,500	$29,660	$46,000	1.27212
2313	10	19	4	$710	$25,180	$32,900	1.27076
2314	10	19	4	$980	$30,600	$39,900	1.26346
2315	10	19	5	$5,600	$35,320	$51,900	1.26833
2316	10	19	6	$5,000	$39,190	$55,900	1.26499
2317	10	19	6	$5,000	$27,930	$41,900	1.27240
2318	10	19	8	$5,900	$39,250	$57,500	1.27353
2319	10	19	20	$6,950	$23,090	$38,000	1.26498
2320	10	19	20	$8,250	$31,430	$50,000	1.26008

REAL ESTATE SALES FOR 1978
IN A MID-SIZED FLORIDA CITY (CONTINUED)

OBS	TOWNSHIP	RANGE	SECTION	LANDVAL	IMPROVAL	SALEPRIC	SALTOAPR
2321	10	19	0	$3,000	$28,320	$39,900	1.27395
2322	10	19	0	$2,800	$29,570	$41,000	1.26660
2323	10	19	0	$3,100	$24,780	$35,500	1.27331
2324	10	19	0	$1,500	$31,930	$42,500	1.27131
2325	10	19	2	$3,500	$17,230	$26,000	1.25422
2326	10	19	2	$3,600	$36,540	$50,000	1.24564
2327	10	19	2	$3,970	$35,480	$49,500	1.25475
2328	10	19	2	$3,500	$33,920	$47,000	1.25601
2329	10	19	3	$6,160	$45,740	$65,000	1.25241
2330	10	19	5	$6,840	$51,690	$73,500	1.25577
2331	10	19	5	$5,000	$32,660	$47,000	1.24801
2332	10	19	5	$5,000	$33,380	$48,000	1.25065
2333	10	19	5	$5,500	$37,400	$53,500	1.24709
2334	10	19	6	$6,000	$27,620	$42,300	1.25818
2335	10	19	6	$6,000	$29,360	$44,000	1.24434
2336	10	19	6	$6,000	$29,200	$44,000	1.25000
2337	10	19	6	$7,500	$32,380	$50,000	1.25376
2338	10	19	8	$5,800	$25,440	$39,200	1.25480
2339	10	19	8	$5,600	$29,190	$43,500	1.25036
2340	10	19	8	$5,500	$24,730	$38,000	1.25703
2341	10	19	8	$5,600	$38,340	$54,700	1.24488
2342	10	19	8	$6,000	$35,290	$51,400	1.24485
2343	10	19	29	$5,000	$25,480	$38,000	1.24672
2344	10	19	1	$6,640	$31,300	$46,900	1.23616
2345	10	19	2	$3,680	$24,590	$35,000	1.23806
2346	10	19	5	$5,500	$36,560	$52,000	1.23633
2347	10	19	8	$5,600	$25,070	$37,900	1.23574
2348	10	19	8	$5,800	$24,740	$37,900	1.24100
2349	10	19	8	$5,700	$27,000	$40,200	1.22936
2350	10	19	8	$5,750	$27,910	$41,700	1.23886
2351	10	19	0	$5,800	$37,310	$53,300	1.23637
2352	10	19	0	$2,000	$34,640	$45,500	1.24181
2353	10	19	3	$3,400	$30,000	$41,000	1.22754
2354	10	19	5	$8,050	$41,060	$59,900	1.21971
2355	10	19	5	$5,200	$61,600	$81,500	1.22006
2356	10	19	6	$6,000	$42,930	$60,000	1.22624
2357	10	19	6	$6,000	$36,310	$51,500	1.21721
2358	10	19	6	$5,000	$31,450	$44,500	1.22085
2359	10	19	8	$5,800	$27,730	$41,000	1.22279
2360	10	19	8	$5,900	$28,590	$41,900	1.21484
2361	10	19	8	$5,800	$25,300	$38,000	1.22186
2362	10	19	8	$5,400	$27,390	$40,100	1.22293
2363	10	19	29	$5,000	$20,940	$31,500	1.21434
2364	10	19	1	$3,500	$27,840	$38,000	1.21251
2365	10	19	3	$3,900	$40,050	$53,000	1.20592
2366	10	19	7	$7,500	$52,510	$72,000	1.19980
2367	10	19	8	$5,700	$29,130	$41,800	1.20011
2368	10	19	8	$5,400	$30,480	$43,000	1.19844
2369	10	19	20	$6,950	$22,740	$36,000	1.21253
2370	10	19	0	$6,000	$28,790	$42,000	1.20724
2371	10	19	0	$2,500	$29,160	$38,000	1.20025
2372	10	19	1	$5,700	$29,700	$42,000	1.18644
2373	10	19	2	$3,500	$33,910	$44,500	1.18952
2374	10	19	2	$3,700	$29,700	$40,000	1.19760
2375	10	19	2	$4,600	$36,550	$49,000	1.19077
2376	10	19	8	$5,600	$25,640	$37,100	1.18758
2377	10	19	17	$4,000	$40,590	$53,000	1.18861
2378	10	19	1	$5,850	$35,450	$48,900	1.18402
2379	10	19	1	$3,500	$27,840	$36,700	1.17103
2380	10	19	4	$890	$26,020	$31,500	1.17057
2381	10	19	4	$790	$23,010	$28,000	1.17647
2382	10	19	6	$6,000	$45,940	$61,000	1.17443
2383	10	19	6	$5,000	$30,730	$42,000	1.17548
2384	10	19	6	$5,000	$35,320	$47,500	1.17808
2385	10	19	6	$5,000	$37,490	$50,000	1.17675
2386	10	19	8	$3,000	$34,770	$44,500	1.17818
2387	10	19	8	$5,600	$32,780	$45,000	1.17249
2388	10	19	8	$5,600	$26,210	$37,300	1.17259
2389	10	19	8	$5,800	$43,270	$58,000	1.18198
2390	10	19	8	$6,250	$36,200	$50,000	1.17786
2391	10	19	20	$6,950	$24,740	$37,500	1.18334
2392	10	19	29	$5,000	$23,910	$34,100	1.17952
2393	10	19	2	$3,500	$45,730	$57,400	1.16596
2394	10	19	6	$5,000	$33,860	$45,000	1.15800
2395	10	19	17	$13,000	$82,830	$112,000	1.16874
2396	10	19	0	$3,750	$35,820	$46,000	1.16250
2397	10	19	2	$3,300	$35,370	$44,500	1.15076
2398	10	19	4	$870	$25,090	$30,000	1.15562
2399	10	19	20	$7,200	$30,140	$42,700	1.14355
2400	10	19	2	$3,300	$37,200	$46,200	1.14074

REAL ESTATE SALES FOR 1978
IN A MID-SIZED FLORIDA CITY (CONTINUED)

OBS	TOWNSHIP	RANGE	SECTION	LANDVAL	IMPROVAL	SALEPRIC	SALTOAPR
2401	10	19	2	$3,680	$27,250	$35,000	1.13159
2402	10	19	3	$3,000	$29,590	$37,000	1.13532
2403	10	19	11	$17,800	$84,740	$115,000	1.12151
2404	10	19	3	$6,710	$43,740	$56,300	1.11596
2405	10	19	2	$3,300	$34,470	$40,600	1.07493
2406	10	19	7	$8,100	$22,890	$33,500	1.08099
2407	10	19	2	$3,850	$32,800	$38,500	1.05048
2408	10	19	6	$6,000	$36,520	$44,000	1.03481
2409	10	19	2	$3,570	$35,150	$39,600	1.02273
2410	10	19	21	$500	$1,940	$2,500	1.02459
2411	10	19	0	$1,500	$34,960	$36,200	0.99287
2412	10	19	0	$6,000	$39,850	$45,000	0.98146
2413	10	19	2	$3,850	$22,120	$25,000	0.96265
2414	10	19	7	$4,500	$32,940	$35,000	0.93483
2415	10	20	4	$600	$3,300	$18,000	4.61538
2416	10	20	3	$600	$3,130	$16,000	4.28954
2417	10	20	4	$600	$3,400	$17,500	4.37500
2418	10	20	4	$2,400	$5,110	$32,000	4.26099
2419	10	20	5	$2,160	$4,970	$29,500	4.13745
2420	10	20	7	$1,500	$4,560	$23,000	3.79538
2421	10	20	1	$1,580	$4,450	$22,500	3.73134
2422	10	20	4	$3,000	$7,130	$37,900	3.74136
2423	10	20	4	$1,150	$5,730	$25,500	3.70640
2424	10	20	4	$730	$4,460	$18,500	3.56455
2425	10	20	6	$2,000	$5,970	$28,500	3.57591
2426	10	20	6	$3,300	$9,430	$44,000	3.45640
2427	10	20	1	$1,500	$6,760	$28,000	3.38983
2428	10	20	5	$1,370	$6,530	$26,000	3.29114
2429	10	20	5	$1,830	$16,000	$60,000	3.36511
2430	10	20	4	$2,450	$7,610	$31,500	3.13121
2431	10	20	4	$3,000	$10,560	$41,300	3.04572
2432	10	20	4	$2,700	$8,340	$34,000	3.07971
2433	10	20	4	$2,570	$7,120	$29,500	3.04438
2434	10	20	15	$1,500	$5,580	$21,500	3.03672
2435	10	20	5	$1,300	$7,920	$26,800	2.90672
2436	10	20	5	$2,030	$15,850	$52,000	2.90828
2437	10	20	1	$1,500	$9,290	$31,100	2.88230
2438	10	20	4	$2,930	$9,850	$36,700	2.87167
2439	10	20	4	$3,570	$13,170	$46,000	2.74791
2440	10	20	5	$1,300	$9,450	$29,500	2.74419
2441	10	20	14	$900	$7,390	$23,000	2.77443
2442	10	20	4	$7,000	$18,570	$70,000	2.73758
2443	10	20	5	$1,500	$4,630	$16,500	2.69168
2444	10	20	5	$1,110	$6,140	$19,500	2.68966
2445	10	20	10	$800	$5,880	$18,200	2.72455
2446	10	20	4	$1,100	$12,740	$36,000	2.60116
2447	10	20	5	$11,250	$23,100	$90,000	2.62009
2448	10	20	4	$3,000	$9,880	$33,000	2.56211
2449	10	20	1	$1,500	$10,340	$29,500	2.49155
2450	10	20	4	$2,800	$7,180	$25,000	2.50501
2451	10	20	6	$3,380	$14,480	$44,300	2.48040
2452	10	20	1	$1,500	$9,540	$27,200	2.46377
2453	10	20	4	$6,530	$14,920	$52,500	2.44755
2454	10	20	5	$1,970	$8,900	$26,500	2.43790
2455	10	20	10	$800	$8,130	$22,000	2.46361
2456	10	20	4	$720	$4,900	$13,500	2.40214
2457	10	20	4	$4,500	$10,010	$34,400	2.37078
2458	10	20	6	$5,810	$23,130	$69,500	2.40152
2459	10	20	5	$1,050	$10,730	$27,500	2.33447
2460	10	20	5	$12,500	$102,300	$265,000	2.30836
2461	10	20	5	$1,450	$7,120	$20,000	2.33372
2462	10	20	6	$4,000	$30,030	$80,000	2.35087
2463	10	20	6	$2,300	$9,900	$28,500	2.33607
2464	10	20	6	$4,140	$32,110	$85,000	2.34483
2465	10	20	15	$1,200	$9,310	$24,600	2.34063
2466	10	20	3	$600	$8,610	$21,000	2.28013
2467	10	20	5	$1,500	$11,160	$29,000	2.29068
2468	10	20	5	$2,750	$12,180	$33,900	2.27060
2469	10	20	12	$2,500	$11,690	$32,000	2.25511
2470	10	20	1	$1,500	$9,220	$23,900	2.22948
2471	10	20	9	$500	$6,200	$15,000	2.23881
2472	10	20	11	$2,100	$11,890	$31,000	2.21587
2473	10	20	3	$1,000	$11,030	$26,000	2.16126
2474	10	20	4	$1,890	$6,370	$18,000	2.17918
2475	10	20	5	$2,740	$35,140	$82,000	2.16473
2476	10	20	1	$1,580	$8,630	$21,900	2.14496
2477	10	20	3	$1,200	$9,820	$23,500	2.13249
2478	10	20	4	$1,020	$5,130	$13,000	2.11382
2479	10	20	5	$1,970	$6,750	$18,400	2.11009
2480	10	20	8	$1,800	$12,850	$31,000	2.11604

REAL ESTATE SALES FOR 1978
IN A MID-SIZED FLORIDA CITY (CONTINUED)

OBS	TOWNSHIP	RANGE	SECTION	LANDVAL	IMPROVAL	SALEPRIC	SALTOAPR
2481	10	20	1	$1,500	$12,960	$30,000	2.07469
2482	10	20	5	$1,510	$15,700	$35,900	2.08600
2483	10	20	6	$3,800	$17,980	$45,000	2.06612
2484	10	20	4	$1,530	$11,600	$26,900	2.04874
2485	10	20	5	$5,100	$15,900	$42,500	2.02381
2486	10	20	5	$630	$2,280	$6,000	2.06186
2487	10	20	4	$6,300	$18,140	$50,000	2.04583
2488	10	20	5	$2,300	$9,910	$25,000	2.04750
2489	10	20	11	$2,600	$12,830	$31,300	2.02852
2490	10	20	1	$2,250	$10,770	$26,200	2.01229
2491	10	20	1	$1,500	$8,430	$20,000	2.01410
2492	10	20	4	$500	$10,670	$22,500	2.01432
2493	10	20	4	$1,320	$5,360	$13,300	1.99102
2494	10	20	4	$4,820	$19,660	$49,000	2.00163
2495	10	20	4	$2,400	$10,840	$26,500	2.00151
2496	10	20	4	$6,200	$14,610	$42,000	2.01826
2497	10	20	6	$2,100	$10,420	$25,000	1.99681
2498	10	20	4	$770	$3,340	$8,000	1.94647
2499	10	20	5	$5,880	$11,980	$35,000	1.95969
2500	10	20	6	$4,500	$28,310	$64,000	1.95062
2501	10	20	11	$2,100	$13,710	$31,000	1.96078
2502	10	20	14	$2,000	$13,800	$31,000	1.96203
2503	10	20	15	$1,500	$10,640	$23,900	1.96870
2504	10	20	3	$1,200	$6,140	$14,000	1.90736
2505	10	20	4	$3,200	$12,940	$31,000	1.92069
2506	10	20	4	$2,720	$15,950	$35,800	1.91751
2507	10	20	4	$5,250	$18,230	$45,000	1.91652
2508	10	20	4	$840	$9,260	$19,000	1.88119
2509	10	20	4	$5,400	$13,220	$35,000	1.87970
2510	10	20	5	$7,980	$48,940	$108,000	1.89740
2511	10	20	5	$1,650	$6,240	$15,000	1.90114
2512	10	20	6	$4,140	$18,960	$43,500	1.88312
2513	10	20	9	$1,200	$12,810	$26,500	1.89151
2514	10	20	12	$2,500	$10,120	$24,000	1.90174
2515	10	20	1	$1,500	$9,790	$20,800	1.84234
2516	10	20	4	$2,880	$9,180	$22,300	1.84909
2517	10	20	4	$3,200	$15,170	$34,000	1.85084
2518	10	20	5	$2,820	$13,860	$31,000	1.85851
2519	10	20	12	$2,500	$16,250	$35,000	1.86667
2520	10	20	1	$1,500	$8,100	$17,500	1.82292
2521	10	20	4	$2,250	$7,660	$18,000	1.81635
2522	10	20	4	$2,920	$12,650	$28,500	1.83044
2523	10	20	5	$2,880	$7,750	$19,500	1.83443
2524	10	20	11	$2,100	$13,780	$28,800	1.81360
2525	10	20	12	$900	$8,640	$17,500	1.83438
2526	10	20	15	$1,200	$10,000	$20,300	1.81250
2527	10	20	4	$2,700	$18,100	$37,500	1.80288
2528	10	20	4	$3,200	$16,530	$35,300	1.78915
2529	10	20	5	$2,930	$20,870	$42,900	1.80252
2530	10	20	0	$16,490	$160,600	$315,000	1.77876
2531	10	20	9	$1,200	$14,320	$27,500	1.77191
2532	10	20	11	$3,000	$14,720	$31,500	1.77765
2533	10	20	1	$2,060	$13,520	$27,400	1.75866
2534	10	20	1	$1,650	$15,500	$30,000	1.74927
2535	10	20	1	$3,150	$9,300	$21,800	1.75100
2536	10	20	3	$600	$14,450	$26,500	1.76080
2537	10	20	6	$4,830	$15,550	$36,000	1.76644
2538	10	20	10	$1,300	$12,950	$25,000	1.75439
2539	10	20	11	$2,000	$14,540	$28,900	1.74728
2540	10	20	11	$2,100	$13,710	$27,900	1.76471
2541	10	20	12	$2,500	$16,050	$32,600	1.75741
2542	10	20	15	$1,200	$13,020	$24,900	1.75105
2543	10	20	1	$2,000	$19,520	$37,300	1.73327
2544	10	20	1	$2,000	$15,940	$30,700	1.71126
2545	10	20	3	$1,340	$11,440	$22,000	1.72144
2546	10	20	3	$600	$5,240	$10,000	1.71233
2547	10	20	4	$1,920	$11,430	$23,000	1.72285
2548	10	20	4	$2,880	$9,860	$22,140	1.73783
2549	10	20	4	$3,400	$12,600	$27,500	1.71875
2550	10	20	6	$5,460	$32,740	$66,000	1.72775
2551	10	20	8	$4,200	$24,560	$49,800	1.73157
2552	10	20	9	$1,300	$17,320	$32,000	1.71858
2553	10	20	9	$1,200	$13,620	$25,500	1.72065
2554	10	20	11	$2,100	$13,560	$26,900	1.71775
2555	10	20	12	$900	$8,370	$16,100	1.73679
2556	10	20	16	$1,200	$14,510	$26,900	1.71229
2557	10	20	1	$1,500	$15,680	$29,000	1.68801
2558	10	20	5	$1,650	$3,690	$9,000	1.68539
2559	10	20	6	$3,780	$13,720	$29,900	1.70857
2560	10	20	6	$4,050	$25,360	$50,000	1.70010

REAL ESTATE SALES FOR 1978
IN A MID-SIZED FLORIDA CITY (CONTINUED)

OBS	TOWNSHIP	RANGE	SECTION	LANDVAL	IMPROVAL	SALEPRIC	SALTOAPR
2561	10	20	6	$3,800	$16,650	$34,900	1.70660
2562	10	20	6	$3,220	$22,040	$43,000	1.70230
2563	10	20	12	$900	$8,600	$16,000	1.68421
2564	10	20	1	$2,060	$17,600	$32,600	1.65819
2565	10	20	1	$1,840	$16,340	$30,500	1.67767
2566	10	20	5	$2,210	$11,800	$23,500	1.67737
2567	10	20	10	$1,200	$10,650	$19,900	1.67932
2568	10	20	11	$2,000	$14,540	$27,500	1.66264
2569	10	20	11	$2,000	$13,710	$26,000	1.65500
2570	10	20	4	$2,420	$13,540	$26,000	1.62907
2571	10	20	5	$1,250	$7,340	$14,000	1.62980
2572	10	20	6	$3,740	$26,800	$50,000	1.63720
2573	10	20	6	$4,050	$21,220	$41,500	1.64226
2574	10	20	11	$3,200	$13,310	$27,000	1.63537
2575	10	20	11	$3,000	$13,570	$27,000	1.62945
2576	10	20	11	$2,200	$15,710	$29,500	1.64712
2577	10	20	11	$2,100	$14,270	$27,000	1.64936
2578	10	20	11	$2,700	$12,370	$24,900	1.65229
2579	10	20	12	$2,500	$12,730	$25,000	1.64150
2580	10	20	12	$1,350	$13,470	$24,200	1.63293
2581	10	20	12	$1,350	$13,190	$23,900	1.64374
2582	10	20	1	$2,090	$17,420	$31,600	1.61968
2583	10	20	5	$2,100	$7,200	$15,100	1.62366
2584	10	20	6	$20,800	$120,740	$228,000	1.61085
2585	10	20	0	$5,250	$16,920	$36,000	1.62382
2586	10	20	16	$1,300	$16,740	$29,000	1.60754
2587	10	20	11	$3,000	$14,280	$28,000	1.62037
2588	10	20	11	$2,200	$15,260	$28,000	1.60367
2589	10	20	11	$2,000	$15,140	$27,700	1.61610
2590	10	20	11	$2,600	$15,160	$28,500	1.60473
2591	10	20	12	$2,500	$14,750	$28,000	1.62319
2592	10	20	12	$2,700	$13,340	$26,000	1.62095
2593	10	20	14	$3,150	$27,030	$48,500	1.60702
2594	10	20	14	$3,000	$24,720	$45,000	1.62338
2595	10	20	1	$2,140	$18,240	$32,200	1.57998
2596	10	20	1	$2,060	$21,290	$37,100	1.58887
2597	10	20	4	$3,800	$12,550	$26,000	1.59021
2598	10	20	6	$2,590	$24,520	$43,000	1.58613
2599	10	20	6	$5,500	$32,030	$59,900	1.59606
2600	10	20	10	$800	$17,220	$28,500	1.58158
2601	10	20	12	$2,250	$15,500	$28,000	1.57746
2602	10	20	12	$3,000	$14,290	$27,600	1.59630
2603	10	20	21	$1,200	$17,800	$30,000	1.57895
2604	10	20	1	$1,880	$14,520	$25,500	1.55488
2605	10	20	4	$2,680	$16,580	$30,000	1.55763
2606	10	20	4	$4,720	$16,160	$32,800	1.57088
2607	10	20	4	$3,200	$20,380	$36,800	1.56064
2608	10	20	4	$6,000	$50,570	$88,400	1.56267
2609	10	20	6	$3,780	$18,700	$35,000	1.55694
2610	10	20	12	$2,500	$15,490	$28,000	1.55642
2611	10	20	12	$2,500	$12,160	$22,900	1.56207
2612	10	20	14	$2,000	$20,020	$34,500	1.56676
2613	10	20	14	$2,000	$15,570	$27,500	1.56517
2614	10	20	1	$2,400	$14,580	$26,000	1.53121
2615	10	20	1	$1,500	$14,550	$24,900	1.55140
2616	10	20	3	$780	$5,530	$9,700	1.53724
2617	10	20	3	$1,650	$5,460	$11,000	1.54712
2618	10	20	16	$1,200	$12,920	$21,700	1.53683
2619	10	20	11	$3,150	$16,880	$31,000	1.54768
2620	10	20	11	$2,100	$13,420	$23,800	1.53351
2621	10	20	12	$2,700	$13,340	$24,600	1.53367
2622	10	20	14	$1,800	$20,310	$34,000	1.53777
2623	10	20	4	$3,800	$20,050	$36,000	1.50943
2624	10	20	4	$1,000	$5,580	$10,000	1.51976
2625	10	20	5	$13,000	$33,340	$70,000	1.51057
2626	10	20	6	$17,520	$51,780	$105,000	1.51515
2627	10	20	6	$5,460	$30,440	$54,400	1.51532
2628	10	20	9	$1,500	$15,350	$25,500	1.51335
2629	10	20	10	$1,200	$13,470	$22,400	1.52693
2630	10	20	11	$2,100	$15,120	$26,200	1.52149
2631	10	20	12	$2,500	$12,600	$23,000	1.52318
2632	10	20	14	$2,000	$19,080	$32,000	1.51803
2633	10	20	3	$500	$13,420	$20,700	1.48707
2634	10	20	0	$8,000	$43,720	$77,000	1.48879
2635	10	20	0	$7,500	$32,660	$60,000	1.49402
2636	10	20	9	$1,300	$18,840	$30,100	1.49454
2637	10	20	11	$2,100	$18,800	$31,100	1.48804
2638	10	20	1	$3,000	$16,450	$28,500	1.46530
2639	10	20	5	$2,150	$4,660	$10,000	1.46843
2640	10	20	8	$6,500	$26,440	$48,600	1.47541

REAL ESTATE SALES FOR 1978
IN A MID-SIZED FLORIDA CITY (CONTINUED)

OBS	TOWNSHIP	RANGE	SECTION	LANDVAL	IMPROVAL	SALEPRIC	SALTOAPR
2641	10	20	11	$2,200	$14,200	$24,300	1.48171
2642	10	20	11	$2,500	$16,730	$28,500	1.48206
2643	10	20	11	$2,000	$18,320	$30,000	1.47638
2644	10	20	12	$2,500	$14,470	$24,900	1.46730
2645	10	20	12	$3,000	$17,010	$29,500	1.47426
2646	10	20	14	$3,000	$23,030	$38,200	1.46754
2647	10	20	1	$2,060	$16,870	$27,500	1.45272
2648	10	20	9	$1,300	$19,260	$30,000	1.45914
2649	10	20	10	$1,600	$3,330	$7,100	1.44016
2650	10	20	12	$2,500	$23,670	$38,000	1.45204
2651	10	20	12	$3,000	$14,280	$25,000	1.44676
2652	10	20	14	$5,100	$28,230	$48,500	1.45515
2653	10	20	21	$1,200	$16,540	$25,600	1.44307
2654	10	20	16	$1,200	$18,750	$28,900	1.44862
2655	10	20	4	$2,800	$16,350	$27,500	1.43603
2656	10	20	5	$3,900	$30,850	$50,000	1.43885
2657	10	20	12	$2,500	$9,120	$16,500	1.41997
2658	10	20	12	$2,500	$16,150	$26,800	1.43700
2659	10	20	1	$2,250	$16,820	$27,000	1.41584
2660	10	20	4	$3,870	$13,430	$24,500	1.41618
2661	10	20	4	$3,000	$18,890	$31,000	1.41617
2662	10	20	4	$1,550	$6,990	$12,000	1.40515
2663	10	20	1	$1,840	$24,070	$35,900	1.38557
2664	10	20	6	$4,830	$24,400	$40,500	1.38556
2665	10	20	15	$1,200	$17,950	$26,800	1.39948
2666	10	20	1	$2,300	$21,890	$33,000	1.36420
2667	10	20	1	$2,090	$13,960	$22,000	1.37072
2668	10	20	4	$2,400	$14,780	$23,700	1.37951
2669	10	20	4	$8,680	$74,920	$114,600	1.37081
2670	10	20	8	$6,500	$31,350	$51,600	1.36328
2671	10	20	0	$6,000	$41,310	$65,000	1.37392
2672	10	20	9	$2,050	$19,800	$30,000	1.37300
2673	10	20	12	$2,500	$12,540	$20,500	1.36303
2674	10	20	15	$1,200	$3,930	$7,000	1.36452
2675	10	20	16	$1,400	$23,430	$34,000	1.36931
2676	10	20	16	$1,500	$22,200	$32,500	1.37131
2677	10	20	1	$2,060	$22,260	$32,900	1.35280
2678	10	20	0	$6,900	$43,920	$69,000	1.35773
2679	10	20	11	$3,500	$22,180	$34,900	1.35903
2680	10	20	12	$2,500	$19,680	$30,000	1.35257
2681	10	20	14	$2,000	$22,370	$33,000	1.35412
2682	10	20	14	$2,000	$19,220	$28,800	1.35721
2683	10	20	15	$1,200	$16,170	$23,500	1.35291
2684	10	20	1	$2,060	$21,670	$31,500	1.32743
2685	10	20	3	$1,000	$10,540	$15,500	1.34315
2686	10	20	4	$750	$16,950	$23,500	1.32768
2687	10	20	8	$6,500	$32,390	$52,000	1.33710
2688	10	20	14	$2,000	$20,430	$30,000	1.33749
2689	10	20	14	$2,500	$22,460	$33,500	1.34215
2690	10	20	16	$1,200	$21,270	$30,000	1.33511
2691	10	20	1	$2,090	$18,290	$27,000	1.32483
2692	10	20	3	$500	$18,560	$25,000	1.31165
2693	10	20	3	$720	$4,210	$6,500	1.31846
2694	10	20	8	$6,300	$32,070	$50,500	1.31613
2695	10	20	10	$1,420	$16,920	$24,000	1.30862
2696	10	20	11	$3,000	$18,230	$28,000	1.31889
2697	10	20	11	$12,000	$124,670	$180,000	1.31704
2698	10	20	1	$1,500	$7,290	$11,350	1.29124
2699	10	20	5	$2,120	$5,150	$9,500	1.30674
2700	10	20	8	$6,500	$28,870	$46,100	1.30336
2701	10	20	9	$300	$6,920	$9,400	1.30194
2702	10	20	11	$3,500	$22,700	$34,000	1.29771
2703	10	20	14	$2,000	$24,780	$34,800	1.29948
2704	10	20	15	$1,490	$17,720	$25,000	1.30141
2705	10	20	1	$2,500	$22,390	$32,000	1.28566
2706	10	20	1	$2,090	$19,920	$28,100	1.27669
2707	10	20	3	$1,000	$3,910	$6,300	1.28310
2708	10	20	8	$6,500	$31,750	$49,300	1.28889
2709	10	20	11	$3,000	$21,800	$32,000	1.29032
2710	10	20	15	$1,200	$9,960	$14,400	1.29032
2711	10	20	11	$3,000	$21,430	$30,900	1.26484
2712	10	20	11	$2,100	$10,600	$16,000	1.25984
2713	10	20	1	$2,300	$21,930	$30,200	1.24639
2714	10	20	1	$2,090	$21,590	$29,500	1.24578
2715	10	20	4	$2,400	$49,310	$65,000	1.25701
2716	10	20	0	$8,000	$60,330	$85,000	1.24396
2717	10	20	12	$800	$2,400	$4,000	1.25000
2718	10	20	16	$1,300	$22,080	$29,000	1.24038
2719	10	20	10	$1,200	$16,100	$21,500	1.24277
2720	10	20	11	$2,900	$21,780	$30,500	1.23582

REAL ESTATE SALES FOR 1978
IN A MID-SIZED FLORIDA CITY (CONTINUED)

OBS	TOWNSHIP	RANGE	SECTION	LANDVAL	IMPROVAL	SALEPRIC	SALTOAPR
2721	10	20	12	$2,700	$19,280	$27,000	1.22839
2722	10	20	16	$1,500	$26,110	$34,000	1.23144
2723	10	20	1	$2,060	$22,430	$30,000	1.22499
2724	10	20	4	$3,500	$30,690	$41,500	1.21381
2725	10	20	10	$1,300	$18,370	$24,000	1.22013
2726	10	20	1	$2,060	$22,830	$30,025	1.20631
2727	10	20	4	$3,870	$17,550	$25,900	1.20915
2728	10	20	11	$3,150	$17,400	$24,900	1.21168
2729	10	20	4	$2,500	$22,600	$30,000	1.19522
2730	10	20	1	$2,000	$25,070	$32,000	1.18212
2731	10	20	11	$2,100	$17,450	$23,000	1.17647
2732	10	20	12	$2,500	$18,050	$24,100	1.17275
2733	10	20	4	$770	$4,180	$5,700	1.15152
2734	10	20	11	$3,500	$25,610	$33,300	1.14394
2735	10	20	11	$3,000	$23,470	$30,400	1.14847
2736	10	20	11	$2,000	$13,660	$18,000	1.14943
2737	10	20	13	$7,300	$64,210	$81,600	1.14110
2738	10	20	12	$2,500	$24,310	$30,000	1.11899
2739	10	20	4	$2,560	$41,920	$49,700	1.11736
2740	10	20	1	$2,200	$25,030	$30,000	1.10173
2741	10	20	3	$900	$4,540	$6,000	1.10294
2742	10	20	1	$1,610	$21,960	$25,500	1.08188
2743	10	20	3	$2,900	$7,970	$11,700	1.07636
2744	10	20	14	$2,000	$22,920	$26,000	1.04334
2745	10	20	3	$500	$5,780	$6,500	1.03503
2746	10	20	4	$3,740	$15,880	$20,000	1.01937
2747	10	20	1	$2,090	$24,990	$26,900	0.99335
2748	10	20	1	$2,300	$19,110	$21,300	0.99486
2749	10	20	3	$500	$19,960	$20,000	0.97752
2750	10	20	4	$600	$6,050	$6,500	0.97744
2751	10	20	6	$4,280	$16,320	$20,250	0.98301
2752	10	20	3	$500	$6,530	$6,500	0.92461
2753	10	20	21	$1,200	$19,440	$18,700	0.90601
2754	10	20	10	$1,200	$16,160	$15,300	0.88134
2755	10	20	5	$1,680	$3,570	$4,500	0.85714
2756	10	20	3	$1,500	$12,030	$11,000	0.81301
2757	10	20	4	$1,270	$17,210	$14,900	0.8063
2758	10	20	5	$1,120	$9,100	$8,000	0.7828
2759	10	20	12	$5,400	$20,180	$20,000	0.7819
2760	10	21	2	$500	$1,150	$16,800	10.1818
2761	10	21	6	$500	$5,730	$23,000	3.6918
2762	10	21	2	$960	$3,470	$14,000	3.1603
2763	10	21	28	$600	$3,500	$13,000	3.1707
2764	10	21	25	$600	$8,910	$25,000	2.6288
2765	10	21	6	$500	$6,940	$18,300	2.4597
2766	10	21	6	$1,000	$3,910	$10,000	2.0367
2767	10	21	6	$1,300	$17,300	$37,000	1.9892
2768	10	21	6	$1,300	$13,590	$26,000	1.7461
2769	10	21	6	$600	$15,160	$23,500	1.4911
2770	10	21	6	$600	$4,140	$6,000	1.2658
2771	10	21	2	$1,010	$6,060	$8,500	1.2023
2772	10	21	7	$12,000	$40,630	$63,000	1.1970
2773	10	21	7	$5,500	$28,840	$38,500	1.1211
2774	10	22	26	$450	$1,200	$6,500	3.9394
2775	10	22	27	$2,250	$5,260	$28,600	3.8083
2776	10	22	26	$740	$7,800	$27,500	3.2201
2777	10	22	29	$800	$6,220	$17,100	2.4359
2778	10	22	29	$900	$8,740	$22,000	2.2822
2779	10	22	27	$800	$6,580	$15,000	2.0325
2780	10	22	1	$1,000	$11,600	$24,500	1.9444
2781	10	22	27	$200	$3,990	$8,000	1.9093
2782	10	22	27	$1,400	$7,200	$15,200	1.7674
2783	10	22	26	$2,350	$19,980	$31,000	1.3883
2784	10	22	26	$1,400	$15,730	$22,500	1.3135
2785	10	22	26	$1,400	$16,390	$23,000	1.2929
2786	10	22	26	$1,400	$20,810	$28,000	1.2607
2787	10	22	26	$1,400	$17,300	$22,500	1.2032
2788	10	22	26	$1,400	$19,910	$25,500	1.1966
2789	10	22	26	$1,400	$21,950	$25,000	1.0707
2790	10	22	26	$2,400	$70,000	$68,100	0.9406
2791	11	18	17	$1,300	$7,550	$42,300	4.7797
2792	11	18	16	$1,500	$5,360	$25,000	3.6443
2793	11	18	22	$1,900	$5,280	$27,000	3.7604
2794	11	18	16	$1,800	$14,090	$43,300	2.7250
2795	11	18	16	$600	$9,060	$24,500	2.5362
2796	11	18	1	$630	$12,800	$29,000	2.1593
2797	11	18	2	$2,500	$12,940	$30,000	1.9430
2798	11	18	2	$2,500	$12,730	$28,000	1.8385
2799	11	18	2	$2,500	$12,730	$28,000	1.8385
2800	11	18	2	$5,860	$29,680	$59,800	1.6826

REAL ESTATE SALES FOR 1978
IN A MID-SIZED FLORIDA CITY (CONTINUED)

OBS	TOWNSHIP	RANGE	SECTION	LANDVAL	IMPROVAL	SALEPRIC	SALTOAPR
2801	11	18	2	$2,500	$19,950	$37,500	1.6704
2802	11	18	16	$3,000	$15,320	$30,000	1.6376
2803	11	18	16	$750	$13,560	$23,000	1.6073
2804	11	18	16	$950	$13,560	$22,500	1.5507
2805	11	18	17	$250	$6,950	$11,000	1.5278
2806	11	18	2	$2,130	$17,910	$28,900	1.4421
2807	11	18	1	$3,030	$21,800	$34,900	1.4056
2808	11	18	1	$3,030	$21,800	$34,900	1.4056
2809	11	18	1	$4,230	$23,100	$37,700	1.3794
2810	11	18	2	$2,500	$19,530	$30,100	1.3663
2811	11	18	1	$3,330	$25,330	$37,700	1.3154
2812	11	18	2	$2,500	$21,450	$31,500	1.3152
2813	11	18	1	$3,300	$24,970	$34,900	1.2345
2814	11	18	16	$1,800	$18,180	$24,500	1.2262
2815	11	18	2	$2,500	$22,110	$28,700	1.1662
2816	11	18	16	$1,600	$17,860	$22,500	1.1562
2817	11	18	16	$1,600	$18,280	$22,500	1.1318
2818	11	18	1	$3,300	$22,970	$29,000	1.1039
2819	11	18	16	$1,600	$19,670	$23,200	1.0907
2820	11	18	17	$300	$25,680	$28,000	1.0778
2821	11	18	34	$350	$4,460	$5,000	1.0395
2822	11	18	1	$4,500	$29,470	$34,800	1.0244
2823	11	18	4	$1,050	$20,710	$22,000	1.0110
2824	11	18	22	$1,700	$8,600	$10,000	0.9709
2825	11	19	30	$1,020	$4,960	$25,000	4.1806
2826	11	19	10	$3,890	$34,510	$70,000	1.8229
2827	11	19	20	$5,010	$36,410	$67,500	1.6296
2828	11	19	15	$3,550	$42,120	$70,000	1.5327
2829	11	19	5	$7,200	$36,220	$65,000	1.4970
2830	11	19	5	$6,500	$28,200	$50,800	1.4640
2831	11	19	5	$6,300	$28,710	$48,500	1.3853
2832	11	19	5	$6,900	$32,010	$52,000	1.3364
2833	11	20	26	$800	$7,810	$23,000	2.6713
2834	11	20	26	$300	$13,530	$37,000	2.6753
2835	11	20	0	$1,500	$3,460	$12,500	2.5202
2836	11	20	27	$100	$3,260	$8,500	2.5298
2837	11	20	26	$3,000	$7,940	$25,000	2.2852
2838	11	20	26	$700	$7,820	$19,000	2.2300
2839	11	20	0	$2,860	$38,810	$83,000	1.9918
2840	11	20	26	$1,000	$9,140	$20,000	1.9724
2841	11	20	26	$1,200	$5,680	$12,900	1.8750
2842	11	20	26	$670	$3,490	$7,700	1.8510
2843	11	20	26	$1,000	$16,500	$30,500	1.7429
2844	11	20	26	$700	$14,750	$27,000	1.7476
2845	11	20	26	$2,000	$32,200	$60,000	1.7544
2846	11	20	0	$800	$1,630	$4,100	1.6872
2847	11	20	26	$1,000	$10,320	$19,000	1.6784
2848	11	20	0	$9,100	$38,260	$74,500	1.5731
2849	11	20	25	$1,380	$19,590	$32,600	1.5546
2850	11	20	0	$1,500	$28,840	$44,000	1.4502
2851	11	20	26	$500	$3,610	$6,000	1.4599
2852	11	20	25	$1,150	$21,070	$31,300	1.4086
2853	11	21	36	$1,000	$7,780	$30,000	3.4169
2854	11	21	36	$6,070	$40,230	$140,000	3.0238
2855	11	21	31	$800	$7,170	$22,500	2.8231
2856	11	21	31	$10	$860	$28,500	32.7586
2857	11	21	36	$3,000	$21,230	$44,000	1.8159
2858	11	21	36	$2,100	$22,070	$33,500	1.3860
2859	11	21	36	$1,500	$16,700	$25,000	1.3736
2860	11	21	36	$2,100	$21,940	$32,500	1.3519
2861	11	22	27	$500	$4,580	$8,000	1.5748
2862	12	22	16	$1,400	$4,960	$12,000	1.8868

Appendix B

Data Set: Real Estate Appraisals and Sales Data for Six Neighborhoods in a Midsized Florida City

1978 APPRAISED VALUES AND SALE PRICES FOR PROPERTIES IN SIX NEIGHBORHOODS

NEIGHBORHOOD   A

OBS	LANDVAL	IMPROVAL	SALEPRIC	OBS	LANDVAL	IMPROVAL	SALEPRIC	OBS	LANDVAL	IMPROVAL	SALEPRIC
1	$5,600	$19,410	$44,000	2	$5,600	$21,040	$45,000	3	$8,600	$35,560	$69,900
4	$5,600	$22,020	$44,000	5	$6,260	$39,700	$72,000	6	$6,040	$52,460	$90,000
7	$7,500	$47,940	$83,500	8	$6,050	$30,770	$56,000	9	$5,800	$18,570	$36,900
10	$6,270	$20,000	$40,000	11	$5,600	$19,680	$37,500	12	$6,500	$36,830	$64,000
13	$7,300	$53,110	$86,500	14	$7,170	$32,040	$56,300	15	$8,450	$43,820	$74,500
16	$8,600	$68,770	$110,000	17	$5,500	$31,150	$52,200	18	$7,680	$45,180	$75,000
19	$7,040	$51,530	$82,500	20	$7,170	$34,740	$58,000	21	$5,600	$19,420	$35,000
22	$6,160	$22,270	$39,700	23	$7,200	$38,890	$62,000	24	$7,360	$52,300	$80,000
25	$7,200	$40,190	$63,000	26	$9,600	$50,560	$80,000	27	$7,260	$39,340	$60,000
28	$7,200	$45,360	$66,900	29	$6,160	$17,550	$29,700	30	$8,320	$70,850	$97,000
31	$6,500	$40,950	$55,600								

NEIGHBORHOOD   B

OBS	LANDVAL	IMPROVAL	SALEPRIC	OBS	LANDVAL	IMPROVAL	SALEPRIC	OBS	LANDVAL	IMPROVAL	SALEPRIC
				32	$6,200	$31,640	$70,300	33	$5,500	$22,360	$48,200
34	$7,020	$40,790	$80,000	35	$5,000	$56,520	$97,500	36	$5,500	$34,430	$63,000
37	$6,200	$46,750	$84,500	38	$6,200	$35,270	$65,800	39	$8,150	$44,030	$82,000
40	$7,020	$42,150	$77,000	41	$5,000	$41,990	$73,800	42	$5,500	$32,520	$59,500
43	$6,890	$39,310	$70,900	44	$6,890	$39,670	$69,900	45	$6,890	$43,300	$74,500
46	$7,200	$44,880	$76,900	47	$5,000	$44,220	$72,000	48	$5,880	$41,200	$68,000
49	$8,190	$57,350	$95,000	50	$7,020	$50,150	$83,200	51	$5,000	$39,990	$65,000
52	$5,800	$49,960	$80,000	53	$8,100	$35,450	$62,500	54	$8,050	$36,820	$64,500
55	$6,800	$39,660	$66,800	56	$7,020	$45,120	$74,600	57	$5,500	$34,890	$58,000
58	$5,700	$46,780	$75,000	59	$8,100	$38,280	$65,000	60	$8,100	$38,310	$65,000
61	$7,200	$49,580	$80,000	62	$5,500	$35,660	$57,000	63	$7,200	$40,600	$66,500
64	$5,800	$52,780	$81,700	65	$5,500	$37,460	$59,500	66	$8,200	$39,830	$65,500
67	$7,020	$53,440	$82,500	68	$5,000	$64,010	$95,000	69	$9,500	$67,810	$105,000
70	$8,050	$36,020	$59,500	71	$8,050	$40,550	$64,800	72	$7,200	$38,620	$60,800
73	$7,920	$44,570	$70,000	74	$5,700	$41,310	$62,000	75	$8,200	$47,780	$73,000
76	$5,000	$35,710	$52,000	77	$5,600	$35,320	$51,900	78	$6,840	$51,690	$73,500
79	$5,000	$32,660	$47,000	80	$5,000	$33,380	$48,000	81	$5,500	$37,400	$53,500
82	$5,500	$36,560	$52,000	83	$8,050	$41,060	$59,900				

NEIGHBORHOOD   C

OBS	LANDVAL	IMPROVAL	SALEPRIC	OBS	LANDVAL	IMPROVAL	SALEPRIC	OBS	LANDVAL	IMPROVAL	SALEPRIC
								84	$2,000	$7,340	$25,000
85	$2,000	$9,130	$27,600	86	$2,500	$13,300	$39,000	87	$4,000	$13,630	$40,500
88	$3,000	$14,020	$37,500	89	$3,080	$7,240	$22,800	90	$5,040	$13,230	$40,000
91	$4,000	$8,580	$25,500	92	$4,320	$9,130	$27,500	93	$3,600	$7,690	$22,000
94	$3,080	$11,430	$28,000	95	$4,000	$14,840	$36,600	96	$4,000	$8,510	$24,200
97	$4,320	$11,510	$30,300	98	$3,150	$12,060	$28,200	99	$4,000	$13,150	$32,000
100	$4,000	$9,980	$26,000	101	$4,500	$10,370	$27,500	102	$3,660	$12,580	$29,500
103	$4,260	$11,960	$29,600	104	$4,320	$12,200	$30,000	105	$3,400	$14,580	$31,900
106	$3,570	$14,990	$33,000	107	$3,400	$15,330	$32,800	108	$4,100	$12,650	$29,500
109	$4,100	$15,990	$35,000	110	$4,310	$12,030	$28,500	111	$3,000	$12,800	$27,900
112	$3,190	$15,060	$32,200	113	$4,000	$12,550	$28,900	114	$3,400	$13,430	$29,000
115	$3,400	$18,250	$37,500	116	$3,080	$13,470	$28,500	117	$3,460	$18,820	$38,400
118	$3,500	$13,130	$28,900	119	$3,570	$12,130	$27,200	120	$3,400	$13,720	$28,800
121	$3,400	$15,840	$32,500	122	$3,510	$14,210	$30,000	123	$4,320	$25,370	$50,000
124	$4,100	$14,120	$30,900	125	$3,570	$15,410	$32,450	126	$3,230	$14,660	$29,800
127	$3,460	$15,470	$31,550	128	$3,290	$13,710	$28,500	129	$3,540	$18,430	$36,800
130	$3,230	$15,810	$31,500	131	$3,650	$14,080	$28,900	132	$3,210	$17,670	$34,000
133	$3,800	$15,400	$31,500	134	$4,040	$14,020	$29,800	135	$4,300	$15,210	$31,900
136	$3,190	$14,200	$28,300	137	$3,190	$11,490	$24,000	138	$4,000	$15,080	$31,500
139	$3,400	$19,200	$36,300	140	$3,230	$15,780	$30,600	141	$3,150	$23,340	$42,500
142	$3,540	$14,480	$29,000	143	$4,260	$12,400	$27,000	144	$3,320	$15,200	$29,900
145	$3,190	$16,030	$31,000	146	$4,000	$12,870	$27,400	147	$3,400	$14,380	$28,200
148	$3,400	$13,150	$26,200	149	$3,400	$18,620	$35,000	150	$4,000	$20,550	$39,000
151	$3,460	$17,550	$33,500	152	$3,510	$13,870	$27,600	153	$3,660	$14,640	$29,000
154	$4,600	$11,820	$25,900	155	$4,000	$14,700	$29,900	156	$4,000	$14,210	$28,700
157	$3,400	$18,170	$33,500	158	$3,400	$14,540	$28,000	159	$3,460	$16,380	$31,000
160	$3,460	$19,590	$35,900	161	$3,150	$19,980	$36,400	162	$3,150	$20,070	$36,400
163	$3,300	$14,350	$27,700	164	$3,540	$15,850	$30,100	165	$3,660	$17,780	$33,500
166	$4,260	$12,510	$26,400	167	$2,000	$8,500	$16,300	168	$3,320	$13,020	$25,500
169	$4,000	$13,640	$27,400	170	$4,000	$15,080	$30,000	171	$4,300	$18,680	$35,500
172	$3,460	$13,980	$27,000	173	$3,150	$17,790	$32,000	174	$3,390	$14,350	$27,500
175	$4,100	$12,560	$25,500	176	$3,440	$17,880	$33,000	177	$4,000	$15,380	$29,700
178	$3,510	$14,360	$27,000	179	$3,540	$15,840	$29,500	180	$4,000	$21,560	$38,500
181	$4,000	$15,050	$29,000	182	$3,400	$14,410	$26,500	183	$3,080	$17,540	$31,000
184	$3,080	$15,070	$27,000	185	$3,510	$19,820	$35,000	186	$3,460	$16,830	$30,500
187	$3,780	$15,830	$29,500	188	$4,180	$12,880	$25,350	189	$4,260	$13,240	$26,000
190	$4,100	$14,610	$28,000	191	$2,000	$9,340	$17,000	192	$4,310	$12,260	$24,900
193	$3,400	$15,530	$28,000	194	$3,510	$16,900	$30,000	195	$4,000	$15,730	$29,000
196	$3,460	$15,560	$28,000	197	$4,200	$20,680	$36,400	198	$3,360	$16,010	$28,500
199	$2,040	$21,040	$34,000	200	$4,000	$19,120	$33,900	201	$4,300	$22,950	$39,400
202	$4,200	$19,800	$34,900	203	$3,600	$14,930	$27,000	204	$3,470	$17,160	$30,000

NEIGHBORHOOD C (CONTINUED)

OBS	LANDVAL	IMPROVAL	SALEPRIC	OBS	LANDVAL	IMPROVAL	SALEPRIC	OBS	LANDVAL	IMPROVAL	SALEPRIC
205	$3,600	$7,360	$16,000	206	$3,190	$17,170	$29,500	207	$4,000	$15,290	$28,000
208	$3,080	$19,020	$31,500	209	$3,510	$18,630	$31,500	210	$3,780	$16,010	$28,200
211	$3,150	$16,010	$27,500	212	$3,470	$15,880	$27,500	213	$3,500	$16,710	$28,900
214	$4,000	$25,390	$42,000	215	$4,000	$24,120	$39,700	216	$3,880	$26,600	$43,000
217	$3,780	$14,350	$25,400	218	$3,650	$15,850	$27,500	219	$4,000	$14,130	$25,700
220	$3,230	$17,410	$29,000	221	$3,870	$16,770	$29,100	222	$3,400	$16,070	$27,000
223	$3,510	$21,410	$34,800	224	$3,150	$16,020	$26,500	225	$4,400	$15,740	$28,000
226	$4,100	$17,600	$30,000	227	$3,460	$16,860	$28,000	228	$3,290	$17,610	$28,700
229	$3,470	$15,260	$25,700	230	$4,000	$19,630	$32,500	231	$4,100	$17,130	$29,000
232	$4,100	$14,170	$25,000	233	$4,390	$14,220	$25,500	234	$4,310	$16,400	$28,500
235	$3,700	$16,030	$27,000	236	$4,300	$16,740	$28,500	237	$3,470	$15,880	$26,000
238	$3,650	$15,840	$26,500	239	$3,540	$15,840	$26,100	240	$15,000	$95,990	$150,000
241	$5,580	$17,800	$31,500	242	$4,320	$20,370	$33,500	243	$4,200	$19,390	$31,500
244	$4,000	$19,330	$31,100	245	$3,780	$16,740	$27,500	246	$4,400	$14,350	$24,900
247	$4,000	$15,840	$26,500	248	$4,180	$13,490	$23,600	249	$4,100	$22,280	$35,000
250	$3,570	$17,780	$28,300	251	$4,300	$16,880	$28,000	252	$3,880	$25,560	$38,900
253	$4,160	$21,430	$33,500	254	$4,100	$17,720	$28,900	255	$4,000	$16,000	$26,300
256	$3,600	$18,540	$28,300	257	$4,800	$20,390	$32,300	258	$3,780	$21,210	$31,600
259	$3,570	$20,170	$30,000	260	$3,190	$24,410	$34,900	261	$3,080	$18,600	$27,000
262	$4,000	$20,890	$31,100	263	$5,580	$27,680	$41,500	264	$3,230	$13,120	$20,100
265	$4,000	$19,960	$29,700	266	$4,300	$16,740	$25,900	267	$4,100	$16,180	$25,000
268	$4,000	$20,310	$29,900	269	$3,230	$20,020	$28,000	270	$3,200	$20,570	$28,800
271	$4,000	$17,780	$26,000	272	$3,470	$15,850	$22,700	273	$3,230	$20,940	$28,500
274	$4,000	$23,090	$32,000	275	$4,100	$21,740	$30,000	276	$4,000	$15,370	$22,500
277	$4,000	$21,190	$26,500	278	$3,400	$16,350	$20,000	279	$4,240	$25,160	$28,000

NEIGHBORHOOD D

OBS	LANDVAL	IMPROVAL	SALEPRIC	OBS	LANDVAL	IMPROVAL	SALEPRIC	OBS	LANDVAL	IMPROVAL	SALEPRIC
280	$4,300	$22,070	$50,000	281	$3,600	$18,060	$39,500	282	$3,600	$19,220	$41,500
283	$3,600	$14,970	$32,500	284	$3,500	$17,000	$35,500	285	$8,370	$62,850	$120,000
286	$4,300	$21,740	$42,500	287	$4,770	$30,960	$58,500	288	$3,990	$25,270	$48,200
289	$4,200	$25,220	$47,900	290	$4,300	$20,130	$39,500	291	$5,500	$27,120	$52,600
292	$3,600	$23,160	$43,000	293	$4,000	$16,420	$32,500	294	$3,990	$17,930	$34,600
295	$3,990	$24,350	$45,300	296	$3,990	$20,430	$38,500	297	$5,000	$31,550	$58,000
298	$3,600	$18,750	$35,500	299	$900	$15,770	$25,900	300	$5,600	$29,310	$55,000
301	$3,950	$21,390	$39,900	302	$3,990	$20,480	$38,500	303	$4,300	$18,500	$35,500
304	$5,000	$29,310	$53,800	305	$3,810	$26,410	$47,000	306	$4,500	$16,890	$33,000
307	$4,300	$24,720	$45,000	308	$3,910	$17,020	$32,100	309	$3,990	$21,910	$39,900
310	$4,000	$29,240	$50,900	311	$4,300	$20,840	$37,900	312	$5,400	$33,420	$59,200
313	$4,100	$17,340	$32,400	314	$4,100	$17,550	$32,900	315	$3,910	$20,290	$36,500
316	$4,820	$29,880	$51,900	317	$4,300	$22,820	$40,800	318	$4,370	$19,910	$36,400
319	$3,990	$19,510	$35,000	320	$3,990	$24,120	$41,800	321	$4,200	$21,050	$37,700
322	$4,100	$23,690	$41,300	323	$4,200	$36,220	$60,000	324	$1,000	$12,000	$19,300
325	$5,200	$24,050	$43,900	326	$4,300	$19,480	$34,900	327	$4,500	$21,750	$38,500
328	$4,300	$23,010	$39,900	329	$4,300	$20,370	$36,500	330	$4,200	$25,490	$43,500
331	$3,910	$16,620	$30,000	332	$5,060	$34,460	$58,300	333	$3,630	$20,970	$36,000
334	$5,270	$36,990	$61,000	335	$5,500	$30,260	$52,000	336	$4,600	$18,540	$33,700
337	$4,100	$20,020	$34,900	338	$4,400	$24,150	$41,500	339	$4,000	$18,280	$32,500
340	$4,000	$32,030	$51,900	341	$7,600	$46,600	$78,900	342	$4,300	$21,790	$37,500
343	$4,300	$18,790	$32,900	344	$4,300	$21,300	$36,500	345	$4,500	$20,670	$36,000
346	$900	$15,770	$23,900	347	$4,000	$21,440	$36,500	348	$4,600	$24,100	$41,000
349	$4,300	$18,540	$32,500	350	$4,300	$26,210	$43,500	351	$3,990	$19,880	$33,900
352	$4,200	$22,980	$38,900	353	$3,810	$26,700	$43,500	354	$3,790	$21,370	$36,000
355	$3,790	$28,140	$45,900	356	$4,100	$27,820	$45,500	357	$4,300	$22,310	$37,500
358	$4,960	$35,600	$57,000	359	$4,210	$27,330	$44,500	360	$5,400	$35,320	$57,000
361	$4,100	$21,270	$36,000	362	$4,300	$25,090	$41,200	363	$4,300	$22,320	$37,300
364	$3,910	$18,880	$32,300	365	$3,910	$19,810	$33,500	366	$3,910	$19,960	$33,700
367	$3,990	$18,400	$31,500	368	$3,930	$23,640	$39,000	369	$3,930	$18,430	$31,300
370	$3,990	$22,540	$37,500	371	$3,990	$23,350	$38,500	372	$3,900	$31,600	$49,900
373	$4,100	$26,760	$43,500	374	$7,600	$46,920	$77,200	375	$7,840	$35,620	$61,000
376	$7,840	$36,590	$62,700	377	$4,400	$21,030	$35,500	378	$5,160	$29,110	$47,500
379	$4,740	$37,160	$58,200	380	$3,850	$20,700	$34,000	381	$4,300	$21,070	$35,400
382	$4,200	$20,530	$34,500	383	$4,300	$23,530	$38,900	384	$3,910	$18,670	$31,600
385	$3,990	$25,640	$41,300	386	$3,950	$20,890	$34,500	387	$3,990	$19,680	$33,000
388	$3,990	$23,280	$38,000	389	$3,990	$21,640	$35,500	390	$4,300	$20,740	$34,900
391	$4,200	$30,850	$48,500	392	$3,600	$31,000	$48,000	393	$4,100	$33,570	$52,700
394	$4,200	$34,610	$54,000	395	$5,180	$29,740	$48,500	396	$4,000	$28,470	$45,000
397	$3,900	$27,940	$44,000	398	$4,300	$17,910	$30,600	399	$4,300	$20,800	$34,600
400	$3,600	$33,990	$51,300	401	$3,810	$27,360	$43,000	402	$4,600	$20,060	$34,000
403	$4,300	$20,530	$34,000	404	$4,300	$19,560	$32,500	405	$4,300	$20,140	$40,100
406	$4,400	$29,860	$46,900	407	$4,300	$27,270	$43,000	408	$3,910	$22,640	$36,200
409	$3,910	$23,160	$37,300	410	$3,910	$20,050	$33,000	411	$3,910	$18,570	$30,900
412	$4,120	$23,540	$38,000	413	$3,990	$25,570	$40,500	414	$4,100	$25,190	$40,000
415	$3,810	$27,540	$42,800	416	$3,810	$29,240	$45,500	417	$3,810	$23,170	$37,000
418	$4,300	$23,040	$37,000	419	$4,400	$21,080	$34,500	420	$900	$15,770	$22,500
421	$5,290	$33,730	$52,500	422	$5,510	$31,400	$49,900	423	$5,510	$34,540	$54,000
424	$5,160	$29,700	$47,000	425	$4,100	$20,800	$33,500	426	$4,400	$29,580	$46,000
427	$4,400	$28,670	$44,900	428	$4,400	$20,620	$34,000	429	$4,300	$24,740	$39,300
430	$3,910	$25,180	$39,200	431	$3,930	$27,680	$42,500	432	$3,930	$25,100	$39,000
433	$3,930	$18,670	$30,500	434	$3,990	$24,080	$37,900	435	$3,990	$24,120	$37,800
436	$3,990	$19,470	$31,600	437	$3,990	$23,290	$37,000	438	$3,990	$23,240	$36,600

NEIGHBORHOOD D (CONTINUED)

OBS	LANDVAL	IMPROVAL	SALEPRIC	OBS	LANDVAL	IMPROVAL	SALEPRIC	OBS	LANDVAL	IMPROVAL	SALEPRIC
439	$3,990	$19,320	$31,400	440	$3,950	$25,110	$39,400	441	$3,950	$23,510	$37,200
442	$3,990	$24,030	$38,000	443	$4,510	$23,800	$38,500	444	$4,200	$32,890	$50,000
445	$4,200	$27,660	$43,300	446	$3,500	$23,560	$36,500	447	$4,830	$33,430	$52,000
448	$4,300	$20,970	$33,900	449	$4,960	$27,760	$43,500	450	$5,270	$32,090	$49,900
451	$4,300	$21,550	$34,500	452	$3,990	$24,030	$37,500	453	$3,930	$27,530	$42,000
454	$3,930	$22,140	$34,600	455	$3,930	$25,290	$39,000	456	$4,120	$25,810	$39,900
457	$3,990	$18,100	$29,500	458	$3,990	$24,440	$38,100	459	$3,990	$23,510	$36,560
460	$5,500	$29,600	$46,900	461	$5,300	$32,300	$50,000	462	$4,400	$28,150	$43,700
463	$3,810	$26,770	$41,000	464	$4,000	$27,470	$42,000	465	$3,790	$24,250	$37,500
466	$4,830	$28,660	$44,900	467	$3,810	$25,400	$39,000	468	$3,900	$28,580	$43,500
469	$4,100	$27,440	$42,000	470	$5,400	$32,150	$49,500	471	$5,520	$26,670	$42,500
472	$5,500	$32,400	$50,000	473	$4,000	$22,850	$35,400	474	$4,300	$26,870	$41,000
475	$3,930	$29,200	$43,900	476	$3,930	$28,880	$43,000	477	$3,930	$23,440	$36,000
478	$3,990	$27,340	$41,100	479	$3,600	$31,760	$46,500	480	$3,600	$33,210	$48,500
481	$4,830	$29,830	$45,500	482	$4,600	$28,770	$43,800	483	$4,300	$23,100	$35,500
484	$5,280	$32,220	$48,500	485	$5,510	$34,420	$51,900	486	$5,380	$29,930	$46,000
487	$4,740	$32,360	$48,000	488	$5,400	$33,060	$49,900	489	$4,600	$26,210	$39,900
490	$4,200	$22,730	$34,870	491	$3,930	$27,480	$41,000	492	$4,370	$25,020	$38,000
493	$3,990	$25,320	$37,900	494	$3,990	$19,100	$29,900	495	$3,950	$24,730	$37,500
496	$3,960	$24,900	$37,700	497	$3,990	$18,950	$29,900	498	$4,400	$27,730	$42,000
499	$4,000	$22,780	$35,000	500	$4,000	$24,570	$37,000	501	$4,100	$29,150	$43,000
502	$4,610	$28,550	$42,900	503	$3,810	$29,430	$43,000	504	$4,830	$32,280	$48,300
505	$4,400	$23,970	$36,500	506	$5,520	$27,420	$42,000	507	$5,270	$34,480	$51,000
508	$4,100	$27,880	$41,000	509	$4,000	$23,120	$35,000	510	$5,000	$33,490	$49,500
511	$4,400	$28,700	$42,500	512	$3,910	$25,040	$37,000	513	$4,200	$29,210	$42,700
514	$4,700	$31,460	$46,500	515	$7,600	$34,130	$53,300	516	$5,180	$31,050	$46,000
517	$5,290	$31,910	$47,000	518	$3,850	$24,510	$35,800	519	$4,300	$24,710	$36,900
520	$4,300	$31,330	$45,000	521	$4,300	$24,070	$36,000	522	$4,300	$29,220	$42,500
523	$4,300	$24,760	$37,000	524	$3,990	$24,710	$36,500	525	$3,990	$20,810	$31,400
526	$3,990	$26,760	$39,100	527	$3,990	$26,750	$39,000	528	$4,300	$24,890	$37,000
529	$4,830	$30,100	$44,000	530	$5,280	$40,570	$57,000	531	$4,200	$25,450	$37,100
532	$4,300	$27,840	$40,000	533	$4,300	$28,480	$40,900	534	$3,990	$24,890	$36,300
535	$3,910	$23,240	$34,000	536	$3,930	$27,930	$40,000	537	$3,990	$25,170	$36,500
538	$3,990	$25,610	$36,900	539	$3,990	$28,240	$40,200	540	$3,990	$25,710	$37,000
541	$3,990	$26,340	$38,000	542	$4,550	$24,220	$36,000	543	$4,100	$26,880	$38,800
544	$4,500	$32,540	$46,500	545	$3,900	$25,700	$36,800	546	$4,300	$27,920	$40,000
547	$3,600	$24,820	$35,000	548	$5,060	$29,330	$42,500	549	$3,900	$26,840	$38,000
550	$5,380	$24,080	$36,500	551	$7,600	$39,960	$58,900	552	$7,760	$40,140	$59,200
553	$5,520	$32,540	$46,500	554	$5,000	$30,180	$42,900	555	$3,990	$23,030	$33,000
556	$3,990	$19,690	$29,000	557	$4,000	$30,260	$42,000	558	$3,500	$33,580	$45,000
559	$3,790	$25,240	$35,500	560	$3,810	$32,360	$44,000	561	$4,700	$23,780	$34,800
562	$3,810	$24,150	$34,000	563	$4,900	$34,320	$47,600	564	$5,210	$30,660	$44,000
565	$5,270	$34,420	$47,700	566	$3,990	$27,080	$37,500	567	$3,810	$27,890	$38,000
568	$5,060	$34,640	$48,000	569	$4,400	$32,830	$44,500	570	$4,200	$30,870	$42,000
571	$4,300	$24,040	$33,500	572	$3,910	$25,820	$34,800	573	$3,910	$24,080	$33,000
574	$4,400	$24,120	$33,500	575	$5,400	$32,710	$44,500	576	$4,370	$28,110	$37,300
577	$5,500	$30,990	$41,900	578	$5,000	$29,900	$40,000	579	$5,520	$37,790	$49,500
580	$3,990	$29,850	$38,500	581	$4,200	$27,530	$36,100	582	$3,500	$32,960	$41,600
583	$5,060	$28,440	$38,300	584	$4,500	$25,640	$34,000	585	$4,300	$25,700	$33,300
586	$3,500	$31,250	$38,500	587	$7,760	$40,890	$53,500	588	$4,300	$35,020	$39,900
589	$4,300	$27,420	$30,900								

NEIGHBORHOOD E

OBS	LANDVAL	IMPROVAL	SALEPRIC	OBS	LANDVAL	IMPROVAL	SALEPRIC	OBS	LANDVAL	IMPROVAL	SALEPRIC
				590	$3,630	$19,200	$44,500	591	$3,490	$14,680	$32,500
592	$3,450	$21,630	$43,000	593	$3,490	$19,100	$38,000	594	$3,490	$17,260	$35,500
595	$3,500	$21,950	$42,500	596	$3,490	$22,230	$42,000	597	$5,400	$16,430	$35,900
598	$3,400	$18,680	$35,800	599	$3,590	$16,760	$33,000	600	$3,590	$23,260	$43,000
601	$3,600	$20,510	$39,000	602	$3,570	$17,630	$33,700	603	$3,490	$14,530	$28,500
604	$5,000	$27,000	$49,900	605	$4,490	$21,270	$38,500	606	$3,440	$18,830	$34,900
607	$3,420	$17,710	$33,000	608	$3,500	$21,820	$39,800	609	$3,970	$18,360	$34,900
610	$6,100	$18,680	$37,900	611	$3,440	$18,790	$34,300	612	$3,900	$21,590	$39,400
613	$3,800	$22,190	$40,000	614	$3,490	$17,190	$31,500	615	$6,400	$18,680	$37,900
616	$6,000	$18,400	$36,900	617	$2,400	$21,780	$36,000	618	$2,900	$25,060	$41,500
619	$3,490	$21,270	$37,000	620	$6,000	$18,100	$36,000	621	$6,000	$17,670	$35,100
622	$6,000	$17,480	$35,500	623	$4,370	$18,200	$33,500	624	$3,440	$21,070	$36,800
625	$3,420	$23,060	$39,700	626	$3,500	$18,510	$32,900	627	$3,550	$20,350	$35,900
628	$2,900	$29,300	$47,500	629	$4,040	$18,760	$33,500	630	$6,000	$16,510	$33,200
631	$6,300	$17,580	$35,100	632	$4,000	$16,050	$29,500	633	$4,280	$18,980	$34,000
634	$4,800	$19,920	$36,500	635	$3,900	$20,120	$35,200	636	$3,450	$16,720	$29,800
637	$3,420	$26,010	$43,500	638	$3,500	$26,670	$44,500	639	$3,420	$26,170	$43,500
640	$4,070	$22,520	$38,900	641	$2,400	$21,780	$34,900	642	$4,280	$17,290	$31,500
643	$3,460	$18,010	$31,100	644	$3,440	$20,730	$35,000	645	$3,440	$20,570	$34,900
646	$3,600	$24,270	$40,400	647	$3,500	$26,310	$43,200	648	$3,970	$22,670	$38,500
649	$6,000	$17,090	$33,000	650	$5,000	$19,310	$34,700	651	$4,100	$26,520	$43,500
652	$3,500	$26,970	$43,800	653	$4,100	$30,390	$49,000	654	$3,970	$24,800	$41,000
655	$6,000	$18,810	$35,000	656	$6,000	$18,190	$34,100	657	$6,000	$18,190	$34,300
658	$6,000	$17,510	$33,300	659	$6,000	$16,740	$32,100	660	$6,100	$16,590	$32,200
661	$6,500	$19,680	$36,900	662	$3,570	$15,700	$27,300	663	$3,610	$18,450	$31,200
664	$4,100	$24,130	$39,750	665	$2,900	$29,880	$45,500	666	$6,000	$18,990	$34,900

NEIGHBORHOOD E (CONTINUED)

OBS	LANDVAL	IMPROVAL	SALEPRIC	OBS	LANDVAL	IMPROVAL	SALEPRIC	OBS	LANDVAL	IMPROVAL	SALEPRIC
667	$6,200	$21,660	$38,700	668	$6,500	$22,110	$39,500	669	$6,000	$22,600	$40,000
670	$6,000	$17,780	$33,185	671	$6,000	$18,050	$33,300	672	$6,200	$16,420	$31,600
673	$7,150	$25,080	$45,000	674	$3,500	$27,700	$43,200	675	$3,610	$30,370	$47,100
676	$3,420	$26,150	$41,200	677	$3,970	$28,290	$44,900	678	$3,750	$24,160	$38,600
679	$3,630	$24,980	$40,000	680	$3,800	$28,910	$45,700	681	$2,300	$28,870	$43,000
682	$6,800	$17,120	$32,600	683	$7,000	$23,590	$41,700	684	$6,000	$18,900	$34,100
685	$6,000	$21,960	$38,200	686	$6,000	$16,820	$31,430	687	$6,000	$20,180	$36,100
688	$6,000	$21,550	$37,900	689	$5,400	$23,510	$39,600	690	$6,000	$18,220	$33,000
691	$6,600	$23,160	$41,000	692	$5,800	$25,880	$43,600	693	$4,300	$19,320	$32,400
694	$3,500	$27,620	$42,900	695	$3,500	$27,100	$41,900	696	$3,420	$23,870	$37,500
697	$4,000	$27,170	$42,600	698	$2,300	$28,870	$42,000	699	$6,000	$23,440	$39,900
700	$6,100	$22,770	$39,000	701	$3,500	$25,830	$39,500	702	$3,500	$24,240	$37,500
703	$3,440	$25,370	$38,700	704	$3,500	$18,450	$29,900	705	$3,870	$26,460	$40,800
706	$3,690	$23,120	$36,000	707	$3,570	$25,160	$38,500	708	$6,000	$22,920	$38,500
709	$6,000	$22,570	$38,000	710	$6,100	$22,940	$38,900	711	$6,100	$18,760	$33,100
712	$5,900	$18,540	$32,500	713	$3,570	$16,660	$27,000	714	$3,420	$24,430	$37,000
715	$4,100	$27,400	$42,900	716	$4,070	$26,550	$40,800	717	$3,970	$25,900	$40,000
718	$4,100	$28,000	$43,000	719	$2,200	$26,190	$37,500	720	$3,570	$25,690	$38,700
721	$6,400	$22,360	$37,900	722	$7,000	$16,590	$30,900	723	$6,800	$24,200	$40,900
724	$6,000	$18,880	$32,700	725	$6,000	$21,960	$36,700	726	$6,000	$17,370	$30,900
727	$6,000	$19,630	$33,000	728	$3,420	$23,080	$34,900	729	$4,000	$24,980	$38,000
730	$3,500	$26,100	$38,800	731	$6,500	$29,870	$47,000	732	$2,900	$29,880	$42,500
733	$6,000	$22,610	$37,200	734	$6,400	$28,630	$45,600	735	$6,000	$22,820	$37,600
736	$6,000	$22,350	$36,800	737	$6,000	$24,500	$39,500	738	$6,000	$20,090	$33,900
739	$6,100	$18,920	$32,400	740	$5,400	$24,060	$38,500	741	$3,610	$27,340	$40,000
742	$3,500	$22,420	$33,500	743	$3,440	$25,970	$38,000	744	$2,300	$30,640	$42,500
745	$2,300	$28,870	$40,000	746	$2,900	$29,880	$42,000	747	$2,900	$29,880	$42,000
748	$5,000	$32,020	$47,200	749	$6,000	$19,410	$32,800	750	$4,800	$20,460	$32,500
751	$3,500	$28,960	$41,500	752	$3,500	$26,810	$39,000	753	$2,400	$30,030	$41,100
754	$6,500	$32,170	$49,000	755	$2,900	$25,060	$35,500	756	$6,000	$23,740	$37,800
757	$6,000	$18,250	$30,900	758	$6,000	$19,170	$31,900	759	$6,000	$22,270	$35,900
760	$5,700	$23,530	$37,000	761	$3,510	$23,740	$34,500	762	$3,670	$23,710	$34,500
763	$2,200	$26,720	$36,000	764	$6,600	$23,370	$37,300	765	$6,100	$20,200	$32,800
766	$6,000	$22,630	$35,800	767	$4,280	$21,600	$32,500	768	$4,000	$30,320	$42,800
769	$6,100	$22,080	$34,900	770	$6,100	$23,650	$36,700	771	$5,800	$19,120	$30,700
772	$6,000	$19,500	$31,000	773	$6,000	$18,500	$30,000	774	$5,500	$21,630	$33,000
775	$3,990	$27,530	$38,500	776	$3,990	$30,230	$42,000	777	$5,000	$41,580	$56,100
778	$6,000	$22,740	$34,700	779	$6,400	$23,470	$36,200	780	$6,500	$22,690	$35,000
781	$5,800	$21,120	$32,500	782	$5,500	$19,310	$30,000	783	$6,000	$23,140	$35,300
784	$4,000	$28,080	$38,500	785	$6,500	$44,450	$61,000	786	$6,000	$21,920	$33,200
787	$6,000	$22,500	$33,800	788	$4,100	$30,940	$41,500	789	$5,000	$30,820	$42,200
790	$6,000	$22,920	$34,000	791	$5,000	$37,880	$49,800	792	$3,500	$25,280	$33,500
793	$6,500	$42,900	$56,900	794	$6,500	$38,540	$51,000	795	$5,000	$38,090	$47,700
796	$6,100	$24,700	$32,900	797	$6,000	$27,780	$34,000				

NEIGHBORHOOD F

OBS	LANDVAL	IMPROVAL	SALEPRIC	OBS	LANDVAL	IMPROVAL	SALEPRIC	OBS	LANDVAL	IMPROVAL	SALEPRIC
								798	$2,500	$10,680	$28,500
799	$2,500	$10,010	$26,000	800	$2,500	$10,520	$26,000	801	$3,000	$13,640	$30,500
802	$3,500	$9,020	$22,900	803	$2,500	$11,710	$25,000	804	$3,000	$12,510	$25,500
805	$3,000	$13,810	$27,500	806	$5,500	$26,150	$51,500	807	$4,000	$32,980	$59,500
808	$2,500	$16,510	$29,000	809	$8,060	$37,070	$68,900	810	$7,200	$32,730	$59,500
811	$8,100	$33,630	$62,000	812	$3,000	$18,700	$31,900	813	$7,700	$41,970	$72,700
814	$6,200	$19,150	$36,600	815	$2,850	$15,890	$27,000	816	$7,000	$38,930	$66,900
817	$8,140	$24,180	$46,600	818	$8,100	$36,590	$64,000	819	$8,630	$39,280	$68,300
820	$8,250	$38,580	$66,000	821	$3,000	$20,730	$33,000	822	$3,000	$13,140	$22,500
823	$4,000	$28,000	$44,500	824	$4,000	$28,240	$44,500	825	$8,250	$31,880	$55,500
826	$8,250	$51,210	$82,500	827	$4,200	$27,830	$44,000	828	$9,500	$40,020	$67,500
829	$8,250	$32,850	$56,000	830	$8,700	$36,940	$62,400	831	$8,480	$43,620	$71,500
832	$3,200	$21,110	$33,000	833	$5,700	$29,120	$47,000	834	$5,700	$31,770	$51,000
835	$8,140	$35,660	$59,500	836	$8,630	$44,060	$71,000	837	$4,000	$28,890	$43,900
838	$7,150	$48,310	$74,000	839	$7,500	$29,450	$49,500	840	$8,250	$38,960	$62,600
841	$8,100	$47,830	$75,000	842	$7,500	$35,690	$58,000	843	$9,780	$42,990	$70,000
844	$2,500	$21,040	$30,800	845	$7,000	$35,710	$56,500	846	$8,630	$40,720	$65,000
847	$6,700	$37,880	$57,000	848	$7,150	$47,830	$70,500	849	$6,500	$31,140	$48,000
850	$7,440	$43,770	$66,000	851	$8,030	$46,710	$70,000	852	$3,200	$24,840	$35,200
853	$8,060	$38,560	$58,000	854	$3,000	$24,290	$33,600	855	$5,700	$30,730	$44,800
856	$6,500	$31,230	$46,500	857	$6,960	$34,190	$51,000	858	$7,700	$40,590	$60,000
859	$8,140	$35,870	$54,700	860	$8,250	$50,960	$72,000	861	$6,500	$37,260	$53,000
862	$8,100	$47,710	$66,900	863	$8,630	$43,580	$63,000	864	$6,500	$37,800	$52,500
865	$7,500	$38,460	$55,000	866	$9,000	$42,740	$62,000	867	$8,250	$46,430	$64,000
868	$6,000	$28,170	$39,900	869	$4,000	$29,860	$39,500	870	$9,000	$41,710	$59,000
871	$7,730	$50,570	$68,000	872	$8,630	$48,040	$66,000	873	$6,700	$41,130	$55,000
874	$8,100	$40,100	$55,000	875	$9,780	$53,730	$72,000	876	$6,500	$43,460	$54,900
877	$5,700	$32,080	$40,000								

Appendix C

Data Set: Daily Closing Prices and Daily Changes of the Standard & Poor's Stock Index, 1975–1979

STANDARD AND POORS
STOCK INDEX, 1975-1979

DATE	INDEX	CHANGE	DATE	INDEX	CHANGE	DATE	INDEX	CHANGE	DATE	INDEX	CHANGE	DATE	INDEX	CHANGE
02JAN75	$70.23	1.67	24MAR75	$81.42	-1.97	12JUN75	$90.08	-0.47	03SEP75	$85.48	-1.40	19NOV75	$89.98	-1.02
03JAN75	$70.71	0.48	25MAR75	$83.06	1.64	13JUN75	$90.52	0.44	04SEP75	$86.03	0.55	20NOV75	$89.64	-0.34
06JAN75	$71.07	0.36	26MAR75	$83.59	0.53	16JUN75	$91.46	0.94	05SEP75	$86.20	0.17	21NOV75	$89.53	-0.11
07JAN75	$71.02	-0.05	27MAR75	$83.85	0.26	17JUN75	$91.46	0.00	08SEP75	$85.62	-0.58	24NOV75	$89.70	0.17
08JAN75	$70.04	-0.98	31MAR75	$83.36	-0.49	18JUN75	$90.58	-0.88	09SEP75	$85.89	0.27	25NOV75	$90.71	1.01
09JAN75	$71.17	1.13	01APR75	$82.64	-0.72	19JUN75	$90.39	-0.19	11SEP75	$84.60	-1.29	28NOV75	$90.94	0.23
10JAN75	$72.61	1.44	02APR75	$82.61	-0.00	20JUN75	$92.02	1.63?	11SEP75	$83.79	-0.81	01DEC75	$91.24	0.30
13JAN75	$72.31	-0.30	03APR75	$81.51	-1.13	23JUN75	$92.61	0.59	12SEP75	$83.45	-0.34	02DEC75	$90.67	-0.57
14JAN75	$71.68	-0.63	04APR75	$80.88	-0.63	24JUN75	$93.62	1.01	15SEP75	$83.30	-0.15	03DEC75	$89.73	-0.94
15JAN75	$72.14	0.46	07APR75	$80.35	-0.53	25JUN75	$94.19	0.57	16SEP75	$82.88	-0.42	04DEC75	$89.60	-0.13
16JAN75	$72.05	-0.09	08APR75	$80.99	0.64	26JUN75	$94.81	0.63	17SEP75	$82.09	-0.79	04DEC75	$87.84	-1.73
17JAN75	$70.96	-1.09	09APR75	$82.84	1.85	27JUN75	$94.81	-0.00	18SEP75	$82.37	0.28	05DEC75	$86.07	-1.24
20JAN75	$71.08	0.12	10APR75	$84.18	1.42	30JUN75	$95.19	0.38	19SEP75	$84.06	1.69	05DEC75	$87.07	1.02
21JAN75	$70.70	-0.38	11APR75	$85.60	1.42	01JUL75	$94.85	-0.34	22SEP75	$85.88	1.82	08DEC75	$87.30	0.23
22JAN75	$70.70	-0.12	14APR75	$86.30	0.70	02JUL75	$94.18	-0.67	23SEP75	$85.07	-0.81	09DEC75	$87.80	0.50
23JAN75	$71.74	1.04	15APR75	$86.60	0.30	03JUL75	$94.36	0.18	24SEP75	$84.94	-0.13	10DEC75	$87.80	-0.28
24JAN75	$72.07	0.33	16APR75	$86.05	-0.55	07JUL75	$93.54	-0.82	26SEP75	$85.64	0.80	11DEC75	$87.83	0.03
27JAN75	$72.98	0.91	17APR75	$87.23	1.18	08JUL75	$93.20	-0.15	29SEP75	$86.19	0.55	12DEC75	$86.93	-0.84
28JAN75	$72.44	-0.39	18APR75	$87.09	-0.93	09JUL75	$94.80	0.41	30SEP75	$85.03	-1.16	15DEC75	$86.93	-0.22
29JAN75	$75.03	0.27	21APR75	$86.12	-0.97	10JUL75	$94.66	-0.15	01OCT75	$83.87	-1.16	16DEC75	$89.15	0.22
30JAN75	$77.26	-0.66	23APR75	$86.04	-0.08	11JUL75	$95.19	0.53	02OCT75	$82.93	-0.94	17DEC75	$89.43	-0.28
31JAN75	$76.21	1.23	24APR75	$86.62	0.58	15JUL75	$95.61	0.42	03OCT75	$83.82	0.89	18DEC75	$88.80	-0.63
03FEB75	$76.98	-1.05	25APR75	$86.23	-0.39	16JUL75	$94.61	-1.00	06OCT75	$85.95	2.13	19DEC75	$86.14	-0.66
04FEB75	$77.82	0.77	28APR75	$85.64	-0.59	17JUL75	$93.63	-0.98	07OCT75	$86.88	0.93	22DEC75	$85.73	-0.59
05FEB75	$77.61	0.84	29APR75	$86.30	0.66	18JUL75	$93.20	-0.43	08OCT75	$86.46	-0.42	23DEC75	$85.46	0.73
06FEB75	$78.95	-0.21	30APR75	$89.22	1.86	21JUL75	$92.44	-0.76	09OCT75	$86.77	0.11	24DEC75	$86.25	-0.12
07FEB75	$78.56	1.34	01MAY75	$88.64	1.12	22JUL75	$90.18	-1.99	10OCT75	$87.94	1.17	26DEC75	$90.17	-0.16
10FEB75	$78.36	-0.39	02MAY75	$89.08	0.44	23JUL75	$90.66	0.16	13OCT75	$87.37	-0.13	30DEC75	$90.17	-0.42
11FEB75	$78.58	-0.27	05MAY75	$89.56	0.48	24JUL75	$90.29	-0.86	14OCT75	$88.21	-0.16	31DEC75	$90.19	0.71
12FEB75	$79.92	0.22	07MAY75	$90.53	0.97	28JUL75	$88.29	-1.44	15OCT75	$89.46	1.25	02JAN76	$90.90	0.42
13FEB75	$81.01	1.34	08MAY75	$90.61	0.08	29JUL75	$88.69	0.44	16OCT75	$89.28	-0.18	05JAN76	$92.58	1.68
14FEB75	$81.50	-1.09	09MAY75	$91.58	0.97	30JUL75	$88.19	-0.50	17OCT75	$89.23	-0.11	06JAN76	$93.53	0.95
18FEB75	$80.93	0.49	12MAY75	$91.27	-0.97	31JUL75	$88.83	0.64	20OCT75	$88.86	-0.60	07JAN76	$93.95	0.42
19FEB75	$81.44	-0.57	13MAY75	$90.43	-0.84	01AUG75	$88.75	-0.08	21OCT75	$88.37	-0.51	08JAN76	$94.58	0.63
20FEB75	$82.21	0.51	14MAY75	$90.53	0.10	07AUG75	$87.99	-0.76	22OCT75	$90.56	-0.96	09JAN76	$94.95	-0.37
21FEB75	$82.62	0.77	16MAY75	$90.07	-0.46	08AUG75	$88.82	0.82	23OCT75	$90.82	-0.74	12JAN76	$95.33	-0.38
25FEB75	$82.44	-0.41	19MAY75	$89.06	-1.01	08AUG75	$86.23	0.28	23OCT75	$90.71	0.24	13JAN76	$95.53	-1.56
26FEB75	$81.13	-1.31	20MAY75	$90.58	0.33	11AUG75	$86.30	0.05	24OCT75	$89.83	-1.41	15JAN76	$95.61	-0.52
27FEB75	$80.37	0.84	22MAY75	$90.39	-0.19	12AUG75	$86.02	-0.28	27OCT75	$89.73	-0.10	16JAN76	$96.00	-0.39
28FEB75	$80.77	0.40	23MAY75	$90.34	-0.03	13AUG75	$86.55	0.53	28OCT75	$90.51	-0.78	19JAN76	$98.36	1.32
03MAR75	$81.59	1.44	27MAY75	$90.71	0.72	14AUG75	$87.12	0.57	29OCT75	$89.39	-1.12	20JAN76	$98.82	-0.54
04MAR75	$83.03	-0.82	28MAY75	$89.68	0.61	14AUG75	$85.97	-1.15	30OCT75	$89.31	-0.08	21JAN76	$98.24	-0.62
05MAR75	$83.74	0.53	29MAY75	$90.34	-0.66	19AUG75	$85.06	-0.19	31OCT75	$89.04	-0.27	22JAN76	$98.21	1.17
06MAR75	$83.56	-0.66	30MAY75	$90.71	0.79	20AUG75	$85.36	-0.23	03NOV75	$88.09	-0.95	23JAN76	$99.68	1.17
07MAR75	$82.90	0.79	02JUN75	$91.15	0.61	21AUG75	$86.20	1.47	06NOV75	$88.15	0.64	26JAN76	$99.07	-0.61
10MAR75	$83.69	0.61	03JUN75	$92.58	-0.23	22AUG75	$84.95	0.31	06NOV75	$89.55	0.40	28JAN76	$98.53	-0.54
11MAR75	$84.19	-0.23	04JUN75	$92.89	-0.59	25AUG75	$83.07	-0.29	07NOV75	$89.33	-0.22	29JAN76	$100.11	1.58
12MAR75	$83.96	-0.59	05JUN75	$92.60	-0.21	26AUG75	$84.28	-0.09	10NOV75	$89.34	0.01	30JAN76	$100.86	0.75
13MAR75	$84.36	-0.77	06JUN75	$92.69	-0.21	27AUG75	$83.36	-0.15	11NOV75	$89.87	0.53	02FEB76	$100.87	0.01
14MAR75	$83.59	0.15	09JUN75	$92.48	-1.27	28AUG75	$84.43	-0.47	12NOV75	$91.19	1.32	03FEB76	$101.18	0.31
17MAR75	$84.76	1.02	10JUN75	$90.21	0.97	29AUG75	$86.88	0.48	13NOV75	$91.04	-0.15	04FEB76	$101.92	0.74
18MAR75	$86.01	1.25	11JUN75	$90.55	0.11				17NOV75	$90.46	-0.47	05FEB76	$90.36	0.53
19MAR75	$85.13	-0.88							18NOV75	$91.00	-0.46	09FEB76	$99.62	0.16
20MAR75	$84.61	0.13												
21MAR75	$83.39	-0.22												

DATE	INDEX	CHANGE
10FEB76	$100.47	0.85
11FEB76	$100.92	0.30
12FEB76	$100.25	-0.52
13FEB76	$99.67	-0.58
17FEB76	$99.05	0.62
18FEB76	$99.85	-0.80
19FEB76	$101.41	1.56
20FEB76	$102.10	0.69
23FEB76	$102.61	0.49
24FEB76	$101.01	-0.42
25FEB76	$101.69	-0.34
26FEB76	$100.11	-1.58
27FEB76	$99.71	-0.40
01MAR76	$100.02	0.31
02MAR76	$100.56	0.54
03MAR76	$99.98	-0.58
04MAR76	$98.92	-1.06
05MAR76	$99.11	0.19
08MAR76	$99.19	-1.08
09MAR76	$100.58	0.39
10MAR76	$100.94	0.36
11MAR76	$100.86	0.95
12MAR76	$99.85	-1.03
15MAR76	$99.86	-0.95
16MAR76	$100.92	-1.12
17MAR76	$100.86	0.06
18MAR76	$100.58	-0.13
19MAR76	$100.71	1.53
22MAR76	$102.24	1.18
23MAR76	$103.42	-0.57
24MAR76	$102.85	-1.06
25MAR76	$102.21	-1.15
26MAR76	$101.28	-0.93
29MAR76	$100.35	-0.80
30MAR76	$100.20	-0.15
31MAR76	$100.31	-0.74
01APR76	$100.67	0.36
05APR76	$101.44	0.77
06APR76	$102.21	0.15
07APR76	$101.28	1.00
08APR76	$100.35	-1.15
09APR76	$100.20	-0.93
12APR76	$103.42	-0.45
13APR76	$103.32	0.92
14APR76	$102.29	-0.23
15APR76	$102.98	0.69
16APR76	$102.83	0.28
19APR76	$102.13	-0.51
20APR76	$102.13	0.46
21APR76	$100.67	0.39
22APR76	$100.57	0.57
23APR76	$103.54	0.00
26APR76	$102.87	0.27
27APR76	$102.98	
28APR76	$102.13	
29APR76	$102.13	

DATE	INDEX	CHANGE
30APR76	$101.64	-0.49
03MAY76	$100.92	-0.72
04MAY76	$100.46	-0.54
05MAY76	$100.88	-0.58
06MAY76	$101.16	0.28
07MAY76	$101.88	0.72
10MAY76	$103.10	1.22
11MAY76	$102.95	-0.15
12MAY76	$102.16	-0.18
13MAY76	$101.34	-0.61
14MAY76	$101.09	-0.82
17MAY76	$101.09	-0.25
18MAY76	$101.18	0.17
19MAY76	$101.26	-0.08
20MAY76	$102.00	0.82
21MAY76	$101.26	-0.58
24MAY76	$99.44	-1.82
25MAY76	$99.49	-0.15
27MAY76	$99.34	0.39
28MAY76	$99.38	-0.04
01JUN76	$100.18	0.80
02JUN76	$99.85	-0.33
03JUN76	$100.22	0.37
04JUN76	$100.13	-0.09
07JUN76	$99.15	-0.98
08JUN76	$98.63	-0.52
09JUN76	$98.90	0.26
10JUN76	$99.56	0.66
11JUN76	$100.71	-0.06
14JUN76	$101.95	1.53
15JUN76	$101.46	-0.49
16JUN76	$102.85	-0.57
17JUN76	$102.41	-0.44
18JUN76	$103.61	0.76
21JUN76	$103.47	-0.13
22JUN76	$103.25	-0.22
23JUN76	$103.79	0.54
24JUN76	$103.43	-0.07
25JUN76	$103.86	0.29
28JUN76	$103.43	-1.15
29JUN76	$104.28	0.42
30JUN76	$104.28	-0.93
01JUL76	$104.59	-0.62
02JUL76	$103.54	0.57
06JUL76	$103.98	0.29
07JUL76	$104.98	-0.74
08JUL76	$103.21	0.77
09JUL76	$101.44	0.43
12JUL76	$103.32	-0.45
13JUL76	$105.90	0.92
14JUL76	$105.67	-0.23
15JUL76	$105.95	0.69
16JUL76	$105.20	-0.54
19JUL76	$104.28	0.27
20JUL76	$103.72	0.00

DATE	INDEX	CHANGE
21JUL76	$103.82	0.10
22JUL76	$103.93	0.11
23JUL76	$104.06	0.13
26JUL76	$104.07	0.01
27JUL76	$103.48	-0.59
28JUL76	$103.05	-0.43
29JUL76	$102.93	-0.12
30JUL76	$102.95	0.25
02AUG76	$103.14	-0.51
03AUG76	$102.16	-0.95
04AUG76	$101.34	-0.61
05AUG76	$104.43	0.29
06AUG76	$103.79	-0.58
09AUG76	$103.49	-0.06
10AUG76	$104.41	-0.92
11AUG76	$104.06	-0.35
12AUG76	$104.22	0.16
13AUG76	$104.43	-0.18
16AUG76	$104.80	0.37
17AUG76	$104.38	-0.24
18AUG76	$104.56	1.17
19AUG76	$103.35	-1.02
20AUG76	$102.37	-0.41
23AUG76	$101.96	-0.69
24AUG76	$101.27	-0.76
25AUG76	$102.03	-0.16
26AUG76	$102.03	-0.57
27AUG76	$101.48	-0.84
30AUG76	$102.07	0.59
31AUG76	$102.91	1.15
01SEP76	$104.06	-0.14
02SEP76	$103.92	-0.38
03SEP76	$104.30	-0.09
07SEP76	$104.08	-0.52
08SEP76	$105.03	-0.60
09SEP76	$105.15	-0.73
10SEP76	$105.07	-0.54
13SEP76	$102.49	-0.25
14SEP76	$102.65	-0.36
15SEP76	$104.29	-0.35
16SEP76	$104.21	-0.27
17SEP76	$105.34	1.13
20SEP76	$106.32	-0.05
21SEP76	$107.83	0.51
22SEP76	$104.26	-0.37
23SEP76	$106.92	-0.54
24SEP76	$106.80	-0.12
27SEP76	$107.26	-0.46
28SEP76	$105.14	-1.34
29SEP76	$105.37	-0.55
30SEP76	$105.90	1.07
01OCT76	$104.17	-0.13
04OCT76	$104.71	-0.49
05OCT76	$104.04	1.13
06OCT76	$105.66	1.12
07OCT76	$106.34	-0.43

DATE	INDEX	CHANGE
08OCT76	$102.56	-0.98
11OCT76	$103.93	-0.92
12OCT76	$100.81	-0.83
13OCT76	$102.12	1.31
14OCT76	$100.85	-1.27
15OCT76	$100.88	0.03
18OCT76	$101.47	0.59
19OCT76	$101.45	-0.02
20OCT76	$100.77	-0.67
21OCT76	$99.96	-0.81
22OCT76	$100.07	0.11
25OCT76	$101.06	0.99
26OCT76	$101.76	-0.70
27OCT76	$101.61	-0.15
28OCT76	$102.90	1.29
29OCT76	$102.90	1.20
01NOV76	$103.10	-0.18
02NOV76	$102.92	0.49
03NOV76	$102.41	-1.59
04NOV76	$102.82	-1.22
05NOV76	$100.82	-0.24
08NOV76	$99.60	-0.55
09NOV76	$99.36	-0.24
10NOV76	$98.81	-0.83
11NOV76	$99.24	-0.41
15NOV76	$99.24	-0.40
16NOV76	$99.90	0.66
17NOV76	$100.61	0.64
18NOV76	$100.89	1.28
19NOV76	$101.92	-1.03
22NOV76	$102.59	0.67
23NOV76	$101.96	-0.63
24NOV76	$102.41	-0.45
26NOV76	$103.15	0.74
29NOV76	$103.44	-0.34
30NOV76	$102.10	-0.71
01DEC76	$102.49	-0.39
02DEC76	$102.12	-0.37
03DEC76	$102.76	0.64
06DEC76	$102.49	-0.27
07DEC76	$103.49	1.13
08DEC76	$104.08	-0.07
09DEC76	$104.51	0.43
10DEC76	$104.26	-0.05
13DEC76	$105.07	-0.54
14DEC76	$105.14	-0.12
15DEC76	$104.80	-0.34
16DEC76	$105.26	-0.61
17DEC76	$103.65	-0.13
20DEC76	$105.37	1.07
21DEC76	$104.22	0.49
22DEC76	$104.71	1.12
23DEC76	$104.84	0.06
27DEC76	$104.77	0.71
28DEC76	$106.08	
29DEC76	$106.34	-0.43

DATE	INDEX	CHANGE
30DEC76	$106.88	0.54
31DEC76	$107.46	0.58
03JAN77	$107.00	-0.46
04JAN77	$105.70	-1.30
05JAN77	$104.76	-0.94
06JAN77	$105.02	0.26
07JAN77	$105.01	-0.01
10JAN77	$105.20	0.19
11JAN77	$104.72	-0.48
12JAN77	$104.20	-0.72
13JAN77	$103.40	-0.80
14JAN77	$103.73	-0.19
17JAN77	$104.01	0.28
18JAN77	$103.73	-0.41
19JAN77	$103.32	-0.53
20JAN77	$102.97	-0.35
21JAN77	$103.32	-0.77
24JAN77	$103.13	-0.12
25JAN77	$102.34	-0.79
26JAN77	$101.79	-0.55
27JAN77	$101.93	0.14
31JAN77	$102.03	0.10
01FEB77	$102.54	0.51
02FEB77	$102.36	-0.18
03FEB77	$101.88	-0.03
04FEB77	$101.80	0.01
07FEB77	$101.00	-0.87
08FEB77	$100.73	-0.60
09FEB77	$100.82	0.09
10FEB77	$100.22	-0.52
11FEB77	$100.74	0.30
14FEB77	$101.50	0.18
15FEB77	$101.04	-0.13
16FEB77	$100.49	-0.43
17FEB77	$100.19	-0.30
18FEB77	$99.60	-0.59
22FEB77	$99.48	-0.12
23FEB77	$99.82	0.34
24FEB77	$100.66	0.84
25FEB77	$100.39	-0.27
28FEB77	$100.66	0.32
01MAR77	$101.20	0.05
02MAR77	$101.25	-0.38
03MAR77	$100.87	0.32
04MAR77	$100.01	-0.86
07MAR77	$100.67	0.66
08MAR77	$100.65	-0.02
09MAR77	$101.42	0.77
10MAR77	$102.97	-0.56
11MAR77	$102.08	-0.09
14MAR77	$101.86	-0.22
15MAR77	$102.97	1.13
16MAR77	$102.08	1.12
17MAR77	$102.08	-4.09
18MAR77	$101.86	-0.22

DATE	INDEX	CHANGE	DATE	INDEX	CHANGE	DATE	INDEX	CHANGE	DATE	INDEX	CHANGE	DATE	INDEX	CHANGE
21MAR77	$101.31	-0.55	09JUN77	$98.14	-0.06	30AUG77	$96.38	-0.54	17NOV77	$95.16	-0.29	08FEB78	$90.83	0.50
22MAR77	$101.00	-0.31	10JUN77	$98.46	0.32	31AUG77	$96.77	0.39	18NOV77	$95.33	0.17	09FEB78	$90.30	-0.53
23MAR77	$100.20	-0.80	13JUN77	$98.74	0.28	01SEP77	$96.83	0.06	21NOV77	$95.25	-0.08	10FEB78	$90.08	-0.22
24MAR77	$99.06	-0.64	14JUN77	$98.62	-0.12	02SEP77	$97.45	0.62	22NOV77	$96.09	0.84	13FEB78	$89.84	-0.24
25MAR77	$99.02	-0.06	15JUN77	$98.85	0.23	06SEP77	$97.71	0.26	23NOV77	$96.49	0.40	14FEB78	$89.62	-0.22
28MAR77	$99.85	0.69	16JUN77	$99.97	0.12	07SEP77	$98.01	0.30	25NOV77	$96.69	0.20	15FEB78	$88.83	-0.21
29MAR77	$99.69	-1.15	17JUN77	$100.42	0.45	08SEP77	$97.28	-0.73	28NOV77	$96.04	-0.65	16FEB78	$88.08	-0.75
30MAR77	$98.54	-0.12	20JUN77	$100.74	0.32	09SEP77	$96.37	-0.91	29NOV77	$94.55	-1.49	17FEB78	$87.96	-0.12
31MAR77	$98.42	-0.79	21JUN77	$100.46	-0.28	12SEP77	$96.03	-0.34	30NOV77	$94.83	0.28	21FEB78	$87.59	-0.37
01APR77	$99.21	-0.98	23JUN77	$100.62	0.16	13SEP77	$96.09	0.06	01DEC77	$94.69	-0.14	22FEB78	$87.64	-0.03
04APR77	$98.23	-0.22	23JUN77	$100.19	-0.21	14SEP77	$96.55	0.46	02DEC77	$94.67	-0.02	23FEB78	$87.64	-0.08
05APR77	$98.01	0.44	28JUN77	$100.98	0.84	15SEP77	$96.80	0.25	05DEC77	$94.27	-0.40	24FEB78	$88.42	0.85
06APR77	$98.35	0.53	28JUN77	$100.14	-0.03	16SEP77	$96.48	-0.14	06DEC77	$92.78	-1.44	28FEB78	$87.04	-0.77
07APR77	$98.88	1.27	29JUN77	$100.10	-0.38	20SEP77	$95.89	-0.63	07DEC77	$92.96	0.18	01MAR78	$87.19	0.15
08APR77	$100.15	0.01	01JUL77	$100.16	0.01	21SEP77	$95.85	-0.04	08DEC77	$93.65	-0.69	02MAR78	$87.45	0.26
11APR77	$100.16	0.04	05JUL77	$100.09	0.38	22SEP77	$95.10	-0.79	09DEC77	$93.63	-0.02	03MAR78	$87.32	-0.13
12APR77	$101.04	0.04	06JUL77	$99.58	-0.51	26SEP77	$95.04	-0.06	12DEC77	$93.65	-0.07	06MAR78	$86.90	-0.55
13APR77	$100.54	-0.50	07JUL77	$99.93	0.35	27SEP77	$95.24	0.14	13DEC77	$93.56	-0.48	07MAR78	$87.36	0.46
14APR77	$100.40	-0.84	08JUL77	$99.55	-0.14	28SEP77	$95.10	-0.94	14DEC77	$94.03	-0.15	08MAR78	$87.84	0.48
15APR77	$99.75	-0.31	11JUL77	$99.59	0.10	29SEP77	$95.85	0.61	15DEC77	$93.55	0.19	09MAR78	$87.89	0.05
18APR77	$98.44	-1.31	12JUL77	$100.18	0.59	30SEP77	$95.53	0.68	16DEC77	$93.40	-0.55	13MAR78	$88.88	-0.07
20APR77	$97.15	-1.29	13JUL77	$100.95	0.77	03OCT77	$96.03	-0.71	19DEC77	$93.05	-0.89	14MAR78	$88.35	-0.39
21APR77	$97.96	-0.04	15JUL77	$101.79	0.84	04OCT77	$96.05	0.07	20DEC77	$93.80	0.75	15MAR78	$89.12	-0.23
22APR77	$98.20	0.85	18JUL77	$101.59	-0.14	05OCT77	$95.75	-0.37	21DEC77	$93.52	-0.93	16MAR78	$89.51	0.63
25APR77	$98.44	0.24	19JUL77	$100.27	-0.82	07OCT77	$94.69	-0.08	22DEC77	$92.74	0.00	17MAR78	$90.20	0.69
26APR77	$99.43	0.50	20JUL77	$98.64	-1.63	10OCT77	$94.94	-0.22	27DEC77	$91.62	0.06	20MAR78	$89.79	0.62
27APR77	$99.96	0.53	21JUL77	$98.79	0.15	11OCT77	$92.75	-0.89	28DEC77	$90.69	-0.19	21MAR78	$89.47	-1.03
28APR77	$100.11	0.15	22JUL77	$98.85	0.06	13OCT77	$93.04	0.11	29DEC77	$90.17	-0.52	24MAR78	$88.37	-0.11
29APR77	$99.49	-0.62	25JUL77	$98.16	-0.27	14OCT77	$93.46	-0.30	30DEC77	$89.74	-0.78	27MAR78	$88.51	0.14
02MAY77	$99.18	-0.31	26JUL77	$98.05	-0.62	17OCT77	$93.56	-1.30	04JAN78	$89.82	-1.12	28MAR78	$89.50	-0.63
03MAY77	$99.47	-0.29	27JUL77	$98.92	0.13	18OCT77	$93.47	0.15	05JAN78	$93.52	-0.93	29MAR78	$89.64	0.14
04MAY77	$98.78	-0.69	28JUL77	$98.37	-0.32	20OCT77	$92.38	-0.27	06JAN78	$92.74	-0.52	30MAR78	$89.41	-0.23
05MAY77	$98.73	-0.95	29JUL77	$98.76	0.69	20OCT77	$92.67	-0.13	09JAN78	$91.62	-0.20	31MAR78	$89.21	-0.20
06MAY77	$96.07	-0.48	01AUG77	$97.99	-0.02	25OCT77	$92.32	-0.03	10JAN78	$90.17	-0.65	03APR78	$88.46	-0.75
09MAY77	$97.21	-0.20	02AUG77	$98.05	0.30	27OCT77	$91.00	-0.77	11JAN78	$89.74	0.01	04APR78	$88.86	0.40
10MAY77	$97.48	-0.74	03AUG77	$98.92	0.42	27OCT77	$92.10	0.87	12JAN78	$89.82	0.81	05APR78	$89.64	0.78
11MAY77	$96.12	-0.15	08AUG77	$98.16	-0.43	28OCT77	$92.34	-0.76	13JAN78	$89.43	0.00	06APR78	$89.47	-0.18
12MAY77	$96.93	0.30	09AUG77	$98.15	-1.30	31OCT77	$91.35	-0.30	17JAN78	$89.88	0.46	07APR78	$90.49	-0.32
13MAY77	$96.74	-0.81	10AUG77	$98.85	-0.20	01NOV77	$90.71	-0.45	18JAN78	$89.25	-0.09	10APR78	$90.25	-0.24
16MAY77	$97.69	-0.19	11AUG77	$97.88	-0.43	02NOV77	$90.76	-0.82	19JAN78	$90.56	-0.47	11APR78	$90.11	-0.14
17MAY77	$97.23	-0.39	12AUG77	$97.73	-1.30	03NOV77	$91.58	-0.11	23JAN78	$90.89	-0.20	13APR78	$90.98	0.87
18MAY77	$97.73	-1.08	15AUG77	$96.07	-0.20	04NOV77	$97.48	0.00	24JAN78	$89.24	-0.65	14APR78	$92.92	1.94
19MAY77	$98.20	0.47	16AUG77	$96.21	-0.45	08NOV77	$97.51	-0.17	25JAN78	$90.39	0.05	17APR78	$94.45	1.53
			17AUG77	$96.12	-0.06	09NOV77	$97.46	-0.28	26JAN78	$88.58	0.14	18APR78	$93.86	-1.02
			18AUG77	$96.93	-0.81	10NOV77	$94.71	1.73	30JAN78	$88.34	0.00	20APR78	$93.86	0.43
			22AUG77	$96.74	-0.19	11NOV77	$95.98	1.27	31JAN78	$89.25	0.08	24APR78	$94.54	-0.28
			23AUG77	$97.23	0.17	14NOV77	$95.13	-0.39	01FEB78	$89.93	0.68	24APR78	$95.77	1.43
			24AUG77	$97.69	-0.17	15NOV77	$95.32	-1.08	02FEB78	$90.11	-0.14	25APR78	$96.11	0.87
			25AUG77	$97.73	1.27		$95.45	0.86	03FEB78	$90.98	0.87	26APR78	$95.86	0.18
			26AUG77	$96.06	-0.50				06FEB78	$89.50	-0.51	27APR78	$95.86	-0.96
			29AUG77	$96.92	0.47				07FEB78	$90.33	0.83	28APR78	$96.83	0.97

DATE	INDEX	CHANGE
01MAY78	$97.67	0.84
02MAY78	$97.25	-0.42
03MAY78	$96.26	-0.99
04MAY78	$95.93	-0.33
05MAY78	$96.53	0.60
08MAY78	$96.19	-0.34
09MAY78	$95.90	-0.29
10MAY78	$95.92	0.02
11MAY78	$97.20	1.28
12MAY78	$98.07	0.87
15MAY78	$98.76	0.69
16MAY78	$99.35	0.59
17MAY78	$99.60	0.25
18MAY78	$98.62	-0.98
19MAY78	$98.12	-0.50
22MAY78	$98.05	-0.07
23MAY78	$97.08	-0.97
24MAY78	$96.80	-0.28
25MAY78	$96.86	0.28
26MAY78	$97.25	0.38
30MAY78	$98.12	-0.79
31MAY78	$98.05	-0.28
01JUN78	$100.12	1.81
02JUN78	$100.21	0.09
05JUN78	$99.93	-0.28
06JUN78	$99.55	-0.38
07JUN78	$99.57	0.02
08JUN78	$99.48	-0.09
09JUN78	$97.49	0.07
12JUN78	$96.01	-0.50
13JUN78	$95.85	-0.39
14JUN78	$94.60	-1.25
15JUN78	$94.98	0.38
16JUN78	$95.40	0.42
19JUN78	$95.53	-0.04
20JUN78	$94.27	-0.44
21JUN78	$94.32	-0.82
22JUN78	$94.89	0.57
23JUN78	$95.27	-0.38
26JUN78	$95.24	0.31
27JUN78	$95.25	0.01
28JUN78	$97.58	1.33
29JUN78	$96.87	-0.91
30JUN78	$98.12	1.25

DATE	INDEX	CHANGE
20JUL78	$98.03	-0.09
21JUL78	$97.75	-0.28
24JUL78	$97.72	-0.03
25JUL78	$98.44	0.72
26JUL78	$99.08	0.64
28JUL78	$99.54	0.46
31JUL78	$100.00	0.46
01AUG78	$100.68	0.68
02AUG78	$100.66	-0.02
03AUG78	$102.92	2.26
04AUG78	$103.51	0.59
07AUG78	$103.92	0.41
08AUG78	$103.55	-0.37
09AUG78	$104.01	0.46
10AUG78	$103.50	-0.49
11AUG78	$103.66	-0.84
14AUG78	$103.96	-0.30
15AUG78	$103.97	0.01
16AUG78	$104.85	0.80
17AUG78	$104.65	-0.12
18AUG78	$105.08	0.43
21AUG78	$104.73	-0.35
23AUG78	$104.31	-0.42
24AUG78	$105.08	0.77
25AUG78	$104.90	-0.18
28AUG78	$103.96	-0.94
29AUG78	$103.39	-0.57
30AUG78	$103.47	0.08
31AUG78	$103.29	-0.18
01SEP78	$103.68	0.39?
05SEP78	$104.49	0.81
06SEP78	$105.38	0.89
07SEP78	$105.42	0.04
08SEP78	$106.79	1.37
11SEP78	$106.98	0.19
13SEP78	$106.34	-0.65
14SEP78	$105.10	-1.24
15SEP78	$104.12	-0.98
18SEP78	$104.66	0.68
20SEP78	$101.73	-0.80
21SEP78	$101.90	0.17
22SEP78	$101.84	-0.06
25SEP78	$101.86	0.02
26SEP78	$102.62	0.76
27SEP78	$101.66	-0.96
28SEP78	$101.08	-0.58
29SEP78	$102.54	0.42
02OCT78	$102.60	-0.36
03OCT78	$103.06	0.46
05OCT78	$103.27	0.21
06OCT78	$103.52	0.25

DATE	INDEX	CHANGE
09OCT78	$104.59	1.07
10OCT78	$104.46	-0.13
11OCT78	$105.39	0.93
12OCT78	$104.88	-0.51
13OCT78	$104.66	-0.22
16OCT78	$102.61	0.35
17OCT78	$101.26	-1.35
18OCT78	$100.49	-0.77
19OCT78	$99.33	-1.16
20OCT78	$97.95	-1.38
23OCT78	$98.18	0.23
24OCT78	$97.49	-0.69
25OCT78	$97.31	-0.18
27OCT78	$96.03	-1.28
30OCT78	$95.06	-0.47
31OCT78	$93.15	-1.91
01NOV78	$96.85	3.70
02NOV78	$95.61	-1.24
03NOV78	$96.18	0.57
06NOV78	$95.15	-0.99
07NOV78	$93.85	-1.34
08NOV78	$94.42	0.57
09NOV78	$94.31	-0.63
10NOV78	$93.96	-0.35
13NOV78	$94.17	0.21
14NOV78	$92.13	-1.64
15NOV78	$92.71	0.58
16NOV78	$93.71	1.00
17NOV78	$94.42	0.71
20NOV78	$95.01	-0.83
21NOV78	$95.25	0.24
22NOV78	$95.01	-0.24
24NOV78	$95.99	0.31
27NOV78	$95.15	-0.20
28NOV78	$93.75	-0.84
29NOV78	$94.28	0.19
01DEC78	$96.28	-1.40
04DEC78	$96.15	1.58
05DEC78	$97.44	-0.13
06DEC78	$97.08	1.29
07DEC78	$96.63	-0.98
08DEC78	$96.90	0.68
11DEC78	$101.90	-0.45
12DEC78	$101.84	0.17
13DEC78	$101.86	0.02
14DEC78	$96.04	-0.06
15DEC78	$95.33	-0.71
18DEC78	$93.24	-0.58
19DEC78	$94.71	0.44
20DEC78	$96.06	0.03
21DEC78	$96.31	1.60
22DEC78	$97.52	1.21
26DEC78	$96.66	-0.86

DATE	INDEX	CHANGE
28DEC78	$96.28	-0.38
29DEC78	$96.25	-0.17
02JAN79	$96.73	0.62
03JAN79	$97.80	1.07
04JAN79	$98.58	0.78
05JAN79	$99.13	0.55
08JAN79	$98.80	-0.33
09JAN79	$99.33	0.53
10JAN79	$98.77	-0.56
11JAN79	$99.10	0.33
12JAN79	$99.93	0.83
15JAN79	$100.69	0.76
16JAN79	$99.46	-1.23
17JAN79	$99.48	0.02
18JAN79	$99.72	0.24
19JAN79	$99.75	0.03
22JAN79	$99.90	0.15
23JAN79	$100.60	0.70
24JAN79	$100.16	-0.44
25JAN79	$101.19	1.03
26JAN79	$101.86	0.67
29JAN79	$101.55	-0.31
30JAN79	$101.75	0.20
31JAN79	$99.93	-0.03
01FEB79	$99.96	-0.46
02FEB79	$98.67	-1.41
05FEB79	$98.05	-0.04
06FEB79	$97.16	-0.89
07FEB79	$97.65	0.49
08FEB79	$97.87	0.22
09FEB79	$98.20	0.33
13FEB79	$98.23	-0.06
14FEB79	$98.73	-0.14
15FEB79	$98.67	-0.06
16FEB79	$99.42	-0.75
20FEB79	$99.07	-0.35
21FEB79	$98.52	-0.74
22FEB79	$98.33	-0.55
23FEB79	$97.67	-0.13
26FEB79	$97.44	1.54
27FEB79	$96.28	-0.62
28FEB79	$96.90	1.09
01MAR79	$100.14	0.07
02MAR79	$100.51	0.37
05MAR79	$99.88	-0.63
06MAR79	$99.93	0.05
07MAR79	$100.22	0.29
08MAR79	$99.58	-0.14
09MAR79	$99.67	-0.17
12MAR79	$99.84	-0.13
13MAR79	$99.71	0.15
14MAR79	$100.69	0.83
16MAR79	$101.06	0.37

DATE	INDEX	CHANGE
20MAR79	$100.50	-0.56
21MAR79	$101.25	0.75
22MAR79	$101.67	0.42
23MAR79	$101.60	-0.07
26MAR79	$102.04	0.44
28MAR79	$102.48	-0.36
29MAR79	$102.13	-0.09
30MAR79	$102.03	-0.44
02APR79	$101.59	-0.69
03APR79	$100.90	1.50
04APR79	$102.40	0.25
05APR79	$102.65	0.61
06APR79	$103.26	-0.08
09APR79	$103.18	0.16
10APR79	$103.34	-0.47
11APR79	$102.31	-1.03
12APR79	$102.00	-0.31
16APR79	$101.12	-0.88
17APR79	$101.24	0.12
18APR79	$101.70	0.46
19APR79	$101.76	0.06
20APR79	$101.57	-0.19
23APR79	$102.20	0.63
24APR79	$102.50	0.30
25APR79	$102.01	-0.49
26APR79	$101.80	-0.21
27APR79	$101.76	-0.04
30APR79	$101.68	-0.08
01MAY79	$101.72	0.04
02MAY79	$100.60	-1.12
03MAY79	$101.27	1.67
07MAY79	$99.02	0.15
08MAY79	$99.17	-0.29
09MAY79	$99.46	-0.94
10MAY79	$98.52	0.52
11MAY79	$99.87	-0.90
14MAY79	$98.06	0.06
15MAY79	$98.14	-0.46
16MAY79	$98.42	0.28
17MAY79	$96.28	0.42
21MAY79	$96.90	1.67
22MAY79	$100.51	0.21
23MAY79	$99.88	0.37
24MAY79	$99.93	-0.63
25MAY79	$100.22	0.05
29MAY79	$100.05	0.29
30MAY79	$99.58	-0.27
31MAY79	$99.67	-0.14
01JUN79	$99.84	-0.03
04JUN79	$99.71	0.15
05JUN79	$99.32	0.15
06JUN79	$100.62	1.30
07JUN79	$101.30	0.68
08JUN79	$101.79	0.49

DATE	INDEX	CHANGE		DATE	INDEX	CHANGE		DATE	INDEX	CHANGE
08JUN79	$101.49	0.30		28AUG79	$109.02	-0.12		15NOV79	$104.13	0.74
11JUN79	$101.91	0.94		29AUG79	$109.02	-0.00		16NOV79	$103.79	-0.34
12JUN79	$102.85	0.94		30AUG79	$109.02	0.00		19NOV79	$104.23	0.44
13JUN79	$102.31	-0.54		31AUG79	$109.32	0.30		20NOV79	$103.69	-0.54
14JUN79	$102.20	-0.11		04SEP79	$107.44	-1.88		21NOV79	$103.85	0.20
15JUN79	$102.09	-0.11		05SEP79	$106.40	-1.04		23NOV79	$104.67	0.78
18JUN79	$101.56	-0.53		06SEP79	$106.85	0.45		26NOV79	$106.80	2.13
19JUN79	$101.58	0.02		07SEP79	$107.66	0.81		27NOV79	$106.38	-0.42
20JUN79	$102.63	1.05		10SEP79	$107.51	-0.15		28NOV79	$106.77	0.39
21JUN79	$102.64	0.55		11SEP79	$107.82	0.31		29NOV79	$106.81	0.04
22JUN79	$102.09	-0.55		12SEP79	$107.51	-0.31		30NOV79	$106.16	-0.65
25JUN79	$102.09	0.05		13SEP79	$107.82	0.03		03DEC79	$105.83	-0.33
26JUN79	$101.66	-0.43		14SEP79	$107.85	0.91		04DEC79	$106.79	0.96
27JUN79	$102.27	0.61		17SEP79	$108.76	0.08		05DEC79	$107.25	0.46
28JUN79	$102.80	0.53		18SEP79	$108.84	-0.84		06DEC79	$108.00	0.75
29JUN79	$102.91	0.11		19SEP79	$108.00	0.28		07DEC79	$107.52	-0.48
02JUL79	$101.99	-0.92		20SEP79	$108.28	2.23		10DEC79	$107.49	-0.18
03JUL79	$102.43	0.40		24SEP79	$110.51	-0.04		12DEC79	$107.52	-0.03
05JUL79	$103.62	1.19		25SEP79	$110.47	-0.86		13DEC79	$107.67	0.15
06JUL79	$104.47	0.85		26SEP79	$109.68	0.07		14DEC79	$108.92	1.25
09JUL79	$104.20	-0.27		27SEP79	$109.96	0.28		17DEC79	$109.33	0.41
10JUL79	$103.64	-0.56		28SEP79	$110.21	0.25		18DEC79	$108.30	-1.03
11JUL79	$102.32	-0.95		01OCT79	$109.32	-0.89		19DEC79	$108.20	-0.10
13JUL79	$102.74	0.42		02OCT79	$108.56	-0.76		20DEC79	$108.26	0.06
16JUL79	$101.83	-0.91		03OCT79	$109.59	1.03		21DEC79	$107.55	-0.67
17JUL79	$101.61	-0.14		04OCT79	$110.17	0.58		24DEC79	$107.66	-0.07
18JUL79	$101.82	0.21		05OCT79	$109.88	-1.10		26DEC79	$107.78	0.12
19JUL79	$101.59	-0.23		08OCT79	$106.63	-1.39		27DEC79	$107.96	0.18
20JUL79	$101.97	0.38		09OCT79	$105.30	-3.25		28DEC79	$107.84	-0.12
23JUL79	$103.08	1.11		10OCT79	$105.05	-1.33		31DEC79	$107.96	0.12
24JUL79	$103.10	0.02		11OCT79	$104.49	-0.25				
25JUL79	$103.15	0.05		15OCT79	$103.36	-0.56				
26JUL79	$103.61	0.66		16OCT79	$103.19	-0.17				
27JUL79	$104.17	0.36		17OCT79	$103.39	-1.13				
30JUL79	$104.10	-0.07		18OCT79	$103.61	-0.20				
31JUL79	$104.04	-0.06		19OCT79	$101.60	-2.01				
01AUG79	$104.30	0.26		22OCT79	$100.71	-0.89				
02AUG79	$105.65	1.35		23OCT79	$100.28	-0.43				
03AUG79	$105.98	0.33		24OCT79	$100.44	0.16				
06AUG79	$105.49	-0.49		25OCT79	$100.00	-0.44				
08AUG79	$106.40	0.91		26OCT79	$100.57	0.57				
09AUG79	$107.52	1.12		29OCT79	$100.71	0.14				
10AUG79	$107.42	-0.10		30OCT79	$102.67	1.96				
14AUG79	$108.25	0.73		31OCT79	$101.82	-0.85				
15AUG79	$108.09	-0.16		01NOV79	$102.57	0.75				
16AUG79	$108.30	0.21		02NOV79	$102.51	-0.06				
17AUG79	$108.83	0.53		05NOV79	$101.82	-0.69				
20AUG79	$108.91	0.08		06NOV79	$101.20	-0.62				
21AUG79	$108.99	0.08		07NOV79	$99.87	-1.33				
22AUG79	$108.63	-0.36		08NOV79	$100.30	0.43				
23AUG79	$108.60	-0.03		09NOV79	$101.51	1.21				
27AUG79	$109.14	0.54		12NOV79	$103.51	2.00				
				13NOV79	$103.54	0.03				
				14NOV79	$103.39	0.45				

Appendix D

Data Set: Supermarket Customer Checkout Times for Mechanical and Automated Checking

CUSTOMER CHECKOUT TIMES(SECONDS)
AT SUPERMARKETS WITH MECHANICAL AND AUTOMATED CHECKERS

SUPERMARKET A (MECHANICAL)

OBS	CHKTIME	OBS	CHKTIME	OBS	CHKTIME	OBS	CHKTIME	OBS	CHKTIME	OBS	CHKTIME	OBS	CHKTIME	OBS	CHKTIME	OBS	CHKTIME	OBS	CHKTIME
1	62	51	112	101	115	151	40	201	77	251	56	301	144	351	100	401	137	451	38
2	133	52	132	102	147	152	65	202	64	252	87	302	75	352	85	402	145	452	27
3	190	53	93	103	63	153	147	203	36	253	112	303	138	353	185	403	80	453	100
4	25	54	270	104	130	154	125	204	131	254	135	304	75	354	95	404	132	454	96
5	80	55	130	105	135	155	112	205	123	255	145	305	56	355	112	405	52	455	70
6	57	56	85	106	40	156	192	206	48	256	90	306	90	356	204	406	55	456	87
7	35	57	70	107	105	157	190	207	72	257	134	307	168	357	208	407	65	457	58
8	135	58	50	108	95	158	130	208	75	258	137	308	100	358	62	408	100	458	106
9	150	59	45	109	70	159	130	209	138	259	116	309	95	359	58	409	170	459	112
10	110	60	135	110	152	160	76	210	87	260	148	310	185	360	75	410	65	460	49
11	152	61	75	111	177	161	138	211	58	261	160	311	132	361	125	411	76	461	147
12	27	62	55	112	113	162	157	212	113	262	97	312	147	362	200	412	25	462	92
13	96	63	85	113	85	163	34	213	160	263	172	313	58	363	149	413	78	463	72
14	145	64	60	114	205	164	96	214	145	264	49	314	21	364	70	414	45	464	145
15	102	65	65	115	75	165	74	215	75	265	53	315	62	365	130	415	115	465	160
16	35	66	95	116	15	166	132	216	73	266	160	316	108	366	116	416	95	466	96
17	147	67	125	117	52	167	148	217	178	267	84	317	105	367	145	417	139	467	84
18	238	68	85	118	20	168	73	218	60	268	48	318	18	368	85	418	112	468	106
19	53	69	70	119	85	169	57	219	206	269	84	319	80	369	46	419	49	469	70
20	77	70	85	120	70	170	197	220	84	270	80	320	125	370	138	420	112	470	55
21	33	71	25	121	47	171	53	221	81	271	102	321	84	371	70	421	96	471	85
22	90	72	80	122	84	172	222	222	156	272	125	322	96	372	85	422	88	472	112
23	275	73	72	123	132	173	70	223	139	273	165	323	170	373	135	423	70	473	130
24	142	74	140	124	80	174	146	224	111	274	90	324	85	374	85	424	172	474	192
25	177	75	135	125	200	175	117	225	57	275	200	325	130	375	72	425	112	475	100
26	32	76	155	126	80	176	94	226	165	276	95	326	144	376	60	426	106	476	114
27	137	77	55	127	64	177	58	227	137	277	80	327	125	377	147	427	70	477	58
28	132	78	124	128	91	178	125	228	125	278	138	328	115	378	155	428	155	478	78
29	147	79	170	129	27	179	160	229	64	279	85	329	28	379	107	429	147	479	147
30	112	80	160	130	125	180	137	230	26	280	172	330	83	380	64	430	167	480	116
31	145	81	75	131	95	181	132	231	72	281	135	331	66	381	155	431	202	481	148
32	327	82	145	132	75	182	107	232	220	282	90	332	72	382	108	432	106	482	85
33	130	83	100	133	65	183	35	233	37	283	98	333	87	383	92	433	78	483	115
34	45	84	97	134	56	184	205	234	80	284	118	334	176	384	116	434	165	484	165
35	72	85	120	135	130	185	215	235	128	285	154	335	94	385	114	435	105	485	75
36	93	86	135	136	85	186	27	236	65	286	60	336	96	386	115	436	144	486	162
37	80	87	52	137	27	187	85	237	95	287	70	337	58	387	130	437	75	487	278
38	215	88	50	138	35	188	75	238	138	288	155	338	84	388	136	438	48	488	220
39	186	89	80	139	162	189	85	239	127	289	146	339	85	389	97	439	75	489	175
40	85	90	67	140	117	190	125	240	75	290	200	340	170	390	170	440	85	490	173
41	142	91	127	141	72	191	129	241	83	291	171	341	87	391	65	441	146	491	162
42	80	92	142	142	63	192	84	242	96	292	98	342	143	392	152	442	82	492	138
43	215	93	70	143	105	193	95	243	220	293	45	343	310	393	100	443	100	493	110
44	186	94	80	144	157	194	185	244	165	294	65	344	75	394	75	444	75	494	175
45	85	95	245	145	208	195	76	245	154	295	146	345	172	395	42	445	70	495	84
46	142	96	98	146	112	196	69	246	96	296	132	346	135	396	156	446	100	496	95
47	77	97	245	147	112	197	125	247	220	297	45	347	310	397	75	447	75	497	110
48	70	98	80	148	157	198	185	248	165	298	65	348	75	398	100	448	152	498	84
49	72	99	75	149	130	199	76	249	165	299	146	349	172	399	75	449	70	499	95
50	194	100	98	150	112	200	69	250	154	300	132	350	135	400	156	450	144	500	85

SUPERMARKET B (AUTOMATED)

OBS	CHKTIME	OBS	CHKTIME	OBS	CHKTIME	OBS	CHKTIME	OBS	CHKTIME	OBS	CHKTIME	OBS	CHKTIME	OBS	CHKTIME	OBS	CHKTIME	OBS	CHKTIME
501	18	551	25	601	25	651	40	701	30	751	20	801	4	851	35	901	30	951	100
502	37	552	7	602	12	652	47	702	15	752	135	802	45	852	30	902	50	952	25
503	63	553	30	603	45	653	13	703	215	753	40	803	40	853	25	903	45	953	80
504	116	554	8	604	26	654	3	704	150	754	57	804	15	854	15	904	2	954	20
505	53	555	73	605	48	655	35	705	120	755	145	805	45	855	70	905	17	955	35
506	65	556	10	606	65	656	120	706	57	756	7	806	15	856	17	906	57	956	70
507	35	557	39	607	44	657	44	707	43	757	159	807	50	857	10	907	30	957	10
508	229	558	61	608	38	658	45	708	35	758	62	808	15	858	35	908	22	958	5
509	8	559	126	609	8	659	26	709	40	759	15	809	5	859	55	909	100	959	60
510	67	560	44	610	35	660	38	710	25	760	115	810	5	860	80	910	23	960	120
511	13	561	8	611	22	661	40	711	22	761	292	811	10	861	70	911	52	961	23
512	63	562	120	612	17	662	50	712	40	762	85	812	105	862	40	912	45	962	7
513	20	563	80	613	78	663	25	713	24	763	33	813	40	863	45	913	95	963	13
514	77	564	36	614	24	664	25	714	350	764	99	814	100	864	15	914	300	964	15
515	3	565	17	615	113	665	70	715	107	765	34	815	15	865	120	915	5	965	15
516	77	566	156	616	17	666	20	716	80	766	103	816	30	866	90	916	37	966	40
517	16	567	31	617	25	667	25	717	110	767	99	817	30	867	30	917	30	967	28
518	98	568	16	618	30	668	110	718	155	768	45	818	100	868	5	918	40	968	13
519	12	569	47	619	6	669	49	719	185	769	57	819	30	869	100	919	30	969	25
520	57	570	36	620	20	670	180	720	153	770	50	820	105	870	30	920	70	970	4
521	81	571	57	621	32	671	190	721	55	771	303	821	5	871	100	921	70	971	3
522	124	572	23	622	7	672	169	722	50	772	135	822	8	872	55	922	80	972	26
523	53	573	60	623	18	673	75	723	120	773	130	823	50	873	35	923	80	973	65
524	124	574	22	624	20	674	40	724	10	774	30	824	100	874	50	924	75	974	65
525	53	575	39	625	15	675	39	725	10	775	130	825	18	875	25	925	45	975	30
526	18	576	93	626	10	676	40	726	123	776	60	826	10	876	2	926	60	976	4
527	57	577	20	627	63	677	60	727	90	777	353	827	70	877	55	927	35	977	70
528	84	578	96	628	30	678	85	728	40	778	110	828	10	878	35	928	45	978	50
529	65	579	237	629	36	679	24	729	63	779	25	829	40	879	30	929	35	979	87
530	124	580	210	630	237	680	91	730	25	780	10	830	25	880	80	930	17	980	30
531	53	581	124	631	145	681	50	731	15	781	25	831	20	881	13	931	12	981	13
532	18	582	53	632	10	682	13	732	57	782	35	832	85	882	42	932	20	982	135
533	18	583	18	633	52	683	10	733	30	783	30	833	20	883	21	933	125	983	36
534	15	584	18	634	33	684	6	734	35	784	35	834	15	884	48	934	3	984	130
535	27	585	18	635	10	685	32	735	40	785	10	835	8	885	90	935	10	985	75
536	34	586	27	636	50	686	143	736	35	786	15	836	50	886	30	936	75	986	35
537	51	587	12	637	143	687	16	737	50	787	20	837	70	887	100	937	40	987	40
538	14	588	74	638	16	688	135	738	16	788	15	838	100	888	7	938	80	988	55
539	25	589	101	639	135	689	27	739	23	789	20	839	110	889	10	939	30	989	65
540	43	590	142	640	101	690	28	740	120	790	8	840	95	890	7	940	65	990	97
541	216	591	100	641	142	691	27	741	23	791	15	841	100	891	40	941	97	991	65
542	66	592	73	642	100	692	13	742	23	792	20	842	30	892	5	942	65	992	45
543	12	593	25	643	73	693	24	743	140	793	8	843	95	893	35	943	97	993	55
544	25	594	14	644	25	694	4	744	15	794	15	844	10	894	60	944	65	994	70
545	66	595	43	645	66	695	39	745	20	795	20	845	45	895	50	945	45	995	85
546	12	596	216	646	12	696	71	746	40	796	8	846	85	896	70	946	55	996	10
547	25	597	12	647	66	697	76	747	55	797	35	847	30	897	20	947	97	997	27
548	66	598	66	648	12	698	6	748	110	798	243	848	45	898	10	948	100	998	25
549	145	599	66	649	66	699	40	749	228	799	35	849	85	899	45	949	35	999	—
550	15	600	12	650	12	700	53	750	127	800	50	850	30	900	10	950	—	1000	—

Appendix E
Statistical Tables

Contents:

TABLE 1   Binomial Probabilities

TABULATED VALUES ARE P(X)

N = 5

P

X	0.01	0.05	0.1	0.2	0.3	0.4	0.5	0.6	0.7	0.8	0.9	0.95	0.99	X
0	.9510	.7738	.5905	.3277	.1681	.0778	.0313	.0102	.0024	.0003	.0000	.0000	.0000	0
1	.0480	.2036	.3280	.4096	.3601	.2592	.1563	.0768	.0283	.0064	.0005	.0000	.0000	1
2	.0010	.0214	.0729	.2048	.3087	.3456	.3125	.2304	.1323	.0512	.0081	.0011	.0000	2
3	.0000	.0011	.0081	.0512	.1323	.2304	.3125	.3456	.3087	.2048	.0729	.0214	.0010	3
4	.0000	.0000	.0004	.0064	.0283	.0768	.1563	.2592	.3601	.4096	.3280	.2036	.0480	4
5	.0000	.0000	.0000	.0003	.0024	.0102	.0313	.0778	.1681	.3277	.5905	.7738	.9510	5

TABULATED VALUES ARE P(X)

N = 6

P

X	0.01	0.05	0.1	0.2	0.3	0.4	0.5	0.6	0.7	0.8	0.9	0.95	0.99	X
0	.9415	.7351	.5314	.2621	.1176	.0467	.0156	.0041	.0007	.0001	.0000	.0000	.0000	0
1	.0571	.2321	.3543	.3932	.3025	.1866	.0938	.0369	.0102	.0015	.0001	.0000	.0000	1
2	.0014	.0305	.0984	.2458	.3241	.3110	.2344	.1382	.0595	.0154	.0012	.0001	.0000	2
3	.0000	.0021	.0146	.0819	.1852	.2765	.3125	.2765	.1852	.0819	.0146	.0021	.0000	3
4	.0000	.0001	.0012	.0154	.0595	.1382	.2344	.3110	.3241	.2458	.0984	.0305	.0014	4
5	.0000	.0000	.0001	.0015	.0102	.0369	.0938	.1866	.3025	.3932	.3543	.2321	.0571	5
6	.0000	.0000	.0000	.0001	.0007	.0041	.0156	.0467	.1176	.2621	.5314	.7351	.9415	6

TABULATED VALUES ARE P(X)

N = 7

P

X	0.01	0.05	0.1	0.2	0.3	0.4	0.5	0.6	0.7	0.8	0.9	0.95	0.99	X
0	.9321	.6983	.4783	.2097	.0824	.0280	.0078	.0016	.0002	.0000	.0000	.0000	.0000	0
1	.0659	.2573	.3720	.3670	.2471	.1306	.0547	.0172	.0036	.0004	.0000	.0000	.0000	1
2	.0020	.0406	.1240	.2753	.3177	.2613	.1641	.0774	.0250	.0043	.0002	.0000	.0000	2
3	.0000	.0036	.0230	.1147	.2269	.2903	.2734	.1935	.0972	.0287	.0026	.0002	.0000	3
4	.0000	.0002	.0026	.0287	.0972	.1935	.2734	.2903	.2269	.1147	.0230	.0036	.0000	4
5	.0000	.0000	.0002	.0043	.0250	.0774	.1641	.2613	.3177	.2753	.1240	.0406	.0020	5
6	.0000	.0000	.0000	.0004	.0036	.0172	.0547	.1306	.2471	.3670	.3720	.2573	.0659	6
7	.0000	.0000	.0000	.0000	.0002	.0016	.0078	.0280	.0824	.2097	.4783	.6983	.9321	7

TABULATED VALUES ARE P(X)

N = 8

P

X	0.01	0.05	0.1	0.2	0.3	0.4	0.5	0.6	0.7	0.8	0.9	0.95	0.99	X
0	.9227	.6634	.4305	.1678	.0576	.0168	.0039	.0007	.0001	.0000	.0000	.0000	.0000	0
1	.0746	.2793	.3826	.3355	.1977	.0896	.0313	.0079	.0012	.0001	.0000	.0000	.0000	1
2	.0026	.0515	.1488	.2936	.2965	.2090	.1094	.0413	.0100	.0011	.0000	.0000	.0000	2
3	.0001	.0054	.0331	.1468	.2541	.2787	.2187	.1239	.0467	.0092	.0004	.0000	.0000	3
4	.0000	.0004	.0046	.0459	.1361	.2322	.2734	.2322	.1361	.0459	.0046	.0004	.0000	4
5	.0000	.0000	.0004	.0092	.0467	.1239	.2167	.2787	.2541	.1468	.0331	.0054	.0001	5
6	.0000	.0000	.0000	.0011	.0100	.0413	.1094	.2090	.2965	.2936	.1488	.0515	.0026	6
7	.0000	.0000	.0000	.0001	.0012	.0079	.0313	.0896	.1977	.3355	.3826	.2793	.0746	7
8	.0000	.0000	.0000	.0000	.0001	.0007	.0039	.0168	.0576	.1678	.4305	.6634	.9227	8

TABULATED VALUES ARE P(X)

N=9

P

X	0.01	0.05	0.1	0.2	0.3	0.4	0.5	0.6	0.7	0.8	0.9	0.95	0.99	X
0	.9135	.6302	.3874	.1342	.0404	.0101	.0020	.0003	.0000	.0000	.0000	.0000	.0000	0
1	.0330	.2985	.3874	.3020	.1556	.0605	.0176	.0035	.0004	.0000	.0000	.0000	.0000	1
2	.0034	.0629	.1722	.3020	.2668	.1612	.0703	.0212	.0039	.0003	.0000	.0000	.0000	2
3	.0001	.0077	.0446	.1762	.2668	.2508	.1641	.0743	.0210	.0028	.0001	.0000	.0000	3
4	.0000	.0006	.0074	.0661	.1715	.2508	.2461	.1672	.0735	.0165	.0008	.0000	.0000	4
5	.0000	.0000	.0008	.0165	.0735	.1672	.2461	.2508	.1715	.0661	.0074	.0006	.0000	5
6	.0000	.0000	.0001	.0028	.0210	.0743	.1641	.2508	.2668	.1762	.0446	.0077	.0001	6
7	.0000	.0000	.0000	.0003	.0039	.0212	.0703	.1612	.2668	.3020	.1722	.0629	.0034	7
8	.0000	.0000	.0000	.0000	.0004	.0035	.0176	.0605	.1556	.3020	.3874	.2985	.0830	8
9	.0000	.0000	.0000	.0000	.0000	.0003	.0020	.0101	.0404	.1342	.3874	.6302	.9135	9

TABULATED VALUES ARE P(X)

N=10

P

X	0.01	0.05	0.1	0.2	0.3	0.4	0.5	0.6	0.7	0.8	0.9	0.95	0.99	X
0	.9044	.5987	.3487	.1074	.0282	.0060	.0010	.0001	.0000	.0000	.0000	.0000	.0000	0
1	.0914	.3151	.3874	.2684	.1211	.0403	.0098	.0016	.0001	.0000	.0000	.0000	.0000	1
2	.0042	.0746	.1937	.3020	.2335	.1209	.0439	.0106	.0014	.0001	.0000	.0000	.0000	2
3	.0001	.0105	.0574	.2013	.2668	.2150	.1172	.0425	.0090	.0008	.0000	.0000	.0000	3
4	.0000	.0010	.0112	.0881	.2001	.2508	.2051	.1115	.0368	.0055	.0001	.0000	.0000	4
5	.0000	.0001	.0015	.0264	.1029	.2007	.2461	.2007	.1029	.0264	.0015	.0001	.0000	5
6	.0000	.0000	.0001	.0055	.0368	.1115	.2051	.2508	.2001	.0881	.0112	.0010	.0000	6
7	.0000	.0000	.0000	.0008	.0090	.0425	.1172	.2150	.2668	.2013	.0574	.0105	.0001	7
8	.0000	.0000	.0000	.0001	.0014	.0106	.0439	.1209	.2335	.3020	.1937	.0746	.0042	8
9	.0000	.0000	.0000	.0000	.0001	.0016	.0098	.0403	.1211	.2684	.3874	.3151	.0914	9
10	.0000	.0000	.0000	.0000	.0000	.0001	.0010	.0060	.0282	.1074	.3487	.5987	.9044	10

TABULATED VALUES ARE P(X)

N=15

P

X	0.01	0.05	0.1	0.2	0.3	0.4	0.5	0.6	0.7	0.8	0.9	0.95	0.99	X
0	.8601	.4633	.2059	.0352	.0047	.0005	.0000	.0000	.0000	.0000	.0000	.0000	.0000	0
1	.1303	.3658	.3432	.1319	.0305	.0047	.0005	.0000	.0000	.0000	.0000	.0000	.0000	1
2	.0092	.1348	.2669	.2309	.0516	.0219	.0032	.0003	.0000	.0000	.0000	.0000	.0000	2
3	.0004	.0307	.1285	.2501	.1700	.0634	.0139	.0016	.0001	.0000	.0000	.0000	.0000	3
4	.0000	.0049	.0423	.1876	.2186	.1268	.0417	.0074	.0006	.0000	.0000	.0000	.0000	4
5	.0000	.0006	.0105	.1032	.2061	.1859	.0916	.0245	.0030	.0001	.0000	.0000	.0000	5
6	.0000	.0000	.0019	.0430	.1472	.2066	.1527	.0612	.0116	.0007	.0000	.0000	.0000	6
7	.0000	.0000	.0003	.0138	.0811	.1771	.1964	.1181	.0348	.0035	.0000	.0000	.0000	7
8	.0000	.0000	.0000	.0035	.0348	.1181	.1964	.1771	.0811	.0138	.0003	.0000	.0000	8
9	.0000	.0000	.0000	.0007	.0116	.0612	.1527	.2066	.1472	.0430	.0019	.0000	.0000	9
10	.0000	.0000	.0000	.0001	.0030	.0245	.0916	.1859	.2061	.1032	.0105	.0006	.0000	10
11	.0000	.0000	.0000	.0000	.0006	.0074	.0417	.1268	.2186	.1876	.0428	.0049	.0000	11
12	.0000	.0000	.0000	.0000	.0001	.0016	.0139	.0634	.1700	.2501	.1285	.0307	.0004	12
13	.0000	.0000	.0000	.0000	.0000	.0003	.0032	.0219	.0916	.2309	.2669	.1348	.0092	13
14	.0000	.0000	.0000	.0000	.0000	.0000	.0005	.0047	.0305	.1319	.3432	.3658	.1303	14
15	.0000	.0000	.0000	.0000	.0000	.0000	.0000	.0005	.0047	.0352	.2059	.4633	.8601	15

TABLE 1 *Continued*   TABULATED VALUES ARE P(X)

N=20

P

X	0.01	0.05	0.1	0.2	0.3	0.4	0.5	0.6	0.7	0.8	0.9	0.95	0.99	X
0	.8179	.3585	.1216	.0115	.0008	.0000	.0000	.0000	.0000	.0000	.0000	.0000	.0000	0
1	.1652	.3774	.2702	.0576	.0068	.0005	.0000	.0000	.0000	.0000	.0000	.0000	.0000	1
2	.0159	.1887	.2852	.1369	.0278	.0031	.0002	.0000	.0000	.0000	.0000	.0000	.0000	2
3	.0010	.0596	.1901	.2054	.0716	.0123	.0011	.0000	.0000	.0000	.0000	.0000	.0000	3
4	.0000	.0133	.0898	.2182	.1304	.0350	.0046	.0003	.0000	.0000	.0000	.0000	.0000	4
5	.0000	.0022	.0319	.1746	.1789	.0746	.0148	.0013	.0000	.0000	.0000	.0000	.0000	5
6	.0000	.0003	.0089	.1091	.1916	.1244	.0370	.0049	.0002	.0000	.0000	.0000	.0000	6
7	.0000	.0000	.0020	.0545	.1643	.1659	.0739	.0146	.0010	.0000	.0000	.0000	.0000	7
8	.0000	.0000	.0004	.0222	.1144	.1797	.1201	.0355	.0039	.0001	.0000	.0000	.0000	8
9	.0000	.0000	.0001	.0074	.0654	.1597	.1602	.0710	.0120	.0005	.0000	.0000	.0000	9
10	.0000	.0000	.0000	.0020	.0308	.1171	.1762	.1171	.0308	.0020	.0000	.0000	.0000	10
11	.0000	.0000	.0000	.0005	.0120	.0710	.1602	.1597	.0654	.0074	.0001	.0000	.0000	11
12	.0000	.0000	.0000	.0001	.0039	.0355	.1201	.1797	.1144	.0222	.0004	.0000	.0000	12
13	.0000	.0000	.0000	.0000	.0010	.0146	.0739	.1659	.1643	.0545	.0020	.0000	.0000	13
14	.0000	.0000	.0000	.0000	.0002	.0049	.0370	.1244	.1916	.1091	.0089	.0003	.0000	14
15	.0000	.0000	.0000	.0000	.0000	.0013	.0148	.0746	.1789	.1746	.0319	.0022	.0000	15
16	.0000	.0000	.0000	.0000	.0000	.0003	.0046	.0350	.1304	.2182	.0898	.0133	.0000	16
17	.0000	.0000	.0000	.0000	.0000	.0000	.0011	.0123	.0716	.2054	.1901	.0596	.0010	17
18	.0000	.0000	.0000	.0000	.0000	.0000	.0002	.0031	.0278	.1369	.2852	.1887	.0159	18
19	.0000	.0000	.0000	.0000	.0000	.0000	.0000	.0005	.0068	.0576	.2702	.3774	.1652	19
20	.0000	.0000	.0000	.0000	.0000	.0000	.0000	.0000	.0008	.0115	.1216	.3585	.8179	20

TABULATED VALUES ARE P(X)

N=25

P

X	0.01	0.05	0.1	0.2	0.3	0.4	0.5	0.6	0.7	0.8	0.9	0.95	0.99	X
0	.7778	.2774	.0718	.0038	.0001	.0000	.0000	.0000	.0000	.0000	.0000	.0000	.0000	0
1	.1964	.3650	.1994	.0236	.0014	.0000	.0000	.0000	.0000	.0000	.0000	.0000	.0000	1
2	.0233	.2305	.2659	.0708	.0074	.0004	.0000	.0000	.0000	.0000	.0000	.0000	.0000	2
3	.0018	.0930	.2265	.1358	.0243	.0019	.0001	.0000	.0000	.0000	.0000	.0000	.0000	3
4	.0001	.0269	.1384	.1867	.0572	.0071	.0004	.0000	.0000	.0000	.0000	.0000	.0000	4
5	.0000	.0060	.0646	.1960	.1030	.0199	.0016	.0000	.0000	.0000	.0000	.0000	.0000	5
6	.0000	.0010	.0239	.1633	.1472	.0442	.0053	.0002	.0000	.0000	.0000	.0000	.0000	6
7	.0000	.0001	.0072	.1108	.1712	.0800	.0143	.0009	.0000	.0000	.0000	.0000	.0000	7
8	.0000	.0000	.0018	.0623	.1651	.1200	.0322	.0031	.0001	.0000	.0000	.0000	.0000	8
9	.0000	.0000	.0004	.0294	.1336	.1511	.0609	.0088	.0004	.0000	.0000	.0000	.0000	9
10	.0000	.0000	.0001	.0118	.0916	.1612	.0974	.0212	.0013	.0000	.0000	.0000	.0000	10
11	.0000	.0000	.0000	.0040	.0536	.1465	.1328	.0434	.0042	.0001	.0000	.0000	.0000	11
12	.0000	.0000	.0000	.0012	.0268	.1140	.1550	.0760	.0115	.0003	.0000	.0000	.0000	12
13	.0000	.0000	.0000	.0003	.0115	.0760	.1550	.1140	.0268	.0012	.0000	.0000	.0000	13
14	.0000	.0000	.0000	.0001	.0042	.0434	.1328	.1465	.0536	.0040	.0000	.0000	.0000	14
15	.0000	.0000	.0000	.0000	.0013	.0212	.0974	.1612	.0916	.0118	.0001	.0000	.0000	15
16	.0000	.0000	.0000	.0000	.0034	.0088	.0609	.1511	.1336	.0294	.0004	.0000	.0000	16
17	.0000	.0000	.0000	.0000	.0001	.0031	.0322	.1200	.1651	.0623	.0018	.0000	.0000	17
18	.0000	.0000	.0000	.0000	.0000	.0009	.0143	.0800	.1712	.1108	.0072	.0001	.0000	18
19	.0000	.0000	.0000	.0000	.0000	.0002	.0053	.0442	.1472	.1633	.0239	.0010	.0000	19
20	.0000	.0000	.0000	.0000	.0000	.0000	.0016	.0199	.1030	.1960	.0646	.0060	.0000	20
21	.0000	.0000	.0000	.0000	.0000	.0000	.0004	.0071	.0572	.1867	.1384	.0269	.0001	21
22	.0000	.0000	.0000	.0000	.0000	.0000	.0001	.0019	.0243	.1358	.2265	.0930	.0018	22
23	.0000	.0000	.0000	.0000	.0000	.0000	.0000	.0004	.0074	.0708	.2659	.2305	.0233	23
24	.0000	.0000	.0000	.0000	.0000	.0000	.0000	.0000	.0014	.0236	.1994	.3650	.1964	24
25	.0000	.0000	.0000	.0000	.0000	.0000	.0000	.0000	.0001	.0038	.0718	.2774	.7778	25

TABLE 2   Cumulative Binomial Probabilities

N=5

P

x	0.01	0.05	0.1	0.2	0.3	0.4	0.5	0.6	0.7	0.8	0.9	0.95	0.99	x
0	.9510	.7738	.5905	.3277	.1681	.0778	.0313	.0102	.0024	.0003	.0000	.0000	.0000	0
1	.9990	.9774	.9185	.7373	.5282	.3370	.1875	.0870	.0308	.0067	.0005	.0000	.0000	1
2	1.0000	.9988	.9914	.9421	.8369	.6826	.5000	.3174	.1631	.0579	.0086	.0012	.0000	2
3	1.0000	1.0000	.9995	.9933	.9692	.9130	.8125	.6630	.4718	.2627	.0815	.0226	.0010	3
4	1.0000	1.0000	1.0000	.9997	.9976	.9898	.9687	.9222	.8319	.6723	.4095	.2262	.0490	4

N=6

P

x	0.01	0.05	0.1	0.2	0.3	0.4	0.5	0.6	0.7	0.8	0.9	0.95	0.99	x
0	.9415	.7351	.5314	.2621	.1176	.0467	.0156	.0041	.0007	.0001	.0000	.0000	.0000	0
1	.9985	.9672	.8357	.6554	.4202	.2333	.1094	.0410	.0109	.0016	.0001	.0000	.0000	1
2	1.0000	.9978	.9841	.9011	.7443	.5443	.3437	.1792	.0705	.0170	.0013	.0001	.0000	2
3	1.0000	.9999	.9987	.9830	.9295	.8208	.6562	.4557	.2557	.0989	.0158	.0022	.0000	3
4	1.0000	1.0000	.9999	.9984	.9891	.9590	.8906	.7667	.5798	.3446	.1143	.0328	.0015	4
5	1.0000	1.0000	1.0000	.9999	.9993	.9959	.9844	.9533	.8824	.7379	.4686	.2649	.0585	5

N=7

P

x	0.01	0.05	0.1	0.2	0.3	0.4	0.5	0.6	0.7	0.8	0.9	0.95	0.99	x
0	.9321	.6983	.4783	.2097	.0824	.0280	.0078	.0016	.0002	.0000	.0000	.0000	.0000	0
1	.9980	.9556	.8503	.5767	.3294	.1586	.0625	.0188	.0038	.0004	.0000	.0000	.0000	1
2	1.0000	.9962	.9743	.8520	.6471	.4199	.2266	.0963	.0288	.0047	.0002	.0000	.0000	2
3	1.0000	.9998	.9973	.9667	.8740	.7102	.5000	.2898	.1260	.0333	.0027	.0002	.0000	3
4	1.0000	1.0000	.9998	.9953	.9712	.9037	.7734	.5801	.3529	.1480	.0257	.0038	.0000	4
5	1.0000	1.0000	1.0000	.9996	.9962	.9812	.9375	.8414	.6706	.4233	.1497	.0444	.0020	5
6	1.0000	1.0000	1.0000	1.0000	.9998	.9984	.9922	.9720	.9176	.7903	.5217	.3017	.0679	6

N=8

P

x	0.01	0.05	0.1	0.2	0.3	0.4	0.5	0.6	0.7	0.8	0.9	0.95	0.99	x
0	.9227	.6634	.4305	.1678	.0576	.0168	.0039	.0007	.0001	.0000	.0000	.0000	.0000	0
1	.9973	.9428	.8131	.5033	.2553	.1064	.0352	.0085	.0013	.0001	.0000	.0000	.0000	1
2	.9999	.9942	.9619	.7969	.5518	.3154	.1445	.0498	.0113	.0012	.0000	.0000	.0000	2
3	1.0000	.9996	.9950	.9437	.8059	.5941	.3633	.1737	.0580	.0104	.0004	.0000	.0000	3
4	1.0000	1.0000	.9996	.9896	.9420	.8263	.6367	.4059	.1941	.0563	.0050	.0004	.0000	4
5	1.0000	1.0000	1.0000	.9988	.9887	.9502	.8555	.6346	.4482	.2031	.0381	.0058	.0001	5
6	1.0000	1.0000	1.0000	.9999	.9987	.9915	.9648	.8936	.7447	.4967	.1869	.0572	.0027	6
7	1.0000	1.0000	1.0000	1.0000	.9999	.9993	.9961	.9832	.9424	.8322	.5695	.3366	.0773	7

N=9

P

x	0.01	0.05	0.1	0.2	0.3	0.4	0.5	0.6	0.7	0.8	0.9	0.95	0.99	x
0	.9135	.6302	.3874	.1342	.0404	.0101	.0020	.0003	.0000	.0000	.0000	.0000	.0000	0
1	.9966	.9288	.7748	.4362	.1960	.0705	.0195	.0038	.0004	.0000	.0000	.0000	.0000	1
2	.9999	.9916	.9470	.7382	.4628	.2318	.0898	.0250	.0043	.0003	.0000	.0000	.0000	2
3	1.0000	.9994	.9917	.9144	.7297	.4826	.2539	.0994	.0253	.0031	.0001	.0000	.0000	3
4	1.0000	1.0000	.9991	.9804	.9012	.7334	.5000	.2666	.0988	.0196	.0009	.0000	.0000	4
5	1.0000	1.0000	.9999	.9969	.9747	.9006	.7461	.5174	.2703	.0856	.0083	.0006	.0000	5
6	1.0000	1.0000	1.0000	.9997	.9957	.9750	.9102	.7682	.5372	.2618	.0530	.0084	.0001	6
7	1.0000	1.0000	1.0000	1.0000	.9996	.9962	.9805	.9295	.8040	.5638	.2252	.0712	.0034	7
8	1.0000	1.0000	1.0000	1.0000	1.0000	.9997	.9980	.9899	.9596	.8658	.6126	.3698	.0865	8

TABLE 2 *Continued*

N=10

P

x	0.01	0.05	0.1	0.2	0.3	0.4	0.5	0.6	0.7	0.8	0.9	0.95	0.99	x
0	.9044	.5987	.3487	.1074	.0282	.0060	.0010	.0001	.0000	.0000	.0000	.0000	.0000	0
1	.9957	.9139	.7361	.3758	.1493	.0464	.0107	.0017	.0001	.0000	.0000	.0000	.0000	1
2	.9999	.9885	.9298	.6778	.3828	.1673	.0547	.0123	.0016	.0001	.0000	.0000	.0000	2
3	1.0000	.9990	.9872	.8791	.6496	.3823	.1719	.0548	.0106	.0009	.0000	.0000	.0000	3
4	1.0000	.9999	.9984	.9672	.8497	.6331	.3770	.1662	.0473	.0064	.0001	.0000	.0000	4
5	1.0000	1.0000	.9999	.9936	.9527	.8338	.6230	.3669	.1503	.0328	.0016	.0001	.0000	5
6	1.0000	1.0000	1.0000	.9991	.9894	.9452	.8281	.6177	.3504	.1209	.0128	.0010	.0000	6
7	1.0000	1.0000	1.0000	.9999	.9984	.9877	.9453	.8327	.6172	.3222	.0702	.0115	.0001	7
8	1.0000	1.0000	1.0000	1.0000	.9999	.9983	.9893	.9536	.8507	.6242	.2639	.0861	.0043	8
9	1.0000	1.0000	1.0000	1.0000	1.0000	.9999	.9990	.9940	.9718	.8926	.6513	.4013	.0956	9

N=15

P

x	0.01	0.05	0.1	0.2	0.3	0.4	0.5	0.6	0.7	0.8	0.9	0.95	0.99	x
0	.8601	.4633	.2059	.0352	.0047	.0005	.0000	.0000	.0000	.0000	.0000	.0000	.0000	0
1	.9904	.8290	.5490	.1671	.0353	.0052	.0005	.0000	.0000	.0000	.0000	.0000	.0000	1
2	.9996	.9638	.8159	.3980	.1268	.0271	.0037	.0003	.0000	.0000	.0000	.0000	.0000	2
3	1.0000	.9945	.9444	.6482	.2969	.0905	.0176	.0019	.0001	.0000	.0000	.0000	.0000	3
4	1.0000	.9994	.9873	.8358	.5155	.2173	.0592	.0093	.0007	.0000	.0000	.0000	.0000	4
5	1.0000	.9999	.9978	.9389	.7216	.4032	.1509	.0338	.0037	.0001	.0000	.0000	.0000	5
6	1.0000	1.0000	.9997	.9819	.8689	.6098	.3036	.0950	.0152	.0008	.0000	.0000	.0000	6
7	1.0000	1.0000	1.0000	.9958	.9500	.7869	.5000	.2131	.0500	.0042	.0000	.0000	.0000	7
8	1.0000	1.0000	1.0000	.9992	.9848	.9050	.6964	.3902	.1311	.0181	.0003	.0000	.0000	8
9	1.0000	1.0000	1.0000	.9999	.9963	.9662	.8491	.5568	.2784	.0611	.0022	.0001	.0000	9
10	1.0000	1.0000	1.0000	1.0000	.9993	.9907	.9408	.7827	.4845	.1642	.0127	.0006	.0000	10
11	1.0000	1.0000	1.0000	1.0000	.9999	.9981	.9824	.9095	.7031	.3518	.0556	.0055	.0000	11
12	1.0000	1.0000	1.0000	1.0000	1.0000	.9997	.9963	.9729	.8732	.6020	.1841	.0362	.0004	12
13	1.0000	1.0000	1.0000	1.0000	1.0000	1.0000	.9995	.9948	.9647	.8329	.4510	.1710	.0096	13
14	1.0000	1.0000	1.0000	1.0000	1.0000	1.0000	1.0000	.9995	.9953	.9648	.7941	.5367	.1399	14

N=20

P

x	0.01	0.05	0.1	0.2	0.3	0.4	0.5	0.6	0.7	0.8	0.9	0.95	0.99	x
0	.8179	.3585	.1216	.0115	.0008	.0000	.0000	.0000	.0000	.0000	.0000	.0000	.0000	0
1	.9831	.7358	.3917	.0692	.0076	.0005	.0000	.0000	.0000	.0000	.0000	.0000	.0000	1
2	.9990	.9245	.6769	.2061	.0355	.0036	.0002	.0000	.0000	.0000	.0000	.0000	.0000	2
3	1.0000	.9841	.8670	.4114	.1071	.0160	.0013	.0000	.0000	.0000	.0000	.0000	.0000	3
4	1.0000	.9974	.9568	.6296	.2375	.0510	.0059	.0003	.0000	.0000	.0000	.0000	.0000	4
5	1.0000	.9997	.9887	.8042	.4164	.1256	.0207	.0016	.0000	.0000	.0000	.0000	.0000	5
6	1.0000	1.0000	.9976	.9133	.6080	.2500	.0577	.0065	.0003	.0000	.0000	.0000	.0000	6
7	1.0000	1.0000	.9996	.9679	.7723	.4159	.1316	.0210	.0013	.0000	.0000	.0000	.0000	7
8	1.0000	1.0000	.9999	.9900	.8867	.5956	.2517	.0565	.0051	.0001	.0000	.0000	.0000	8
9	1.0000	1.0000	1.0000	.9974	.9520	.7553	.4119	.1275	.0171	.0006	.0000	.0000	.0000	9
10	1.0000	1.0000	1.0000	.9994	.9829	.8725	.5881	.2447	.0480	.0026	.0000	.0000	.0000	10
11	1.0000	1.0000	1.0000	.9999	.9949	.9435	.7483	.4044	.1133	.0100	.0001	.0000	.0000	11
12	1.0000	1.0000	1.0000	1.0000	.9987	.9790	.8684	.5841	.2277	.0321	.0004	.0000	.0000	12
13	1.0000	1.0000	1.0000	1.0000	.9997	.9935	.9423	.7500	.3920	.0867	.0024	.0000	.0000	13
14	1.0000	1.0000	1.0000	1.0000	1.0000	.9984	.9793	.8744	.5836	.1958	.0113	.0003	.0000	14
15	1.0000	1.0000	1.0000	1.0000	1.0000	.9997	.9941	.9490	.7625	.3704	.0432	.0026	.0000	15
16	1.0000	1.0000	1.0000	1.0000	1.0000	1.0000	.9987	.9840	.8929	.5886	.1330	.0159	.0000	16
17	1.0000	1.0000	1.0000	1.0000	1.0000	1.0000	.9998	.9964	.9645	.7939	.3231	.0755	.0010	17
18	1.0000	1.0000	1.0000	1.0000	1.0000	1.0000	1.0000	.9995	.9924	.9308	.6083	.2642	.0169	18
19	1.0000	1.0000	1.0000	1.0000	1.0000	1.0000	1.0000	1.0000	.9992	.9885	.8784	.6415	.1821	19

N = 25

X	0.01	0.05	0.1	0.2	0.3	0.4	0.5	0.6	0.7	0.8	0.9	0.95	0.99	X
0	.7778	.2774	.0718	.0038	.0001	.0000	.0000	.0000	.0000	.0000	.0000	.0000	.0000	0
1	.9742	.6424	.2712	.0274	.0016	.0001	.0000	.0000	.0000	.0000	.0000	.0000	.0000	1
2	.9980	.8729	.5371	.0982	.0090	.0004	.0000	.0000	.0000	.0000	.0000	.0000	.0000	2
3	.9999	.9659	.7636	.2340	.0332	.0024	.0001	.0000	.0000	.0000	.0000	.0000	.0000	3
4	1.0000	.9928	.9020	.4207	.0905	.0095	.0005	.0000	.0000	.0000	.0000	.0000	.0000	4
5	1.0000	.9988	.9666	.6167	.1935	.0294	.0020	.0001	.0000	.0000	.0000	.0000	.0000	5
6	1.0000	.9998	.9905	.7800	.3407	.0736	.0073	.0003	.0000	.0000	.0000	.0000	.0000	6
7	1.0000	1.0000	.9977	.8909	.5118	.1536	.0216	.0012	.0000	.0000	.0000	.0000	.0000	7
8	1.0000	1.0000	.9995	.9532	.6769	.2735	.0539	.0043	.0001	.0000	.0000	.0000	.0000	8
9	1.0000	1.0000	.9999	.9827	.8106	.4246	.1148	.0132	.0005	.0000	.0000	.0000	.0000	9
10	1.0000	1.0000	1.0000	.9944	.9022	.5858	.2122	.0344	.0018	.0000	.0000	.0000	.0000	10
11	1.0000	1.0000	1.0000	.9985	.9558	.7323	.3450	.0778	.0060	.0001	.0000	.0000	.0000	11
12	1.0000	1.0000	1.0000	.9996	.9825	.8462	.5000	.1538	.0175	.0004	.0000	.0000	.0000	12
13	1.0000	1.0000	1.0000	.9999	.9940	.9222	.6550	.2677	.0442	.0015	.0000	.0000	.0000	13
14	1.0000	1.0000	1.0000	1.0000	.9982	.9656	.7878	.4142	.0978	.0056	.0000	.0000	.0000	14
15	1.0000	1.0000	1.0000	1.0000	.9995	.9868	.8852	.5754	.1894	.0173	.0001	.0000	.0000	15
16	1.0000	1.0000	1.0000	1.0000	.9999	.9957	.9461	.7265	.3231	.0468	.0005	.0000	.0000	16
17	1.0000	1.0000	1.0000	1.0000	1.0000	.9988	.9784	.8464	.4882	.1091	.0023	.0000	.0000	17
18	1.0000	1.0000	1.0000	1.0000	1.0000	.9997	.9927	.9264	.6593	.2200	.0095	.0002	.0000	18
19	1.0000	1.0000	1.0000	1.0000	1.0000	.9999	.9980	.9706	.8065	.3333	.0334	.0012	.0000	19
20	1.0000	1.0000	1.0000	1.0000	1.0000	1.0000	.9995	.9905	.9095	.5793	.0980	.0072	.0000	20
21	1.0000	1.0000	1.0000	1.0000	1.0000	1.0000	.9999	.9976	.9668	.7660	.2364	.0341	.0001	21
22	1.0000	1.0000	1.0000	1.0000	1.0000	1.0000	1.0000	.9996	.9910	.9018	.4629	.1271	.0020	22
23	1.0000	1.0000	1.0000	1.0000	1.0000	1.0000	1.0000	.9999	.9984	.9726	.7288	.3576	.0258	23
24	1.0000	1.0000	1.0000	1.0000	1.0000	1.0000	1.0000	1.0000	.9999	.9962	.9282	.7226	.2222	24

TABLE 3
Normal Curve Areas

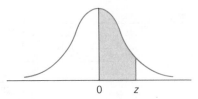

z	.00	.01	.02	.03	.04	.05	.06	.07	.08	.09
0.0	.0000	.0040	.0080	.0120	.0160	.0199	.0239	.0279	.0319	.0359
0.1	.0398	.0438	.0478	.0517	.0557	.0596	.0636	.0675	.0714	.0753
0.2	.0793	.0832	.0871	.0910	.0948	.0987	.1026	.1064	.1103	.1141
0.3	.1179	.1217	.1255	.1293	.1331	.1368	.1406	.1443	.1480	.1517
0.4	.1554	.1591	.1628	.1664	.1700	.1736	.1772	.1808	.1844	.1879
0.5	.1915	.1950	.1985	.2019	.2054	.2088	.2123	.2157	.2190	.2224
0.6	.2257	.2291	.2324	.2357	.2389	.2422	.2454	.2486	.2517	.2549
0.7	.2580	.2611	.2642	.2673	.2704	.2734	.2764	.2794	.2823	.2852
0.8	.2881	.2910	.2939	.2967	.2995	.3023	.3051	.3078	.3106	.3133
0.9	.3159	.3186	.3212	.3238	.3264	.3289	.3315	.3340	.3365	.3389
1.0	.3413	.3438	.3461	.3485	.3508	.3531	.3554	.3577	.3599	.3621
1.1	.3643	.3665	.3686	.3708	.3729	.3749	.3770	.3790	.3810	.3830
1.2	.3849	.3869	.3888	.3907	.3925	.3944	.3962	.3980	.3997	.4015
1.3	.4032	.4049	.4066	.4082	.4099	.4115	.4131	.4147	.4162	.4177
1.4	.4192	.4207	.4222	.4236	.4251	.4265	.4279	.4292	.4306	.4319
1.5	.4332	.4345	.4357	.4370	.4382	.4394	.4406	.4418	.4429	.4441
1.6	.4452	.4463	.4474	.4484	.4495	.4505	.4515	.4525	.4535	.4545
1.7	.4554	.4564	.4573	.4582	.4591	.4599	.4608	.4616	.4625	.4633
1.8	.4641	.4649	.4656	.4664	.4671	.4678	.4686	.4693	.4699	.4706
1.9	.4713	.4719	.4726	.4732	.4738	.4744	.4750	.4756	.4761	.4767
2.0	.4772	.4778	.4783	.4788	.4793	.4798	.4803	.4808	.4812	.4817
2.1	.4821	.4826	.4830	.4834	.4838	.4842	.4846	.4850	.4854	.4857
2.2	.4861	.4864	.4868	.4871	.4875	.4878	.4881	.4884	.4887	.4890
2.3	.4893	.4896	.4898	.4901	.4904	.4906	.4909	.4911	.4913	.4916
2.4	.4918	.4920	.4922	.4925	.4927	.4929	.4931	.4932	.4934	.4936
2.5	.4938	.4940	.4941	.4943	.4945	.4946	.4948	.4949	.4951	.4952
2.6	.4953	.4955	.4956	.4957	.4959	.4960	.4961	.4962	.4963	.4964
2.7	.4965	.4966	.4967	.4968	.4969	.4970	.4971	.4972	.4973	.4974
2.8	.4974	.4975	.4976	.4977	.4977	.4978	.4979	.4979	.4980	.4981
2.9	.4981	.4982	.4982	.4983	.4984	.4984	.4985	.4985	.4986	.4986
3.0	.4987	.4987	.4987	.4988	.4988	.4989	.4989	.4989	.4990	.4990

Source: Abridged from Table I of A. Hald, *Statistical Tables and Formulas* (New York: John Wiley & Sons, Inc.), 1952. Reproduced by permission of A. Hald and the publisher.

TABLE 4
Critical Values for
Student's t

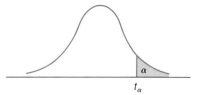

DEGREES OF FREEDOM	$t_{.100}$	$t_{.050}$	$t_{.025}$	$t_{.010}$	$t_{.005}$
1	3.078	6.314	12.706	31.821	63.657
2	1.886	2.920	4.303	6.965	9.925
3	1.638	2.353	3.182	4.541	5.841
4	1.533	2.132	2.776	3.747	4.604
5	1.476	2.015	2.571	3.365	4.032
6	1.440	1.943	2.447	3.143	3.707
7	1.415	1.895	2.365	2.998	3.499
8	1.397	1.860	2.306	2.896	3.355
9	1.383	1.833	2.262	2.821	3.250
10	1.372	1.812	2.228	2.764	3.169
11	1.363	1.796	2.201	2.718	3.106
12	1.356	1.782	2.179	2.681	3.055
13	1.350	1.771	2.160	2.650	3.012
14	1.345	1.761	2.145	2.624	2.977
15	1.341	1.753	2.131	2.602	2.947
16	1.337	1.746	2.120	2.583	2.921
17	1.333	1.740	2.110	2.567	2.898
18	1.330	1.734	2.101	2.552	2.878
19	1.328	1.729	2.093	2.539	2.861
20	1.325	1.725	2.086	2.528	2.845
21	1.323	1.721	2.080	2.518	2.831
22	1.321	1.717	2.074	2.508	2.819
23	1.319	1.714	2.069	2.500	2.807
24	1.318	1.711	2.064	2.492	2.797
25	1.316	1.708	2.060	2.485	2.787
26	1.315	1.706	2.056	2.479	2.779
27	1.314	1.703	2.052	2.473	2.771
28	1.313	1.701	2.048	2.467	2.763
29	1.311	1.699	2.045	2.462	2.756
∞	1.282	1.645	1.960	2.326	2.576

Source: From M. Merrington, "Table of Percentage Points of the t-Distribution," *Biometrika,* 1941, *32,* 300. Reproduced by permission of the *Biometrika* Trustees.

TABLE 5 Critical Values for the F Statistic: $F_{.10}$

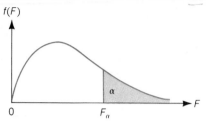

ν_1	NUMERATOR DEGREES OF FREEDOM								
ν_2	1	2	3	4	5	6	7	8	9
1	39.86	49.50	53.59	55.83	57.24	58.20	58.91	59.44	59.86
2	8.53	9.00	9.16	9.24	9.29	9.33	9.35	9.37	9.38
3	5.54	5.46	5.39	5.34	5.31	5.28	5.27	5.25	5.24
4	4.54	4.32	4.19	4.11	4.05	4.01	3.98	3.95	3.94
5	4.06	3.78	3.62	3.52	3.45	3.40	3.37	3.34	3.32
6	3.78	3.46	3.29	3.18	3.11	3.05	3.01	2.98	2.96
7	3.59	3.26	3.07	2.96	2.88	2.83	2.78	2.75	2.72
8	3.46	3.11	2.92	2.81	2.73	2.67	2.62	2.59	2.56
9	3.36	3.01	2.81	2.69	2.61	2.55	2.51	2.47	2.44
10	3.29	2.92	2.73	2.61	2.52	2.46	2.41	2.38	2.35
11	3.23	2.86	2.66	2.54	2.45	2.39	2.34	2.30	2.27
12	3.18	2.81	2.61	2.48	2.39	2.33	2.28	2.24	2.21
13	3.14	2.76	2.56	2.43	2.35	2.28	2.23	2.20	2.16
14	3.10	2.73	2.52	2.39	2.31	2.24	2.19	2.15	2.12
15	3.07	2.70	2.49	2.36	2.27	2.21	2.16	2.12	2.09
16	3.05	2.67	2.46	2.33	2.24	2.18	2.13	2.09	2.06
17	3.03	2.64	2.44	2.31	2.22	2.15	2.10	2.06	2.03
18	3.01	2.62	2.42	2.29	2.20	2.13	2.08	2.04	2.00
19	2.99	2.61	2.40	2.27	2.18	2.11	2.06	2.02	1.98
20	2.97	2.59	2.38	2.25	2.16	2.09	2.04	2.00	1.96
21	2.96	2.57	2.36	2.23	2.14	2.08	2.02	1.98	1.95
22	2.95	2.56	2.35	2.22	2.13	2.06	2.01	1.97	1.93
23	2.94	2.55	2.34	2.21	2.11	2.05	1.99	1.95	1.92
24	2.93	2.54	2.33	2.19	2.10	2.04	1.98	1.94	1.91
25	2.92	2.53	2.32	2.18	2.09	2.02	1.97	1.93	1.89
26	2.91	2.52	2.31	2.17	2.08	2.01	1.96	1.92	1.88
27	2.90	2.51	2.30	2.17	2.07	2.00	1.95	1.91	1.87
28	2.89	2.50	2.29	2.16	2.06	2.00	1.94	1.90	1.87
29	2.89	2.50	2.28	2.15	2.06	1.99	1.93	1.89	1.86
30	2.88	2.49	2.28	2.14	2.05	1.98	1.93	1.88	1.85
40	2.84	2.44	2.23	2.09	2.00	1.93	1.87	1.83	1.79
60	2.79	2.39	2.18	2.04	1.95	1.87	1.82	1.77	1.74
120	2.75	2.35	2.13	1.99	1.90	1.82	1.77	1.72	1.68
∞	2.71	2.30	2.08	1.94	1.85	1.77	1.72	1.67	1.63

DENOMINATOR DEGREES OF FREEDOM

| v_1 | NUMERATOR DEGREES OF FREEDOM | | | | | | | | | |
v_2	10	12	15	20	24	30	40	60	120	∞
1	60.19	60.71	61.22	61.74	62.00	62.26	62.53	62.79	63.06	63.33
2	9.39	9.41	9.42	9.44	9.45	9.46	9.47	9.47	9.48	9.49
3	5.23	5.22	5.20	5.18	5.18	5.17	5.16	5.15	5.14	5.13
4	3.92	3.90	3.87	3.84	3.83	3.82	3.80	3.79	3.78	3.76
5	3.30	3.27	3.24	3.21	3.19	3.17	3.16	3.14	3.12	3.10
6	2.94	2.90	2.87	2.84	2.82	2.80	2.78	2.76	2.74	2.72
7	2.70	2.67	2.63	2.59	2.58	2.56	2.54	2.51	2.49	2.47
8	2.54	2.50	2.46	2.42	2.40	2.38	2.36	2.34	2.32	2.29
9	2.42	2.38	2.34	2.30	2.28	2.25	2.23	2.21	2.18	2.16
10	2.32	2.28	2.24	2.20	2.18	2.16	2.13	2.11	2.08	2.06
11	2.25	2.21	2.17	2.12	2.10	2.08	2.05	2.03	2.00	1.97
12	2.19	2.15	2.10	2.06	2.04	2.01	1.99	1.96	1.93	1.90
13	2.14	2.10	2.05	2.01	1.98	1.96	1.93	1.90	1.88	1.85
14	2.10	2.05	2.01	1.96	1.94	1.91	1.89	1.86	1.83	1.80
15	2.06	2.02	1.97	1.92	1.90	1.87	1.85	1.82	1.79	1.76
16	2.03	1.99	1.94	1.89	1.87	1.84	1.81	1.78	1.75	1.72
17	2.00	1.96	1.91	1.86	1.84	1.81	1.78	1.75	1.72	1.69
18	1.98	1.93	1.89	1.84	1.81	1.78	1.75	1.72	1.69	1.66
19	1.96	1.91	1.86	1.81	1.79	1.76	1.73	1.70	1.67	1.63
20	1.94	1.89	1.84	1.79	1.77	1.74	1.71	1.68	1.64	1.61
21	1.92	1.87	1.83	1.78	1.75	1.72	1.69	1.66	1.62	1.59
22	1.90	1.86	1.81	1.76	1.73	1.70	1.67	1.64	1.60	1.57
23	1.89	1.84	1.80	1.74	1.72	1.69	1.66	1.62	1.59	1.55
24	1.88	1.83	1.78	1.73	1.70	1.67	1.64	1.61	1.57	1.53
25	1.87	1.82	1.77	1.72	1.69	1.66	1.63	1.59	1.56	1.52
26	1.86	1.81	1.76	1.71	1.68	1.65	1.61	1.58	1.54	1.50
27	1.85	1.80	1.75	1.70	1.67	1.64	1.60	1.57	1.53	1.49
28	1.84	1.79	1.74	1.69	1.66	1.63	1.59	1.56	1.52	1.48
29	1.83	1.78	1.73	1.68	1.65	1.62	1.58	1.55	1.51	1.47
30	1.82	1.77	1.72	1.67	1.64	1.61	1.57	1.54	1.50	1.46
40	1.76	1.71	1.66	1.61	1.57	1.54	1.51	1.47	1.42	1.38
60	1.71	1.66	1.60	1.54	1.51	1.48	1.44	1.40	1.35	1.29
120	1.65	1.60	1.55	1.48	1.45	1.41	1.37	1.32	1.26	1.19
∞	1.60	1.55	1.49	1.42	1.38	1.34	1.30	1.24	1.17	1.00

DENOMINATOR DEGREES OF FREEDOM

TABLE 6   Critical Values for the F Statistic: $F_{.05}$

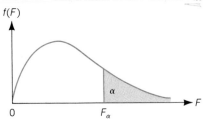

$f(F)$

α

F

0   F_α

ν_1	NUMERATOR DEGREES OF FREEDOM								
ν_2	1	2	3	4	5	6	7	8	9
1	161.4	199.5	215.7	224.6	230.2	234.0	236.8	238.9	240.5
2	18.51	19.00	19.16	19.25	19.30	19.33	19.35	19.37	19.38
3	10.13	9.55	9.28	9.12	9.01	8.94	8.89	8.85	8.81
4	7.71	6.94	6.59	6.39	6.26	6.16	6.09	6.04	6.00
5	6.61	5.79	5.41	5.19	5.05	4.95	4.88	4.82	4.77
6	5.99	5.14	4.76	4.53	4.39	4.28	4.21	4.15	4.10
7	5.59	4.74	4.35	4.12	3.97	3.87	3.79	3.73	3.68
8	5.32	4.46	4.07	3.84	3.69	3.58	3.50	3.44	3.39
9	5.12	4.26	3.86	3.63	3.48	3.37	3.29	3.23	3.18
10	4.96	4.10	3.71	3.48	3.33	3.22	3.14	3.07	3.02
11	4.84	3.98	3.59	3.36	3.20	3.09	3.01	2.95	2.90
12	4.75	3.89	3.49	3.26	3.11	3.00	2.91	2.85	2.80
13	4.67	3.81	3.41	3.18	3.03	2.92	2.83	2.77	2.71
14	4.60	3.74	3.34	3.11	2.96	2.85	2.76	2.70	2.65
15	4.54	3.68	3.29	3.06	2.90	2.79	2.71	2.64	2.59
16	4.49	3.63	3.24	3.01	2.85	2.74	2.66	2.59	2.54
17	4.45	3.59	3.20	2.96	2.81	2.70	2.61	2.55	2.49
18	4.41	3.55	3.16	2.93	2.77	2.66	2.58	2.51	2.46
19	4.38	3.52	3.13	2.90	2.74	2.63	2.54	2.48	2.42
20	4.35	3.49	3.10	2.87	2.71	2.60	2.51	2.45	2.39
21	4.32	3.47	3.07	2.84	2.68	2.57	2.49	2.42	2.37
22	4.30	3.44	3.05	2.82	2.66	2.55	2.46	2.40	2.34
23	4.28	3.42	3.03	2.80	2.64	2.53	2.44	2.37	2.32
24	4.26	3.40	3.01	2.78	2.62	2.51	2.42	2.36	2.30
25	4.24	3.39	2.99	2.76	2.60	2.49	2.40	2.34	2.28
26	4.23	3.37	2.98	2.74	2.59	2.47	2.39	2.32	2.27
27	4.21	3.35	2.96	2.73	2.57	2.46	2.37	2.31	2.25
28	4.20	3.34	2.95	2.71	2.56	2.45	2.36	2.29	2.24
29	4.18	3.33	2.93	2.70	2.55	2.43	2.35	2.28	2.22
30	4.17	3.32	2.92	2.69	2.53	2.42	2.33	2.27	2.21
40	4.08	3.23	2.84	2.61	2.45	2.34	2.25	2.18	2.12
60	4.00	3.15	2.76	2.53	2.37	2.25	2.17	2.10	2.04
120	3.92	3.07	2.68	2.45	2.29	2.17	2.09	2.02	1.96
∞	3.84	3.00	2.60	2.37	2.21	2.10	2.01	1.94	1.88

DENOMINATOR DEGREES OF FREEDOM

Source: From M. Merrington and C. M. Thompson, "Tables of Percentage Points of the Inverted Beta (F)-Distribution," *Biometrika*, 1943, *33*, 73–88. Reproduced by permission of the *Biometrika* Trustees.

ν_2 \ ν_1	NUMERATOR DEGREES OF FREEDOM									
	10	12	15	20	24	30	40	60	120	∞
1	241.9	243.9	245.9	248.0	249.1	250.1	251.1	252.2	253.3	254.3
2	19.40	19.41	19.43	19.45	19.45	19.46	19.47	19.48	19.49	19.50
3	8.79	8.74	8.70	8.66	8.64	8.62	8.59	8.57	8.55	8.53
4	5.96	5.91	5.86	5.80	5.77	5.75	5.72	5.69	5.66	5.63
5	4.74	4.68	4.62	4.56	4.53	4.50	4.46	4.43	4.40	4.36
6	4.06	4.00	3.94	3.87	3.84	3.81	3.77	3.74	3.70	3.67
7	3.64	3.57	3.51	3.44	3.41	3.38	3.34	3.30	3.27	3.23
8	3.35	3.28	3.22	3.15	3.12	3.08	3.04	3.01	2.97	2.93
9	3.14	3.07	3.01	2.94	2.90	2.86	2.83	2.79	2.75	2.71
10	2.98	2.91	2.85	2.77	2.74	2.70	2.66	2.62	2.58	2.54
11	2.85	2.79	2.72	2.65	2.61	2.57	2.53	2.49	2.45	2.40
12	2.75	2.69	2.62	2.54	2.51	2.47	2.43	2.38	2.34	2.30
13	2.67	2.60	2.53	2.46	2.42	2.38	2.34	2.30	2.25	2.21
14	2.60	2.53	2.46	2.39	2.35	2.31	2.27	2.22	2.18	2.13
15	2.54	2.48	2.40	2.33	2.29	2.25	2.20	2.16	2.11	2.07
16	2.49	2.42	2.35	2.28	2.24	2.19	2.15	2.11	2.06	2.01
17	2.45	2.38	2.31	2.23	2.19	2.15	2.10	2.06	2.01	1.96
18	2.41	2.34	2.27	2.19	2.15	2.11	2.06	2.02	1.97	1.92
19	2.38	2.31	2.23	2.16	2.11	2.07	2.03	1.98	1.93	1.88
20	2.35	2.28	2.20	2.12	2.08	2.04	1.99	1.95	1.90	1.84
21	2.32	2.25	2.18	2.10	2.05	2.01	1.96	1.92	1.87	1.81
22	2.30	2.23	2.15	2.07	2.03	1.98	1.94	1.89	1.84	1.78
23	2.27	2.20	2.13	2.05	2.01	1.96	1.91	1.86	1.81	1.76
24	2.25	2.18	2.11	2.03	1.98	1.94	1.89	1.84	1.79	1.73
25	2.24	2.16	2.09	2.01	1.96	1.92	1.87	1.82	1.77	1.71
26	2.22	2.15	2.07	1.99	1.95	1.90	1.85	1.80	1.75	1.69
27	2.20	2.13	2.06	1.97	1.93	1.88	1.84	1.79	1.73	1.67
28	2.19	2.12	2.04	1.96	1.91	1.87	1.82	1.77	1.71	1.65
29	2.18	2.10	2.03	1.94	1.90	1.85	1.81	1.75	1.70	1.64
30	2.16	2.09	2.01	1.93	1.89	1.84	1.79	1.74	1.68	1.62
40	2.08	2.00	1.92	1.84	1.79	1.74	1.69	1.64	1.58	1.51
60	1.99	1.92	1.84	1.75	1.70	1.65	1.59	1.53	1.47	1.39
120	1.91	1.83	1.75	1.66	1.61	1.55	1.50	1.43	1.35	1.25
∞	1.83	1.75	1.67	1.57	1.52	1.46	1.39	1.32	1.22	1.00

DENOMINATOR DEGREES OF FREEDOM

TABLE 7   Critical Values for the F Statistic: $F_{.025}$

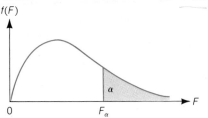

v_1 v_2	NUMERATOR DEGREES OF FREEDOM								
	1	2	3	4	5	6	7	8	9
1	647.8	799.5	864.2	899.6	921.8	937.1	948.2	956.7	963.3
2	38.51	39.00	39.17	39.25	39.30	39.33	39.36	39.37	39.39
3	17.44	16.04	15.44	15.10	14.88	14.73	14.62	14.54	14.47
4	12.22	10.65	9.98	9.60	9.36	9.20	9.07	8.98	8.90
5	10.01	8.43	7.76	7.39	7.15	6.98	6.85	6.76	6.68
6	8.81	7.26	6.60	6.23	5.99	5.82	5.70	5.60	5.52
7	8.07	6.54	5.89	5.52	5.29	5.12	4.99	4.90	4.82
8	7.57	6.06	5.42	5.05	4.82	4.65	4.53	4.43	4.36
9	7.21	5.71	5.08	4.72	4.48	4.32	4.20	4.10	4.03
10	6.94	5.46	4.83	4.47	4.24	4.07	3.95	3.85	3.78
11	6.72	5.26	4.63	4.28	4.04	3.88	3.76	3.66	3.59
12	6.55	5.10	4.47	4.12	3.89	3.73	3.61	3.51	3.44
13	6.41	4.97	4.35	4.00	3.77	3.60	3.48	3.39	3.31
14	6.30	4.86	4.24	3.89	3.66	3.50	3.38	3.29	3.21
15	6.20	4.77	4.15	3.80	3.58	3.41	3.29	3.20	3.12
16	6.12	4.69	4.08	3.73	3.50	3.34	3.22	3.12	3.05
17	6.04	4.62	4.01	3.66	3.44	3.28	3.16	3.06	2.98
18	5.98	4.56	3.95	3.61	3.38	3.22	3.10	3.01	2.93
19	5.92	4.51	3.90	3.56	3.33	3.17	3.05	2.96	2.88
20	5.87	4.46	3.86	3.51	3.29	3.13	3.01	2.91	2.84
21	5.83	4.42	3.82	3.48	3.25	3.09	2.97	2.87	2.80
22	5.79	4.38	3.78	3.44	3.22	3.05	2.93	2.84	2.76
23	5.75	4.35	3.75	3.41	3.18	3.02	2.90	2.81	2.73
24	5.72	4.32	3.72	3.38	3.15	2.99	2.87	2.78	2.70
25	5.69	4.29	3.69	3.35	3.13	2.97	2.85	2.75	2.68
26	5.66	4.27	3.67	3.33	3.10	2.94	2.82	2.73	2.65
27	5.63	4.24	3.65	3.31	3.08	2.92	2.80	2.71	2.63
28	5.61	4.22	3.63	3.29	3.06	2.90	2.78	2.69	2.61
29	5.59	4.20	3.61	3.27	3.04	2.88	2.76	2.67	2.59
30	5.57	4.18	3.59	3.25	3.03	2.87	2.75	2.65	2.57
40	5.42	4.05	3.46	3.13	2.90	2.74	2.62	2.53	2.45
60	5.29	3.93	3.34	3.01	2.79	2.63	2.51	2.41	2.33
120	5.15	3.80	3.23	2.89	2.67	2.52	2.39	2.30	2.22
∞	5.02	3.69	3.12	2.79	2.57	2.41	2.29	2.19	2.11

DENOMINATOR DEGREES OF FREEDOM

v_1 v_2	NUMERATOR DEGREES OF FREEDOM									
	10	12	15	20	24	30	40	60	120	∞
1	968.6	976.7	984.9	993.1	997.2	1001	1006	1010	1014	1018
2	39.40	39.41	39.43	39.45	39.46	39.46	39.47	39.48	39.49	39.50
3	14.42	14.34	14.25	14.17	14.12	14.08	14.04	13.99	13.95	13.90
4	8.84	8.75	8.66	8.56	8.51	8.46	8.41	8.36	8.31	8.26
5	6.62	6.52	6.43	6.33	6.28	6.23	6.18	6.12	6.07	6.02
6	5.46	5.37	5.27	5.17	5.12	5.07	5.01	4.96	4.90	4.85
7	4.76	4.67	4.57	4.47	4.42	4.36	4.31	4.25	4.20	4.14
8	4.30	4.20	4.10	4.00	3.95	3.89	3.84	3.78	3.73	3.67
9	3.96	3.87	3.77	3.67	3.61	3.56	3.51	3.45	3.39	3.33
10	3.72	3.62	3.52	3.42	3.37	3.31	3.26	3.20	3.14	3.08
11	3.53	3.43	3.33	3.23	3.17	3.12	3.06	3.00	2.94	2.88
12	3.37	3.28	3.18	3.07	3.02	2.96	2.91	2.85	2.79	2.72
13	3.25	3.15	3.05	2.95	2.89	2.84	2.78	2.72	2.66	2.60
14	3.15	3.05	2.95	2.84	2.79	2.73	2.67	2.61	2.55	2.49
15	3.06	2.96	2.86	2.76	2.70	2.64	2.59	2.52	2.46	2.40
16	2.99	2.89	2.79	2.68	2.63	2.57	2.51	2.45	2.38	2.32
17	2.92	2.82	2.72	2.62	2.56	2.50	2.44	2.38	2.32	2.25
18	2.87	2.77	2.67	2.56	2.50	2.44	2.38	2.32	2.26	2.19
19	2.82	2.72	2.62	2.51	2.45	2.39	2.33	2.27	2.20	2.13
20	2.77	2.68	2.57	2.46	2.41	2.35	2.29	2.22	2.16	2.09
21	2.73	2.64	2.53	2.42	2.37	2.31	2.25	2.18	2.11	2.04
22	2.70	2.60	2.50	2.39	2.33	2.27	2.21	2.14	2.08	2.00
23	2.67	2.57	2.47	2.36	2.30	2.24	2.18	2.11	2.04	1.97
24	2.64	2.54	2.44	2.33	2.27	2.21	2.15	2.08	2.01	1.94
25	2.61	2.51	2.41	2.30	2.24	2.18	2.12	2.05	1.98	1.91
26	2.59	2.49	2.39	2.28	2.22	2.16	2.09	2.03	1.95	1.88
27	2.57	2.47	2.36	2.25	2.19	2.13	2.07	2.00	1.93	1.85
28	2.55	2.45	2.34	2.23	2.17	2.11	2.05	1.98	1.91	1.83
29	2.53	2.43	2.32	2.21	2.15	2.09	2.03	1.96	1.89	1.81
30	2.51	2.41	2.31	2.20	2.14	2.07	2.01	1.94	1.87	1.79
40	2.39	2.29	2.18	2.07	2.01	1.94	1.88	1.80	1.72	1.64
60	2.27	2.17	2.06	1.94	1.88	1.82	1.74	1.67	1.58	1.48
120	2.16	2.05	1.94	1.82	1.76	1.69	1.61	1.53	1.43	1.31
∞	2.05	1.94	1.83	1.71	1.64	1.57	1.48	1.39	1.27	1.00

DENOMINATOR DEGREES OF FREEDOM

TABLE 8
Critical Values for
the χ^2 Statistic

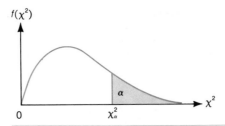

DEGREES OF FREEDOM	$\chi^2_{.995}$	$\chi^2_{.990}$	$\chi^2_{.975}$	$\chi^2_{.950}$	$\chi^2_{.900}$
1	0.0000393	0.0001571	0.0009821	0.0039321	0.0157908
2	0.0100251	0.0201007	0.0506356	0.102587	0.210720
3	0.0717212	0.114832	0.215795	0.351846	0.584375
4	0.206990	0.297110	0.484419	0.710721	1.063623
5	0.411740	0.554300	0.831211	1.145476	1.61031
6	0.675727	0.872085	1.237347	1.63539	2.20413
7	0.989265	1.239043	1.68987	2.16735	2.83311
8	1.344419	1.646482	2.17973	2.73264	3.48954
9	1.734926	2.087912	2.70039	3.32511	4.16816
10	2.15585	2.55821	3.24697	3.94030	4.86518
11	2.60321	3.05347	3.81575	4.57481	5.57779
12	3.07382	3.57056	4.40379	5.22603	6.30380
13	3.56503	4.10691	5.00874	5.89186	7.04150
14	4.07468	4.66043	5.62872	6.57063	7.78953
15	4.60094	5.22935	6.26214	7.26094	8.54675
16	5.14224	5.81221	6.90766	7.96164	9.31223
17	5.69724	6.40776	7.56418	8.67176	10.0852
18	6.26481	7.01491	8.23075	9.39046	10.8649
19	6.84398	7.63273	8.90655	10.1170	11.6509
20	7.43386	8.26040	9.59083	10.8508	12.4426
21	8.03366	8.89720	10.28293	11.5913	13.2396
22	8.64272	9.54249	10.9823	12.3380	14.0415
23	9.26042	10.19567	11.6885	13.0905	14.8479
24	9.88623	10.8564	12.4011	13.8484	15.6587
25	10.5197	11.5240	13.1197	14.6114	16.4734
26	11.1603	12.1981	13.8439	15.3791	17.2919
27	11.8076	12.8786	14.5733	16.1513	18.1138
28	12.4613	13.5648	15.3079	16.9279	18.9392
29	13.1211	14.2565	16.0471	17.7083	19.7677
30	13.7867	14.9535	16.7908	18.4926	20.5992
40	20.7065	22.1643	24.4331	26.5093	29.0505
50	27.9907	29.7067	32.3574	34.7642	37.6886
60	35.5346	37.4848	40.4817	43.1879	46.4589
70	43.2752	45.4418	48.7576	51.7393	55.3290
80	51.1720	53.5400	57.1532	60.3915	64.2778
90	59.1963	61.7541	65.6466	69.1260	73.2912
100	67.3276	70.0648	74.2219	77.9295	82.3581

Source: From C. M. Thompson, "Tables of the Percentage Points of the χ^2-Distribution," *Biometrika*, 1941, *32*, 188–189. Reproduced by permission of the *Biometrika* Trustees.

DEGREES OF FREEDOM	$\chi^2_{.100}$	$\chi^2_{.050}$	$\chi^2_{.025}$	$\chi^2_{.010}$	$\chi^2_{.005}$
1	2.70554	3.84146	5.02389	6.63490	7.87944
2	4.60517	5.99147	7.37776	9.21034	10.5966
3	6.25139	7.81473	9.34840	11.3449	12.8381
4	7.77944	9.48773	11.1433	13.2767	14.8602
5	9.23635	11.0705	12.8325	15.0863	16.7496
6	10.6446	12.5916	14.4494	16.8119	18.5476
7	12.0170	14.0671	16.0128	18.4753	20.2777
8	13.3616	15.5073	17.5346	20.0902	21.9550
9	14.6837	16.9190	19.0228	21.6660	23.5893
10	15.9871	18.3070	20.4831	23.2093	25.1882
11	17.2750	19.6751	21.9200	24.7250	26.7569
12	18.5494	21.0261	23.3367	26.2170	28.2995
13	19.8119	22.3621	24.7356	27.6883	29.8194
14	21.0642	23.6848	26.1190	29.1413	31.3193
15	22.3072	24.9958	27.4884	30.5779	32.8013
16	23.5418	26.2962	28.8454	31.9999	34.2672
17	24.7690	27.5871	30.1910	33.4087	35.7185
18	25.9894	28.8693	31.5264	34.8053	37.1564
19	27.2036	30.1435	32.8523	36.1908	38.5822
20	28.4120	31.4104	34.1696	37.5662	39.9968
21	29.6151	32.6705	35.4789	38.9321	41.4010
22	30.8133	33.9244	36.7807	40.2894	42.7956
23	32.0069	35.1725	38.0757	41.6384	44.1813
24	33.1963	36.4151	39.3641	42.9798	45.5585
25	34.3816	37.6525	40.6465	44.3141	46.9278
26	35.5631	38.8852	41.9232	45.6417	48.2899
27	36.7412	40.1133	43.1944	46.9630	49.6449
28	37.9159	41.3372	44.4607	48.2782	50.9933
29	39.0875	42.5569	45.7222	49.5879	52.3356
30	40.2560	43.7729	46.9792	50.8922	53.6720
40	51.8050	55.7585	59.3417	63.6907	66.7659
50	63.1671	67.5048	71.4202	76.1539	79.4900
60	74.3970	79.0819	83.2976	88.3794	91.9517
70	85.5271	90.5312	95.0231	100.425	104.215
80	96.5782	101.879	106.629	112.329	116.321
90	107.565	113.145	118.136	124.116	128.299
100	118.498	124.342	129.561	135.807	140.169

TABLE 9   Random Numbers

COLUMN / ROW	1	2	3	4	5	6	7	8	9	10	11	12	13	14
1	10480	15011	01536	02011	81647	91646	69179	14194	62590	36207	20969	99570	91291	90700
2	22368	46573	25595	85393	30995	89198	27982	53402	93965	34095	52666	19174	39615	99505
3	24130	48360	22527	97265	76393	64809	15179	24830	49340	32081	30680	19655	63348	58629
4	42167	93093	06243	61680	07856	16376	39440	53537	71341	57004	00849	74917	97758	16379
5	37570	39975	81837	16656	06121	91782	60468	81305	49684	60672	14110	06927	01263	54613
6	77921	06907	11008	42751	27756	53498	18602	70659	90655	15053	21916	81825	44394	42880
7	99562	72905	56420	69994	98872	31016	71194	18738	44013	48840	63213	21069	10634	12952
8	96301	91977	05463	07972	18876	20922	94595	56869	69014	60045	18425	84903	42508	32307
9	89579	14342	63661	10281	17453	18103	57740	84378	25331	12566	58678	44947	05585	56941
10	85475	36857	53342	53988	53060	59533	38867	62300	08158	17983	16439	11458	18593	64952
11	28918	69578	88231	33276	70997	79936	56865	05859	90106	31595	01547	85590	91610	78188
12	63553	40961	48235	03427	49626	69445	18663	72695	52180	20847	12234	90511	33703	90322
13	09429	93969	52636	92737	88974	33488	36320	17617	30015	08272	84115	27156	30613	74952
14	10365	61129	87529	85689	48237	52267	67689	93394	01511	26358	85104	20285	29975	89868
15	07119	97336	71048	08178	77233	13916	47564	81056	97735	85977	29372	74461	28551	90707
16	51085	12765	51821	51259	77452	16308	60756	92144	49442	53900	70960	63990	75601	40719
17	02368	21382	52404	60268	89368	19885	55322	44819	01188	65255	64835	44919	05944	55157
18	01011	54092	33362	94904	31273	04146	18594	29852	71585	85030	51132	01915	92747	64951
19	52162	53916	46369	58586	23216	14513	83149	98736	23495	64350	94738	17752	35156	35749
20	07056	97628	33787	09998	42698	06691	76988	13602	51851	46104	88916	19509	25625	58104
21	48663	91245	85828	14346	09172	30168	90229	04734	59193	22178	30421	61666	99904	32812
22	54164	58492	22421	74103	47070	25306	76468	26384	58151	06646	21524	15227	96909	44592
23	32639	32363	05597	24200	13363	38005	94342	28728	35806	06912	17012	64161	18296	22851
24	29334	27001	87637	87308	58731	00256	45834	15398	46557	41135	10367	07684	36188	18510
25	02488	33062	28834	07351	19731	92420	60952	61280	50001	67658	32586	86679	50720	94953
26	81525	72295	04839	96423	24878	82651	66566	14778	76797	14780	13300	87074	79666	95725
27	29676	20591	68086	26432	46901	20849	89768	81536	86645	12659	92259	57102	80428	25280

28	00742	57392	39064	66432	84673	40027	32832	61362	98947	96067	64760	64584	96096	98253
29	05366	04213	25669	26422	44407	44048	37937	63904	45766	66134	75470	66520	34693	90449
30	91921	26418	64117	94305	26766	25940	39972	22209	71500	64568	91402	42416	07844	69618
31	00582	04711	87917	77341	42206	35126	74087	99547	81817	42607	43808	76655	62028	76630
32	00725	69884	62797	56170	86324	88072	76222	36086	84637	93161	76038	65855	77919	88006
33	69011	65795	95876	55293	18988	27354	26575	08625	40801	59920	29841	80150	12777	48501
34	25976	57948	29888	88604	67917	48708	18912	82271	65424	69774	33611	54262	85963	03547
35	09763	83473	73577	12908	30883	18317	28290	35797	05998	41688	34952	37888	38917	88050
36	91576	42595	27958	30134	04024	86385	29880	99730	55536	84855	29080	09250	79656	73211
37	17955	56349	90999	49127	20044	59931	06115	20542	18059	02008	73708	83517	36103	42791
38	46503	18584	18845	49618	02304	51038	20655	58727	28168	15475	56942	53389	20562	87338
39	92157	89634	94824	78171	84610	82834	09922	25417	44137	48413	25555	21246	35509	20468
40	14577	62765	35605	81263	39667	47358	56873	56307	61607	49518	89656	20103	77490	18062
41	98427	07523	33362	64270	01638	92477	66969	98420	04880	45585	46565	04102	46880	45709
42	34914	63976	88720	82765	34476	17032	87589	40836	32427	70002	70663	88863	77775	69348
43	70060	28277	39475	46473	23219	53416	94970	25832	69975	94884	19661	72828	00102	66794
44	53976	54914	06990	67245	68350	82948	11398	42878	80287	88267	47363	46634	06541	97809
45	76072	29515	40980	07391	58745	25774	22987	80059	39911	96189	41151	14222	60697	59583
46	90725	52210	83974	29992	65831	38857	50490	83765	55657	14361	31720	57375	56228	41546
47	64364	67412	33339	31926	14883	24413	59744	92351	97473	89286	35931	04110	23726	51900
48	08962	00358	31662	25388	61642	34072	81249	35648	56891	69352	48373	45578	78547	81788
49	95012	68379	93526	70765	10592	04542	76463	54328	02349	17247	28865	14777	62730	92277
50	15664	10493	20492	38391	91132	21999	59516	81652	27195	48223	46751	22923	32261	85653
51	16408	81899	04153	53381	79401	21438	83035	92350	36693	31238	59649	91754	72772	02338
52	18629	81953	05520	91962	04739	13092	97662	24822	94730	06496	35090	04822	86674	98289
53	73115	35101	47498	87637	99016	71060	88824	71013	18735	20286	23153	72924	35165	43040
54	57491	16703	23167	49323	45021	33132	12544	41035	80780	45393	44812	12515	98931	91202
55	30405	83946	23792	14422	15059	45799	22716	19792	09983	74353	68668	30429	70735	25499
56	16631	35006	85900	98275	32388	52390	16815	69298	82732	38480	73817	32523	41961	44437
57	96773	20206	42559	78985	05300	22164	24369	54224	35083	19687	11052	91491	60383	19746
58	38935	64202	14349	82674	66523	44133	00697	35552	35970	19124	63318	29686	03387	59846
59	31624	76384	17403	53363	44167	64486	64758	75366	76554	31601	12614	33072	60332	92325
60	78919	19474	23632	27889	47914	02584	37680	20801	72152	39339	34806	08930	85001	87820
61	03931	33309	57047	74211	63445	17361	62825	39908	05607	91284	68833	25570	38818	46920
62	74426	33278	43972	10119	89917	15665	52872	73823	73144	88662	88970	74492	51805	99378
63	09066	00903	20795	95452	92648	45454	09552	88815	16553	51125	79375	97596	16296	66092
64	42238	12426	87025	14267	20979	04508	64535	31355	86064	29472	47689	05974	52468	16834
65	16153	08002	26504	41744	81959	65642	74240	56302	00033	67107	77510	70625	28725	34191
66	21457	40742	29820	96783	29400	21840	15035	34537	33310	06116	95240	15957	16572	06004

Continued

TABLE 9 *Continued*

ROW \ COLUMN	1	2	3	4	5	6	7	8	9	10	11	12	13	14
67	21581	57802	02050	89728	17937	37621	47075	42080	97403	48626	68995	43805	33386	21597
68	55612	78095	83197	33732	05810	24813	86902	60397	16489	03264	88525	42786	05269	92532
69	44657	66999	99324	51281	84463	60563	79312	93454	68876	25471	93911	25650	12682	73572
70	91340	84979	46949	81973	37949	61023	43997	15263	80644	43942	89203	71795	99533	50501
71	91227	21199	31935	27022	84067	05462	35216	14486	29891	68607	41867	14951	91696	85065
72	50001	38140	66321	19924	72163	09538	12151	06878	91903	18749	34405	56087	82790	70925
73	65390	05224	72958	28609	81406	39147	25549	48542	42627	45233	57202	94617	23772	07896
74	27504	96131	83944	41575	10573	08619	64482	73923	36152	05184	94142	25299	84387	34925
75	37169	94851	39117	89632	00959	16487	65536	49071	39782	17095	02330	74301	00275	48280
76	11508	70225	51111	38351	19444	66499	71945	05422	13442	78675	84081	66938	93654	59894
77	37449	30362	06694	54690	04052	53115	62757	95348	78662	11163	81651	50245	34971	52924
78	46515	70331	85922	38329	57015	15765	97161	17869	45349	61796	66345	81073	49106	79860
79	30986	81223	42416	58353	21532	30502	32305	86482	05174	07901	54339	58861	74818	46942
80	63798	64995	46583	09785	44160	78128	83991	42865	92520	83531	80377	81250	81250	54238
81	82486	84846	99254	67632	43218	50076	21361	64816	51202	88124	41870	52689	51275	83556
82	21885	32906	92431	09060	64297	51674	64126	62570	26123	05155	59194	52799	28225	85762
83	60336	98782	07408	53458	13564	59089	26445	29789	85205	41001	12535	12133	14645	23541
84	43937	46891	24010	25560	86355	33941	25786	54990	71899	15475	95434	98227	21824	19585
85	97656	63175	89303	16275	07100	92063	21942	18611	47348	20203	18534	03862	78095	50136
86	03299	01221	05418	38982	55758	92237	26759	86367	21216	98442	08303	56613	91511	75928
87	79626	06486	03574	17668	07785	76020	79924	25651	83325	88428	85076	72811	22717	50585
88	85636	68335	47539	03129	65651	11977	02510	26113	99447	68645	34327	15152	55230	93448
89	18039	14367	61337	06177	12143	46609	32989	74014	64708	00533	35398	58408	13261	47908
90	08362	15656	60627	36478	65648	16764	53412	09013	07832	41574	17639	82163	60859	75567
91	79556	29068	04142	16268	15387	12856	66227	38358	22478	73373	88732	09443	82558	05250
92	92608	82674	27072	32534	17075	27698	98204	63863	11951	34648	88022	56148	34925	57031
93	23982	25835	40055	67006	12293	02753	14827	23235	35071	99704	37543	11601	35503	85171
94	09915	96306	05908	97901	28395	14186	00821	80703	70426	75647	76310	88717	37890	40129
95	59037	33300	26695	62247	69927	76123	50842	43834	86654	70959	79725	93872	28117	19233
96	42488	78077	69882	61657	34136	79180	97526	43092	04098	73571	80799	76536	71255	64239
97	46764	86273	63003	93017	31204	36692	40202	35275	57306	55543	53203	18098	47625	88684
98	03237	45430	55417	63282	90816	17349	88298	90183	36600	78406	06216	95787	42579	90730
99	86591	81482	52667	61582	14972	90053	89534	76036	49199	43716	97548	04379	46370	28672
100	38534	01715	94964	87288	65680	43772	39560	12918	62738	19636	51132	25739	25739	56947

Source: Abridged from W. H. Beyer, Ed., CRC *Standard Mathematical Tables*, 24th ed. (Cleveland: The Chemical Rubber Company), 1976. Reproduced by permission of the publisher. Copyright The Chemical Rubber Co., CRC Press, Inc.

SAMPLE SIZE n	$r_{.050}$	$r_{.025}$	$r_{.010}$	$r_{.005}$
3	.988	.969	.951	.988
4	.900	.950	.980	.900
5	.805	.878	.934	.959
6	.729	.811	.882	.917
7	.669	.754	.833	.875
8	.621	.707	.789	.834
9	.582	.666	.750	.798
10	.549	.632	.715	.765
11	.521	.602	.685	.735
12	.497	.576	.658	.708
13	.476	.553	.634	.684
14	.457	.532	.612	.661
15	.441	.514	.592	.641
16	.426	.497	.574	.623
17	.412	.482	.558	.606
18	.400	.468	.543	.590
19	.389	.456	.529	.575
20	.378	.444	.516	.561
21	.369	.433	.503	.549
22	.360	.423	.492	.537
27	.323	.381	.445	.487
32	.296	.349	.409	.449
37	.275	.325	.381	.418
42	.257	.304	.358	.393
47	.243	.288	.338	.372
52	.231	.273	.322	.354
62	.211	.250	.295	.325
72	.195	.232	.274	.302
82	.183	.217	.257	.283
92	.173	.205	.242	.267
102	.164	.195	.230	.254

TABLE 10
Critical Values of the
Sample Coefficient of
Correlation, r

Answers to Selected Exercises

2.1a. Quantitative   **b.** Qualitative   **c.** Qualitative
2.2a. Quantitative   **b.** Quantitative   **c.** Qualitative
2.4a. Qualitative   **b.** Qualitative   **c.** Quantitative   **d.** Quantitative   **e.** Qualitative
2.6b. .40   **c.** .16

2.9a.

CATEGORY	1981	1982
Interest on debt	12.1%	12.2%
Health	10.0%	10.1%
Energy	1.3%	1.6%
Environment	2.1%	1.9%
Veterans' benefits	3.4%	3.3%
Transportation	3.6%	2.9%
Education	4.8%	4.7%
Defense	24.3%	24.9%
Social Security	35.0%	34.5%
Other	3.4%	3.9%

c. Defense   **2.15** Approx. 52%

*Numbers rounded and based on 1981 budget of 662.8 and 1982 budget of 739.3 (billions of $)

2.16a. Quantitative   **b.** Qualitative   **c.** Quantitative   **d.** Qualitative   **e.** Qualitative   **f.** Quantitative
g. Quantitative   **h.** Qualitative
2.17a. Qualitative   **c.** 21.04%   **2.19b.** Cola   **c.** 37.8%
2.22a. Quantitative   **b.** Relative frequency distribution   **2.23a.** Bar graph   **c.** 0%
2.24a. Quantitative   **b.** Frequency distribution   **c.** Approx. 28%
d. Yes; no diameters recorded in the interval (.9985, .9995)
2.25a. Quantitative

3.1a. 12   **b.** 40   **c.** 7   **d.** 21   **3.2a.** 33   **b.** 175   **c.** 20   **d.** 71   **3.3a.** 11.2   **b.** 12
3.4a. 19.43   **b.** 20   **3.5a.** 6   **b.** 50   **c.** 42.8   **3.6** Mean = 4.6, Median = 4
3.7 Mean = 4.33, Median = 4.5   **3.8** Mean = 42,730, Median = 37,550   **3.9** 35,050–45,050; Mode = 40,050

3.10 Larger, yes   **3.12** Range $= 9$, St. dev. $= 3.51$, Var. $= 12.3$ **3.13** Range $= 6$, St. dev. $= 2.16$, Var. $= 4.67$
3.14 Range $= 8$, Var. $= 3.66$, St. dev. $= 1.91$
3.15 4.64 ± 1.91 (proportion $= .72$), 4.64 ± 3.82 (proportion $= .96$), 4.64 ± 5.73 (proportion $= 1.00$)
3.17 $\bar{x} = 380.4$, $s = 217.59$; 380.4 ± 217.59 (proportion $= .657$), 380.4 ± 435.18 (proportion $= .971$),
380.4 ± 652.77 (proportion $= 1.00$)
3.18b. Approx. 95%   **c.** Approx. 60–80%
3.19 70% of the residential prices lie below \$45,000 and 30% lie above \$45,000
3.20a. $-.86$ **b.** .75, negative z values lie to the left or below the mean
3.21a. \$28.75   **b.** -1.12 **c.** $-.38$, skewed to the right
3.22b. 3.05   **c.** No; most likely, otherwise we have observed a very rare event   **3.23b.** $z = 2.0$ **c.** No
3.24b. $\bar{x} = 377.5$, $s = 207.89$ **3.25a.** $\bar{x} = 8.21$, $s = 9.72$ **3.26** $\bar{x} = 32.42$, $s = 18.37$
3.27 $\bar{x} = 3.07$, $s^2 = 51.80$, $s = 7.20$
3.28a. 37, 341, 1,369   **b.** 470, 86,138, 220,900   **c.** -10, 58, 100   **d.** 89, 1,651, 7,921
3.29a. 6.17, 7.5, 8   **b.** 117.5, 111.5, all 4 numbers are the mode   **c.** -1.43, -2, bimodal (-2 and -3)
d. 17.8, 17, 17
3.30a. 14, 22.6, 4.75   **b.** 247, 10,304.3, 101.5   **c.** 8, 7.29, 2.70   **d.** 11, 16.7, 4.09
3.31a. .76, .836, .914   **b.** 4.15, 15.32, 3.91   **c.** 2, 9.67, 3.11
3.32a. 5, 35.2, 5.93   **b.** 3, 140, 11.8   **c.** 2, 17.8, 4.21   **d.** 1,000, 407,679.33, 638.5
3.34 Standard deviation   **3.35** Percentiles, z-scores
3.36a. 1.4, 1, bimodal (0 and 1), 4, 1.82, 1.35   **b.** Range, variance, standard deviation; mean, median, mode
3.37 67.88, 382.0, 19.5   **3.38** Superior: stock 2, inferior: stock 3
3.39a. Skewed to the right   **b.** Median   **c.** Mean   **3.41a.** 199   **b.** 174   **c.** Bimodal; 174 and 162
3.42 627, 17,661.48, 132.90
3.43 199 ± 132.90 (proportion $= .80$), 199 ± 265.8 (proportion $= .95$), 199 ± 398.7 (proportion $= .975$)   **3.44** 82
3.45b. Approx. 95%   **c.** Approx. 20—40%   **3.46a.** 1, $-.5$, .67, $-.33$, $-.67$ **b.** Highest: #1, lowest: #5
3.47a. Approx. 60–80% within 273.51 ± 78.35; approx. 95% within 273.51 ± 156.70; almost all within 273.51 ± 235.05
b. Approx. 95%   **c.** Approx. 50%   **d.** Not likely, $z = 2.25$
3.49a. Approx. 95%   **b.** Almost 100%   **3.50a.** $z = -3.43$ **b.** Yes   **3.51a.** 36.36   **b.** $s = 12.39$
3.52a. 9.07, 5.65   **b.** 9.07 ± 11.30; 54   **3.53b.** Approx. 60–80%   **c.** $z = -1.25$ **d.** Greater than
3.54a. Approx. 60–80% within 5.0 ± 1.5; approx. 95% within 5.0 ± 3.0; almost all within 5.0 ± 4.5 **b.** No
3.55a. 8.05–8.35   **b.** 7.74, .53   **c.** At least $^{182}/_{200}$
3.56a. $\bar{x} = 410.347$, $s = 143.886$, $s^2 = 20,703,161$ (in thousands)   **b.** Median $= 375,700$, Range $= 488,900$
c. $z = -.12$ **d.** Boeing
e. 410.35 ± 143.89 (proportion $= .87$), 410.35 ± 287.78 (proportion $= .93$), 410.35 ± 431.67 (proportion $= 1.00$)
3.57b. Approx. 95%   **c.** No   **3.59a.** 22.2, 54.92, 7.41   **c.** $z = -.30$
3.60a. Approx. 60–80% within 8.5 ± 2.0; approx. 95% within 8.5 ± 4.0; almost all within 8.5 ± 6.0
b. Yes; on approx. 95% of nonholiday weekends, the number of no-shows will fall between 4.5 and 12.5

▬▬▬▬▬ Chapter 4

4.1 A and C are mutually exclusive   **4.2** (A and B) and (B and C) are mutually exclusive
4.3 No pair is mutually exclusive   **4.4** (A and C) and (B and C) are mutually exclusive
4.5a. WES, WSE, EWS, ESW, SWE, SEW   **b.** Yes   **4.7** $^2/_{365} = .0054795$ **4.9** .08
4.11a. $\frac{1}{4}$ **b.** $\frac{1}{4}$ **c.** $\frac{3}{4}$ **d.** Observe at most one head; $\frac{3}{4}$ **4.12a.** $\frac{1}{36}$ **b.** $\frac{3}{36}$ **c.** $\frac{2}{36}$
4.14 $\frac{1}{6}$ **4.16a.** 10   **4.17a.** $\frac{3}{10}$ **b.** No   **4.18** 26   **4.19** $\frac{8}{26}$
4.20b. $\frac{1}{16}$ **c.** Either the public prefers A or we have observed a rare event.   **4.21** $\frac{1}{36}$ **4.22** .000125
4.23a. .2   **b.** $^{10}/_{49}$ **c.** $^{10}/_{46}$ **4.24a.** .00000001   **b.** Claim is probably false
4.25a. $\frac{8}{36}$ **b.** $\frac{4}{36}$ **c.** $\frac{8}{36}$ **d.** $\frac{4}{36}$ **4.26a.** .10   **b.** .8   **c.** .08

4.27a. .63   **b.** .57   **c.** .21   **d.** .41   **e.** 0   **f.** .79   **g.** $^{41}/_{63}$ **4.28** .99
4.29b. .15   **d.** .90   **4.30a.** $^{242}/_{515}$ **b.** 0   **c.** $^{3}/_{1000}$ **d.** $^{826}/_{1000}$ **e.** $^{428}/_{1000}$ **f.** $^{556}/_{1000}$
4.31 (A and B), (A and C), (B and C), (B and D)   **4.32** (A and B) and (B and C) are mutually exclusive
4.33b. ¼   **c.** ½   **4.34** ½   **4.35** No   **4.36** .62
4.37a. .15   **b.** .80   **c.** .60   **d.** None are mutually exclusive
4.38a. $^{410}/_{500}$ **b.** $^{125}/_{500}$ **c.** $^{375}/_{500}$ **d.** $^{205}/_{500}$ **e.** 1   **f.** $^{61}/_{500}$ **g.** 0   **h.** $^{10}/_{125}$
i. $^{80}/_{90}$ **j.** No   **k.** Yes   **4.39** .675   **4.40a.** .01   **b.** .99   **c.** .0001   **d.** Most likely false
4.41 2,598,960   **4.42a.** .30   **b.** .90   **4.43a.** 20   **c.** $^{4}/_{20}$ **d.** $^{16}/_{20}$ **e.** $^{4}/_{10}$
4.44a. .81   **b.** .1296   **4.45b.** $^{5}/_{9}$ **c.** $^{3}/_{9}$ **4.46a.** $^{17}/_{50}$ **b.** $^{21}/_{50}$ **c.** $^{38}/_{50}$ **d.** $^{8}/_{50}$ **e.** $^{17}/_{33}$
4.47a. .40   **b.** .12   **c.** .70   **d.** $^{18}/_{40}$
4.48a. .216   **b.** .064   **c.** Probably not; highly unlikely to observe 3 incorrect predictions if the claim is true
4.49a. .06   **b.** .94   **4.50a.** .5   **b.** .1   **4.51a.** $^{1}/_{6}$ **b.** $^{1}/_{11}$ **c.** $^{1}/_{66}$ **d.** Yes, good chance
4.52a. 120   **b.** .0083   **c.** .9917   **d.** Yes   **4.53a.** 10 ways   **b.** $^{4}/_{10}$
4.54a. .729   **b.** .081   **c.** .001   **d.** .81   **e.** 0   **f.** 0   **g.** No   **4.55a.** .45   **b.** .9   **c.** 0
4.56a. $^{24}/_{36}$ **b.** $^{5}/_{36}$ **c.** $^{6}/_{36}$ **4.57b.** No

Chapter 5

5.1 Yes   **5.2** No   **5.3** No   **5.4** Yes   **5.5** Yes   **5.6** Yes   **5.7a.** Yes   **b.** $p > .5$ **c.** $p = .5$
5.8 .0625, .25, .375, .25, .0625   **5.9** .4096, .4096, .1536, .0256, .0016   **5.11a.** .3125   **b.** .6875
5.12a. .8192   **b.** .1808   **c.** Complementary   **d.** Probabilities sum to 1
5.13a. .008   **b.** .384   **c.** .488   **5.14a.** .8   **c.** $x = 0$ **d.** $x = 2$ **e.** x is at most 2
5.15b. .6   **c.** .48   **5.16b.** .4   **c.** .48   **5.17a.** .3241   **b.** .3125   **c.** .0001
5.18a. .3487   **b.** .3874   **c.** .1937   **5.19a.** .1172   **b.** .2051   **c.** .2461
5.22a. .8369   **b.** .9976   **c.** 1   **5.23a.** .9983   **b.** .9877   **c.** .0017   **5.24a.** .9298   **b.** .0702
5.25a. .8125   **b.** .1875   **c.** .1875   **d.** .5000   **5.26a.** .5987   **b.** .9139   **c.** .9139   **d.** .0861
5.27a. .3833   **b.** .0056   **c.** .9827   **5.28a.** .8725   **b.** .5955   **c.** .0510
5.29a. 1.5, 1.16   **b.** 7.5, 1.94   **5.30** Approx. 95%   **5.31a.** 944   **b.** .964, yes
5.32a. 99, .995   **b.** 80, 4   **c.** 50, 5   **d.** 20, 4   **e.** 1, .995
5.34a. 891, 2.98   **b.** 720, 12   **c.** 450, 15   **d.** 180, 12   **e.** 9, 2.98
5.36a. 120   **b.** 120 ± 20.78   **c.** Yes, yes   **5.37a.** 1960   **b.** 6.26   **c.** 1960 ± 12.52   **d.** Yes
5.39a. .50   **b.** 500, 15.8   **c.** 500 ± 31.6   **5.40** .729, .243, .027, .001   **5.41** .343, .441, .189, .027
5.42 .125, .375, .375, .125   **5.43** .027, .189, .441, .343   **5.44** .001, .027, .243, .729
5.45a. .2734   **b.** .3633   **c.** .0352
5.46a. .071   **b.** Yes   **c.** Yes, claim is most likely false
5.47a. .0523   **b.** Yes; if $p = .1$, the observed event is rare   **5.48** Yes   **5.49** No
5.50a. Yes   **b.** No   **c.** No   **5.51a.** Approx. 0   **b.** .0702   **c.** .6513   **5.52** .1821
5.54a. 3, 1.225   **b.** 3 ± 2.45   **5.55a.** .5793   **b.** .1091   **c.** .0982
5.56a. 75   **b.** 7.98   **c.** Possibly, because 55 is more than 2 standard deviations from the mean
5.57a. Yes   **b.** .0715   **c.** .9285   **d.** .3199   **5.58** No

Chapter 6

6.1a. .3849   **b.** .4319   **c.** .1844   **d.** .4147   **e.** .0918
6.2a. .4750   **b.** .4750   **c.** .95   **d.** .2912   **e.** .1075
6.3a. .0934   **b.** .5   **c.** .9115   **d.** .9066   **e.** .8164

6.4α. .0869   **b.** .0099   **c.** .0099   **d.** .8965
6.5α. .25   **b.** .92   **c.** 1.28   **d.** 1.65   **e.** 1.96
6.6α. 1.13   **b.** 2.33   **c.** .67   **d.** .84   **e.** 1.00
6.7α. 1.96   **b.** 1.65   **c.** 2.58   **d.** 2.33   **e.** 1.28
6.8α. .75   **b.** −1.00   **c.** −1.625   **d.** 2.00   **e.** −2.00
6.9α. .75   **b.** 1.46   **c.** 1.82   **d.** .38   **e.** .99   **6.10α.** 1.28   **b.** 1.04   **c.** .84   **d.** .67
6.11α. −1.28   **b.** −1.04   **c.** −.52   **d.** .00   **6.12α.** .0985   **b.** .3745   **c.** .0262
6.13α. .0436   **b.** .1271   **c.** .6141   **6.14α.** .50   **b.** .1056   **c.** .1056   **6.15** .0475   **6.16** .2033
6.17 .0294, no   **6.18** 4.58 minutes   **6.19** $360.60
6.20α. .1721   **b.** .2372   **c.** .8257   **d.** .9441   **e.** .7794
6.21α. .0   **b.** 1.18   **c.** .13   **d.** .67   **6.22α.** −1.65   **b.** −1.96   **c.** −.99   **d.** −.77
6.23α. .0712   **b.** .2483   **c.** .0559   **6.24α.** .9808   **b.** .0032   **c.** 10.21 ounces
6.25α. .7642   **b.** .2037   **c.** 65,825 miles   **6.26α.** .0228   **b.** .1587   **c.** .8413
6.27α. .6736   **b.** .3264   **c.** .50   **d.** .3264   **6.28** 19.08 minutes

Chapter 7

7.2α. 35   **7.6** Method B, Method A   **7.8** Statistic B
7.12α. Approx. normal, $\mu_{\bar{x}} = 8{,}000$, $\sigma_{\bar{x}} = 237.17$ **b.** .0174   **c.** .9652
7.13α. Approx. normal, $\mu_{\bar{x}} = 9.8$, $\sigma_{\bar{x}} = .078$ **b.** .8997   **c.** No, $z = -3.21$
7.15α. Approx. normal, $\mu_{\bar{x}} = 22{,}500$, $\sigma_{\bar{x}} = 1{,}095.44$ **b.** .9774   **7.16α.** It will be larger   **b.** Approx. 1, yes
7.17α. .0062   **b.** Yes   **7.18α.** 15   **7.19α.** Approx. normal, $\mu_{\bar{x}} = 170$, $\sigma_{\bar{x}} = 15$ **b.** .069   **c.** .2514
7.20α. Approx. normal, $\mu_{\bar{x}} = 29.5$, $\sigma_{\bar{x}} = .339$ **b.** .0016   **c.** Yes   **7.22α.** 20   **c.** No
7.23α. Approx. normal, $\mu_{\bar{x}} = 200$, $\sigma_{\bar{x}} = 4$ **b.** .1587   **c.** .9938   **d.** .1974
7.24α. (1.452, 2.548)   **b.** .0026   **7.25α.** Approx. normal   **b.** 80,000   **c.** 4,518.5   **d.** .0040   **e.** No
7.26α. .3023   **b.** .0668   **7.27b.** .0013   **c.** Probably wrong; yes
7.28α. Approx. normal, $\mu_{\bar{x}_{25}} = 17$, $\sigma_{\bar{x}_{25}} = 2$ **b.** Approx. normal, $\mu_{\bar{x}_{100}} = 17$, $\sigma_{\bar{x}_{100}} = 1$
c. $P(15 < \bar{x}_{100} < 19)$ **d.** .6826, .9544
7.29α. .0179   **b.** Yes   **7.30α.** .0139   **b.** Yes   **7.31** .0062

Chapter 8

8.2α. 1.44   **b.** 1.96   **c.** 2.24   **8.4** 3,412 ± 225.23   **8.6** 37.1 ± .464
8.7α. 3.2 ± .082   **c.** Increase n or decrease confidence coefficient
8.9α. $425   **b.** $425 ± 18.21   **c.** .97   **d.** No   **8.10α.** 2.898   **b.** 2.262   **c.** 1.761
8.12α. 54.8 ± 12.74 mph   **8.13α.** 14.71 ± .83 hours   **b.** Decrease   **8.14α.** $31,000 ± $1,857.6
8.16b. 10.1 ± 3.85 bushels   **8.17α.** $41.75 ± $2.65   **c.** No   **8.18α.** .12 ± .064   **c.** Increase
8.19 .612 ± .062   **8.20** .3 ± .195   **8.21α.** .45 ± .126   **8.22** .24 ± .078
8.23α. .086   **b.** .086 ± .016   **c.** No; .074 is included in the interval   **8.24** 21.4 ± 4.45   **8.25α.** 214 ± 70.16
8.26α. 8.4 ± 3.63   **b.** Yes   **8.27α.** −61   **b.** −61 ± 10.65   **d.** Yes   **8.28α.** −4.6 ± 2.87   **b.** Yes
8.30α. 21.4 ± 14.01   **8.32** −3.75 ± 2.89   **8.33α.** −.08 ± .269   **8.34α.** −4.8 ± 23.38   **c.** No
8.35 −.024 ± .121   **8.36α.** −.227 ± .218   **b.** Japan   **c.** Decrease   **8.37α.** .18 ± .148   **b.** Yes, Ration A
8.38 −.03 ± .054   **8.39α.** −.046 ± .133   **b.** Yes   **8.42α.** 7.5 ± 1.11   **b.** 3.7 ± 1.59   **8.43** 8.5 ± 1.04
8.44α. 29.6 ± 43.91   **b.** No   **c.** Decrease   **8.45** .328 ± .049   **8.46α.** −.028 ± .069   **b.** No
8.47 27.5 ± 1.42 millimeters   **8.48α.** 7.5 ± 10.23 hours   **b.** No   **8.49α.** 47.17 ± 3.74   **b.** No
8.50 −.08 ± .098   **8.51** .615 ± .033   **8.52α.** −25 ± 26.56   **b.** No   **8.53α.** .02 ± .019   **b.** Yes

8.55 112 ± 134.85, no   **8.57a.** $.014 \pm .024$ **b.** No evidence of a difference between proportions
8.58a. $86,890 \pm 27,668$ **b.** Claim is false, since the interval includes only positive differences.

Chapter 9

9.2 H_0: $(p_1 - p_2) = 0$, H_a: $(p_1 - p_2) < 0$ **9.3** H_0: $\mu = \$35.00$, H_a: $\mu > \$35.00$
9.4 H_0: $(\mu_1 - \mu_2) = 0$, H_a: $(\mu_1 - \mu_2) \neq 0$ **9.5** H_0: $\mu = .04$, H_a: $\mu < .04$
9.6 9.2, 9.3, 9.5 are one-tailed, 9.4 is two-tailed   **9.11c.** Type II error, Type I error
9.12 $z < -2.33$ or $z > 2.33$ **9.13** $z > 1.645$ **9.14a.** $\alpha = .025$ **b.** $\alpha = .05$ **c.** $\alpha = .01$
9.15a. $z < -2.33$ **b.** $z < -2.05$ **c.** $z < -1.645$ **d.** $z < -1.28$
9.16a. $z = -2.65$ **b.** $z < -2.33$ **c.** Reject H_0 at $\alpha = .01$
9.17a. $z < -1.96$ or $z > 1.96$ **b.** $z = .81$ **c.** Do not reject H_0 at $\alpha = .05$ **9.20** Reject H_0, do not reject H_0
9.21 Decreases   **9.24a.** $z < -2.58$ or $z > 2.58$ **b.** $z < -2.33$ or $z > 2.33$ **c.** $z < -2.05$ or $z > 2.05$
9.25a. .005   **b.** .0985   **c.** .10   **9.26** H_0: $\mu = 22$, H_a: $\mu < 22$
9.27 H_0: $(p_1 - p_2) = 0$, H_a: $(p_1 - p_2) \neq 0$ **9.28** H_0: $(\mu_1 - \mu_2) = 0$, H_a: $(\mu_1 - \mu_2) > 0$
9.29 H_0: $p = \frac{1}{6}$, H_a: $p \neq \frac{1}{6}$ **9.30a.** $z > 2.33$ **b.** $z = 1.57$ **c.** Do not reject H_0
9.31a. $z = -3.13$ **b.** $z < -1.645$ or $z > 1.645$ **c.** Reject H_0
9.32a. $z < -2.33$ or $z > 2.33$ **b.** $z = 4.03$ **c.** Yes

Chapter 10

10.1 Yes, $z = -1.93$ **10.2** Yes, $z = 1.94$ **10.3** Yes, $z = 2.53$ **10.4** No, $z = 1.43$ **10.6** No, $t = -1.29$
10.7 $t = .14$, do not reject H_0: $\mu = 50,000$ **10.8** Yes, $t = -2.96$ **10.9** No, $t = -1.31$
10.10 $z = 2.00$, do not reject H_0: $p = .1$ **10.11** No, $z = -1.27$ **10.12** Yes, $z = 2.14$
10.13 $z = -.97$, do not reject H_0: $p = .95$ **10.14** Yes, $z = 9.43$ **10.15** Yes, $z = -4.60$ **10.16** Yes, $z = 6.83$
10.17 Yes, $z = -1.83$ **10.18** $t = -3.47$, reject H_0 **10.19** No, $t = -1.53$ **10.20** Yes, $t = 3.19$
10.21 $t = 2.97$, reject H_0 **10.22** Yes, $z = 2.99$ **10.23** No, $z = 1.32$ **10.24** No, $z = .69$
10.25 Yes, $z = -2.70$ **10.26a.** .0250   **b.** .05   **c.** .0038   **d.** .1056
10.27a. .3124   **b.** .0178   **c.** 0   **d.** .147   **10.28** .0268   **10.29** p-value $> .10$, do not reject H_0
10.30 Approx. 0, reject H_0 **10.31** .2451, do not reject H_0 **10.32** Yes, $z = -2.97$ **10.33** No, $t = -.17$
10.34 Yes, $z = 2.31$ **10.35** $z = 2.95$, reject H_0 **10.36** $z = -3.38$, reject H_0 **10.37** $z = -3.56$, reject H_0
10.38 No, $z = 1.33$ **10.39** $t = -2.56$, reject H_0 **10.40** No, $z = -.60$ **10.41** $t = .52$, do not reject H_0
10.42 $z = 1.39$, p-value $= .0823$, do not reject H_0 at $\alpha = .05$ **10.43** $t = 1.10$, do not reject H_0
10.44 Yes (at $\alpha = .05$), $z = 1.74$, p-value $= .0409$ **10.45** $t = -.46$, do not reject H_0 **10.46** No, $z = -1.35$
10.47 No, $t = .35$ **10.48** No, $z = .92$, p-value $= .1788$ **10.49** $t = 1.11$, do not reject H_0 **10.50** No, $z = .53$
10.51 Yes, $z = 6.67$ **10.52** Yes, $z = -2.47$

Chapter 11

11.1a. 2.40   **b.** 3.35   **c.** 1.65   **d.** 5.86   **11.2a.** 3.18   **b.** 2.62   **c.** 2.10
11.3a. $\text{MST} = 3.111$ **b.** $\text{MSE} = 1.405$ **c.** 2   **d.** 7   **e.** $F = 2.21$ **f.** Reject H_0 if $F > 4.74$
g. Do not reject H_0: $\mu_1 = \mu_2 = \mu_3$
11.4a. H_0: $\mu_1 = \mu_2 = \mu_3 = \mu_4$, H_a: At least 2 means are different   **b.** $\text{MST} = 375.6$
c. $\text{MSE} = 140.775$ **d.** $F = 2.67$ **e.** 3   **f.** 16   **g.** Reject H_0 if $F > 4.08$ **h.** No, do not reject H_0
11.5 Reject H_0, $F = 9.50$ **11.6** Reject H_0, $F = 17.66$ **11.7** Reject H_0, $F = 13.00$ **11.8** -15 ± 15.91

11.9a. 34.3 ± 4.97 **b.** 6.25 ± 7.03; no evidence of a difference between means, zero is included in the interval
11.10a. 90% CI for μ_1: 340.9 ± 36.76, 90% CI for μ_2: 462.7 ± 36.76, 90% CI for μ_3: 286.1 ± 36.76,
90% CI for μ_4: 534.25 ± 36.76, 90% CI for μ_5: 374.9 ± 36.76 **b.** Possibly location IV
11.11a. 99% CI for $(\mu_1 - \mu_2)$: $-.97 \pm .702$, 99% CI for $(\mu_1 - \mu_3)$: $.148 \pm .702$, 99% CI for $(\mu_2 - \mu_3)$: $1.118 \pm .702$
b. Firm 2 (theory Y)

11.12

SOURCE	df	SS	MS	F
City	3	1126.8	375.60	2.67
Error	16	2252.4	140.775	
Total	19	3379.2		

11.13

SOURCE	df	SS	MS	F
Theory	2	4.42714	2.21357	13.00
Error	15	2.5535	0.17023	
Total	17	6.98064		

11.14 SST = .0992333, SSE = .0450625, SS(Total) = .14429583, MST = .04961667, MSE = .00214583, $F = 23.12$,
df(Drugs) = 2, df(Error) = 21; Reject H_0: $\mu_1 = \mu_2 = \mu_3$, p-value = .0001
11.15a. SST = 7.015, SSE = 1.88333333, MST = 2.33833333, MSE = .09416667, $F = 24.83$
b. Yes; reject H_0: $\mu_1 = \mu_2 = \mu_3 = \mu_4$, p-value = .0001
11.16a. 2   **b.** 42   **11.17a.** 7   **b.** 24

11.18

SOURCE	df	SS	MS	F
Treatment	9	136.8	15.2	2.27
Error	30	200.7	6.69	
Total	39	337.5		

11.19

SOURCE	df	SS	MS	F
Treatment	1	28	28.0	14.0
Error	16	32	2.0	
Total	17	60		

11.20a.

SOURCE	df	SS	MS	F
Plan	3	117.642	39.214	7.79
Error	13	65.417	5.032	
Total	16	183.059		

b. Yes, reject H_0: $\mu_1 = \mu_2 = \mu_3 = \mu_4$; $F_{.025} = 4.35$ **c.** 95% CI for $(\mu_1 - \mu_3)$: -5.65 ± 3.25

11.21a.

SOURCE	df	SS	MS	F
Day	2	76.778	38.389	0.47
Error	15	1233.500	82.233	
Total	17	1310.278		

b. No, do not reject H_0: $\mu_8 = \mu_{10} = \mu_{12}$; $F_{.10} = 2.70$ **c.** 79.333 ± 6.490 **d.** 3.167 ± 9.178

11.22a.

SOURCE	df	SS	MS	F
Treatment	5	55.546867	11.1094	5.49
Error	12	24.286733	2.0239	
Total	17	79.8336		

b. Yes, reject H_0: $\mu_A = \mu_B = \cdots = \mu_F$; $F_{.05} = 3.11$ **c.** 5.12 ± 2.531 **d.** 12.443 ± 1.790

11.23a.

SOURCE	df	SS	MS	F
Watch	2	2.0720533	1.03602667	1.33
Error	12	9.34104	.77842	
Total	14	11.4130933		

b. No, do not reject H_0; $F_{.025} = 5.10$ **c.** $.116 \pm .994$

Chapter 12

12.1 Negative   **12.2** Yes, negative
12.3a. Positive: price of steel and price of car   **b.** Negative: price of gas and gallons of gas sold
12.4a. Yes, positive   **b.** $r = .971$ **c.** Yes, $r_{.025} = .878$
12.5a. Yes, positive   **b.** $r = .963$ **c.** Yes, $r_{.025} = .754$
12.6a. Yes, negative   **b.** $r = -.929$ **c.** Yes, $-r_{.025} = -.632$
12.7a. Yes, negative   **b.** $r = -.962$ **c.** Yes, $-r_{.025} = -.632$
12.8a. Negative   **b.** $r = -.914$ **c.** Yes, $-r_{.025} = -.576$
12.9a. 3.5   **b.** 5.5   **d.** 4.5   **e.** Points fall exactly on the line
12.10a. 1.5   **b.** 2   **c.** Increase by 2   **d.** Decrease by 2   **e.** 1.5
12.11a. $-.5$ **b.** -2.5 **d.** -1.5 **e.** Points fall exactly on the line
12.12a. 1.5   **b.** -2 **c.** Decrease by 2   **d.** 1.5   **e.** Same y-intercepts, different slopes
12.14a. $\beta_0 = 1$, $\beta_1 = 3$ **b.** $\beta_0 = 1$, $\beta_1 = -3$ **c.** $\beta_0 = -1$, $\beta_1 = \frac{1}{2}$ **d.** $\beta_0 = -1$, $\beta_1 = -3$
e. $\beta_0 = 2$, $\beta_1 = -\frac{1}{2}$ **f.** $\beta_0 = -1.5$, $\beta_1 = 1$ **g.** $\beta_0 = 0$, $\beta_1 = 3$ **h.** $\beta_0 = 0$, $\beta_1 = -2$
12.15b. $\hat{y} = .35 + 1.05x$ **12.16b.** $\hat{y} = 4.986 - 1.934x$ **12.17b.** $\hat{y} = 3.343 + .576x$ **12.18b.** $\hat{y} = 1.255 - .398x$
12.19b. $\hat{y} = 124.9 - .2x$ **d.** 28.9   **12.20b.** $\hat{y} = 69.65 - 2.285x$ **d.** 17.095
12.21a. SSE = .675, $s^2 = .225$ **b.** 3   **c.** $t = 7.00$, reject H_0 **d.** .0060   **e.** $1.05 \pm .353$
12.22a. SSE = 1.816, $s^2 = .363$ **b.** 5   **c.** $t = 7.99$, reject H_0 **d.** .0005   **e.** $.576 \pm .142$
12.23a. SSE = 78.9, $s^2 = 9.8625$ **b.** 8   **c.** Yes, $t = -7.12$, reject H_0
12.24a. SSE = 68.585, $s^2 = 6.8585$ **b.** 10   **c.** Yes; reject H_0, $t = -7.12$, p-value = .0001
12.25 Yes, reject H_0, $t = 3.79$, p-value = .0161
12.26a. $\hat{y} = 20.599 + 5.638x$ **b.** SSE = 562.997, $s^2 = 140.749$ **c.** 5.638 ± 1.448
12.28 $r^2 = .942$ **12.29** $r^2 = .927$ **12.30** $r^2 = .864$ **12.31** $r^2 = .835$
12.32a. $1.4 \pm .499$ **b.** 1.4 ± 1.223 **c.** Prediction interval is wider
12.33a. $2.767 \pm .481$ **b.** 2.767 ± 1.306 **c.** Prediction interval is wider
12.34a. 17.095 ± 1.383 **b.** 17.095 ± 4.944
12.35a. $\hat{y} = 153.930 - 7.465x$ **b.** 49.42 ± 3.334 **c.** 49.42 ± 8.283
12.36a. $\hat{\beta}_0 = 0$, $\hat{\beta}_1 = .857$ **c.** Yes; reject H_0: $\beta_1 = 0$, $t = 6.71$
12.37a. Positive; as x increases y increases   **b.** $r = .958$ **c.** $r^2 = .918$ **d.** Yes
e. $r = .958$, hence reject H_0; yes
12.38a. $1.714 \pm .619$ **b.** 1.714 ± 1.297 **12.39a.** $\hat{\beta}_0 = 2$, $\hat{\beta}_1 = -1.2$ **c.** Yes; reject H_0: $\beta_1 = 0$, $t = -5.20$

12.40α. Negative; as x increases y decreases   **b.** $r = -.949$ **c.** $r^2 = .900$ **d.** Yes
e. $r = -.949$, hence reject H_0; yes
12.41α. $-.04 \pm 1.331$ **b.** $-.04 \pm 2.714$ **12.42** $\hat{y} = -.1927 + 1.2206x$; $r^2 = .5921$
12.43α. $r = .843$ **b.** No, $r_{.025} = .878$, do not reject H_0
12.44α. $\hat{y} = 16.283 + 2.078x$ **c.** Yes; $t = 6.67$, p-value $= .0026$ **d.** 57.839 ± 6.145
12.45α. $\hat{y} = 17.8774 + 1.2907x$ **c.** $r = .9993$, $r^2 = .9987$ **d.** $28.203 \pm .244$ **e.** $26.912 \pm .642$

▬▬▬▬ Chapter 13

13.1α. $\hat{y} = .04564705 + .00078505x_1 + .23737262x_2 - .00003809x_1x_2$ **b.** SSE $= 2.71515039$, $s^2 = .16969690$
13.2α. Yes; $F = 84.86$, p-value $= .0001$ **13.3** $(7.323, 9.449)$ **13.4α.** No, $F = 1.28$ **b.** No
13.5α. 13.6812   **b.** Yes   **13.6α.** $F = 52.21$, reject H_0: $\beta_1 = \beta_2 = 0$ **c.** 2.65%
13.7α. $\hat{y} = 69.75354 - 10.09196x_1 - 5.334766x_2$ **b.** $R^2 = .95917$ **c.** Yes, $F = 46.99$
d. Do not reject H_0: $\beta_1 = 0$, $t = \sqrt{F} = -2.23$; reject H_0: $\beta_2 = 0$, $t = \sqrt{F} = -8.48$
13.8α. $\hat{y} = -1,180 + 6,808x$ **b.** Yes, reject H_0: $\beta_1 = 0$, $t = 19.0$ **c.** $R^2 = .984$

▬▬▬▬ Chapter 14

14.1α. Production: 66.02%; Clerical: 68.47%; Management: 78.79%   **b.** Yes

14.2α.

Expected number	Production	Clerical	Management
Favor	173.4	75.2	22.4
Do not favor	82.6	35.8	10.6

b.

Observed – Expected	Production	Clerical	Management
Favor	−4.4	.8	3.6
Do not favor	4.4	−.8	−3.6

c. $\chi^2 = 2.219$

14.3α.

Percentage in each expectation category	Accounting	Economics	Finance	Management
High	54.84	57.69	51.19	63.16
Modest	29.03	34.62	36.90	26.31
Poor	16.13	7.69	11.91	10.53

b. Yes

14.4α.

Expected	Accounting	Economics	Finance	Management
High	35.1	44.2	47.6	43.1
Modest	19.8	25.0	26.9	24.3
Poor	7.0	8.8	9.5	8.6

b.

Observed – Expected	Accounting	Economics	Finance	Management
High	−1.1	.8	−4.6	4.9
Modest	−1.8	2.0	4.1	−4.3
Poor	3.0	−2.8	.5	−.6

c. $\chi^2 = 5.035$

14.5α. 14.0671   **b.** 23.5418   **c.** 23.2093   **d.** 17.5346   **e.** 16.7496
14.6α. .025   **b.** .01   **c.** .05   **14.7α.** 1   **b.** 3   **c.** 4   **d.** 6
14.8α. H_0: The two directions of classification Employment Category and Opinion are independent;
H_a: The two directions of classification are dependent   **b.** 2   **c.** No; $\chi^2 = 2.219$, do not reject H_0
14.9 p-value $> .10$ (p-value $= .3298$)
14.10α. H_0: The two directions of classification College Major and Employment Expectations are independent;
H_a: The two directions of classification are dependent   **b.** 6   **c.** $\chi^2 = 5.035$, do not reject H_0
14.11 p-value $> .10$ (p-value $= .5393$)   **14.12** .6775 $\pm$ .0384
14.13 No; $z = -.46$, do not reject H_0: $(p_1 - p_2) = 0$ **14.14** p-value $= .6456$
14.15α. 17.5346   **b.** 11.0705   **c.** 18.3070   **d.** 6.25139   **e.** 9.21034
14.16 $\chi^2_{.10} = 4.60517$, $\chi^2_{.05} = 5.99147$, $\chi^2_{.025} = 7.37776$, $\chi^2_{.01} = 9.21034$, $\chi^2_{.005} = 10.5966$
14.17α. Yes; $\chi^2 = 5.136$, $.01 < p$-value $< .025$ (p-value $= .0235$)   **b.** $z = 2.28$, reject H_0: $(p_1 - p_2) = 0$ **c.** No
14.18 Yes; $\chi^2 = 40.701$, p-value $< .005$ **14.19α.** Yes, $\chi^2 = 46.248$, p-value $< .005$ **b.** .825 $\pm$ .026
14.20 Yes, $\chi^2 = 31.855$ **14.21** .12 $\pm$ .095   **14.22** p-value $< .005$

Chapter 15

15.2

1970	1971	1972	1973	1974	1975
96.97	89.52	100.00	110.27	116.94	124.40

1976	1977	1978	1979	1980	1981
128.48	110.82	85.16	94.26	117.74	133.69

15.3α.

	Jan	Feb	Mar	Apr	May	Jun
1978	202.09	201.74	201.58	202.37	204.43	207.19
1979	270.33	276.77	289.41	305.22	321.65	346.98
1980	445.28	470.56	484.39	485.58	487.55	488.34

	Jul	Aug	Sep	Oct	Nov	Dec
1978	210.59	219.59	215.45	216.08	218.81	222.72
1979	367.80	382.62	391.27	394.19	399.45	422.76
1980	487.95	487.16				

15.4

1973	1974	1975	1976	1977	1978	1979
92.53	97.26	100.00	101.81	106.16	111.46	114.45

15.5α.

1967	1968	1969	1970	1971	1972	1973
100.00	109.54	118.48	126.45	136.56	149.79	165.26

1974	1975	1976	1977	1978	1979	1980
181.05	198.90	220.66	247.25	276.05	308.77	341.55

15.6

Jan	Feb	Mar	Apr	May
89.10	92.10	98.09	95.10	100.00

Jun	Jul	Aug	Sep	Oct
100.82	94.01	94.01	97.28	100.00

15.7

1970	1971	1972	1973	1974
80.40	90.53	100.00	110.53	118.27

1975	1976	1977	1978
127.96	143.97	160.18	170.59

15.8

	I	II	III	IV
1979	100.00	95.76	136.20	135.28
1980	143.70	154.03	149.13	187.61

15.9

1975	1976	1977	1978	1979
100.00	86.21	70.75	77.74	81.86

15.10

1972	1973	1974	1975	1976	1977	1978
100.00	109.08	120.92	130.44	142.46	156.54	173.28

15.11

1975	1976	1977	1978	1979
100.00	123.81	152.87	173.80	216.93

15.12b.

	I	II	III	IV
1977	—	—	496.8	478.0
1978	460.6	435.1	412.6	413.8
1979	416.8	410.5	401.5	381.9
1980	323.9	—	—	—

15.13a.

	I	II	III	IV
1972	—	—	110.74	111.82
1973	111.10	110.57	105.44	101.06
1974	96.49	85.27	78.02	75.37
1975	77.66	82.75	90.15	95.01
1976	97.28	102.62	104.94	103.85
1977	102.90	100.72	97.63	95.33
1978	94.09	95.60	95.85	98.94
1979	100.79	102.48	105.44	—

15.14

1971	1972	1973	1974	1975
45.42	65.89	105.37	139.64	148.63

1976	1977	1978	1979
144.83	155.53	216.53	369.10

15.15a.

1965	1966	1967	1968	1969	1970	1971	1972
—	95.7	101.2	105.5	107.7	108.0	109.5	115.9

1973	1974	1975	1976	1977	1978	1979	1980
121.9	122.7	124.1	128.6	138.0	145.5	145.7	—

b.

1965	1966	1967	1968	1969	1970	1971	1972
—	—	100.7	104.2	106.0	109.0	113.0	115.8

1973	1974	1975	1976	1977	1978	1979	1980
118.0	122.6	127.2	131.3	136.8	141.0	—	—

c.

1965	1966	1967	1968	1969	1970	1971	1972
—	—	—	102.4	106.1	110.1	113.6	115.4

1973	1974	1975	1976	1977	1978	1979	1980
118.1	122.6	128.2	133.5	135.4	—	—	—

15.16b. $Y_t = \beta_0 + \beta_1 t + \text{Random error}$ **c.** $\hat{Y}_t = 74.4 + 1.8909t$ **d.** $r^2 = .965$

15.17b. $\hat{Y}_t = 39.48791209 + 19.13031674t - 1.31528765t^2$

15.18a. Railroads, air carriers   **b.** Railroads: $\hat{Y}_t = 81.3964 - 10.205t$; buses: $\hat{Y}_t = 33.221 - 1.855t$; air carriers: $\hat{Y}_t = -17.107 + 12.032t$; inland waterways: $\hat{Y}_t = 2.489 + .0274t$

15.19 95.2; 95% prediction interval: (91.983, 98.417)   **15.20** -15.415; 90% prediction interval: (-52.554, 21.724)

15.21 Railroads: -20.651, (-43.462, 2.159); buses: 14.674, (-7.625, 36.972); air carriers: 103.214, (86.842, 119.587); inland waterways: 2.763, ($-.082$, 5.609)

15.22 Secular trend, cyclical fluctuation, seasonal variation, irregular variation

15.27a.

1965	1966	1967	1968	1969	1970	1971	1972
240.73	153.47	147.67	54.62	34.39	100.00	−7.99	−199.93

1973	1974	1975	1976	1977	1978	1979
140.83	120.50	550.10	323.77	−319.08	−310.32	164.46

15.28

1965	1966	1967	1968	1969	1970	1971	1972
—	5357.3	3517.3	2340.0	1868.7	1249.7	−1067.0	−663.3

1973	1974	1975	1976	1977	1978	1979
607.0	8022.3	9831.0	5485.0	−3021.7	−4596.7	—

15.29

1975	1976	1977	1978	1979
100.000	84.220	69.270	57.899	66.165

15.30α.

1979			1980		
Nov	Dec	Jan	Feb	Mar	Apr
101.85	100.08	100.00	105.23	102.06	97.80

			1980		
May	Jun	Jul	Aug	Sep	Oct
99.47	94.29	120.38	123.05	136.43	125.17

b.

1979			1980		
Nov	Dec	Jan	Feb	Mar	Apr
102.00	100.16	100.00	105.19	101.85	97.83

			1980		
May	Jun	Jul	Aug	Sep	Oct
99.66	94.15	121.04	123.72	137.58	125.89

15.31b. 3 Point Moving Average

1960	1961	1962	1963	1964	1965	1966
—	1581	2644.67	4122	5611	6814.33	7250.33

1967	1968	1969	1970	1971	1972	1973
7181.33	6728.67	6143.67	5594.33	5074.67	4830	4781.67

1974	1975	1976	1977	1978	1979
4821.33	5019.67	5396	5927	6613.67	—

5 Point Moving Average

1960	1961	1962	1963	1964	1965	1966
—	—	2944.4	4137.6	5381.8	6346	6859.6

1967	1968	1969	1970	1971	1972	1973
6945.8	6665.6	6127.6	5640.4	5254.8	4959.4	4847.0

1974	1975	1976	1977	1978	1979
4910.0	5152.2	5505.2	6009.2	—	—

7 Point Moving Average

1960	1961	1962	1963	1964	1965	1966
—	—	—	4180.71	5083.57	5823.43	6386.86

1967	1968	1969	1970	1971	1972	1973
6583.14	6454.43	6157.00	5732.71	5396.43	5145.57	5000.29

1974	1975	1976	1977	1978	1979	
5076.00	5288.14	5659.86	—	—	—	

15.32a. $\hat{Y}_t = 143.014 + 5.754t$ **b.** 189.043 **c.** (183.534, 194.551)

15.33

	Jan	Feb	Mar	Apr	May	Jun
1976	—	—	—	—	—	—
1977	55.90	56.29	56.88	57.39	57.90	58.45
1978	62.36	62.92	63.62	64.28	64.93	65.70
1979	70.10	70.56	71.29	71.82	72.47	73.10
1980	76.02	76.59	76.84	77.17	—	—

	Jul	Aug	Sep	Oct	Nov	Dec
1976	53.54	53.71	54.03	54.52	54.96	55.43
1977	59.03	59.39	59.79	60.42	60.85	61.61
1978	66.57	67.29	67.88	68.50	69.05	69.62
1979	73.68	74.31	75.06	75.29	75.60	75.89
1980	—	—	—	—	—	—

15.34a. $\hat{Y}_t = 35.61602324 + .99400831t - .01156288t^2$ **c.** $t = 40$: (42.015, 71.737); $t = 45$: (35.805, 78.058)

15.35b.

	Jan	Feb	Mar	Apr	May	Jun
1978	76.60	76.60	110.64	117.02	127.66	103.19
1979	100.00	88.30	135.11	129.79	161.70	123.40
1980	87.23	94.68	105.32	106.38	130.85	115.96

	Jul	Aug	Sep	Oct	Nov	Dec
1978	115.96	118.09	91.49	123.40	118.09	85.11
1979	122.34	142.55	120.21	130.85	106.38	62.77
1980	163.83	165.96	175.53	137.23	102.13	—

c.

	Jan	Feb	Mar	Apr	May	Jun
1978	—	—	—	—	—	—
1979	10.89	10.94	11.13	11.36	11.42	11.33
1980	10.38	10.71	10.89	11.33	11.38	11.34

	Jul	Aug	Sep	Oct	Nov	Dec
1978	9.90	10.08	10.18	10.37	10.47	10.73
1979	11.15	11.05	11.10	10.87	10.68	10.44
1980	—	—	—	—	—	—

d. Multiple regression

15.36a.

	I	II	III	IV
1977	—	—	33.95	34.74
1978	35.78	36.74	38.46	39.72
1979	41.17	42.67	44.27	45.62
1980	46.90	47.65	48.13	—

15.37b. $\hat{Y}_t = 8375.49699035 + 21.36690744t - 740.774779061(\cos 2\pi t/12) - 813.41233482(\sin 2\pi t/12)$

c. (6,462.592, 10,798.693)

Chapter 16

16.1 Actions, states of nature, outcomes, objective variable

16.2 Actions: a_1 = Grant loan, a_2 = Do not grant loan; States: S_1 = Customer repays, S_2 = Customer defaults; Outcomes: Grant loan/Customer repays = +\$3,000, Grant loan/Customer defaults = −\$13,000, Do not grant loan = \$0; Objective variable: Net profit

16.3 Actions: a_1 = Settle out of court, a_2 = Go to court; States: S_1 = Win court case, S_2 = Lose court case; Outcomes: Settle out/Win = −\$800,000, Settle out/Lose = −\$800,000, Go to court/Win = −\$50,000, Go to court/Lose = −\$2,000,000; Objective variable: Net loss

16.4 Actions: a_1 = Buy 1 box, a_2 = Buy 2 boxes, . . . , a_5 = Buy 5 boxes; States: S_1 = Sell 1 box, S_2 = Sell 2 boxes, . . . , S_5 = Sell 5 boxes; Outcomes: Buy 1/Sell 1 = \$10, Buy 1/Sell 2 = \$10, . . . , Buy 5/Sell 4 = \$35, Buy 5/Sell 5 = \$50; Objective variable: Net profit

16.5 Actions: a_1 = Buy restaurant, a_2 = Do not buy restaurant; States: S_1 = Low demand, S_2 = Medium demand, S_3 = High demand; Outcomes: Buy/Low = −\$125,000, Buy/Medium = +\$50,000, Buy/High = +\$200,000, Do not buy/Low = \$0, Do not buy/Medium = \$0, Do not buy/High = \$0; Objective variable: Net profit

16.6a.

		STATE OF NATURE	
		Research successful	Research unsuccessful
ACTION	Adopt proposal	700	−8.5
	Reject proposal	1	1

b.

		STATE OF NATURE	
		Research successful	Research unsuccessful
ACTION	Adopt proposal	0	9.5
	Reject proposal	699	0

16.7a.

		STATE OF NATURE				
		.5	10	15	20	25
ACTION	Market wine	−2.85	0	1.5	3	4.5
	Do not market wine	0	0	0	0	0

b.

		STATE OF NATURE				
		.5	10	15	20	25
ACTION	Market wine	2.85	0	0	0	0
	Do not market wine	0	0	1.5	3	4.5

16.8a.

		STATES OF NATURE		
		Poor	Mediocre	Successful
ACTION	Limited	−150,000	0	200,000
	Unlimited	−70,000	20,000	95,000

b.

		STATES OF NATURE		
		Poor	Mediocre	Successful
ACTION	Limited	80,000	20,000	0
	Unlimited	0	0	105,000

16.9a.

		STATES OF NATURE	
		Repay	Default
ACTION	Grant loan	3,000	−13,000
	Do not grant loan	0	0

b.

		STATES OF NATURE	
		Repay	Default
ACTION	Grant loan	0	13,000
	Do not grant loan	3,000	0

16.10a.

		STATES OF NATURE	
		Win	Lose
ACTION	Go to court	−50,000	−2,000,000
	Settle	−800,000	−800,000

b.

		STATES OF NATURE	
		Win	Lose
ACTION	Go to court	0	1,200,000
	Settle	750,000	0

16.11a.

	Sell	STATE OF NATURE				
		1	2	3	4	5
	Buy 1	10	10	10	10	10
	2	5	20	20	20	20
ACTION	3	0	15	30	30	30
	4	−5	10	25	40	40
	5	−10	5	20	35	50

b.

	Sell	STATE OF NATURE				
		1	2	3	4	5
	Buy 1	0	10	20	30	40
	2	5	0	10	20	30
ACTION	3	10	5	0	10	20
	4	15	10	5	0	10
	5	20	15	10	5	0

16.12a.

		STATE OF NATURE		
		Low	Medium	High
ACTION	Buy	−125,000	50,000	200,000
	Do not buy	0	0	0

b.

		STATE OF NATURE		
		Low	Medium	High
ACTION	Buy	125,000	0	0
	Do not buy	0	50,000	200,000

16.18a. $EP(a_1) = 4$, $EP(a_2) = -2.5$; choose a_1
b. Expected opportunity loss for a_1 is 2.5; expected opportunity loss for a_2 is 9.0; choose a_1

		STATE OF NATURE		
		S_1	S_2	S_3
ACTION	a_1	5	4	0
	a_2	0	0	20

c. Yes

16.19 $EP(a_1) = 25,500$, $EP(a_2) = 41,000$, $EP(a_3) = 26,500$; choose a_2 **16.20** a_1 **16.21** a_3
16.22a. $EP(a_1) = 34,000$, $EP(a_2) = 22,000$, $EP(a_3) = 22,000$; choose a_1 **b.** Choose a_1

		STATE OF NATURE			
		S_1	S_2	S_3	$EP(a_i)$
	a_1	0	110,000	60,000	56,000
ACTION	a_2	150,000	0	40,000	68,000
	a_3	150,000	20,000	0	68,000

16.23 Adopt proposal
16.24 $EP(a_1) = 10$, $EP(a_2) = 17.75$, $EP(a_3) = 22.5$, $EP(a_4) = 22$, $EP(a_5) = 17.75$; choose a_3 (buy 3 boxes)

16.25a. a_4 **b.** a_1 **c.**

		STATE OF NATURE		
		S_1	S_2	S_3
	a_1	0	0	105
ACTION	a_2	50	20	105
	a_3	125	70	85
	a_4	25	15	0

d. a_4

16.26a. a_3 **b.** a_1 **16.27** a_1 **16.28a.** Limited tickets   **b.** Unlimited tickets   **c.** Limited tickets

16.29a.

		STATE OF NATURE		
		S_1	S_2	S_3
	a_1	28	0	107
	a_2	16	75	68
ACTION	a_3	60	36	0
	a_4	15	72	10
	a_5	0	27	70

b.

	a_1	a_2	a_3	a_4	a_5	
Expected payoffs	23.7	15	18.3	28	37	Choose a_5
Expected opportunity losses	35.4	44.1	40.8	31.1	22.1	Choose a_5

c. Maximax: a_3; Maximin: a_5; Minimax: a_3

16.30a. Actions: Go to court, Settle out of court; States of nature: Win, lose; Outcomes: Go to court/Win = 0, Go to court/Lose = $-1,000,000$, Settle out of court/Win = $-250,000$, Settle out of court/Lose = $-250,000$; Objective variable: Loss

b.

		STATE OF NATURE	
		Win	**Lose**
ACTION	**Go to court**	0	$-1,000,000$
	Settle out of court	$-250,000$	$-250,000$

d. Settle **e.** Go to court **f.** Settle **g.** Settle

16.31a. Actions: Investment A, Investment B; States of nature: Rezoning approved, Rezoning rejected; Outcomes: Investment A/Rezoning = $450,000, Investment A/No rezoning = $450,000, Investment B/Rezoning = $580,000, Investment B/No rezoning = $80,000; Objective variable: Profit

c. Investment A

16.32b.

		STATE OF NATURE					
	Sell	**3**	**4**	**5**	**6**	**7**	**8**
	Buy 3	60	60	60	60	60	60
	4	55	80	80	80	80	80
	5	50	75	100	100	100	100
ACTION	**6**	45	70	95	120	120	120
	7	40	65	90	115	140	140
	8	35	60	85	110	135	160

c.

		STATE OF NATURE					
	Sell	**3**	**4**	**5**	**6**	**7**	**8**
	Buy 3	0	20	40	60	80	100
	4	5	0	20	40	60	80
	5	10	5	0	20	40	60
ACTION	**6**	15	10	5	0	20	40
	7	20	15	10	5	0	20
	8	25	20	15	10	5	0

d. Buy 6 dozen **f.** Buy 8 dozen **g.** Buy 3 dozen **h.** Buy 7 dozen

16.33a. Actions: Sponsor, Do not sponsor; States of nature: Favorable, Fair, Unfavorable;
Outcomes: Sponsor/Favorable = 400,000, Sponsor/Fair = 150,000, Sponsor/Unfavorable = −85,000,
Do not sponsor/Favorable = 150,000, Do not sponsor/Fair = 150,000, Do not sponsor/Unfavorable = 150,000;
Objective variable: Profit

b. PAYOFF TABLE

		STATE OF NATURE		
		Favorable	**Fair**	**Unfavorable**
ACTION	**Sponsor**	400,000	150,000	−85,000
	Do not sponsor	150,000	150,000	150,000

OPPORTUNITY LOSS TABLE

		STATE OF NATURE		
		Favorable	**Fair**	**Unfavorable**
ACTION	**Sponsor**	0	0	235,000
	Do not sponsor	250,000	0	0

c. Sponsor   **d.** Maximax: Sponsor; maximin: Do not sponsor; minimax: Sponsor

16.34a. Actions: Issue, Do not issue; States of nature: Favorable, No reaction, Unfavorable;
Outcomes: Issue/Favorable = 5, Issue/No reaction = 0, Issue/Unfavorable = −7, Do not issue/Favorable = 0,
Do not issue/No reaction = 0, Do not issue/Unfavorable = 0; Objective variable: Point increase in poll

b.

		STATE OF NATURE		
		Favorable	**No reaction**	**Unfavorable**
ACTION	**Issue**	5	0	−7
	Do not issue	0	0	0

c. Maximax: Issue; maximin: Do not issue

d.

		STATE OF NATURE		
		Favorable	**No reaction**	**Unfavorable**
ACTION	**Issue**	0	0	7
	Do not issue	5	0	0

Minimax decision: Do not issue

Index

Normal Curve Areas

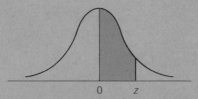

z	.00	.01	.02	.03	.04	.05	.06	.07	.08	.09
0.0	.0000	.0040	.0080	.0120	.0160	.0199	.0239	.0279	.0319	.0359
0.1	.0398	.0438	.0478	.0517	.0557	.0596	.0636	.0675	.0714	.0753
0.2	.0793	.0832	.0871	.0910	.0948	.0987	.1026	.1064	.1103	.1141
0.3	.1179	.1217	.1255	.1293	.1331	.1368	.1406	.1443	.1480	.1517
0.4	.1554	.1591	.1628	.1664	.1700	.1736	.1772	.1808	.1844	.1879
0.5	.1915	.1950	.1985	.2019	.2054	.2088	.2123	.2157	.2190	.2224
0.6	.2257	.2291	.2324	.2357	.2389	.2422	.2454	.2486·	.2517	.2549
0.7	.2580	.2611	.2642	.2673	.2704	.2734	.2764	.2794	.2823	.2852
0.8	.2881	.2910	.2939	.2967	.2995	.3023	.3051	.3078	.3106	.3133
0.9	.3159	.3186	.3212	.3238	.3264	.3289	.3315	.3340	.3365	.3389
1.0	.3413	.3438	.3461	.3485	.3508	.3531	.3554	.3577	.3599	.3621
1.1	.3643	.3665	.3686	.3708	.3729	.3749	.3770	.3790	.3810	.3830
1.2	.3849	.3869	.3888	.3907	.3925	.3944	.3962	.3980	.3997	.4015
1.3	.4032	.4049	.4066	.4082	.4099	.4115	.4131	.4147	.4162	.4177
1.4	.4192	.4207	.4222	.4236	.4251	.4265	.4279	.4292	.4306	.4319
1.5	.4332	.4345	.4357	.4370	.4382	.4394	.4406	.4418	.4429	.4441
1.6	.4452	.4463	.4474	.4484	.4495	.4505	.4515	.4525	.4535	.4545
1.7	.4554	.4564	.4573	.4582	.4591	.4599	.4608	.4616	.4625	.4633
1.8	.4641	.4649	.4656	.4664	.4671	.4678	.4686	.4693	.4699	.4706
1.9	.4713	.4719	.4726	.4732	.4738	.4744	.4750	.4756	.4761	.4767
2.0	.4772	.4778	.4783	.4788	.4793	.4798	.4803	.4808	.4812	.4817
2.1	.4821	.4826	.4830	.4834	.4838	.4842	.4846	.4850	.4854	.4857
2.2	.4861	.4864	.4868	.4871	.4875	.4878	.4881	.4884	.4887	.4890
2.3	.4893	.4896	.4898	.4901	.4904	.4906	.4909	.4911	.4913	.4916
2.4	.4918	.4920	.4922	.4925	.4927	.4929	.4931	.4932	.4934	.4936
2.5	.4938	.4940	.4941	.4943	.4945	.4946	.4948	.4949	.4951	.4952
2.6	.4953	.4955	.4956	.4957	.4959	.4960	.4961	.4962	.4963	.4964
2.7	.4965	.4966	.4967	.4968	.4969	.4970	.4971	.4972	.4973	.4974
2.8	.4974	.4975	.4976	.4977	.4977	.4978	.4979	.4979	.4980	.4981
2.9	.4981	.4982	.4982	.4983	.4984	.4984	.4985	.4985	.4986	.4986
3.0	.4987	.4987	.4987	.4988	.4988	.4989	.4989	.4989	.4990	.4990

Source: Abridged from Table I of A. Hald, *Statistical Tables and Formulas* (New York: John Wiley & Sons, Inc.), 1952. Reproduced by permission of A. Hald and the publisher.